Contemporary Business (Select Chapters)

Authors

Brahm M. Canzer • David L. Kurtz • Louis E. Boone • Michael H. Khan

ISBN 9781119335122

List of Titles

Contemporary Business, 2nd edition
by Louis E. Boone, David L. Kurtz, Michael H. Khan, and Brahm M. Canzer
Copyright © 2016, ISBN: 978-1-119-19433-0

Table of Contents

WileyPLUS Learning Space

Includes **ORION** Adaptive Practice

An easy way to help your students learn, collaborate, and grow.

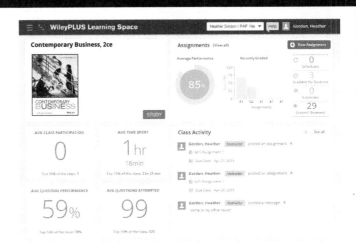

Diagnose Early

Educators assess the real-time proficiency of each student to inform teaching decisions. Students always know what they need to work on.

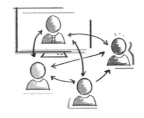

Facilitate Engagement

Educators can quickly organize learning activities, manage student collaboration, and customize their course. Students can collaborate and have meaningful discussions on concepts they are learning.

Measure Outcomes

With visual reports, it's easy for both educators and students to gauge problem areas and act on what's most important.

Instructor Benefits

- Assign activities and add your own materials
- Guide students through what's important in the interactive e-textbook by easily assigning specific content
- Set up and monitor collaborative learning groups
- Assess learner engagement
- Gain immediate insights to help inform teaching

Student Benefits

- Instantly know what you need to work on
- Create a personal study plan
- Assess progress along the way
- Participate in class discussions
- Remember what you have learned because you have made deeper connections to the content

www.wileypluslearningspace.com

WILEY

SECOND CANADIAN EDITION

CONTEMPORARY BUSINESS

LOUIS E. BOONE
University of South Alabama

MICHAEL H. KHAN
University of Toronto

DAVID L. KURTZ
University of Arkansas

BRAHM M. CANZER
John Abbott College

WILEY

Library and Archives Canada Cataloguing in Publication

Boone, Louis E., author
      Contemporary business / Louis E. Boone, David L. Kurtz, Michael H. Khan, Brahm M. Canzer. — Second Canadian Edition.

Includes bibliographical references and index.
Issued in print and electronic formats.
ISBN 978-1-119-19433-0 (loose leaf).—ISBN 978-1-119-24506-3 (paperback).—ISBN 978-1-119-24038-9 (ebook)

      1. Management—Textbooks.   2. Business—Textbooks.   I. Kurtz, David L., author   II. Khan, Michael H., author   III. Canzer, Brahm, author   IV. Title.

HD31.B626 2015   658   C2015-906812-6
                                                         C2015-906813-4

Production Credits

V.P. & Director Market Solutions: Veronica Visentin	Production and Media Specialist: Meaghan MacDonald
Executive Editor: Darren Lalonde	Assistant Editor: Ashley Patterson
Senior Marketing Manager: Anita Osborne	Typesetting: SPi Global
Editorial Manager: Karen Staudinger	Cover Design: Joanna Vieira
Developmental Editor: Gail Brown	Cover Image: © Mel Yates/Getty
Media Editor: Luisa Begani	

Printing and binding: Quad Graphics
Printed and bound in the United States.
1 2 3 4 5 QG 19 18 17 16 15

WILEY

90 Eglinton Avenue East, Suite 300
Toronto, Ontario, M4P 2Y3 Canada
Visit our website at: www.wiley.ca

PREFACE

Canadian college and university students have questions about business and the role business-people play. Some questions relate to their personal experiences, and others concern understanding issues we all face as Canadians living in an increasingly global society. Students want answers to these questions and more:

- What products are "made in Canada" and why can't we make more?

- Why do Canadian consumers pay more than Americans for many products and services?

- Why did BlackBerry lose its global leadership role in smartphone technology?

- Why are some countries wealthy and others not?

- Which Canadian businesses will provide job opportunities for me when I graduate?

- Should I start my own business?

Contemporary Business, Second Canadian Edition, is a comprehensive introductory textbook. Rooted in the basics of business, this textbook provides students with a foundation upon which to build a greater understanding of current business practices and issues that affect their lives.

Chapter 1 opens with a close-up look at the role of the Internet and social media in launching Drake's and Justin Bieber's career. The changes brought on by Internet and other technologies are illustrated throughout the textbook. As regular users of the Internet, students understand first-hand how the Internet has changed their behaviour—starting with communications and digital media. We use this familiarity to build an understanding of businesses that have been affected by the Internet, such as BlackBerry, discussed in Chapter 7. We also examine Canadian businesses that have succeeded in large part due to the marketing power of the Internet, such as StockTrak in Chapter 14.

Another theme throughout the textbook is globalization and the growing challenges facing Canadian businesses as they compete not only against American and Mexican firms in North America but against firms everywhere in the world. We look at changes in production of tangibles and intangibles, the use of automation, and outsourcing to lower-cost countries, such as China and India. Chapter 8 opens with a closer examination of the decline of the Canadian apparel industry and how some apparel companies have managed to succeed by focusing on niche markets.

Responsible Business

A current topic of major interest is the use of business ethics and corporate social responsibility (CSR). Chapter 2 is rich in content related to CSR. It opens with a look at Canada's world-renowned Cirque du Soleil and its model of global CSR. Throughout the textbook, and particularly in each chapter's *"Solving an Ethical Controversy"* feature, we focus on ethical issues and CSR. Similarly, each chapter's *"Going Green"* feature looks at green issues, including conservation, pollution, recycling, and reusing. The *"Hit & Miss"* feature shines a spotlight on companies, business leaders, and entrepreneurs.

Student-Focused

We present Canadian content that speaks directly to students about the world of business. Many examples included in this textbook were inspired by student peers. From companies such as Cirque du Soleil to lesser-known success stories across Canada, this textbook brings Canadian business and businesspeople face-to-face with students so that the roles played by businesspeople in our economy can be better understood, questioned, and debated. New to this edition is a running case featuring the Canadian company Beau's All Natural Brewing Company. The case is presented in six parts, corresponding to the six parts of the textbook, and is located following the last chapter of each part. Beau's takes students through the decision-making that resulted in the establishment of a successful family-run micro-brewery based in Vankleek Hill, in the Ottawa region. Instructors may choose to use some or all of the parts in sequence or as one longer case assignment. As well, the *"Career Kickstart"* feature provides useful tips and information for students who will embark on a business career. Students said they wanted to understand business beyond the simple concepts of profit as a goal or maximizing the provision of services for not-for profit organizations. We believe we have produced a textbook that meets these needs.

Contemporary Business, Second Canadian Edition, is written in a conversational style that has been thoroughly edited for plain language to ensure readability for all students, including students for whom English is their second language.

ACKNOWLEDGEMENTS

Contemporary Business, Second Canadian Edition, is the result of the efforts of many people who rightfully need acknowledgement. We would first like to thank our publishing team, beginning with our developmental editor, Gail Brown, for her suggestions on style and content throughout the writing effort. We thank Leanne Rancourt for an excellent job on the copy edit, Leslie Saffrey for her accurate proofreading, Hadi Ahmad for providing editorial insight, and Martin Eichler for his dedicated work as a research coordinator on the project.

We wish to thank the Wiley team on the business side of the project, beginning with Darren Lalonde, Veronica Visentin, and all of the marketing and sales representatives for their field knowledge and support of this book.

We thank the faculty members who contributed to the development of the textbook's resources and ancillaries, specifically Cheryl Dowell, Algonquin College (instructor's manual), Philip Eng, George Brown College (quizzes), Joyce Manu, George Brown College (test bank), and Wendy Tarrel, Nova Scotia Community College (quizzes and clicker questions), and a special thank you to Deanna Durnford for coordinating these ancillaries..

We especially want to thank our academic colleagues for their suggestions and constructive criticisms—both for the previous Canadian edition and this second Canadian edition. We know we could not have produced a textbook of this quality and calibre without their contributions.

Editorial Advisory Board

Reviewers

Peggy Carter, Nova Scotia Community
    College
Scott Cawfield, York University
David Delcorde, University of Ottawa
Joyce Manu, George Brown College
Gordon McFarlane, Langara College
Donna McRae-Murphy, Eastern College
Peter Mombourquette, Mount Saint Vincent
    University

Paul Myers, St. Clair College
Hyacinth Randall, Seneca College
Andrea Rennie, Seneca College
Al Ruggero, Seneca College
Ronnalee Rylance, CDI College
Drew Smylie, Centennial College
Michael Wade, Seneca College
Claudia Zhang, Grant MacEwan University

Finally, we extend special thanks to the following group of University of Toronto students for their insightful and invaluable contributions to the text.

From the left: Mouri Khan, Martin Eichler, Zachary Bunting, Elliot Spicer, Daouii Abouchere. Absent: Pascal Elliott Chong

This book is lovingly dedicated to my growing family: my wife Carole; my son Matthew and his wife Leslie Grenier; and my daughter Sarah and her husband James Wiseman.

Brahm Canzer

This book is dedicated to my parents, for providing my foundation; my wife Asma, who encourages me in all of my endeavours; my children, Khadijah and Zakariyah, who can always bring a smile to my face; and finally, all of my friends, family, and students who have supported me throughout the years.

Michael Khan

SUPPLEMENTS

WileyPLUS Learning Space

Learning experts have shown greater gains in outcomes and improved retention when students are able to read, interact with, discuss, and write about course content. Research also shows that when students collaborate with each other, they make deeper connections to the content. Typically, when students work together, they also feel part of a community. This sense of community helps them grow in areas beyond topics in the course—they are able to develop skills like critical thinking and teamwork that can be applied down the road in future careers and life.

WileyPLUS Learning Space will transform any course into a vibrant, collaborative, learning community. This exciting online platform invites students to experience learning activities, work through self-assessment, ask questions and share insights. As they interact with the course content, their peers, and their instructor, *WileyPLUS Learning Space* creates a personalized study guide for each student.

Through a flexible course design, you can quickly organize learning activities, manage student collaboration, and customize your course—having full control over content as well as the amount of interactivity between students.

WileyPLUS Learning Space lets you:

- Assign activities and add your own materials
- Guide your students through what's important in the interactive e-textbook by easily assigning specific content
- Set up and monitor group learning
- Assess student engagement
- Gain immediate insights to help inform teaching

Defining a clear path to action, the visual reports in *WileyPLUS Learning Space* help both you and your students gauge problem areas and act on what's most important.

With the visual reports, you can:

- See exactly where your students are struggling and intervene as needed
- Help students see what they don't know to better prepare for exams
- Give students insight into their strengths and weaknesses to succeed in the course

Integrated with *WileyPLUS Learning Space* is ORION. Based on cognitive science, ORION is a personalized, adaptive learning experience that helps students build proficiency on topics while using their study time most effectively.

Resources

Contemporary Business, Second Canadian Edition, is accompanied by a suite of instructor and student resources and ancillaries designed to facilitate teaching and learning.

Resources can be found within the *Contemporary Business*, Second Canadian Edition, *WileyPLUS Learning Space* course. Selected resources are available on the textbook's companion website, www.wiley.com/go/boonecanada. Consistent with the first edition of *Contemporary Business*, the instructor resources are designed to propel the instructor into the classroom with all the materials needed to engage students and help them understand concepts.

For Instructors

CBC Videos. Two sets of CBC Videos are available for *Contemporary Business*, Second Canadian Edition—short clips with discussion questions to generate interest and initiate discussion into relevant business topics and longer video cases with discussion questions that take an in-depth look at key subjects of interest to students, such as entrepreneurship and sustainability.

Test Bank. The Test Bank contains a variety of question types—matching, essay/short answer, multiple choice, and true/false. The Test Bank is available in a Word® document format, as well as a Computerized Test Bank. Instructors can generate multiple test versions, rearrange question order, or customize tests for specific content.

Instructor's Manual. This Instructor's Manual is designed to help instructors maximize student learning and encourage critical thinking. It presents a lecture outline for each section and objective in each chapter, and includes answers to review questions and suggested responses to the Project and Teamwork Applications in the textbook. The instructor's manual also includes collaborative learning exercises.

PowerPoint® Presentations. PowerPoint® Presentations are provided for each chapter and include an outline of key points (with accompanying lecture notes), learning objectives, key terms, and figures and tables from the textbook.

Clicker Questions. This resource offers questions about key chapter concepts and can be used with a variety of personal response (or "clicker") systems.

Wiley Contemporary Business Weekly Updates Site, http://contemporarybusinessupdates.ca. This weekly update site provides highlights of the very latest in business news and current affairs. Each week's update includes links to relevant business news articles and video clips, with discussion questions to help guide an understanding of the news item and to encourage classroom analysis and discussion. Instructors who wish to receive email alerts with each week's highlights can subscribe directly on the website. New to the Weekly Updates are Video Case Exercises that correspond to the six parts of the textbook.

For Students

Free Study Guide. The *Study Guide to Accompany Contemporary Business*, Second Canadian Edition, is available free to students and provides a solid review of the concepts covered in the textbook and in a contemporary business course. The study guide includes a variety of question material and application exercises and is available in *WileyPLUS Learning Space*.

Practice Quizzes. This resource allows students to test their knowledge and understanding of key chapter content. Practices quizzes are available in *WileyPLUS Learning Space*.

Video Summaries. This resource is an author-presented summary and overview of the key concepts and learning objectives in each chapter.

AP Photo/Julio Cortez/The Canadian Press

7 | MANAGEMENT, LEADERSHIP, AND THE INTERNAL ORGANIZATION

LEARNING OBJECTIVES

LO 7.1 Describe *management*.

LO 7.2 Explain the role of vision and ethical standards in business success.

LO 7.3 Summarize the importance of planning and the three types of planning.

LO 7.4 Describe the strategic planning process.

LO 7.5 Describe the two major types of business decisions and the steps in the decision-making process.

LO 7.6 Define *leadership*, and compare different leadership styles.

LO 7.7 Discuss the meaning and importance of corporate culture.

LO 7.8 Identify the five major forms of departmentalization and the four main types of organization structures.

INSIDE BUSINESS

Can John S. Chen Save BlackBerry?

It is hard for many people to understand how Waterloo, Ontario-based BlackBerry Ltd. (formerly Research In Motion Ltd. [RIM]) could fall from the height of success. It was even harder for shareholders and industry analysts who watched as the firm's management seemed unable to cope in a competitive environment where once it was the leader.

By 2012, BlackBerry had an estimated 75 million global subscribers and was generating $20 billion in revenues. The company was profitable, posting more than $3.4 billion in profit in 2011. But analysts could see that the firm was losing customers to new-product offerings from Apple, Google, and others.

The company had early success with its 1998 introduction of the device called the BlackBerry. The product's reliability and the firm's superior customer support made it popular and led to its success. To use a BlackBerry device, wireless service providers need to buy into the system that the firm is selling. The individual customer buys a BlackBerry device, but the wireless service provider must buy the software and other technology from the company. Then, the software and technology together make it possible for customers to use these products and products licensed to other manufacturers by BlackBerry.

The business model worked well. In fact, it still works well in many markets around the world where voice and data (text) communication meet the primary needs of mostly business subscribers. But then Apple introduced the iPhone. Software developers began creating hundreds and hundreds of special applications (apps) to run on the iPhone. BlackBerry's smartphone devices lost their appeal as more and more consumers purchased iPhones instead.

By the time the late Steve Jobs introduced the iPad, Apple's mobile tablet device, BlackBerry was trying to catch up. BlackBerry launched its PlayBook, but it was poorly received. The trend for future growth—especially in the bigger consumer market—pointed away from BlackBerry and toward Apple and other producers. Apple and Google chose to focus on digital content sales. It seemed that BlackBerry's management was losing touch with what customers wanted. The hardware device was less important to generating revenue. Instead, digital content was becoming the source of growth.

By January 2012, unhappy shareholders had seen their stock value fall to $15 per share from highs of more than $150 per share in 2008. The shareholders demanded major leadership changes at the firm. The board of directors removed the two top management figures, who had led BlackBerry's original success. Mike Lazaridis and Jim Balsillie were not out, but they were no longer setting the vision and direction for the company they had built from scratch. Thorsten Heins was named president and chief executive officer replacing Mike Lazaridis. Jim Balsillie stepped down as co-CEO. He initially remained on the board of directors, but then stepped down from that position in late March 2012. Thorsten Heins's time at the helm was brief. He was replaced by John S. Chen, a Silicon Valley success story, in 2013 to dramatically change the company. The board had recognized that time was running out for BlackBerry and drastic change in direction was needed if the company was to have any chance of a future in an industry that it had helped create.[1]

CHAPTER 7 OVERVIEW

Many students in introductory business courses dream about the challenges of a management career. When you ask business students about their career goals, many will say, "I want to be a manager." You may think that being a manager means being the boss. But in today's business world, companies want managers to be more than bosses. They want managers who understand technology, adapt quickly to change, can skillfully motivate employees, and realize the importance of satisfying customers. Managers who can master those skills will be in great demand. Managers who have strong commitments can improve their firms' performance.

This chapter begins by looking at how successful organizations use management to turn visions into reality. It describes the levels of management, the skills that managers need, and the functions that managers perform. The chapter explains how the first of these functions—planning—helps managers in two ways: to meet the challenges of a rapidly changing business environment and to develop strategies that guide a company's future. Other sections of the chapter explore the types of decisions that managers make, the role of managers as leaders, and the importance of corporate culture. The chapter concludes by examining the second function of management—organizing.

LO 7.1 Describe *management.*

management the process of achieving organizational goals through people and other resources.

WHAT IS MANAGEMENT?

Management is the process of achieving organizational goals through people and other resources. The manager's job is to combine human and technical resources in the best way possible to achieve the company's goals.

Management principles and concepts apply to both not-for-profit organizations and for-profit firms. The managerial functions described in this chapter are performed by a city mayor, the president of the YMCA, and a superintendent of schools. Management takes place at many levels, from the level of a manager at a family-owned restaurant to the level of a national sales manager for a major manufacturer.

The Management Hierarchy

Your local grocery store has a fairly simple organization: a store manager, several assistant managers or department managers, and employees who may be baggers, cashiers, or stock clerks. If your grocery store is part of a regional or national chain, it will also have corporate managers who are ranked above the store manager. Loblaw is Canada's largest food distribution company. It operates more than 1,000 grocery stores across Canada. It has headquarters in Brampton, Ontario. Each store has managers for everything, from the meat department to human resources. At Loblaw headquarters, you'll find top-level managers for finance, consumer affairs, real estate, information technology, sales and operations, pharmacy, and other areas.[2]

All these managers combine human and other resources to meet Loblaw goals. But their jobs differ because they work at different levels of the organization.

A firm's management usually has three levels: top, middle, and supervisory. These levels of management form a management hierarchy, as shown in **Figure 7.1**. The hierarchy is the traditional structure found in most organizations. Managers at each level perform different activities.

The highest level of management is *top management.* Top managers include such positions as chief executive officer (CEO), chief financial officer (CFO), and executive vice-president. Top managers spend most of their time developing long-range plans for their organizations. They decide whether to introduce new products, purchase other companies, or enter new geographical markets. Top

FIGURE 7.1 The Management Hierarchy

Top Management	• Chief Executive Officer • Chief Financial Officer • Premier, Mayor
Middle Management	• Regional Manager • Division Head • Director, Dean
Supervisory (First-Line) Management	• Supervisor • Department Chairperson • Program Manager

managers set a direction for their organization. They also inspire the company's executives and employees to achieve their vision for the company's future.

The job isn't easy. Many top managers must steer their firms through an economic downturn, a slump in sales, or a crisis in quality. TD Bank's Ed Clark was recently named outstanding CEO of the Year. This recognition was, in part, because of his success in steering Canada's second-largest bank through one of the worst global financial crises in history (2008–2010) and back to continued growth. The bank's stock market value returned to pre-crisis levels, likely because of two factors: uninterrupted dividend payouts to shareholders and investors' confidence in future growth. In 2012 and 2013, Ed was named to *Barron's* prestigious annual list of the world's 30 best CEOs. He retired from TD Bank in 2014 after 12 years as CEO.[3]

Middle management is the second level in the management hierarchy. It includes general managers, plant managers, division managers, and branch managers. Middle managers focus their attention on specific operations, products, or customer groups. They develop detailed plans and procedures to carry out the firm's strategic plans. For example, suppose top management decides to increase distribution of a product. A sales manager will decide on how many salespeople are needed. Middle managers will focus on the products to be sold and on the customers who will buy the products and lead to the profit growth the CEO expects. The middle managers might budget money for product development, identify new uses for existing products, and improve the ways they train and motivate salespeople. Middle managers are more familiar with day-to-day operations than CEOs. That's why middle managers often come up with new ways to increase sales or solve company problems.

Supervisory management, or first-line management, includes supervisors, section chiefs, and team leaders. These managers assign specific jobs to nonmanagerial employees and assess their performance. Managers at this first level of the hierarchy work directly with the employees who produce and sell the firm's goods and services. They carry out middle managers' plans by motivating workers to accomplish daily, weekly, and monthly goals. In a study of top-ranked customer service firms, all firms had first-line managers who carried out the firms' strategies to provide superior customer service.[4]

For the past six years, TD Canada Trust has ranked highest in customer satisfaction among the big five Canadian retail banks, according to J.D. Power and Associates. The first-line managers make sure that customer service is the main concern for all employees.

Skills Needed for Managerial Success

Managers at every level in the management hierarchy use three basic types of skills: technical, human, and conceptual. All managers must acquire these skills, but the importance of each skill changes at each management level.

Technical skills are the manager's ability to understand and use the techniques, knowledge, tools, and equipment of a specific department or area of study. Technical skills are especially important for first-line managers. They are less important at higher levels of the management hierarchy. But most top executives started out as technical experts. The résumé of a vice-president for information systems probably lists jobs as a computer analyst. A vice-president for marketing usually has a background in sales. Many firms, such as The Home Depot and Dell, have increased their training programs for first-line managers to increase their technical skills and productivity. Cold Stone Creamery operates franchises for its premium ice cream stores in Alberta and Saskatchewan. This company carefully trains managers and crew members in the art of preparing its specialty ice cream for hungry customers. "We set high standards and provide world-class training," says the company.[5]

Human skills are interpersonal skills that help managers to work effectively with people. Human skills include the ability to communicate with, motivate, and lead employees to complete their assigned activities. Managers need human skills to interact with people both inside and outside the organization. People without these skills will probably have a difficult time trying to be a successful manager. Human skills must be adapted to different forms. For example, human skills include mastering and communicating effectively with staff using email, cellphones, pagers, faxes, and text messaging. All these forms of communication are widely used in today's offices. As you can imagine, managers at Cold Stone Creamery ice cream stores need to have excellent human skills, not only with customers but also with employees.

Conceptual skills help a manager to see the organization as a single unit and to understand how each part of the overall organization interacts with other parts. People with conceptual skills can see the big picture by acquiring, analyzing, and interpreting information. Conceptual skills are especially important for top-level managers, who must develop long-range plans for the future direction of their organization. Tony Hsieh sold his own company, LinkExchange, to Microsoft for $265 million. He then joined Zappos as an advisor and later became its CEO. Hsieh's conceptual skills helped Zappos to grow its sales to more than $1 billion annually while also winning praises for being an excellent place to work. Recently, Hsieh sold Zappos to Amazon in a deal worth $1.2 billion.[6]

Managerial Functions

In the course of a typical day, managers meet and talk with people, read, think, and send text or email messages. As they perform these activities, managers carry out four basic functions: planning, organizing, directing, and controlling. Planning activities set out the basics for activity, and the other functions carry out the plans.

Planning

planning the process of looking forward to future events and conditions and deciding on the courses of action for achieving organizational goals.

Planning is the process of looking forward to future events and conditions and deciding on the courses of actions for achieving organizational goals. Effective planning helps a business to focus its vision, avoid costly mistakes, and seize opportunities. Planning should be flexible and responsive to changes in the business environment. It should also involve managers from all levels of the organization. Planning for the future is more important than ever because global competition is getting stronger, technology continues to expand, and firms are bringing new innovations to market faster. For example, a CEO and other top-level managers need to plan for succession—for those who will follow in their footsteps. Some CEOs don't want to do this kind of planning, fearing that it might shorten their time leading a company. Management experts advise firms to plan ahead for the next generation of management, so they can keep the company's position in the marketplace.[7]

Frank Stronach led Magna International from its start in 1969 to become the largest automotive parts manufacturer in North America with sales over $23 billion. Stronach decided to step down as CEO. He announced his decision before a shareholders' vote on his position. Although the company had returned to profitability after the financial crisis, which hit the auto industry hard, many thought that it was time for new leadership at the firm.[8]

Organizing

After plans have been developed, the next step in the management process is **organizing**—the process of blending human and material resources through a formal structure of tasks and authority: arranging work, dividing tasks among employees, and coordinating them to ensure plans are carried out and goals are met. Organizing involves classifying and dividing work into manageable units with a structure that makes sense. Managers staff the organization with the best possible employees for each job. Sometimes, the organizing function requires studying a company's existing structure and deciding whether to restructure it to operate more efficiently, cost effectively, or sustainably.

> **organizing** the process of blending human and material resources through a formal structure of tasks and authority: arranging work, dividing tasks among employees, and coordinating them to ensure plans are carried out and goals are met.

Directing

After an organization has been set up, managers focus on **directing**, or guiding and motivating employees to accomplish organizational goals. Directing can include training (or retraining), setting up schedules, assigning tasks, and monitoring progress. For example, an office manager might need to meet the goal of reducing the office electricity bill. This manager might do the following: assign incandescent light bulbs to be replaced by compact fluorescents, ask employees to turn off the lights when they leave a room, and direct the information technology (IT) staff to program all computer screens to turn off after 15 minutes of inactivity.[9]

> **directing** guiding and motivating employees to accomplish organizational goals.

Some managers take time to listen to their employees. These managers gain an understanding of their employees, and the employees feel that the manager cares about their work. Weekly meetings with employees allow for the exchange of information, and individuals can make their views known. Such meetings can help to motivate employees and provide an opportunity for comments about the direction the firm is moving.

Controlling

The **controlling** function assesses an organization's performance against its goals. Controlling assesses the success of the planning function and provides feedback for future rounds of planning.

> **controlling** the function of assessing an organization's performance against its goals.

Controlling has four basic steps: setting performance standards, monitoring actual performance, comparing actual performance with the standards, and making corrections if needed. For example, according to the Sarbanes-Oxley Act, CEOs and CFOs must monitor the performance of the firm's accounting staff more closely than was done in the past. CEOs and CFOs must personally confirm the truth of financial reports filed with the U.S. Securities and Exchange Commission. Many Canadian firms, such as Magna International, are listed on American stock exchanges. These Canadian firms are also required to comply with Sarbanes-Oxley.

✓ **ASSESSMENT CHECK**

7.1.1 What is management?

7.1.2 Describe the differences in the jobs of top managers, middle managers, and supervisory managers.

7.1.3 What is the relationship between the manager's planning and controlling functions?

SETTING A VISION AND ETHICAL STANDARDS FOR THE FIRM

> **LO 7.2** Explain the role of vision and ethical standards in business success.

A business begins with a **vision**, its founder's ability to perceive marketplace needs and what an organization must do to satisfy them. Vision is a focus for a firm's actions. Vision helps to direct the company toward opportunities and sets it apart from its competitors. The current vision for Facebook is not very different from the original vision proposed by founder Mark Zuckerberg— "Giving people the power to share, and make the world more open and connected."[10]

> **vision** the ability to perceive marketplace needs and what an organization must do to satisfy them.

A firm's vision is a focus for its actions. Vision helps to direct the company toward opportunities and sets it apart from its competitors. The current vision for Facebook is not very different from the original vision proposed by founder Mark Zuckerberg—"Giving people the power to share, and make the world more open and connected."

A company's vision must be focused. It must also be flexible enough to adapt to changes in the business environment. The ethical standards set by top management are also important to a firm's long-term relationships with its customers, suppliers, and the general public. Sometimes, ethical standards are made to comply with industry or federal regulations, such as safety or quality standards. Other times, new standards are set after unethical actions have been taken by managers, such as the financial accounting wrongdoings that led to the Sarbanes-Oxley Act. Many firms are now taking a closer look at large compensation packages received by their CEOs and other top executives. Because of public demands, compensation committees are reassessing their guidelines for salaries, bonuses, and other benefits.[11]

The ethical tone set by a top management team can lead to financial and nonfinancial rewards. Setting a high ethical standard does not just keep employees from doing wrong but it also encourages, motivates, and inspires them to achieve goals they never thought possible. Such satisfaction creates a more productive, stable workforce—one that can create a long-term competitive advantage for the organization. In practice, ethical decisions are not always clear, and managers must make difficult decisions. Sometimes, a firm operates in a country where standards differ from our standards in Canada. Other times, a manager might have to make an ethical decision that reduces profits or leads to job losses. You might think that a large firm—because of its size—will have a harder time adopting ethical practices than a small firm. But consider toymaker giant Mattel, which has earned recognition again and again for its ethical standards. Named one of the "World's Most Ethical Companies" by the Ethisphere Institute, Mattel consistently demonstrates high standards. "Our commitment to 'play fair' is at the core of our organization's culture and is the cornerstone of our ethical compliance program," notes chairman and CEO Robert A. Eckert.

Alex Brigham, executive director of the Ethisphere Institute, sees the connection between ethics and good business. "Mattel's promotion of a sound ethical environment shines within its industry and shows a clear understanding that operating under the highest standards for business behaviour goes beyond goodwill and is intimately linked to performance and profitability," he says.[12]

Taking an ethical stand can actually cost a firm in lost revenues and other support. When Google announced a reversal of its original stance on censorship in China—by shutting down operations there and rerouting traffic to an uncensored site in Hong Kong—not only did the company lose business, it found itself standing alone on the issue. Google's decision and the consequences are discussed in the "Solving an Ethical Controversy" feature.

✔ **ASSESSMENT CHECK**

7.2.1 What is meant by a vision for the firm?

7.2.2 Why is it important for a top executive to set high ethical standards?

SOLVING AN **ETHICAL** CONTROVERSY

Google Stands Alone: When Ethics and Business Don't Mix

When Google first entered the Chinese market, the firm was criticized. Google had agreed to the censorship guidelines set out by the Chinese government, which controls the distribution of information to the Chinese public. Google made this agreement in the hope that the Chinese government would later relax its stand and allow Chinese citizens to have the same open access to Internet information as others have. But that didn't happen. In fact, the censorship seemed to grow tighter. And it also seemed that someone was using Google to identify Chinese citizens who actively disagreed with the government. So, Google decided to shut down operations in China and rerouted Chinese users to a safe site in Hong Kong. Google received praise from the Internet community for its move to Hong Kong, but received only mild support from the business world.

(continued)

SOLVING AN **ETHICAL** CONTROVERSY *(continued)*

Should the ethical standards set by a business have more weight than undemocratic laws and regulations in the countries where it operates?

PRO

1. Many multinational firms now have global ethics policies. These policies apply to each country where these firms do business, regardless of national law. Global ethics policies help managers to make consistent decisions, even if they have to lose some profits.

2. Firms and their employees must always put ethical standards ahead of practices that restrict human rights. "If any corporate executive finds that he or she is actually thinking about putting profit ahead of humanity," argues Mickey Edwards, vice-president of the international not-for-profit Aspen Institute, "it is time for that person to reflect seriously on how and when the moral compass, and one's own claim to humanity, got lost."

CON

1. Ethical standards are not always the same from one country to the next. Google's move may have a negative impact on Chinese consumers. They at least had access to some information when Google was there. "Leaving may look and feel great to those of us in the West, but exiting a market may not always have the desired impact," writes one expert.

2. Companies that are willing to work with such governments can actually use their influence with consumers to make change happen. For example, companies can create demand for their goods and services. They can also become active in the community through service projects, such as building schools.

Summary

Google's exit from China was a clear decision to some people; to others, it was not clear at all. "China is a very important market," noted one analyst. "What's the incentive for a government or another company to join with Google? There is none and that's why you haven't seen it happen." Others point out that China has a market of more than 1 billion consumers, so it is hard to know how open that market will be in the next five or 10 years. And things are getting tougher, not easier for companies wanting to operate in China. "There is a barrage of new rules and regulations for foreign companies operating in China," notes a businessperson with experience in China. "And everybody is trying to figure out what it means."

Sources: Alexei Oreskovic and Paul Eckert, "Google Finds Few Allies in China Battle," *Reuters*, March 25, 2010, accessed July 2, 2015, www.reuters.com/article/2010/03/25/us-google-china-analysis-idUSTRE6205FS20100325; Steve Pearlstein and Raju Narisetti, "Doing Right at What Cost?" *The Washington Post*, March 25, 2010, accessed July 2, 2015, http://views.washingtonpost.com/leadership/2010/03/doing_right_at_what_cost/all.html; Aron Cramer and Dunstan Allison Hope, "Google and China: When Should Business Leave on Human Rights Grounds?" *Huffington Post*, March 22, 2010, accessed July 2, 2015, www.huffingtonpost.com/aron-cramer/google-and-china-when-sho_b_508675.html.

IMPORTANCE OF PLANNING

LO 7.3 Summarize the importance of planning and the three types of planning.

Good planning can turn a vision into reality. When Reid Hoffman first got the idea for the professional social network LinkedIn, he was "very interested in this whole notion of each of us as individual professionals who are on the Internet and how that changes the way we do business, our careers, our brand identity. I realized that the world was transforming every individual into a small business." As Hoffman worked on the idea, he thought about how a professional social network could be used. He asked himself and others questions to help develop his plan. "How do you positively influence your brand on the Net? How do you assemble a team fast? Who has the expertise to guide you?" The answers to these questions and more became the plan for LinkedIn.[13]

Types of Planning

Planning can be categorized by scope, or how widely the plan affects other factors. Planning can also be categorized by breadth, or how far into the future the plan extends. For example, some plans are very broad and long range. Other plans are short range and very narrow, affecting only some parts of the organization, not the whole firm. Planning can be divided into four categories: strategic, tactical, operational, and contingency planning. Each step includes more specific information than the step before. Each planning step must also fit into an overall plan, from the mission statement (described in the next section) to objectives to specific plans. This overall plan must also

As part of its strategic planning, Home Depot has introduced mobile apps with location-based technology that provides shoppers with real-time inventory, pricing, and information about where to find products in a specific store.

include narrow, functional plans aimed at individual employees and work areas that relate to individual tasks. These plans must fit within the firm's overall plan and help it to reach objectives and achieve its mission.

Strategic Planning

The most far-reaching level of planning is *strategic planning*—the process of deciding on the primary objectives of an organization and then taking action and setting aside resources to achieve those objectives. Generally, strategic planning is done by the top executives in a company. As customers use multiple channels for retail shopping, Home Depot has implemented a strategy called "interconnected retailing." The company wants to create a seamless experience for customers—whether they browse online, open promotional emails on their smartphones, or visit brick-and-mortar locations in person.[14]

Tactical Planning

Tactical planning involves implementing the activities specified by strategic plans. Tactical plans guide the current and near-term activities required to implement overall strategies. As part of Home Depot's strategy to create a multi-channel customer shopping experience, the company has recently introduced an optimized mobile redesign, which integrates location-based technology in smartphones. The technology allows promotions to be sent to in-store shoppers while giving them access to real-time inventory, location, and pricing by store. How-to videos are offered for mobile shoppers doing research on products. The tactical plan keeps customers in contact with the retailer across multiple points of the shopping process.[15]

Operational Planning

Operational planning sets the detailed standards that help to carry out tactical plans. This activity involves choosing specific work targets and assigning employees and teams to carry out plans. Unlike strategic planning, which focuses on the organization as a whole, operational planning deals with developing and implementing tactics in specific functional areas. If customers make purchases online and pick up or return merchandise to the retailer, Home Depot will need staff at its stores to take care of these transactions. This will require additional planning on the part of management that might include additional staffing in shipping, separate customer service teams, and different delivery strategies.

Contingency Planning

Planning cannot foresee every possibility. Even the best plans may face major accidents, natural disasters, and rapid economic downturns. To handle these disruptions, many firms use *contingency planning*. This type of planning helps firms to resume operations as quickly and as smoothly as possible after a crisis. It also makes it easier for them to openly tell the public what happened. Contingency planning activity involves two components: continuing the business and communicating to the public. Many firms have management strategies that make it easier to recover from the loss of data, breaches of security, product failures, and natural disasters such as floods or fire. When a major disaster occurs or business is disrupted, a company can turn to its contingency plan. This plan usually outlines a chain of command for crisis management and assigns specific emergency functions to some or all managers and employees. But a crisis usually occurs on a smaller scale—a product delivery might get lost, a key person might be sick and unable to attend

Table 7.1 Planning at Different Management Levels

PRIMARY TYPE OF PLANNING	MANAGERIAL LEVEL	EXAMPLES
Strategic	Top management	Organizational objectives, fundamental strategies, long-term plans
Tactical	Middle management	Quarterly and semi-annual plans, departmental policies and procedures
Operational	Supervisory management	Daily and weekly plans, rules, and procedures for each department
Contingency	Primarily top management, but all levels contribute	Ongoing plans for actions and communications in an emergency

an important meeting, or the electricity might go out for a day. These events also need contingency planning. For example, when British Airways (BA) cabin crews walked off their jobs, the airline had to cancel or delay hundreds of flights. Many travellers were stranded or rerouted. Others tried to find flights on different airlines. By the second day of the strike, many BA flights were back on schedule. BA said that its contingency planning was successful. Because it sensed a possible strike, BA had retrained some on-ground staffers to work as cabin crew. It also leased planes and crew from some of its competitors. "Our contingency plans are continuing to work well . . . around the world," stated an airline spokesperson.[16]

Planning at Different Organizational Levels

Managers spend time planning every day. The total time spent and the type of planning depends on the level of the manager. As shown in **Table 7.1**, top managers, including a firm's board of directors and CEO, spend a great deal of time on long-range planning. Middle-level managers and supervisors focus on short-term, tactical, and operational planning. Employees at all levels can help themselves and their company by making plans to meet their own specific goals.

ASSESSMENT CHECK

7.3.1 Outline the planning process.

7.3.2 Describe the purpose of tactical planning.

7.3.3 Compare the types of plans made by top managers and middle managers. How does their focus differ?

THE STRATEGIC PLANNING PROCESS

LO 7.4 Describe the strategic planning process.

Strategic planning can make the difference between success and failure. Strategic planning forms the basis of many management decisions. Successful strategic planners often follow the six steps shown in **Figure 7.2**: defining a mission, assessing the organization's competitive position, setting organizational objectives, creating strategies for competitive differentiation, implementing the strategy, and assessing the results and refining the plan.

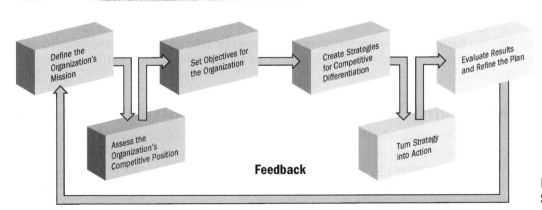

FIGURE 7.2 Steps in the Strategic Planning Process

GOING GREEN — JOHNSON & JOHNSON: CARING FOR THE WORLD

In its company statement of values and company credo, Johnson & Johnson promises, "We must maintain in good order the property we are privileged to use, protecting the environment and natural resources." Johnson & Johnson makes consumer products such as Band-Aids, Listerine, and Johnson's Baby Lotion, as well as medical devices and prescription drugs. Doing so can result in a giant carbon footprint made by manufacturing emissions, chemicals in products and processes, and a tremendous use of energy. Yet Johnson & Johnson has put strategies in place to reach its environmental goals.

The firm sets new long-term goals every five years, under its "Healthy Planet" program, for example, using direct purchase of low-impact hydro and wind power, onsite solar power and landfill gas, and purchasing renewable energy certificates. Johnson & Johnson also operates the largest fleet of hybrid and alternative fuel vehicles owned by any corporation in the world.

Part of the "Healthy Planet" program also involves being truthful about green advertising and being specific about sustainability measures. The company is the second-largest producer of solar panels in the United States, and it has received the Leadership in Energy and Environmental Design (LEED) Gold certification for its Spring House research facility in Pennsylvania.

None of these goals could be achieved without support from Johnson & Johnson's leadership. Chairman and CEO Alex Gorsky writes, "I am proud to continue to lead our legacy of commitment to sustainable ideals, born from our Credo commitments and in line with our purpose of caring for the world, one person at a time."

Questions for Critical Thinking

1. What role does the CEO's leadership play in meeting Johnson & Johnson's green goals?

2. How does the company's mission relate to sustainability?

Sources: Johnson & Johnson, accessed February 11, 2014, www.jnj.com; Michael Christel, "J&J's New Lean, Green Lab to Be Key R&D Hub," *PharmaLive*, accessed January 25, 2014, http://blog.rddirections.com; Johnson & Johnson, "To Our Shareholders," Annual Report, accessed January 25, 2014, http://files.shareholder.com/downloads/JNJ/266540474x0x815170/816798CD-60D9-4653-BB5A-50A66FD5B9E7/JNJ_2014_Annual_Report_bookmarked_.pdf; "Partner Profile," Green Power Partnership, accessed January 25, 2014, www.epa.gov.

Defining the Organization's Mission

mission statement a written description of an organization's overall business purpose and aims.

The first step in strategic planning is to translate the firm's vision into a **mission statement**. A mission statement is a written description of an organization's overall business purpose and aims. It is a statement of a firm's reason for being. It can highlight the range of its operations, the market it will serve, and how it will try to set itself apart from competitors. A mission statement guides the actions of employees.

Mission statements can be short or long:

- Starbucks: "To inspire and nurture the human spirit—one person, one cup and one neighbourhood at a time."
- Disney: "We create happiness by providing the finest in entertainment for people of all ages, everywhere."
- Nike: "To bring inspiration and innovation to every athlete in the world."
- Sony: "To experience the joy of advancing and applying technology for the benefit of the public."

A good mission statement states the firm's purpose for being in business and its overall goal. The most effective mission statements are those that people remember. The "Going Green" feature describes the mission of Johnson & Johnson, a global manufacturer of medicinal drugs and healthcare products.

Assessing Your Competitive Position

SWOT analysis SWOT is a short form for *strengths, weaknesses, opportunities,* and *threats.* By assessing all four factors one by one, a firm can then develop the best strategies for gaining a competitive advantage.

After a mission statement has been created, the next step in the planning process is to decide on the firm's current—or hoped-for—position in the marketplace. The company's founder or top managers assess the factors that can help it grow or cause it to fail. The **SWOT analysis** is a tool that is often used in this part of strategic planning. SWOT is a short form for *strengths, weaknesses, opportunities,* and *threats.* By assessing all four factors one by one, a firm can then develop the best strategies for gaining a competitive advantage. The framework for a SWOT analysis is shown in **Figure 7.3**.

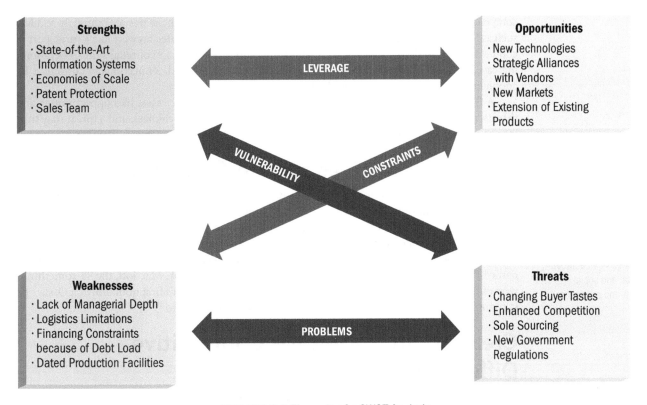

Strengths
- State-of-the-Art Information Systems
- Economies of Scale
- Patent Protection
- Sales Team

Opportunities
- New Technologies
- Strategic Alliances with Vendors
- New Markets
- Extension of Existing Products

LEVERAGE

VULNERABILITY

CONSTRAINTS

Weaknesses
- Lack of Managerial Depth
- Logistics Limitations
- Financing Constraints because of Debt Load
- Dated Production Facilities

Threats
- Changing Buyer Tastes
- Enhanced Competition
- Sole Sourcing
- New Government Regulations

PROBLEMS

FIGURE 7.3 Elements of a SWOT Analysis

To assess a firm's strengths and weaknesses, its managers may look at each functional area, such as finance, marketing, information technology, and human resources. Or they might look at the strengths and weaknesses of each office, plant, or store. Entrepreneurs may use a SWOT analysis to focus on the individual skills and experience they bring to a new business.

For Starbucks, a key strength is consumers' positive view of the company's brand. After all, it gets them to stand in line to pay premium prices for coffee. That positive view comes from Starbucks being one of the best 100 companies to work for according to *Fortune*. It also comes from its socially responsible corporate policies. The company's strategic plans have included various ways to build on Starbucks's strong brand loyalty by attaching it to new products and expanding into new markets. The expansion efforts have included the purchase of Evolution Fresh cold-pressed juices, La Boulange Café and Bakery, and Teavana, a high-end tea store found in shopping malls. Starbucks remains focused on overseas retail expansion; its online, mobile, and digital loyalty program; and its gift card business. Weaknesses include a premium-priced product in a challenging economy, saturating some markets with too many stores, and not paying attention to store design. Starbucks eventually addressed these weaknesses by lowering the price of bagged coffee, closing some stores, and redesigning others.[17]

SWOT analysis continues with an attempt to define the major opportunities and threats the firm is likely to face. Threats might include rising coffee bean prices, trademark infringements, increased competition from local cafes and lower-priced fast-food chains, and increased online shopping, particularly during holiday seasons, thus reducing foot traffic in stores. Starbucks addressed the threat of the challenging economy and lower-priced

Starbucks extends its strong brand loyalty to new products and markets. This activity is one example of the company's strategic turnaround plan.

competitors by beginning to offer less-expensive, instant coffee in its stores and through retailers such as Costco and Walmart. An additional threat includes single coffee brewers like Keurig, part of competitor Green Mountain Roasters. Opportunities include expansion of retail stores' operations, increased product offerings, expansion to emerging economies, and connections to customers by continuing to build online communities.[18]

A SWOT analysis can change. After all, strengths and weaknesses, like opportunities and threats, may shift over time. A strength may eventually become a weakness, and a threat may turn into an opportunity. But the SWOT analysis gives managers a place to start.

Setting Objectives for the Organization

objectives guideposts by which managers define the organization's desired performance in such areas as new-product development, sales, customer service, growth, environmental and social responsibility, and employee satisfaction.

The next step in planning is to develop objectives for the firm. **Objectives** set guideposts by which managers define the organization's desired performance in such areas as new-product development, sales, customer service, growth, environmental and social responsibility, and employee satisfaction. While the mission statement identifies a company's overall goals, objectives are more concrete.

As part of its growth strategy, Marriott Corporation recently opened its first boutique hotel, named *Edition*, in London. "We're trying to get some flash," says J.W. Marriott, the 80-something-year-old son of the company's founder. Arne M. Sorenson, Marriott's first nonfamily CEO, says he is committed to broadening the company's overall business portfolio.[19]

Creating Strategies for Competitive Differentiation

When managers develop a mission statement and set objectives, they help their business to move in a specific direction. But the firm also needs to decide on the strategies it will use to reach its target ahead of the competition. The basic goal of developing a strategy is *competitive differentiation*—the unique mix of a company's abilities and resources that set it apart from its competitors. A firm might differentiate itself, or set itself apart, by being the first to introduce a product. For example, Apple introduced the iPad to a global market, WestJet decided to focus on providing exceptional customer service, and Costco chose to offer bargains. Becel is the leading margarine brand in Canada. The company has a strong commitment to heart health innovation and education. The firm sets itself apart from other brands by highlighting its association with reducing cholesterol through proper diet and exercise.[20]

Implementing the Strategy

After the first four phases of the strategic planning process are complete, managers are ready to put those plans into action. The middle managers or supervisors are often the people who actually implement a strategy. But studies show that many top company officials don't want to give these managers the power to make decisions that could be helpful for the company. Companies that *are* willing to empower employees usually profit from that decision.[21]

Many firms have a strategy of cutting costs and maintaining a high level of customer service. A strategy that makes sense is to cross-train call centre representatives. When customers phone in, they don't need to be transferred to someone else if the person who answers the call has been trained to answer the most frequently asked questions. This idea may seem like an obvious strategy that won't have much effect. But research shows that cross-training can reduce the cost of running a call centre, increase customer satisfaction, and improve employee morale.[22]

Monitoring and Adapting Strategic Plans

The final step in the strategic planning process is to monitor and adapt plans when the actual performance fails to meet goals. Monitoring involves gathering feedback about performance. Managers might compare actual sales against forecast sales; compile information from surveys; listen to complaints from the customer hot line; interview employees who are involved; and review reports prepared by production, finance, marketing, or other company units. If an Internet advertisement doesn't result in enough customers or sales, managers might look at whether to continue

ASSESSMENT CHECK

7.4.1 What is the purpose of a mission statement?

7.4.2 Which of a firm's characteristics are compared in a SWOT analysis?

7.4.3 How do managers use objectives?

the advertisement, change it, or discontinue it. If a retailer sees that customers buy more jeans when they are displayed near the front door, the display area will probably stay near the door—and may even be made bigger. Managers can continue to use of such tools as SWOT analysis and forecasting to help adapt their objectives and functional plans as changes occur.

MANAGERS AS DECISION MAKERS

LO 7.5 Describe the two major types of business decisions and the steps in the decision-making process.

Managers make decisions every day. Some decisions may involve shutting down a manufacturing plant. Other decisions may deal with adding grilled cheese sandwiches to a lunch menu. **Decision making is the process of seeing a problem or opportunity, assessing possible solutions, selecting and carrying out the best-suited plan, and assessing the results.** Managers make two basic kinds of decisions: programmed decisions and nonprogrammed decisions.

decision making the process of seeing a problem or opportunity, assessing possible solutions, selecting and carrying out the best-suited plan, and assessing the results.

Programmed and Nonprogrammed Decisions

A *programmed decision* involves simple, common, and frequently occurring problems that already have solutions. For example, programmed decisions include reordering office supplies, renewing a lease, and referring to an already-decided-on discount for bulk orders. Programmed decisions are made in advance. The firm sets rules, policies, and procedures for managers and employees to follow on a routine basis. Programmed decisions save managers time and save companies money because new decisions don't have to be made each time the situation arises.

A *nonprogrammed decision* involves a complex and unique problem or opportunity and has important results for the organization. Nonprogrammed decisions include entering a new market, deleting a product from the line, or developing a new product. Apple's decision to develop and launch the iPad was a nonprogrammed decision that involved research and development, finances, technology, production, and marketing. Decisions were made about everything, from what kinds of apps and accessories the iPad would offer, to how much the new device would cost consumers.[23]

Apple made a nonprogrammed decision when it released the iPad. The decision involved a complex and unique opportunity and had important results for the company.

How Managers Make Decisions

In a simple view, decision making is choosing from two or more options, and the chosen option becomes the decision. In a larger view, decision making is a step-by-step process that helps managers to make effective choices. This process begins when someone sees a problem or an opportunity, develops possible ways of taking action, evaluates the options, selects and carries out one option, and assesses the outcome. It's important to remember that managers are *human* decision makers. Managers may follow the decision-making process shown in **Figure 7.4** step-by-step, but the outcome of their decisions depends on many factors: the quality of the information they used and their experience, creativity, and wisdom. Warren Buffett, billionaire investor and CEO of Berkshire Hathaway, empowers his managers to make decisions without his input. See the "Hit & Miss" feature for more on Buffet's management style.

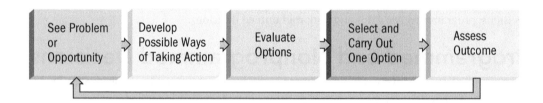

FIGURE 7.4 Steps in the Decision-Making Process

HIT & MISS

Hands-Off Approach Works for Buffett

Warren Buffett, billionaire investor and CEO of Berkshire Hathaway, is known for his hands-off management style. Buffett prefers to give his chief lieutenants the autonomy to make decisions on their own about the companies they run—even if he doesn't agree with them.

Buffett believes that giving people autonomy motivates them to do the best possible job. In his company's annual letter to shareholders, he writes, "there are managers to whom I have not talked in the last year, while there is one with whom I talk almost daily. Our trust is in people rather than process. A 'hire well, manage little' code suits both them and me."

In Berkshire Hathaway's more than 40 businesses, the CEOs are experienced and competent, and understand Buffett's management approach. Tracy Cool, a 29-year-old business-school graduate, is one of Buffett's most recent recruits and has become one of his most trusted advisors. Cool chairs four of Buffett's subsidiaries, with combined sales exceeding $4 billion and more than 10,000 employees. When Cool hires employees, she tries to hire individuals who are committed to the job, who understand Berkshire's unique culture, and who can function in a hands-off environment. She also believes that making mistakes is a great way to learn, and Buffett is very supportive of his management team. Buffett echoes Cool's comments.

He believes in hiring self-starters who love what they do. "Talented people can accomplish a whole lot," he says.

Questions for Critical Thinking

1. What are the advantages and disadvantages of a hands-off management style like Buffett's approach?

2. Buffett states there are managers to whom he has not talked with over the last year, and those with whom he talks almost daily. As one of Buffett's lieutenants, how often would you communicate with your boss? Explain your reasoning.

Sources: Company website Berkshire Hathaway, accessed January 26, 2014, http://berkshirehathaway.com; Anupreeta Das, "Tracy Britt Cool on Management Lessons from Warren Buffett," *The Wall Street Journal*, October 16, 2013, accessed July 2, 2015, http://blogs.wsj.com/moneybeat/2013/10/16/tracy-britt-cool-on-management-lessons-from-warren-buffett; Noah Buhayar and Laura Colby, "Buffett Leans on 29-Year-Old Cool to Oversee Problems," *Bloomberg Business*, January 21, 2014, accessed July 2, 2015, www.bloomberg.com/news/articles/2014-01-21/buffett-leans-on-29-year-old-cool-to-oversee-problems; Andrew Ross Sorkin, "Warren Buffett, the Delegator in Chief," *The New York Times*, April 23, 2011, accessed July 2, 2015, http://dealbook.nytimes.com/2011/04/23/warren-buffett-the-delegator-in-chief; Timothy R. Clark, "Why We Trust Warren Buffett," *Deseret News*, April 11, 2011, accessed July 2, 2015, www.deseretnews.com/article/705370243/Why-we-trust-Warren-Buffett.html?pg=allwww.deseretnews.com.

Making good decisions is never easy. A decision might hurt or help the sales of a product; it might insult or disappoint a customer or co-worker; it might affect the manager's own career or reputation. Managers' decisions can have legal and ethical effects. In Canada, *Corporate Knights Magazine* publishes an annual list of "The Best 50 Corporate Citizens." In the United States, *CRO Magazine* publishes an annual list of "The 100 Best Corporate Citizens." The companies on these lists make decisions that are ethical, environmentally responsible, fair toward employees, and accountable to local communities. These companies also provide responsible goods and services to customers and a healthy return to investors. These organizations prove that good corporate citizenship is good behaviour. The top 10 Canadian corporate citizens named one recent year were Mountain Equipment Co-op, Co-operators Group, Vancouver City Savings Credit Union, Bombardier, Tim Hortons, Mouvement des caisses Desjardins (The Desjardins Group), Teck Resources, Husky Energy, Toronto-Dominion Bank, and Cenovus Energy. The top 10 U.S. corporate citizens named were AT&T, Mattel, Bristol-Myers Squibb, Eaton, Intel, The Gap, Hasbro, Merck & Co., Campbell Soup Company, and Coca-Cola Enterprises.[24]

> ✓ **ASSESSMENT CHECK**
>
> **7.5.1** Distinguish between programmed and nonprogrammed decisions.
>
> **7.5.2** What are the steps in the decision-making process?

MANAGERS AS LEADERS

> **LO 7.6** Define *leadership*, and compare different leadership styles.

A manager must show **leadership**, by directing or inspiring others to reach goals. All great leaders do not share the same qualities, but three personal qualities are often mentioned: empathy (the ability to imagine being in someone else's position), self-awareness, and objectivity. Empathy and objectivity may seem like opposites, but they do balance each other. Many leaders share other qualities, such as courage, passion, commitment, innovation, and flexibility.

leadership the ability to direct or inspire people to reach goals.

Leadership involves the use of influence or power. This influence may come from one or more sources. One source of power is the leader's position in the company. A national sales manager has the authority to direct the activities of the sales force. Another source of power is a leader's expertise and experience. A first-line supervisor with expert machinist skills will likely be respected by employees in the machining department. Some leaders derive power from their personalities. Employees may admire a leader because they see a person who is exceptionally kind and fair, humorous, energetic, or enthusiastic. Admiration, inspiration, and motivation are especially important during difficult economic times or when a leader needs to make tough decisions for the company, as was the case at General Motors. See the accompanying "Hit & Miss" feature for an introduction to Mary Barra, the company's first female CEO.

When Doug Conant, former CEO at Campbell Soup Company, took over the company in 2001, the company was decidedly a little boring. Instead of being filled with new ideas, the firm wasn't thinking about doing anything new. Conant looked around the company. It produces one of the best-known brands in the world. Conant was frustrated. "The microwave was invented in 1947, but it took us until 2002 to put together a microwaveable soup pack," he told the company's researchers, marketers, and managers. Conant got to work on updating the world's largest soup company. He cut all products that were not number one or number

Doug Conant, Campbell Soup Company's former CEO, believed that action was the best way to show leadership.

(HIT) & MISS

GM's First Female CEO Faces Challenges and Opportunities

Mary Barra, GM's first female CEO, knows cars. She has worked for the Detroit automaker for more than 30 years in a variety of positions. She began her GM career as an intern while in college. After graduation, Barra's first job was a plant engineer at the assembly factory in Pontiac, Michigan.

Before being tapped for the CEO post, Barra spent time in several different divisions of the company, including global manufacturing, purchasing, supply chain management, and human resources. Most recently, she headed up the $15 billion global product development group, where she and her team were responsible for the design and engineering of GM vehicles worldwide. *Motor Trend Magazine* recently named the Cadillac CTS Car of the Year, and *Consumer Reports* named the Chevy Impala the best sedan and the Silverado the best pickup truck.

In her new position as CEO, Barra has already faced several challenges, including a safety recall of millions of GM vehicles caused by a faulty ignition switch that resulted in multiple deaths. She appeared before a congressional committee to discuss the recall, authorized an in-depth internal investigation by a former federal prosecutor, and subsequently fired 15 employees for misconduct and incompetence.

Despite the recall and associated issues, Barra continues to see opportunities for GM, particularly in Asia. Of the 2.4 million cars sold in GM's most recent financial quarter, more than 30 percent were sold in China. She plans to continue the company's global expansion with sales of the Chevrolet and Cadillac brands and is optimistic that new product launches will keep the auto giant on a successful business path.

Questions for Critical Thinking

1. How do Barra's previous job experiences at GM help her in her role as the company's CEO?

2. What challenges will Barra encounter as she guides the company's global expansion into other markets?

Sources: Kyle Stock, "GM's Mary Barra Fires 15, Says More Recalls Are Coming," *Bloomberg Business*, June 6, 2014, accessed July 2, 2015, www.bloomberg.com/bw/articles/2014-06-05/gms-mary-barra-fires-15-says-more-recalls-are-coming; Chris Isidore and Katie Lobosco, "GM CEO Barra: 'I Am Deeply Sorry,'" *CNN Money*, April 1, 2014, accessed July 5, 2015, http://money.cnn.com/2014/04/01/news/companies/barra-congress-testimony; Joann Muller, "Exclusive Q&A: GM CEO Mary Barra on Crisis Management, Culture Change and the Future of GM," *Forbes*, May 29, 2014, accessed July 2, 2015, www.forbes.com/sites/joannmuller/2014/05/29/exclusive-qa-gm-ceo-mary-barra-on-crisis-management-culture-change-and-the-future-of-gm; General Motors company website, www.gm.com, accessed February 11, 2014; Sherri Welch, "By Naming Mary Barra CEO, GM Sends Strong Message about Talent, Opportunity," *Crain's Detroit Business*, December 10, 2013, accessed July 2, 2015, www.crainsdetroit.com/article/20131210/NEWS/131219986/analysis-by-naming-mary-barra-ceo-gm-sends-strong-message-about; Tim Higgins, "GM CEO Barra Aims to Accelerate Strategies Set Under Akerson," *Bloomberg Business*, January 23, 2014, accessed July 2, 2015, www.bloomberg.com/news/articles/2014-01-23/gm-s-barra-seeks-to-accelerate-strategy-set-under-akerson; Tim Higgins and Brian Urstadt, "Exclusive: The Inside Story of GM's Comeback and Mary Barra's Rise," *Bloomberg Business*, December 12, 2013, accessed July 2, 2015, www.bloomberg.com/bw/articles/2013-12-12/exclusive-the-inside-story-of-gms-comeback-and-mary-barras-rise.

With more than 30 years of experience at GM, Mary Barra recently became the company's first female CEO.

two in their categories. He poured resources into developing products that offered value, nutrition, and convenience. And he engineered a new focus on two of the world's largest soup-eating nations: China and Russia. Conant believed that action was the best demonstration of leadership. "You can't talk your way out of something you behaved your way into," he says.[25]

Leadership Styles

A person's leadership style depends on how that person uses power to lead others. Leadership styles range from autocratic leadership at one extreme to free-rein leadership at the other extreme. *Autocratic leadership* is centred on the boss. Autocratic leaders make decisions on their own without consulting employees. They make decisions, communicate the decisions to employees, and expect the decisions to be carried out right away.

Democratic leadership includes employees in the decision-making process. This leadership style centres on employees' contributions. Democratic leaders assign projects, ask employees for suggestions, and encourage participation. An important outcome of democratic leadership in business is the concept of

Stan Honda/AFP/Getty Images

empowerment, where employees share authority, responsibility, and decision making with their managers.

At the opposite extreme from autocratic leadership is *free-rein leadership*. Free-rein leaders believe in minimal supervision. They allow employees to make most of their own decisions. Free-rein leaders communicate with employees frequently. For its first decade in business, Google was proud of its free-rein leadership style. Engineers were encouraged to pursue any and all ideas, teams formed or disbanded on their own, and employees spent as much or as little time as they wanted to on any given project. But then the firm entered its second decade. Not every innovation was worth pursuing—and some valuable ideas were getting lost. CEO Eric Schmidt noted, "We were concerned that some of the biggest ideas were getting squashed." So the firm set up a process for reviewing new project ideas to focus on those ideas most likely to succeed.[26]

> **empowerment** giving employees shared authority, responsibility, and decision making with their managers.

Which Leadership Style Is Best?

No single leadership style is right for every firm in every situation. Leadership styles sometimes need to be changed for a company to grow. That was the situation for Google. In a crisis, an autocratic leadership style might save the company—and sometimes the lives of customers and employees. That's what happened when US Airways flight 1549 was forced to land in the Hudson River in New York. Quick, autocratic decisions made by pilot Chesley Sullenberger meant that everyone on the flight survived. But US Airways management on the ground used a democratic style of leadership: managers at many levels were empowered to take actions to help the passengers and their families. For example, one executive arrived on the scene with a bag of emergency cash for passengers and credit cards for employees so they could purchase medicines, food, or anything else they needed.[27] Some companies know which leadership style works best for their employees, customers, and business conditions. Those companies are most likely to choose the best leaders for their needs.

> ✔ **ASSESSMENT CHECK**
>
> **7.6.1** How is *leadership* defined?
>
> **7.6.2** Identify the styles of leadership as they range from the most to the least amount of employee participation.

CORPORATE CULTURE

>  **LO 7.7** Discuss the meaning and importance of corporate culture.

An organization's **corporate culture** is its collection of principles, beliefs, and values. The corporate culture is influenced by the leadership style of its managers, the way the firm communicates, and the overall work environment. A corporate culture is typically shaped by the leaders who founded and developed the company and by the leaders who were appointed since the founders left. For example, look at Google. It has grown by leaps and bounds since its launch. The firm tries to continue the culture of innovation, creativity, and flexibility that its co-founders, Larry Page and Sergey Brin, promoted from the beginning. Google now has offices around the world, staffed by thousands of workers who speak many different languages. "We are aggressively inclusive in our hiring, and we favour ability over experience," states the website. "The result is a team that reflects the global audience Google serves. When not at work, Googlers pursue interests from cross-country cycling to wine tasting, from flying to Frisbee."[28]

> **corporate culture** an organization's collection of principles, beliefs, and values.

Managers sometimes use symbols, rituals, ceremonies, and stories to strengthen a corporate culture. The corporate culture at the Walt Disney Company is almost as famous as the Disney characters themselves. In fact, every Disney employee is known as a cast member. All new employees attend training seminars to learn the language, customs, traditions, stories, product lines—everything about the Disney culture and its original founder, Walt Disney.[29]

Corporate cultures can be very strong and lasting. But sometimes they need to change to meet new demands in the business world. A firm that is filled with tradition and bureaucracy might need to shift to a leaner, more flexible culture to respond to shifts in technology or customer

(HIT)& MISS

WestJet Airlines: Most Admired Corporate Culture in Canada

WestJet Airlines was named a J.D. Power 2011 Customer Service champion. The company was also inducted into the Corporate Cultures Hall of Fame after being named one of Canada's Most Admired Corporate Cultures every year from 2005 to 2010. The airline is well known for its reasonable fares, cheerful service, convenient schedules, and genuine interest in its passengers. WestJet is both successful and profitable. It is the business model that other service-oriented businesses study to learn how WestJet sets itself apart through its superior customer service.

WestJet's strategic plan is built on four pillars for long-term success:

- People and Culture: Investing in and fostering the growth, development, and commitment of our people.

- Guest Experience: Consistently and continuously providing an amazing guest experience.

- Revenue and Growth: Achieving an average annual compound growth rate in available seat miles of between four and seven per cent.

- Costs: Achieving a targeted, sustainable profit margin that will be number one among North American airlines.

Together, these pillars describe the corporate focus and culture that directs the firm. WestJet is also known to have a corporate culture filled with humour and energy that spills over to its customers. When you fly WestJet, the hosts tell jokes over the public address system before giving the formal instructions about flight safety. The jokes help to get passengers' attention and create a more relaxed atmosphere for the flight. Employees are empowered and convey the culture of the company to customers. The idea is that if the company's 8,000 employees are happy, they will want to make sure their customers are happy, too. This simple strategy has been very effective. There's another reason employees feel differently about the company they work for. About 85 percent of eligible employees own shares of the company through an employee share purchase plan.

Questions for Critical Thinking

1. How would you describe the principles, beliefs, and values at WestJet?

2. How important is employee ownership to creating and maintaining the corporate culture?

Sources: WestJet website, "About WestJet," accessed January 23, 2012, www.westjet.com/guest/en/about/index.shtml; WestJet, Fact Sheet, accessed January 23, 2012, www.westjet.com/pdf/investorMedia/investorFactSheet.pdf; Canada Newswire, "WestJet Named to Corporate Culture Hall of Fame," February 1, 2010, accessed July 2, 2015, www.newswire.ca/en/story/692931/westjet-named-to-corporate-culture-hall-of-fame; "WestJet Culture Seen as Tops in Country," *Calgary Herald*, October 11, 2006, accessed January 12, 2012, www.canada.com/calgaryherald/news/calgarybusiness/story.html?id=1cec87b5-bbab-4e1 e-a63a-e64f91 b15fa6&k=24339.

✓ ASSESSMENT CHECK

7.7.1 What is the relationship between leadership style and corporate culture?

7.7.2 What is a strong corporate culture?

LO 7.8 Identify the five major forms of departmentalization and the four main types of organization structures.

organization a structured group of people working together to achieve common goals.

demands. A firm that grows quickly—like Google—usually needs to make some adjustments in its culture to make room for more customers and more employees.

In an organization with a strong culture, everyone knows and supports the same principles, beliefs, and values. That's the culture at WestJet Airlines, described in the "Hit & Miss" feature. To reach its goals, a business must also provide structure, which results from the management function of organizing.

ORGANIZATIONAL STRUCTURES

An **organization** is a structured group of people working together to achieve common goals. An organization features three key elements: human interaction, goal-directed activities, and structure. The organizing process is mostly led by managers. It should result in an overall structure that makes it easier for individuals and departments to work together to achieve company goals.

The steps involved in the organizing process are shown in **Figure 7.5**. Managers first decide on the specific activities needed to carry out plans and achieve goals. Next, they group these work activities into a structure that makes sense. Then, they assign work to specific employees and give them the resources they need. Managers coordinate the work of different groups and employees

Imp.

| 1. Decide on the Specific Work Activities Needed to Carry Out Plans and Achieve Objectives | → | 2. Group All Work Activities into a Pattern or Structure that Makes Sense | → | 3. Assign Activities to Specific Employees and Give Them the Resources They Need | → | 4. Coordinate the Activities of Different Groups and Individuals | → | 5. Evaluate the Results of the Organizing Process |

FIGURE 7.5 Steps in the Organizing Process

within the firm. Finally, they evaluate the results of the organizing process to ensure effective and efficient progress toward planned goals. Evaluation sometimes results in changes to the way work is organized.

Many factors can affect the results of organizing. The list includes a firm's goals and competitive strategy, the type of product it offers, the way it uses technology to accomplish work, and its size. Small firms typically create very simple structures. For example, the owner of a dry-cleaning business is often the top manager, who hires several employees to process orders, clean the clothing, and make deliveries. The owner purchases supplies such as detergents and hangers, hires and trains employees, coordinates employees' work, prepares advertisements for the local newspaper, and keeps the accounting records.

As a company grows, its structure becomes more complex. Increased size often means specialization and growing numbers of employees. A larger firm may need to hire many salespeople and a sales manager to direct and coordinate their work, or it may need to organize an accounting department.

An effective structure is clear and easy to understand: employees know what they are expected to do, and they know whom they report to. They also know how their jobs help to achieve the company's mission and overall strategic plan. An *organization chart* can help people to understand the structure of a firm. **Figure 7.6** shows a sample organization chart.

Not-for-profit organizations also organize themselves using formal structures. These structures help them to function efficiently and to carry out their goals. The organizational structure of

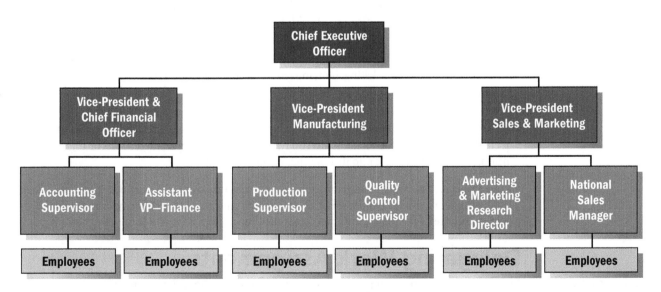

FIGURE 7.6 Sample Organization Chart

not-for-profits, such as the Salvation Army and the Alberta Society for Prevention of Cruelty to Animals, sometimes includes a mix of paid staff and volunteers.

Departmentalization

departmentalization
the process of dividing work activities into units within the organization.

Departmentalization is the process of dividing work activities into units within the organization. In this arrangement, employees specialize in certain jobs—such as marketing, finance, or design. Depending on the size of the firm, usually an executive heads the department, followed by middle-level managers and supervisors. The five major forms of departmentalization divide work by product, geographical area, customer, function, and process.

These familiar office products represent only one of 3M Corporation's many product lines. Because 3M serves a broad range of customers, it is organized on the basis of customer departmentalization.

© R. Alcorn, photographed for JohnWiley & Sons

- *Product departmentalization.* This approach organizes work units based on the goods and services a company offers. Activision Blizzard Inc. recently restructured its organization by product. The videogame publisher is now divided into four divisions: "Call of Duty," a military game; internally owned games, such as "Guitar Hero" and "Tony Hawk"; licensed properties; and Blizzard Entertainment, maker of the online game "World of Warcraft."[30]

- *Geographical departmentalization.* This form organizes units by geographical regions within a country or, for a multinational firm, by region throughout the world. Enterprise Rent-A-Car is organized by geography, staffing 7,000 rental locations in the United States, Canada, Germany, Ireland, and England.[31]

- *Customer departmentalization.* Customer departmentalization might be used by a firm that offers a variety of goods and services for different types of customers. For example, 3M's wide range of products is divided among six business units: consumer and office; display and graphics; electro and communications; healthcare; industrial and transportation; and safety, security, and protection services.[32]

- *Functional departmentalization.* Some firms organize work units according to business functions, such as finance, marketing, human resources, and production. An advertising agency may create departments for creative personnel (for example, copywriters), media buyers, and account executives.

- *Process departmentalization.* Some goods and services require multiple work processes to complete their production. A manufacturer may set up separate departments for cutting material, heat-treating it, forming it into its final shape, and painting it.

As **Figure 7.7** shows, a single company may use several forms of departmentalization. When deciding on a form of departmentalization, managers take into account the type of product they produce, the size of their company, their customer base, and the locations of their customers.

Delegating Work Assignments

delegation the managerial process of assigning work to employees.

Managers assign work to employees, a process called **delegation**. For example, employees might be assigned to answer customer calls, scoop ice cream, process returns, make deliveries, open or close a store, cook or serve food, contribute to new-product design, calculate a return on investment,

FIGURE 7.7 Different Forms of Departmentalization within One Company

or any of thousands of other tasks. Just as important as the tasks themselves, employees are usually given some authority to make decisions.

Companies like Zappos, the online shoe retailer, give their workers the power to make decisions to better serve their customers. The result is generally happier employees and more satisfied customers.[33] As employees receive more power to make decisions, they also must be accountable for their actions and decisions—that is, they receive credit when things go well and must accept responsibility when things don't go well. Managers also must decide on the best way to delegate responsibilities when employees belong to different age groups, as discussed in the "Career Kickstart" feature.

CAREER **KICKSTART**

Managing a Multigenerational Workforce

Today's firms employ workers who span a wide range of ages. Management experts warn against stereotyping, or treating people on the basis of an overly simple idea of their characteristics or qualities. The experts do suggest making an effort to understand each group. They suggest taking steps to open up communications so that everyone in the workforce works well together. Baby boomers, those people born between 1946 and 1964, tend to be competitive. Most of them believe that younger employees should work their way up the company ladder. Gen-Xers, born between 1965 and 1977, are more skeptical, independent thinkers. Gen-Yers—also called the Millennials—were born in 1978 or later. They prefer teamwork, feedback, and technology.

Managers can use the following tips to effectively assign work to employees in these groups:

- Offer—and encourage—mentoring, an informal relationship between younger and older employees to guide and advise younger employees. Communication and support that crosses age groups can increase understanding among employees.

- Understand different learning styles and work styles, and make workplace changes to help employees who learn and work differently.

- Involve employees in the workplace through training, education, and career development opportunities.

- Discard strict routines for those who work best without them.

- Use different forms of communication. Older employees may prefer chatting on the phone or in person. Millennials might prefer emails, text messages, or social networking.

- Give everyone an equal voice. Everyone wants to be heard and understood. Offer opportunities for all employees to voice their opinions.

Sources: Sally Kane, "The Multigenerational Workforce," About.com, accessed March 29, 2010, http://legalcareers.about.com/od/practicetips/a/multigeneration.htm; "How to Manage Different Generations," *Wall Street Journal*, accessed March 29, 2010, http://guides.wsj .com/management/managing-your-people/how-to-manage-different-generations; Tammy Erickson, "Finally, Gen X Takes Over," *Harvard Business Review*, January 12, 2009, accessed March 29, 2010, https://hbr.org/2009/01/across-the-ages-in-2009.

Span of Management

The *span of management*, or span of control, is the number of employees a manager supervises. These employees are often referred to as *direct reports*. First-line managers often have the widest spans of management because they monitor the work of many employees. The span of management varies, depending on many factors, including the type of work performed and employees' training. In recent years, a growing trend has brought wider spans of control. Many companies have reduced their layers of management to flatten their organizational structures. This process usually increases employees' decision-making responsibility.

Centralization and Decentralization

How widely should managers assign decision-making authority throughout an organization? A company that emphasizes *centralization* keeps decision making at the top of the management hierarchy. A company that emphasizes *decentralization* shifts decision making to lower levels. A trend toward decentralization has pushed decision making down to operating employees in many companies. Firms decentralize because they believe the change will improve their service to customers. For example, a hotel's front desk clerk is better able to help a guest who needs a crib or a wake-up call than the hotel's general manager.

Types of Organization Structures

The four basic types of organization structures are line, line-and-staff, committee, and matrix. Some companies use one type of structure, but most use a mix of two or more types.

Line Organizations

The oldest and simplest organization structure is a *line organization*. It sets up a direct flow of authority from the chief executive to the employees. The line organization defines a simple, clear *chain of command*—a hierarchy of managers and workers. Everyone knows who is in charge, and decisions can be made quickly. This structure is very effective in a crisis situation. But a line organization also has its downsides. Each manager has complete responsibility for a range of activities. But in a medium-sized or large organization, the manager can't be an expert in all of the tasks. In a small organization, such as a local hair salon or a dentist's office, a line organization is probably the most efficient way to run the business.

Line-and-Staff Organizations

A *line-and-staff organization* combines the direct flow of authority of a line organization with staff departments that support the line departments. Line departments help to make decisions that affect the firm's core operations. Staff departments lend specialized technical support. **Figure 7.8** shows a line-and-staff organization. Accounting, engineering, and human resources are staff departments. They support the line authority that extends from the plant manager to the production manager and supervisors.

A line manager and a staff manager have different authority relationships. A line manager forms part of the primary line of authority that flows throughout the organization. Line managers work directly with the production, financing, or marketing departments—the areas that are needed to produce and sell goods and services. A staff manager provides information, advice, or technical assistance to help the line managers. Staff managers do not have authority to give orders outside their own departments or to assign actions to the line managers.

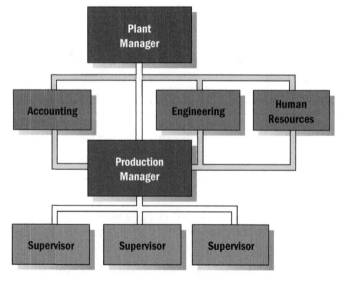

— Line Relationships
▭ Staff Relationships

FIGURE 7.8 Line-and-Staff Organization

The line-and-staff organization is common in mid-size and large organizations. It is an effective structure because it combines the line organization's rapid decision making and direct communication with the expert knowledge of the staff departments.

Committee Organizations

A *committee organization* is a structure that places authority and responsibility in a group of individuals, not a manager. This model often appears as part of a regular line-and-staff structure.

Committees also work in areas such as new-product development. A new-product committee may include managers from accounting, engineering, finance, manufacturing, marketing, and technical research. Having representatives from all areas involved in creating and marketing products is a good idea. It usually improves both the planning process and employee morale because decisions reflect very different viewpoints.

Committees tend to act slowly and make conservative, or safe, decisions. They may make decisions by compromising, or by coming to an agreement with conflicting interests, instead of choosing the best alternative. The definition of a camel as "a racehorse designed by committee" provides a fitting description of the imperfections of committee decisions.

Matrix Organizations

Some organizations use a matrix or product management design to make their structures more suitable to their business. The *matrix structure* links employees from different parts of the organization who work together on specific projects. **Figure 7.9** shows a matrix structure. A project manager assembles a group of employees from different functional areas. The employees keep their ties to the line-and-staff structure, as shown by the vertical white lines. As the horizontal gold lines show, employees are also members of project teams. When the project is completed, employees return to their "regular" jobs.

[Handwritten annotations in right margin:]

[Advantages]
- Flexibility in adapting to changes
- Focus on major problems / products

Disadvantages.
- Integrating skills of many specialists into a coordinated team
- Regular workloads.

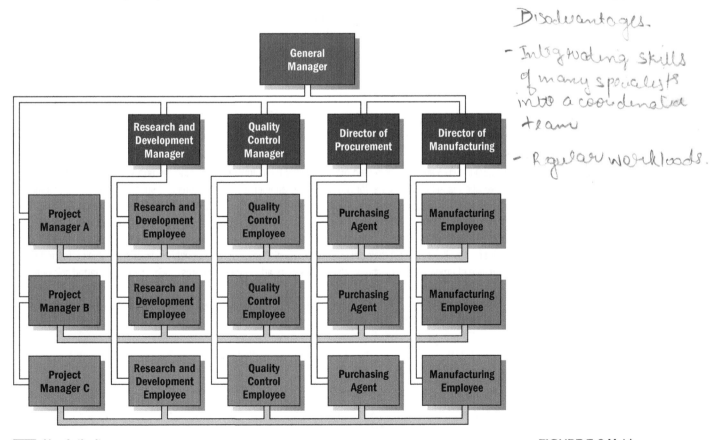

— Line Authority
═══ Project Authority

FIGURE 7.9 Matrix Organizations

In the matrix structure, each employee reports to two managers: one line manager and one project manager. Employees who are working on a special project receive instructions from the project manager (horizontal authority), but they continue as employees in their permanent functional departments (vertical authority). The term *matrix* refers to the intersecting grid of horizontal and vertical lines of authority.

The matrix structure is popular at high-technology and multinational corporations, and in hospitals and consulting firms. Dow Chemical and Procter & Gamble have both used matrix structures. The major upsides of the matrix structure come from its flexibility to adapt quickly to rapid changes in the environment. It also focuses resources on major problems or products. The matrix structure also provides an outlet for employees' creativity and initiative. But it challenges project managers to take the skills of specialists from many departments and form a coordinated team. Team members' permanent functional managers must adjust their employees' regular workloads.

The matrix structure is most effective when company leaders give project managers the authority to use whatever resources are available to achieve the project's objectives. Good project managers know how to make the project goals clear and how to keep team members focused. A firm that truly adopts the matrix structure will also encourage a project culture by making sure staffing is adequate, the workload is reasonable, and other company resources are available to project managers.[34]

✔ ASSESSMENT CHECK

7.8.1 What is the purpose of an organization chart?

7.8.2 What are the five major forms of departmentalization?

7.8.3 What does *span of management* mean?

WHAT'S AHEAD

In the next chapter, we focus on the importance of people in shaping the growth and profitability of the organization. We examine how firms recruit, select, train, evaluate, and compensate employees as they try to attract, retain, and motivate a high-quality workforce. The concept of motivation is examined, and we will discuss how managers apply theories of motivation in the modern workplace. The next chapter also looks at the important topic of labour-management relations.

RETURN TO INSIDE BUSINESS

Can John S. Chen Save BlackBerry?

John S. Chen replaced Thorsten Heins as CEO in 2013 and has redirected management's focus toward developing the firm's software and other proprietary technology. Many observers believe Chen is setting the stage for a merger with another technology company such as Microsoft. BlackBerry remains synonymous with leading security software in wireless communications. When first introduced in 1998, the BlackBerry was a hit with mobile business people who liked the value-added feature of a pager they could securely use to instantly receive, read, and reply to email from their office computers. Laptops were larger, more expensive, and not as easy to connect for communicating with others. The BlackBerry is small, costs under $500, and allows business people to receive their email while away from their office. Their connection fees were reasonably inexpensive, which attracted the business market that believed in the importance of timely communications. When BlackBerry added more features, such as voice, it started competing with cellphones.

As we all know now, Apple's iPhone and iPad offered consumers even more functions. Some people questioned the firm's leadership and management decision making. Today, many are watching to see if John Chen can revitalize the company in a global market where many are concerned with secure communications.

QUESTIONS FOR CRITICAL THINKING

1. Is top management responsible for the decline of BlackBerry share value?

2. Can a restructuring of management alone return the firm to a leadership position?

SUMMARY OF LEARNING OBJECTIVES

LO 7.1 Describe *management*.

Management is the process of achieving organizational goals through people and other resources. The management hierarchy usually has three levels: top managers who provide overall direction for company activities, middle managers who carry out the strategies of top managers and direct the activities of supervisors, and supervisors who deal directly with workers. The three basic managerial skills are technical, human or interpersonal, and conceptual. The four basic managerial functions are planning, organizing, directing, and controlling.

✔ ASSESSMENT CHECK ANSWERS

7.1.1 What is management? Management is the process of achieving organizational goals through people and other resources. The manager's job is to combine human and technical resources in the best way possible to achieve the company's goals.

7.1.2 Describe the differences in the jobs of top managers, middle managers, and supervisory managers. Top managers develop long-range plans, set a direction for their organization, and inspire all employees to achieve the company's vision. Middle managers focus their attention on specific operations, products, or customers. They develop plans and procedures to carry out the firm's strategic plans. Supervisory managers deal directly with nonmanagerial employees who produce and sell the firm's goods and services. These managers are responsible for carrying out the plans developed by middle managers and for motivating workers to accomplish immediate goals.

7.1.3 What is the relationship between the manager's planning and controlling functions? Controlling is assessing an organization's performance to decide whether it is achieving its goals. The basic purpose of controlling is to assess the success of the planning function. Controlling also provides feedback for future rounds of planning.

LO 7.2 Explain the role of vision and ethical standards in business success.

Vision is the founder's ability to perceive marketplace needs and what an organization must do to satisfy them. Vision helps to clarify a firm's purpose and the actions it can take to make the most of opportunities. High ethical standards can help build success for a firm through job satisfaction and customer loyalty.

✔ ASSESSMENT CHECK ANSWERS

7.2.1 What is meant by a vision for the firm? A vision is a focus for a firm's actions. Vision helps to direct the company toward opportunities and sets it apart from its competitors.

7.2.2 Why is it important for a top executive to set high ethical standards? High ethical standards often result in a stable workforce, job satisfaction, and customer loyalty.

LO 7.3 Summarize the importance of planning and the three types of planning.

The planning process identifies organizational goals and develops the actions needed to reach those goals. Planning helps a company to turn its vision into action. It also helps it to take advantage of opportunities and to avoid costly mistakes. Strategic planning is a far-reaching process. It takes a broad view of the world to decide on the organization's long-range focus and activities. Tactical planning focuses on the current and short-range activities required to carry out the organization's strategies. Operational planning sets the standards and work targets for functional areas such as production, human resources, and marketing.

✔ ASSESSMENT CHECK ANSWERS

7.3.1 Outline the planning process. Some plans are very broad and long range. These plans focus on the main organizational goals. Other plans are more detailed and show how particular goals will be met. Each planning step—from the mission statement to objectives to specific plans—must fit into an overall plan.

7.3.2 Describe the purpose of tactical planning. The purpose of tactical planning is to decide which short-term activities should be carried out to meet the firm's overall strategy.

7.3.3 Compare the types of plans made by top managers and middle managers. How does their focus differ? Top managers focus on long-range, strategic plans. In contrast, middle-level managers and supervisors focus on short-term, tactical planning.

LO 7.4 Describe the strategic planning process.

The first step in strategic planning is to translate the firm's vision into a mission statement that describes the firm's overall purpose and aims. Next, planners assess the firm's current competitive position using tools such as a SWOT analysis. Managers then set specific objectives. The next step is to develop strategies for reaching objectives that will differentiate the firm, or set it apart, from its competitors. Managers then develop an action plan. This plan outlines the specific ways for carrying out the strategy. Finally, the results achieved by the plan are assessed, and the plan is adjusted as needed.

 **ASSESSMENT CHECK ANSWERS**

7.4.1 What is the purpose of a mission statement? A mission statement is a public description of a firm's purpose, the reason it exists, the customers it will serve, and the way it is different from competitors. A mission statement guides the actions of company managers and employees.

7.4.2 Which of a firm's characteristics are compared in a SWOT analysis? A SWOT analysis assesses a firm's strengths, weaknesses, opportunities, and threats, compared with its competitors. A SWOT analysis helps to decide on a firm's competitive position in the marketplace.

7.4.3 How do managers use objectives? Objectives result from the firm's mission statement. They are used to set performance levels in areas such as profitability, customer service, and employee satisfaction.

LO 7.5 Describe the two major types of business decisions and the steps in the decision-making process.

A programmed decision applies a company rule or policy to solve a frequently occurring problem. A nonprogrammed decision responds to a complex and unique problem that has important results for the organization. The five-step approach to decision making includes seeing a problem or opportunity, developing possible ways of taking action, evaluating the options, selecting and carrying out one option, and assessing the outcome.

 **ASSESSMENT CHECK ANSWERS**

7.5.1 Distinguish between programmed and nonprogrammed decisions. Programmed decisions involve simple problems that occur frequently, such as reordering office supplies. The firm usually sets policies and procedures for dealing with these problems to make the process easier. Nonprogrammed decisions require more individual evaluation. For example, buying real estate or equipment is a nonprogrammed decision that needs some research.

7.5.2 What are the steps in the decision-making process? The decision-making steps are seeing a problem or opportunity, developing possible ways of taking action, evaluating the options, selecting and carrying out one option, and assessing the outcome.

LO 7.6 Define *leadership,* and compare different leadership styles.

Leadership is the ability to direct or inspire others to reach goals. The basic leadership styles are autocratic, democratic, and free-rein leadership. The best leadership style depends on three elements: the leader, the followers, and the situation.

ASSESSMENT CHECK ANSWERS

7.6.1 How is *leadership* defined? Leadership means the ability to direct or inspire people to reach organizational goals. Effective leaders share several personal qualities, such as empathy, self-awareness, and objectivity in dealing with others. Leaders also use the power of their jobs, expertise, and experience to influence others.

7.6.2 Identify the styles of leadership as they range from the least to the most amount of employee participation. At one extreme, autocratic leaders make decisions on their own without consulting employees. At the opposite extreme, free-rein leaders leave most decisions to their employees. In the middle are democratic leaders who ask employees for suggestions and encourage participation.

LO 7.7 Discuss the meaning and importance of corporate culture.

Corporate culture refers to an organization's principles, beliefs, and values. It is typically shaped by a firm's founder and is communicated to all employees through formal programs, such as training, rituals, and ceremonies, and through informal discussions among employees. Corporate culture can influence a firm's success by giving it a competitive advantage.

ASSESSMENT CHECK ANSWERS

7.7.1 What is the relationship between leadership style and corporate culture? The best leadership style to adopt often depends on the organization's corporate culture, its system of principles, beliefs, and values. Corporate culture is influenced by managers' philosophies, the firm's communications networks, its workplace environments, and its practices.

7.7.2 What is a strong corporate culture? A corporate culture is an organization's collection of principles, beliefs, and values. In an organization with a strong culture, everyone knows and supports the same principles, beliefs, and values.

LO 7.8 Identify the five major forms of departmentalization and the four main types of organization structures.

The division of work activities into units within the organization is called *departmentalization*. The units may be based on products, geographical locations, customers, functions, or processes. Most firms implement one or more of four organization structures: line, line-and-staff, committee, and matrix structures.

✓ ASSESSMENT CHECK ANSWERS

7.8.1 What is the purpose of an organization chart? An organization chart is a visual diagram of a firm's structure that shows job positions, job functions, and the reporting hierarchy.

7.8.2 What are the five major forms of departmentalization? Product departmentalization organizes units by the goods and services a company offers. Geographical departmentalization organizes units by geographical regions. Customer departmentalization organizes units by different types of customers. Functional departmentalization organizes units by business functions such as finance, marketing, human resources, and production. Process departmentalization organizes units by the steps or work processes needed to complete production or provide a service.

7.8.3 What does *span of management* mean? The span of management, or span of control, is the number of employees a manager supervises.

BUSINESS TERMS YOU NEED TO KNOW

controlling 183

corporate culture 195

decision making 191

delegation 198

departmentalization 198

directing 183

empowerment 195

leadership 193

management 180

mission statement 188

objectives 190

organization 196

organizing 183

planning 182

SWOT analysis 188

vision 183

REVIEW QUESTIONS

1. What are the three levels of management hierarchy? Which management skills are the most important at each level? Why?

2. Identify the four basic managerial functions. Suppose you were hired to be the manager of a local restaurant. Which managerial functions would the biggest part of your job? Why?

3. Describe the link between a company's vision and its ethical standards. Why is it important for top management to communicate a clear vision and ethical standards for a company?

4. Identify the four types of planning. Suppose you planned a barbecue with your friends. When you woke up on the morning of the party, it was pouring rain. What type of planning would help you to deal with the rain? What are your options for the barbecue?

5. What is the link between a firm's vision and its mission statement? Think about your own dream of a career as an entrepreneur. What is your vision? What might be your mission statement?

6. Define *objectives*. Outline objectives you might have for your own college or university education and your career. How can an outline help you carry out your own career strategy?

7. Identify each of the following as a programmed or nonprogrammed decision:

   a. Reordering printer cartridges

   b. Selecting a cellphone provider

   c. Buying your favourite toothpaste or shampoo

   d. Selecting a college or university to attend

   e. Filling your car with gasoline

8. From what sources does a leader gain power? Which leadership style works best for a manager whose firm is making cost-cutting decisions? Why?

9. Why is a strong corporate culture important to a company's success? How is the corporate culture linked to leadership style?

10. Which type of organization structure provides the most flexibility to respond to changes in the marketplace and to be innovative? What are the downsides of this structure?

PROJECTS AND TEAMWORK APPLICATIONS

1. Imagine that you've been hired as a supervisor at a bakery shop called Claire's Cakes. The founder, Claire, wants to increase production, expand deliveries, and eventually open several more shops. Create a job description for yourself. Include the managerial functions and the skills you'll need to be successful.

2. On your own or with a classmate, write a mission statement for Claire's Cakes. Think about the type of company it is, the products it offers customers (cakes for special occasions), and the type of growth it is planning.

3. Contingency planning requires a combination of looking ahead and being adaptable. Josh James is the founder of Omniture, the Web analytics firm he recently sold to Adobe. James recalls the importance of being adaptable when his company was having difficulties. "There were times when I lay down on the floor at night, close to crying. Then my wife would come over and kick me and say, 'Get up and figure it out.'"[35] Research the news headlines for situations that required contingency planning. Report to the class what the challenge was and how the managers handled it. Discuss whether the planning was effective or successful.

4. Identify a person you think is a good leader. It can be someone you know personally or a public figure. Describe the personal qualities that are most important in making this person an effective leader. Would this person's leadership style work in situations other than his or her current position? Why or why not?

5. Research a firm whose goods or services you purchase or admire. Learn what you can about the organization's culture. Would you be an effective manager in this culture? Why or why not? Share your findings with the class.

WEB ASSIGNMENTS

1. **Strategic planning.** Visit the website listed below. It summarizes Johnson & Johnson's strategic planning philosophy. Read up on several recent acquisitions by Johnson & Johnson. Prepare a brief report to discuss how the acquisitions resulted from the company's strategic planning process.

    www.investor.jnj.com/strategic.cfm

2. **Mission statements.** Go to the websites of two organizations: one for-profit firm and one not-for-profit organization. Print out the mission statements from both organizations. Take the material with you to class to participate in a discussion on mission statements.

3. **Management structure.** Visit the website listed below. Click on "corporate governance" and answer the following questions:

    a. How would you characterize Target's organizational structure?

    b. What is the composition of Target's board of directors?

    http://investors.target.com/phoenix.zhtml?c=65828&p=irol-IRHome

---

Note: Internet Web addresses change frequently. If you don't find the exact sites listed, you may need to access the organization's home page and search from there or use a search engine such as Bing or Google.

Echo/Getty Images

10 | PRODUCTION AND OPERATIONS MANAGEMENT

LEARNING OBJECTIVES

LO 10.1 Explain the strategic importance of production.

LO 10.2 Describe the four main categories of production processes.

LO 10.3 Explain the role of technology in the production process.

LO 10.4 Identify the factors involved in a plant location decision.

LO 10.5 Outline the job of production managers.

LO 10.6 Identify the steps in the production control process.

LO 10.7 Discuss the importance of quality control.

INSIDE BUSINESS

Building a 3D Future at GE

General Electric (GE), one of the world's largest manufacturers, is creating parts for its jet engines using a new technology called 3D printing or additive manufacturing. Unlike many conventional manufacturing processes that are subtractive—for example, drilling a hole in a block of metal—3D printing is an additive manufacturing process that creates the metal block around the hole. Expected to be one of the biggest changes in industrial production methods in decades, 3D printing is a process that is capable of creating almost any solid shape.

As with a 2D printer, the 3D printing process begins with the creation of a product design on a computer. Designers use computer-aided design (CAD) programs to specify the product size, shape, tolerances, colour, and materials. This information is then transferred to a 3D printer, which creates the shape from plastic or metal material one layer at a time. One method uses thin layers of powdered metals or plastics with an epoxy to adhere the powder particles together. Other methods use extruded plastics or a liquid material that solidifies when exposed to ultraviolet light to make the desired solid shapes.

This process allows firms like GE to create structures that were unimaginable just a few years ago. For its advanced jet engine, the LEAP-1, GE has created a new fuel nozzle using 3D printing. What had been a 20-piece assembly is now a single metal part printed in one piece that is 25 percent lighter than the original version. Printing in one piece also gives the new fuel nozzle a life estimated to be five times greater than the 20-piece assembly. And the design and prototyping time required for building these types of structures is greatly reduced, as engineers can design and fabricate test products in a matter of hours.

Maybe best of all, the cost of producing complex fuel nozzles via 3D printing is 20 percent less than a conventionally made one, according to GE. This translates into lower labour costs because less time is spent assembling and inspecting the various parts of the fuel nozzles. GE believes that 3D printing is the manufacturing technology of the future and estimates it will produce more than 40,000 fuel nozzles annually using this new process.[1]

CHAPTER 10 OVERVIEW

Businesses satisfy their commitment to society by producing and marketing the goods and services that people want. They create what economists call *utility*—the want-satisfying power of a good or service. Businesses can create or improve four basic kinds of utility: time, place, ownership, and form. A firm's marketing department creates time, place, and ownership utility by offering products to customers at a time and place that are convenient for purchase.

Production creates form utility by converting raw materials and other inputs into finished products, such as GE's 3D fuel nozzles. **Production** uses resources, including workers and machinery, to convert materials into finished goods and services. This process can either make major changes to raw materials or combine two or more already finished parts into new products. The task of **production and operations management** is to oversee the firm's production process by managing the people and machinery that convert materials and resources into finished goods and services. This process is shown in **Figure 10.1**.

People sometimes use the terms *production* and *manufacturing* to mean the same thing, but the two are actually different. Production is used in both manufacturing and nonmanufacturing industries. For example, fishing and mining companies are involved in production, as are firms that deliver packages or offer hotel rooms. **Figure 10.2** lists five examples of production systems for goods and services.

The production process can result in a tangible good such as a car or an intangible service such as cable television. The production process always converts inputs into outputs. A cabinetmaker combines wood, tools, and skill to create finished kitchen cabinets. A transit system combines buses, trains, and employees to create its output: passenger transportation. Both production processes create a useful good or service.

This chapter describes the process of producing goods and services. It looks at the importance of production and operations management. It also discusses the new technologies that are changing the production function. The chapter then discusses the tasks of the production and operations manager, the importance of quality, and the methods businesses use to ensure high quality.

production the use of resources, such as workers and machinery, to convert materials into finished goods and services.

production and operations management the process of overseeing the production process by managing the people and machinery that convert materials and resources into finished goods and services.

FIGURE 10.1 The Production Process: Converting Inputs into Outputs

INPUTS	CONVERSION PROCESS	OUTPUTS
· Resources · Raw Materials	· Add Value	· Goods · Services

LO 10.1 Explain the strategic importance of production.

THE STRATEGIC IMPORTANCE OF PRODUCTION

Production is a vital business activity, as are marketing and finance. Without products to sell, companies cannot generate money to pay their employees, lenders, and shareholders. And without the profits from products, firms quickly fail. The production process is just as important in not-for-profit organizations, such as The Hospital for Sick Children (SickKids) and Goodwill Industries. These organizations offer goods or services that are tied to their existence. When production and operations management are effective, they can lower a firm's costs of production, increase the quality of its goods and services, allow it to be dependable when meeting customer demands, and enable it to renew itself by providing new products. Let's look at the differences among three kinds of production: mass, flexible, and customer-driven production.

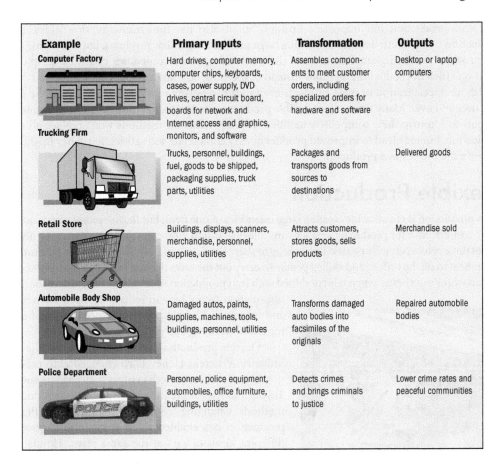

Example	Primary Inputs	Transformation	Outputs
Computer Factory	Hard drives, computer memory, computer chips, keyboards, cases, power supply, DVD drives, central circuit board, boards for network and Internet access and graphics, monitors, and software	Assembles components to meet customer orders, including specialized orders for hardware and software	Desktop or laptop computers
Trucking Firm	Trucks, personnel, buildings, fuel, goods to be shipped, packaging supplies, truck parts, utilities	Packages and transports goods from sources to destinations	Delivered goods
Retail Store	Buildings, displays, scanners, merchandise, personnel, supplies, utilities	Attracts customers, stores goods, sells products	Merchandise sold
Automobile Body Shop	Damaged autos, paints, supplies, machines, tools, buildings, personnel, utilities	Transforms damaged auto bodies into facsimiles of the originals	Repaired automobile bodies
Police Department	Personnel, police equipment, automobiles, office furniture, buildings, utilities	Detects crimes and brings criminals to justice	Lower crime rates and peaceful communities

FIGURE 10.2 Typical Production Systems

Mass Production

Canada began as a colonial supplier of raw materials to Europe and has become an industrial giant. Much of this change has resulted from **mass production**, a system for manufacturing products in large quantities by using effective combinations of employees with *specialized skills, mechanization*, and *standardization*. Because of mass production, outputs (goods and services) are available in large quantities at lower prices than individually made items. Mass production has brought us cars, computers, televisions, books, and even homes.

Mass production begins with the specialization of labour skills, by dividing work into its simplest forms so that each worker can focus on one task. By separating jobs into small tasks, managers create the right conditions for high productivity through mechanization. In mechanization, machines do much of the work previously done by people. Standardization, the third element of mass production, involves producing identical, interchangeable goods and parts. Standardized parts make it easier to replace substandard or worn-out parts. For example, if your car's windshield wiper blades wear out, you can easily buy replacements at a local auto parts store, such as Canadian Tire.

These principles of specialization, mechanization, and standardization led to development of the *assembly line*. This manufacturing method moves the product along a conveyor belt past many workstations, where workers perform specialized tasks, such as welding, painting, installing individual parts, and tightening bolts. Henry Ford's application of the assembly line greatly changed auto assembly. Before the assembly line, Ford's workers took 12 hours to assemble a Model T car. With an assembly line, the same car could be made in just 1.5 hours. Not surprisingly, many other industries soon adopted the assembly-line process.

mass production a system for manufacturing products in large quantities by using effective combinations of employees with specialized skills, mechanization, and standardization.

Mass production has important upsides, but it also has limitations, or downsides. Mass production is highly efficient for producing large numbers of similar products, but it is highly inefficient when producing small batches of different items. Some companies might be tempted to focus on efficient production methods instead of focusing on making what customers want. Also, the labour specialization of mass production can lead to boring jobs, as workers repeat the same task over and over. Many firms adopt flexible production systems and customer-driven production systems to improve their competitive abilities. These production methods won't replace all mass production, but may lead to improved product quality and greater job satisfaction. They might also improve the use of mass production.

Flexible Production

Mass production is effective for creating large quantities of one item, but *flexible production* is usually more cost-effective for producing smaller runs. Flexible production can take many forms. Generally, it uses three resources: information technology to share the details of customer orders, programmable equipment to fill the orders, and skilled people to carry out the tasks needed to complete an order. This system works even better when it is combined with lean production methods that use automation and information technology to reduce the need for workers and inventory. Flexible production needs a lot of communication among everyone in the organization.

Nathan Denette/The Canadian Press

This Honda auto plant uses flexible production techniques to produce different models. The auto industry developed mass production methods, but now finds more efficiency in flexible production.

Flexible production is now widely used in the auto industry. Whereas Henry Ford changed auto production in the early twentieth century, automakers such as Toyota and Honda are innovating with new production methods. Changing from mass production to flexible production has enabled these companies to produce different kinds of cars at the same plant. Honda now builds 15 different models spread across four plants in North America. "Using our flexible manufacturing capacity, we plan to continue to maintain our local production levels at approximately 80 percent of our annual sales," states a company spokesperson.[2] Honda's news is good news for North American workers and consumers.

Customer-Driven Production

A *customer-driven production* system assesses customer demands to make a connection between the products that are manufactured and the products people want to buy. Many firms use this approach with great success. One method is to set up computer links between factories and retailers' scanners. Data about sales are then used to create short-term forecasts and design production schedules to meet those forecasts. Another approach to customer-driven production systems is to wait until a customer orders a product and then produce it—whether it's a taco or a computer. Shibui Designs creates custom-made dresses in high-end fabrics for female executives and other women over 40. Each item of clothing is made to fit a single customer's measurements. Founder Elizabeth Nill, who is over 60, started the business because she couldn't find clothing that fit well. "I don't have the body of a model, and the bulges are real. Truly made classic clothing that is custom made-to-measure helps camouflage these inevitable imperfections and makes me feel more elegant." Nill's customers agree.[3]

 **ASSESSMENT CHECK**

10.1.1 What is mass production?

10.1.2 What is the difference between flexible production and customer-driven production?

LO 10.2 Describe the four main categories of production processes.

PRODUCTION PROCESSES

It probably won't surprise you that an Apple iPad and a litre of gasoline use different production processes and take different amounts of time to make. Production processes use either an analytic or a synthetic system; time requirements use either a continuous or an intermittent process.

An analytic production system reduces a raw material to its component, or individual, parts to extract one or more marketable products. Petroleum refining breaks down crude oil into several marketable products, including gasoline, heating oil, and aviation fuel. When corn is processed, it results in marketable food products, including animal feed and corn-based sweetener.

A synthetic production system is the reverse of an analytic system. It combines two or more raw materials or parts, or transforms raw materials, to produce finished products. Canon's assembly line produces a camera by assembling various parts such as a shutter or a lens cap. Other synthetic production systems make drugs, chemicals, computer chips, and canned soup.

A continuous production process creates finished products over a long period of time. The steel industry is a good example. Its blast furnaces never completely shut down except for repairs. Other firms that use continuous production are petroleum refineries, chemical plants, and nuclear power facilities. A shutdown can damage sensitive equipment and lead to a costly outcome.

An intermittent production process creates products in short production runs. Machines may be shut down frequently or may be changed so they produce different products. Most services result from intermittent production systems. For example, accountants, plumbers, and dentists do not try to standardize their services because each customer offers a different situation that needs an individual approach. But some companies, such as Mr. Lube (auto service), H&R Block (tax preparation service), and GreenLawn (lawn-care service), offer standardized services. This offering is part of a strategy to operate more efficiently and to compete by offering lower prices. McDonald's is well known for its nearly continuous production of food. This company has moved toward a more intermittent production model. The fast-food chain invested millions of dollars in new cooking equipment to set up kitchens for preparing sandwiches quickly to order. McDonald's prefers this method instead of producing large batches ahead of time and then keeping them warm under heat lamps.

✔ **ASSESSMENT CHECK**

10.2.1 What are the two main production systems?

10.2.2 What are the two time-related production processes?

TECHNOLOGY AND THE PRODUCTION PROCESS

LO 10.3 Explain the role of technology in the production process.

Production changes rapidly as computer technologies continue to develop. Many manufacturing plants are now known as "lights out" facilities. These facilities are completely automated. That means no workers are needed to build or make the products. This type of manufacturing plant means a big change in the types of jobs available in manufacturing. It also means that companies can design, produce, and adapt products more quickly to meet customers' changing needs.

Green Manufacturing Processes

More and more manufacturing firms are investing resources into developing processes that result in less waste, lower energy use, and little or no pollution. Companies as big as Walmart and as small as your local café are learning to operate in a more sustainable manner. Some companies may use biofuel to power a fleet of delivery trucks or may stop using unnecessary packaging. Firms are proud of the steps they take to be more sustainable. Seventh Generation makes household goods and cleaning products. This company has used sustainable manufacturing processes since it started. The firm's approach is to look at its operations as a whole, by considering the entire impact of its processes and products on the environment. Seventh Generation consistently assesses its processes and makes changes. For example, it might cut emissions from its distribution system or redesign its packages. "It's the best insurance any company can have for long-term success," notes co-founder and top executive Jeffrey Hollender.[4] The "Going Green" feature describes energy firms that are working on new methods for drilling for natural gas. The new methods are much less damaging to the environment than traditional methods.

GOING GREEN

DRILLING FOR NATURAL GAS—CLEAN ALTERNATIVES

Drilling for natural gas doesn't usually lead to images of an undisturbed landscape. In fact, studies by the government and by private environmental groups show that the main method for extracting natural gas from the earth—hydraulic fracturing—can result in contaminated water supplies. Hydraulic fracturing involves injecting millions of litres of water, sand, and chemicals deep into the ground to crack open the beds of shale that contain natural gas. Then, the gas can rise to the surface. Environmental scientists and the people who live near the drilling sites are concerned about two things: the amount of water being used and the possible contamination of their water supplies by the chemicals used in the process. These concerns have been voiced in many communities across Canada. In Quebec, the provincial government decided to go ahead with its planned natural gas development. The Quebec government's handling of the decision and how it dealt with public opinion led to much criticism.

But many energy companies *are* paying attention to these concerns—including those that drill for oil and natural gas. Environmental Technologies Ltd. makes a nontoxic alternative to the toxic chemicals. This firm says that its product kills bacteria just as effectively as the toxic chemicals. Ecosphere Technologies Inc. claims antibacterial chemicals aren't needed because its product can completely kill the bacteria at the surface before water is injected into the gas wells. Ecosphere also reduces water use and

water waste by helping energy producers to reuse the water used in hydraulic fracturing. That means companies no longer need to pay to ship millions of litres of waste water to treatment plants or disposal sites.

None of these firms suggests that the drilling should stop. Instead, the firms are researching and developing greener technologies. New companies—and divisions or subsidiaries of the larger energy firms—are forming rapidly to take advantage of this business opportunity.

Questions for Critical Thinking

1. What type of production system is used by natural gas drilling companies? Explain your answer.

2. Do you predict that the firms that are investing in greener processes will ultimately be successful? Why or why not?

Sources: Marianne White, "Quebec Moved Too Fast on Shale Gas: Watchdog," *Montreal Gazette*, March 31, 2011, accessed April 14, 2011, http://www.montrealgazette.com/news/decision-canada/Quebec+moved+fast+shale+watchdog/4532660/story.html#ixzz1JW9Ku1zL; "Hydraulic Fracturing," EPA website, accessed April 29, 2010, www.epa.gov; "Sustainable Technology," Baker Hughes website, accessed April 29, 2010, www.bakerhughes.com/company/corporate-social-responsibility/sustainable-technology; Ben Casselman, "Firms See 'Green' in Natural-Gas Production," *The Wall Street Journal*, March 30, 2010, www.wsj.com/articles/SB10001424052748704094104575143771963721284; "EPA Launches Hydraulic Fracturing Study," *Environmental Leader*, March 19, 2010, www.environmentalleader.com/2010/03/19/epa-launches-hydraulic-fracturing-study.

LEED (Leadership in Energy and Environmental Design) a voluntary certification program administered by the Canada Green Building Council, aimed at promoting the most sustainable construction processes available.

Firms that are involved in building construction—or are thinking of building new offices or manufacturing plants—are turning their attention to LEED (**Leadership in Energy and Environmental Design**) certification. LEED is a voluntary certification program offered by the Canada Green Building Council (CaGBC). It is aimed at promoting the most sustainable construction processes available. The LEED certification process is tough. It involves meeting standards in energy savings, water efficiency, carbon dioxide (CO_2) emissions reduction, improved indoor environmental quality (including air and natural light), and other categories.[5]

Robots

More and more manufacturers have freed workers from boring and sometimes dangerous jobs by replacing them with robots. A *robot* is a machine that can be programmed to perform tasks that require the repeated use of materials and tools. Robots can repeat the same tasks many times without changing their movements. Many factories use robots to stack their products on pallets and shrink-wrap them for shipping. Consolidated Technologies Inc. is located in Vaudreuil, Quebec, near Montreal. It produces robotic corrugated paper-box assemblers and product-packaging machines. One machine can assemble more than 120 cartons per minute. Another machine fills the cartons at a rate of 20 cases of products per minute. Both machines work much faster than humans.[6]

In the past, robots were most common in automotive and electronics manufacturing. Today, more and more industries are adding robots to their production lines. Because of improvements in technology, robots are now less expensive and more useful than they once were. Firms operate many different types of robots. The simplest is a pick-and-place robot. It moves in only two or three directions, picking up one item from one spot and placing it in another spot. So-called field robots assist people in nonmanufacturing, often dangerous, environments, such as nuclear power plants, the International Space Station, and even on battlefields. Police use remote-controlled robots to pick up and deal with suspected bombs. The same technology can also be used in factories. By using vision systems, infrared sensors, and bumpers on mobile platforms, robots can move parts or finished goods from one place to another. They can either follow or avoid people, whichever is needed to do the job. For example, machine vision systems are used for complex applications, such as quality assurance in the manufacturing of medical devices. Innovations in machine vision parts, such as cameras, lighting systems, and processors have greatly improved what these systems can do.

Robots are used in manufacturing as well as in many other fields. In auto manufacturing, robots can perform a variety of tasks that have freed workers from boring and sometimes dangerous jobs.

Computer-Aided Design and Manufacturing

Computer-aided design (CAD) is a process used by engineers to design parts and entire products on the computer. Engineers who use CAD can work faster and with fewer mistakes than those who use traditional drafting systems. An engineer can use an electronic pen to sketch three-dimensional (3D) designs on an electronic drafting board or directly on the computer screen. The engineer can then use software tools to make major and minor design changes. The computer can also analyze the results for certain characteristics or problems. Engineers can put a new car design through a simulated road test to project its real-world performance. For example, if they find a problem with weight distribution, the necessary changes can be made virtually—without actually test-driving the car. With advanced CAD software, creating a prototype, or a trial model, is as much "virtual" as it is "hands-on." Actual prototypes or parts aren't built until the engineers are satisfied that the virtual designs are as perfect as they can be. Dentistry has also benefited from CAD, which can design and create, at the dentist's office, such products as caps and crowns that perfectly fit a patient's mouth or jaw.[7]

computer-aided design (CAD) a process used by engineers to design parts and entire products on the computer. Engineers who use CAD can work faster and with fewer mistakes than those who use traditional drafting systems.

The process of **computer-aided manufacturing (CAM)** picks up where the CAD system leaves off. A manufacturer can use CAM to analyze the steps that a machine must take to produce a needed product or part. Electronic signals send instructions to the processing equipment to perform the needed production steps in the correct order. Both CAD and CAM technologies are now used together at most modern production facilities. These so-called CAD/CAM systems are linked electronically so they can automatically transfer computerized designs to the production facilities. These systems save both time and effort. They also allow firms to produce parts that need more precise manufacturing.

computer-aided manufacturing (CAM) a computer tool that a manufacturer uses to analyze CAD output and the steps that a machine must take to produce a needed product or part.

Flexible Manufacturing Systems

A **flexible manufacturing system (FMS)** is a production facility that workers can quickly change to manufacture different products. The typical system uses computer-controlled machining centres to produce metal parts, robots to handle the parts, and remote-controlled carts to deliver the materials. All steps of the process are linked by electronic controls that direct activities at each stage of manufacturing. The system can even replace broken or worn-out drill bits and other tools.

Flexible manufacturing systems have been improved by powerful new software that allows machine tools to be reprogrammed while they are running. This capability means that the same

flexible manufacturing system (FMS) a production facility that workers can quickly change to manufacture different products.

machine can make hundreds of different parts, and the operator doesn't need to shut the machine down to load each new program. The software also connects to the Internet to receive updates and to control machine tools at other sites. The software resides on a company's computer network. That means that engineers can use the software to locate production problems any time, from anywhere they can access the network. Nissan Motor Company recently expanded its flexible manufacturing system to join its plants in emerging markets, including China, Thailand, and India. In general, Nissan's expanded FMS cuts its new-vehicle lead time and investment in half. But the new system is not without its flaws that will take time to work out.[8]

computer-integrated manufacturing (CIM) an integrated production system that uses computers to help workers design products, control machines, handle materials, and control the production function.

Computer-Integrated Manufacturing

Companies use robots, CAD/CAM, FMS, computers, and other technologies together to apply **computer-integrated manufacturing (CIM)**. This integrated production system uses computers to help workers design products, control machines, handle materials, and control the production function. This type of manufacturing does not always lead to more automation and fewer people than other options. But it does involve a new type of automation that is organized around the computer. The key to CIM is a centralized computer system running software that integrates and controls separate processes and functions. The advantages of CIM include increased productivity, decreased design costs, increased equipment utilization, and improved quality.

CIM is widely used in the printing industry to coordinate thousands of printing jobs, some very small. CIM saves money by combining many small jobs into one larger job and by automating the printing process from design to delivery. Global printing company manroland uses CIM to provide printing solutions for its business customers. One of its products, PrintValue, offers a complete line of solutions for every aspect of a pressroom.[9]

ASSESSMENT CHECK

10.3.1 List some of the reasons businesses invest in robots.

10.3.2 What is a flexible manufacturing system (FMS)?

10.3.3 What are the major benefits of computer-integrated manufacturing (CIM)?

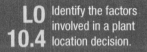

LO 10.4 Identify the factors involved in a plant location decision.

THE LOCATION DECISION

The decision of where to locate a production facility depends on transportation, human, and physical factors, as shown in **Table 10.1**. Transportation factors include the closeness to markets and raw materials and the availability of transportation options for both inputs and outputs. Automobile assembly plants are usually located near major rail lines. Inputs—such as engines, plastics, and metal

TABLE 10.1 Factors in the Location Decision

LOCATION FACTOR	EXAMPLES OF AFFECTED BUSINESSES
Transportation	
Closeness to markets	Baking companies and manufacturers of other perishable products, dry cleaners, hotels, other services
Closeness to raw materials	Paper mills
Availability of transportation options	Brick manufacturers, retail stores
Physical Factors	
Water supply	Computer chip fabrication plants
Energy	Aluminum, chemical, and fertilizer manufacturers
Hazardous wastes	All businesses
Human Factors	
Labour supply	Auto manufacturers, software developers
Local zoning regulations	Manufacturing and distribution companies
Community living conditions	All businesses
Taxes	All businesses

Deciding where to locate a production facility can often depend on the weather. Some theme parks, such as Walt Disney World, are located in warm climates so they can attract visitors year round.

parts—arrive by rail, and the finished vehicles are shipped out by rail. Shopping malls are often located next to major streets and freeways in suburban areas because most shoppers arrive by car.

Physical variables include such issues as weather, water supplies, available energy, and options for disposing of hazardous waste. Theme parks, such as Walt Disney World, are often located in warm climates so they can attract visitors year round. A manufacturing business that wants to locate near a community must prepare an *environmental impact study*. This study analyzes how a proposed plant will affect the quality of life in the surrounding area. Regulatory agencies usually need these studies to report on the impact on transportation facilities; energy requirements; water and sewage treatment needs; the effects on natural plant life and wildlife; and any possible water, air, and noise pollution.

Human factors in the location decision include an area's labour supply, local regulations, taxes, and living conditions. Management considers local labour costs and the availability of workers with the needed qualifications. Software makers and other computer-related firms concentrate in areas that have the technical talent they need, including California's Silicon Valley, Boston, Toronto, Montreal, and Austin, Texas. By contrast, some labour-intensive industries have located their plants in rural areas, where there is readily available labour and few other high-wage jobs. Some firms that have headquarters in Canada, the United States, and other industrialized countries have moved their production offshore in search of low wages. But no matter what type of industry a firm is in, when deciding on a location, a production and operations manager must consider the following factors:

- Closeness to suppliers, warehouses, and service operations
- Costs of insurance and taxes
- Availability of employee needs such as housing, schools, mass transportation, day care, shopping, and recreational facilities
- Size, skills, and costs of the local labour force
- Enough space for current and future needs of the firm

- Distance to the market for goods
- Receptiveness of the community
- Economical transportation for incoming materials and supplies and for outgoing finished goods
- Climate and environment that matches the industry's needs and employees' lifestyle
- Amount and cost of energy services
- Government incentives

A recent trend in location strategy is bringing production facilities closer to the final markets where the goods will be sold. One reason is the reduced time and cost for shipping. Another reason is a closer cultural relationship between the parent company and the supplier (in cases where production remains overseas). This trend has led some business developers to label Central America "the new Asia."[10] German automaker Volkswagen decided to build a $1 billion manufacturing plant in North America to make its new midsize sedan. Volkswagen expects to roll 150,000 vehicles out of the plant each year. The plant site includes the possibility of a major expansion that would further increase production capacity. CEO Stefan Jacoby notes that the plant is part of Volkswagen's overall strategy for capturing more of the North American auto market.[11]

Governments sometimes offer incentives to businesses that are willing to locate in their region. These incentives may take the form of tax breaks, agreements to improve infrastructure, and similar activities. Sometimes, location is all about bringing the right people together in the centre of the action. The "Hit & Miss" feature describes how Mexico has become a major hub for automobile manufacturing.

ASSESSMENT CHECK

10.4.1 How does an environmental impact study affect the location decision?

10.4.2 What human factors contribute to the location decision?

HIT & MISS

Mexico Becomes a Major Hub for Auto Manufacturing

When it comes to automobile manufacturing, you probably do not think about Mexico as the destination for billions of investment dollars—but it is. Most automakers, including Ford, General Motors, and Chrysler, have increased their manufacturing assembly lines in Mexico. The country's proximity to the United States and its highly skilled workers match their American and Canadian counterparts at a fraction of the wage cost.

Mexico has become the fastest-growing country worldwide for auto assembly and parts production. General Motors is making its iconic Silverado pickup trucks in central Mexico's Guanajuato state. Audi will invest $1.3 billion to build its assembly plant in the state of Puebla, where it will build its luxury vehicles—a first for Mexico. And Mexico is ground zero for Nissan's expansion plans in the Americas. Honda and Mazda are also adding manufacturing facilities in the country, which has shot past Canada to become the second-largest auto producer in North America.

A German-engineered BMW made in Mexico? The company recently announced a billion-dollar investment to build a new plant there to produce 150,000 vehicles annually, and Toyota recently announced it was going to build a billion-dollar plant in Guanajuato, Mexico, to take over production of the subcompact Corolla, currently assembled in Cambridge, Ontario. The Cambridge plant will be refurbished to build more expensive vehicles.

Questions for Critical Thinking

1. How does this business boom in Mexico impact the future of autoworkers in the United States and Canada?

2. About 80 percent of the cars made in Mexico are for export to the United States and Canada. Do you foresee Mexico's growth trend continuing? Why or why not?

Sources: *FinancialPost.com*, "Toyota moves Corolla production to Mexico with new plant, retools Ontario factory for other models," April 15, 2015, accessed April 15, 2015, http://business.financialpost.com/news/transportation/toyota-moves-corolla-production-to-mexicowith-new-plant-retools-ontario-factory-for-other-models; Nick Parker, "BMW's Billion-Dollar Bet on Mexico," CNN Money, accessed July 13, 2014, http://money.cnn.com; Chris Anderson, "Mexico: The New China," The New York Times, accessed February 24, 2014, www.nytimes.com; Harold L. Sirkin, "The New Mexico," Bloomberg Businessweek, accessed February 24, 2014, www .businessweek.com; Philip LeBeau, "Mexico Stakes Claim as Hottest Hub for Auto Production," CNBC, accessed February 24, 2014, www.cnbc.com; Ben Klayman, "Auto Industry Love for Mexico Grows with New Audi Plant," Reuters, accessed February 24, 2014, www .reuters.com; Juan Montes, "BMW Considers First Plant in Mexico," The Wall Street Journal, accessed February 24, 2014, http://online.wsj.com.

THE JOB OF PRODUCTION MANAGERS

LO 10.5 Outline the job of production managers.

Production and operations managers supervise the work of people and machinery to convert inputs (materials and resources) into finished goods and services. As **Figure 10.3** shows, these managers perform four major tasks.

1. Planning the overall production process
2. Selecting the best layout for the firm's facilities
3. Carrying out the production plan
4. Controlling the manufacturing process to maintain the highest possible quality

Part of the control process involves continuous assessment of the results. If problems occur, managers return to the first step and make adjustments.

PRODUCTION MANAGEMENT TASKS

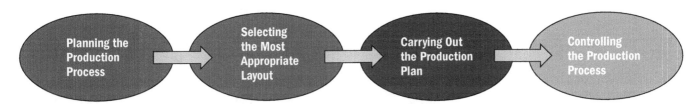

FIGURE 10.3 Tasks of Production Managers

Planning the Production Process

Production planning begins by choosing the goods or services to offer to customers. This decision is the essence, or core, of every company's reason for operating. Other decisions follow product planning, such as machinery purchases, pricing decisions, and selection of retail outlets. In product planning, it's not enough to plan products that satisfy customers. Products must satisfy customers *and* be produced as efficiently and inexpensively as possible. Market research is used to gather consumer reactions to proposed products. It is also used to estimate potential sales and profitability. Production departments focus on planning the production process in two ways: (1) by converting original product ideas into final specifications and (2) by designing the most efficient facilities to produce those products.

Production managers need to understand how a project fits into the company's structure because it can affect the success of the project. In a traditional manufacturing organization, each production manager has a specific area of authority and responsibility, such as purchasing or inventory control. One downside to this structure is that it may actually mean that the purchasing manager will compete against the inventory control manager. More organizations have moved toward team-oriented structures. Some organizations assign team members to specific projects, with all team members reporting to the production manager. Each team is responsible for the quality of its products and has the authority to make changes to improve performance and quality. The two approaches have two major differences: all workers on teams are responsible for their output, and teamwork avoids the competitiveness between managers often found in traditional structures.

Selecting the Facility Layout

The next production management task is selecting the best layout for the facility. An efficient facility layout can reduce material handling, decrease costs, and improve product flow through the facility. This decision requires managers to consider all phases of production and the inputs needed at each step. **Figure 10.4** shows three common layout designs: process, product, and fixed-position layouts. It also shows a customer-oriented layout typical of service providers' production systems.

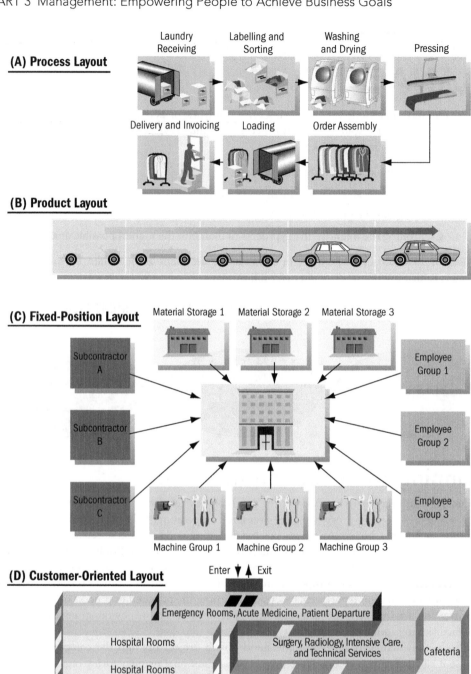

FIGURE 10.4 Basic Facility Layouts

[Product Layout]

7

Product layout refers to a production system where the work stations and equipments are located along the line of production. Usually work units are moved along a line by a conveyor.

A *process layout* groups machinery and equipment according to their functions. The work in process moves around the plant to reach different workstations. A process layout often makes it easier to produce a variety of nonstandard items in relatively small batches.

Its purpose is to process goods and services that have a variety of functions. For example, a typical machine shop has separate departments where machines are grouped by functions such as grinding, drilling, pressing, and lathing. *Process layouts* can suit a variety of production functions and use general-purpose equipment that can be less costly than specialized equipment to purchase and maintain.

A *product layout*, also called an assembly line, sets up production equipment along a product-flow line. The work in process moves along this line past workstations. This type of layout efficiently produces large numbers of similar items, but it may be inflexible, with room for only a few product variations. Although product layouts date back at least to the Model T assembly line, companies are improving this approach with modern touches. Many auto manufacturers continue to use a product layout, but robots perform many of the activities that humans once did. Automation solves one of the major drawbacks of this system—unlike humans, robots don't get bored doing a dull, repetitive job. European automaker Holland Car PLC uses an assembly-line approach called complete knockdown (CKD). In this assembly line, all the auto parts are imported in pieces to be welded, painted, and assembled at its facility in Ethiopia.[12]

A *fixed-position layout* places the product in one spot. The workers, materials, and equipment go to the product's location. This approach suits very large, bulky, heavy, or fragile products. For example, a bridge cannot be built on an assembly line. Fixed-position layouts are used in several industries, including construction, shipbuilding, aircraft and aerospace, and oil drilling. In all of these industries, the nature of the product generally dictates a fixed-position layout.

Service organizations must also decide on suitable layouts for their production processes. A service firm should arrange its facilities to enhance the interactions between customers and its services—also called a *customer-oriented layout*. If you think of patients as inputs, a hospital uses a form of the process layout. Banks, libraries, dental offices, and hair salons also use process layouts. Sometimes the details surrounding a service require a fixed-position layout. For example, doctors, nurses, and medical devices are brought to patients in a hospital emergency room.

Carrying Out the Production Plan

After production managers plan the production process and select the best layout, the next task is to carry out the production plan. This activity involves (1) deciding whether to make, buy, or lease products or parts; (2) selecting the best suppliers for materials; and (3) controlling inventory to keep enough supplies in stock, but not too much.

Make, Buy, or Lease Decision

Every producer faces a **make, buy, or lease decision**—whether to manufacture a product or part in-house, buy it from an outside supplier, or lease it. This decision is critical in many contemporary business situations.

Several factors affect the make, buy, or lease decision, including the costs of leasing or purchasing parts from outside suppliers compared with the costs of producing the parts in-house. The decision sometimes depends on whether outside suppliers can meet a firm's standards for quality and quantity. The need for confidentiality sometimes affects the decision, as does the short- or long-term duration of the firm's need for supplies. A firm might not yet have the technology to produce certain components or materials, or the technology might be too costly. The "Hit & Miss" feature describes some of the difficult production decisions Harley-Davidson had to make to help it rebound from a sluggish economy.

When a firm decides to buy goods from outside suppliers, production managers should still keep a relationship going with other supply sources. Having an alternative supplier means that the firm can get the materials it needs even during strikes or when quality-assurance problems or other situations affect the inputs. Outsourcing has its downsides, too. Companies say the main reason they use outsourcing is to reduce costs and focus on their core business activities. But outsourcing can also lead to layoffs and a decrease in the quality of the firm's outputs.[13]

make, buy, or lease decision choosing whether to manufacture a product or part in-house, buy it from an outside supplier, or lease it.

(HIT) & MISS

Harley-Davidson Turns Lean

For more than a century, Harley-Davidson, the iconic motorcycle brand, has embodied everything American. In its heyday, Harley-Davidson had such a following that consumers would wait patiently for 18 months to get their hands on a new bike. More recently, however, a combination of a slow economy and global competition created some tough decisions for the company. Like other manufacturers that opted for low-cost overseas or domestic nonunion production, the company was forced to decide whether to eliminate its union. Rather than scrap the union, the company redesigned the production system to allow for fewer workers in its York, Pennsylvania, plant—with the union's blessing. In addition, Harley-Davidson tore down the York plant and built a brand-new one. Instead of replacing experienced employees with state-of-the-art robotic technology, the company developed a lean manufacturing operation, complete with teams of five to six workers who manually build each of its core four motorcycle styles, complete with more than 1,200 customizable options.

With its lean manufacturing process and new facility, the company has reduced costs by $100 million while increasing quality and customer demand. In addition, it retained the union—experienced workers who are able to solve problems and search for better ways to make motorcycles that robots cannot. With a new motorcycle starting on the assembly line every 80 seconds, Harley-Davidson remains optimistic that its H.O.G. members (Harley Owner's Group) worldwide will continue to be happy, while now only waiting a few weeks for a new bike.

Questions for Critical Thinking

1. What do you think might have been the outcome had the company decided to follow other manufacturers overseas in pursuit of lower production costs?

2. Discuss the relationship between the iconic Harley-Davidson brand and the company's production decisions.

Sources: Company website, "Harley Owners Group," www.Harley-Davidson.com, accessed February 5, 2014; Adam Davidson, "Building a Harley Faster," The New York Times, accessed February 5, 2014, www.nytimes.com; Ginger Christ-Martin, "2013 IW Best Plants Winner: Harley-Davidson—Driving a Future of Excellence," Industry Week, accessed February 5, 2014, www.industryweek.com; James Hagerty, "Harley Goes Lean to Build Hogs," The Wall Street Journal, accessed February 5, 2014, http://online.wsj.com.

Selection of Suppliers

After a company decides what inputs to buy, it must choose the best suppliers for its needs. To make this choice, production managers compare several factors: quality, prices, dependability of delivery, and services offered by competing companies. Different suppliers may offer the same quality and the same prices. The final decision often depends on the firm's past experience with each supplier, speed of delivery, warranties on purchases, and other services.

When a firm is planning for a major purchase, negotiations with suppliers may take several weeks or months. The buying decision may need several managers to look at all the options before the final selection is made. For example, the selection of a supplier for an industrial drill press may require a joint decision by the production, engineering, purchasing, and quality-control departments. These departments often must sort out their different views before they agree on a purchasing decision.

The Internet provides powerful tools for finding and comparing suppliers. Buyers can log on to business exchanges to compare specifications, prices, and availability. Ariba offers online software and other tools that organizations can use to source $120 billion worth of goods and services from suppliers around the world.[14]

Firms often purchase raw materials and parts on long-term contracts. If a manufacturer needs a continuous supply of materials, a one-year or two-year contract with a supplier can ensure availability. Today, many firms build long-term relationships with suppliers and reduce the number of companies they deal with. At the same time, many organizations ask their suppliers to expand their roles in the production process.

Production managers use networking to learn about suppliers and to get to know them personally. Managers also meet suppliers, competitors, and colleagues at trade shows, conferences,

CAREER KICKSTART

Making the Most of Business Meetings

Some people love business meetings because they are a nice change from boring tasks. Others find meetings to be tiresome disruptions from more important work they need to do. But business meetings are sometimes necessary. You might enjoy meetings more if you look at how they can help you to build your career. Think of all meetings—including staff meetings, sales meetings, appointments with customers, and conferences with colleagues—as part of your overall networking strategy. Use these tips to make the most of your next business meeting:

- *Be on time.* Being on time shows that you value your own time and that of others. It also shows that you take the meeting seriously.

- *Turn off your cellphone and any other electronic devices.* Unless you are a doctor on call for emergencies, keep your cellphone turned off. Beeps and ringtones can distract others. They also show that your attention is elsewhere.

- *Pay attention.* Listen actively to what others are saying. Take notes when it is suitable.

- *Participate.* Ask questions and make brief points when appropriate. Stay on the subject. Avoid controlling a discussion.

- *Conduct yourself professionally.* Be polite to others at the meeting. Thank the others for their time at the end of the meeting.

- *Exchange business cards.* At the end of the meeting, exchange business cards or contact information with others that you may want to contact later.

Sources: Karyn Hill, "Business Meeting Etiquette—5 Essential Tips," Business Coach site, accessed April 26, 2010, www.bellaonline.com; Donna Reynolds, "Practice Business Meeting Etiquette," *How To Do Things*, accessed April 26, 2010, www.howtodothings.com, accessed April 26, 2010; Shaun Mangan, "7 Tips for More Effective Business Meetings," *Ezine Articles*, accessed April 26, 2010, http://ezinearticles.com.

and seminars, and other meetings. The "Career Kickstart" feature provides tips for making the most of these meetings.

Inventory Control

Production and operations managers are responsible for **inventory control**. They need to balance the costs of storing inventory with the need to have stock on hand to meet demand. Several costs are involved in storing inventory: warehousing costs, taxes, insurance, and maintenance. Firms waste money if they store more inventory than they need. But having too little inventory may lead to a shortage of raw materials, parts, or goods that can be sold. The outcome can be delays and unhappy customers.

Firms lose business when they keep missing promised delivery dates or turn away orders. When farmer Jay Armstrong ordered a combine attachment—just as his family had done for 50 years—the dealer told Armstrong he wouldn't receive the equipment until August, when the farm's growing season would nearly be over. Armstrong was forced to make his purchase from a competitor, who promised delivery in May.[15]

Efficient inventory control can save money. Many firms use *perpetual inventory* systems to continuously assess the amount of their stock and where it is stored. These inventory control systems usually rely on computers, and many automatically generate orders when stock is low. Many grocery stores link their scanning devices to perpetual inventory systems that reorder goods without the need for a human. When the system records a shopper's purchase, it reduces the inventory count stored in the computer. When inventory drops to a certain level, the system automatically reorders the merchandise. Canada's largest supermarket chain, Loblaw, uses a software system designed by SAP. The network of more than 1,000 corporate and franchised Loblaw stores use the SAP system to manage stock. The system is responsible for ordering and receiving inventory. It also counts and selects inventory in the stockrooms. The software can update and confirm the perpetual inventory balances.[16]

Some companies hand over their inventory control functions to suppliers. This concept is known as *vendor-managed inventory*. At Dell Computer assembly plants, almost all the parts suppliers also handle Dell's inventory control functions.

inventory control a function that balances the costs of storing inventory with the need to have stock on hand to meet demand.

JIT— is an inventory strategy companies employ to increase efficiency and decrease waste by receiving goods only as they are needed in the production process, thereby reducing inventory costs.

© Andy Sotiriou/Getty Images

JIT systems are being used in a wide range of industries, including the medical supplies field.

Just-in-Time Systems

just-in-time (JIT) system a broad management philosophy that reaches beyond the narrow activity of inventory control to affect the entire system of production and operations management.

A **just-in-time (JIT) system** is based on a broad management philosophy that reaches beyond the narrow activity of inventory control. A JIT system affects all production and operations management. A JIT system tries to use only items that add value to operations activities. It does this by providing the right part at the right place at just the right time—just before it is needed in production.

JIT systems are used in a wide range of industries, including the medical supplies field. Hospitals can use a JIT system to manage the distribution of supplies, equipment, and clinical materials. Hospitals partner with their key distributors to keep an inventory of certain emergency supplies on hand. Other supplies are distributed on a JIT basis, which saves time and money.[17]

Production that uses a JIT system shifts most of the responsibility for carrying inventory to suppliers. The suppliers use forecasts to decide how much inventory to carry. They keep stock on hand to respond to manufacturers' needs. When suppliers do not keep enough high-quality parts on hand, the purchasers may hand them penalties. When manufacturers underestimate demand for a product, the JIT system may have trouble adapting. Strong demand can overtax JIT systems. Suppliers and their customers may struggle to keep up with orders without having an inventory of goods to meet the extra demand.

Materials Requirement Planning

materials requirement planning (MRP) a computer-based production planning system that ensures a firm has all the parts and materials it needs to produce its output at the right time and place and in the right amounts.

Effective inventory control requires efficiency. It also needs careful planning to ensure the firm has all the inputs it needs to make its products. How do production and operations managers work through all of this information? They use **materials requirement planning (MRP)**, a computer-based production planning system that ensures a firm has all the parts and materials it needs to produce its output at the right time and place and in the right amounts.

Production managers use MRP programs to create schedules that list the specific parts and materials needed to produce an item. These schedules show the exact quantities needed. They also show the dates to order those quantities from suppliers so that they will be delivered at the correct time in the production cycle. A small company might get by without an MRP system. If a firm makes a simple product with only a few parts, a production manager can phone in an order for an overnight delivery of crucial parts. But for a complex product, such as a high-definition TV or aircraft, longer lead times are needed.

The Allan Candy Company is a large Canadian candy manufacturer. It uses MRP software from Microsoft to streamline and integrate all of its processes. The software figures out which materials are needed and automatically generates the purchase orders. CEO Steven Dakowsky believes this system gives his firm a competitive edge in the candy market. "I believe in the power of technology and that it is a differentiating factor, especially for companies our size," he says. "So, for me, it is critically important that we are ahead of the game."[18]

✔ **ASSESSMENT CHECK**

10.5.1. List the four major tasks of production and operations managers.

10.5.2 What is the difference between a traditional manufacturing structure and a team-based structure?

10.5.3 What factors affect the make, buy, or lease decision?

CONTROLLING THE PRODUCTION PROCESS

LO 10.6 Identify the steps in the production control process.

The final task of production and operations managers is controlling the production process to maintain the highest possible quality. **Production control** creates well-defined procedures for coordinating people, materials, and machinery to provide the greatest production efficiency. Suppose that a watch factory must produce 80,000 watches during October. Production control managers divide this total into a daily production assignment of 4,000 watches for each of the month's 20 working days. Next, they decide on the number of workers, raw materials, parts, and machines the plant needs to meet the production schedule. This work is much like the work of a manager in a service business such as a restaurant. A restaurant manager must estimate how many dinners will be served each day. The manager then decides what food to buy and how many people are needed to prepare and serve the food.

production control creating well-defined procedures for coordinating people, materials, and machinery to provide the greatest production efficiency.

Figure 10.5 shows production control as a five-step process: planning, routing, scheduling, dispatching, and follow-up. These steps are part of the firm's overall emphasis on total quality management.

Planning → Routing → Scheduling → Dispatching → Follow-Up

FIGURE 10.5 Steps in Production Control

Production Planning

The first step of production control is *production planning*. In this step, managers decide on the amount of resources (including raw materials and other items) needed to produce a certain output. The production planning process leads to a list of all needed parts and materials. Purchasing staff can compare this list with the firm's perpetual inventory data to identify which items need to be purchased. Employees or automated systems set up the delivery schedules so the needed parts and materials will arrive when they are needed during the production process. Production planning also ensures the availability of needed machines and personnel. At the Wilson Sporting Goods Company factory in Ohio, there's a special excitement leading up to the Super Bowl each year. Workers there have made every football that has ever been used in a Super Bowl game. Each January, construction on the balls begins. The footballs are about 70 percent complete before the final playoff games are decided. When workers know which two team names will be printed on the balls, production speeds up. The plant makes about 120 official game balls and about 6,000 versions for sale to fans. "The market determines how many balls we will make," notes Gregory Miller, the plant controller.[19]

Material inputs contribute to service-production systems, but production planning for services tends to focus on human resources more than materials.

In the routing phase of production control, managers decide on the sequence of work throughout the facility, who should perform each operation in the production process, and where it should be done.

Routing

The second step of production control is *routing*. In this step, the manager decides on the sequence of work throughout the facility, who will perform each part of the work, and where the work will be done. Routing choices depend on two factors: the nature of the good or service and the facility layout. As discussed earlier in the chapter, the common layout designs are product, process, fixed-position, and customer-oriented layouts. Some routing decisions make sense, such as dipping an automobile body into a rust-proofing bath before painting it. Other decisions may need more study. For example, what is the best sequence when mixing ingredients to make a salad dressing?

Scheduling

The next stage of production control is the *scheduling* phase. In this stage, managers develop timetables that show how long each operation in the production process takes and when workers should perform it. Efficient scheduling means that production will meet the delivery schedules and make efficient use of resources.

Scheduling is important whether the product is complex or simple to produce and whether it is a good or a service. A pencil is simpler to produce than a computer, but each production process has scheduling needs. A stylist may take 25 minutes to complete each haircut using just one or two tools, but every day a hospital schedules procedures and treatments, from x-rays to surgery to follow-up appointments. Sleepmaster is a medium-sized firm that recently moved some of its production from its Australian headquarters to China. But the company's MRP system had very little capacity for scheduling, and the workers in China did not know how to use the technology. Sleepmaster's operations manager set up a new scheduling program called Resource Manager. The new program is easier to use and organize, costs little to operate, and has support available via Skype.[20]

Production managers use several analytical methods for scheduling. One of the oldest methods is the *Gantt chart*. This method tracks projected and actual work progress over time. Many people use Gantt charts, like the one shown in **Figure 10.6**. One glance at the chart quickly shows the progress of any project. Gantt charts are most effective for scheduling simple projects.

A complex project might require a *PERT (program evaluation and review technique)* chart. This chart tries to reduce the number of delays by coordinating all parts of the production process. PERT was first developed for the military and has been adapted for use in industry. The simplified PERT diagram in **Figure 10.7** shows the schedule for purchasing and installing a new robot. The heavy gold line indicates the *critical path*—the sequence of operations that requires the longest time for completion. In this case, the project cannot be completed in less than 17 weeks.

A PERT network may be made up of thousands of events and may take place over months of time. Complex computer programs help production managers to develop a PERT network and to find the critical path among all the events and activities. This type of complex production planning is needed when constructing a huge office building.

David Burton/Fuse/Getty Images

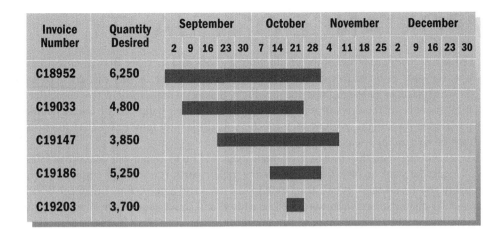

Invoice Number	Quantity Desired	September					October				November				December				
		2	9	16	23	30	7	14	21	28	4	11	18	25	2	9	16	23	30
C18952	6,250																		
C19033	4,800																		
C19147	3,850																		
C19186	5,250																		
C19203	3,700																		

FIGURE 10.6 Sample Gantt Chart

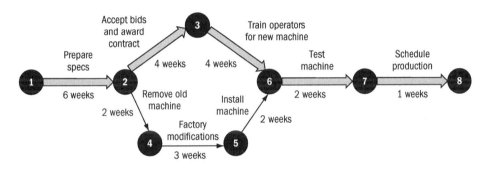

1. Project started
2. Specs completed
3. Contract awarded
4. Old machine removed
5. Plant modifications completed
6. Training and installation completed
7. Testing completed
8. Project completed

 Critical path

FIGURE 10.7 PERT Diagram for the Purchase and Installation of a New Robot

Dispatching

In the *dispatching* phase of production control, management instructs each department on the work it needs to do and how long it has to do the work. The dispatcher authorizes performance, provides instructions, and lists job priorities. Dispatching may be the responsibility of a manager or a self-managed work team.

Follow-Up

Sometimes even the best plans fail. That's why production managers need to be aware of any problems. In the *follow-up* phase of production control, managers and employees, or team members, spot problems in the production process and come up with solutions. Problems can take many forms: machinery malfunctions, delayed shipments, and absent employees can all affect production. The production control system must identify and report these delays to managers or work teams so they can adjust schedules and correct the underlying problems.

✔ ASSESSMENT CHECK

10.6.1 What five steps are involved in controlling the production process?

10.6.2 What is the difference between a PERT chart and a Gantt chart?

LO 10.7 Discuss the importance of quality control.

quality the state of being free of deficiencies or imperfections.

IMPORTANCE OF QUALITY

Next we look at quality in terms of the production of goods and services. In this sense, **quality** is defined as the state of being free of deficiencies or imperfections. Quality matters because it is costly to fix, replace, or redesign imperfect products. If Seagate makes a defective computer hard drive, it must either fix the drive or replace it to keep a customer happy. If Air Canada books too many passengers for a flight, it must offer vouchers worth several hundred dollars to encourage passengers to give up their seats and take a later flight.

For most companies, the costs of poor quality can add up to 20 percent or more of sales revenue. The costs of poor quality include downtime, repair costs, rework, and employee turnover. Low-quality goods and services can also result in lost sales and a poor company image. Facebook experienced a quality crisis when users were confused and upset about its new privacy settings. "Many of you thought our controls were too complex," wrote CEO Mark Zuckerberg in a letter to users. "Our intention was to give you lots of granular controls, but that may not have been what many of you wanted. We just missed the mark."[21]

Companies can use benchmarking to ensure that they always produce high-quality products. When a company uses **benchmarking**, it looks at how well other companies perform business functions or tasks and uses their performance as a standard for measuring its own performance. In other words, benchmarking is the process of comparing one firm's standards and practices to other firms' standards and best practices. Automobile companies routinely purchase each other's cars and then take them completely apart to examine and compare the design, components, and materials used to make even the smallest part. These companies then make improvements to match or exceed the quality found in their competitors' cars. Companies may use many different benchmarks, depending on their objectives. For example, organizations that want to make more money may compare their operating profits or expenses to those of other firms. Retailers concerned with productivity may want to benchmark their sales per square metre.

When a firm is benchmarking, it needs to decide what it wants to accomplish, what it wants to measure, and which company can provide the most useful benchmarking information. A firm might choose a direct competitor for benchmarking, or it might choose a company in an entirely different industry that has processes the firm wants to study and copy.[22]

benchmarking the process of looking at how well other companies perform business functions or tasks and using their performance as a standard for measuring another company's performance.

Quality Control

Quality control involves measuring output against quality standards. Firms use quality control to spot defective or imperfect products and to avoid delivering poor-quality goods to customers. Quality standards should be set high enough to meet customer expectations. A 90 or 95 percent success rate might seem to be good, but would you want your phone service or Internet network to work only 90 percent of the time? You would likely feel frustrated, and you would probably switch your phone service or your Internet service provider.

Manufacturing firms can check on quality levels by using visual inspections, electronic sensors, robots, and x-rays. Service organizations can gather quality-control information from surveys. Negative feedback from customers or a high rejection rate on a product or part may mean that production is not meeting quality standards. Firms that outsource their operations face a greater challenge in checking on quality levels. They also have a tougher time assuring customers of the quality of their goods or services, especially when they are highly visible companies, such as airlines. The "Solving an Ethical Controversy" feature discusses the quality of multivitamins manufactured in China for North American companies.

A typical factory can spend up to half its operating budget identifying and fixing mistakes. That means that a company should not rely just on inspections to meet its quality goals. Instead, production managers should identify all processes involved in producing goods and services and then work to increase the efficiency of these processes. They need to find and correct the causes of

quality control measuring output against quality standards.

problems in the processes. A company needs to focus its efforts on better designs of products and processes and to set clear quality targets. These efforts can lead to higher-quality, error-free production.

The Six Sigma concept to achieving quality goals is used by more and more large organizations, including Rogers Communications, the Ontario Lottery and Gaming Corporation, General Electric, Heinz, 3M, and Sears. When a company uses *Six Sigma*, it tries to make error-free products 99.9997 percent of the time. That means it is allowed to make only 3.4 errors for every 1 million opportunities. The goal of Six Sigma programs is for companies to eliminate nearly all defects in output, processes, and transactions.[23]

ISO Standards

For many organizations, an important measure of quality is being able to meet the standards of the **International Organization for Standardization**, known as **ISO** for short. ISO doesn't stand for anything; that is, it is not an acronym but is a shorter name from the Greek word *isos*, meaning "equal." ISO started in 1947 and is a network of national standards bodies from 163 countries. Its mission is to develop and promote international standards for business, government, and society. The aim is to improve and encourage global trade and cooperation. ISO has developed voluntary standards for all sorts of tasks, from the format of banking and telephone cards to freight containers to paper sizes to metric screw threads. The Standards Council of Canada (SCC) is the Canadian member body, and the American National Standards Institute is the U.S. member. Canadian firms typically deal with both bodies.

The ISO 9000 standards help organizations to ensure that their products and services (1) are of high quality and (2) provide a basis for continual improvement. The ISO 14000 standards for

International Organization for Standardization (ISO) an international organization whose mission is to develop and promote international standards for business, government, and society. The aim is to improve and encourage global trade and cooperation.

SOLVING AN **ETHICAL** CONTROVERSY

Multivitamins Produced in China: Are Stricter Quality Controls Necessary?

Chinese-made multivitamins reportedly contain dangerous levels of lead and toxic bacteria—and are showing up in North American stores. Some people have called for stricter quality standards.

PRO

1. According to the Chinese Ministry of Commerce, 85 percent of Chinese citizens rank quality concerns high for food and drugs made in their own country. Tighter controls would also benefit Chinese consumers.

2. Vitamins stamped "Made in Germany" or "Made in the USA" might still contain ingredients from China. Because it has already been demonstrated that these products contain high levels of toxic substances, tighter quality controls must be put into place.

CON

1. Many vitamins contain ingredients from multiple sources, so it is impossible to target China as the sole source of contamination.

2. Chinese production offers companies good value. With lower-cost labour and other services, savings can be passed along to the consumer.

Summary

Despite ongoing concerns, Swiss manufacturer Lonza recently announced it would locate its vitamin B3 manufacturing in China. Meanwhile, China is considering new production regulations on vitamin C—but with an emphasis on pricing power.

Sources: Steve Kelman, "Secret Chinese Vitamins," Federal Computer Week, accessed February 4, 2014, www.fcw.com; "Lonza to Build Vitamin B3 Plant in China," All about Feed, accessed February 4, 2014, www.allaboutfeed.net; "New Multivitamins Target Concern over China's Quality Problems," Bio-Medicine, accessed February 4, 2014, http://news.bio-medicine.org.

Many consumers prefer to buy from companies that are ISO certified.

environmental management help organizations to ensure that their operations (1) cause as little harm as possible to the environment and (2) continually improve their environmental performance.

ISO 9001:2008 and ISO 14001:2004 respectively give the requirements for a quality management system and an environmental management system. Both can be used for certification. An organization gains certification when its management system (the way it manages its processes) is independently audited by a certification body (also known in North America as a registration body, or registrar) and is confirmed as meeting the requirements of the standard. The organization is then issued with an ISO 9001:2008 or an ISO 14001:2004 certificate.

Certification is not a requirement of either standard. An organization can follow ISO standards to gain benefits for the organization and its customers—without certification. But many organizations want to be certified because many managers, consumers, and shareholders see an independent audit as adding confidence to a firm's abilities. Business partners, customers, suppliers, and shareholders may prefer to deal with certified organizations. Certifications need to be renewed every few years, which means audits are also needed every few years.

The ISO itself develops standards but does not carry out the auditing and certification. These tasks are done independently of ISO by hundreds of certification organizations around the world. The certificates they issue carry their own logo, not that of the ISO because the ISO does not approve or control the activities of the certification organizations.

Many organizations report significant benefits from using ISO's management system standards, such as increased efficiency, better teamwork, improved customer satisfaction, and reduced consumption of resources.[24]

✓ ASSESSMENT CHECK

10.7.1 What are some ways that a company can track the quality of its output?

10.7.2 List some of the benefits of ISO 9000 certification.

WHAT'S AHEAD

Maintaining high quality is an important part of satisfying customers. The business function of marketing also has the objectives of product quality and customer satisfaction. The next part consists of three chapters that explore the many activities involved in customer-driven marketing. These activities include product development, distribution, promotion, and pricing.

RETURN TO INSIDE BUSINESS

Building a 3D Future at GE

3D printing technology is changing the way many industries think about production planning and inventory control. Instead of mass production of rarely needed parts, customized products can be made with short production runs on a demand basis eliminating inventory and storage costs. This emerging technology is also providing opportunities for small businesses that can service industries who only require occasional production services much the way a printing service company works today.

QUESTIONS FOR CRITICAL THINKING

1. Which industries would likely do well to adopt 3D technology production?

2. How might 3D technology development affect management relations with employees?

SUMMARY OF LEARNING OBJECTIVES

LO 10.1 Explain the strategic importance of production.

Production and operations management is a vital business function. A company needs a quality good or service to create profits; otherwise, it soon fails. The production process is also important in not-for-profit organizations. These organizations offer goods or services that are tied to why they exist. Production and operations management plays an important strategic role. It can lower the costs of production, increase output quality, and allow the firm to respond flexibly and dependably to customers' demands.

✓ ASSESSMENT CHECK ANSWERS

10.1.1 **What is mass production?** Mass production is a system for manufacturing products in large quantities by using effective combinations of mechanization, standardization, and employees with specialized skills.

10.1.2 **What is the difference between flexible production and customer-driven production?** Flexible production generally involves using three resources: information technology to receive and share orders, programmable equipment to fill the orders, and skilled people to carry out tasks needed to complete an order. Customer-driven production assesses customer demands to make a connection between the products that are manufactured and the products people want to buy.

LO 10.2 Describe the four main categories of production processes.

The four main categories of production processes are the analytic production system, the synthetic production system, the continuous production process, and the intermittent production process. The analytic production system reduces a raw material to its component, or individual, parts to extract one or more marketable products. The synthetic production system combines two or more raw materials or parts to produce finished products. The continuous production process creates finished products over a long period of time. The intermittent production process creates products in short production runs.

✓ ASSESSMENT CHECK ANSWERS

10.2.1 **What are the two main production systems?** The two main production systems are analytic production and synthetic production. An analytic production system reduces a raw material to its component, or individual, parts to extract one or more marketable products. A synthetic production system combines two or more raw materials or parts, or transforms raw materials, to produce finished products.

10.2.2 **What are the two time-related production processes?** The two time-related production processes are the continuous production process and the intermittent production process. The continuous production process creates finished products over a long period of time. The intermittent production process creates products in short production runs.

LO 10.3 Explain the role of technology in the production process.

Computer-driven automation allows companies to design, create, and adapt products quickly. Companies can also produce products in ways that meet customers' changing needs. Important design and production technologies include robots, computer-aided design (CAD), computer-aided manufacturing (CAM), and computer-integrated manufacturing (CIM). Many manufacturing firms invest resources into developing processes that result in less waste, lower energy use, and little or no pollution.

✓ ASSESSMENT CHECK ANSWERS

10.3.1 **List some of the reasons businesses invest in robots.** Businesses use robots to free workers from sometimes dangerous jobs and to move heavy items from one place to another in a factory.

10.3.2 **What is a flexible manufacturing system (FMS)?** An FMS is a production facility that workers can quickly change to manufacture different products.

10.3.3 **What are the major benefits of computer-integrated manufacturing (CIM)?** The main benefits are increased productivity, decreased design costs, increased equipment utilization, and improved quality.

LO 10.4 Identify the factors involved in a plant location decision.

The factors for choosing the best site for a production facility fall into three categories: transportation, human, and physical factors. Transportation factors include the availability of transportation options and the closeness to markets and raw materials. Physical variables involve such issues as water supply, available energy, and options for disposing of hazardous wastes. Human factors include the area's labour supply, local regulations, taxes, and living conditions.

✓ ASSESSMENT CHECK ANSWERS

10.4.1 **How does an environmental impact study affect the location decision?** An environmental impact study analyzes how a proposed plant will affect the quality of life in the surrounding area. The study reports on how transportation, energy use, water and sewer treatment needs, and other factors will affect plants, wildlife, water, air, and other features of the natural environment.

10.4.2 **What human factors contribute to the location decision?** Human factors in the location decision include an area's labour supply, labour costs, local regulations, taxes, and living conditions.

LO 10.5 Outline the job of production managers.

Production and operations managers use people and machinery to convert inputs (materials and resources) into finished goods and services. Four major tasks are involved. First, the managers must plan the overall production process. Next, they must select the best layout for their facilities. Then they carry out their production plans. Finally, they control the production process and assess the results to maintain the highest possible quality.

Carrying out the production plan involves deciding whether to make, buy, or lease products or parts; selecting the best suppliers for materials; and controlling inventory to keep enough supplies in stock, but not too much.

 **ASSESSMENT CHECK ANSWERS**

10.5.1 **List the four major tasks of production and operations managers.** The four tasks are planning overall production, selecting a layout for the firm's facilities, carrying out the production plan, and controlling manufacturing to achieve high quality.

10.5.2 **What is the difference between a traditional manufacturing structure and a team-based structure?** In the traditional structure, each manager is responsible for a specific area. In a team-based structure, all workers are responsible for their output.

10.5.3 **What factors affect the make, buy, or lease decision?** Several factors affect this decision, including the need for confidentiality, whether outside suppliers can meet a firm's standards, and the costs of leasing or purchasing parts from outside suppliers compared with the costs of producing them in-house.

LO 10.6 Identify the steps in the production control process.

The production control process has five steps: planning, routing, scheduling, dispatching, and follow-up. Quality control is an important consideration throughout this process. Coordination of each of these phases should result in high production efficiency and low production costs.

 **ASSESSMENT CHECK ANSWERS**

10.6.1 **What five steps are involved in controlling the production process?** The five steps are planning, routing, scheduling, dispatching, and follow-up.

10.6.2 **What is the difference between a PERT chart and a Gantt chart?** PERT charts try to reduce the number of delays by coordinating all parts of the production process. PERT charts are used for more complex projects. Gantt charts track projected and actual work progress over time. Gantt charts are used for scheduling simple projects.

LO 10.7 Discuss the importance of quality control.

Quality control involves measuring goods and services against quality standards. Firms use quality control to spot defective or imperfect products and to avoid delivering poor-quality goods to customers. Devices for monitoring quality levels of the firm's output include visual inspection, electronic sensors, robots, and x-rays. Companies can increase the quality of their goods and services by using Six Sigma techniques and by becoming ISO 9000 and 14000 certified.

✔ **ASSESSMENT CHECK ANSWERS**

10.7.1 **What are some ways that a company can track the quality of its output?** Companies can track quality by using benchmarking, quality control, Six Sigma, and ISO standards.

10.7.2 **List some of the benefits of ISO 9000 certification.** These standards show how a company can ensure that its products meet customers' requirements. Studies show that business partners, customers, suppliers, and shareholders prefer to deal with companies that are ISO 9000 certified.

BUSINESS TERMS YOU NEED TO KNOW

benchmarking 278

computer-aided design (CAD) 265

computer-aided manufacturing (CAM) 265

computer-integrated manufacturing (CIM) 266

flexible manufacturing system (FMS) 265

International Organization for Standardization (ISO) 279

inventory control 273

just-in-time (JIT) system 274

LEED (Leadership in Energy and Environmental Design) 264

make, buy, or lease decision 271

mass production 261

materials requirement planning (MRP) 274

production 260

production and operations management 260

production control 275

quality 278

quality control 278

REVIEW QUESTIONS

1. What is utility? How does production create utility?

2. Why is production such an important business activity? How does production create value for the company and its customers?

3. Why are firms moving toward flexible production and customer-driven production instead of mass production? Describe a product that is better suited to flexible production or customer-driven production than mass production. Explain your choice.

4. Identify whether an analytic production system or a synthetic production system applies to each of the following products:

    a. logging

    b. medical care

    c. cotton farming

    d. fishing

    e. construction

5. The home construction industry and the dental industry benefit from the use of CAD. Both industries can also benefit from using CAM—to manufacture home construction parts and to create dental implants and crowns. Choose another industry that would benefit from the use of both CAD and CAM systems. Explain how the industry can use both systems.

6. The Vancouver Aquarium is the largest aquarium in Canada and one of the five largest in North America. What specific factors might have contributed to the selection and success at this location?

7. What is the best facility layout for each of the following?

    a. movie rental shop

    b. a nail salon

    c. a car wash

    d. a sandwich shop

8. What factors might be involved in selecting suppliers for a steakhouse restaurant?

9. What is inventory control? Why is the management of inventory crucial to a company's success?

10. What is benchmarking? How can it help a firm improve the quality of its goods and services?

PROJECTS AND TEAMWORK APPLICATIONS

1. Imagine that you recently became the owner of a popular ice cream shop. You want to attract more customers and expand the business. What type of production process—continuous or intermittent—is better for your business? Create a plan that shows the details of how you will use this process and why it will help you to meet your goals as a business owner.

2. On your own or with a classmate, imagine that you've been hired to help a business group design a shopping mall. Using the location factors discussed in the chapter, recommend where the mall should be located—and why. Present your plan to the class.

3. On your own or with a classmate, select one of the following businesses and sketch out or describe the layout that would be best for attracting and serving customers:

    a. a Mexican restaurant

    b. a home furnishings store

    c. a pet store

    d. a motorcycle dealership

    e. a dentist office

4. Suppose you and your best friend decide to start a house-painting service. Draft a production plan for your business, including the following decisions: (a) make, buy, or lease; (b) suppliers; and (c) inventory control.

5. Choose two firms to compare (one firm should provide a good benchmarking opportunity for its production processes). The benchmarking firm doesn't need to be in the same industry as the other firm. Present your decisions to the class and explain why you made both choices.

WEB ASSIGNMENTS

1. **Just-in-time inventory management systems.** Go to the websites listed below to learn more about just-in-time inventory management systems. Make some notes on what you learned and bring them to class to participate in a class discussion.

    www.wisegeek.com/what-is-a-just-in-time-inventory.htm

    www.smcdata.com/software-choices/just-in-time-inventory-control-systems-1.html

2. **Plant location decision.** Using an Internet news service, such as Google news (http://news.google.com) or Yahoo! news (http://news.yahoo.com), search for news about a recent decision on a plant location. An example is Toyota's recent decision to expand its production facilities in Woodstock and Cambridge, Ontario. Research the decisions. Prepare a brief report that shows the factors that the firm considered in making its decision to expand in Canada.

    www.theglobeandmail.com/report-on-business/toyota-eyes-expansion-of-ontario-plants/article2341364

3. **ISO certification.** Visit the website of the International Organization for Standardization (www.iso.org). Click on one of the popular standards and summarize the information presented.

Note: Internet Web addresses change frequently. If you don't find the exact sites listed, you may need to access the organization's home page and search from there or use a search engine such as Bing or Google.

PART 3: CASE STUDY Beau's All Natural Brewing Company

Managing the Pains of Early Growth

Steve Beauchesne had written over 100 business plans while working for an Ontario government agency. He understood the importance of thinking out the details in a strategic plan that would guide management before launching the business. Once the business was functional, time would be in short supply, especially since he and his small team would be doing everything necessary to kickstart the brewery. Looking back, 70 hour workweeks were the norm for Steve and Tim. No one else managing the firm had as much invested in the brewery and no one else was as motivated to make Beau's succeed.

From the beginning Steve and Tim were guided by a desire to make Beau's different than its competitors in ways that would guide how the company would be managed and seen by their customers and employees. Their mission statement focuses on five key ideas: quality beer production, local focus, family run, organic and sustainable, and a DIY-entrepreneurial spirit. Each of these ideas would be the starting point for their future SWOT analyses and efforts to develop competitive advantage over their competitors.

Quality Beer Production

Steve and Tim believed that the beer they produced had to be unique and offer an alternative taste to the traditional beers produced by the big brewers. They also believed their beer had to be more than different—it had to be "better" if they were going to establish themselves as an alternative to the craft brew customer. Beau's efforts have been recognized by the dozens of industry awards earned in competitions.

Local Focus

Beau's is managed with a strong and active commitment to the community it serves, supporting more than 100 independent arts and music, community building, and charitable organizations every year. Giving back to the community reflects the understanding that the Beauchesne's are also members of the community. Beginning with the handful of employees hired to start the company, new employees are made welcome to a growing fun place to work.

Family Run

Like Beau's, most of the customers Steve and Tim called on to introduce their beer were also family-owned restaurants, pubs, and bars. According to Steve, there was instant recognition of the family effort to get Beau's started and help it grow. Letting retailers and their customers know that Beau's was the real-deal family-run business was a distinguishing plus for the firm.

Organic and Sustainable

Perhaps Steve and Tim's commitment to brewing outstanding award-winning beer is explained by their use of only the finest-quality certified organic ingredients. These ingredients may cost more, but they

(continued)

PART 3: CASE STUDY **Beau's All Natural Brewing Company**

help make for better beer taste and are worth the extra expense, according to Steve. This way of thinking also guides managerial decision making when it comes to issues related to sustainability and the environment. For example, the company uses enviro-friendly packaging and solar-generated electricity to run the plant.

DIY-Entrepreneurial Spirit

Starting any business is a challenge. Especially when there are so many tasks to be concerned with and many of those that require specialized expertise and knowledge. As mentioned in part two of the case study, Beau's lucked out when one of the most talented brew masters in the country, Matthew O'Hara, joined them. Matthew developed Beau's flagship beer, a lagered ale called Lug Tread, and hasn't stopped experimenting with new recipes. In fact, the spirit of developing new ideas for products or marketing is part of the DIY (do-it-yourself) culture at Beau's where everyone is encouraged to explore their interests. "When someone comes forward with an idea we encourage them to run with it. Rather than going outside the company, we allocate a bit of money to test the idea out, and if it

works we allocate more money and resources the next time," according to Steve. As a result, the 130 employees understand there are opportunities to develop their interests and grow with the firm.

As the firm grew from humble beginnings and a handful of employees into a going concern with over 130 employees, Steve and Tim have gradually expanded the organization structure with defined managerial lines of command and communications. Although the family-oriented open management style is still at the core of the firm's culture, the challenge remains to move forward without undermining what works so well today.

Questions for Critical Thinking

1. As the company continues to grow, how can Steve and Tim maintain the corporate culture and core values that are at the heart of their success?

2. Going forward, what do you think an ideal organization structure would look like?

3. How can Steve and Tim maintain control over decision making as the firm grows?

3 LAUNCHING YOUR . . .

MANAGEMENT CAREER

Part 3, "Management: Empowering People to Achieve Business Goals," covers Chapters 7 through 10. These four chapters discuss management, leadership, and the internal organization; human resource management, motivation, and labour–management relations; improving performance through empowerment, teamwork, and communication; and production and operations management. In those chapters, you read about top executives and company founders who directed their companies' strategy and led others in their day-to-day tasks to keep them on track. You also read about middle managers who make plans to turn the strategies into realities, and supervisors who work directly with employees to create strong teams that satisfy customers. A variety of jobs are available to people who choose management careers. And the demand for managers will continue to grow.

So what kinds of jobs can you choose from if you decide on a management career? As you learned in Chapter 7, three types of management jobs exist: supervisory managers, middle managers, and top managers. Supervisory management, or first-line management, includes positions such as supervisor, office manager, department manager, section chief, and team leader. Managers at this level work directly with the employees who produce and sell a firm's goods and services.

Middle management includes positions such as general managers, plant managers, division managers, and regional or branch managers. These managers are responsible for setting objectives that work with top management's goals. They also plan and carry out strategies for meeting those objectives.

Top managers include such positions as chief executive officer (CEO), chief operating officer (COO), chief financial officer (CFO), chief information officer (CIO), and executive vice-president. Top managers spend most of their time developing long-range plans, setting a direction for their organization, and inspiring a company's executives and employees to achieve their vision for the company's future. Top managers travel frequently between local, national, and global offices so they can meet and work with customers, suppliers, company managers, and employees.

Most managers start their careers in sales, production, or finance. If you are interested in a management career, you will likely start in a similar entry-level job. When you perform that job and other jobs well, you may be considered for a supervisory position. Then, if you are interested in supervising others and you have the technical, human, and conceptual skills to succeed, you'll begin your management career path. But what kinds of supervisory management jobs are available? Let's review the exciting possibilities.

Administrative services managers manage basic services that all organizations need—such as clerical work, payroll, travel, printing and copying, data records, telecommunications, security, parking, and supplies.

Construction managers plan, schedule, and coordinate the building of homes, commercial buildings such as offices and stores, and industrial facilities such as manufacturing plants and distribution centres. While administrative service managers work in offices, construction managers usually work on building sites with architects, engineers, construction workers, and suppliers.

Food service managers run restaurants and services that prepare and offer meals to customers. They coordinate workers and suppliers in kitchens, dining areas, and banquet operations; are responsible for those who order and purchase food inventories; maintain kitchen equipment; and recruit, hire, and train new workers. Food service managers can work for restaurant chains such as Swiss Chalet, for small locally owned restaurants, or for corporate food service departments in organizations.

Human resource managers help organizations to follow federal and provincial labour laws; effectively recruit, hire, train, and retain talented workers; administer corporate pay and benefits plans; develop and administer organizational human resource policies; and, when necessary, participate in contract negotiations or handle disputes. Human resource management jobs vary widely, depending on how specialized the requirements are.

Lodging managers work in hotels and motels but also help run camps, ranches, and recreational resorts. They may supervise employees that work in guest services, the front desk, the kitchen, the restaurant, banquets, house cleaning, and building maintenance. Because they are expected to help satisfy customers around the clock, they often work long hours and may be on call when not at work.

Medical and health services managers work in hospitals, nursing homes, doctors' offices, and corporate and university settings. They run departments that offer clinical services; ensure that provincial and federal laws are followed; and handle decisions related to the management of patient care, nursing, surgery, therapy, medical records, and financial payments.

Purchasing managers lead and control organizational supply chains that ensure companies purchase materials at reasonable prices and have the materials they need to produce the goods and services they sell. They also oversee deliveries when and where they are needed. Purchasing managers work with wholesale and retail buyers, to buy goods that are then resold to others; purchasing agents, who buy supplies and raw materials for their organizations; and contract specialists, who negotiate and supervise purchasing contracts with key suppliers and vendors.

Production managers direct and coordinate operations that manufacture goods. They work with employees who produce parts and assemble products and help decide which new machines should be purchased and when existing machines need maintenance. They are also responsible for meeting production goals that specify the quality, cost, schedule, and quantity of units to be produced.

The website "Living in Canada" provides a survey of salaries paid for a wide variety of managerial and other positions. You can find out more about managerial salaries by visiting www.livingin-canada.com/wages-for-management-jobs-canada.html. The average manager's salary appears to be about $60,000 per year.[1]

CAREER ASSESSMENT EXERCISES IN MANAGEMENT

1. The Canadian Institute of Management (CIM) is a not-for-profit professional organization that provides a range of management development and educational services to individuals, companies, and government agencies. Access the CIM's website at www.cim.ca. Write a one-page summary of CIM's services.

2. Go online to a business news service, such as Yahoo! News or Google News, or look at the business section of your local newspaper. Find a story relating to a first-line supervisor, a middle manager, or a top executive. Write a summary of that person's duties. What decisions does the manager make? How do those decisions affect the manager's organization?

3. From the descriptions above, pick a management position that interests you. Research the career field. What skills do you have that would make you a good candidate for a management position in that field? What work and other experience do you need to help you get started? List your strengths and weaknesses. Draw up a plan to improve your strengths.

11 | CUSTOMER-DRIVEN MARKETING

LEARNING OBJECTIVES

LO 11.1 Explain what marketing is and how it creates utility.

LO 11.2 Discuss the evolution of the marketing concept.

LO 11.3 Describe not-for-profit marketing and nontraditional marketing.

LO 11.4 Outline the basic steps in developing a marketing strategy.

LO 11.5 Describe the marketing research function.

LO 11.6 Discuss the methods used to segment consumer and business markets.

LO 11.7 Outline the determinants of consumer behaviour.

LO 11.8 Discuss the benefits of, and tools for, relationship marketing.

INSIDE BUSINESS

Handmade Items: Etsy.com Has Them All

Lisa Lutz, of Kelowna, British Columbia, promotes her handmade beaded jewellery and accessories from her own website, BeadCrazed.com. But she sells to customers online through her personal Etsy.com shop. Unique, handmade items have always been popular alternatives to mass-market products. Not very long ago, many craftspeople physically carried their creations to craft fairs or sold their work through friends and associates. Some still do, but now they also have access to potentially unlimited global markets through websites such as ArtFire, 1000 Markets, and Etsy.

Unlike eBay, where independent artisans compete directly with mass producers and importers, Etsy caters to customers who are looking for one-of-a-kind jewellery, a handmade quilt, or a pair of hand-carved bookends. Think of a craft fair online. Artisans use these sites to set up online "shops"; many have shops at more than one website to increase their exposure. These sites also carry knitted goods, clothing for adults and children, vintage items, photographs and other visual artworks, paper goods, spices and other food items, services such as custom DVDs of your special event, and craft supplies for making your own project. Shoppers can see photographs of individual items and ratings of different sellers. They also can choose from various payment options.

Etsy is now the largest online artisan and vintage market. Etsy got a boost from the craft boom. But when the collapse of the job market drove many hobbyists to try to make a living from their crafts, Etsy's membership soared. Etsy now has 19.8 million active buyers connecting to 1.4 million active sellers listing 29 million items. In a recent year, it had gross sales of $1.93 billion from which the company of 650 employees generated revenues of $195 mil-

lion. Looking for a piece of jewellery, maybe a new ring? A jewellery search on Etsy turned up 86,237 rings on 4,107 pages. Their prices range from pennies to almost a hundred thousand dollars for an opulent diamond engagement ring. The Etsy community spans the globe with buyers and sellers coming from more than 150 countries, including Canada.

Opening an online shop is cheaper and easier than opening a bricks-and-mortar store. Most websites allow sellers to set up shop for free, charge a small fee to post an item, and take a percentage of each sale. For example, Etsy charges 20 cents to post one item for four months, and takes 3.5 percent when that item is sold. That isn't very much, but if sellers want their items to stay high in search results, they need to renew the listings often. Some sellers renew their listings daily, so the fees can add up. Etsy also offers sellers a support system through blogs and links to social networking sites such as Facebook and Twitter. It is working to improve its search functions and is planning to set up a customer service phone line.

Many people dream of quitting their day jobs to make a living from selling their handmade products online, but selling online is not easy and is getting harder. Competition has become extreme as more artisans are joining these websites. Working from home or a studio often means spending long hours knitting or sewing or making jewellery—especially during the holiday rush—then more long hours standing in line at the post office waiting to ship the items sold. And of course, sellers have to spend time promoting their products in every possible medium, from blogs to magazines to, yes, that network of friends and associates.[1]

CHAPTER 11 OVERVIEW

Business success in the twenty-first century is directly tied to a company's ability to identify and serve its target markets. In fact, all organizations—profit-oriented and not-for-profit, manufacturing, and retailing—*must* serve customer needs to succeed. And that's what Etsy does by offering a wide range of unique, handmade items. Marketing is the link between the organization and the people who buy and use its goods and services. Organizations use marketing to figure out buyer needs. They also use marketing to show that they can meet those needs by supplying a quality product at a reasonable price. Marketing is the path to developing loyal, long-term customers.

Consumers purchase goods for their own use and enjoyment. Business purchasers look for products for their firms to use in their business operations. Both types of buyers may seem to be made up of a large number of similar people. But marketers see the separate wants and needs for each group. Buyers can be manufacturers, Web surfers, and shoppers in the grocery aisles. Companies gather huge amounts of data on every detail of consumer lifestyles and buying behaviours. Marketers use the data to understand the needs and wants of both final customers and business buyers. When buyers can satisfy customers, they are on their way toward building relationships with them. But it's not always easy. To start a relationship with the buying public, Whole Foods CEO John Mackey invites emails from consumers who may—or may not—be customers. Mackey spent several weeks in an email debate with an animal welfare activist about Whole Foods selling duck meat from a particular source. Mackey then asked the activist to help rewrite his firm's policies on farm animal treatment. This relationship developed through direct communication between the CEO and a consumer. Mackey's open email invitation helps Whole Foods to build a relationship with customers who have certain food-source concerns.

This chapter begins with an examination of the marketing concept and how businesspeople develop a marketing strategy. We then turn to marketing research techniques and an explanation of how businesses apply data to market segmentation to better understand customer behaviour. The chapter closes with a detailed look at the important role customer relationships play in today's highly competitive business world.

WHAT IS MARKETING?

LO 11.1 Explain what marketing is and how it creates utility.

marketing an organizational function and set of processes for creating, communicating, and delivering value to customers and for managing customer relationships in ways that benefit the organization and its stakeholders.

To succeed, every organization must serve customer needs—from profit-seeking firms such as McDonald's and Bell Canada to not-for-profits such as the Make-a-Wish Foundation of Canada and the Canadian Cancer Society. According to the American Marketing Association, **marketing** is "an organizational function and a set of processes for creating, communicating, and delivering value to customers and for managing customer relationships in ways that benefit the organization and its stakeholders."[2] Marketing techniques don't just sell goods and services, they also help people support ideas or viewpoints and educate others. The Canadian Diabetes Association mails out questionnaires that ask, "Are you at risk for diabetes?" The documents help educate the general public about this widespread disease by listing its risk factors and common symptoms and by describing the work of the association.

The best marketers not only give consumers what they want but anticipate and expect consumers' needs even before consumers see those needs themselves. Ideally, marketers can get ahead of the competition by helping consumers create a link between their new need and the fulfillment of that need by the marketers' products. ScotiaBank and Bank of Montreal promote pre-approved mortgages at low interest rates so customers know what they can borrow before they shop for a house. NetJets offers fractional (or shared) jet ownership to executives who want the luxury and flexibility of private ownership without the cost of owning their own plane. Samsung offers its next generation of high-definition TV with its trademarked Internet@TV. Owners connect their televisions to their home Internet connection, then add widgets to track the weather, check eBay, view Flickr albums, and check for Twitter updates—all in real time. Consumers can also sign up for Video-on-Demand service through Rogers, Bell, and other service providers. "Get the best of the Web right on your TV!" their promotion says.

Lexington Herald-Leader, Frank Anderson/AP/Wide World Photos

The best marketers give consumers what they want and anticipate their needs. NetJets offers fractional (shared) jet ownership to executives who want the luxury and flexibility of private ownership without the cost of owning their own plane.

As these examples show, marketing is more than just selling. Marketing is a process that begins with discovering unmet customer needs and continues with several tasks: researching the potential market; producing a good or service that can satisfy the targeted customers; and promoting, pricing, and distributing that good or service. Throughout the entire marketing process, a successful organization focuses on building customer relationships.

When two or more parties benefit from trading something of value (such as goods, services, or cash), they have entered into an **exchange process**. When you purchase a cup of coffee, the other party in the exchange may be a convenience store clerk, a vending machine, or a Tim Hortons server. The exchange seems simple—you hand over some money, and you receive your cup of coffee. But the exchange process is more complex. The exchange happens because you felt the need for a cup of coffee. It also happens because you saw the convenience store or the vending machine. You might not choose Tim Hortons unless you had heard of the brand. Because of marketing, your desire for a flavoured blend, a decaf, or a plain black coffee is identified—and the coffee manufacturer's business is successful.

exchange process an activity in which two or more parties trade something of value (such as goods, services, or cash) that satisfies each other's needs.

How Marketing Creates Utility

Marketing affects many parts of an organization. It also affects an organization's dealings with its customers. **Utility** is the ability of a good or service to satisfy the wants and needs of customers. A company's production function creates *form utility* by converting raw materials, component parts, and other inputs into finished goods and services. But the marketing function creates three types of utility: time utility, place utility, and ownership utility. *Time utility* is created by making a good or service available when customers want to purchase it. *Place utility* is created by making a product available in a location convenient for customers. *Ownership utility* refers to an organized

utility the power of a good or service to satisfy a want or need.

HIT & MISS

Beyoncé Thrills Fans and Surprises Marketers

Grammy Award–winning entertainer Beyoncé recently took the music industry—and marketing strategists—by storm. Without any advance warning, she released a new self-titled album by simply posting a trailer on her Instagram account with the caption "Surprise!" Beyoncé announced her latest release exclusively on iTunes. And in its first three days, consumers downloaded the album with its 14 songs and 17 videos more than 828,000 times.

Stunned by this approach, some executives believe that Beyoncé has changed music marketing forever. Others think her strategy worked because the singer's superstar brand allowed her to bypass traditional marketing channels. Some marketing experts have compared Beyoncé's album release to a form of relationship marketing. Beyoncé's surprise announcement about her new album catapulted its release to the top of iTune's all-time down-

loads list because she has a very loyal fan base with whom she has built a rock-solid relationship.

Questions for Critical Thinking

1. How will Beyoncé's move to bypass traditional marketing channels impact future projects?

2. What is the downside to Beyoncé's marketing strategy?

Sources: "Did Beyoncé's Album Just Prove Marketing Is Dead?" *CNBC*, December 17, 2013, accessed July 3, 2015, www.cnbc.com/id/101277017; Lyneka Little, "Target Doesn't Plan on Carrying New Beyoncé Album," *Wall Street Journal*, December 17, 2013, accessed July 3, 2015, http://blogs.wsj.com/speakeasy/2013/12/17/target-doesnt-plan-on-carrying-new-beyonce-album; Abigail Tracy, "Beyoncé Shows How Social Media Is Changing Marketing," *Inc.*, December 16, 2013, accessed July 3, 2015, www.inc.com/abigail-tracy/beyonce-shows-the-true-power-of-social-media.html; Lyneka Little, "Beyoncé Surprises Fans with Sudden Release of New 'Visual Album,'" *Wall Street Journal*, December 13, 2013, accessed July 3, 2015, http://blogs.wsj.com/speakeasy/2013/12/13/beyonce-surprises-fans-with-sudden-release-of-new-visual-album.

---

transfer of goods and services from the seller to the buyer. Some firms can create all three forms of utility. Target was the first American retailer to offer bar-coded, scannable mobile coupons direct to cellphones. Guests can sign on to the program either on their personal computers or on their cellphones. Each month, they receive either an email or a text message with a link to a mobile website page where they find offers for various products. They can use the mobile coupons at any Target store because Target is the first retailer to have point-of-sale scanning technology for the coupons in all of its stores.[3] Technology is also having a major impact on the entertainment industry. See the "Hit & Miss" feature for more details.

✔ ASSESSMENT CHECK

11.1.1 What is utility?

11.1.2 Identify how marketing creates utility.

LO 11.2 Discuss the evolution of the marketing concept.

EVOLUTION OF THE MARKETING CONCEPT

Marketing has always been a part of business, from the earliest village traders to large twenty-first century organizations that produce and sell complex goods and services. Over time, marketing activities have evolved through the five eras shown in **Figure 11.1**: the production, sales, marketing, relationship, and now the social era. These eras run similar to some of the time periods discussed in Chapter 1.

For centuries, organizations of the *production era* stressed their efficiency in producing quality products. Their philosophy could be summed up by the remark, "A good product will sell itself." This focus on production continued into the twentieth century, then it gradually gave way to the *sales era*. In the sales era, businesses assumed that consumers would buy as a result of energetic sales efforts. Organizations didn't fully recognize the importance of their customers until the *marketing era* of the 1950s. Then, organizations began to adopt a consumer orientation. This focus has grown stronger in recent years, leading to the *relationship era* in the 1990s. In the relationship era, companies focus on customer satisfaction and building long-term business relationships. Today, the social era continues to grow exponentially, thanks to the Internet and social media sites

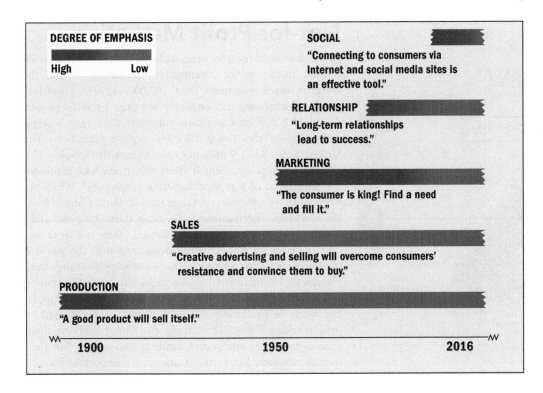

FIGURE 11.1 Five Eras in the History of Marketing

like Facebook, Twitter, and LinkedIn. Companies now routinely use mobile, social media, and the Web as a way of marketing their goods and services to consumers.

Emergence of the Marketing Concept

The term **marketing concept** refers to a companywide customer focus with the goal of achieving long-term success. The basic idea of the marketing concept is that marketplace success begins with the customer. A firm should analyze each customer's needs and then work backward to offer products that fulfill those needs. The emergence of the marketing concept can be explained best by the shift from a *seller's market,* a market with a shortage of goods and services, to a *buyer's market,* a market with too many goods and services. During the 1950s, North America became a strong buyer's market. As a result, companies were forced to satisfy customers rather than just producing and selling goods and services.

Today, much competition among firms centres on the effort to satisfy customers. Apple's iPhone followed on the heels of its wildly successful iPod. Apple introduced the iWatch, which has launched a new category of "wearable" devices that connect to iPhones. As with other devices, an entire industry of programmers has sprung up to take advantage of the Apple software platform to produce apps that will cater to a variety of customers' needs and wants.[4]

marketing concept a companywide consumer focus on promoting long-term success.

 **ASSESSMENT CHECK**

11.2.1 What is the marketing concept?

11.2.2 How is the marketing concept tied to the relationship and social eras of marketing?

NOT-FOR-PROFIT AND NONTRADITIONAL MARKETING

LO 11.3 Describe not-for-profit marketing and nontraditional marketing.

The marketing concept has traditionally been associated with profit-seeking organizations. But today the marketing concept is also applied to the not-for-profit sector and to other nontraditional areas, such as religious organizations and political campaigns.

Courtesy of United Way Toronto

In some cases, not-for-profit organizations form a partnership with a for-profit company to promote the firm's message or to distribute its goods and services. This partnership usually benefits both organizations. Scotiabank is the title sponsor for the annual Rat Race for the United Way Toronto.[7]

Not-for-Profit Marketing

Every continent receives benefits from the approximately 20 million not-for-profit organizations operating around the world. Canada has more than 160,000 registered not-for-profit organizations that employ more than 2 million people. About 12.5 million Canadians volunteer their time, energy, and skills with charities and not-for-profit organizations. The United States has 1.9 million organizations that employ 12.9 million workers and benefit from volunteers who represent the equivalent of 9 million full-time employees.[5] When the value of those volunteers is taken into account, Canada leads the world in contributions to its gross domestic product by not-for-profit organizations; the United States is a close second.[6] The largest not-for-profit organization in the world is the Red Cross/Red Crescent. Other not-for-profits range from Habitat for Humanity to the Alberta Society for the Prevention of Cruelty to Animals. These organizations benefit by applying many of the strategies and business concepts used by profit-seeking firms. They apply marketing tools to reach audiences, attract and secure funding, and accomplish their overall missions. Marketing strategies are important for not-for-profit organizations because, just like for-profit businesses, they also compete for dollars. Not-for-profit organizations compete for dollars from individuals, foundations, and corporations.

Not-for-profit organizations operate in both public and private sectors. Public groups include government units and agencies that receive tax funding. For example, a municipal swimming pool receives funding from the local municipal government and might be operated by volunteers. The private not-for-profit sector comprises many different types of organizations, including the Canadian Olympic Committee and the Canadian Medical Association. Although some private not-for-profits generate surplus revenue, their primary goals are not about earning profits. If they earn funds beyond their expenses, they invest the excess in their organizational missions.

Celebrities are particularly visible in their campaigns for not-for-profit organizations—both their own organizations and those of others. The actress Reese Witherspoon is the Avon Global Ambassador and Honorary Chairperson of the Avon Foundation for Women. Witherspoon helped present a $500,000 grant to the Fund for Global Women's Leadership. The grant was intended to help the worldwide movement to end violence toward women.[8]

Nontraditional Marketing

Not-for-profit organizations often use one or more of five major categories of nontraditional marketing: person marketing, place marketing, event marketing, cause marketing, and organization marketing. **Figure 11.2** shows examples of these types of marketing. As described in the "Going Green" feature, an organization uses each of these types of marketing to connect with the audience that is most likely to offer time, money, or other resources. In some cases, the effort may reach the market the organization intends to serve. In the case of ice cream maker Häagen-Dazs, the company has chosen to support research related to the disappearing honey bee.

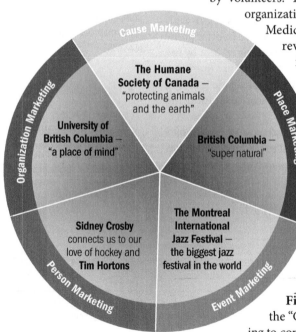

FIGURE 11.2 Categories of Nontraditional Marketing

GOING GREEN | HÄAGEN-DAZS FOCUSES ON HONEY BEE RESEARCH

You may not immediately make an association between premium ice cream and honey bees. Pollinating many of the fruits, vegetables, and nuts we eat, honey bees are integral to more than half of the all-natural fruits, nuts, and berries used to produce Häagen-Dazs ice creams, sorbets, and frozen yogurts. Mysteriously, honey bees have been disappearing over the last decade.

Häagen-Dazs decided to take action by contributing to research to preserve honey bee colonies. The company has created the Häagen-Dazs Ice Cream Bee Board to provide insight and consultation into the causes of colony collapse disorder (CCD), which occurs when bees mysteriously die after leaving their hives.

Scientists and researchers are not certain what causes CCD. Environmental factors like chemical exposure, parasites, and pesticides are believed to be contributors, along with viruses, mites, and poor nutrition.

To date, Häagen-Dazs has contributed over $700,000 to support a California-based honey bee research facility, one of the largest of its kind in North America. In addition, the company has made a gift of $250,000 to Penn State University to provide funds for research, education, outreach, and student training. "We want to keep these little heroes buzzing. We hope you'll join our mission," reads the Häagen-Dazs website.

Questions for Critical Thinking

1. Häagen-Dazs has introduced an ice cream flavour called Vanilla Honey Bee, and partial proceeds go to CCD research. How can the company make consumers aware of its efforts to save the bees?

2. Discuss how Häagen-Dazs is attempting to use cause marketing. Whose interests are being served in the company's attempt to save honey bees?

Sources: Häagen-Dazs, "Honey, Please Don't Go," accessed February 9, 2014, www.haagendazs.us/Learn/HoneyBees/; University of California, Davis, "Laidlaw Facility: Häagen-Dazs Honey Bee Haven," accessed February 9, 2014, http://beebiology.ucdavis.edu; Michael Wines, "Bee Deaths May Stem from Virus, Study Says," *New York Times*, January 14, 2014, accessed www.nytimes.com/2014/01/22/us/bee-deaths-may-stem-from-virus-study-says.html?_r=0; Parija B. Kavilanz, "Disappearing Bees Threaten Ice Cream Sellers," *CNNMoney*, February 20, 2008, accessed July 3, 2015, http://money.cnn.com/2008/02/17/news/companies/bees_icecream.

Person Marketing — *Example — Political campaigns to urge people to vote to that person.*

Person marketing refers to efforts designed to attract the attention, interest, and preference of a target market toward a person. Campaign managers for a political candidate conduct marketing research to identify groups of voters and financial supporters. They design advertising campaigns, fundraising events, and political rallies to reach that target group. In another example of person marketing, Canon Canada's television advertising campaign spokeswoman Avril Lavigne showed her creative use of Canon's PowerShot camera to a young potential market that knew her more for her musical talents. The message was clear—PowerShot makes creative photography simple and easy, even for people who know very little about the mechanics of a camera.

> **person marketing** efforts that are designed to attract the attention, interest, and preference of a target market toward a person.

Many successful job seekers use the tools of person marketing. They research the wants and needs of prospective employers, and they identify ways they can meet those wants and needs. They look for employers through a variety of channels and send messages that focus on how they can benefit the employer.

Place Marketing

As the term suggests, **place marketing** attempts to attract people to a particular area, such as a city, region, or country. This marketing may focus on a place that may appeal to consumers as a tourist destination or to businesses as a desirable business location. A strategy for place marketing often includes advertising.

> **place marketing** an attempt to attract people to a particular area, such as a city, region, or country.

Place marketing may be combined with event marketing, such as the Olympics. For example, Vancouver used three mythical cartoon critters, named Quatchi, Miga, and Sumi, to promote the Olympic and Paralympic Winter Games. Merchandise featuring the mascots was available for sale to the public for more than two years before the actual games took place.[9]

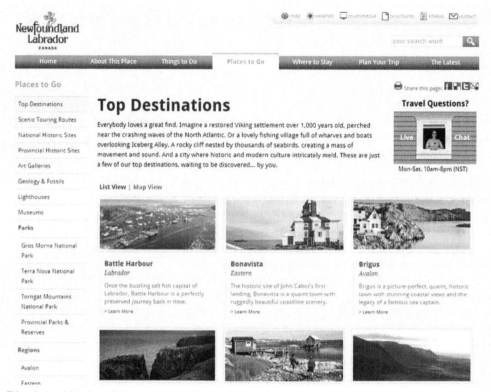

This webpage sightseeing guide is an example of *place marketing*. It is published by the government of Newfoundland and Labrador to encourage tourism.

Courtesy of Newfoundland and Labrador Tourism

Event Marketing

event marketing marketing or sponsoring of short-term events such as athletic competitions and cultural and charitable performances.

Event marketing refers to marketing or sponsoring short-term events such as athletic competitions and cultural and charitable performances. The Canadian Diabetes Association sponsors "Walk, Run, Cycle for Diabetes" events throughout the year. This event offers Canadian communities an opportunity to get active while also raising awareness and funds for the Canadian Diabetes Association. These volunteer-led events target local communities, promote a healthy and active lifestyle, and are dedicated to exposing the reality of diabetes and the importance of the cause.[10]

Event marketing often leads to partnerships between not-for-profit and for-profit organizations. Many businesses sponsor events such as 10K runs to raise funds for health-related charities. These occasions require a marketing effort to plan the event and attract participants and sponsors. Events may be intended to raise money or awareness, or both.

Cause Marketing

cause marketing marketing that promotes a cause or social issue, such as preventing child abuse, anti-littering efforts, and stop-smoking campaigns.

Cause marketing is marketing that promotes awareness of a cause or social issue or raises money for a cause or social issue, such as drug abuse prevention or childhood hunger. Cause marketing tries to educate the public and may or may not try to raise funds. An advertisement often contains a phone number or website address where people can get more information about the organization or issue. People can either donate money or take other actions of support. The Royal Bank of Canada sponsors the University of Western Ontario's Alternative Spring Break program. This program provides funds that help young adults and student volunteers participate in community activities in Canada and in other locations in need. Projects range from rebuilding housing damaged by natural disaster to teaching health care and English to children.[11]

For-profit companies look for ways to contribute to their communities by joining forces with charities and causes to provide financial resources, marketing resources, and human resources. Timberland is well known for participating in the City Year program, where young adults contract to perform a year of volunteer service in their communities. For-profit firms can also combine their goods and services with a cause. Seventh Generation makes household cleaning and paper products and is committed to educating consumers about how "green" products can make their homes healthier and safer.[12]

organization marketing a marketing strategy that influences consumers to accept the goals of an organization, receive the services of an organization, or contribute in some way to an organization.

Organization Marketing

The final category of nontraditional marketing, **organization marketing,** focuses on an organization. It influences consumers to accept the goals of an organization, receive the services of an organization, or contribute in some way to an organization. Examples of organizations that use marketing include the college or university you are attending, the Canadian Cancer Society, and Oprah Winfrey's Angel Network. These organizations use their own websites, advertise in magazines, and send mail directly to consumers in their efforts to market their organizations. The Angel Network was established by Oprah Winfrey more than a decade ago to "encourage people around the world to make a difference in the lives of others." The organization runs its own charitable projects and supports the projects of other not-for-profits such as Habitat for Humanity.[13]

✓ **ASSESSMENT CHECK**

11.3.1 Why do not-for-profit organizations use marketing?

11.3.2 What are the five types of nontraditional marketing used by not-for-profit organizations?

DEVELOPING A MARKETING STRATEGY

LO 11.4 Outline the basic steps in developing a marketing strategy.

In any successful organization, for-profit or not-for-profit, decision makers follow a two-step process to develop a *marketing strategy*. First, decision makers study and analyze all possible target markets and choose the most suitable market. Second, they create a marketing mix to satisfy the chosen market. **Figure 11.3** shows the relationships among the target market, the marketing mix variables, and the marketing environment. This section describes the development of a marketing strategy that is designed to attract and build relationships with customers. Sometimes, in an effort to attract customers, marketers use questionable methods, as described in the "Solving an Ethical Controversy" feature.

Earlier chapters of this book introduced many environmental factors that affect the success or failure of a firm's business strategy, including today's rapidly changing and highly competitive world of business, a wide range of social and cultural factors, economic challenges, political and legal factors, and technological innovations. Although these external forces often operate outside managers' control, marketers must still consider the impact of environmental factors on their decisions.

A marketing plan is a key part of a firm's overall business plan. The marketing plan outlines a firm's marketing strategy. It also includes information about the target market, sales and revenue goals, the marketing budget, and the timing for implementing the elements of the marketing mix.

Selecting a Target Market

The two elements of a marketing strategy are best described by the expression "find a need and fill it." A firm's marketers study the individuals and business decision makers in its potential market to find a need. A market consists of people who have purchasing power, a willingness to buy, and the authority to make purchase decisions.

Markets can be classified by type of product. Consumer products—often known as **business-to-consumer (B2C)** products—are goods and services that are purchased by end users. Some examples

business-to-consumer (B2C) product a good or service that is purchased by end users.

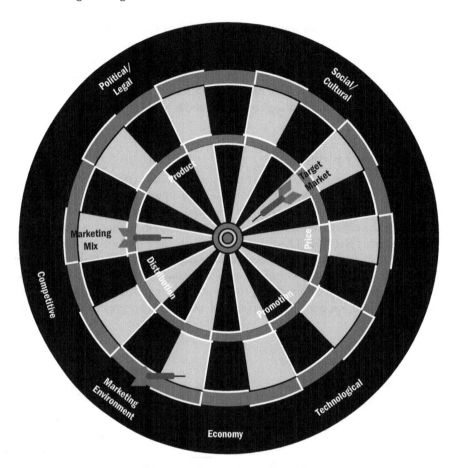

FIGURE 11.3 Target Market and Marketing Mix within the Marketing Environment

---

SOLVING AN **ETHICAL** CONTROVERSY

When Free Credit Reports Aren't Free

When times are tough and credit is tight, consumers are more likely to want to look up their credit scores and see what they can do about them. In Canada, the way that credit reporting companies handle a person's personal information is governed by the federal Personal Information Protection and Electronic Document Act (PIPEDA) and Credit Reporting Act and by such provincial acts as the Personal Information Protection Act (PIPA). In the United States, the Fair Credit Reporting Act (FCRA) governs the industry, which deals with the three major consumer reporting companies in North America—Equifax, Experian, and TransUnion. Credit reporting companies often advertise offers for a free credit report on the Internet. But many offers have hidden costs or will lead customers to other services that have costs.

Should firms be allowed to use the word *free* when advertising for credit reports if the service contains hidden costs?

PRO

1. If the credit score itself is free, but related services are not, then the advertising is truthful. Ty Taylor, the president of Experian's Consumer Direct Division, says, "You get a free credit report and free score for test-driving our services."

2. Some promotional offers include free credit scores, with a tie-in to additional services for a fee. Other industries make similar offers for a free month of phone, cable, or Internet service.

CON

1. The word *free* is a powerful invitation in advertising. Some companies provide "free" reports, then bill consumers for services they have to cancel.

2. Consumer advocates say that firms work on people's fears. Edgar Dworsky, the founder of ConsumerWorld.org and former member of Experian's consumer advisory panel, says, "Does the average person really need to see their credit reports more than once every four months? Do you need to look at it daily? That's paranoia."

(continued)

SOLVING AN **ETHICAL** CONTROVERSY (*continued*)

Summary

Most consumers know that the use of the word *free* in any advertising is generally attached to some kind of cost at some point in time. However, should consumers have to figure out exactly when they might be charged a cost for their dealings with consumer reporting companies—or with any company?

Sources: Federal Trade Commission, "Free Annual Credit Reports," accessed February 11, 2014, www.consumer.ftc.gov/articles/0155-free-credit-reports; Ron Lieber, "Free Credit on Credit? No Longer," *New York Times*, April 17, 2010, accessed February 11, 2014, www.nytimes.com/2010/04/08/your-money/credit-scores/08credit.html; Joe Taylor Jr., "New Laws Crack Down on Free Credit Report Marketing," *CardRatings*, updated March 22, 2015, accessed February 11, 2014, www.cardratings.com/free-credit-report-legislation.html; Michelle Singletary, "Free Credit Reports Get Easier to Find," *Washington Post*, March 4, 2010, accessed February 11, 2014, www.boston.com/business/personalfinance/articles/2010/03/04/free_credit_reports_get_easier_to_find.

are ice skates, tomato sauce, and a haircut. Business products—or **business-to-business (B2B)** products—are goods and services purchased to be used, either directly or indirectly, in making other goods that will be resold. Some products can fit either classification depending on who buys them and why. For example, a computer and a credit card can be used by both a business and a consumer.

A **target market** is the group of possible customers that an organization directs its marketing efforts toward. Customer needs and wants differ, and no single organization can satisfy everyone. For example, *Popular Science* is a magazine geared toward readers who are interested in science and technology, whereas *Bon Appétit* is aimed at readers who are interested in fine food and cooking.

Decisions about marketing involve strategies for four areas of marketing activity: product, distribution, promotion, and pricing. A firm's **marketing mix** blends the four strategies to fit the needs and preferences of a specific target market. Marketing success depends not on the four individual strategies but on their unique combination.

Product strategy involves more than just designing a good or service by adding needed qualities. It also includes decisions about package design, brand names, trademarks, warranties, product image, new-product development, and customer service. Think about your favourite pair of jeans. Do you like them because they fit the best, or do other qualities—such as styling and overall image—play a role in your brand preference? *Distribution strategy*, the second marketing mix variable, ensures that customers receive their purchases in the proper quantities at the right times and locations. *Promotional strategy*, another marketing mix element, effectively blends advertising, personal selling, sales promotion, and public relations to achieve its goals of informing, persuading, and influencing purchase decisions.

Pricing strategy, the final mix element, is also one of the most difficult areas of marketing decision making. Firms need to set profitable and justifiable prices for their product offerings. Such actions must sometimes comply with government regulation and may receive considerable public criticism. They also represent a powerful competitive strategy. Pricing strategies frequently lead to responses by the other firms in the industry, which may match price changes to avoid losing customers. Think about your jeans again. Would you continue to purchase them if they were priced much higher or much lower?

Developing a Marketing Mix for International Markets

Marketing a good or service in foreign markets means deciding whether to offer the same marketing mix in every market (*standardization*) or to develop a unique mix to fit each market (*adaptation*). Standardizing the marketing mix can have upsides such as reliable marketing performance and low costs. This approach works best with B2B goods, such as steel, chemicals, and aircraft. These products need little sensitivity to a nation's culture.

business-to-business (B2B) product a good or service purchased to be used, either directly or indirectly, in the production of other goods for resale.

target market a group of people that an organization markets its goods, services, or ideas toward, using a strategy designed to satisfy this group's specific needs and preferences.

marketing mix a blending of the four elements of marketing strategy—product, distribution, promotion, and pricing—to satisfy chosen customer segments.

Adaptation allows marketers to vary their marketing mix to suit local competitive conditions, consumer preferences, and government regulations. Consumer products tend to be more culture dependent than business products. For that reason, they often need adaptation. SUBWAY, which already has 144 stores in China, plans to open 500 new stores there.

In contrast, adaptation lets marketers vary their marketing mix to suit local competitive conditions, consumer preferences, and government regulations. Consumer tastes are often shaped by local cultures. Consumer products tend to be more culture dependent than business products. For that reason, they often need adaptation. SUBWAY, which already has 425 stores in China, plans to open 600 new stores in the next few years. SUBWAY hopes to match the Chinese presence of McDonald's in 10 years, and with 40,000 stores worldwide has surpassed McDonald's 33,000 units. As SUBWAY opens stores in different regions, it plans to adapt its menu to local tastes with such offerings as Beijing roast duck sandwiches and "hot spicy Szechuan sauce." Why do these firms go out of their way to adapt to Chinese preferences? China is a market with 1.3 billion potential consumers.[14]

Marketers also try to build adaptability into the designs of standardized goods and services for international and domestic markets. *Mass customization* allows a firm to mass-produce goods and services while also adding unique features to individual or small groups of orders. For example, online firm Blank Label (www.blanklabel.com) specializes in custom-made men's dress shirts. Customers can choose their own fabric, style, individual features, and size. Spreadshirt (www.spreadshirt.com) specializes in customized casual wear, accessories, and even personalized underwear.[15]

✓ **ASSESSMENT CHECK**

11.4.1 Distinguish between consumer products and business products.

11.4.2 What are the steps in developing a marketing strategy?

LO 11.5 Describe the marketing research function.

marketing research the process of collecting and evaluating information to support marketing decision making.

MARKETING RESEARCH

Marketing research involves more than just collecting data. Researchers must decide how to collect data, interpret the results, convert the data into decision-oriented information, and communicate those results to managers for use in decision making. **Marketing research** is the process of collecting and evaluating information to help marketers make effective decisions. It links business decision makers to the marketplace by providing data about potential target markets that help them design effective marketing mixes.

Obtaining Marketing Research Data

Marketing researchers need both internal and external data. Firms generate *internal data* within their organizations. Financial records provide useful information, such as changes in unpaid bills; inventory levels; sales generated by different categories of customers or product lines; profitability of particular divisions; or comparisons of sales by territories, salespeople, customers, or product lines.

Researchers gather *external data* from outside sources, including previously published data. Trade associations publish reports on activities in specific industries. Advertising agencies collect information on the audiences reached by various media. National marketing research firms offer information through subscription services. Some professional research firms specialize in specific markets, such as youth or ethnic groups. This information helps companies to make decisions about developing or modifying products. The largest consumer-goods manufacturer in the world, Procter & Gamble, has excelled in marketing research for a long time; it created its own marketing research department in 1923 and began conducting its research online in 2001. To help the company recover from the global recession and focus on the future, the company's CEO, A.G. Lafley, continues to rely on his inquisitive nature and commitment to understanding how consumers live. Early in his career, Lafley spent time in households in various countries to observe and listen and to understand what delights customers. As the consumer products giant moves forward with expansion plans to reach customers in developing regions, Procter & Gamble continues its sharply focused marketing research efforts.[16]

Secondary data, or previously published data, are low cost and easy to obtain. Government publications are excellent data sources, and most are available online. The most frequently used government statistics are census data, which contain the population's age, gender, education level, household size and composition, occupation, employment status, and income. Even private research firms such as TRU-Insight (formerly Teenage Research Unlimited), which studies the purchasing habits of teens, provide some free information on their websites. This information helps firms evaluate consumers' buying behaviour, look ahead to possible changes in the marketplace, and identify new markets.[17]

Even though secondary data are a quick and inexpensive resource, this information sometimes is not specific or current enough for marketing researchers' needs. Researchers may decide that they need to collect *primary data*—data collected firsthand through such methods as observation and surveys.

Observational studies view the actions of consumers either directly or by using mechanical devices. More retailers are watching their customers by way of video cameras. This kind of observation can solve problems such as widening a too-narrow aisle to allow shoppers easier access. But such close observation has also raised privacy concerns.[18] Procter & Gamble spends about $200 million on consumer observation each year and says it is the firm's most important type of marketing research. Retired CEO Robert McDonald said, "If we can continue to innovate and continue to mind consumer needs and delight consumers, that ability outweighs any macroeconomic force."[19]

Observing customers cannot provide all the information a marketing researcher needs. For example, a researcher might observe a customer buying a red sweater, but have no idea why the purchase was made—or for whom. When researchers need information about consumers' attitudes, opinions, and motives, they need to ask the consumers themselves. They may conduct surveys by telephone, in person, online, or in focus groups.

A *focus group* gathers 8 to 12 people in a room or over the Internet to discuss a specific topic. A focus group can lead to new ideas, address consumers' needs, and even point out flaws in existing products. Campbell Soup Company held nationwide focus groups in which respondents reviewed ingredients from two soups. Two of three focus group participants overwhelmingly chose the Campbell's brand. Marketing researchers have also begun to take advantage of mobile marketing and social media outlets such as Facebook, Twitter, and blogs.[20]

Applying Marketing Research Data

Market researchers now collect information that is more accurate than in the past. That means the resulting marketing strategies are also more effective. One field of research, known as **business intelligence**, uses various activities and technologies to gather, store, and analyze data to make better competitive decisions. Unilever, maker of consumer products including Dove soap, Axe deodorant, and Ben and Jerry's ice cream, has a highly regarded global research staff and values input from outside sources. The company has adopted a crowdsourced, open-idea platform, where external contributions are sought for diverse projects. Unilever's "challenges and wants" webpage solicits ideas for new designs and technologies to help improve the way its products are made. If Unilever decides to pursue a submitted idea, the originator might benefit financially.[21]

business intelligence a field of research that uses activities and technologies for gathering, storing, and analyzing data to make better competitive decisions.

Data Mining

data mining the use of computer searches of customer data to detect patterns and relationships.

After a company has built a database, marketers must be able to analyze the data and use the information it provides. **Data mining** is part of the broader field of business intelligence. It refers to the task of using computer-based technology to evaluate data in a database and identify useful trends. These trends or patterns may suggest models of real-world business activities. Accurate data mining can help researchers forecast recessions and pinpoint sales prospects.

data warehouse a customer database that allows managers to combine data from several different organizational functions.

Data mining uses a **data warehouse,** a sophisticated customer database that allows managers to combine data from several different organizational functions. Rapleaf Inc. collects publicly available personal information from social networking sites such as Facebook, Twitter, and other forums. Rapleaf then sells this information to airlines and credit card companies that view those individuals as potential customers. Such information can include everything from your blogging or posting habits to your credit rating. Among the issues arising from data mining are ownership of Web user data, the targeting capabilities of the Web, government supervision—and, of course, privacy.

Some observers feel that privacy norms are changing. They see confidentiality giving way to increasing openness.[22] Playnomics's segmentation technology and predictive analysis mine and analyze the behaviour of online and app game players by tracking the number of hours they spend on games and creating behavioural profiles. App and game developers pay a monthly fee for the resulting data. The company's CEO says providing information about user activity gives marketers a way to find and engage the right player for greater retention and increased revenues.[23]

✔ **ASSESSMENT CHECK**

11.5.1 What is the difference between primary data and secondary data?

11.5.2 What is data mining?

LO 11.6 Discuss the methods used to segment consumer and business markets.

market segmentation the process of dividing a total market into several relatively similar groups.

MARKET SEGMENTATION

Market segmentation is the process of dividing a market into several relatively similar groups. Both for-profit and not-for-profit organizations use segmentation to help them reach desirable target markets. Market segmentation is often based on the results of research, which tries to identify trends among certain groups of people. For instance, one recent survey revealed that social media use among Internet-using baby boomers—those North Americans between 50 and 64 years old—grew from 52 to 65 percent. Younger adults—those under age 30—are still the heaviest users, with 90 percent visiting a social networking site on any given day. Overall, 73 percent of adult Internet users visit social networking sites, but the rise in use by older consumers is important information for businesses.[24] This kind of information helps marketers to decide what types of products to develop and to whom these products should be marketed.

Market segmentation attempts to isolate the traits that set a certain group of customers apart from the overall market. However, segmentation doesn't automatically produce marketing success. **Table 11.1** lists several criteria that marketers should consider. The effectiveness of a segmentation strategy depends on how well the market meets these criteria. Once marketers identify a market segment to target, they can create an appropriate marketing strategy.

Table 11.1 Criteria for Market Segmentation

CRITERION	EXAMPLE
A segment must be a measurable group.	Data can be collected on the dollar amount and number of purchases made by college and university students.
A segment must be accessible for communication.	More and more seniors are now online, so many more seniors can now be reached through Internet channels.
A segment must be large enough to offer profit potential.	In a small community, a store carrying only large-size shoes might not be profitable. For similar reasons, a specialty retail chain may prefer to locate in a large market.

Companies that can identify trends in consumer preferences before their rivals can benefit greatly; those that miss the boat generally suffer the consequences. There is an expanding opportunity for mobile apps and Internet-based services to make their way into consumers' cars. Pandora Internet Radio is now being used in 5 million cars and 100 models through its partnerships with auto brands and stereo manufacturers. Apple hopes to integrate Siri technology and maps into car navigation systems, and Ford already uses voice, steering wheel, or touchscreen-activated controls for mobile apps.[25]

How Market Segmentation Works

The first segmentation distinction involves whether a firm offers goods and services to customers for their own use or to purchasers who will use them directly or indirectly in providing other products for resale (the so-called B2B market). Depending on whether their firms offer consumer or business products, marketers segment their target markets differently. Four common bases for segmenting consumer markets are geographical segmentation, demographic segmentation, psychographic segmentation, and product-related segmentation. By contrast, business markets can segment on three criteria: customer-based segmentation, end-use segmentation, and geographical segmentation. **Figure 11.4** illustrates the segmentation methods for these two types of markets.

Segmenting Consumer Markets

Market segmentation has been practised since people first began selling products. Tailors made some clothing items for men and others for women. Tea was imported from India for tea drinkers in England and other European countries. In addition to demographic and geographical segmentation, today's marketers also define customer groups based on product-related differences and criteria that are psychographic—relating to lifestyle and values.

Geographical Segmentation

The oldest segmentation method is **geographical segmentation**—dividing a market into similar groups on the basis of their locations. Geographical location does not guarantee that consumers in a certain region will all buy the same kinds of products, but it does provide some information about needs. For example, people who live in the suburbs buy more lawn-care products than those

geographical segmentation dividing an overall market into similar groups on the basis of their locations.

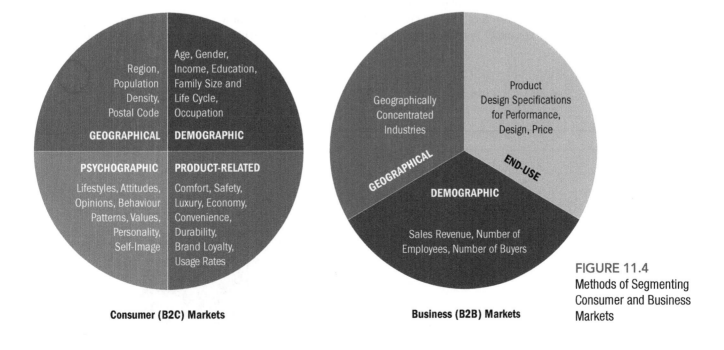

Consumer (B2C) Markets

Business (B2B) Markets

FIGURE 11.4
Methods of Segmenting Consumer and Business Markets

who live in city centres. But many people in the suburbs choose instead to purchase the services of a lawn maintenance firm. Consumers who live where winter is more severe are more likely than those who live in warmer areas to buy ice scrapers, snow shovels, and snow blowers. They are also more likely to contract with firms to remove the snow from driveways. Marketers also look at the size of the population of an area and who lives there—are the residents old or young? Do they reflect an ethnic background? What is the level of their income?

Job growth and migration patterns are also important to consider. Some businesses combine areas or even entire countries that share similar population and product-use patterns, instead of treating each as an independent segment.

Demographic Segmentation

demographic segmentation dividing markets on the basis of various demographic or socioeconomic characteristics, such as gender, age, income, occupation, household size, stage in family life cycle, education, or ethnic group.

The most common method of market segmentation is **demographic segmentation.** This type of segmentation separates markets on the basis of various demographic or socioeconomic characteristics. Common demographic measures include gender, income, age, occupation, household size, stage in the family life cycle, education, and racial or ethnic group. Statistics Canada and the U.S. Census Bureau are the best sources of demographic information for their markets. **Figure 11.5** lists some of the measures used in demographic segmentation.

North American police departments are a highly specialized occupational demographic group. Popular for its durability, the Ford Crown Victoria has long held 75 percent of the patrol-car market share. Ford has phased out the "Crown Vic," replacing it with the Police Interceptor, modelled on the Taurus sedan but modified for the extreme circumstances of police work. The Interceptor's fuel efficiency is 25 percent better than the Crown Vic's. Its 365-horsepower engine outguns the Crown Vic's by 115 horsepower. Its newest model, the Explorer Police Interceptor, has a 3.5-liter, twin turbocharged engine, which helps the company compete with similar models from GM and Dodge.[26]

Gender used to be a simple way to define markets for certain products—jewellery and skin care products for women; tools and motorcycles for men. Much of that has changed—dramatically. Men now buy jewellery and skin care products, and women buy tools and motorcycles. But marketers have also found that even though these shifts have blurred the lines between products, there are still differences in the *way* that women and men shop. A recent study of online shopping habits revealed that men are more likely to make a purchase from a desktop or laptop computer, while women are more likely to use a mobile device to complete a purchase. Marketers should be sure a website has an easy-to-use mobile interface. Other data suggests that women were slightly more intent on getting the best available price, so easy page-browsing and in-page price comparisons from a mobile device should be a top priority.[27]

Another shift involves purchasing power. Women now control an estimated 80 percent of consumer spending, estimated between $5 and $15 trillion per year.[28] With this knowledge in

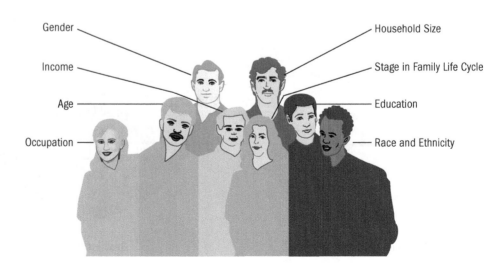

FIGURE 11.5 Common Demographic Measures

hand, Amazon purchased online retailer Zappos and launched a program called Amazon Mom, a free membership program for parents of small children.[29]

Age may be the most unstable factor in demographic segmentation in Canada and the United States because of our rapidly aging population. Of the 340-plus million people who live in North America, more than one-third will be age 55 or older by the year 2020.[30] Because of these statistics, marketers for travel and leisure products, and marketers for retirement and business investments, are working hard to attract the attention of this age group, the aging baby boomers—those born between 1946 and 1964. Active-adult housing communities are one result of these efforts. Some developers have built communities with a resort-style atmosphere in desirable locations such as Whistler, British Columbia, ski country or the outskirts of a large city such as Toronto or Montreal. But, because of the recession, many such communities have actually

The millennials are a rapidly growing consumer market. They are characterized as tech-savvy shoppers who influence the purchases of their families and friends.

seen their populations decrease. According to Mark Mather, associate vice-president of the Population Reference Bureau, "Baby boomers helped fuel housing and population growth in retirement areas earlier in the decade, and now they are playing an important role in the decline."[31]

Teens are another rapidly growing market. The entire scope of Generation Y—those born between 1976 and 1997—takes in about one-third of the total North American population. These consumers, often called the millennials, are tech-savvy shoppers. They influence not only their own purchases but also those of their families and friends. They are educated consumers who comparison shop and usually avoid impulse purchases, partly because of the recession and partly because they are spending their own money. According to a Nielsen survey, compared with older generations, such as the "greatest generation" (those who lived through World War II) and the baby boomers, Generation Y consumers shop less often but when they do shop, they buy more, preferring megastores and big box-retailers.[32]

Statistics can be helpful, but they don't tell the whole story. To serve customers well, marketers must also learn where people live, how old they are, what languages they speak, how much income they have, and their cultural tastes and preferences. Sometimes, marketers must do intensive research to reach a particular age group or gender group, or both, as described in the "Hit & Miss" feature.

(HIT) & MISS

Disney XD TV: Marketing to Boys

Disney marketing aimed at young girls has been highly successful. Just think of the "Princesses" products, the Jonas Brothers, and *High School Musical*. But the Disney Channel audience is 40 percent male. *(Pirates of the Caribbean* and *Toy Story* have both had successful sequels.)

In North America, about 10 percent of the population are males aged 5 to 19 years old. Worldwide, boys (or their parents) spend $50 billion every year on clothes, toys, and video games.

Recently, Disney bought Marvel Entertainment. It is hoping that Marvel's superheroes will draw viewers to Disney's XD TV channel. The channel is aimed at boys but doesn't exclude girls from its

offerings of animation, action-adventure, comedy, movies, sports-themed shows, and music videos. The Disney XD website provides access to games, videos, and TV episodes.

How did Disney research a demographic that is known for not talking about their feelings? It hired a team of social scientists, who learned the following:

- Boys identify with main characters who are trying to grow, and they want to see more characters like themselves in TV shows.

- Boys personalize the undersides of their skateboards and carry them so the tag shows.

- Boys like to share small accomplishments.

(continued)

HIT & MISS *(continued)*

- Boys shuttle quickly from one activity to another, moving from TV to video games to sports, and so on.

- Boys want more variety and reality in TV shows, not just all action or all cartoons.

Disney used these results to add a trophy room to the games page at the XD website and by advising its actors to carry their skateboards so the tagging showed, for realism. Viewership at XD increased more than 25 percent—but most of the new audience was girls. Boys aged 6 to 14 increased only 10 percent. The economic downturn also hurt advertising, but didn't discourage Rich Ross, the president of Disney Channels Worldwide. "We've seen cultural resonance, and it doesn't come overnight," he said.

Questions for Critical Thinking

1. What type(s) of segmentation strategy is Disney applying? Will it be effective? Why or why not?

2. What steps can Disney take to increase viewership of Disney XD among boys?

Sources: Disney XD, accessed April 17, 2015, www.disneyxd.ca; Disney, accessed April 11, 2010, http://disney.com; Tom Lowry and Ronald Grover, "Disney's Marvel Deal and the Pursuit of Boys," *Bloomberg Business*, March 9, 2010, accessed July 3, 2015, www.bloomberg.com/bw/magazine/content/09_38/b4147066139865.htm; Seth Lubove and Andy Fixmer, "Disney Beefs Up Marketing to Boys," *Ledger*, March 4, 2010, accessed July 3, 2015, www.theledger.com/article/20100304/news/3045052.

Psychographic Segmentation

psychographic segmentation dividing consumer markets into groups with similar attitudes, values, and lifestyles.

Lifestyle is the sum of a person's needs, preferences, motives, attitudes, social habits, and cultural background. In recent years, marketing researchers have tried to put together lifestyle portraits of consumers. This effort has led to another strategy for segmenting target markets, **psychographic segmentation,** which divides consumer markets into groups with similar psychological characteristics, values, and lifestyles.

Psychographic studies are used to evaluate motivations for purchases of hundreds of goods and services, ranging from soft drinks to healthcare services. Firms use the resulting data to tailor their marketing strategies to carefully chosen market segments. A frequently used way of developing psychographic profiles uses *AIO statements*—people's verbal descriptions of their various attitudes, interests, and opinions. Researchers survey a sample of consumers, asking them whether they agree or disagree with each statement. The answers are then organized and analyzed for use in identifying various lifestyle categories.

Another way to get consumers to provide current information about their lifestyles is for organizations to create *blogs* in the hope that consumers may respond. Companies including Lululemon Athletica, *Globe and Mail*, and Microsoft have hired bloggers to run online Web journals as a way to connect with consumers and receive information from them. Other firms encourage employees at all levels to use blogs to communicate with consumers. General Motors has several blogs at its GMblogs.com site, each set up for a specific brand or consumer interest. The FastLane blog discusses GM cars and trucks and invites consumers to offer their thoughts and ideas. Chevrolet Voltage is aimed at fans of the Volt and other electric vehicles. The Lab is where GM's advanced design team talks about its work and invites feedback from community members.[33] Although demographic classifications such as age, gender, and income are relatively easy to identify and measure, researchers also need to define psychographic categories. Marketing research firms often conduct wide studies of consumers and then share their psychographic data with clients. Businesses sometimes look to studies done by sociologists and psychologists to help them understand their customers. For example, while children may belong to one age group and their parents to another, both live certain lifestyles together. Recent marketing research shows that today's parents are willing and able to spend more on goods and services for their children than parents were willing and able to spend a generation or two ago. Spending on toys and video games for children topped $38 billion for a recent year in North America.[34] These are just a few trends identified by the researchers, but they provide valuable information to firms that may be considering developing games, designing the interiors of family vehicles, or offering new wireless plans.

Product-Related Segmentation

product-related segmentation dividing consumer markets into groups that are based on benefits sought by buyers, usage rates, and loyalty levels.

Sellers who use **product-related segmentation** divide a consumer market into groups that are based on buyers' relationships to the good or service. The three most popular approaches to product-related segmentation are based on benefits sought, usage rates, and brand loyalty levels.

WRAP DRESS
$99.00 USD

COLOR   Black

SIZE   XS

QUANTITY   1   Buy Now

Flattering, always a classic and always on trend. Designed for the seated frame, hemline in the back has more length than usual, so it matches length in the front when seated. Easy dressing with simple wrap and tie. Stretch fabric for added comfort and fit.

Full-length sleeves.

V-neck.

Tie closure.

95% rayon, 5% spandex.

Machine wash warm, tumble dry low, medium iron.

Share: f Facebook   Twitter   Pinterest

PARKA
$529.00 USD

COLOR   Black

SIZE   S

QUANTITY   1   Reserve

The ultimate in warmth and style. Longer in the front to drape smoothly over your lap. Hemline at back finishes at the seat of your chair, makes it easier to get dressed while seated. Water-resistant shell. Lined with Kasha and Thinsulate for serious warmth. Hood with removable coyote fur-trim.

Two front pockets.

Elastic cuffs.

Zipper & Velcro closures.

Hood.

Removable coyote fur trim.

Shell: 100% nylon.

Fill: Thinsulate.

Courtesy of IZ Collection

Canadian businesses can compete in a crowded fashion industry by developing and producing products that cater to niche markets. IZ Collection produces adaptive fashions for wheelchair users. Its clothing is cut and designed to fit a seated body shape, while maintaining comfort and style.

Segmenting by *benefits sought* focuses on the qualities that people look for in a good or service and the benefits they expect to receive. As more firms shift toward consumer demand for products that are eco-friendly, marketers find ways to emphasize the benefits of these products. Home-goods retailer Crate & Barrel has begun to offer tables and chairs made of mango wood. The wood is harvested only after the trees can no longer produce fruit. Consumers can also select a sofa whose cushions are made of recycled fibres that are filled with a natural, soy-based foam. According to the company's website, "While our collection has featured renewable woods and sustainable materials for a number of years, we are now introducing important initiatives that will help make our homes more thoughtful environments."[35]

Consumer markets can also be segmented according to the amounts of a product that people buy and use. Segmentation by *product usage rate* usually defines such categories as heavy users, medium users, and light users. The 80/20 principle states that roughly 80 percent of a product's revenues come from only 20 percent of its buyers. Companies can now pinpoint which of their customers are the heaviest users and even the most profitable customers. Companies then direct most of their marketing efforts to those customers.

The third technique for product-related segmentation divides customers by *brand loyalty*—the degree to which consumers recognize, prefer, and insist on a particular brand. Marketers define groups of consumers with similar degrees of brand loyalty. They then try to tie loyal customers to a good or service by giving away premiums, anything from a logo-imprinted T-shirt to a pair of tickets to a concert or sports event.

Segmenting Business Markets

In many ways, the segmentation process for business markets is like the segmentation process for consumer markets. But some specific methods are different. Business markets can be divided in three ways: through geographical segmentation; demographic, or customer-based, segmentation; and end-use segmentation.

Geographical segmentation methods for business markets are like the geographic segmentation methods used for consumer markets. Many B2B marketers target geographically concentrated industries, such as aircraft manufacturing, automobiles, and oil field equipment. The marketing mix may need to be changed to adapt to the customer needs, languages, and other variables of a different location. These changes will likely be needed when the company is marketing itself internationally.

Demographic, or customer-based, segmentation begins with a good or service being designed to suit a specific organizational market. Sodexho Marriott Services is the largest provider of food services in North America. Its customers include healthcare institutions, business and government offices, schools, colleges, and universities. Within these broad business segments, Sodexho identifies more specific segments, which might include government offices on the west coast or universities that have culturally diverse populations—and their different food preferences or dining styles. Sodexho uses survey data that cover students' lifestyles, attitudes, preferences for consumer products in general, services, and media categories. In addition, Sodexho uses targeted surveys that identify preferences for restaurant brands or certain foods, meal habits, and the amount spent on meals. Marketers evaluate the data, which sometimes reveal surprising trends. At one university, students said that they liked foods with an international flavour. So Sodexho adapted its offerings.[36]

To make it easier to focus on a specific type of business customer, the federal government has developed a system for subdividing the business marketplace into detailed segments. The six-digit *North American Industry Classification System (NAICS)* provides a common classification system used by the United States, Canada, and Mexico, the member nations of the North American Free Trade Agreement (NAFTA). This system divides industries into broad categories such as agriculture, forestry, and fishing; manufacturing; transportation; and retail and wholesale trade. Each major category is further subdivided into smaller segments, such as gas stations with convenience food and warehouse clubs. The smaller segments provide more detailed information and make it easier to compare data among the member nations.

Another way to group firms by their demographics is to segment them by size, such as by their sales revenues or number of employees. Some firms collect data from visitors to its website and use the data to segment customers by size. Modern information processing also means that companies can segment business markets based on how much they buy, not just how big they are.

End-use segmentation focuses on the precise way a B2B purchaser will use a product. This method is similar to the benefits-sought segmentation used for consumer markets. End-use segmentation helps small and mid-size companies target specific end-user markets instead of competing directly with large firms for wider customer groups. A company might also design a marketing mix based on certain criteria for making a purchase.

end-use segmentation a marketing strategy that focuses on the precise way a B2B purchaser will use a product.

ASSESSMENT CHECK

11.6.1 What is the most common form of segmentation for consumer markets?

11.6.2 What are the three approaches to product-related segmentation?

11.6.3 What is end-use segmentation in the B2B market?

CONSUMER BEHAVIOUR

LO 11.7 Outline the determinants of consumer behaviour.

A fundamental marketing task is to find out why people buy one product and not another. The answer requires an understanding of consumer behaviour: the activities of end consumers that are directly involved in obtaining, consuming, and disposing of products, and the decision processes before and after these activities.

consumer behaviour end consumers' activities that are directly involved in obtaining, consuming, and disposing of products, and the decision processes before and after these activities.

Determinants of Consumer Behaviour

Businesses study people's purchasing behaviour to identify their attitudes toward products and to learn how they use products. This information also helps marketers reach their targeted customers. Both personal and interpersonal factors affect the way buyers behave. Personal influences on consumer behaviour include individual needs and motives, perceptions, attitudes, learned experiences, and self-concept. For example, people are constantly looking for ways to save time, so firms do everything they can to provide goods and services that are designed for convenience. But when it comes to products such as dinner foods, consumers don't just want convenience—they also want the flavour of a home-cooked meal and quality time with their families. So companies such as Stouffer's offer frozen lasagna and manicotti in family sizes, and grocery stores have entire sections of freshly prepared take-out meals, including roast turkey and filet mignon.

McDonald's is betting that consumers who drink premium coffee beverages will also like to buy them at bargain prices. In many locations, McDonald's has placed McCafé coffee bars near the cash register. These coffee bars offer cappuccinos, lattes, and mochas. Most McDonald's stores now serve these beverages, putting the company in direct competition with Starbucks.[37]

The interpersonal determinants of consumer behaviour include cultural, social, and family influences. In the area of convenience foods, cultural, social, and family influences come into play as much as an individual's need to save time. Marketers understand that many consumers value the time they spend with their families and want to provide them with good nutrition. Marketers often emphasize these values when advertising convenience food products.

Sometimes external events influence consumer behaviour. One study suggests that because of the recession, consumers may have permanently changed their buying and spending behaviour. The survey found that 72 percent of consumers said that they had significantly or somewhat changed their shopping habits; only 7 percent said they had made no change. Manufacturers and retailers—and especially small businesses—will need to create new marketing strategies in response to these challenges.[38]

Determinants of Business Buying Behaviour

When business buyers need to make a purchase, they have to deal with their own preferences, which may not be their firm's preference. They must also deal with a variety of influences from their organizations because many people can be involved in the decision to purchase B2B products. For example, a design engineer may help set the specifications that potential suppliers must meet. A procurement manager may invite selected companies to bid on a purchase. A production supervisor may evaluate the operational qualities of the proposals that the firm receives, and the vice-president of manufacturing may head a committee making the final decision.

Steps in the Consumer Behaviour Process

Consumer decision making follows the sequential process shown in **Figure 11.6**. Interpersonal and personal influences affect every step. The process begins when the consumer recognizes a problem or opportunity. For example, if someone needs a new pair of shoes, that need becomes a problem to solve. If you receive a promotion at work and a 20 percent salary increase, that change may lead to a purchase opportunity.

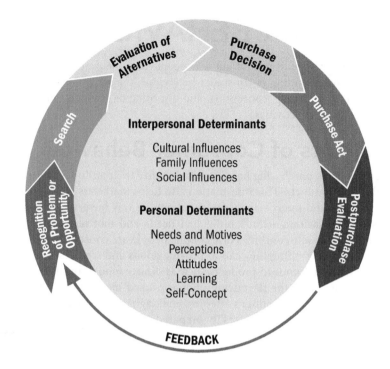

FIGURE 11.6 Steps in the Consumer Behaviour Process

✓ ASSESSMENT CHECK

11.7.1 Define *consumer behaviour.*

11.7.2 What are some determinants of consumer behaviour?

To solve the problem or take advantage of the opportunity, the consumer looks for information about his or her intended purchase and evaluates options, such as the available brands. The goal is to find the best response to the problem or opportunity.

In the end, the consumer usually reaches a decision and completes the transaction. Later, the customer evaluates the experience by making a postpurchase evaluation. Feelings about the experience serve as feedback that will affect future purchase decisions. The various steps in the sequence are affected by both interpersonal and personal factors.

LO 11.8 Discuss the benefits of, and tools for, relationship marketing.

RELATIONSHIP MARKETING

The past decade has brought rapid change to most industries. Customers have become better informed and more demanding purchasers by closely comparing competing goods and services. They expect, even demand, new benefits from the companies that supply them. These expectations make it harder for firms to gain a competitive advantage on the basis of product features alone.

relationship marketing
developing and maintaining long-term, cost-effective exchange relationships with partners.

In today's hypercompetitive era, businesses need to find new ways of relating to customers to maintain long-term success. Businesses are developing strategies and tactics that create closer relationships with their customers, suppliers, and even employees. As a result, many firms are turning their attention to relationship marketing. **Relationship marketing** goes beyond an effort toward making the sale. This type of marketing develops and maintains long-term, cost-effective exchange relationships with partners. These partners include individual customers, suppliers, and employees. As its ultimate goal, relationship marketing seeks to achieve customer satisfaction.

When businesses manage their relationships instead of just completing sales transactions, they can often develop creative partnerships. But customers will enter into relationships with firms only when they are assured that the relationship will be of benefit to them. As the intensity of commitment increases, so does the likelihood of a business continuing a long-term relationship with its customers. Businesses build relationships by partnering with customers, suppliers, and other businesses. Timberland, maker of footwear and clothing, creates many partnerships that foster long-term relationships. Timberland partners with not-for-profit organizations such as CARE, City Year, and Clean Air–Cool Planet to complete service projects for communities and the environment.

Through its Serv-a-Palooza, hundreds of Timberland employees sign up for volunteer tasks in their communities. Those opportunities even extend to customers who have expressed an interest in participating in programs in their own regions. If you want to volunteer for a food drive or to help restore a marsh, just log on to the Timberland website to see what's available. All of these activities help build relationships with customers, communities, and other organizations.[39]

Benefits of Relationship Marketing

Relationship marketing helps all parties involved. Businesses that create solid relationships with suppliers and customers protect themselves against competitors. These businesses are also often rewarded with lower costs and higher profits than they would generate on their own. Long-term agreements with a few high-quality suppliers can reduce a firm's production costs. Unlike one-time sales, these ongoing relationships encourage suppliers to offer customers preferred treatment. For example, suppliers might quickly correct any quality problems and be willing to adjust shipments to accommodate changes in orders.

Encouraging good relationships with customers can be a vital strategy for a firm. By identifying current purchasers and maintaining positive relationships with them, organizations can efficiently target their best customers. Studying current customers' buying habits and preferences can help marketers to identify potential new customers and establish ongoing contact with them. Attracting a new customer can cost five times as much as keeping an existing customer. Long-term customers do not just reduce marketing costs; they usually buy more, require less service, refer other customers, and provide valuable feedback. Together, these elements contribute to a higher **lifetime value of a customer**—the revenues and intangible benefits (such as referrals and customer feedback) from the customer over the life of the relationship, minus the amount the company must spend to acquire and serve that customer. Keeping that customer may occasionally require some extra effort, especially when the customer has become upset or dissatisfied with a good or service. But good marketers can overcome this particular challenge, as described in the "Career Kickstart" feature.

lifetime value of a customer the revenues and intangible benefits (such as referrals and customer feedback) from a customer over the life of the relationship, minus the amount the company must spend to acquire and serve that customer.

CAREER KICKSTART

Calming the Angry Customer

In any business, an angry customer is a challenge. An upset customer represents not only an immediate problem but also a potential loss of future business. The customer may be upset over poor service or a broken product, frustrated by lack of attention from the company, or just plain demanding. You, the businessperson, should look at this customer not as a disruption but as an opportunity to see your company from the outside. With a little bit of common sense, good personal skills, and knowledge of your company and its products, you can turn the customer's dissatisfaction into satisfaction.

- *Remain calm and professional.* The customer isn't angry with you personally. Let the customer speak first, and listen carefully as he or she states the problem. Make written notes. Acknowledge the customer's anger, then assure him or her that you will correct the situation.

- *Repeat the customer's stated problem.* Using your own words assures the customer that you have been listening. For example, you might say, "The shoes you received were the right colour but the wrong size." Make sure you understand the problem before offering a solution.

- *Focus on the solution.* Having procedures in place beforehand can help you resolve a problem quickly. If you can't solve the problem yourself, immediately refer it to someone who can. Fast action will let the customer know that you are on his or her side.

- *Thank the customer for his or her patience.* By bringing the problem to your attention, the customer is actually giving you an opportunity to improve service to all your clients.

- *Follow up.* If appropriate, send an email or make a phone call to make sure the correct pair of shoes arrived. Your professionalism will strengthen the customer's relationship with your firm—and positive word of mouth may even bring you new customers.

Sources: Lynne McClure, "Handling Customers," *Impact Publications*, accessed February 25, 2014, www.impactpublications.com; Katy Tynan, "Conflict Management Part 2—Calming an Irate Customer," *Ezinearticles.com*, accessed February 25, 2014, http://ezinearticles.com/?Conflict-Management-Part-2---Calming-an-Irate-Customer&id=3656834; "How to Calm an Angry Customer," *Business Knowledge Source*, accessed February 25, 2014, http://businessknowledgesource.com/blog/how_to_calm_an_angry_customer_024261.html.

Businesses also benefit from having strong relationships with other companies. Purchasers who repeatedly buy from one business may find that they save time and gain service quality as the business learns more about their specific needs. Some relationship-oriented companies also customize items based on customer preferences. Because many businesses reward loyal customers with discounts or bonuses, some buyers may even find that they save money by developing long-term relationships. Alliances, or working with other firms, to serve the same customers also can be rewarding. The partners combine their capabilities and resources to accomplish goals that they could not reach on their own. Alliances with other firms may also help businesses to develop the skills and experience they need to improve service to current customers or to successfully enter new markets.

Tools for Nurturing Customer Relationships

Relationship marketing has important benefits for both customers and businesses. Most relationship-oriented businesses quickly learn that some customers generate more profitable business than others. The 80/20 principle mentioned earlier in the chapter suggests that 20 percent of a firm's customers account for 80 percent of its sales and profits. A customer in that category has a higher lifetime value than a customer who buys only once or twice, or a customer who makes small purchases.

Businesses shouldn't ignore any customer, but they do need to distribute their marketing dollars wisely. A firm may choose to customize goods or services for high-value customers while working to increase repeat sales of standardized products to less valuable customers. Differentiating between these two groups also helps marketers to focus on each group in an effort to increase their commitment.

Frequency Marketing and Affinity Marketing Programs

frequency marketing a marketing initiative that rewards frequent purchases with cash, rebates, merchandise, or other premiums.

affinity program a marketing effort sponsored by an organization that targets people who share common interests and activities.

co-marketing a cooperative arrangement where two businesses jointly market each other's products.

co-branding a cooperative arrangement where two or more businesses team up to closely link their names on a single product.

Firms try to build and protect customer relationships by using popular techniques, including frequent-buyer or frequent-user programs. These so-called **frequency marketing** programs reward purchasers with cash, rebates, merchandise, or other premiums. Frequency programs have grown more sophisticated over the years. They offer more personalization and customization than in the past. Airlines, hotel groups, restaurants, and many retailers, including grocery stores, use frequency programs. Customers who join the Marriott Rewards program have the option to spend their earned points at nearly 3,000 hotels, resorts, spas, and golf locations in 67 countries and territories worldwide.[40]

Affinity programs are another tool for building emotional links with customers. An affinity program is an organization's marketing effort that targets people who share common interests and activities. Affinity programs are common in the credit card industry. For example, a person can sign up for a credit card that is printed with the logo of a favourite charity, a sports or entertainment celebrity, or a photograph of his or her college or university. MBNA Canada Bank is the largest independent credit card issuer in the world and offers an affinity MasterCard credit card for the University of Toronto.

Many businesses also use co-marketing and co-branding. In a **co-marketing** deal, two businesses jointly market each other's products. When two or more businesses link their names to a single product, **co-branding** occurs. Sometimes, two unlikely businesses team up. When that happens, the marketing sparks can fly—and two very different groups of consumers may come together to buy the same product. For example, Nike and Apple have marketed the Nike + iPod Sport kit. To use this kit, a runner

Affinity programs are a tool for building emotional links with customers. These programs are common in the credit card industry. For example, MBNA Canada Bank offers an affinity MasterCard credit card for the University of Toronto.

© Jon Stokes/Alamy Stock Photo

inserts a special sensor into a built-in pocket in a Nike + shoe. The sensor matches the runner's activity with workout data and music that plays through the iPod. Consumers can also purchase specially designed Nike workout clothing that has pockets designed to hold an iPod nano itself.[41]

One-on-One Marketing

The ability to customize products and rapidly deliver goods and services is increasingly dependent on technology, such as computer-aided design and computer-aided manufacturing (CAD/CAM). The Internet offers a way for businesses to connect with customers in a direct and personal manner. Companies can take orders for customized products, gather data about buyers, and predict what items a customer might want in the future. Computer databases provide strong support for effective relationship marketing. Marketers can maintain databases on customer tastes, price-range preferences, and lifestyles. They can also quickly obtain names and other information about possible customers. Amazon.com greets each online customer with a list of suggested books he or she might like to purchase. Many online retailers send their customers emails about upcoming sales, new products, and special events.

Small and large companies often use *customer relationship management (CRM)* software technology to help them gather, sort, and interpret data about customers. Software firms develop this software to help businesses build and manage their relationships with customers. For example, QueueBuster is a software product that offers callers the choice of receiving an automated return call instead of waiting on hold for the next available representative. After putting the software in place, travel agency STA reported that its customer satisfaction ratings had improved to 98 percent. This simple solution to customers' frustration helped STA to build customer loyalty. It also helped save STA from lost business.[42]

ASSESSMENT CHECK

11.8.1 What is the lifetime value of a customer?

11.8.2 Discuss the increasing importance of one-on-one marketing efforts.

WHAT'S AHEAD

The next two chapters examine each of the four elements of the marketing mix that marketers use to satisfy their selected target markets. Chapter 12 focuses on products and their distribution through various channels to different outlets. Chapter 13 covers promotion and the various methods marketers use to communicate with their target customers, and strategies for setting prices for different products.

RETURN TO INSIDE BUSINESS

Handmade Items: Etsy.com Has Them All

Lisa Lutz creates her own jewellery and uses Etsy.com to help build her brand recognition and distribution. She also uses Facebook and other social media platforms such as blogs to link online readers back to her business, Bead Crazed, and its website at www.beadcrazed.com/. She writes online, "I love to learn and have taken classes in wirework, ArtClay silver and metalsmithing. While looking for the 'perfect' bead, I discovered lampworking. My hobby quickly turned into a bead crazed obsession, and I have been making lampwork beads for about 4 years now." Although she is a full-time medical technician in microbiology and mother of four, she says that she is happily busy producing and selling her creations online as well as creating customized pieces for customers.

QUESTIONS FOR CRITICAL THINKING

1. How can Bead Crazed and Lisa Lutz generate more attention online?

2. Does Lutz have an advantage producing and selling jewellery online instead of some other art form?

3. What sort of customer is drawn to the artisans selling on Etsy.com?

SUMMARY OF LEARNING OBJECTIVES

LO 11.1 Explain what marketing is and how it creates utility.

Utility is the ability of a good or service to satisfy the wants and needs of customers. The production function creates form utility by converting inputs to finished goods and services. Marketing creates three types of utility—time utility, place utility, and ownership utility—by making the product available when consumers want to buy it, where consumers want to buy it, and arranging for an organized transfer of ownership.

 ASSESSMENT CHECK ANSWERS

11.1.1 **What is utility?** Utility is the ability of a good or service to satisfy the wants and needs of customers.

11.1.2 **Identify how marketing creates utility.** Marketing creates time utility by making a good or service available when customers want to purchase it, place utility by making the product available in a convenient location, and ownership utility by transferring the product from the buyer to the seller.

LO 11.2 Discuss the evolution of the marketing concept.

The marketing concept refers to a companywide customer focus with the goal of achieving long-term success. This concept is much needed in today's marketplace, which is mainly a buyer's market, where buyers can choose from many goods and services. Marketing now centres on satisfying customers and building long-term relationships with them.

 ASSESSMENT CHECK ANSWERS

11.2.1 **What is the marketing concept?** The marketing concept is a companywide customer focus with the goal of achieving long-term success. According to the marketing concept, success begins with the customer.

11.2.2 **How is the marketing concept tied to the relationship and social eras of marketing?** Most marketing now centres on the satisfaction of customers and building long-term relationships with them through several channels including the Internet and social media, rather than simply producing and selling goods and services.

LO 11.3 Describe not-for-profit marketing and nontraditional marketing.

Not-for-profit organizations use marketing just as for-profit firms do. Not-for-profit organizations operate in both the public and private sectors. They use marketing to attract volunteers and donations, to make people aware of their existence, and to achieve certain goals for society. Not-for-profit organizations may use several types of nontraditional marketing—person, place, event, cause, or organization marketing. They may use only one type of marketing or a combination of two or more types.

 ASSESSMENT CHECK ANSWERS

11.3.1 **Why do not-for-profit organizations use marketing?** Not-for-profit organizations use marketing to attract volunteers and donors, communicate their message, and achieve their societal goals.

11.3.2 **What are the five types of nontraditional marketing used by not-for-profit organizations?** The five types of nontraditional marketing are person, place, event, cause, and organization marketing.

LO 11.4 Outline the basic steps in developing a marketing strategy.

All organizations develop marketing strategies to reach their customers. This process involves two steps: first, analyzing the overall market and selecting a target market; and, second, developing a marketing mix that blends elements related to product, distribution, promotion, and pricing decisions.

 ASSESSMENT CHECK ANSWERS

11.4.1 **Distinguish between consumer products and business products.** Business products are goods and services purchased to be used, either directly or indirectly, in the production of other goods for resale. Consumer products are goods and services purchased by the end users.

11.4.2 **What are the steps in developing a marketing strategy?** The steps in developing a marketing strategy are analyzing the overall market, selecting a target market, and developing a marketing mix.

LO 11.5 Describe the marketing research function.

Marketing research is the information-gathering function that links marketers to the marketplace. It provides valuable information about potential target markets. Firms may generate internal data or gather external data. They may use secondary data or conduct research to obtain primary data. Data mining involves computer searches through customer data to detect patterns or relationships. It is a helpful tool in forecasting various trends such as sales revenues and consumer behaviour.

ASSESSMENT CHECK ANSWERS

11.5.1 What is the difference between primary data and secondary data? Primary data are collected firsthand through observation or surveys. Secondary data are previously published facts that are inexpensive to retrieve and easy to obtain.

11.5.2 What is data mining? Data mining involves using computer searches of customer data to evaluate the data and identify useful trends that may suggest models of real-world business activities.

LO 11.6 Discuss the methods used to segment consumer and business markets.

Consumer markets can be divided according to four criteria: geographical factors; demographic characteristics, such as age and family size; psychographic variables, which involve behavioural and lifestyle profiles; and product-related variables, such as the benefits consumers look for when buying a product or the degree of brand loyalty they feel toward it. Business markets are segmented according to three criteria: geographical characteristics, customer-based specifications for products, and end-user applications.

ASSESSMENT CHECK ANSWERS

11.6.1 What is the most common form of segmentation for consumer markets? The most commonly used consumer market segmentation method is demographics.

11.6.2 What are the three approaches to product-related segmentation? The three approaches to product-related segmentation are by benefits sought, product usage rate, and brand loyalty.

11.6.3 What is end-use segmentation in the B2B market? End-use segmentation focuses on the precise way a B2B purchaser will use a product.

LO 11.7 Outline the determinants of consumer behaviour.

Consumer behaviour refers to end consumers' activities that have direct effects on obtaining, consuming, and disposing of products, and the decision processes before and after these actions. Personal influences on consumer behaviour include an individual's needs and motives, perceptions, attitudes, learned experiences, and self-concept. The interpersonal determinants include cultural influences, social influences, and family influences. Many people within a firm

may take part in business purchase decisions, so business buyers must consider a variety of organizational influences in addition to their own preferences.

ASSESSMENT CHECK ANSWERS

11.7.1 Define *consumer behaviour.* Consumer behaviour refers to end consumers' activities that are directly involved in obtaining, consuming, and disposing of products, and the decision processes before and after these actions.

11.7.2 What are some determinants of consumer behaviour? Determinants of consumer behaviour include both personal influences and interpersonal influences. Personal influences include an individual's needs and motives; perceptions, attitudes, and experiences; and self-concept. Interpersonal influences include cultural, social, and family influences.

LO 11.8 Discuss the benefits of, and tools for, relationship marketing.

Relationship marketing is an organization's attempt to develop long-term, cost-effective links with individual customers for mutual benefit. Encouraging good relationships with customers can be part of a firm's vital strategy. By identifying current purchasers and encouraging a positive relationship with them, an organization can efficiently target its best customers, fulfill their needs, and create loyalty. Information technologies, frequency and affinity programs, and one-on-one efforts all help build relationships with customers.

ASSESSMENT CHECK ANSWERS

11.8.1 What is the lifetime value of a customer? The lifetime value of a customer is the total of the revenues and intangible benefits from the customer over the life of the customer's relationship with a firm, minus the amount the company must spend to acquire and serve the customer.

11.8.2 Discuss the increasing importance of one-on-one marketing efforts. One-on-one marketing is increasing in importance as consumers demand more customization in goods and services. One-on-one marketing is also increasingly dependent on technology such as computer-aided design and computer-aided manufacturing (CAD/CAM). The Internet also offers a way for businesses to connect with customers in a direct and personal manner.

BUSINESS TERMS YOU NEED TO KNOW

affinity program 314

business intelligence 303

business-to-business (B2B)
   product 301

business-to-consumer (B2C)
   product 299

cause marketing 298

co-branding 314

co-marketing 314

consumer behaviour 311

data mining 304

data warehouse 304

demographic segmentation 306

end-use segmentation 310

event marketing 298

exchange process 293

frequency marketing 314

geographical segmentation 305

lifetime value of a customer 313

marketing 292

marketing concept 295

marketing mix 301

marketing research 302

market segmentation 304

organization marketing 299

person marketing 297

place marketing 297

product-related
   segmentation 308

psychographic
   segmentation 308

relationship marketing 312

target market 301

utility 293

REVIEW QUESTIONS

1. Define the four different types of utility and explain how marketing contributes to the creation of utility. Then choose one of the following companies and describe how it creates each type of utility with its goods or services:

   a. Burger King

   b. Polo Ralph Lauren

   c. Indigo bookstore

   d. Supercuts hair salons

   e. Adobe Systems

2. Describe the shift from a seller's market to a buyer's market. Why was this move important to marketers?

3. Describe how an organization might combine person marketing and event marketing. Give an example.

4. Describe how an organization might combine cause marketing and organization marketing. Give an example.

5. Identify each of the following as a consumer product or a business product, or classify it as both:

   a. a cup of coffee

   b. iPad

   c. gasoline

   d. a boat trailer

   e. hand sanitizer

   f. hair gel

6. Identify and describe the four strategies that blend to create a marketing mix.

7. What is a target market? Why is target market selection usually the first step in the development of a marketing strategy?

8. Identify the two strategies that a firm can use to develop a marketing mix for international markets. What are the upsides and downsides of each?

9. Describe the types of data that might be gathered by someone who is thinking of starting an accounting service. How might this businessperson use the data in making the startup decision?

10. Explain each of the methods used to segment consumer and business markets. Which methods are most effective for each of the following and why? (Note that more than one method might be suitable.)

   a. a grocery store featuring organic foods

   b. hair-care products

   c. a tour bus company

   d. a line of baby food

   e. dental insurance

   f. a dry cleaner

11. What are the three major determinants of consumer behaviour? Give an example of how each one might influence a person's purchasing decision.

12. What are the benefits of relationship marketing? Describe how frequency and affinity programs work toward building relationships.

PROJECTS AND TEAMWORK APPLICATIONS

1. On your own or with a classmate, choose one of the following products and create an advertisement that illustrates how your firm creates time, place, and form utility in its delivery of the product to the customer.

   a. an auto repair service

   b. hiking tours

   c. a craft supply store

   d. a pet-sitting service

2. Choose one of the following not-for-profit organizations or find one on your own. Research the organization online to learn more about it. Outline your proposal for a fundraising event. You can base your event on the chapter discussion of nontraditional marketing, such as cause marketing or organization marketing.

   a. Alberta Society for the Prevention of Cruelty to Animals

   b. Prostate Cancer Foundation

   c. Canadian Red Cross

   d. Salvation Army

3. As a marketer, you may be able to classify your firm's goods and services as both business and consumer products. Your company's sales will likely increase because you will build relationships with a new category of customers. On your own or with a classmate, choose one of the following products, and outline a marketing strategy for attracting the classification of customer that is *opposite* from the one listed in parentheses.

   a. a hybrid car (consumer)

   b. an LCD TV (consumer)

   c. a limousine service (business)

   d. office furniture (business)

4. Think of two situations where you were a customer: one situation when you were satisfied with the merchandise you received and one situation when you were not satisfied. List the reasons you were satisfied in the first case and list the reasons you were not satisfied in the second case. Did the failure occur because the seller did not understand your needs?

5. Co-marketing and co-branding are techniques that organizations often use to market their own and each other's products, such as Nike running shoes and the Apple iPod. On your own or with a classmate, choose two firms with goods and/or services you think would work well together for co-marketing separate products or co-branding a single product. Create an advertisement for your co-marketing or co-branding effort.

WEB ASSIGNMENTS

1. **Demographic trends**. The Canadian Census and the *Statistical Abstract of the United States* are excellent sources of demographic and economic data. Visit the websites listed below. On the StatsCan website, click on "By topic" from the list on the left and then view the population data. On the U.S. website, scroll down the list on the left and select "Population." What do the Canadian and American populations currently look like in terms of age and race? What will the population look like in the decades to come?

   www12.statcan.ca/census-recensement/index-eng.cfm
   www.census.gov/compendia/statab

2. **Market segmentation**. Go to the website of Canon Canada and review the company's range of product offerings. Prepare a brief report on how Canon segments its markets.

   www.canon.ca

3. **Customer loyalty programs**. Airlines and hotel chains offer customer loyalty programs. Pick an airline and hotel chain and print out information on the firm's customer loyalty program (two examples are listed here). Bring the material to class to participate in a discussion on this topic.

   www.westjet.com/guest/en/rewards/index.shtml
   www.marriott.com/rewards/rewards-program.mi

Note: Internet Web addresses change frequently. If you don't find the exact sites listed, you may need to access the organization's home page and search from there or use a search engine such as Bing or Google.

Echo/Getty Images

12 | PRODUCT AND DISTRIBUTION STRATEGIES

LEARNING OBJECTIVES

LO 12.1 Explain product strategy and how to classify goods and services.

LO 12.2 Describe the four stages of the product life cycle and their marketing implications.

LO 12.3 Explain how firms identify their products.

LO 12.4 Outline the major components of an effective distribution strategy.

LO 12.5 Explain the concept of wholesaling.

LO 12.6 Describe the types of retailers and retail strategies used.

LO 12.7 Discuss distribution channel decisions and logistics.

INSIDE BUSINESS

Montreal's Fitness City Complex: Bringing Fitness Businesses Together Under One Roof

It is a well-established business model—bring competing businesses together at one location for the convenience of the customer. If customers don't find what they are looking for at one business, they can easily check out the others. That's why we often find car dealerships grouped together in a "car-shopping district." Customers can easily visit a few car dealers and compare their products before making a purchase decision. Car dealerships outside of the main car-shopping district need to offer something very special if they expect shoppers to travel to their business.

This clustering, or grouping, strategy is familiar to us. We see it in large cities in their restaurant districts, fashion districts, and theatre districts. The same idea might be successful for other businesses, too. Think about the possibilities for businesses that do not compete directly, but complement each other by offering related services. These businesses tend to be scattered. Because of their locations, they are not very visible to potential customers. But, by clustering together in one location, customers of one business are more likely to become customers of a complementary business.

An example of this kind of strategic thinking is Fitness City, located near the Trans-Canada Highway in Montreal's suburban area known as the West Island. Fitness City instantly became the largest fitness facility in Quebec when it recently opened its doors. The facility brings together a variety of fitness businesses under one 73,000-square-foot roof to serve customers who are both fitness-conscious and health-conscious.

Fitness City's largest fitness provider is Monster Gym, which takes up 45,000 square feet. Monster Gym has been owned and managed by Carmine Petrillo for more than 20 years. His original gym would have been considered large enough at 8,000 square feet. But the move to the new building provides space to offer even more facilities to Monster Gym's 6,000 members. Monster Gym acts as the "anchor" for the complex because of its 24/7 operating hours, its size, and its large and diverse clientele.

As members walk through the building's main entrance, they pass Cielos Studios, the 9,000-square-foot space dedicated to yoga, Pilates, pole dancing, Zumba, tai chi, erotic dance, meditation, and other equipment-free classes. Like Monster Gym, Cielos was an established West Island business that brought along its diverse customers when it relocated to Fitness City.

The same scenario was true for Grant Brothers Boxing and MMA Gyms, operated by former Canadian Middleweight Champion Otis Grant and his brother Howard, a 1988 Olympian and former Canadian Lightweight Champion. (Another brother, Ryan, operates a Grant Brothers Boxing Gym in Toronto.) These gyms offer boxing, which tends to attract young men. They also offer kick-boxing, which appeals to women because of the aerobic workout and defensive training. According Howard Grant, men and women are often more likely to try boxing and other classes when they see someone of their own age in the ring working out. This is especially true for young adults who look at boxing and other contact sports as part of an overall effort to build and discipline both their bodies and their minds.

The Fitness City complex also offers the services of the Nuance Spa and massage facility, professional physiotherapists, dieticians, trainers, and coaches to help fitness-minded individuals reach their goals. Le Bistro Fit is the new restaurant located in the centre of the complex. It provides healthy meals and beverages for clients to enjoy after their workouts. Each of these individually owned businesses hopes to gain new customers—and revenue—from the mix of clientele that use the complex. In time, each business will see how much it benefits from the success of its neighbours.[1]

CHAPTER 12 OVERVIEW

In this chapter we examine the many ways that organizations design and carry out marketing strategies that address customers' needs and wants. Two of the most powerful tools are strategies that relate to products (which include both goods and services) and strategies that relate to the distribution of those products.

As the Fitness City complex shows, successful companies are deeply aware of their customers' needs. Fitness City continues to build business by adding new service providers, such as food supplements stores and more martial arts specialists. The creation of new products is the lifeblood, or life force, of an organization. Companies must constantly develop new products to ensure their survival and long-term growth.

This chapter focuses on the first two elements of the marketing mix: product and distribution. We begin our discussion of product strategy by describing the classifications of goods and services, customer service, product lines and the product mix, and the product life cycle. Companies often shape their marketing strategies differently depending on the stage of the product life cycle: when they are introducing a new product, when the product has established itself in the marketplace, and when the product is declining in popularity. We also discuss product identification through brand name and distinctive packaging. We then look at how companies foster, or encourage, loyalty to their brands to keep customers coming back for more.

Distribution is the second mix variable discussed. It focuses on moving goods and services from producer to wholesaler to retailer to buyers. Managing the distribution process includes making decisions such as what kind of wholesaler to use and where to offer products for sale. Retailers can range from specialty stores to factory outlets and everything in between. To succeed, retailers must choose suitable customer service, pricing, and location strategies. The chapter ends with a look at logistics, the process of coordinating the flow of information, goods, and services among suppliers and on to final consumers.

LO 12.1 Explain product strategy and how to classify goods and services.

product a bundle of physical, service, and symbolic characteristics designed to satisfy consumer wants.

PRODUCT STRATEGY

What is a product? Most people answer this question by listing a product's physical features. But marketers take a broader view. To marketers, a **product** is a bundle of physical, service, and symbolic characteristics designed to satisfy consumer wants. The chief executive officer of a major tool manufacturer once startled his shareholders when he said, "Last year our customers bought over 1 million quarter-inch drill bits, and none of them wanted to buy the product. They all wanted quarter-inch holes." Product strategy involves much more than just producing a good or service; it focuses on the benefits of a good or service. The marketing conception of a product includes decisions about package design, brand name, trademarks, warranties, product image, new-product development, and customer service. For example, think about your favourite soft drink. Do you like it for its taste alone? Or are you attracted by other qualities, such as clever ads, attractive packaging, overall image, and ease of purchase from vending machines and other convenient locations? These other qualities may influence your choice more than you think.

Classifying Goods and Services

Marketers have found it useful to classify goods and services as either B2C or B2B, depending on whether the purchasers of the particular item are consumers or businesses. These classifications can be subdivided further. Each classification type needs a different competitive strategy.

Classifying Consumer Goods and Services

Consumer goods and services—that is, goods and services used by end consumers who purchase products for their own use and enjoyment and not for resale—are usually classified on the basis of how consumers buy them. Convenience products are items that *consumers purchase* frequently, immediately, and with little effort. For example, such convenience products as newspapers, snacks, candy, coffee, and bread are usually for sale in gas-station stores, vending machines, and local newsstands.

Shopping products are those products that are usually purchased only after the buyer has compared competing products in competing stores. A person who wants to buy a new sofa or dining room table may visit many stores, examine dozens of pieces of furniture, and spend days making the final decision. *Specialty products* are the third category of consumer products. These are products that a purchaser is willing to make a special effort to obtain. The purchaser is already familiar with the item and considers it to have no reasonable substitute. For example, the nearest Mini Cooper dealer may be 75 kilometres away, but if you have decided you want one, you will make the trip.

Note that a shopping product for one person may be a convenience item for someone else. Each item's product classification is based on the buying patterns of most of the people who purchase it.

The interrelationship of the marketing mix factors is shown in **Figure 12.1**. Marketing decision makers need to know the best classification for a specific product. Knowing the most suitable classification helps marketers to understand how the other mix variables will adapt to create a profitable, customer-driven marketing strategy.

Buying a *specialty product* takes extra effort. The Fiat 500 is sold in a limited number of places.

Classifying Business Goods

Business products are goods and services such as paycheque services and huge multifunction copying machines used in operating an organization. They also include machinery, tools, raw materials, components, and buildings used to produce other items for resale. While consumer products are classified by how consumers buy them, business products are classified by their basic characteristics

Marketing Strategy Factor	Convenience Product	Shopping Product	Specialty Product
· **Purchase Frequency**	· Frequent	· Relatively infrequent	· Infrequent
· **Store Image**	· Unimportant	· Very important	· Important
· **Price**	· Low	· Relatively high	· High
· **Promotion**	· By manufacturer	· By manufacturer and retailers	· By manufacturer and retailers
· **Distribution Channel**	· Many wholesalers and retailers	· Relatively few wholesalers and retailers	· Very few wholesalers and retailers
· **Number of Retail Outlets**	· Many	· Few	· Very small number; often one per market area

FIGURE 12.1 Marketing Impacts of Consumer Product Classification

and by how they are used. Products that are long lived and relatively expensive are called *capital items*. Less costly products that are consumed within a year are referred to as *expense items*.

B2B products have five basic categories: installations, accessory equipment, component parts and materials, raw materials, and supplies. *Installations* are major capital items, such as new factories, heavy equipment and machinery, and custom-made equipment. Installations are expensive and often involve buyer and seller negotiations that may last for more than a year before a purchase is made. Purchase approval often involves the agreement of many different people—production specialists, purchasing department representatives, and members of top management.

Although *accessory equipment* also includes capital items, these items are usually less expensive and shorter lived than installations, and involve fewer decision makers. Examples include hand tools and fax machines. *Component parts and materials* are finished business goods that become part of a final product, such as disk drives that are sold to computer manufacturers or batteries purchased by automakers. *Raw materials* are farm and natural products used to produce other final products. Examples include milk, wood, leather, and soybeans. *Supplies* are expense items used in a firm's daily operation that do not become part of the final product. Supplies are often referred to as MRO (maintenance, repair, and operating supplies). They include paper clips, light bulbs, and copy paper.

Classifying Services

Services can be classified as either B2C or B2B. Examples of services for consumers include childcare and eldercare centres and auto detail shops. Examples of services for businesses include the Pinkerton security patrol at a local factory and Kelly Services' temporary office workers. Sometimes, a service works in both consumer and business markets. For example, when ServiceMaster cleans the upholstery in a home, it is a B2C service, but when it spruces up the painting system and robots in a manufacturing plant, it is a B2B service.

Services can also be convenience products, shopping products, or specialty products. Which type of product it is will depend on the buying patterns of customers. Services can be distinguished from goods in several ways. First, services are intangible, or immaterial; in contrast, goods are tangible, or material. In addition, services are perishable, or short-lived, because firms cannot store them in inventory. They are also difficult to standardize because they must meet individual customers' needs. Finally, from a buyer's perspective, the service provider is the service; the two are inseparable in the buyer's mind.

Marketing Strategy Implications

The consumer-product classification system is a useful tool in marketing strategy. As shown in Figure 12.1, a new refrigerator is classified as a shopping good. That classification gives its marketers a better idea of how it needs to be promoted, priced, and distributed.

Each group of business products needs a different marketing strategy. Most installations and many component parts are marketed directly from manufacturer to business buyer. That means the promotional emphasis is on personal selling, not on advertising. In contrast, marketers of supplies and accessory equipment rely more on advertising because their products are often sold through an intermediary, such as a wholesaler. Producers of installations and component parts may involve their customers in new-product development, especially when the business product is custom made. Finally, firms selling supplies and accessory equipment place greater emphasis on competitive pricing strategies than do other B2B marketers, who tend to focus more on product quality and customer service.

Product Lines and Product Mix

Few firms do business with only a single product. If their first market entry is successful, they tend to increase their chances for profit and growth by adding new offerings. The iPhone and iPad, with their touch-screen technology and apps, have expanded Apple's product line.

PepsiCo product mix includes Rockstar energy drinks, which are distributed in the United States and Canada by various Pepsi bottling enterprises.

Although most main-stream knowledge workers will probably continue to use conventional computers for some time, touch-screen technology is fast becoming a standard feature in consumer electronics.[2]

A company's **product line** is a group of related products that share physical similarities or are targeted toward a similar market. A **product mix** is the assortment of product lines and individual goods and services that a firm offers to consumers and business users. The Coca-Cola Company and PepsiCo both have product lines that include old standards—Coke Classic and Diet Coke, Pepsi and Diet Pepsi. But recently, Rockstar Energy Drink switched distributors from The Coca-Cola Company to PepsiCo, as a result of The Coca-Cola Company's distribution agreement with competitor Monster energy drink. As part of a multiyear agreement, Rockstar energy drinks are distributed in the United States and Canada by Pepsi Bottling Group, PepsiAmericas, and Pepsi Bottling Ventures, as well as other independent Pepsi bottlers.[3]

Marketers must continually assess their product mix for a few reasons: to ensure company growth, to satisfy changing consumer needs and wants, and to adjust to competitors' offerings. To remain competitive, marketers look for gaps in their product lines and fill them with new offerings or modified versions of existing products. A helpful tool that is frequently used in making product decisions is the product life cycle.

product line a group of related products that share physical similarities or are targeted toward a similar market.

product mix the assortment of product lines and individual goods and services that a firm offers to consumers and business users.

✔ **ASSESSMENT CHECK**

12.1.1 How do consumer products differ from business products?

12.1.2 Differentiate among convenience products, shopping products, and specialty products.

PRODUCT LIFE CYCLE

After a product is on the market, it usually goes through four stages known as the **product life cycle**: introduction, growth, maturity, and decline. As **Figure 12.2** shows, industry sales and profits vary depending on the product's life-cycle stage.

Product life cycles are not set in stone; that is, not all products follow this pattern precisely, and some products may spend different amounts of time in each stage. But the idea of a product life cycle helps the marketing planner to look ahead to new developments throughout the various stages of a product's life. Profits take on a predictable pattern through the stages, and the promotional focus shifts from communicating product information in the early stages to heavy brand promotion in the later stages.

LO 12.2 Describe the four stages of the product life cycle and their marketing implications.

product life cycle the four basic stages in the development of a successful product—introduction, growth, maturity, and decline.

Stages of the Product Life Cycle

In the *introduction stage*, the firm tries to promote demand for its new offering; inform the market about it; give free samples to entice consumers to make a trial purchase; and explain its features, uses, and benefits. Sometimes companies partner at this stage to promote new products. California-based Fuhu is the maker of the Nabi, a first-of-its-kind Android tablet for children. The company

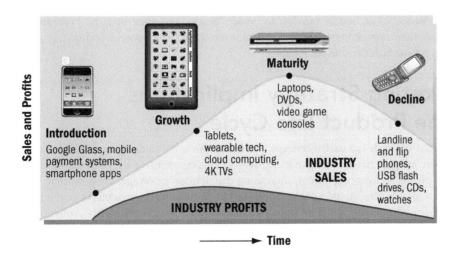

FIGURE 12.2 Stages in the Product Life Cycle

sees the Nabi as a distribution channel for content geared to children and has signed agreements with Nickelodeon and Disney. With retailers Walmart, Target, and Best Buy on board to sell the tablet, the company is developing an audio dock attachment that converts the Nabi into a karaoke machine. Fuhu has announced it will produce an original animated TV series on the BabyFirst cable network that will feature a character modelled after its Nabi tablet.[4]

New-product development costs and extensive introductory promotional campaigns to acquaint prospective buyers with the merits of the innovation, though essential to later success, are expensive and commonly lead to losses in the introductory stage. Some firms are seeking to lower these costs through ultra-low-cost product development, which involves meeting customer needs with the lowest-cost innovations possible, designing from scratch with a stripped-down budget, and the simplest engineering possible. But all these expenditures are necessary if the firm is to profit later.

During the *growth stage*, sales climb quickly as new customers join early users who now are repurchasing the item. Word-of-mouth referrals and continued advertising and other special promotions by the firm induce others to make trial purchases. At this point, the company begins to earn profits on the new product. This success encourages competitors to enter the field with similar offerings, and price competition develops. After its initial success with the Kindle, Amazon faced competition from Barnes & Noble's Nook. Amazon rushed to launch its Kindle for the iPad app, then Barnes & Noble countered with its Nook Color. Since then, the tablet market has become increasingly crowded, with the iPad still dominating the sector. Recent statistics reveal Apple with a 37 percent share of the tablet market, Samsung with 18 percent, and Amazon with 3 percent.[5]

In the *maturity stage,* industry sales at first increase, but they eventually reach a saturation level at which further expansion is difficult. Competition also intensifies, increasing the availability of the product. Firms concentrate on capturing competitors' customers, often dropping prices to further the appeal. Smartphones are in the maturity stage: competitors compete not only on price but also on features such as operating systems, size, weight, battery life, camera and video specifications, and messaging. When flat-screen TVs reached the maturity stage, companies tried to entice customers to buy new ones by offering even bigger screen sizes than before, topping the 90-inch mark. Today, there are continuing developments in colour accuracy, higher resolution, and brighter displays for better screen visibility.[6]

Sales volume fades late in the maturity stage, and some of the weaker competitors leave the market. During this stage, firms promote mature products aggressively to protect their market share and to distinguish their products from those of competitors.

Sales continue to fall in the *decline stage,* the fourth phase of the product life cycle. Profits decline and may become losses as further price cutting occurs in the reduced overall market for the item. Competitors gradually exit, making some profits possible for the remaining firms in the shrinking market. The decline stage usually is caused by a product innovation or a shift in consumer preferences. Sometimes technology change can accelerate the decline stage for a product. For example, at one time more than 90 percent of U.S. homes contained at least one DVD player. Once touted as the ultimate in DVD technology, high-definition DVDs have now been superseded by Blu-ray technology and online streaming sites. Online sites like Amazon, Netflix, and Hulu, where consumers can watch movies, television shows, or other original programming, have become another major competitor for entertainment as the link between technology and distribution has become faster and more reliable.[7]

Marketing Strategy Implications of the Product Life Cycle

The product life cycle is a useful concept. Marketers can use it to design a flexible marketing strategy that can adapt to the changing marketplace. A firm's competitive activities may involve developing new products, lowering prices, increasing distribution coverage, creating new promotional campaigns, or any combination of these approaches. In general, the marketer's goal is to extend the product life cycle as long as the item is profitable. Some products are highly profitable during the later stages of their life cycle because all the initial development costs have already been recovered.

A commonly used strategy for extending the life cycle is to increase customers' frequency of use. (See the "Hit & Miss" feature for a description of Canadian Tire's life cycle and the current upgrades

HIT & MISS

Canadian Tire: Changing with the Times

From coast to coast across Canada, the long-respected Canadian Tire Corporation is a retailing institution. About 85 percent of Canadians live within a 15-minute drive of a store. More than 10,000 Canadians have their cars serviced there every day. Canadian Tire is visited by 40 percent of the adult population at least once a week. It is the most visited nongrocery retailer in the country. Not surprising, Canadian Tire is the top national retailer in gardening, home appliances, home-improvement products, power tools—and, of course, auto parts and accessories. Today, Canadian Tire has 487 associated dealer-owned and corporate-owned stores across Canada employing more 68,000 people.

But it wasn't always this way. It may be hard to imagine, but in 1922 Ontario had about 200,000 automobiles. The same year, brothers John W. and Alfred J. Billes bought the Hamilton Tire & Garage Ltd. in Toronto. Just when Canadians were starting to think about the automobile as a serious form of personal transportation, the Billes brothers were offering parts, a repair service, storage in the winter, and fuel to keep local motorists on the move. As the popularity of automobiles ownership increased, companies like Canadian Tire competed for the attention of customers who would need services for their automobiles and farm vehicles. The Canadian Tire Corporation has grown tremendously. Over the years, it has become a retail centre for auto, sports, leisure, and home products.

The Canadian Tire catalogue was first introduced in 1928 to reach customers in rural and remote areas of the country. The catalogue is still popular today: 9 million copies are printed each year. One thing may be more appreciated by Canadians than the convenience of their local Canadian Tire store or catalogue—finding a stack of Canadian Tire money in their glove compartment. Canadian Tire money was first introduced in 1961 to reward cash-paying customers and to encourage return visits. It has proven to be a huge success as a customer-loyalty plan.

Today, Canadian Tire stores in major city centres and regional shopping malls don't look anything like the small retailer that seemed to show up in every small Canadian town, where it sold sports gear and provincial hunting and fishing licences. The pace of store renovations has been increased to attract more shoppers after early results showed customers' quick acceptance of the new look and product selections. Canadian Tire has introduced financial services, including bank savings accounts, guaranteed investment certificates, credit cards, and mortgages. In 2002, the company acquired Mark's Work Wearhouse casual clothing. In 2011, it bought The Forzani Group of sports shops. Both acquisitions have helped position the firm for future revenue growth. As customers continue to respond to new, larger store formats, Canadian Tire earnings and profits reach ever higher levels. In 2014, gross revenues rose to $12.4 billion. From humble beginnings, the Billes's small family enterprise has grown to become the huge Canadian franchise corporation we know today.

Questions for Critical Thinking

1. What are the greatest challenges facing Canadian Tire today?

2. Which future retailing acquisition would fit well within the Canadian Tire organization?

Sources: Canadian Tire, accessed April 20, 2015, http://corp.canadiantire.ca/EN/Pages/default.aspx; Canadian Tire Annual Report 2014, accessed April 26, 2015, http://corp.canadiantire.ca/EN/Investors/Documents/2014%20Annual%20Report-EN.pdf.

the store is making to attract new customers.) Walmart and Shoppers Drug Mart (Pharmaprix in Quebec) offer grocery sections in their stores. Both firms added groceries to increase the frequency of shopper visits. Another strategy is to add new users. Marketers for Old Spice grooming products decided that Old Spice didn't need to be an old-fashioned product. They came up with a campaign to freshen up the product line's image and attract younger men. The new campaign was called "The Man Your Man Could Smell Like." It cleverly poked fun at the idea that merely using Old Spice would make younger men irresistible to women—while promising, with a wink, that it would.[8]

Arm & Hammer used a third approach: it found new uses for its products. The original use of the firm's baking soda was for baking. But Arm & Hammer now promotes its newer uses as a toothpaste, refrigerator freshener, and flame extinguisher. A fourth product life cycle extension strategy is changing package sizes, labels, and product designs. Changing the product design can often mean finding a way to give it an online application. For example, Mattel's doll sales had declined almost 20 percent. The toymaker increased sales by teaming its Barbie doll with the White House Project and the Take Our Daughters and Sons to Work Foundation. Consumers were invited to celebrate Barbie's 125th career by voting online to choose from among architect, computer engineer, environmentalist, news anchor, and surgeon. The winners, announced at the New York Toy Fair, were Computer Engineer Barbie (by popular vote) and News Anchor Barbie (by girls' vote). Both were part of Barbie's "I Can Be" series.[9]

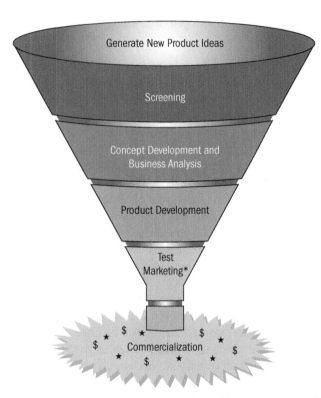

Generate New Product Ideas

Screening

Concept Development and Business Analysis

Product Development

Test Marketing*

Commercialization

* Some firms skip this step and move directly from product development to commercialization.

FIGURE 12.3 Process for Developing New Goods and Services

Stages in New-Product Development

New-product development is expensive, time-consuming, and risky. Only about one-third of all new products become success stories. Products can fail for many reasons. Some have not been properly developed and tested, some are poorly packaged, and others don't have enough promotional support or distribution or do not satisfy a consumer need or want. Even successful products reach the end of the decline stage and must be replaced with new-product offerings.

Most of today's newly developed items are aimed at satisfying specific consumer demands. New-product development is more efficient and cost effective because marketers use a systematic, or organized, approach to develop new products. As **Figure 12.3** shows, the new-product development process has six stages. Each stage requires a "go/no-go" decision by management before moving on to the next stages. The development of new products needs large investments in both time and money. The sooner that decision makers can identify a weak product and drop it from further steps, the less time and money will be wasted.

The starting point in the new-product development process is generating ideas for new offerings. Ideas come from many sources, including customer suggestions, suppliers, employees, research scientists, marketing research, inventors outside the firm, and competitive products. The most successful ideas are directly related to satisfying customer needs. Procter & Gamble recently expanded its Febreze home collection by adding the Flameless Luminary In-Home Scent Delivery System. Instead of lighting a potentially dangerous candle, consumers can use a battery-operated, flameless light that distributes fragrance from a decorative, scented shade. The light automatically turns off after four hours. The design was a finalist in the Consumer Packaged Goods—Household Segment category of the Edison Best New Product Awards.[10]

In the second stage, screening removes ideas that do not work with overall company goals or that cannot be developed given the company's resources. Some firms hold open discussions of new-product ideas with specialists who work in different functional areas in the organization.

During the concept development and business analysis phase, further screening occurs. The analysis involves assessing the new product's potential sales, profits, growth rate, and competitive strengths. It also tries to determine whether the new product fits with the company's product, distribution, and promotional resources. At this stage, some companies use *concept testing*—marketing research designed to attract consumers' first reactions to new-product ideas. For example, potential consumers might be asked about proposed brand names and other methods of product identification. *Focus groups* are formal sessions where consumers meet with marketers to discuss what they like or dislike about current products. Sometimes the consumers can test or sample a new offering to provide immediate feedback.

Next, an actual product is developed, subjected to a series of tests, and revised. At this stage, developers may create functioning prototypes, or test models, or detailed descriptions of the product. These designs are the joint responsibility of the firm's development staff and its marketers. The marketers provide feedback on consumer reactions to the proposed product design, colour, and other physical features.

test marketing the introduction of a new product and a complete marketing campaign to a selected city or TV coverage area.

Test marketing introduces a new product and a complete marketing campaign to a selected city or TV coverage area. When marketers look for a test location, they prefer a location or television coverage area with a manageable size, where residents match their target market's demographic profile. During the test marketing stage, the item is sold in a limited area while the company examines both consumer responses to the new offering and the marketing effort used to support the product. Test market results can help managers to decide on the product's likely performance in a full-scale introduction. Some firms skip test marketing because of concerns that the test could reveal their

Table 12.1 Examples of Products That Failed

PRODUCT	WHY IT FLOPPED
New Coke	Facing stiff competition from other soft drink producers in the mid-1980s, executives at The Coca-Cola Company stopped production on the original Coke and introduced a new, sweeter formula of the soft drink. Consumers were outraged and flooded the company with complaints. Three months later, the company went back to the original Coke formula.
Sony Betamax	Sony's Betamax video recorder was introduced in the mid-1970s. Soon after, a rival company introduced VHS technology, which became the standard for video recordings, and several other competitors introduced VHS machines quickly. Because Sony chose not to license its Betamax technology, and the two technologies were not compatible, consumers needed to choose between Betamax and VHS. As a result, Sony lost its market share.
Pepsi A.M. and Crystal Pepsi	In the late 1980s, Pepsi A.M. was marketed as an alternative to coffee for people who wanted a caffeinated beverage in the morning. Crystal Pepsi was introduced about the same time and was a clear cola drink. Neither product caught on with consumers.
Harley-Davidson Perfume	Fans of the Harley-Davidson brand are considered very loyal to the motorcycle maker. Trying to leverage this loyalty and extend its brand, the company introduced perfume, but consumers didn't buy it.
Colgate Kitchen Entrees	Colgate tried to capitalize on its popular brand by introducing a line of frozen dinners in the early 1980s. Unfortunately, consumers thought of Colgate as a toothpaste brand and not a food company.

Sources: "Top 25 Biggest Product Flops of All Time," *Daily Finance*, accessed March 12, 2014, www.dailyfinance.com/photos/top-25-biggest-product-flops-of-all-time; Len Penzo, "10 Grocery Products That Flopped," accessed March 12, 2014, http://lenpenzo.com/blog/id12478-10-grocery-store-products-that-flopped.html; "Top 10 Bad Beverage Ideas," *Time*, accessed March 12, 2014, http://content.time.com/time/specials/packages/article/0,28804,1913612_1913610_ 1913608,00.html.

product strategies to the competition. Also, many expenses are involved in doing limited production runs of complex products such as a new auto or refrigerator. Sometimes, these costs are so high that the test marketing stage is skipped, and the development process moves directly to the next stage.

In the final stage, commercialization, the product is made available in the marketplace. This stage is also known as a product launch. Much planning goes into this stage. The firm's strategies for distribution, promotion, and pricing must all work together to support the new product. The videogame-maker Electronic Arts (EA) announced a new distribution strategy for future games. EA will release premium downloadable content (PDLC) for a game before releasing the complete, packaged version. The PDLC will be priced at $15 and will include three to four hours of playing time. The company will invite comments from reviewers and players. It will then make changes to the final version before releasing it for sale.[11]

New-product development is a vital process for twenty-first-century firms: firms need a steady stream of new products to offer their customers; the risks of product failure can be very expensive; and tens of millions of dollars are needed to complete a successful new-product launch. But, as **Table 12.1** shows, success is not guaranteed until the new product achieves customer acceptance. Microsoft introduced a new operating system, Windows Vista, but it never caught on. The next version of Windows, Windows 7, did much better. Another company, DigiScent, launched a new computer device. It was intended to bring the sense of smell to online shopping or browsing. But DigiScent didn't think through its plan carefully. Consumers rejected the idea of having to deal with unwanted aromas. Consumers also gave a thumbs-down on the product's name—iSmell.[12]

✓ ASSESSMENT CHECK

12.2.1 What are the stages of the product life cycle?

12.2.2 What are the marketing implications of each stage?

PRODUCT IDENTIFICATION

LO 12.3 Explain how firms identify their products.

A major part of developing a successful new product is choosing how to identify the product and distinguish it from other products. Both tangible goods and intangible services are identified by brands, brand names, and trademarks. A **brand** is a name, term, sign, symbol, design, or some combination that identifies the products of one firm and shows how they differ from competitors' products. Tropicana, Pepsi, and Gatorade are all made by PepsiCo, but the unique combinations of names and symbols used to market these products sets them apart from other similar products.

brand a name, term, sign, symbol, design, or some combination that identifies the products of one firm and shows how they differ from competitors' offerings.

brand name the part of the brand that is made up of words or letters that form a name. It is used to identify a firm's products and show how they differ from the products of competitors.

trademark a brand that has been given legal protection.

A **brand name** is that part of the brand that is made up of words or letters that form a name. It is used to identify a firm's products and show how they differ from the products of competitors. The brand name is the part of the brand that can be spoken. Many brand names are well known around the world, such as Coca-Cola, McDonald's, American Express, Google, and Nike. McDonald's brand mark, the "golden arches," is also familiar around the world. In 2013, Research In Motion changed its corporate name to BlackBerry, the brand for which it was recognized around the world.

A **trademark** is a brand that has been given legal protection. The protection is granted only to the brand's owner. Trademark protection includes the brand name, design logos, slogans, packaging elements, and product features such as colour and shape. A well-designed trademark, such as the Nike "swoosh," can make a difference in how positively consumers perceive a brand.

Selecting an Effective Brand Name

Good brand names are easy to say, easy to recognize, and easy to remember: Crest, Visa, and Dell are good examples. Global firms face a real problem when selecting brand names. An excellent brand name in one country may be a poor choice in another country. Most languages have a short *a*, so *Coca-Cola* is easy to say almost anywhere. But an advertising campaign for E-Z washing machines failed in the United Kingdom. The British pronounce *z* as "zed." They are not as familiar with American "pronunciation" as Canadians are.

Brand names should also send the right image to the buyer. One effective way to create a name is to link the product with its positioning strategy. The name Purell reinforces the concept of sanitizing hands to protect against germs. Dove soap and beauty products link to the idea of mildness. Taster's Choice instant coffee links to its promotional claim "Tastes and smells like ground roast coffee."

Brand names also must be legally protectable. Trademark law does not allow brand names that contain words in general use, such as *television* or *automobile*. Generic words—words that describe a type of product—cannot be used exclusively by any organization. But sometimes a brand name becomes so popular that it passes into common language and turns into a generic word. Then, the company can no longer use it as a brand name. A long time ago, aspirin, linoleum, and zipper were exclusive brand names. But these words have become generic terms and no longer have legal protection.

To be effective, *brand names* must be easy for consumers to say, recognize, and remember.

Brand Categories

A brand that is offered and promoted by a manufacturer is known as a *manufacturer's* (or *national*) *brand*. Examples are Tide, Cheerios, Windex, Fossil, and Nike. But not all brand names belong to manufacturers; some are the property of retailers or distributors. A *private* (or *store*) *brand* identifies a product that is not linked to the manufacturer; instead, it carries a wholesaler's or retailer's label. Two examples are Sears's Craftsman tools and Loblaw's President's Choice foods.

Another branding decision that marketers must make is whether to use a family branding strategy or an individual branding strategy. A *family brand* is a single brand name used for several related products. Lululemon, Kraft, KitchenAid, Johnson & Johnson, Hewlett-Packard, and Arm & Hammer use a family name for their entire line of products. When a firm using family branding introduces a new product, both customers and retailers recognize the familiar brand name. The promotion of individual products within a product line benefits all the products because the family brand is well known.

Other firms use an *individual branding* strategy by giving a different brand name to each product within a product line. For example, Procter & Gamble has individual brand names for its different laundry detergents—Tide, Cheer, and Gain. Each brand targets a unique market segment. Consumers who want a cold-water detergent can choose Cheer over Tide or Gain, instead of purchasing a competitor's brand. Individual branding also builds competition within a firm and enables the company to increase its overall sales.

Brand Loyalty and Brand Equity

Brands achieve different levels of consumer familiarity and acceptance. For example, a homeowner may insist on Andersen windows when renovating, but may not prefer any brand when buying a loaf of bread. Consumer loyalty can increase a brand's value, so marketers try to strengthen brand loyalty. When a brand image suffers, marketers try to recreate a positive image.

Brand Loyalty

Marketers measure brand loyalty in three stages: brand recognition, brand preference, and brand insistence. *Brand recognition* is brand acceptance that is strong enough that the consumer is aware of the brand, but not strong enough to lead a customer to prefer it over other brands. A consumer might have heard of L'Oréal hair care products, without necessarily preferring those products to Redken products. Marketers can often increase brand recognition through advertising, free samples, and discount coupons.

Brand preference occurs when a consumer chooses one firm's brand over a competitor's. At this stage, the consumer usually uses his or her previous experience when selecting the product. Furniture and other home furnishings fall into this category. Suppose a shopper purchased an IKEA dining room table and chairs and was satisfied with them. This shopper is likely to return to IKEA to purchase a bedroom set. While there, this shopper might also pick up a set of mixing bowls for the kitchen or a lamp for the family room—because this shopper knows and likes the IKEA brand.

During Design Week in New York City, IKEA installed this clever display, which is meant to look like a bus stop. IKEA, the retailer of affordable, well-designed contemporary furniture enjoys *brand insistence*—the ultimate expression of brand loyalty. For devoted IKEA fans, no other brand will do.

Brand insistence is the ultimate degree of brand loyalty. Consumers who have brand insistence will look for a product at another outlet, special-order it from a dealer, order by mail, or search the Internet. Shoppers who insist on IKEA products for their homes may drive an hour or two—making a day excursion of the venture—to visit an IKEA store. The combination of value for the money and the concept of IKEA as a shopping destination have given the brand a unique appeal for shoppers.[13]

Brand-building strategies were once limited to consumer goods, but they are becoming more important for B2B brands. Intel, Xerox, IBM, and service providers such as ServiceMaster and Cisco are among the suppliers who have built brand names among business customers.

Brand Equity

Brand loyalty is at the heart of **brand equity**, the added value that a respected and successful name gives to a product. This value results from a combination of factors: awareness, loyalty, perceived quality, and feelings or images the customer associates with the brand. High brand equity offers financial advantages to a firm because the product represents a large market share. High brand equity can also reduce price sensitivity, which can lead to higher profits. **Figure 12.4** shows the world's 10 most valuable brands and their estimated worth.

Brand awareness is high when the product is the first one that comes to mind when you hear a product category. If someone says "coffee," do you think of Starbucks, Dunkin' Donuts, or Tim Hortons? Brand association is the link between a brand and other favourable images.

Large companies usually assign the task of managing a brand's marketing strategies to a *brand manager*, also called a *product manager*. This marketing professional plans and puts in place the other promotional, pricing, distribution, and product arrangements that lead to strong brand

brand equity the added value that a respected and successful name gives to a product.

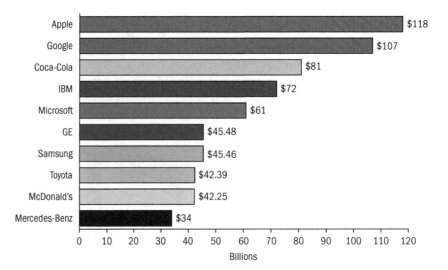

FIGURE 12.4 The World's Ten Most Valuable Brands and Their Worth (in billions of dollars)

Source: Data from "Best Global Brands 2014," *Interbrand*, http://interbrand.com/best-brands/best-global-brands/2014/ranking.

equity. A *category manager*, a newer type of professional, oversees an entire group of products. Unlike traditional brand managers or product managers, category managers have profit responsibility for their product group. These managers are assisted by associates, usually called *analysts*. Part of the shift to category management was started by large retailers. They realized they could benefit from the marketing power of large grocery and household goods producers such as Kraft and Procter & Gamble. As a result, producers began to focus their attention on in-store merchandising instead of mass-market advertising. A few years ago, Kraft reorganized its sales force so that each representative was responsible for a retailer's needs instead of just promoting a single brand.

category advisor the individual that the business customer assigns as the major supplier to deal with all the other suppliers for a project. The category advisor also presents the entire package to the business buyer.

A **category advisor** functions in the B2B context. This individual is the major supplier that a business customer assigns to deal with all the other suppliers for a project. The category advisor also presents the entire package to the business buyer.

Packages and Labels

Mary Altaffer/AP Photo/The Canadian Press

Consumer demand has led to more environmentally friendly packages. Box manufacturers and chemical companies are working to create more compact packaging that is made from renewable sources and is recyclable. Frito-Lay introduced compostable packaging for its SunChips multigrain snacks.

Packaging and labels are needed for product identification. They also play an important role in a firm's overall product strategy. Packaging affects an item's durability, image, and convenience. It is also one of the biggest costs in many consumer products. Consumer demand has led to smaller, more environmentally friendly packages. Box manufacturers and chemical companies are working to create more compact packaging that is made from renewable sources and is recyclable. As explained in the "Going Green" feature, Frito-Lay introduced compostable packaging for its SunChips multigrain snacks. One-third of North America's waste consists of containers and packaging, much of it from fast-food chains. Quiznos recently launched its "Eat Toasty, Be Green" campaign to introduce its new, environmentally friendly packaging. The restaurant chain now uses 100 percent compostable, wax-coated paper cups; salad containers made of renewable sugar cane; napkins made from 100 percent recycled materials; and plastic lids made from 30 percent recycled polyethylene terephthalate (PET) bottles. Even the employees' uniforms were changed—the hats and aprons are now made from 100 percent recycled soda bottles.[14]

Choosing the right package is especially important in international marketing. Marketers need to be aware of language variations and cultural preferences. Consumers in African nations

SUNCHIPS **INTRODUCES GREENER PACKAGING**

Everybody loves to snack on chips. But nobody can love what happens to the empty bag. It eventually ends up in a landfill—and may never decompose. Frito-Lay's brand SunChips aimed to change all that. On Earth Day 2009, it introduced what it called "the world's first compostable chip bag."

In a recent survey, 75 percent of those questioned thought that recyclable packaging was "somewhat important," and 51 percent felt that compostable packaging was "somewhat important." A recyclable item can be used repeatedly, whereas a compostable item breaks down in the presence of water and oxygen.

The company had to meet the challenge of developing packaging that was ecologically sound while also preserving the contents. After four years of research and testing, the company had a bag made of more than 90 percent plant-based, and therefore renewable, materials. The outer layer is made of corn-based polylactic acid (PLA). Although the bag is 100 percent compostable, researchers are working on an environmentally friendly inner layer that will keep the contents crisp and edible. Frito-Lay makes it clear that the bag decomposes most quickly—in about 14 weeks—in a hot, active composting bin. If the bag is simply left on the ground, it will still break down, but less quickly.

The new bag sounds a little different from its old packaging. But Frito-Lay assured its customers that SunChips still taste the same. It even promoted the difference as the "new sound of green" and included a clip of the sound on its website, along with a link to Facebook.

The Biodegradable Products Institute certified the new packaging, but getting North Americans to recognize the need for composting is another matter. A Frito-Lay executive acknowledged the challenge—and the opportunity to educate consumers. What was not expected was an 11 percent drop in sales and public ridicule over the "noise" made when consumers handled the new packaging material. Marketers learned a hard lesson: Although the socially responsible green packaging was popular with most consumers and most of society, many customers avoided the product because of this effect. As a result, the company returned to the original packaging for all but the original flavour chips. Frito-Lay continues to search for new materials that are not quite so noisy.

Questions for Critical Thinking

1. What role did the new, compostable packaging play in the overall marketing strategy for SunChips?

2. How do you think SunChips can most effectively educate North Americans about the importance of composting?

Sources: Bruce Horovitz, "Frito-Lay Sends Noisy, 'Green' SunChips Bag to the Dump," *USA Today,* October 5, 2010, accessed May 9, 2012, www.usatoday.com/money/industries/food/2010-10-05-sunchips05_ST_N.html; SunChips, accessed April 20, 2015, www.sunchips.com; Kate Galbraith, "A Compostable Chips Bag Hits the Shelves," *New York Times,* March 16, 2010, http://green.blogs.nytimes.com/2010/03/16/a-compostable-chips-bag-hits-the-shelves/?_r=0; Kathryn Siranosian, "New SunChips Bag: 90% Plant-Based, 100% Compostable," *Triple Pundit,* February 22, 2010, www.triplepundit.com/2010/02/new-sunchips-bag-compostable.

often prefer bold colours, but use of the country's flag colours can lead to problems. Some countries don't like to see other uses of their flag. Also, Africans often associate red with death or witchcraft. Package size can vary depending on a country's purchasing patterns and market conditions. In countries where many people have only small refrigerators, consumers may want to buy their beverages one at a time instead of in six-packs. Package weight is another important issue because shipping costs are often based on weight.

Labelling is another important part of the packaging process. In Canada, companies must meet labelling laws by providing enough information so that consumers can compare competitive products. In the case of food packaging, labelling must include nutritional information. Marketers who ship products to other countries must meet the labelling requirements in those nations. They need to know the answers to the following questions:

- Does the information on the labels need to be in more than one language?

- Do ingredients need to be listed?

- Do the labels give enough information about the product to meet government standards?

Another important part of packaging and labelling is the *universal product code (UPC)*. This bar code is read by the optical scanners that link the UPC to a product and print the name of the item and the price on a receipt. For many stores, these identifiers are useful for packaging and labelling, for simplifying and speeding retail transactions, and for evaluating customer purchases and controlling inventory. Radio-frequency identification (RFID) technology uses embedded chips that can broadcast their product information to receivers. It is unlikely, however, that they will replace bar codes.

✓ ASSESSMENT CHECK

12.3.1 Differentiate among a brand, a brand name, and a trademark.

12.3.2 Define *brand equity.*

LO 12.4 Outline the major components of an effective distribution strategy.

DISTRIBUTION STRATEGY

distribution strategy a plan that deals with the marketing activities and institutions that get the right good or service to the firm's customers.

distribution channels the paths that products—and their legal ownership—follow from producer to consumers or business users.

physical distribution the actual movement of products from producer to consumers or business users.

The second element of the marketing mix is the **distribution strategy**. This strategy is a plan that deals with the marketing activities and institutions that get the right good or service to the firm's customers. Distribution decisions involve selecting the suitable types of transportation, warehousing, inventory control, order processing, and marketing channels. Marketing channels are usually made up of intermediaries such as retailers and wholesalers that move a product from producer to final purchaser.

Two major parts of an organization's distribution strategy are distribution channels and physical distribution. **Distribution channels** are the paths that products—and their legal ownership—follow from producer to consumer or business user. All organizations use these channels to distribute their goods and services. **Physical distribution** is the actual movement of products from producer to consumers or business users. Physical distribution covers a broad range of activities, including customer service, transportation, inventory control, materials handling, order processing, and warehousing. As explained in the "Hit & Miss" feature, Gourmet Chips and Sauces, a Montreal food distributor, is building a distribution network of retailers across Canada for its imported and domestic lines of all-natural extremely hot products.

Distribution Channels

Marketers' first decision in distribution channel selection is to choose which type of channel will best meet both their firm's marketing objectives and the needs of their customers. As shown in **Figure 12.5**, marketers can choose to use either a *direct distribution channel* or a *marketing intermediary*. A distribution channel carries goods directly from producer to the consumer or business user. A *marketing intermediary* (also called a *middleman*) is a business firm that moves goods from their producers to consumers or business users. It usually involves several different marketing intermediaries. Marketing intermediaries help the distribution channel operate smoothly through

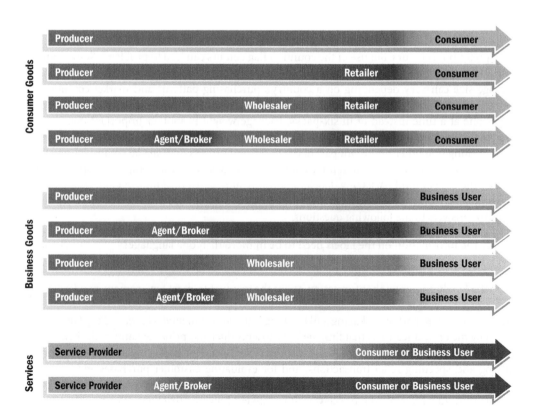

FIGURE 12.5 Alternative Distribution Channels

HIT & MISS

Gourmet Chips & Sauces Targets a Niche Market

The "heat levels" of these products differ. Some are mild, like Aubrey D.'s Condiments, Sweet Death, Jalapeño Death Sauces, and Chipotle Death Rain Potato Chips. Others are insanely hot, like Ultra Death Sauce and XXX Hot Habañero Salsa. And when Gourmet Chips & Sauces talks about the "heat level," they're talking about the "extreme end" of the market. With every bite, warning labels and fire alarm bells go off.

The gourmet market for high-quality "extremely hot" and spicy chips and sauces is small when compared with the variety and sales volumes offered by the industry's leaders, such as PepsiCo. PepsiCo leads the market by selling products with highly visible and recognizable brands such as Frito-Lay, Tostitos, and Doritos.

To compete with companies like PepsiCo, smaller firms can choose to focus on a niche in the marketplace. They can try to set themselves apart to attract customers who want something that is different from all the mass-market products.

Montreal-based Gourmet Chips & Sauces produces its own line of Aubrey D.'s Gourmet Condiments. It also imports a select line of Blair's sauces and chips from the United States and distributes this product for sale across Canada. This line of hot and spicy potato chips and sauces are all handcrafted to ensure top quality. They are made from natural ingredients, contain no preservatives or trans fats, and are gluten-free. The chips are kettle-cooked in canola or sunflower oil. Along with the sauces, they are a healthier alternative to the mass-market snacks typically found.

The limited distribution is a problem. Customers need to make more of an effort to buy these products, compared with the PepsiCo products that seem to be for sale everywhere. But the limited distribution has led to a growing niche market of premium customers and retailers who recognize the superior quality and unique product value. As a result, many customers who have tried the products are prepared to spend time looking for them. They are also prepared to pay a small premium in price. Retailers want to offer their customers something unique. The premium price is also a welcome contribution to their businesses.

Questions for Critical Thinking

1. How can Gourmet Chips & Sauces build its distribution network of grocery and convenience stores across Canada?

2. What other products could the firm add to its line?

Sources: Gourmet Chips & Sauces, accessed April 20, 2015, www.gourmetchip.com; interviews with company owner, Aubrey Zelman, March 15, 2015, and November 15, 2011.

several activities: buying, selling, storing, and transporting products; sorting and grading bulky items; and providing information to other channel members. The two main categories of marketing intermediaries are wholesalers and retailers.

No one channel suits every product. The best channel depends on the circumstances of the market and on customer needs. The most suitable channel choice may also change over time as new opportunities arise and marketers try to maintain their competitiveness.

Direct Distribution

The shortest and simplest way to connect producers and customers is by direct contact between the two parties. This method is most commonly used in the B2B market. Other examples of direct distribution occur when consumers buy fresh fruits and vegetables at roadside stands or farmers markets. Direct distribution can also be found in services, such as banking, 10-minute oil changes, and ear piercing.

Direct distribution is often found in the marketing of relatively expensive, complex products that may require demonstrations. Direct contacts between producers and business buyers are used to market most major B2B products, such as installations, accessory equipment, component parts, business services, and even raw materials. The Internet has also made direct distribution an attractive option for many retail companies and service providers. FedEx customers have long used online tools to track conventional shipments. FedEx's new International Priority Direct Distribution service allows users to ship more than one package from a single country of origin to different recipients in a single destination country. The packages are cleared through customs as a single shipment. In addition, multiple shipments to multiple recipients in multiple European

16 Contacts

FIGURE 12.6 Reducing
Transactions through
Marketing Intermediaries

✔ **ASSESSMENT CHECK**

12.4.1 Define *distribution channels*.

12.4.2 What is a marketing intermediary?

Union countries can be cleared through customs as a single shipment through Charles de Gaulle Airport near Paris.[15]

Distribution Channels Using Marketing Intermediaries

Direct channels allow producers to have simple and straightforward connections with their customers. But the list of channel alternatives in Figure 12.5 suggests that direct distribution is not always the best choice. Some products sell in small quantities for relatively low prices to thousands of widely scattered consumers. Makers of such products cannot cost-effectively contact each of their customers. Instead, they distribute products through specialized intermediaries called *wholesalers* and *retailers*.

You might think that adding intermediaries to the distribution process would increase the final cost of products. But adding intermediaries often lowers consumer prices. Intermediaries such as wholesalers and retailers often add significant value to a product as it moves through the distribution channel. They add value by creating utility, providing additional services, and reducing costs.

Marketing utility is created when intermediaries help ensure that products are available for sale when and where customers want to purchase them. For example, if you want something warm to eat on a cold winter night, you don't call Campbell's Soup and ask them to ship a can of chicken noodle soup. Instead, you go to the nearest grocery store, where you find utility in the form of product availability—a can of Campbell's chicken noodle soup on the grocery store shelf. Intermediaries perform important services such as transporting merchandise to convenient locations. Finally, a marketing intermediary represents numerous producers, which can cut the costs of buying and selling. As **Figure 12.6** illustrates, four manufacturers each selling directly to four consumers requires 16 separate transactions. Adding a marketing intermediary, such as a retailer, cuts the number of necessary transactions to eight.

LO 12.5 Explain the concept of wholesaling.

WHOLESALING

wholesaler a distribution channel member that sells primarily to retailers, other wholesalers, or business users.

A **wholesaler** is a distribution channel member that sells primarily to retailers, other wholesalers, or business users. For example, Sysco is a wholesaler that buys food products from producers and then resells them to restaurants, hotels, and other institutions in the United States and Canada.

Wholesaling is a crucial part of the distribution channel for many products, especially consumer goods and business supplies. Wholesaling intermediaries can be classified on the basis of ownership: some are owned by manufacturers, some are owned by retailers, and others are independently owned. Statistics Canada reports that Canada has approximately 111,500 wholesale enterprises located mostly in Ontario (39 percent) and Quebec (23 percent). The United States has about 486,000 wholesalers, and two-thirds of them have fewer than 20 employees. In many product categories, Canadian wholesalers compete with American wholesalers for customers anywhere in North America.[16]

Manufacturer-Owned Wholesaling Intermediaries

A manufacturer's marketing manager may decide to distribute goods directly through company-owned facilities to control distribution or customer service. Firms operate two main types of manufacturer-owned wholesaling intermediaries: sales branches and sales offices.

Sales branches stock the products they distribute and fill orders from their inventories. They also provide offices for sales representatives. Sales branches are common in the chemical, petroleum products, motor vehicle, and machine and equipment industries.

A *sales office* is exactly what its name implies: an office for a producer's salespeople. Manufacturers set up sales offices in various regions to support local selling efforts and improve customer service. Some kitchen and bath fixture manufacturers maintain showrooms to display their products. Builders and decorators can visit these showrooms to see how the finished items will look. Unlike sales branches, sales offices do not store any inventory. When a customer orders from a showroom or other sales office, the merchandise is delivered from a separate warehouse.

Independent Wholesaling Intermediaries

An independent wholesaling intermediary is a business that represents several different manufacturers and sells to retailers, manufacturers, and other business accounts. Independent wholesalers can be either merchant wholesalers or agents and brokers, depending on whether they take title to (legal ownership of) the products they handle.

Merchant wholesalers, like apparel wholesaler WholesaleSarong.com, are independently owned wholesaling intermediaries. They take title to, or legal ownership of, the goods they handle. Within this category, a *full-function merchant wholesaler* provides an assortment of services for retailers or industrial buyers, such as warehousing, shipping, and even financing. A subtype of full-function merchant is a *rack jobber*. This type of firm stocks, displays, and services specific retail products, such as paperback books or greeting cards in a drugstore or supermarket. The retailer usually receives a commission that is based on actual sales. This commission is considered to be payment for providing merchandise space to a rack jobber.

A *limited-function merchant wholesaler* also takes legal title to the products it handles, but it provides fewer services to the retailers it sells to. Some limited-function merchant wholesalers only warehouse products and do not offer delivery services. Others may warehouse products and deliver them but provide no financing. One type of limited-function merchant wholesaler is a *drop shipper*. Drop shippers operate in the coal and lumber industries and in other industries that deal in bulky products, where no single producer can provide a complete assortment. Drop shippers provide access to many related goods by contacting numerous producers and negotiating the best possible prices. To control costs, producers usually ship such products directly to the drop shipper's customers.

Another category of independent wholesaling intermediaries consists of *agents* and *brokers*. They may or may not take physical possession of the goods they handle, but they never take title, or ownership. They work mainly to bring buyers and sellers together. Stockbrokers, such as Scotiabank's ScotiaMcLeod investment dealers, and real estate agents, such as RE/MAX realtors, perform functions similar to those of agents and brokers, but at the retail level. They do not take title to the sellers' property; instead, they create time and ownership utility for both buyer and seller by helping to carry out buying and selling transactions.

Manufacturers' reps act as independent sales forces by representing the manufacturers of related but noncompeting products. These agent intermediaries are sometimes referred to as *manufacturers' agents*. They receive commissions that are based on a percentage of the sales they make.

Retailer-Owned Cooperatives and Buying Offices

Retailers sometimes work together to form their own wholesaling organizations. Such organizations can take the form of either a buying group or a cooperative. The retailers set up the new operation to reduce costs or to provide some service that is not readily available in the marketplace.

ASSESSMENT CHECK

12.5.1 Define *wholesaling.*

12.5.2 Differentiate between a merchant wholesaler and an agent or broker in terms of title to the goods.

For example, to achieve cost savings through quantity purchases, independent retailers may form a buying group that negotiates bulk sales with manufacturers. Federated Co-operatives Limited (FCL) is a Western Canada-based cooperative that is owned by approximately 250 retail cooperatives. These retail co-ops are the "members" of FCL. FCL provides central wholesaling, manufacturing, and administrative services to its member owners. Together, FCL and its member owners are known as the Co-operative Retailing System (CRS).[17] In a cooperative, an independent group of retailers may decide to work together to share functions such as shipping or warehousing.

LO 12.6 Describe the types of retailers and retail strategies used.

retailers distribution channel members that sell goods and services to individuals for their own use, not for resale.

RETAILING

Retailers, in contrast to wholesalers, are distribution channel members that sell goods and services to individuals for their own use, not for resale. Consumers usually buy their food, clothing, shampoo, furniture, and appliances from some type of retailer. Your grocery store may have bought some of its dairy products from a cooperative wholesaler, such as Quebec-based Agropur, and then resold them to you.

Retailers are the final link—the so-called "last three feet"—of the distribution channel. Retailers are often the only channel members that deal directly with consumers. That means retailers need to remain alert to changing consumer needs. For example, soaring gas prices affect consumers' budgets: they may make fewer trips to the mall and may cut back on nonessential purchases. As a result, retailers may need to offer special sales or events to encourage customers to visit their shops. Retailers also need to keep pace with developments in the fast-changing business environment, such as disruptions in the delivery of supplies because of widespread wildfires or storms.

Nonstore Retailers

Retailers are divided into two categories: store retailers and nonstore retailers. As **Figure 12.7** illustrates, nonstore retailing includes four forms: direct-response retailing, Internet retailing, automatic merchandising, and direct selling. *Direct-response retailing* reaches consumers through catalogues; telemarketing; and even magazine, newspaper, and television ads. Shoppers order goods by mail, telephone, computer, and fax machine. Their purchases are delivered to their home, or shoppers pick up their purchases at a local store.

Internet retailing is the second form of nonstore retailing. Tens of thousands of retailers have set up shop online. Internet sales are growing at a rate of about 5 percent a year (as total retail sales decline). Today, North American online sales account for about 6 percent of total retail sales.[18] Hundreds of Internet enterprises shut down during the first few years of the twenty-first century. The firms that survived have stronger business models than those that failed. Two examples of successful pure dot-com businesses are Amazon and eBay. Retailing has seen a major shift: many traditional bricks-and-mortar retailers have set up online shopping through their own websites to compete with pure dot-com start-ups. Best Buy and Walmart report strong online sales. Shopping sites are among the most popular Internet destinations, and the most common products purchased online include electronics, clothing, household goods, and office supplies.

The last two forms of nonstore retailing are automatic merchandising and direct selling. *Automatic merchandising* provides convenience through the use of vending machines. Automated teller machines (ATMs) may soon join vending machines as banks find new ways to compete for customers. In the United States, NCR Corporation, a leading manufacturer of ATMs, will soon be putting human tellers on its screens. The new interactive teller includes human help to assist customers with transactions in English or Spanish, with more languages to be added in the future. Bank of

Internet Retailing Examples: sales through virtual storefronts, Web-based sellers, and the websites of bricks-and-mortar retailers

Direct-Response Retailing Examples: sales through catalogues; telemarketing; and magazine, newspaper, and television ads

Nonstore Retailers

Direct Selling Examples: direct manufacturer-to-consumer sales through party plans and direct contact by Amway, Home & Garden Party decorations, and Electrolux vacuum cleaner salespeople

Automatic Merchandising Examples: sales of such consumer products as candy, soft drinks, ice, chewing gum, sandwiches, and soup through vending machines

FIGURE 12.7 Types of Nonstore Retailing

America hopes the use of remote tellers at its ATMs will help build deeper customer relationships.[19] *Direct selling* includes direct-to-consumer sales by Pampered Chef kitchen representatives and salespeople for Silpada sterling silver jewellery through party-plan selling methods. Both are forms of direct selling.

Companies that once used telemarketing to attract new customers have been faced with consumer resistance to intrusive phone calls. Among the growing barriers are caller ID, call-blocking devices such as the TeleZapper, and the National Do Not Call List (DNCL). The DNCL makes it illegal for most companies to call people who have registered their phone number. As a result, many companies, including telecommunications and regional utilities, now send direct-mail pieces to promote such services as phones, cable television, and natural gas.

Bank of America hopes the use of remote human tellers at its ATMs will build stronger customer relationships.

HO Marketwire Photos/Newscom

Store Retailers

In-store sales still result in more sales than nonstore retailing such as direct-response retailing and Internet selling. Store retailers range in size from tiny newsstands to multi-storey department stores and large warehouse-style retailers such as Costco. **Table 12.2** lists the different types of store retailers with examples of each type. Clearly, retailing can take many approaches. Retail outlets must choose among these approaches to sell a variety of services and product lines offered at a range of prices.

Table 12.2 **Types of Retail Stores**

STORE TYPE	DESCRIPTION	EXAMPLE
Specialty store	Offers a complete selection in a narrow line of merchandise	Choices Markets, Bass Pro Shops, Golf Town, Williams-Sonoma
Convenience store	Offers staple convenience goods, easily accessible locations, extended store hours, and rapid checkouts	7-Eleven, Boni Soir, Mac's
Discount store	Offers wide selection of merchandise at low prices; off-price discounters offer designer or brand-name merchandise	Walmart, Giant Tiger, Army & Navy
Warehouse club	Large, warehouse-style store selling food and general merchandise at discount prices to membership card-holders	Costco, DirectBuy
Factory outlet	Manufacturer-owned store selling seconds, production overruns, or discontinued lines	Adidas, Tommy Hilfiger, Pottery Barn, Ralph Lauren
Supermarket	Large, self-service retailer offering a wide selection of food and nonfood merchandise	Safeway, Whole Foods Market, Loblaw
Supercentre	Giant store offering food and general merchandise at discount prices	Walmart Supercentre, Real Canadian Superstore
Department store	Offers a wide variety of merchandise selections (furniture, cosmetics, housewares, clothing) and many customer services	Hudson's Bay

The Wheel of Retailing

Retailers face constant change as new stores replace older stores. In a process called the *wheel of retailing*, new retailers enter the market by reducing services so they can offer lower prices. For example, supermarkets and discount stores gained their market position by offering low prices and limited service. Some of these new retailers slowly add services as they grow. In a few years, they become "older stores" and are the targets of new retailers.

As **Figure 12.8** illustrates, most major developments in retailing appear to fit the wheel pattern. The low-price, limited-service strategy describes supermarkets, catalogue retailers, discount stores, Internet retailers, and "big-box" stores, such as PetSmart and Office Depot. Corner grocery stores have led to supermarkets and then to warehouse clubs such as Costco. Department stores have lost market share to discount clothing retailers such as Target and Winners. Independent bookstores have lost business to giant chains such as Chapters Indigo and online-only sellers such as Amazon.ca and Buy.ca. But the wheel of retailing does not fit every pattern of retail evolution. For example, automatic merchandising has always been a relatively high-priced retail method. The wheel of retailing has benefits for retailers. It gives retail managers a general idea of what to expect during the evolution of retailing. It also shows that business success involves the "survival of the fittest." Retailers that fail to change will fail to survive.

Mid-1900s
Supermarkets;
Discount
Stores

Early 1900s
Self-Service
Grocers;
Sears
Catalogue

Early 2000s
Internet Retailers;
Big-Box Stores;
Lifestyle Shopping
Centres

Late 1800s
Department
Stores;
Five & Dime
Variety Stores

FIGURE 12.8 The Wheel of Retailing

How Retailers Compete

Retailers compete with each other in many ways. Nonstore retailers focus on making the shopping experience as convenient as possible. Shoppers at store retailers such as Holt Renfrew enjoy a luxurious atmosphere and personal service.

Like manufacturers, retailers must develop marketing strategies that are based on goals and strategic plans. Successful retailers use images that alert consumers to the stores' identities and the shopping experiences they provide. To create that image, all parts of a retailer's strategy must work together and complement each other. Retailers must first identify their target markets, and then choose the strategies for merchandising, customer service, pricing, and location that will attract customers in their target market segments.

Seventh Generation identified its *target market* as those people who are committed to using environmentally safe products for household cleaning.

Identifying a Target Market

The first step in developing a competitive retailing strategy is to select a target market. This choice requires careful evaluation of the market segment's size, profit potential, and its current level of competition. For example, bargain stores, such as Dollar Store, target consumers who are extremely price-conscious; while convenience stores, such as 7-Eleven, target consumers who want an easy way to purchase items they buy frequently. Seventh Generation makes "green" products for household cleaning and personal care. It began as a mail-order company, then started selling at natural-food stores. It grew into a major business whose products were featured at supermarkets nationwide and at Amazon.ca. Seventh Generation is committed to increasing consumer awareness of environmentally safe cleaning and household products. It recently began its "Protecting Planet Home" campaign. The company plans to build on its 45 percent profits by launching its first national marketing campaign online, in print, and in TV commercials. The company's goal is to get 45 percent of North American households to try at least one Seventh Generation product.[20]

Selecting a Product Strategy

Next, the retailer must develop a product strategy to decide on the best mix of merchandise to carry to satisfy its target market. Retail strategists must decide on the general product categories, product lines, and the variety to offer. Sometimes this decision involves expanding or reducing the product mix. Almost 20 years ago, Under Armour began making tee shirts to help athletes stay cool and dry. Since then, the company has expanded its brand to include women's and children's clothing, as well as football cleats and running shoes.[21]

Shaping a Customer Service Strategy

A retailer's customer service strategy focuses on attracting and retaining target customers to maximize sales and profits. Some stores offer a wide variety of services, such as gift wrapping, alterations, returns, interior design services, and delivery. Other stores offer only basic customer service, and they feature their low prices instead. Some grocery shoppers find convenience online, by using a service that selects grocery items, packs the products, and delivers the purchases to the door. Other grocery shoppers choose to visit a bricks-and-mortar store and make their own selections.

Selecting a Pricing Strategy

Retailers base their pricing decisions on their costs of purchasing products from other channel members and offering services to customers. Pricing can play a major role in consumers' view of a retailer. Consumers don't always choose the lower-priced products. For example, Loblaw offers three choices: high-quality products under its President's Choice private brand, lower-priced no-name brands, and higher-priced national brands. Loblaw provides these options, and customers can choose the products they prefer. Pricing strategy is covered in more detail in Chapter 13.

Choosing a Location

A good retail location can often make the difference between success and failure. The location decision depends on the retailer's size, financial resources, product offerings, competition, and, of course, its target market. The decision is also influenced by traffic patterns, the visibility of the store's signage, parking, and the location of complementary stores. Consider the competition between PetSmart and Mondou. Mondou tends to have smaller stores than PetSmart and in greater numbers. Their stores are mostly located in strip malls. In contrast, PetSmart's strategy is to build bigger "power centres" right beside other large discount chains. Some PetSmart stores offer added pet services—adoption, grooming, daycare, and boarding. Mondou stores are thought of more as "convenience stores" for pet supplies—especially food. Both companies have implemented "green" initiatives.[22]

A *planned shopping centre* is a group of retail stores that have been planned, coordinated, and marketed as a unit to shoppers in a geographical trade area. By providing single convenient locations and free parking, shopping centres have replaced downtown shopping in many cities. But time-pressed consumers are always looking for more efficient ways to shop, including using catalogues, Internet retailers, and one-stop shopping at large free-standing stores such as Walmart Supercentres. To lure more customers, shopping centres are now marketing themselves as entertainment destinations, by offering movie theatres, art displays, carousel rides, and musical entertainment. The West Edmonton Mall includes a water park and indoor arena. The giant Mall of America in Bloomington, Minnesota, features a seven-acre amusement park and an aquarium.

Shopping malls attract teens, who often meet there to socialize with friends. Businesses want to welcome their teen customers, but sometimes the group of teens hanging around the mall causes difficulties for other customers and some retailers, as described in the "Solving an Ethical Controversy" feature.

In recent years, some large regional malls have seen a growing shift in shopping centre traffic to smaller strip centres and name-brand outlet centres. Many consumers have also shifted their

SOLVING AN **ETHICAL** CONTROVERSY

Teens at the Mall: Good or Bad for Business?

Some shopping malls have banned unsupervised minors on weekend evenings. Others have initiated a total ban on unaccompanied teens. However, teenagers also spend money at malls. Some merchants who once complained about groups of unsupervised teens have now pinned their revenue hopes on these young spenders.

Should malls lift curfews on teenagers to boost business?

PRO

1. Some studies suggest teenage spending has increased, contrary to expectations after several years of declining figures.

2. Most teenagers are well behaved and should not be banned as a group because of the bad behaviour of a few.

CON

1. Some merchants are still wary because some parents ignore their childrens' bad behaviour.

2. The attractiveness of teenage spending has to be weighed against the reality of crowd behaviour. Malls provide a venue for teen fights, flash mobs, and other disturbances.

Summary

Just as adults spent much less during the recent recession, so did their children. Teenagers have now returned in some measure to previous spending habits, particularly if they are carrying credit cards. Mall owners and civic leaders will need to find a balance between maintaining order and encouraging tomorrow's consumers.

Sources: Thomas Tracy and Mark Morales, "Brooklyn Mall Lifts Ban on Teens after Post-Christmas Flash Mob Trouble," *New York Daily News*, accessed February 15, 2014, www.nydailynews.com/new-york/brooklyn/brooklyn-mall-lifts-ban-teens-flash-mob-trouble-article-1.1561067; Pattie Kate, "What Are the Characteristics of Teenage Spending?" *wiseGEEK*, accessed February 14, 2014, www.wisegeek.com/what-are-the-characteristics-of-teenage-spending.htm; Andrea Chang, "Free-Spending Teens Return to Malls," *Los Angeles Times*, accessed February 14, 2014, http://articles.latimes.com/2010/mar/28/business/la-fi-cover-teen-spending28-2010mar28; Erica Shaffer, "City Leaders Recommend Total Ban of Unsupervised Teens at Mall," *Toledo News NOW*, accessed February 14, 2014, www.toledonewsnow.com/story/12008127/city-leaders-recommend-total-ban-of-unsupervised-teens-at-mall; Fran Daniel, "Mall May Limit Teens: Policy Expected to Require Parental Supervision on Friday, Saturday Evenings," *Winston-Salem Journal*, accessed February 14, 2014, www.journalnow.com/business/mall-may-limit-teens-policy-expected-to-require-parental-supervision/article_d893f606-4926-5a40-8004-04e9a01acf4d.html.

shopping to so-called *lifestyle centres*. These open-air complexes house retailers that often focus on specific shopper segments and specific product interests.

Building a Promotional Strategy

A retailer designs advertisements and develops other promotions for two reasons: to create demand and to provide information, such as the store's location, its offerings, prices, and hours. When a recent year proved to be difficult, Starbucks turned to social media for a new promotional strategy. The chain launched MyStarbucksIdea.com. Customers could log onto this forum to ask questions, offer suggestions, and even voice their dislikes. The site's 180,000 registered users have offered 100,000 ideas; Starbucks has carried out 150 of the suggestions. The Starbucks Facebook page has some 36 million fans; the chain also has 7 million Twitter followers. Charles Bruzzo, the chain's vice-president for brand, content, and online, says the company is seeing the beginning of an "intersection between digital and physical."[23]

Nonstore retailers provide their phone numbers and website addresses as part of their promotional strategy. More recently, online retailers have scaled back their big advertising campaigns and worked to build traffic through word of mouth and clever promotions. Promotional strategy is also discussed in depth in Chapter 13.

Creating a Store Atmosphere

A successful retailer designs its merchandising, pricing, and promotion strategies to work with *store atmospherics*, the physical characteristics of a store and its services. The idea is to positively influence consumers' views of the shopping experience. Atmospherics begin with the store's exterior. Eye-catching architectural elements and signage are used to attract customer attention and interest. Interior atmospheric elements include the store layout, merchandise presentation, lighting, colour, sound, and cleanliness. For example, a high-end store like Holt Renfrew may feature high ceilings that highlight tasteful and well-designed displays of high-quality goods. In contrast, Costco stocks an ever-changing offering of moderately priced products in its warehouse-like settings decorated with industrial-style display hardware.

ASSESSMENT CHECK

12.6.1 Define *retailer.*

12.6.2 What are the elements of a retailer's marketing strategy?

DISTRIBUTION CHANNEL DECISIONS AND LOGISTICS

LO 12.7 Discuss distribution channel decisions and logistics.

Every firm faces two major decisions when choosing how to distribute its goods or services: selecting a specific distribution channel and deciding on the level of distribution intensity. When deciding which distribution channel is most efficient, business managers need to consider four factors: the market, the product, the producer, and the competition. These factors are often interrelated and may change over time. In today's global business environment, strong relationships with customers and suppliers are important for survival. One way to help strengthen such relationships online is through the effective use of social media, as explained in the "Career Kickstart" feature.

CAREER KICKSTART

Effective Use of Social Media for Your Small Business

More and more entrepreneurs are using social networking media to promote their small or medium-size businesses. Facebook, Twitter, LinkedIn, and many blogs and forums offer endless marketing opportunities. A recent survey found that 70 percent of small businesses planned to increase their use of social media. Seventy-nine percent did not plan to run TV commercials, and 70 percent didn't use radio ads. Just as in the real business world, good manners, common courtesy, and common sense will take you far in the virtual business world. Here are a few tips for effective use of social media:

1. *Even though you join social networks to promote your business, don't make it too obvious.* Instead of promoting yourself or your business nonstop, post carefully worded messages to show that you have something of value to offer to interested people. Otherwise, you risk being considered a spammer.

2. *Be aware that you are in social networks for the long haul.* Group members or forum members are real people with real interests and ideas. Get to know the members of your forums. Learn about their interests and how the community, as a whole, works.

Virtual networks of "friends" have unwritten rules, just as real networks do.

3. *It's not the numbers that count.* Getting your brand known or achieving other marketing goals doesn't depend on how many Twitter followers you have; it depends on how you connect with them.

4. *Be careful of what you say.* Avoid vulgar language, off-colour jokes, or any hint of racial or gender bias. Don't bring up religion, politics, or other sensitive subjects. Leave any strong opinions out of your marketing profile.

5. *Remember that your customers will be discussing you on their own networks.* Your reputation may travel farther than you know!

Sources: Mickie Kennedy, "Do You Have Good Social Media Manners?" *eReleases,* March 23, 2010, www.ereleases.com/prfuel/good-social-media-manners; Michelle Bowles, "5 Social Media Tips for ecommerce Marketing," Top Rank Online Marketing Blog, March 12, 2010, www.toprankblog.com/2010/03/ecommerce-marketing-social-media-tips; Kim States, "Five Social Media Tips to Connect Small Businesses," *Inside Tucson Business,* January 2, 2010, www.insidetucsonbusiness.com/news/small_business/five-social-media-tips-to-connect-small-businesses/article_45cf1623-afdf-52e4-960f-9fb516a0ae36.html.

Selecting Distribution Channels

Market factors may be the most important consideration when choosing a distribution channel. When a firm needs to reach a target market of a small number of buyers or buyers within a small geographical area, the best option may be a direct channel. In contrast, if the firm must reach customers who live in a wide geographical area or who make frequent small purchases, then the channel may need to use marketing intermediaries to make goods available when and where customers want them.

In general, most standardized products or items with low unit values use relatively long distribution channels. On the other hand, products that are complex, expensive, custom made, or perishable move through shorter distribution channels involving few—or no—intermediaries. The increasing use of ecommerce is resulting in changes in traditional distribution practices. The European Commission recently issued an interesting set of rules, effective until 2022. These rules allow makers of goods with less than a 30 percent market share—usually high-end manufacturers—to block Internet-only retailers from carrying their products. The commission declared that "suppliers should normally be free to decide on the number and type of distributors they want to have in their distribution systems . . . More generally, suppliers may only want to sell to distributors that have one or more physical points of present [actual "bricks-and-mortar" stores] where the suppliers' goods can be touched, smelled, tried, etc." The European Alliance—which represents luxury goods manufacturers such as Louis Vuitton Moët Hennessey (LVMH), Gucci, and Burberry—lobbied for and welcomed the new rules as a way to protect the quality image of their products. Online-only retailers, such as Amazon, eBay, and their European equivalents, called for a reversal of the "bricks-and-mortar" requirement and warned that some manufacturers would use the new rules to "restrict the availability" of their products online and thus keep prices high.[24]

But the Greek entrepreneur Stelios Haji-Ioannou finds the Internet to be the perfect channel for easyGroup, the private investment group for his "easy" brand. The company represents a variety of businesses with the "easy" tag—easyJet.com, easyCar.com, easyJobs.com, easyPizza.com, and even an easyBus route between Gatwick Airport and London. Each business offers a no-frills, low-cost approach to services that consumers can order online. EasyJet is one of Europe's biggest Internet retailers, selling 95 percent of its seats online.[25]

Some producers offer a broad product line and have the financial and marketing resources to distribute and promote their products. These producers are more likely than others to choose a shorter channel. Instead of depending on marketing intermediaries, financially strong manufacturers with broad product lines typically use their own sales representatives, warehouses, and credit departments to serve both retailers and consumers.

In many cases, startup manufacturers turn to direct channels for two reasons: because they can't get intermediaries to carry their products or because they want to extend their sales reach. Some companies use direct channels to carry intangible goods. For example, in New York City, Art Meets Commerce uses the Internet and social networking to promote small Broadway and off-Broadway shows that have tight marketing budgets. The company posts short videos of its clients' shows on YouTube. It also uses Facebook and Twitter to increase traditional word-of-mouth publicity. When celebrities see the shows and post favourable tweets, their followers may also feel encouraged to see the shows.[26]

Competitive performance is the fourth key consideration when choosing a distribution channel. A producer loses customers when an intermediary fails to deliver the promotion or product. Channels used by established competitors and new market entries also can influence decisions. Sometimes a joint venture between competitors can work well. For example, Best Buy and Apple have teamed up to sell their products under the same roof. Under the agreement, Apple controls its own retail space within Best Buy stores. Although Apple has a well-established retail business, it can't match the size of electronics giant Best Buy. Best Buy benefits by generating more traffic from customers who want to see and buy Apple's innovative products in convenient locations. The strategy has worked well—specifically, sales of Macs have increased. Best Buy was the only non-Apple retailer in North America to carry the iPad. All of Best Buy's 673 stores with Apple shops sold out their stock of iPads in four days.[27]

Selecting Distribution Intensity

A second key distribution decision involves *distribution intensity*—the number of intermediaries or outlets a manufacturer uses to distribute its goods. Your community may have only one BMW dealership, but you can likely find Coca-Cola everywhere—in grocery stores, convenience stores, gas stations, vending machines, and restaurants. BMW has chosen a different level of distribution intensity from that used by Coca-Cola. In general, market coverage has three different intensity levels:

Exclusive distribution limits market coverage in a specific geographical region. This approach suits relatively expensive specialty products such as Rolex watches. Retailers are carefully selected to enhance the product's image to the market.

1. *Intensive distribution* involves placing a firm's products in nearly every available outlet. Intensive distribution usually suits low-priced convenience goods such as milk, newspapers, and soft drinks. This kind of market coverage requires cooperation from many intermediaries, including wholesalers and retailers.

2. *Selective distribution* involves a manufacturer selecting only a limited number of retailers to distribute its product lines. Selective distribution can reduce total marketing costs and establish strong working relationships within the channel.

3. *Exclusive distribution* is at the opposite extreme from intensive distribution. This distribution strategy limits market coverage in a specific geographical region. This approach suits relatively expensive specialty products such as Rolex watches. Retailers are carefully selected to enhance the product's image to the market and to ensure that well-trained personnel will contribute to customer satisfaction. Producers may give up some market coverage by granting an exclusive territory to a single intermediary. But the decision usually pays off by developing and maintaining an image of quality and prestige.

When companies are clearing out excess inventory, even high-priced retailers may look to discounters to help them move the merchandise from their warehouses. For example, to satisfy consumers' taste for luxury goods, designer outlet malls offer shoppers a chance to buy originally high-priced items at lower prices. And online vendors like Montreal-based Beyond the Rack provide distributors and manufacturers the opportunity to clear excess merchandise inventories quickly. After all, their fashion-driven shoppers are searching online for the next great deal.[28]

Logistics and Physical Distribution

A firm's choice of distribution channels creates the final link in the **supply chain**, the complete sequence of suppliers that help to create a good or service and deliver it to business users and final consumers. The supply chain begins when the raw materials used in production are delivered to the producer. The supply chain continues with the actual production activities that create finished goods. Finally, the finished goods move through the producer's distribution channels to end customers.

The process of coordinating the flow of goods, services, and information among members of the supply chain is called **logistics**. The term originally referred to strategic movements of military troops and supplies. Today, it describes all of the business activities involved in the supply chain with the ultimate goal of getting finished goods to customers.

supply chain the complete sequence of suppliers that help to create a good or service and deliver it to business users and final consumers.

logistics the process of coordinating the flow of goods, services, and information among members of the supply chain.

Physical Distribution

Physical distribution is a major focus of logistics management. It was identified earlier in the chapter as one of the two basic dimensions of distribution strategy. Physical distribution refers to the activities aimed at efficiently moving finished goods from the production line to the consumer or business

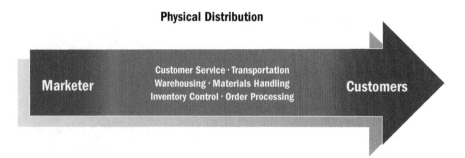

FIGURE 12.9 Elements of a Physical Distribution System

buyer. As **Figure 12.9** shows, physical distribution is a broad concept that includes transportation and many other elements that help link buyers and sellers. An effectively managed physical distribution system can increase customer satisfaction by ensuring reliable movements of products through the supply chain. For example, Walmart studies how quickly goods can be shelved after they arrive at the store. Walmart executives know that strategies that may seem to be efficient in the warehouse, such as completely filling pallets with goods, can actually be time-consuming or costly in the store aisles.

Radio-frequency identification (RFID) technology relies on a computer chip. This chip is implanted on a product or its packaging and emits a low-frequency radio signal to identify the item. The radio signal doesn't need a direct line of sight to register on the store's computers the way a bar code does. That means a hand-held RFID reader can scan crates and cartons before they are unloaded. Because the chip can store information about the product's progress through the distribution channel, RFID can help retailers to better manage inventories, maintain stock levels, reduce loss, track stolen goods, and cut costs. The technology is similar to what is already used to identify lost pets and to help some vehicles move more quickly past toll booths. Walmart, Target, and the German retailer Metro Group already require their suppliers to use RFID technology. Automakers use RFID technology to improve their production processes by tracking parts and other supplies. A new version of the RFID chip can be printed on paper or plastic. The use of RFID technology has led to privacy and counterfeiting concerns. Recently, one company developed a process that uses unique silicon "fingerprints" to generate unclonable RFID chips.[29]

Warehousing is the physical distribution activity that involves the storage of products. *Materials handling* is moving items within factories, warehouses, transportation terminals, and stores. Inventory control involves managing inventory costs, such as storage facilities, insurance, taxes, and handling. The physical distribution activity of *order processing* includes preparing orders for shipment and receiving orders when shipments arrive.

The wide use of electronic data interchange (EDI) and the constant pressure on suppliers to improve their response time have led to **vendor-managed inventory**. It is the process in which the producer and the retailer agree that the producer (or the wholesaler) will decide how much of a product a buyer needs and automatically ship new supplies when needed.

The form of transportation used to ship products depends on the kind of product, the distance involved, and the cost. The logistics manager can choose from several companies and types of transportation. **Table 12.3** shows the five major transport modes: trucks (with about 75 percent

vendor-managed inventory the process in which the producer and the retailer agree that the producer (or the wholesaler) will decide how much of a product a buyer needs and automatically ship new supplies when needed.

Table 12.3 Comparison of Transportation Modes

MODE	SPEED	DEPENDABILITY IN MEETING SCHEDULES	FREQUENCY OF SHIPMENTS	AVAILABILITY IN DIFFERENT LOCATIONS	FLEXIBILITY IN HANDLING	COST
Truck	Fast	High	High	Very Extensive	Average	High
Rail	Average	Average	Low	Low	High	Average
Water	Very slow	Average	Very low	Limited	Very high	Very low
Air	Very fast	High	Average	Average	Low	Very high
Pipeline	Slow	High	High	Very limited	Very low	Low

of total expenditures), railroads (approximately 12 percent), water carriers (6 percent), air freight (4 percent), and pipelines (3 percent). The faster methods usually cost more than the slower methods. When choosing the most suitable method of transportation, the important factors include speed, reliable delivery, shipment frequency, location availability, handling flexibility, and cost.

About 26.4 million trucks operate in the United States, and about 700,000 operate in Canada. They carry most finished goods all or part of the way to the consumer. Nearly 3 million of the U.S. trucks are tractor trailers.[30] Another major form of transportation is the railroads, which compete with many truck routes despite their recent loss of market share. The 565 freight railroads in the United States, Canada, and Mexico operate across more than 325,000 kilometres of track and earn almost $75 billion in revenues. Seventy percent of all autos manufactured in North America travel to their destinations by train. A freight train needs only 3.8 litres of diesel fuel to transport 1 tonne of cargo almost 685 miles.[31]

Customer Service

Customer service is a major part of both product and distribution strategies. *Customer service standards* measure the quality of service a firm provides for its customers. Managers often set quantitative guidelines—for example, that all orders be processed within 24 hours after they are received or that salespeople approach shoppers within two minutes after they enter the store. Sometimes customers set their own service standards and then choose suppliers that meet or exceed those standards.

The customer service portions of product strategy include warranty and repair service programs. *Warranties* are firms' promises to repair a defective product, refund money paid, or replace a product if it proves unsatisfactory. Repair services are also important. Consumers want to know that help is available if something goes wrong. For example, shoppers for home computers often choose retailers that feature low prices *and* offer repair services and tech support centres. Products with poor after-sales service quickly disappear from the market as a result of word-of-mouth criticism.

Consumers' complaints of the impersonal service they received at websites led dot-coms to take several steps to "humanize" their customer interactions and deal with complaints. Many websites include help button icons that link the visitor to a company representative.

 **ASSESSMENT CHECK**

12.7.1 What is distribution intensity?

12.7.2 Define *supply chain*.

12.7.3 What do customer service standards measure?

WHAT'S AHEAD

This chapter covered two of the elements of the marketing mix: product and distribution. It introduced the key marketing tasks of developing, marketing, and packaging want-satisfying goods and services. It also focused on three major parts of an organization's distribution strategy: the design of efficient distribution channels; wholesalers and retailers who make up many distribution channels; and logistics and physical distribution. We now turn to the remaining two elements of the marketing mix—promotion and pricing—in Chapter 13.

RETURN TO INSIDE BUSINESS

Montreal's Fitness City Complex—Bringing Fitness Businesses Together Under One Roof

The concept of clustering fitness businesses under one roof has proven to be successful. Soon after Fitness City opened, a new tenant launched a CrossFit centre catering to a new method of working out with motivational support from group members. This business is a welcomed addition to Fitness City and undoubtedly will benefit from its location at the main entrance of the complex.

The owners of Fitness City continue to seek new tenants that can benefit from the fitness-oriented customers who regularly spend time—and money—at the complex. One idea is to expand health and wellness services by providing space where professionals such as dieticians and physiotherapists can meet with their clients.

QUESTIONS FOR CRITICAL THINKING

1. Which other health-related and wellness-related professionals should be considered as tenants?

2. How can these professional services be marketed within the complex?

SUMMARY OF LEARNING OBJECTIVES

LO 12.1 Explain product strategy and how to classify goods and services.

A product is a bundle of physical, service, and symbolic characteristics designed to satisfy consumer wants. The marketing concept of a product includes the brand, product image, warranty, service attributes, packaging, labelling, and the physical or functional characteristics of the good or service.

Goods and services can be classified as consumer (B2C) or business (B2B) products. Consumer products are those goods and services purchased by end consumers for their own use. They can be convenience products, shopping products, or specialty products, depending on how consumers buy them. Business products are those products purchased for use either directly or indirectly in the production of other goods and services for resale. They can be classified as installations, accessory equipment, component parts and materials, raw materials, and supplies. This classification is based on how the items are used and product characteristics. Services can be classified as either consumer or business services.

A product mix is the assortment of goods and services a firm offers to individual consumers and B2B users. A product line is a series of related products.

 ASSESSMENT CHECK ANSWERS

12.1.1 How do consumer products differ from business products? Business products, such as drill presses, are sold to firms or organizations. Consumer products, such as personal-care items, are sold to end users.

12.1.2 Differentiate among convenience products, shopping products, and specialty products. Convenience products are items the consumer seeks to purchase frequently, immediately, and with little effort. Shopping products are typically purchased after the buyer has compared competing products in competing stores. Specialty products are those products that a purchaser is willing to make a special effort to obtain.

LO 12.2 Describe the four stages of the product life cycle and their marketing implications.

Every successful new product passes through four stages in its product life cycle: introduction, growth, maturity, and decline. In the introduction stage, the firm attempts to create demand for the new product. In the product's growth stage, sales climb, and the company earns its first profits. In the maturity stage, sales reach a saturation level. In the decline stage, both sales and profits decrease. Marketers sometimes use strategies to extend the product life cycle, such as increasing the frequency of use; adding new users; finding new uses for the product; and changing package size, labelling, or product quality.

The new-product development process for most products has six stages: idea generation, screening, concept development and business analysis, product development, test marketing, and commercialization. At each stage, marketers must decide whether to continue to the next stage, make changes to the new product, or discontinue the development process. Some new products may skip the test marketing stage for various reasons: because they want to quickly introduce a new product with excellent potential, because of a desire not to reveal new-product strategies to competitors, or because of the high costs involved in limited production runs.

 ASSESSMENT CHECK ANSWERS

12.2.1 What are the stages of the product life cycle? The product life cycle has four stages: introduction, growth, maturity, and decline. In the introduction stage, the firm tries to attract demand for the new product. In the product's growth stage, sales climb, and the company earns its first profits. In the maturity stage, sales reach a saturation level. In the decline stage, both sales and profits decline.

12.2.2 What are the marketing implications of each stage? Marketers sometimes use strategies to extend the product life cycle, including increasing frequency of use, adding new users, finding new uses for the product, and changing package size, labelling, or product quality.

LO 12.3 Explain how firms identify their products.

Products are identified by brands, brand names, and trademarks. All three are important elements of product images. Effective brand names are easy to say, easy to recognize, and easy to remember. They also project the right images to buyers. Brand names cannot contain generic words. Under certain circumstances, companies can lose the exclusive rights to their brand names if common use transforms the brand names into generic terms for product categories. Some brand names belong to retailers or distributors, not to manufacturers. Brand loyalty is measured in three degrees: brand recognition, brand preference, and brand insistence. Some marketers use family brands to identify several related items in a product line. Other marketers use individual branding strategies by giving a different brand name to each product within a product line.

 ASSESSMENT CHECK ANSWERS

12.3.1 Differentiate among a brand, a brand name, and a trademark. A brand is a name, term, sign, symbol, design, or some combination used to identify the products of one firm and show how they differ from competitive offerings. A brand name is that part of the brand consisting of words or letters. It is used to identify a firm's products and show how they differ from the products of competitors. A trademark is a brand that has been given legal protection.

12.3.2 Define *brand equity.* Brand equity is the added value that a respected and successful brand name gives to a product.

LO 12.4 Outline the major components of an effective distribution strategy.

A firm must decide whether to move products through direct or indirect distribution. After making this decision, the company needs to identify which types of marketing intermediaries, if any, will distribute its goods and services. The Internet has made direct distribution an attractive option for many retail companies.

 ASSESSMENT CHECK ANSWERS

12.4.1 Define *distribution channels.* Distribution channels are the paths that products, and their legal ownership, follow from producer to consumer or business user.

12.4.2 What is a marketing intermediary? A marketing intermediary (also called a middleman) is a business firm that moves goods from their producers to the consumers or business users.

LO 12.5 Explain the concept of wholesaling.

Wholesaling is a crucial part of the distribution channel for many products, especially consumer goods and business supplies. Wholesaling intermediaries can be classified on the basis of ownership: some are owned by manufacturers, some are owned by retailers, and others are independently owned. Firms operate two main types of manufacturer-owned wholesaling intermediaries: sales branches and sales offices.

An independent wholesaling intermediary is a business that represents several different manufacturers and sells to retailers, manufacturers, and other business accounts. Independent wholesalers can be either merchant wholesalers or agents and brokers, depending on whether they take title to (legal ownership of) the products they handle.

Retailers sometimes work together to form their own wholesaling organizations. Such organizations can take the form of either a buying group or a cooperative.

 ASSESSMENT CHECK ANSWERS

12.5.1 Define *wholesaling.* Wholesaling is a crucial part of the distribution channel for many products, especially consumer goods and business supplies.

12.5.2 Differentiate between a merchant wholesaler and an agent or broker in terms of title to the goods. Merchant wholesalers are independently owned wholesaling intermediaries that take title to the goods they handle. Agents and brokers may or may not take physical possession of the goods they handle, but they never take title, or ownership. They work mainly to bring buyers and sellers together.

LO 12.6 Describe the types of retailers and retail strategies used.

Retailers, in contrast to wholesalers, are distribution channel members that sell goods and services to individuals for their own use, not for resale. Nonstore retailing includes four forms: direct-response retailing, Internet retailing, automatic merchandising, and direct selling. Store retailers range in size from tiny newsstands to multi-storey department stores and warehouse-style retailers such as Costco.

The first step in developing a competitive retailing strategy is to select a target market. Next, the retailer must develop a product strategy to determine the best mix of merchandise to carry to satisfy that market. A retailer's customer service strategy focuses on attracting and retaining target customers to maximize sales and profits. Retailers base their pricing decisions on their costs of purchasing products from other channel members and offering services to customers. A good retail location can often make the difference between success and failure. A retailer designs advertisements and develops other promotions to stimulate demand and to provide information such as the store's location, merchandise offerings, prices, and hours. A successful retailer closely matches its merchandising, pricing, and promotion strategies with store atmospherics—the physical characteristics of a store and its amenities. A good match can help to influence consumers' perceptions of the shopping experience.

 ASSESSMENT CHECK ANSWERS

12.6.1 Define *retailer.* A retailer is a distribution channel member that sells goods and services to individuals for their own use, not for resale.

12.6.2 What are the elements of a retailer's marketing strategy? Retailers must first identify their target markets, and then choose the strategies for merchandising, customer service, pricing, and location that will attract customers in their target market segments.

LO 12.7 Discuss distribution channel decisions and logistics.

Marketers can choose either a direct distribution channel or an indirect distribution channel. A direct distribution channel moves goods directly from the producer to the consumer. An indirect distribution channel uses marketing intermediaries to make goods available when and where customers want them. Ideally, the choice of a distribution channel should support a firm's overall marketing strategy. Before selecting distribution channels, firms must consider their target markets, the types of goods being distributed, their own internal systems and concerns, and competitive factors.

A second key distribution decision involves distribution intensity. The business must decide on the market coverage needed to achieve its marketing strategies: intensive distribution, selective distribution, or exclusive distribution.

✓ **ASSESSMENT CHECK ANSWERS**

12.7.1 What is distribution intensity? Distribution intensity is the number of intermediaries or outlets a manufacturer uses to distribute its goods.

12.7.2 Define *supply chain*. A supply chain is the sequence of suppliers that help in creating a good or service and delivering it to business users and end consumers.

12.7.3 What do customer service standards measure? Customer service standards measure the quality of service a firm provides for its customers.

BUSINESS TERMS YOU NEED TO KNOW

brand 329

brand equity 331

brand name 330

category advisor 332

distribution channels 334

distribution strategy 334

logistics 345

physical distribution 334

product 322

product life cycle 325

product line 325

product mix 325

retailers 338

supply chain 345

test marketing 328

trademark 330

vendor-managed inventory 346

wholesaler 336

REVIEW QUESTIONS

1. Classify each of the following products as either a business-to-consumer (B2C) product or a business-to-business (B2B) product. Then choose one product and describe how it can be classified as both a B2C product and a B2B product.

   a. *Runner's World* or *Esquire* magazine

   b. A six-pack of apple juice

   c. A limousine service

   d. Tech support for a communications system

   e. A golf course

   f. A Thai restaurant

2. What is the relationship between a product line and a product mix? Give an example of each.

3. Identify and briefly describe the six stages of new-product development.

4. What is the difference between a manufacturer's brand and a private brand? What is the difference between a family brand and an individual brand?

5. What are the three stages of brand loyalty? Why is it so important to marketers to reach the last stage of brand loyalty?

6. What are the upsides of direct distribution? When is a producer most likely to use direct distribution?

7. What is the wheel of retailing? How has the Internet affected the wheel of retailing?

8. Identify and briefly describe the four different types of nonstore retailers. Give an example of at least one type of good or service that would be suited to each type of nonstore retailer.

9. What are the three intensity levels of distribution? Give an example of two products for each level.

10. Define *logistics*. How does it relate to physical distribution?

PROJECTS AND TEAMWORK APPLICATIONS

1. On your own or with a classmate, choose one of the following goods or services. Decide whether you want to market it as a consumer product or a business product. Create a brand name and marketing strategy for your product.

   a. A lawn mower repair service

   b. A hardware store

   c. A soft drink

   d. An English-language class

   e. An accounting firm

2. Choose one of the following products that is in either the maturity stage or the decline stage of its life cycle (or select one of your own). Develop a marketing strategy for extending the product's life cycle.

   a. Popcorn

   b. A fast-food restaurant chain

   c. A newspaper

   d. Music CDs

   e. Paper stationery or notecards

3. Where do you do most of your shopping—in stores or online? Choose your favourite retailer and analyze why you like it. Outline your reasons for shopping there. Suggest two or three areas for improvement.

4. Choose one of the following products. Select a distribution intensity for the product. Describe specifically where and how the product would be sold. Describe the reasons for your strategy.

   a. A line of furniture manufactured from recycled or reclaimed materials

   b. Custom-designed jewellery

   c. A house-painting service

   d. Handicraft supplies

   e. A radio talk show

WEB ASSIGNMENTS

1. **Product classification.** Review the chapter's discussion on product classification. Visit the website of Johnson & Johnson (www.jnj.com) and click on "Our Products." Classify Johnson & Johnson's wide range of products.

2. **Shopping centres.** The West Edmonton Mall in Edmonton is North America's largest shopping centre. Go to the mall's website (www.wem.ca) to learn more about it. Make a list of five interesting facts you learned about the West Edmonton Mall.

3. **Railroad statistics.** Visit the website of the Railway Association of Canada (www.railcan.ca). Review the material and answer the following questions:

   a. How big is the railway industry in Canada?

   b. How many people do railroads employ?

   c. How much freight did railroads carry during the most recent year for which data are available?

Note: Internet Web addresses change frequently. If you don't find the exact sites listed, you may need to access the organization's home page and search from there or use a search engine such as Bing or Google.

© weareadventurers/iStockphoto

Handwritten notes on image:

$$\# \, FC = 42{,}000$$
$$\# \, VC = 14, \quad \# \, SP = 20.$$

$$\text{In } \$ \text{ amount} = \frac{FC}{1 - VC/SP} = \frac{42{,}000}{0.3} = \boxed{140{,}000}$$
$$\frac{}{1 - 14/20}$$

13 | PROMOTION AND PRICING STRATEGIES

LEARNING OBJECTIVES

LO 13.1 Discuss how integrated marketing communications relates to a firm's overall promotional strategy.

LO 13.2 Summarize the different types of advertising.

LO 13.3 Outline sales promotion.

LO 13.4 Describe pushing and pulling promotional strategies.

LO 13.5 Outline the different types of pricing objectives in the marketing mix.

LO 13.6 Describe how firms set prices in the marketplace and the four alternative pricing strategies.

LO 13.7 Discuss consumer perceptions of price.

Handwritten notes:

Examples

$$BEP_{(U)} = \frac{FC}{\frac{SP}{U} - \frac{VC}{U}}$$

$$= \frac{FC}{SP\,(20) - (14)_{VC}} = \frac{42{,}000}{20 - 14} = \frac{42{,}000}{6} \Rightarrow \boxed{7{,}000 \text{ units}}$$

⟹ if you want profit, add the amount of your profit to the fixed cost

Profit = 24,000

$$42{,}000 + 24{,}000 = \boxed{11{,}000}$$

142

$$P = \frac{Rev - TC}{SxU} = 0$$

FC + VC

INSIDE BUSINESS

WorkSafeBC: Promoting Safety to Young Workers

WorkSafeBC is an insurance agency serving more than 200,000 employers and 2.3 million workers in British Columbia. It is a workers' compensation board that helps workers who have injuries related to the workplace. WorkSafeBC is a quasi-government agency, which means it operates under the guidance of the BC provincial government but is separate from the government. In a recent year, premiums collected from employers totalled about $1 billion and payouts for claims were more than $1.3 billion. About 137,000 claims were made, resulting in 2.8 million lost workdays. The top three causes of injuries that led to lost workdays were strains (excluding back strains) at 1,118,000 days, back strains at 567,000 days, and fractures at 456,000 days. Although the average age of an injured worker is 41 years, 12 percent of young men under age 25 (about 6,300) reported injuries. The agency performance can be improved by reducing the number and the seriousness of worker injuries. One way to achieve this goal is to change people's attitudes toward workplace safety—especially the attitudes of younger men, who are more likely than any other population group to experience an injury.

Back in 2001, Vancouver-based Wasserman & Partners Advertising Inc. first won the contract to create a new promotional program for BC's Workers' Compensation Board (WCB). The agency began with a basic recommendation—make WorkSafeBC the public face of the organization. A total rebrand was needed. The WCB brand referred to claims, insurance, and administration, but it didn't have the heart or the belief that anyone or anything could change workplace behaviour. It also did not capture the passion within the organization that was focused on safety and accident prevention in the workplace.

WorkSafeBC's goal was to change social attitudes toward safety in the workplace. By doing this, it was hoped that workers would learn that work injuries can be avoided. Since putting the rebrand strategy in place, the organization's corporate reputation has increased. WorkSafeBC has a proud internal culture and focus. Statistics show that its promotional campaigns are changing attitudes toward workplace safety—and reducing injuries.

Before developing promotional ideas, research was done to better understand the target audience. This generation of consumers believes that it's cool to care about something; the agency wanted to find an opportunity to use that desire to make a change for the good. This audience also feels in control of their culture, instead of being consumers of culture. They don't want to be spoken at, they want to engage. They are connected 24/7. Technology and community are both important.

Unlike most other safety campaigns that target youth, the firm rejected the traditional "shock and awe" approach of scaring young people into working safely. According to Alvin Wasserman, president and creative strategist:

"Shock and awe" catches attention, but in our current culture of violence as entertainment, it's too easy to say "That's not me" and it doesn't provide tangible information on what to do. Research shows that it is ineffective in changing behaviour. A successful social marketing campaign presents the magnitude of the problem but also gives the audience something tangible to do in order to address the problem. To develop our approach we asked ourselves and our target audience what would be the first step to making the work environment safer. The answer—ask for help if you don't know what to do.

The strategy developed was to tap into the target audience's desire to make a difference. This strategy led to the launch of the Raise Your Hand campaign, as a blueprint, or a plan, for a young worker movement that focuses on workplace safety and rights: the right to know about hazards at your job and how to protect yourself; the right to participate in making sure your job and workplace are safe and healthy; and the right to refuse unsafe work. The idea was to help create a social environment where all young workers in BC would ask for help to be safer on the job and would feel free to "raise their hand" when the workplace did not appear to be safe.

Raise Your Hand engages with young workers by showing up at all of the popular summertime youth cultural events throughout the province. From music events to major sporting events, the Raise Your Hand team is there. In the fall, Raise Your Hand participates in campus crawls at universities and colleges throughout BC to reach more young people.

But connecting online has always been a major strategy of the campaign. The interactivity of rich media online ads has led to record website results. WorkSafeBC's online presence includes distribution strategies that use social media sites such as Facebook, YouTube, and Twitter.[1]

CHAPTER 13 OVERVIEW

This chapter focuses on the different types of promotional activities and how prices are decided on for goods and services. **Promotion** is the function of informing, persuading, and influencing a purchase decision. This activity is as important to not-for-profit organizations as it is to for-profit companies.

Some promotional strategies try to develop *primary demand,* or consumer desire, for a general product category. The objective of such a campaign is to stimulate sales for an entire industry so that individual firms benefit from the total market growth. A popular example is the dairy industry's "Got Milk?" campaign. Print and television messages about the nutritional benefits of milk feature various celebrities. Another very successful promotional campaign aimed at increasing per-capita consumption is the long-running "Get Cracking" campaign by the Egg Farmers of Ontario. This promotion emphasizes the many easy meal preparations that use eggs.

In contrast, most promotional strategies try to stimulate *selective demand*—desire for a specific brand. Just about every adult needs banking and financial services. TD Canada Trust wants consumers to pick its firm from among the many competitors in the marketplace. Banks tend to promote their friendly customer services, expertise, and convenient locations to set themselves apart from competitors. For most customers, the bank brand is understood in terms of the people they actually come in contact with at their local branch. Marketers choose from among many promotional options to communicate with potential customers. Marketing messages can be communicated through a television or radio commercial, a newspaper or magazine ad, a website, a direct-mail flyer, or a sales call. Each marketing message reflects the product, place, person, cause, or organization promoted in the content. Marketers use **integrated marketing communications (IMC)** to coordinate all promotional activities—media advertising, direct mail, personal selling, sales promotion, and public relations—to produce a unified, customer-focused promotional strategy. This coordination is designed to avoid confusing the consumer and to focus positive attention on the promotional message.

This chapter begins by explaining the role of IMC, and then discusses the objectives of promotion and the importance of promotional planning. Next, it examines the elements of the promotional mix: advertising, sales promotion, personal selling, and public relations. Finally, the chapter addresses pricing strategies for goods and services.

promotion the function of informing, persuading, and influencing a purchase decision.

integrated marketing communications (IMC) the coordination of all promotional activities—media advertising, direct mail, personal selling, sales promotion, and public relations—to produce a unified, customer-focused promotional strategy.

LO 13.1 Discuss how integrated marketing communications relates to a firm's overall promotional strategy.

INTEGRATED MARKETING COMMUNICATIONS

An integrated marketing communications strategy focuses on customer needs to create a unified promotional message in the firm's ads, in-store displays, product samples, and presentations by company sales representatives. To gain a competitive advantage, marketers that use IMC need a broad view of promotion. Media options continue to increase, and marketers cannot rely on traditional broadcast, print media, and direct mail. Marketing plans must include all forms of customer contact. Packaging, store displays, sales promotions, sales presentations, and online and interactive media also communicate information about a brand or organization. Marketers that use IMC create a unified personality and message for the good, brand, or service they promote. Coordinated activities also increase the effectiveness of reaching and serving target markets.

Marketing managers set the goals and objectives for the firm's promotional strategy, while keeping in mind the firm's overall organizational objectives and marketing goals. Using these objectives, marketers weave the various elements of the strategy—personal selling, advertising, sales promotion, publicity, and public relations—into an integrated communications plan. This document becomes a central focus of the firm's total marketing strategy to reach its selected target market. Feedback, including marketing research and sales reports, completes the strategy by identifying any activities that differ from the plan and suggesting improvements.

The job-search engine Monster.com combined several marketing promotions to create its stepped-up IMC campaign "Get a Monster Advantage." The campaign's first TV commercial featured a down-on-his-luck boogeyman who goes to Monster.com to find the perfect new job. A second commercial, featuring another character, aired during a recent Super Bowl game. Other spots were aired on national cable networks and were extended to social media. Humorous interactive links on sites such as Facebook and advertising on other sites further reached out to the online audience. Print ads appeared in the *Wall Street Journal,* in more than 100 regional daily newspapers, in monthly business publications, and in human resource publications, such as *HR Executive, Wired,* and *Fast Company.*[2]

The Promotional Mix

Every organization creates a marketing mix by combining product, distribution, promotion, and pricing strategies. In a similar way, each organization also needs to blend the many types of promotion into a unified and organized plan. The **promotional mix** is the combination of personal selling and nonpersonal selling that marketers use to meet the needs of a firm's target customers and to effectively and efficiently communicate its message to them. **Personal selling** is the most basic form of promotion: a direct person-to-person promotional presentation to a potential buyer. The buyer–seller communication can occur in several ways: during a face-to-face meeting, or by telephone, videoconference, or an interactive computer link.

Nonpersonal selling consists of advertising, sales promotion, direct marketing, and public relations. Advertising is the best-known form of nonpersonal selling, but sales promotion accounts for about half of the money spent on nonpersonal selling. Spending is increasing for sponsorships, which involve marketing messages that are delivered in association with another activity, such as a golf tournament or a benefit concert. Marketers need to be careful about the types of promotion they choose because they risk alienating, or isolating, the very people they are trying to reach.

Each element in the promotional mix offers its own advantages and disadvantages, as **Table 13.1** shows. When a firm selects the most effective combination of promotional mix elements, it may reach its promotional objectives. The spending levels within the promotional mix vary by industry. Manufacturers of many business-to-business (B2B) products typically spend more on personal selling than on advertising because those products—such as a new telecommunications system—may require a significant investment. Consumer-goods marketers may focus more on advertising and sponsorships. Later sections of this chapter discuss how the parts of the mix contribute to effective promotion.

promotional mix the combination of personal and nonpersonal selling that marketers use to meet the needs of a firm's target customers and to effectively and efficiently communicate its message to them.

personal selling the most basic form of promotion: a direct person-to-person promotional presentation to a potential buyer.

nonpersonal selling forms of selling such as advertising, sales promotion, direct marketing, and public relations.

Table 13.1 **Comparing the Elements of the Promotional Mix**

ELEMENT	ADVANTAGES	DISADVANTAGES
Advertising	Reaches large consumer audience at low cost per contact Allows strong control of the message Message can be modified to suit different audiences	Difficult to measure effectiveness Limited value for closing sales
Personal selling	Message can be tailored for each customer Produces immediate buyer response Effectiveness is easily measured	High cost per contact High expense and difficulty of attracting and retaining effective salespeople
Sales promotion	Attracts attention and creates awareness Effectiveness is easily measured Produces increases in short-term sales	Difficult to differentiate from similar programs of competitors Nonpersonal appeal
Public relations	Improves trust in a product or firm Creates a positive attitude about the product or company	Difficult to measure effectiveness Often devoted to nonmarketing activities
Sponsorships	Viewed positively by consumers Enhances brand awareness	Difficult to control message

Objectives of Promotional Strategy

Promotional strategy objectives vary among organizations. Some organizations use promotion to expand their markets, while other organizations use promotion to defend their current positions. As **Figure 13.1** illustrates, common objectives include providing information, differentiating a product, increasing sales, stabilizing sales, and highlighting a product's value.

Marketers often pursue more than one promotional objective at the same time. For example, to promote its Microsoft Office software, Microsoft needs to convince two groups that the product is a worthwhile investment: business owners, who buy the software, and the business owners' employees, who use the software.

Providing Information

A major portion of advertising is information-oriented. Credit card ads provide information about benefits and rates. Ads for hair-care products include information about benefits such as shine and volume. Ads for breakfast cereals often mention nutritional information. Television ads for prescription drugs, a nearly $3 billion industry in North America, are sometimes criticized for relying on emotional appeals rather than providing information about the causes, risk factors, and the prevention of disease.[3] But print advertisements for drugs often contain an entire page of warnings, side effects, and usage guidelines.

Differentiating a Product

Promotion can also be used to differentiate a firm's offerings from the competition. By using a concept called **positioning**, marketers try to establish their products in the minds of customers. The idea is to communicate to buyers some meaningful differences about the attributes, price, quality, or use of a good or service.

When you set out to purchase a car, you can choose from hundreds of brands. How do you decide which car to buy? Carmakers do their best to differentiate their vehicles by style, performance, safety features, and price. They must make their vehicles stand out to individual consumers. General Motors intends its new Chevrolet Cruze compact car to replace the discontinued Cobalt model. Traditionally, compact cars have been less expensive than midsize cars but are also known for being pretty ordinary, or average. The Cruze costs more than the Cobalt, but GM is promoting its higher quality and—especially—its high-quality safety engineering and safety features. A version of the Cruze has been on sale in other countries for a few years. The Cruze received the highest crash-safety score ever in the European New Car Assessment Program.[4]

Increasing Sales

Increasing sales volume is the most common objective of a promotional strategy. Naturalizer became the third-largest seller of women's dress shoes by appealing to baby boomers. But as these women have grown older, they have bought fewer pairs of shoes each year. Naturalizer wants to keep these customers but also wants to attract the younger generation. The firm developed a new line of trendy shoes. The promotional strategy included ads in magazines read by younger women—such as *Elle* and *Marie Claire*—featuring young women in beach attire and Naturalizer shoes. The response to this strategy was a large increase in Naturalizer's sales in department stores.

Stabilizing Sales

Sales stabilization is another goal of promotional strategy. During slow sales periods, some firms use employee sales contests. These contests are meant to motivate salespeople by offering prizes such as vacations, TVs, smartphones, and cash to those who meet certain sales goals. During the

FIGURE 13.1 Five Major Promotional Objectives

DIFFERENTIATE PRODUCT
Example: Television ad comparing performance of two leading laundry detergents

PROVIDE INFORMATION
Example: Print ad describing features and availability of a new breakfast cereal

HIGHLIGHT PRODUCT VALUE
Example: Warranty programs and guarantees that make a product more attractive than its major competitors

STABILIZE SALES
Example: Even out sales patterns by promoting low weekend rates for hotels, holding contests during slow sales periods, or advertising cold fruit soups during summer months

INCREASE SALES
Example: End-of-aisle grocery displays, or "end caps," to encourage impulse purchases

positioning a concept whereby marketers try to establish their products in the minds of customers by communicating to buyers the meaningful differences about the attributes, price, quality, or use of a good or service.

off-season, companies may try to stimulate sales from customers by distributing sales promotion materials, such as calendars, pens, and notepads. Jiffy Lube puts that little sticker on your windshield to remind you when to have your car's next oil change. The regular visits help to stabilize sales. A stable sales pattern brings several advantages. It evens out the production cycle and reduces some management and production costs. It also simplifies financial, purchasing, and marketing planning. An effective promotional strategy can contribute to these goals.

Highlighting the Product's Value

Some promotional strategies improve a product's value by explaining the hidden benefits of ownership. For example, carmakers offer long-term warranty programs, and life insurance companies promote certain policies as investments. The creation of brand awareness and brand loyalty improves a product's image and increases its desirability. Advertising that includes luxurious images supports the reputation of premium brands such as Jaguar, Tiffany, and Rolex.

Promotional Planning

Today's marketers can promote their products in many ways, and the lines between the different elements of the promotional mix are blurring. Consider the practice of **product placement**. A growing number of marketers pay placement fees to have their products showcased in various media, ranging from newspapers and magazines to television and movies. The Superman movie *Man of Steel* holds the current record for the number of product placements, with more than 100 companies paying $160 million or about 75 percent of the film's total budget. Brands skillfully integrated into the movie include Sears, IHOP, and 7-Eleven. Product placement can be subtle, as was shown in the TV series *24*, where the lead character, Jack Bauer, drove a Chevrolet. One of the longest-running product placements is Coca-Cola on *American Idol*.[5]

Another type of promotional planning must be considered by firms with small budgets. **Guerrilla marketing** involves innovative, low-cost marketing efforts designed to get consumers' attention in unusual ways. Guerrilla marketing is an increasingly popular tactic for marketers, especially those with limited promotional budgets. Cathay Pacific, a Hong Kong airline, surprised travellers during a recent holiday season by staging a 300-person flash mob at Hong Kong International Airport, which included ground staff, cabin crew, and even pilots. The unannounced dance took place to the tune of "All I Want for Christmas Is You" in the middle of the busy airport.[6]

product placement a form of promotion where marketers pay placement fees to have their products featured in various media, from newspapers and magazines to television and movies.

guerrilla marketing innovative, low-cost marketing efforts designed to get consumers' attention in unusual ways.

Red Bull Stratos/AP Photos

Energy drink maker Red Bull used a space stunt as a guerilla marketing tactic to launch Felix Baumgartner from a capsule approximately 24 miles above New Mexico. Baumgartner's space suit was covered with Red Bull logos.

Marketers for larger companies have caught on and are using guerrilla approaches as well. In addition to online viral campaigns, there is a new breed of guerrilla tactics being used by leading brands like Red Bull. Maker of energy drinks, Red Bull made a huge scene during a Formula 1 event when a driver made a pit stop in the London race. In another guerrilla marketing move, Red Bull's space stunt, complete with the slogan, "Red Bull Gives You Wings," includes Felix Baumgartner's parachute jump from a capsule at the edge of space—24 miles above Roswell, New Mexico. Baumgartner's spacesuit was branded with Red Bull's logo, and the marketing event was viewed live by millions on YouTube.[7]

From this overview of the promotional mix, we now turn to discussions of each of its elements. The following sections detail the major promotional mix elements of advertising, sales promotion, personal selling, and public relations.

LO 13.2 Summarize the different types of advertising.

ADVERTISING

advertising paid nonpersonal communication usually targeted at large numbers of potential buyers.

Consumers receive thousands of marketing messages each day, many of them in the form of advertising.[8] Advertising is the most visible form of nonpersonal promotion—and the most effective for many firms. **Advertising** refers to paid nonpersonal communication usually targeted at large numbers of potential buyers. Although we often think of advertising as a typically North American function, it is a multibillion-dollar global activity. In a recent year, global ad spending was expected to reach $500 billion—an all-time high. The surge is primarily a result of the growth of mobile technologies and the use of social media. Global ad spending is expected to reach levels experienced prior to the global recession. In addition, consumer electronics and technology is the fastest-growing ad category among the top 100 global firms.[9] More than $10 billion is spent on advertising every year in Canada. According to Statistics Canada, about 5,000 advertising agencies are among nearly 12,000 firms involved in advertising and related services. Advertising agencies account for about 40 percent of advertising revenues generated, with the most being revenues sourced in Ontario (57 percent), Quebec (23 percent), and British Columbia (8 percent).[10]

Advertising expenditures vary among industries, companies, and media. The top five categories for global advertisers are consumer goods, health care, industry and services (business services, property, institutions, power, and water), media, and telecommunications. Personal-care marketers make up 25 percent of global ad spending in a recent year, and the three biggest global advertisers are consumer product companies, Procter & Gamble, Unilever, and L'Oréal. Because advertising expenditures are so great, and because consumers around the world are bombarded with messages, advertisers need to be increasingly creative and efficient at attracting consumers' attention.[11]

iPad
A magical and revolutionary product at an unbelievable price. Starting at $499.

iPad with Wi-Fi + 3G is now available. Find an Apple Retail Store ▸ Buy from the Apple Online Store ▸

Watch the Guided Tours ▸
Watch the TV ad ▸
Watch the iPad video ▸

© digitallife/Alamy Inc.

Product advertising consists of messages designed to sell a particular good or service.

Types of Advertising

product advertising messages designed to sell a particular good or service.

institutional advertising messages that promote concepts, ideas, or philosophies. It can also promote goodwill toward industries, companies, organizations, or government entities.

The two basic types of advertisements are product ads and institutional ads. **Product advertising** consists of messages designed to sell a particular good or service. Advertisements for BlackBerry PlayBooks, Apple iPods, and Capital One credit cards are examples of product advertising. **Institutional advertising** involves messages that promote concepts, ideas, or philosophies. It can also promote goodwill toward industries, companies, organizations, or government entities. Each year, the Juvenile Diabetes Research Foundation promotes its "Walk for the Cure," a fundraising event. Your college or university may advertise in local papers or on news shows to promote its activities.

Cause advertising is a form of institutional advertising that is growing in importance. This type of advertising promotes a specific viewpoint on a public issue. It uses advertising to influence public opinion and the political process about such issues as literacy, hunger and poverty, and alternative energy sources. Both not-for-profit organizations and businesses use cause advertising, which is sometimes called *advocacy advertising*. As part of Avon's corporate responsibility, the Avon Foundation promotes its Speak Out Against Domestic Violence program. The ads feature a celebrity endorsement from Reese Witherspoon.[12]

cause advertising a form of institutional advertising that promotes a specific viewpoint on a public issue as a way to influence public opinion and the political process.

Advertising and the Product Life Cycle

Advertising is designed to inform, persuade, or remind. Both types of advertising—product advertising and institutional advertising—belong to one of these three categories depending on the advertising objectives. For example, a firm uses *informative advertising* to build initial demand for a product in the introductory, or beginning, phase of the product life cycle. Highly publicized new-product entries attract the interest of potential buyers. The buyers then look for information about the advantages of the new products over existing products, the new products' warranties, their prices, and locations that offer the new products. Ads for new cellphones try to attract new customers by boasting about their new features, colours, designs, and pricing options.

Persuasive advertising tries to improve the competitive status of a product, institution, or concept. This type of advertising is usually used in the growth and maturity stages of the product life cycle. *Comparative advertising* is one of the most popular types of persuasive product advertising. This type of advertising compares products directly with their competitors—either by naming the competing product or by suggesting it. For example, Tylenol advertisements mention the possible stomach problems that the generic drug aspirin could cause, and then states that its pain reliever does not irritate the stomach. But advertisers need to be careful when they name competing brands; they risk leaving themselves open to controversy or even legal action. Notice that Tylenol does not mention a specific aspirin brand in its promotions.

Reminder-oriented advertising is often used for products in the late maturity or decline stages of the product life cycle. This advertising is used to maintain awareness of the importance and usefulness of a product, concept, or institution. For example, Triscuits have been around for a long time, but Nabisco tries to increase sales by using up-to-date advertising that appeals to health and fitness-conscious consumers. The advertising mentions its new no-trans-fat formula.

Advertising Media

Marketers must choose how to allocate their advertising budgets among various media. All media offer advantages and disadvantages. Cost is an important consideration in media selection, but marketers must also choose the media best suited for communicating their message. As **Figure 13.2** indicates, the three leading media outlets for advertising are television, the Internet, and newspapers. Advertising executives have observed that firms are rethinking traditional ad campaigns and incorporating new media, as well as updated uses of traditional media. Less than a decade ago, the Internet ranked sixth in global ad media behind TV, newspapers, magazines, radio, and outdoor advertising. Today, it is second behind television and ahead of newspapers. Global Internet ad spending has surpassed the 20 percent mark, and over the next several years, analysts expect the Internet to account for more than 27 percent of global ad spending.[13]

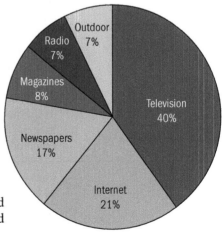

Television

Television continues to be one of North America's leading national advertising media. Television advertising can be classified as network ads, national ads, local ads, or cable ads. Despite a decline in audience share

FIGURE 13.2 Dividing Up the Advertising Media Pie

Sources: "Executive Summary: Advertising Expenditure Forecasts December 2013," *ZenithOptimedia*, accessed February 20, 2014, www.zenithoptimedia. com/wp-content/uploads/2013/12/Adspend-forecasts-December-2013-executive-summary.pdf; "TV Remains the Reigning Champ, but Display Internet Ads Are the MVPs of 3Q," Nielsen, accessed February 20, 2014, www.nielsen.com/us/en/insights/news/2014/tv-remains-the-reigning-champ-but-display-internet-ads-are-the-mvps-of-3q.html.

and growing competition from cable, network television remains the easiest way for advertisers to reach large numbers of viewers—10 million to 20 million North Americans with a single commercial. Automakers, fast-food restaurants, and food manufacturers are heavy users of network TV advertising.

About 80 percent of Canadian households (11.5 million subscribers) and 32 percent of U.S. households with TVs subscribe to cable television. They are attracted to the more than 800 channels available through cable or satellite services. But the cable and satellite networks are facing new competition. One survey indicates that 60 percent of North American homes have one or more videogame consoles. People are using the consoles to download apps and video-on-demand offerings. And a growing number of viewers are discontinuing their cable service and opting instead for online services such as Netflix, Hulu, Apple's iTunes, and the networks' own websites. Recently, 1.3 million people watched at least part of the Masters Golf Tournament online, double the number who watched online the previous year. People still prefer free, advertising-supported downloads, although online network advertising made up only 2.5 percent of the $62 billion in annual North American advertising revenues. But the number of homes with digital video recorders (DVRs) and high-definition (HD) televisions is increasing steadily. Recent research suggests that even people who can use their DVRs to skip TV ads don't always do so. According to the Nielsen Company, many DVR users still watch shows at their scheduled times and watch the ads; even those who record shows for later viewing watch almost half the ads they could skip. As more people watch playbacks of their favourite shows, the networks' ratings—and commercial watching—increase too.[14]

Although—or perhaps because—television reaches the greatest number of consumers at once, it is the most expensive advertising medium. The Super Bowl is widely known for its hefty advertising price tag—and its ability to reach over 100 million people in a three-hour period. Firms such as Budweiser, Frito-Lay, GoDaddy, T-Mobile, and The Coca-Cola Company paid as much as $4 million for a 30-second spot during a recent game, although some of the advertisers posted their ads online in the days leading up to the game. Intuit, a software developer for small businesses, recently sponsored a contest called "Small Business Big Game." The winner was awarded a 30-second commercial spot on the Super Bowl broadcast. Oakland, California–based GoldieBlox, maker of toys intended to get girls interested in science and engineering, has experienced phenomenal success as the winning entry, with more than 100 million viewers exposed to its unique products.[15]

Internet Advertising

The digital ad market is growing faster than the rest of the advertising sector due mainly to the rising number of smartphones and tablets in use and increased social media usage. North American digital advertising, including mobile, rose to about $27 billion in a recent year, making up almost 25 percent of all advertising revenues. Ad types include search and banner, the largest category, along with classified, rich media, video, lead generation, sponsorship, and email.

Second to TV ads in terms of overall dollars, digital ad revenues are expected to reach $42 billion in a few years. Spending on ads delivered to desktops and laptops has slowed in comparison to mobile advertising, which has doubled over the last few years and is expected to top $10 billion in the not-too-distant future. The five companies that dominate digital advertising—Google, Yahoo, Facebook, Microsoft, and AOL—accounted for more than 64 percent of all digital ad expenditures in a recent year.[16]

Viral advertising creates a message that is novel or entertaining enough for consumers to forward to others, spreading it like a virus. The great advantage is that spreading the word online, which often relies on social networking sites such as Facebook, YouTube, and Twitter, costs the advertiser nothing. Although viral marketing can be risky, the best campaigns are edgy or funny. Dove soap's Beauty Sketches campaign, one of the biggest online viral sensations ever, sent the following message to women: "You are more beautiful than you think." The campaign compares a woman's description of herself to a description made by strangers through a series of sketches created by an FBI-trained artist. The stranger's description was typically more attractive than what the women themselves described—with the point being that women tend to be overly critical about the way they look. The viral campaign generated close to 30 million views and 660,000 Facebook shares during its first 10 days online.[17]

Newspapers

As companies shift advertising dollars to other platforms, newspaper print advertising revenues continue to fall. Although one advantage of newspaper advertising is the ease with which marketers can easily tailor ads to local tastes and preferences, a disadvantage comes from the relatively short life span—people usually discard their newspapers soon after reading them. Retailers and automobile dealers rank as the biggest newspaper advertisers. Most newspapers now have websites, which have offset some of the declines in advertising dollars.[18]

Radio

Despite the proliferation of other media, the average North American household owns a number of radios—including those in cars—and this is a market penetration that makes radio, which relies on commercial sponsorship, an important advertising medium. Advertisers like the captive audience of listeners at work or as they commute to and from work. As a result, morning and evening drive-time shows command higher ad rates for airtime. In major markets, many stations, depending on their format, serve different demographic groups with targeted programming. Internet radio programming also offers opportunities for more focused targeting.

A recent study of several music-sharing sites reveals that more than half of people 12 years and older listen to online radio through a computer or smartphone. The top reasons cited for listening to online radio include better variety of music and the ability to skip songs.

Projected ad spending estimates for Internet radio, which includes news, sports, talk, and various music genres, will reach $1.31 billion over the next few years with the number of monthly listeners projected to be over 175 million. Recent marketing research shows that the percentage of people listening to Internet radio will soon surpass traditional platforms like AM and FM stations.[19]

Magazines

Magazines include consumer publications and business trade journals. *Time, Reader's Digest,* and *Sports Illustrated* are consumer magazines. *Advertising Age* and *Oil & Gas Journal* are trade publications.

Magazines sometimes customize their publications and target advertising messages to different regions of the country. One method places local advertising in regional editions of the magazines. Other magazines attach wraparounds—half-size covers on top of full-size covers. These wraparounds highlight articles that relate to particular geographic areas; different wraparounds appear in different parts of the country.

Magazines are a natural choice for targeted advertising. Media buyers study demographics of subscribers and select magazines that attract the desired readers. For example, American Express advertises in *Fortune* and *Forbes* to reach businesspeople. PacSun clothes and Clearasil skin medications are advertised in *Teen Vogue.*

Direct Mail

The average North American household receives about 550 pieces of direct mail each year, including 100 catalogues. The huge growth in the variety of direct-mail offerings and the convenience they offer today's busy, time-pressed shoppers has made direct-mail advertising a multibillion-dollar business. Even consumers who like to shop online often page through a catalogue before placing an online order. Although direct-mail advertising is expensive per person, a small business may be able to afford a limited direct-mail campaign but not a television or radio ad. For businesses with a small advertising budget, a carefully targeted direct-mail effort can be highly effective. Email is a low-cost form of direct marketing. Marketers can target the most interested Internet users by offering website visitors an option to register to receive email. Companies like Amazon.ca, The Home Depot, and Abercrombie & Fitch routinely send emails to regular customers.

Address lists are at the heart of direct-mail advertising. Direct-mail marketers use data-mining techniques to segment markets. They then create profiles that show the types of consumers who are likely to buy their products or donate to their organizations. Catalogue retailers sometimes experiment by sending direct-mail pieces randomly to people who subscribe to particular magazines. Then, they analyze the orders received from the mailings and develop profiles of purchasers. Finally, they rent lists of subscriber names that match the profiles they have developed.

Studies have shown that most consumers are annoyed by the amount of so-called "junk mail" they receive every day, including catalogues, advertising postcards, and flyers. Among Internet users, a major pet peeve is *spam,* or junk email. Many local governments have outlawed sending email promotions without legitimate return addresses, although it is difficult to track down and charge offenders.

The Canadian Marketing Association (CMA; www.the-cma.org) helps marketers by offering its members guidelines on ethical business practices. The American-based Direct Marketing Association (DMA; www.the-dma.org) also provides consumer information at its website. The DMA and Canada Post offer services for consumers to opt out of receiving unsolicited direct mail.

Outdoor Advertising

In one year, outdoor advertising accounted for more than $6.7 billion in North American advertising spending.[20] Most spending on outdoor advertising is for billboards, but spending is growing fast for other types of outdoor advertising, such as signs in transit stations, stores, airports, and sports stadiums. Advertisers are exploring new forms of outdoor media that involve technology: computerized paintings, video billboards, "trivision" that displays three revolving images on a single billboard, and moving billboards mounted on trucks, as well as advertising on taxi tops. To see how some NBA teams are using advertising on their courts, see the "Hit & Miss" feature. Other innovations include ads displayed on the Goodyear blimp, using an electronic system that offers animation and video. Digital, electronic, or LED billboards, introduced less than two decades ago, provide an effective medium for advertisers who want to reach their segment with timely and relevant messages. Digital billboards are dynamic, with content updating every 4 to 10 seconds, with multiple advertisers and messages. But outdoor advertising has several disadvantages. The medium requires brief messages, and billboards are often attacked by preservation and conservation groups.

Advertisers are exploring new forms of outdoor media that involve technology, such as computerized paintings and electronic billboards. At 24 million pixels, this eight story high, one-block long digital billboard in Times Square is the largest and highest resolution sign. Advertisers such as Google pay over $2.5 million USD a month.

HIT & MISS

NBA Says Yes to Floor Ads

Instead of putting corporate logos on its jerseys, the NBA has allowed floor advertising on the courts of its 30 teams. The floor ad space is the idea of NBA commissioner Adam Silver, and it will be evaluated over time to determine if there will be a permanent location to sell ad space in the future. While corporate logos on NBA jerseys would generate about $100 million annually, the NBA management projects the "real estate" on the court floor to be worth far more money from television advertising and exposure.

NBA teams received approval to sell space on part of the basketball court known as the apron—space that covers the out-of-bounds area on the sidelines between the baselines, in front of team benches, and the coaches' box where teams already advertise their websites or Twitter handles. There is a catch, however. Company logos must be removable decals and can only be affixed during games televised locally.

So far, three teams have signed up. The Indiana Pacers signed a deal with the state's Economic Development Corporation; JP Morgan Chase will be on the floor at Madison Square Garden during New York Knicks games, and the Miami Heat has signed a deal with Samsung. Samsung is also one of the NBA's newest league partners, recently signing a reported three-year, $100 million deal. The Toronto Raptors were the first team to experiment with technology that creates a 3D optical illusion of its logo on the baseline, which could potentially be extended to corporate sponsor logos.

While pricing varies among the 30 teams, it is rumoured that one top franchise has an asking price of $3 million for the ad space on the court. Front Row Marketing Services, a company that tracks what appears on-screen in sports broadcasts, estimates that the prime floor space might fetch anywhere between $450,000 and $2.5 million per year, depending on the franchise.

Questions for Critical Thinking

1. Although ad space sales have been slow initially, observers believe that some teams are holding out for blue chip companies that appear to be a good fit for the team. What types of sponsors would be the best fit with top NBA franchises?

2. While this is a unique marketing opportunity for a corporate sponsor, some argue that the cost is on par with national advertising fees for games that will only be televised locally. So far, nationally televised regular season games, NBA All-Star weekend, and playoff games are not included. How would you evaluate the cost versus the marketing exposure?

Sources: Ira Boudway, "Slow Sales at the Outset for NBA Floor Space," *Bloomberg Business*, accessed February 16, 2014, www.bloomberg.com/bw/articles/2013-12-02/slow-sales-at-the-outset-for-nba-floor-space; Darren Rovell, "Limited Use of Ads on Court OK'd," *Hotbox Sports*, accessed February 16, 2014, http://news.hotboxsports.com/NBA/article/30799; Philip Johnson, "The NBA Expects To Make $100 Million with On-Court Ads Next Season," *Business Insider*, accessed February 16, 2014, www.businessinsider.com/nba-on-court-ads-first-time-next-season-2013-6; YouTube, "Toronto Raptors Show Off New 3-D Illusion," accessed April 20, 2015, www.youtube.com/watch?v=Fqc92khwhwU.

Sponsorship

Marketers can use one of the hottest trends in promotion to integrate several elements of the promotional mix. **Sponsorship** involves providing funds for a sporting or cultural event in exchange for a direct association with the event. Sports sponsorships attract two-thirds of all sponsorship dollars in North America. Entertainment, festivals, causes, and the arts divide up the remaining third of sponsorship dollars. Firms may also sponsor charitable or other not-for-profit awards or events such as the CIBC-sponsored Canadian Breast Cancer Foundation's Run for the Cure.

Sponsors benefit in two major ways: they gain exposure to the event's audience and they gain association with the image of the activity. If a celebrity is involved, sponsors usually earn the right to use the celebrity's name and the name of the event in advertisements. They can set up signs at the event, offer sales promotions, and similar activities. Sponsorships play an important role in relationship marketing, by bringing together the event, its participants, and the sponsoring firms. Spending on sponsorships is expected to soon increase to $20.6 billion.[21]

sponsorship providing funds for a sporting or cultural event in exchange for a direct association with the event.

Other Media Options

As consumers filter out familiar advertising messages, marketers look for new ways to catch their attention. Many firms use the major media, but some firms promote through other means, such as infomercials and specialized media. **Infomercials** are a form of broadcast direct marketing, also

infomercials a form of broadcast direct marketing; 30-minute programs resemble regular TV programs, but sell goods or services.

called *direct-response television (DRTV)*. These 30-minute programs resemble regular television programs but sell goods or services, such as exercise equipment, skin-care products, or kitchenware. The long format allows an advertiser to thoroughly present product benefits, increase awareness, and make an impact on consumers. Advertisers also receive immediate responses in the form of sales or inquiries because most infomercials feature toll-free phone numbers. Infomercial stars may become celebrities, attracting more customers wherever they go. The most effective infomercials tend to be for auto-care products, beauty and personal-care items, investing and business opportunities, collectibles, fitness and self-improvement products, housewares, and electronics.[22]

Advertisers use just about any medium they can find. A more recent development is the use of automated teller machines (ATMs) for advertising. Some ATMs can play 15-second commercials on their screens, and many can print advertising messages on receipts. An ATM screen has a captive audience because the user must watch the screen to complete a transaction. Directory advertising includes the familiar Yellow Pages listings in telephone books. Advertising is also available in thousands of other types of directories; most such advertising is for business-related promotions. Besides local and regional directories, publishers also produce special printed and online versions of the Yellow Pages specifically for ethnic groups.

✓ ASSESSMENT CHECK

13.2.1 What are the two basic types of advertising? Into what three categories do they fall?

13.2.2 What is the leading advertising medium in North America?

13.2.3 In what two major ways do firms benefit from sponsorship?

LO 13.3 Outline sales promotion.

sales promotion forms of promotion such as coupons, product samples, and rebates that support advertising and personal selling.

SALES PROMOTION

Sales promotion was traditionally viewed as a supplement, or add-on, to a firm's sales or advertising efforts. But sales promotion has emerged as an important part of the promotional mix. Promotion now accounts for more than half as many marketing dollars as are spent on advertising, and promotion spending is rising faster than ad spending. **Sales promotion** consists of forms of promotion such as coupons, product samples, and rebates that support advertising and personal selling.

Both retailers and manufacturers use sales promotions to offer consumers extra incentives to buy. Sales promotions can lead to the short-term advantage of increased sales. But sales promotions can also help marketers build brand equity and improve their customer relationships. Examples of sales promotion include samples, coupons, contests, displays, trade shows, and dealer incentives.

Consumer-Oriented Promotions

The goal of a consumer-oriented sales promotion is to get new and existing customers to try products, and ultimately, to buy products. Marketers want to increase sales of complementary products, increase impulse purchases, and encourage repeat business by rewarding product purchasers. **Figure 13.3** illustrates how marketers allocate their consumer-oriented spending among the categories of promotions. Total promotions spending in the North America exceeded $584 billion in a recent year, reflecting opportunities for other businesses to produce promotional products for various campaigns.[23]

Promotions can also be used to popularize an idea, such as the growing awareness of plastic shopping bags and the pollution they contribute to the environment. The "Going Green" feature discusses the growing trend of banning plastic shopping bags.

Premiums, Coupons, Rebates, and Samples

Nearly six of every 10 sales promotion dollars are spent on *premiums*—items given away for free or at a reduced price when another product is purchased. For example, cosmetics companies, such as Clinique, offer sample kits with purchases of their products. Fast-food restaurants are also big users of premiums. McDonald's and Burger King include a toy with the purchase of every children's meal. The toys are often tie-ins with new movies or popular cartoon shows. Marketers generally choose premiums that are likely to get consumers thinking about and caring about the brand and

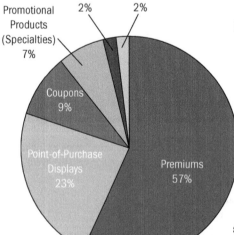

FIGURE 13.3
Spending on Consumer-Oriented Promotions

Sources: Data from Kathleen M. Joyce, "Higher Gear," *Promo Magazine,* accessed April 26, 2010, http://promomagazine.com.

GOING GREEN

HOW **MUCH WOULD YOU PAY FOR A PLASTIC SHOPPING BAG?**

Many stores in Toronto, Montreal, Vancouver, and other Canadian cities now collect a tax or charge about five cents for giving customers a plastic shopping bag at the checkout counter. This cost is meant to discourage the use of plastic bags and instead encourage the use of longer-lasting reusable and recyclable bags.

In North America, it is estimated that almost 4 billion tons of plastic waste—in the form of bags, sacks, and wrapping—were generated in one year. The plastic is made from oil and can take 1,000 years to break down. Only about 1 percent of this waste is ever recycled.

A growing number of people want to reduce these statistics. For example, more city governments have banned the use of plastic bags, required certain retailers to accept plastic bags for recycling, or imposed a tax on plastic.

But such laws have not always been met with approval. In eco-friendly Seattle, voters overturned a law charging 20 cents per plastic bag, perhaps because they were already recycling and reusing the bags. Big retailers like Walmart and Loblaw sell reusable bags for about a dollar. These bags carry the store's logo and name and promote the use of reusable bags. Some retailers have reacted to customer complaints and have stopped charging for plastic bags.

Questions for Critical Thinking

1. Can stores that provide eco-friendly shopping bags or other ways to reduce the polluting effects of plastic gain promotional benefits from their efforts? How can cities that ban or tax plastic bags promote their actions?

2. What other ways can you think of to promote the idea of recycling plastic bags or reducing their use?

Sources: "NYCWasteLe$$," Plastic Bag Recycling, accessed May 11, 2010, www.nyc.gov; Dave Gram, "Vt. Plastic Bag Tax Proposal Seen Coming Too Late," *Rutland Herald*, April 16, 2010, www.rutlandherald.com/article/20100416/NEWS04/4160363; Melissa Eddy, "Plastic Bag Ban: Would You Pay 5 Cents for a Bag?" *Huffington Post*, February 22, 2010, www.huffingtonpost.com/2010/02/22/plastic-bags-ban-would-yo_n_471228.html; Steve Painter, "3 Wal-Marts Testing Purge of Plastic Bags," *Arkansas Online*, January 24, 2010, www.arkansasonline.com/news/2010/jan/24/3-wal-marts-testing-purge-plastic-bags-20100124; Stephen Messenger, "Washington D.C.'s Plastic Bag Tax Takes Effect This Week," *TreeHugger.com*, January 3, 2010, www.treehugger.com.

the product. People who purchase health foods at a grocery store may find an offer for a free personal training session at a local health club printed on the back of their sales receipt.

Customers redeem *coupons* for small price discounts when they purchase the promoted products. Such offers may persuade a customer to try a new or different product. Some large supermarket chains double the face value of manufacturers' coupons. Coupons have the downside of focusing customers on price instead of brand loyalty. Some consumers complain that clipping or printing out coupons is too time-consuming, but others enjoy the savings, especially when money is tight and prices seem high.

Industrywide coupon redemption remained steady in a recent year at 2.9 billion coupons redeemed, while distribution grew more than 3 percent over the previous year. Of the coupons distributed, approximately 40 percent were for food products. As marketers continue to leverage technology when offering coupons, digital coupon redemption increased more than 140 percent in a recent year. Overall, the use of digital coupons continues to grow faster than traditional coupons. Approximately 87 percent of traditional coupons are distributed through free-standing inserts in the newspaper—and represent 41 percent of the coupons redeemed. Some people predict that the growing use of paperless mobile coupons, which consumers access on their smartphones while shopping could make clippable or printed-out coupons obsolete.[24]

Rebates offer cash back to consumers who mail in required proofs of purchase. Today, firms have simplified the rebate mail-in requirement by offering consumers the opportunity to submit rebates online. Rebates help packaged-goods manufacturers increase purchase rates, promote multiple purchases, and reward product users. Other types of companies also offer rebates, especially for electronics, computers and their accessories, and automobiles. Processing rebates gives marketers a way to collect data about their customers, but many shoppers find it awkward to collect the required receipts, forms, and universal product codes (UPCs) and then wait several weeks for the refund. In the past, many manufacturers counted on the fact that consumers would not follow through on rebates.[25]

A *sample* is a gift of a product distributed by mail, door to door, in a demonstration, or inside packages of another product. On any given day, you might receive a sample moisturizer, a bar of soap, or a packet of laundry detergent. Out of every four consumers who receive samples, three will try them.

Games, Contests, and Sweepstakes

Contests, sweepstakes, and games offer cash, merchandise, or travel as prizes to participating winners. Firms often sponsor these activities to introduce new goods and services and to attract new customers. Games and contests require entrants to solve problems or write essays, and they must sometimes provide a proof of purchase. Sweepstakes choose winners by chance and require no product purchase. Consumers typically prefer sweepstakes because they are easy; games and contests require more effort. Companies like sweepstakes, too, because they are inexpensive to run and the number of winners is decided at the beginning. With games and contests, the company doesn't know how many people will correctly complete a puzzle or gather the right number of symbols from scratch-off cards. Sweepstakes, games, and contests can reinforce a company's image and advertising message. But consumer attention may focus on the promotion instead of on the product.

In recent years, court rulings and legal restrictions have limited the use of games and contests. Companies must proceed carefully when advertising their contests and games and the prizes they award. Marketers must show the chances of winning and avoid false promises, such as suggesting that a consumer has already won.

Specialty Advertising

specialty advertising promotional items that prominently display a firm's name, logo, or business slogan.

Have you received any free pens, T-shirts, or refrigerator magnets imprinted with a business name? These offers are examples of **specialty advertising** or *advertising specialties*. This type of sales promotion involves the gift of useful merchandise carrying the name, logo, or slogan of a profit-seeking business or a not-for-profit organization. Because those products are useful and sometimes personalized with recipients' names, people tend to keep and use them, giving advertisers repeated exposure. Advertising specialties were originally designed to identify and create goodwill for advertisers. Now they generate sales leads and develop traffic for stores and trade show exhibitors. Like premiums, these promotions should reinforce the brand's image and its relationship with the recipient.

Trade-Oriented Promotions

trade promotion sales promotion geared to marketing intermediaries, not to final consumers.

Sales promotion techniques can also contribute to campaigns directed to retailers and wholesalers. **Trade promotion** is sales promotion geared to marketing intermediaries, not to consumers. Marketers use trade promotion to encourage retailers to stock new products, continue carrying existing products, and promote both new and existing products effectively to consumers. Successful trade promotions offer financial incentives. They require careful timing, attention to costs, and should be easy for intermediaries to apply. These promotions should bring quick results and improve retail sales. Major trade promotions include point-of-purchase advertising and trade shows.

point-of-purchase (POP) advertising displays or demonstrations that promote products when and where consumers buy them, such as in retail stores.

Point-of-purchase (POP) advertising consists of displays or demonstrations that promote products at checkout areas or in the location where consumers buy the item, such as in retail stores. Displays are in various forms, including shelf-mounted signs and hanging posters. Sunscreen, painting supplies, and snacks are typically displayed this way. POP displays can have a significant impact on sales, as an estimated 70 percent of purchase decisions are made within the retail store itself. Recently, electronic, dynamically updated POP displays have been used to present targeted product information and instant coupons. Marketing research has shown that consumers are more likely to purchase certain products when such displays are present. About 78 percent of Facebook's daily users visit the site via mobile and tablet devices, and 41 percent of ad revenue comes from small screens over laptops and desktops. Location-based advertising will be directed primarily to smartphones.[26]

Manufacturers and other sellers often exhibit at *trade shows* to promote goods or services to members of their distribution channels. These shows are often organized by industry trade associations. Each year, thousands of trade shows attract millions of exhibitors and hundreds of millions of attendees. Such shows are particularly important in fast-changing industries like those for computers, toys, furniture, and fashions. The International Consumer Electronics Show, which is held annually in Las Vegas and attracts more than 3,200 exhibitors and 150,000 attendees, is the largest. Other trade shows are in the construction, consumer goods, energy, entertainment, manufacturing, and sports and outdoors industries. Trade shows are especially effective for introducing new products and generating sales leads.[27]

Personal Selling

Many companies consider personal selling—a person-to-person promotional presentation to a potential buyer—to be the key to marketing effectiveness. Unless a seller matches a firm's goods or services to the needs of a certain client or customer, none of the firm's other activities produces any benefits. Today, sales and sales-related jobs employ about 16 million North American workers and are expected to grow.[28] Businesses often spend five to 10 times as much on personal selling as on advertising. Personal selling includes the significant costs of hiring, training, benefits, and salaries. Because of these costs, businesses are very concerned with the effectiveness of their sales personnel. One of their continuing concerns is with the way representatives communicate with others.

How do marketers decide whether to make personal selling the main focus of their firm's marketing mix? In general, firms are likely to focus on personal selling instead of advertising or sales promotion under four conditions:

Personal selling involves a person-to-person promotional presentation to a potential buyer. At a cosmetics counter, the salesperson provides a free makeup demonstration to reinforce the message of how a company's products enhance a person's looks.

1. Customers are relatively few in number and are geographically concentrated.

2. The product is technically complex, involves trade-ins, or requires special handling.

3. The product carries a relatively high price.

4. The product moves through direct distribution channels.

A good example is selling Piper Cub airplanes. Airplane buyers tend to be wealthy people who value their freedom and privacy—and the luxury of owning their own plane. "It is a way of life I am selling," says veteran sales rep Bruce Keller, "not just aluminum. I want the customer to share that with me. If you look at my airplane and you sit in it, you are going flying."[29]

The sales functions of most companies are going through rapid change. Compared to the past, today's salespeople are more concerned with creating long-term buyer–seller relationships and acting as consultants to their customers. After the recession, salespeople faced a new challenge—consumers who haggle over prices, even on retail items. One survey found that 88 percent of those questioned had haggled over at least one price in the past six months. The survey found that hagglers had better than a 75 percent success rate in making deals on clothing, appliances, and jewellery.[30] The Great Depression of the 1930s was the last time North Americans engaged in serious amounts of haggling. Today's consumers have advantages that would surprise their grandparents. Anyone with a smartphone can search online for competing prices of merchandise while standing in a retail store. Many consumers have become savvy online shoppers, searching for bargains on websites like Overstock, eBay, Expedia, Orbitz, and Priceline.

Personal selling can occur in several settings; each setting can involve either business-to-business (B2B) or business-to-consumer (B2C) selling. *Field selling* refers to sales representatives who make sales calls on prospective customers at their businesses. Companies that sell major industrial equipment typically rely on field selling. *Over-the-counter selling* describes sales activities in retailing and some wholesale locations, where customers visit the seller's facility to purchase items. *Telemarketing* sales representatives make their presentations over the phone. A later section reviews telemarketing in more detail.

Sales Tasks

All sales activities involve helping customers in some way. A salesperson's work can vary from one company or situation to another, but all sales work usually includes a mix of three basic tasks: order processing, creative selling, and missionary selling.

order processing a form of selling used mostly at the wholesale and retail levels; involves identifying customer needs, pointing out products that meet those needs, and completing orders.

Order Processing   Order processing is used in both field selling and telemarketing, but this form of selling is most often related to retail and wholesale firms. In order processing, the salesperson identifies customer needs, points out merchandise to meet those needs, and processes the order. Route-sales personnel process orders for such consumer goods as bread, milk, soft drinks, and snack foods. They check each store's stock, report inventory needs to the store manager, and complete the sale. Most of these jobs include at least minor order-processing functions.

creative selling a persuasive type of promotional presentation.

Creative Selling   Sales representatives for most business products and some consumer items perform **creative selling**, a persuasive type of promotional presentation. Creative selling promotes a good or service whose benefits are not readily seen or whose purchase decision requires a close look at other options. Creative selling is used to sell intangible products such as insurance, but can also be used to sell tangible goods.

Many retail salespeople just process orders, but many consumers want more customer service. That's where creative selling comes in. For example, training sales staff at women's clothing stores might include holding seasonal wardrobe-building workshops. After attending such a workshop, the sales staff can better help customers select and purchase coordinating clothing, accessories, and shoes. Customers might not have purchased these items if they hadn't received such advice.

missionary selling an indirect form of selling where the representative promotes goodwill for a company or provides technical or operational assistance to the customer.

Missionary Selling   Sales work also includes an indirect form of selling, where the representative promotes goodwill for a company or gives the customer technical or operational help. This practice is called **missionary selling**. Many businesses that sell technical equipment, such as Oracle and Fujitsu, provide systems specialists who act as consultants to customers. These salespeople work to solve problems and sometimes help their clients with questions not directly related to their employers' products. Other industries also use missionary selling techniques. Pharmaceutical company representatives—called *detailers*—visit physicians to describe the firm's latest offerings. Some firms are also finding success with less direct methods, including web-based sales calls after office hours. The large pharmaceutical maker Pfizer recently cut back its sales force and is turning toward electronic marketing. The company has found electronic detailing especially helpful. It allows doctors to access the latest information on drugs when and where they choose. The information can also be strictly controlled, and the company runs much less risk of its salespeople being accused of marketing drugs for off-label uses—that is, for treating conditions other than those they were originally intended to help.[31] The actual sales, in any case, are handled through pharmacies, which fill the prescriptions.

telemarketing personal selling by telephone, which provides marketers with a high return on their expenses, an immediate response, and an opportunity for a personalized two-way conversation.

Telemarketing   Telemarketing refers to personal selling by telephone. It provides a firm's marketers with a high return on their expenses, an immediate response, and an opportunity for a personalized two-way conversation. Many firms use telemarketing because expense or other factors keep salespeople from meeting many potential customers in person. Telemarketers can use databases to target prospects based on population data. Telemarketing takes two forms: outbound and inbound. A sales representative who calls you is practising *outbound telemarketing*. On the other hand, *inbound telemarketing* occurs when you call a toll-free phone number to get product information or place an order.

Outbound telemarketers must follow various legal requirements and industry guidelines that guide their behaviour. In general, telemarketers must disclose what they are selling and the organization they represent before making their presentations. Calls are limited to between 9 A.M. and 9:30 P.M. on weekdays and between 10 A.M. and 6 P.M. on weekends. Sellers must also inform the customer about the details of exchange policies. Recent legislation requires telemarketers to respect lists of people who do not want to receive calls. Consumers who want to be on the list must call a special number or visit a website to register. Telemarketers must stop calling registered numbers within 31 days or face stiff fines.[32] Charities, surveys, and political campaign calls are exempt from these restrictions. Also, businesses that already have a relationship with consumers can make telemarketing calls. These businesses include the bank where customers have accounts or the dealership where they bought their car.

The Sales Process

The sales process typically follows the seven-step sequence illustrated in **Figure 13.4**: prospecting and qualifying, the approach, the presentation, the demonstration, handling objections, closing, and the follow-up. Remember the importance of flexibility; a good salesperson will vary the sales process to suit a customer's responses and needs. The process of selling to a potential customer who is unfamiliar with a company's products differs from the process of serving a long-time customer.

Prospecting, Qualifying, and Approaching At the prospecting stage, salespeople identify potential customers. Salespeople may look for leads for prospective sales from such sources as existing customers, friends and family, and business associates. The qualifying process identifies potential customers who have the financial ability and authority to buy.

FIGURE 13.4 Seven Steps in the Sales Process

Companies use different ways to identify and qualify prospects. Some companies rely on business development teams to do this work. They use the responses from direct mail to provide leads to sales reps. Other companies believe in personal visits from sales representatives; others use email, which is inexpensive and usually has a good response rate. Many B2B firms use electronic social media such as electronic newsletters, web events, virtual trade shows, podcasts, videos, online demonstrations, and blogs.[33]

Before making the first contact with a customer, successful salespeople make careful preparations, by analyzing available data about a prospective customer's product lines and other related information. These salespeople know that a good first impression can influence a customer's attitude toward the selling company and its products.

Presentation and Demonstration At the presentation stage, salespeople communicate promotional messages. They may describe the major features of their products, highlight the advantages, and give examples of satisfied consumers. A demonstration is a critical step in the sales process. It helps to reinforce the message that the salesperson has been communicating. For example, department-store shoppers can get a free makeover at the cosmetics counter. And anyone looking to buy a car will take it for a test drive before deciding whether to purchase it.

Some products are too large to transport to prospective buyers or require a special installation to demonstrate. Sales representatives can demonstrate these products for customers by using laptop computers, multimedia presentations, web conferences, podcasts, and graphic programs like SmartDraw.[34] Services, which are intangible, can't be demonstrated in the same way. Salespeople may find it helpful to show a presentation that includes testimonials from satisfied customers or graphs illustrating results.

Handling Objections Some salespeople fear potential customers' objections because they view their questions as criticism. But a good salesperson can use objections as an opportunity to answer questions and explain how the product will benefit the customer. As a general rule, the key is to sell the benefits, not the features: How will this product help the customer?

Closing   The critical point in the sales process is the closing. This is the time when the salesperson asks the prospect to buy. If the presentation has matched the product benefits to customer needs, the closing should be a natural conclusion. If there are some bumps in the process, the salesperson can try some different techniques, such as offering alternative products, offering a special incentive for purchase, or restating the product benefits. The ideal outcome of this interaction is closing the sale—and beginning a relationship where the customer builds loyalty to the brand or product. But even if the sale is not closed, the salesperson should still think of the interaction as the beginning of a potential relationship. The prospect might become a customer in the future. See the "Career Kickstart" feature for tips on how to close the big sale.

Follow-up   A salesperson's actions after the sale may lead to the customer making another purchase. Follow-up is an important part of building a long-lasting relationship. After closing, the salesperson should process the order efficiently. By calling soon after a purchase, the salesperson reassures customers that they made the right decision to buy. The salesperson also creates an opportunity to correct any problems.

Public Relations

A final element of the promotional mix is public relations (PR). Public relations includes publicity and supports advertising, personal selling, and sales promotion, usually by pursuing broader objectives. Companies use PR to try to improve their image with the public by distributing specific messages or ideas to target audiences. Cause-related promotional activities are often backed up by

CAREER KICKSTART

How to Negotiate in a Difficult Economy

Tips for Closing the Next Big Sale

If you enjoy competition, the thrill of victory, and rewards commensurate with your performance, a sales career might be for you. There is no better feeling than closing a deal—and the potential rewards that come with a close. However, with victory comes a fair share of rejection. Here are some tips for closing a sale:

- *Know your customer.* Review everything the customer has told you about the business and the challenges or issues that need to be resolved.

- *Listen.* Always be the best listener you can be. Listening allows you to develop an effective solution, and selling a solution helps close the deal.

- *Be patient.* Whether it is for a large, multimillion dollar deal or not, building solid relationships takes time, sometimes even years.

- *Create value.* Positioning your goods or services to meet customer needs is at the heart of selling. Part of the sales process involves identifying a customer's objectives, strategy, decision process, and timing. It also involves showing the customer how

your good or service will help overcome issues or challenges. Ask probing questions and obtain honest feedback.

- *Summarize the benefits.* Have the conviction and confidence that your good or service will help solve the customer's problem. Provide a final summary with the benefits of your good or service. This is also the time for your customer to bring up any objections.

- *Know how to ask for the business.* There comes a time when it simply makes sense to ask your customer for the sale. If your solution is well thought out, organized, and targeted, asking for the sale should be a time for both parties to agree to move forward.

If you don't succeed and the customer doesn't buy, remember that the last impression is almost as important as the first and be gracious and professional. Most important, always follow up.

Sources: Thomas Phelps, "Why Choose a Career in Sales," About.com, accessed February 16, 2014, http://salescareers.about.com; Geoffrey James "How to Close a Sale," Inc., accessed February 16, 2014, www.inc.com; Sloan Brothers, "5 Tips for Closing a Sales Deal," Startup Nation, accessed February 16, 2014, www.startupnation.com.

public relations and publicity campaigns. In addition, PR helps a firm to increase awareness of goods and services and then builds a positive image of those goods and services.

Public relations refers to an organization's communications and relationships with its various public audiences, such as customers, vendors, news media, employees, shareholders, the government, and the general public. Many of these communication efforts have marketing purposes. Public relations is an efficient, indirect communications channel for promoting products. It can publicize products and help create and maintain a positive image of the company.

The public relations department links a firm with the media. It provides the media with news releases and video and audio clips. It also holds news conferences to announce new products, the formation of strategic alliances, management changes, financial results, and other developments. Publications issued by the department include newsletters, brochures, and reports.

Publicity

The type of public relations that is tied most closely to promoting a company's products is **publicity**— the nonpersonal stimulation of demand for a good, service, place, idea, event, person, or organization by unpaid placement of information in print or broadcast media. Press releases and news coverage generate publicity. Ironically, criticism can sometimes also generate publicity. Spirit Airlines recently got a lot of negative publicity when it started charging fees for carry-on luggage— but the airline's bookings increased 50 percent. The increased bookings resulted from the airline having installed "pre-reclined" seats on its new planes. The new seats meant the airline could add more seating and lower its airfares. Even though "pre-reclined" is a poor name—the seats don't recline but stay permanently upright—some observers say that consumers looking for the cheapest airfares will continue to book on Spirit.[35]

Publicity also benefits not-for-profit organizations when they receive coverage of events such as the 17th Annual Head and Neck Cancer Fundraising Gala for McGill University's Department of Otolaryngology. The event was highly publicized because of the attendance and support of actor and producer Michael Douglas. Douglas has a vacation home in the resort area of Mont Tremblant. When he called his doctor in New York complaining about severe pain, his doctor referred him to his friend and colleague, Dr. Saul Frenkiel, at the Jewish General Hospital in Montreal. Frenkiel diagnosed Douglas as having a tumour. But other health professionals had examined Douglas for the same symptoms and had missed the tumour. After successful treatment in the United States, a grateful Douglas asked how he could show his gratitude. Someone suggested he could help with fundraising. That's how Douglas became the honouree at the event, which raised $2 million. It is an extraordinary amount for what is generally considered to be a little known area of cancer research and treatment. Besides the funds for research, the publicity has helped raise awareness in the general public about this cancer's risks and treatments.[36] When a for-profit firm teams up with a not-for-profit firm in a fundraising effort, the relationship usually generates good publicity for both organizations.

public relations an organization's communications and relationships with its various public audiences.

publicity the nonpersonal stimulation of demand for a good, service, place, idea, event, person, or organization by unpaid placement of information in print or broadcast media.

✔ ASSESSMENT CHECK

13.3.1 Why do retailers and manufacturers use sales promotions?

13.3.2 When does a firm use personal selling instead of nonpersonal selling?

13.3.3 How do public relations serve a marketing purpose?

PUSHING AND PULLING STRATEGIES

LO 13.4 Describe pushing and pulling promotional strategies.

Marketers can choose between two general promotional strategies: a pushing strategy or a pulling strategy. A **pushing strategy** uses personal selling to market an item to wholesalers and retailers in a company's distribution channels. Companies promote the product to members of the marketing channel, not to end users. Sales personnel explain to marketing intermediaries why they should carry particular merchandise. They usually support their promotion by offering special discounts and promotional materials. Some marketers also offer **cooperative advertising** allowances, by sharing with channel partners the cost of local advertising of their firm's product or product line. All these strategies are designed to motivate wholesalers and retailers to push the good or service to their own customers.

pushing strategy personal selling to market an item to wholesalers and retailers in a company's distribution channels.

cooperative advertising allowances that marketers provide to share with channel partners the cost of local advertising of their firm's product or product line.

pulling strategy promotion of a product by generating consumer demand for it, mainly through advertising and sales promotion appeals.

A **pulling strategy** tries to promote a product by generating consumer demand for it, mainly through advertising and sales promotion appeals. Potential buyers will then request that their suppliers—retailers or local distributors—carry the product, which pulls it through the distribution channel. Dove used this strategy when it launched its new Men 1 Care line of men's personal-care products during a recent Super Bowl. The 30-second commercial, with its tagline "Be comfortable in your own skin," generated a large online response. Many consumers searched such terms as "Super Bowl," "ad," and "men" to find retailers that stocked the products.[37]

Most marketing situations require combinations of pushing and pulling strategies, although the main emphasis can vary. Consumer products usually depend more heavily on pulling strategies; and B2B products usually favour pushing strategies.

ASSESSMENT CHECK

13.4.1 Give an example of a pushing strategy.

13.4.2 Give an example of a pulling strategy.

LO 13.5 Outline the different types of pricing objectives in the marketing mix.

PRICING OBJECTIVES IN THE MARKETING MIX

Products offer utility, or want-satisfying power. As consumers, we decide how much value we associate with each product. For example, after a major storm, we may value electricity, food, and water above everything else. If we commute a long distance or are planning a vacation, fuel may be of greater concern. All consumers have limited amounts of money and a variety of possible uses for it. The **price**—the exchange value of a good or service—becomes a major factor in consumer buying decisions.

price the exchange value of a good or service.

Businesspeople try to meet certain objectives through their pricing decisions. Pricing objectives vary from firm to firm, and many companies have multiple pricing objectives. Some firms try to improve profits by setting high prices; others set low prices to attract new business. As **Figure 13.5** illustrates, the four basic categories of pricing objectives are (1) profitability, (2) volume, (3) meeting competition, and (4) prestige.

Profitability
"We want profits to increase by 10 percent a year through 2020."

Volume
"By 2020, we plan to achieve a 28 percent share of the personal watercraft market."

Prestige
"The new perfume has an exquisite package, a beautiful label, and one of the highest retail prices."

Meeting Competition
"We will meet their prices and achieve profit and volume growth by offering better customer service."

Pricing Objectives

FIGURE 13.5 Pricing Objectives

profitability objectives common goals that are included in the strategic plans of most firms.

Profitability Objectives

Profitability objectives are the most common goals listed in most firms' strategic plans. Marketers know that profits are the revenue the company brings in, minus its expenses. Usually a big difference exists between revenue and profit. Most automakers try to produce at least one luxury vehicle. They can charge $50,000 or more for it instead of relying entirely on the sale of cars priced at $15,000 to $25,000.

Some firms maximize profits by reducing costs instead of increasing prices. Companies can maintain prices and increase profitability by operating more efficiently or by changing the product to make it less costly to produce. One strategy is to maintain a steady price while reducing the size or amount of the product in the package. Manufacturers of candy, coffee, and cereal often use this strategy.

Volume Objectives

volume objectives pricing decisions that are based on market share, the percentage of a market controlled by a certain company or product.

A second approach to pricing strategy—**volume objectives**—bases pricing decisions on market share, the percentage of a market controlled by a certain company or product. One firm may want to have a 25 percent market share in a certain product category; another firm may want to maintain or expand its market share for specific products. As a market becomes oversupplied—like the PC market—firms need to find ways to get consumers to upgrade or try new products. Setting a lower price can meet that objective, as long as the firm still makes a profit. Many PC makers—and retailers—have begun to offer their products at lower prices, especially at the start of the school year.[38]

Pricing to Meet Competition

A third set of pricing objectives tries to meet competitors' prices so that price becomes a nonissue. In many lines of business, firms set their own prices to match the prices set by established industry leaders. But companies cannot legally work together to agree on prices.

Price is a highly visible element of a firm's marketing mix. Some businesses may be tempted to use a product's price to gain an advantage over competitors. Sometimes the race to match competitors' prices results in a *price war,* which has happened in the airline and fast-food industries. Because some competitors can match a price cut, many marketers try to avoid price wars by using other strategies, such as adding value, improving quality, educating consumers, and building relationships.

Although price is a major element of the marketing mix, it is not the only one. Electronic readers such as the Kindle and the iPad are in a fierce pricing competition for digital books, as the "Solving an Ethical Controversy" feature explains.

Prestige Objectives

The final category of objectives takes in the effect of prices on prestige. **Prestige pricing** sets a relatively high price to develop and maintain an image of quality and exclusiveness. Marketers set such objectives because they recognize the role of price in communicating an overall image for the firm

prestige pricing setting a relatively high price to develop and maintain an image of quality and exclusiveness.

SOLVING AN **ETHICAL** CONTROVERSY

Free E-books: Good or Bad for Business?

When Amazon's Kindle electronic reader first became available, Amazon charged consumers $9.99 for each e-book they purchased. Publishers insisted that that price was too low to keep their business profitable. But Amazon actually gave some e-books away for free, including those of living authors who earn an income from their writing.

Amazon explained that the free e-books were a way to get consumers to read some unfamiliar writers. The hope was that customers would then buy other works by those writers. But some publishers delay publication of electronic editions for several months after the hardcover books have been issued, in the same way they delay publishing paperback editions.

Should e-books be given away for free?

PRO

1. Some publishers view free e-books as promotions to generate buzz about new or unknown authors.

2. Some publishers that give away e-books on a regular basis have noticed an increase in sales, which, as one executive says, is "all found money."

CON

1. "It is illogical to give books away for free," said David Young of Hachette Book Group, which publishes Stephenie Meyer's *Twilight* series.

2. The relatively low price of e-books may discourage consumers from buying actual books with suggested retail prices of $25 or more.

Summary

Both Amazon's Kindle and Barnes & Noble's Nook continue to offer free e-books. In addition, both offer the capability for customers to lend e-books to friends and family for 14 days by simply inputting a name and email address. Although some publishers might cringe at these practices, it is likely that the trend will continue.

Sources: Hillel Italie, "Amazon Escalates Standoff with Hachette," *USA Today*, accessed June 17, 2014, www.usatoday.com/story/money/business/2014/05/23/amazon-escalates-standoff-with-publisher-hachette/9507621; Alec Liu, "Kindle, Nook, Whatever: Here's How to Get Free E-Books," *Fox News*, accessed February 21, 2014, www.foxnews.com/tech/2011/01/27/kindle-nook-heres-free-e-books; Stan Schroeder, "The E-Book Price War Isn't Over Yet," *Mashable*, accessed February 21, 2014, http://mashable.com/2010/02/18/ipad-ebook-prices; Motoko Rich, "Apple's Prices for E-Books May Be Lower Than Expected," *New York Times*, accessed February 21, 2014, www.nytimes.com/2010/02/18/technology/18apple.html?_r=0; "With Kindle, the Best Sellers Don't Need to Sell," *Hindustantimes*, accessed February 21, 2014, www.hindustantimes.com/world-news/with-kindle-the-best-sellers-don-t-need-to-sell/article1-501400.aspx; "The Kindle Pricing Strategy & the Kindle Pricing History," *Ask Deb*, accessed February 21, 2014, www.askdeb.com.

Prestige pricing sets a relatively high price to develop and maintain an image of quality and exclusiveness. People expect to pay more for a Louis Vuitton bag, just like the rock star in this ad.

and its products. People expect to pay more for a Lexus, a Louis Vuitton purse, or a Caribbean vacation on St. Kitts or Nevis. Despite a recession, the British retailer Selfridges has seen a 60 percent increase in sales of "must-have" handbags by the luxury brand Mulberry. Mulberry even has waiting lists for some of its styles.[39]

Scarcity can also create prestige. Products that are limited in distribution or products that are so popular that they become scarce generate their own prestige. Businesses can then charge more for them. Apple iPhones and iPads always seem to be in short supply when new models are introduced. Eager buyers can be seen camping outside retail locations the day before, in hopes of being among the first to own the latest technological gadgets.

 **ASSESSMENT CHECK**

13.5.1 Define *price.*

13.5.2 What is a second approach to pricing strategy?

LO 13.6 Describe how firms set prices in the marketplace and the four alternative pricing strategies.

PRICING STRATEGIES

People from different areas of a company contribute their expertise to set the most strategic price for a product. Accountants, financial managers, and marketers provide relevant sales data, cost data, and customer feedback. Designers, engineers, and systems analysts also contribute important information.

Prices are determined in two basic ways: by applying the concepts of supply and demand discussed in Chapter 3 and by completing cost-oriented analyses. Economic theory assumes that a market price will be set at the point where the amount of a product desired at a given price equals the amount that suppliers will offer for sale at that price. In other words, the market price occurs at the point where the amount demanded and the amount supplied are equal. Online auctions, such as those on eBay, are a popular application of the demand-and-supply approach.

Price Determination in Practice

cost-based pricing calculating total costs per unit and then adding markups to cover overhead costs and generate profits.

Economic theory might lead to the best pricing decisions, but most businesses do not have all the information they need to make those decisions. Most businesses use **cost-based pricing** formulas. These formulas calculate total costs per unit and then add markups to cover overhead costs and generate profits.

Cost-based pricing totals all costs associated with offering a product in the market, including research and development, production, transportation, and marketing expenses. An added amount, the markup, then covers any unexpected or overlooked expenses and provides a profit.

The total is the selling price. The actual markup used varies depending on such factors as brand image and type of store. The typical markup for clothing is determined by doubling the wholesale price (the cost to the merchant) to arrive at the retail price for the item.

Breakeven Analysis

Businesses often do a **breakeven analysis** to calculate the minimum sales volume a product must generate at a certain price level to cover all costs. This method involves looking at various costs and total revenues. *Total cost* is the sum of total variable costs and total fixed costs. *Variable costs* change with the level of production, as labour and raw materials do. *Fixed costs* such as insurance premiums and utility rates charged by water, natural gas, and electric power suppliers remain stable regardless of the production level. *Total revenue* is calculated by multiplying price by the number of units sold.

breakeven analysis the pricing-related technique used to calculate the minimum sales volume a product must generate at a certain price level to cover all costs.

Finding the Breakeven Point

The *breakeven point* is the level of sales that will generate enough revenue to cover all of the company's fixed and variable costs. It is the point where total revenue just equals total costs. Sales beyond the breakeven point will generate profits; sales volume below the breakeven point will result in losses. This is illustrated in **Figure 13.6**.

The following formulas give the breakeven point in units and dollars:

$$\text{Breakeven Point (in units)} = \frac{\text{Total fixed costs}}{\text{Contribution to fixed costs per unit}}$$

$$\text{Breakeven Point (in dollars)} = \frac{\text{Total fixed costs}}{1 - \text{Variable cost per unit}/\text{Price}}$$

As an example, a product sells for $20. It has a variable cost of $14 per unit and produces a $6 per-unit contribution to fixed costs. If the firm has total fixed costs of $42,000, then it must sell 7,000 units to break even on the product. The calculation of the breakeven point in units and dollars is as follows:

$$\text{Breakeven Point (in units)} = \frac{\$42,000}{\$20 - \$14} = \frac{\$42,000}{\$6} = 7,000 \text{ units}$$

$$\text{Breakeven Point (in dollars)} = \frac{\$42,000}{1 - \$14/\$20} = \frac{\$42,000}{1 - 0.7} = \frac{\$42,000}{0.3} = \$140,000$$

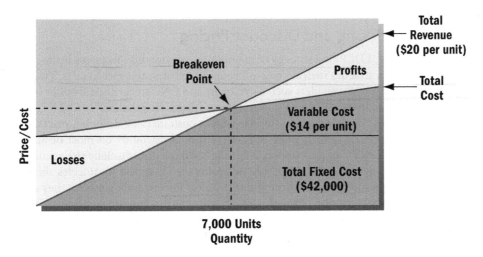

FIGURE **13.6** Breakeven Analysis

Marketers use breakeven analysis to calculate the profits or losses that would result from several different proposed prices. Because different prices produce different breakeven points, marketers can compare their calculations of required sales to break even with the sales estimates from marketing research studies. This comparison can identify the best price—the price that would attract enough customers to exceed the breakeven point and earn profits for the firm.

Most firms want to know whether enough customers will buy the number of units the firm needs to sell at a particular price to break even. They develop estimates of consumer demand through surveys of likely customers, interviews with retailers that would sell the product, and reviewing prices charged by competitors. The breakeven points for several possible prices are then calculated and compared with sales estimates for each price. This practice is referred to as *modified breakeven analysis*.

Alternative Pricing Strategies

The strategy a company uses to set its prices should grow out of the firm's overall marketing strategy. In general, firms can choose from four alternative pricing strategies: skimming, penetration, discount or everyday low pricing, and competitive pricing.

Skimming Pricing

skimming pricing a strategy that sets an intentionally high price relative to the prices of competing products.

A **skimming pricing** strategy sets an intentionally high price relative to the prices of competing products. The term comes from the expression "skimming the cream." This pricing strategy often works when introducing a distinctive good or service that has little or no competition, but it can also be used at other stages of the product life cycle. A skimming strategy can help marketers set a price that separates a firm's high-end product from those of competitors. It can also help a firm recover its product development costs before competitors enter the field. This strategy is often used with prescription drugs.

Penetration Pricing

penetration pricing a strategy that sets a low price as a major marketing tactic.

A **penetration pricing** strategy sets a low price as a major marketing tactic. Businesses may price new products much lower than competing products when they enter new industries that have dozens of competing brands. Once the new product achieves some market success, through purchases encouraged by its low price, marketers may increase the price to the level of competing products. But stiff competition can prevent the price increase.

Everyday Low Pricing and Discount Pricing

everyday low pricing (EDLP) a strategy of maintaining continuous low prices instead of using short-term price-cutting tactics such as cents-off coupons, rebates, and special sales.

Everyday low pricing (EDLP) is a strategy of maintaining continuous low prices instead of using short-term price-cutting tactics such as cents-off coupons, rebates, and special sales. This strategy has been used successfully by retailers such as Walmart and GNC to consistently offer low prices to consumers; manufacturers also use EDLP to set stable prices for retailers.

Businesses that use *discount pricing* hope to attract customers by dropping prices for a set period of time. Automakers usually offer consumers special discounts on most or all of their vehicles during the holiday shopping season. After the holidays, prices usually rise again. Experts warn that discounting must be done carefully, or profits can disappear. Businesses should offer discounts only for a specified period of time and with a clear understanding of what they are trying to accomplish by using the strategy. They should advertise the discount, so customers know it is a special deal. When the time period is over, the discount should be over too.

Selling a product that is well understood by consumers and whose price must fall within a competitive range established by the market is a major challenge for businesses. This strategy is discussed in the "Hit & Miss" feature.

© Randy Duchaine/Alamy Stock Photo

Stores such as Walmart use an everyday low pricing strategy of maintaining continuous low prices instead of using short-term price-cutting tactics such as cents-off coupons, rebates, and special sales.

(HIT) & MISS

A Bis Gourmet—Quality Fast Food At Competitive Prices

A bis, the Latin term for "encore or to repeat a pleasurable experience," suggests the company philosophy that customers will come back for more after tasting the difference quality can make to something as simple as a sandwich.

A Bis Gourmet hand produce and deliver over 20,000 fresh sandwich products, parfait cups, fresh leaf and pasta salads each and every day. The reason for their success is attention to quality, consistency, and customer service. From locations in Montreal, Ottawa, and Toronto, dedicated staff prepare preservative free, high-quality food, wrapped in eco-friendly individual serving containers for sale to customers on-the-go through retail convenience stores.

The market price for these sorts of food items is competitive and A Bis Gourmet must be careful to control costs while delivering the superior quality products and taste it promises its retail distributors. This competitive differentiation allows A Bis Gourmet to confidently promote their brand as a superior choice for retail distributors to offer their customers—and keep them coming back for more too.

Questions for Critical Thinking

1. How much "extra" do think customers would be willing to pay for higher quality sandwiches at say, a convenience store located on the ground floor of a downtown office building?

2. How would you suggest A Bis Gourmet develop new customized menu items in conjunction with retailers that would sell them exclusively?

Sources: A Bis Gourmet, accessed April 20, 2015, www.abisgourmetqc.ca.

Competitive Pricing

Many organizations rely heavily on price as a competitive tactic, but even more organizations use **competitive pricing** strategies. These firms try to reduce the emphasis on price competition by matching other firms' prices and by focusing their own marketing efforts on the product, distribution,

competitive pricing a strategy that tries to reduce the emphasis on price competition by matching other firms' prices and by focusing their own marketing efforts on the product, distribution, and promotional elements of the marketing mix.

 **ASSESSMENT CHECK**

13.6.1 What is a cost-based pricing formula?

13.6.2 Why do companies implement competitive pricing strategies?

LO 13.7 Discuss consumer perceptions of price.

and promotional elements of the marketing mix. In industries with relatively similar products, competitors must match each other's price reductions to maintain market share and remain competitive. By pricing their products to match the prices of competing offerings, marketers largely remove the price variable from their marketing strategies.

CONSUMER PERCEPTIONS OF PRICES

How do you perceive, or view, prices for certain products? Marketers need to consider how customers perceive prices. If large numbers of potential buyers consider a price to be too high or too low, businesses must correct the situation. When setting prices, marketers consider price–quality relationships and the use of odd pricing.

Price–Quality Relationships

Research shows that a consumer's perception of product quality is closely related to an item's price. Most marketers believe that this perceived price–quality relationship remains steady over a relatively wide range of prices, although extremely high or low prices have less credibility. The price–quality relationship can critically affect a firm's pricing strategy.

Many consumers associate prestige, quality, and high price as being related. That is, they believe that paying a high price for an item such as an Infiniti car or a Chanel bag will convey prestige and ensure quality. Others believe that eating at an expensive restaurant means the food will be better than food served at a modestly priced restaurant. The opposite is also true. Many consumers may view an extremely low price as an indication that corners have been cut and quality will be poor. Interestingly, a recent study noted that California wines made from organically grown grapes are less expensive than those made from nonorganic grapes. But this price difference actually seemed to be a disadvantage for the organic wines: labelling a wine as "made from organically grown grapes" drove the price down, but the same wine without the certification notice sold for more. Many factors may contribute to this situation. In the 1970s and 1980s, when organic wines were first produced, the reds gained a bad reputation: many of them quickly turned to vinegar because they were made without preservatives. Some consumers still remember this. Also, "green" consumers are aware of the benefits of organically grown fruits and vegetables, but the benefits of organically grown wines are not so well known. Growers need to communicate to consumers that, in this case at least, price and quality don't necessarily go together.[40]

odd pricing a pricing method that uses uneven amounts to make prices appear to be less than they really are.

Odd Pricing

Have you ever wondered why retailers set prices like $1.99 instead of $2 or $9.95 instead of $10? **Odd pricing** is a pricing method that uses uneven amounts to make prices appear to be less than they really are. Before the age of cash registers and sales taxes, retailers reportedly followed this practice to force clerks to make correct change as part of their cash control efforts. But odd pricing is commonly used today because many retailers believe that consumers prefer uneven amounts or amounts that sound less than they really are. Some retailers also use this method to identify items that have been marked down. The odd price lets people know the item is on sale.

 **ASSESSMENT CHECK**

13.7.1 How does the price–quality relationship affect a firm's pricing strategy?

13.7.2 Why is odd pricing used?

WHAT'S AHEAD

The chapters in Part 4 have explained the main principles of marketing management. These chapters also described how each principle fits a firm's overall business strategy. Part 5 will help you understand how companies manage the technology and information that businesses can use to create value for their customers and improve their competitiveness in the marketplace.

RETURN TO INSIDE BUSINESS

WorkSafeBC: Promoting Safety to Young Workers

For the first two years, Raise Your Hand was expressed simply by using photos of raised hands. Each hand was connected to a story contributed by a young worker. As more and more young workers participated, the website changed daily. The campaign grew to further express the feel of a grassroots movement. It then built on the stories, to give something back to young workers in the form of an empowering message about how to exercise their workplace rights.

Postings to YouTube and other social media sites have exceeded expectations, as measured by the number and quality of stories, event and online interactions, and click-through rates.

QUESTIONS FOR CRITICAL THINKING

1. How would you continue the success of this online program?

2. Describe the concept for a new online promotional campaign.

SUMMARY OF LEARNING OBJECTIVES

LO 13.1 Discuss how integrated marketing communications relates to a firm's overall promotional strategy.

When a firm practises integrated marketing communications, it coordinates promotional activities to produce a unified, customer-focused message. IMC identifies consumer needs and shows how a company's products meet those needs. Marketers select the promotional media that work best to target and reach customers. The programs rely on teamwork and careful promotional planning to coordinate IMC strategies.

A company's promotional mix combines personal selling and nonpersonal selling. Nonpersonal selling includes advertising, sales promotion, and public relations. By selecting the most suitable combination of promotional mix elements, marketers try to achieve the firm's five major promotional objectives: providing information, differentiating a product, increasing demand, stabilizing sales, and highlighting the product's value.

ASSESSMENT CHECK ANSWERS

13.1.1 What is the objective of an integrated marketing communications program? An IMC strategy focuses on customer needs to create a unified promotional message about a firm's goods or services.

13.1.2 Why do firms pursue multiple promotional objectives at the same time? Firms pursue multiple promotional objectives because they may need to convey different messages to different audiences.

13.1.3 What are product placement and guerrilla marketing? Product placement involves paying a fee to have a product featured in certain media. Guerrilla marketing refers to innovative, low-cost marketing efforts designed to get consumers' attention in unusual ways.

LO 13.2 Summarize the different types of advertising.

Advertising is the most visible form of nonpersonal promotion. Advertising is designed to inform, persuade, or remind. Product advertising promotes a good or service, while institutional advertising promotes a concept, idea, organization, or philosophy. Television, newspapers, and magazines are the largest advertising media categories. Other advertising media include direct mail, radio, and outdoor advertising. Interactive advertising directly involves the consumer, who controls the flow of information.

ASSESSMENT CHECK ANSWERS

13.2.1 What are the two basic types of advertising? Into what three categories do they fall? The two basic types are product and institutional. They fall into the categories of informative, persuasive, and reminder-oriented advertising.

13.2.2 What is the leading advertising medium in North America? According to the most recent statistics listed in Figure 13.2, television is the leading advertising medium in North America.

13.2.3 In what two major ways do firms benefit from sponsorship? Firms benefit from sponsorship in two ways: they gain exposure to the event's audience, and they gain from their association with the activity's positive image.

LO 13.3 Outline sales promotion.

Sales promotion accounts for more expenses than advertising. Consumer-oriented sales promotions include coupons, games, rebates, samples, premiums, contests, sweepstakes, and promotional products. This type of sales promotion offers consumers an extra incentive to buy a product. Point-of-purchase advertising displays and trade shows are sales promotions directed to the trade markets. Personal selling involves face-to-face interactions between the seller and buyers. The primary sales tasks are order processing, creative selling, and missionary selling. Public relations is nonpaid promotion that seeks to enhance a company's public image.

ASSESSMENT CHECK ANSWERS

13.3.1 Why do retailers and manufacturers use sales promotions? Retailers and manufacturers use sales promotions to offer consumers extra incentives to buy their products

13.3.2 When does a firm use personal selling instead of nonpersonal selling? Personal selling is generally used when there are few customers who are geographically concentrated, the product is technically complex or requires special handling, the price is high, or the product moves through direct distribution channels.

13.3.3 How do public relations serve a marketing purpose? Public relations are an efficient, indirect communications channel for promoting products. It can publicize products and help create and maintain a positive image of the company.

LO 13.4 Describe pushing and pulling promotional strategies.

A pushing strategy relies on personal selling to market a product to wholesalers and retailers in the company's distribution channels. A pulling strategy promotes the product by generating consumer demand for it, through advertising and sales promotion.

ASSESSMENT CHECK ANSWERS

13.4.1 Give an example of a pushing strategy. A pushing strategy is used by drug manufacturers, who used to market only to physicians and hospitals. Today, drug manufacturers also use a pulling strategy by marketing directly to patients through advertising, which encourages patients to ask their doctors about the medications.

13.4.2 Give an example of a pulling strategy. Pulling strategies are used by retailers and by manufacturers of consumer goods such as cosmetics, automobiles, and clothing.

LO 13.5 Outline the different types of pricing objectives in the marketing mix.

Pricing objectives can be classified as profitability, volume, meeting competition, and prestige. Profitability objectives are the most common goals. Volume objectives base pricing decisions on market share. Meeting competitors' prices makes price a nonissue in competition. Prestige pricing sets a high price to develop and maintain an image of quality or exclusiveness.

ASSESSMENT CHECK ANSWERS

13.5.1 Define *price*. Price is the exchange value of a good or service.

13.5.2 What is a second approach to pricing strategy? A second approach to pricing strategy is volume objectives. This pricing strategy bases pricing decisions on market share.

LO 13.6 Describe how firms set prices in the marketplace and the four alternative pricing strategies.

Economic theory determines prices by using the law of demand and supply. But most firms use cost-based pricing, which adds a markup after totalling all costs. Firms usually do a breakeven analysis to calculate the minimum sales volume a product must generate at a certain price to cover all costs. The four alternative pricing strategies are skimming, penetration, everyday low pricing and discounting, and competitive pricing. A skimming strategy sets a high price initially to recover costs and then lowers the price. A penetration strategy sets a lower price and then raises it later. Everyday low pricing and discounting offer a lower price for a period of time. Competitive pricing matches other firms' prices and highlights a product's nonprice benefits.

ASSESSMENT CHECK ANSWERS

13.6.1 What is a cost-based pricing formula? A cost-based pricing formula calculates the total costs per unit and then adds markups to cover overhead costs and generate profits.

13.6.2 Why do companies implement competitive pricing strategies? Companies use competitive pricing strategies to reduce the emphasis on price competition by matching other firms' prices and by focusing their own marketing efforts on the product, distribution, and promotional elements of the marketing mix.

LO 13.7 Discuss consumer perceptions of price.

When setting prices, marketers must consider how consumers perceive the price–quality relationship of their products. Consumers may be willing to pay a higher price if they perceive a product to be of superior quality. Marketers often use odd pricing to convey a message to consumers.

✔ **ASSESSMENT CHECK ANSWERS**

13.7.1 How does the price–quality relationship affect a firm's pricing strategy? Consumers believe that the price of an item reflects its quality, except in extreme cases. A firm must try to set its prices accordingly.

13.7.2 Why is odd pricing used? Retailers believe that consumers prefer prices that have uneven amounts or amounts that sound like less than they really are. Odd pricing may also be used to indicate a sale item.

BUSINESS TERMS YOU NEED TO KNOW

advertising 358

breakeven analysis 375

cause advertising 359

competitive pricing 377

cooperative advertising 371

cost-based pricing 374

creative selling 368

everyday low pricing (EDLP) 376

guerrilla marketing 357

infomercials 363

institutional advertising 358

integrated marketing communications (IMC) 354

missionary selling 368

nonpersonal selling 355

odd pricing 378

order processing 368

penetration pricing 376

personal selling 355

point-of-purchase (POP) advertising 366

positioning 356

prestige pricing 373

price 372

product advertising 358

product placement 357

profitability objectives 372

promotion 354

promotional mix 355

publicity 371

public relations 371

pulling strategy 372

pushing strategy 371

sales promotion 364

skimming pricing 376

specialty advertising 366

sponsorship 363

telemarketing 368

trade promotion 366

volume objectives 372

REVIEW QUESTIONS

1. What is the purpose of integrated marketing communications?

2. What are the five major objectives of a promotional strategy?

3. Identify and define each of the three categories of advertising based on their purpose. Which of the three categories of advertising would marketers likely use for the following products?

   a. Deodorant

   b. An electronic reader

   c. Organic produce

   d. Healthcare insurance

4. What are the benefits of online and interactive advertising? What might be some drawbacks?

5. For each of the following, describe potential benefits and drawbacks of a sponsorship relationship:

   a. Royal Bank of Canada and professional golfer Jason Day

   b. Bell Canada and Montreal International Jazz Festival

6. If you were a marketer for Rolex, what kind of sales promotion might you use for high-end watches?

7. In what situations are firms likely to emphasize personal selling?

8. Describe the seven-step sales process.

9. Define the four basic categories of pricing objectives.

10. What are the four alternative pricing strategies used by marketers? Give an example of the circumstances under which each might be selected.

PROJECTS AND TEAMWORK APPLICATIONS

1. Choose a product that you purchased recently. Identify the various media that were used to promote the product and analyze the promotional mix. Do you agree with the company's marketing strategy, or would you suggest changes to the promotional mix? Why? Create your own print ad for the product you chose, using any business strategies or knowledge you have learned in this course so far.

2. Evaluate the price of the product you selected in the exercise above. What pricing strategy is the manufacturer using? Do you think the price is fair? Why or why not? Choose a different strategy; develop a new price for the product based on the new strategy. Ask your classmates whether they would purchase the product at the new price. Why or why not?

3. Some schools receive financial benefits by allowing companies to promote their goods and services to students. Others have decided against this practice, and some schools ban this type of promotion. Find some examples of corporate sponsors in public elementary and high schools and on college and university campuses. With your class, discuss the pros and cons of promotion in public schools and on college and university campuses. In your view, is there a difference between a public school and a college or university campus? Why or why not?

4. On your own or with a classmate, research a recent issue that has caused a business, a not-for-profit organization, or a government agency to suffer from bad publicity. Evaluate the situation, outlining the steps the organization might take to build better public relations.

5. You are the marketing manager at a company that is introducing a new line of video games. How would you set the prices for the new products?

WEB ASSIGNMENTS

1. **Top advertisers.** *Advertising Age* compiles data annually on the top national advertisers. Visit the website listed below to access the most recent year. Answer the following questions:

   a. Who were the top 10 advertisers that year?

   b. How much did they spend on advertising?

   c. What was the most advertised brand that year?
   http://adage.com/datacenter/#advertising_spending

2. **Online coupon fraud.** Go to the websites listed to learn about online coupon fraud. Prepare a brief report. Make sure to answer the following questions: How big a problem is online coupon fraud? What changes have marketers made to try to reduce online coupon fraud?
   www.newser.com/story/35962/hackers-spread-coupon-scam.html

   http://online.wsj.com/article/SB124641121217977575.html

   http://multichannelmerchant.com/retail/news/0308-curtailing-online-coupon-fraud

3. **Yield management.** Assume you want to fly from St. John's, Newfoundland and Labrador, to Victoria, British Columbia. Visit some travel sites. Search for fares. Change such factors as advance purchase, day of departure, time of departure, and so on. What did this exercise teach you about yield management?
   www.expedia.ca
   www.ca.kayak.com
   www.travelocity.ca

Note: Internet Web addresses change frequently. If you don't find the exact sites listed, you may need to access the organization's home page and search from there or use a search engine such as Bing or Google.

PART 4 CASE STUDY Beau's All Natural Brewing Company

Building Brand Awareness

Strategic planning today is built upon historical industry knowledge—primarily about competitors and customers that have come before your company. Although many things change over time, industry knowledge is cumulative and often reflects trends in behaviours that may have started long ago. Having researched and written over 100 business plans in his career with the Ontario government before starting up Beau's, Steve Beauchesne was familiar with the importance of industry research. He learned to follow proven strategies in some cases but in others, he found "there were myths about what had to be done, or else."

The first Canadian craft beer venture is generally credited to John Mitchell and Frank Appleton in British Columbia. In the early 1980s, strict provincial control of beer sales prevented a brewery owner from owning a licensed establishment serving beer as well. As a result, only large producers like Molson, Labatt, Carling, and O'Keefe provided product to the beer market. After successfully lobbying politicians to change the laws, Mitchell and Appleton were able to do both.

Mitchell was originally from Britain and was familiar with the brewpub model where local pubs produced and sold their products along with quality food. Appleton knew about craft brewing and taught Mitchell the techniques. Shortly after developing their signature "Bay Ale," the two turned their Troller Pub in Horseshoe Bay, BC in West Vancouver into Canada's first brewpub. They learned what customers liked directly from customer feedback. If it sold well and customers asked for more, they brewed more. In many ways, this empirical research model still drives how craft brewers research customer preferences and plan growth. They have learned that the best way to know what to brew is from customer tasting and feedback. This demands a distribution network that provides a presence in the bars, restaurants and other venues and servers familiar with the competing brands. Distribution means availability and sales will follow.

Generally, each craft brewer would boost its bestselling and banner beer brand and attempt to grow sales and customers through development of other blends. Steve and Tim had developed various brews as hobbyists and had hit on several recipes that they felt were outstanding. Informal testing among friends and family convinced them that these brews would be well received if they could gear up production and provide a distribution network where customers could buy.

Craft beer marketing generally focuses on a unique recipe, freshness of the brew, use of organic ingredients, and the absence of preservatives. There is also a cultural difference in the way the business and its products are offered to customers. The breweries, which are also primary points of sale to customers, are generally presented as fun places to tour, see how the beer is made, and shop. The brewery tour also allows the firm to promote their pride in the production process and develop closer relationships with customers and the communities served.

The primary challenge facing every new business is generating brand recognition by the target market of potential customers. Craft beer customers don't order brands they have never heard of or know nothing about. They are different from regular "big brewery" customers in several ways. For instance, determinants that influence how customers learn about new beers entering the marketplace are different. Whereas big brewery customers are typically made aware of new brands through large-scale advertising campaigns in multiple media platforms, craft beer customers are generally introduced to new brands and breweries by their local bar or restaurant server. So the first order of business Steve and Tim faced, and continue to face as the firm expands into new markets throughout Ontario, Quebec, and the United States, is to establish brand recognition. Once the potential customer understands what the Beau's brand means and is presented with the opportunity to taste the difference themselves—as Steve says, "We've won them over."

Learning how to generate awareness, promote trial tasting, and building brand loyalty with customers is an ongoing effort as conditions are often different in different markets, and craft beer customers don't all behave in the same way. Beau's marketing team has learned to grow sales by trying different low budget strategies and has avoided the industry myth that demands heavy advertising spending to succeed. Instead, great success has come from small promotional events, which often can generate publicity in the local media. For example, Oktoberfest is a popular annual event at Beau's brewery in Vankleek Hill that recently brought together 19,000 visitors and raised over $95,000 for community charities.

This way of thinking and learning from others in the craft beer industry seems to be working as sales recently surpassed 3.5 million litres. With the Ontario government seemingly more open to relaxing strict retail-sales control of beer, Beau's is exploring new ways to generate growth.

Questions for Critical Thinking

1. What other marketing ideas would you suggest Beau's try?

2. How can Beau's communicate with customers who are too far away to actually have direct contact with the Beau's brewery staff?

3. What does the Beau's logo and labels communicate about the company, in your mind?

4 LAUNCHING YOUR . . .

MARKETING CAREER

In Part 4, "Marketing Management," you learned about the goals and functions of marketing. The three chapters in this part emphasized the central role of customer satisfaction in defining value and developing a marketing strategy in traditional and nontraditional marketing settings. You learned about the role of marketing research and the need for relationship marketing in today's competitive environment. You discovered how new products are developed and how they change through the four stages of the product life cycle, from introduction through growth and maturity to decline. You also learned about the role of different channels in creating effective distribution strategies. Finally, you saw the impact of integrated marketing communications on the firm's promotional strategy, the role of advertising, and how pricing affects consumer behaviour. You may have read about some marketing tasks and functions that sounded especially interesting. Here are a few ideas about careers in marketing.

The first thing to remember is that marketing is more than personal selling and advertising. For example, are you curious about why people behave the way they do? Are you good at spotting trends? Marketing research analysts look for answers to a wide range of questions about business competition, customer preferences, market trends, and past and future sales. They often design and conduct their own consumer surveys, using the telephone, mail, the Internet, or personal interviews and focus groups. They collect the data and analyze it. Their recommendations become input for managerial decisions, such as whether to introduce new products, redesign current products, enter new markets, or discontinue products or markets where profitability is low. Marketing researchers may be included in a new-product development team, where they work directly with scientists, production and manufacturing personnel, and finance employees. Marketing researchers are often asked to help clients put their recommendations in place. With today's highly competitive economy, jobs in this area are expected to grow.

Another career path in marketing is sales. Do you work well with others? Are you good at reading other people's feelings? Are you a self-starter? If so, being a sales representative might be for you. Selling jobs exist in every industry. Many of these jobs use a combination of salary and performance-based commissions, so they can pay very well. Sales jobs are also often a first step on the ladder to upper-management positions. Sales representatives work for wholesalers and manufacturing companies (and even for publishers such as the one that produces this book). They sell automobiles, computer systems and technology, pharmaceuticals, advertising, insurance, real estate, commodities and financial services, and all kinds of consumer goods and services.

If you're interested in mass communications, you should know that print and online magazines, newspapers, and broadcast companies generate most of their revenue from advertising. Sales representatives who sell space and time slots in the media contribute to the success of these firms. If you like to travel, consider that many sales jobs involve travel.

Advertising, marketing management, and public relations are other categories of marketing. In large companies, marketing managers, product managers, promotion managers, and public relations managers often work long hours under pressure; they may travel frequently or transfer between jobs at headquarters and positions in regional offices. Their responsibilities include directing promotional programs, supervising advertising campaigns and budgets, and conducting communications such as press releases with the firm's public audiences. Thousands of new positions are expected to open up in the next several years; the field is expected to grow 14 percent over the next decade. Growth of the Internet and new media has increased demand for advertising and public relations specialists.

Advertising and public relations firms employ thousands of people. Most advertising firms develop specialties; many of the largest advertising firms work internationally. Online advertising is one area where new jobs will be opening in the future, especially as more and more client firms expand their online sales operations.

CAREER ASSESSMENT EXERCISES IN MARKETING

1. Select a field that interests you. Use the Internet to research the types of sales positions available in that field. Locate a few entry-level job openings and see what career steps that position can lead to. (You might want to start with a popular job-posting site such as Monster.ca.) Note the job requirements, the starting salary, and the form of compensation—straight salary or salary plus commission? Write a one-page summary of your findings.

2. Use the Internet to identify and research two or three of the leading advertising agencies in Canada, such as Cossette Communications or Wasserman & Partners. What are some of their recent ad campaigns? Who are their best-known clients? Where do the agencies have offices? What job openings do they currently list, and what qualifications do they ask for? Write a brief report comparing the agencies you selected, decide which agency you would prefer to work for, and give your reasons.

3. Test your research skills. Choose an ordinary product, such as toothpaste or soft drinks. Design a survey to find out why people chose the brand they most recently purchased. For instance, suppose you wanted to find out how people choose their shampoo. List as many decision criteria as you can think of, such as availability, scent, price, packaging, benefits from use (conditioning, dandruff-reducing, and so on), brand name, and ad campaign. Ask eight to 10 friends to rank these decision factors, and note some simple demographics about your research subjects such as their age, gender, and occupation. Chart your results. What did you learn about how your friends made their purchase decision? Did any of your findings surprise you? How could you have improved the survey?

14 | USING TECHNOLOGY TO MANAGE INFORMATION

LEARNING OBJECTIVES

LO 14.1 Distinguish between data and information, and discuss the role of information systems in business.

LO 14.2 Describe the components and types of information systems.

LO 14.3 Outline how computer hardware and software are used to manage information.

LO 14.4 Describe networking and telecommunications technology and the types of computer networks.

LO 14.5 Outline the security and ethical issues affecting information systems.

LO 14.6 Explain how companies plan for, and recover from, information systems disasters.

LO 14.7 Review the trends in information systems.

INSIDE BUSINESS

Stock-Trak: Learning about the Stock Market through Simulation

What's the best way to learn about the stock market—a complicated business environment that involves rapidly changing information and special terms that only those involved seem to understand? More importantly, how can someone develop good trading skills, gain a sense of how stocks behave in real time, and experience what they would do in a situation—without actually risking any money?

According to Tom Reti and Mark Brookshire, executives at Stock-Trak Global Portfolio Simulations, there is no better way to learn about investment trading than real-life experience. To get that experience without risking any money, Stock-Trak provides a web-based stock market simulation and training products package. Stock-Trak has sold its products to the academic and financial services markets and to the general public.

Wall Street Survivor (www.wallstreetsurvivor.com) is part of Stock-Trak's consumer division; it targets online investing, trading, and game enthusiasts with an investment-oriented simulation and contest website. Anyone interested in learning and developing their trading skills can sign up and experience online trading without the risk of losing real money. Real-time data are provided so that learners can see the immediate results of their decisions. Learners can also use a variety of learning materials and supplements, such as discussion forums with other learners and tutorials to improve their trading skills. Contest prizes make the experience more exciting and competitive while avoiding the risk of losing money. Stock-Trak's co-branding with newspapers and other media has proven very successful, as shown by the website www.marketwatch.com/game/. If you've ever seen a stock market investment contest, chances are good that Stock-Trak provided the simulation and learning environment.

In the academic market, more than 60,000 students at colleges and universities in 30 countries have used the simulation to learn about trading stocks, options, futures, bonds, and mutual funds. Dedicated websites such as http://nipissing.stocktrak.com/home.aspx at Ontario's Nipissing University are typical of websites Stock-Trak has set up for other universities, such as Montreal's McGill University, the University of Toronto, New York University, Yale University, and Columbia University.

The third market for Stock-Trak is the growing financial services industry that uses simulation training for employees before putting them to work trading with real client's money. Stock-Trak has been providing training to employees of Scottrade Inc. since 2008. Under the terms of their agreement, Stock-Trak manages a web-based employee education and training simulator used by employees of Scottrade's 375 branch offices. Each quarter, new hires are given simulated cash to manage. They are tested for their knowledge of the stock and option markets and their ability to successfully use the various tools and techniques learned through Scottrade's training program.

Stock-Trak has three office locations in Montreal, Quebec; Mississauga, Ontario; and Atlanta, Georgia.[1]

CHAPTER 14 OVERVIEW

This chapter explores how businesses manage information as a resource and how they use technology to help in this task. Today, nearly all business functions—from human resources to production to supply chain management—rely on information systems. The chapter begins by looking at the differences between information and data and then defines an information system. The components of information systems are presented, and two major types of information systems are described. The chapter also discusses databases, which are important to all organizations and are the heart of all information systems. Then the chapter looks at the computer hardware and software that drive information systems. Today, specialized networks make information access and information transmission work smoothly; so the chapter examines different types of telecommunications and computer networks to see how businesses are using them for competitive advantage. The chapter then turns to a discussion of the ethical and security issues affecting information systems, followed by a description of how organizations plan for, and recover from, information system disasters. A review of the current trends in information systems concludes the chapter.

LO 14.1 Distinguish between data and information, and discuss the role of information systems in business.

DATA, INFORMATION, AND INFORMATION SYSTEMS

Every day, businesspeople ask themselves questions such as the following:

- How well is our product selling in Calgary compared to Halifax? Have sales among consumers aged 25 to 45 increased or decreased in the past year?

- How will rising energy prices affect production and distribution costs?

- If employees can access the benefits system through our network, will our benefit costs increase or decrease?

- How can we communicate more efficiently and effectively with our workforce that is spread out across the country?

data raw facts and figures that may or may not be meaningful to a business decision.

information knowledge gained from processing data.

An effective information system can help answer these and many other questions. **Data** consist of raw facts and figures that may or may not be relevant, or meaningful, to a business decision. **Information** is knowledge gained from processing those facts and figures. For example, businesspeople need to gather demographics, or population data, about a target market or the specifications of a certain product. But the data are useless unless they are transformed into relevant information that can be used to make a competitive decision. For example, data might be the sizes of various demographic groups. Information drawn from those data could be how many of those individuals are potential customers for a firm's products. Technology has advanced so quickly that all businesses—large or small, in large cities or in remote areas, now have access to data and information that can make them competitive in a global arena.

information system an organized method for collecting, storing, and communicating past, present, and projected information on internal operations and external intelligence.

chief information officer (CIO) the executive responsible for managing a firm's information systems and related computer technologies.

An **information system** is an organized method for collecting, storing, and communicating past, present, and projected information on internal operations and external intelligence. Most information systems today use computer and telecommunications technology. A large organization typically assigns responsibility for managing its information systems and related operations to an executive called the **chief information officer (CIO)**. The CIO often reports directly to the firm's chief executive officer (CEO). An effective CIO can understand and control technology so that the company can use one seamless operation to communicate both internally and externally. But small companies rely just as much on information systems as do large ones, even if they do not assign a full-time manager to this area.

Today's CIO, closely connected to the company's overall business strategies and marketing efforts, is concerned with how cloud-delivered business services of software and data are transmitted to enterprises, with a focus on sales, customer interfaces, and "consumerization," the reorientation of goods and service designs around the individual end user. Yesterday's CIO, focused on installation and design of software, has become increasingly aware of the need for data security, systems availability, and responsiveness. Their expertise makes CIOs and former CIOs good candidates for corporate boards.[2]

Information systems can be designed to assist many business functions and departments—from marketing and manufacturing to finance and accounting. They can manage a huge flood of information by organizing data in a logical and accessible manner. A company can use the system to monitor all areas of its operations and business strategy and to identify problems and opportunities. Information systems gather data from inside and outside the organization; they then process the data to produce information that is meaningful to all aspects of the organization. The processing steps can include storing data for later use, classifying and analyzing it, and retrieving it easily when needed.

Many companies—and nations—combine high-tech and low-tech solutions to manage the flow of information. Email, wireless communications, and videoconferencing are increasingly common. But they haven't totally replaced paper memos, phone conversations, and face-to-face meetings. Information can make the difference between staying in business and going bankrupt. The right information can help a firm keep up to date with changing consumer demands, competitors' activities, and government regulations. A firm can then apply this information to fine-tune existing products, develop new products, and maintain effective marketing.

✔ **ASSESSMENT CHECK**

14.1.1 Distinguish between data and information.

14.1.2 What is an information system?

COMPONENTS AND TYPES OF INFORMATION SYSTEMS

LO 14.2 Describe the components and types of information systems.

The definition of *information system* in the previous section does not specifically mention the use of computers or technology. Information systems have been around since the beginning of civilization. Of course, by today's standards, the early information systems were very low-tech. Think about your college or university library. At one time, the library probably had a card catalogue to help students find information. The card catalogue was an information system because it stored data about books and periodicals in an organized manner on index cards. Library users could flip through the cards and locate library materials by author, title, or subject. But the process could be difficult and time-consuming.

When today's businesspeople think about information systems, they most likely think about **computer-based information systems.** These systems rely on computer and related technologies to store information electronically in an organized, accessible manner. Instead of a card catalogue, your college or university library probably uses a computerized information system. Users can search through library holdings quickly and easily.

Computer-based information systems consist of four components and technologies:

- Computer hardware
- Computer software
- Telecommunications and computer networks
- Data resource management

computer-based information systems information systems that use computer and related technologies to store information electronically in an organized, accessible manner.

Computer hardware consists of machines that range from supercomputers to smartphones. It also includes the input, output, and storage devices needed to support computing machines. Software includes operating systems, such as Microsoft's Windows 8 or Linux, and application programs, such as Adobe Acrobat and Customer Relationship Management, or CRM. Consumer software includes Dropbox and Evernote, while enterprise software includes Salesforce.com and Workday. In addition, mobile software consists primarily of iOS and Android operating systems. Telecommunications and computer networks encompass the hardware and software needed to provide wired or wireless voice and data communications. This includes support for external networks such as the Internet and private internal networks. Data resource management involves developing and maintaining an organization's databases so that decision makers are able to access the information they need in a timely manner.

In the case of your college or university library, the computer-based information system is usually made up of computer hardware, such as monitors and keyboards, which are linked to the library's network and a database containing information on the library's holdings. Specialized software allows users to access the database. The library's network is likely also connected to a larger private network and the Internet. These connections give users remote access to the library's database and access to other computerized databases, such as LexisNexis.

database a centralized integrated collection of data resources.

Databases

The heart of any information system is its **database**, a centralized integrated collection of data resources. A company designs its databases to meet specific information processing and retrieval needs of its workforce. Businesses obtain databases in many ways. They can hire a staff person to build them onsite, hire an outside source to build them, or buy packaged database programs from specialized vendors, such as Oracle. A database acts as an electronic filing cabinet. It is capable of storing large amounts of data and retrieving a specific piece of data within seconds. A database should be continually updated; otherwise, a firm may find itself with data that are outdated and possibly useless. One problem with databases is that they often contribute to information overload—too much data for people to absorb or data that are irrelevant, or not meaningful, to decision making. Computer processing speed and storage capacity are increasing rapidly, and data have become more abundant—that is, there is more data and it is more easily available. As a result, businesspeople need to be careful that their databases contain only the facts they need. If they aren't careful, much time can be wasted wading through unnecessary data. Another challenge with databases is keeping them safe, as the "Hit & Miss" feature describes.

Decision makers can also look up data online. Online systems give access to large amounts of government data, such as economic data from Statistics Canada. One of the largest online databases is that of the Canadian Census. The Canadian Census of Population is conducted every five years. It collects data on households across Canada and tries to count everyone in the country. Selected participants fill out forms, answering questions about marital status, place of birth, ethnic background, citizenship, workplaces, commuting time, income, occupation, type of housing, number of telephones and vehicles, and even the number of grandparents who are caregivers. Although certain restrictions limit how people can access and use specific census data, the general public may access the data through Statistics Canada's website. Another

A library's *computer-based information system* is generally made up of computer hardware linked to the library's network and a database of information on the library's holdings. Specialized software allows users to access the database.

Purestock/Getty Images, Inc.

(HIT) & MISS

Business Intelligence Software Helps with Information Overload

According to research, about 60 percent of Canadian companies use business intelligence software to help managers deal with all the data they need to process and understand. Sales of analytical software are growing at a 10 percent rate and approaching $11 billion annually.

More than half of executives reported feeling weighed down by the volume of data processing and analysis that they need to do as part of their decision-making responsibilities. But these tasks can be made easier by using software that processes large volumes of data and can produce guidance for management.

For example, most businesses have little if any understanding of their mobile, wireless, and data communications usage. They receive invoices from large telecommunications companies, such as Bell Canada, Rogers, or TELUS, and simply pay the bills. They have no way of knowing if they are paying for unneeded services or if they are overpaying for the services they use. A business intelligence software solution can now help large corporations to save time and money.

Etelesolv is a startup consulting firm in Lachine, Quebec. Its TeleManager system provides managers with details of costs and usage to help them control costs, such as an employee who runs up excessive charges. According to Etelesolv's president, Christopher Thierry, the software identified $800,000 of potential savings for one client.

The young company's clients include RBC Financial Group, Canada Post, RONA, GazMet, and Sun Life Financial. But even smaller firms need help with analyzing and reconciling their telecommunications invoices.

Questions for Critical Thinking

1. What other areas of managerial decision making involve large volumes of data and would likely benefit from a software solution?

2. How might software firms price their software solutions to different companies?

Sources: Etelesolv, accessed May 19, 2011, www.etelesolv.com; Peter Hadekel, "Solving Telecom Mysteries," *Montreal Gazette*, April 7, 2011, B1–B2; Matt Hartley, "Information Overload Burden to Execs: Poll," *National Post*, May 16, 2011, A2.

source of free information is company websites. Anyone who is interested can visit firms' home pages to look for information about customers, suppliers, and competitors. Trade associations and academic institutions also maintain websites with related information.

Types of Information Systems

Many different types of information systems exist. In general, information systems fall into one of two broad categories: operational support systems or management support systems.

Operational Support Systems

Operational support systems are designed to produce a variety of information on an organization's activities for both internal and external users. Examples of operational support systems include transaction processing systems and process control systems. **Transaction processing systems** record and process data from business transactions. For example, major retailers use point-of-sale systems, which link electronic cash registers to the retailer's computer centres. Sales data are transmitted from cash registers to the computer centre either immediately or at regular intervals. **Process control systems** monitor and control physical processes. For example, a steel mill may have electronic sensors linked to a computer system to monitor the entire production process. The system makes necessary changes and alerts operators to potential problems.

Commercial airplane manufacturer Airbus relies on an advanced information system. It uses RFID (radio-frequency identification) technology to track parts and tools used in the production and maintenance of its products, including its new A350 XWB planes. The high-memory RFID tags are placed on parts. The information system then follows the parts from warehouses to production facilities to the specific production lines where they are attached to aircraft. The system also tracks how and where tools are used. Airbus expects the information system to improve overall supply chain management, reduce required inventory levels, and increase productivity.[3]

Management Support Systems

Management support systems are information systems that are designed to provide support for effective decision making. Several different types of management support systems are available. A **management information system (MIS)** is designed to produce reports to managers and other professionals.

A **decision support system (DSS)** gives direct support to businesspeople during the decision-making process. For example, a marketing manager might use a decision support system to analyze

operational support systems information systems designed to produce a variety of information on an organization's activities for both internal and external users.

transaction processing systems operational support systems that record and process data from business transactions.

process control systems operational support systems that monitor and control physical processes.

management support systems information systems that are designed to provide support for effective decision making.

management information system (MIS) an information system that is designed to produce reports to managers and other professionals.

decision support system (DSS) an information system that gives direct support to businesspeople during the decision-making process.

© Cultura Creative (RF)/Alamy

The complex process of airline production and maintenance is critical to passenger safety. Many airlines use an *operational support system* to track parts, schedule inspections, and manage inventory levels.

executive support system (ESS) an information system that lets senior executives access the firm's primary databases, often by touching the computer screen, pointing and clicking a mouse, or using voice recognition.

expert system a computer program that imitates human thinking through complicated sets of "if-then" rules.

✓ ASSESSMENT CHECK

14.2.1 List the four components of a computer-based information system.

14.2.2 What is a database?

14.2.3 What are the two general types of information systems? Give examples of each.

how a product's price change will affect sales and profits. MEI Computer Technology Group provides North American consumer-products producers with a comprehensive sales and trade promotions tracking software called TradeInsight. This software provides real results that are linked to specific promotional efforts, such as an advertising campaign, a special coupon, or another marketing tactic. Clients such as Kellogg's, Heinz, and L'Oreal can track the impact of their promotional spending on sales. They can then use this information when planning their future promotional strategies.[4]

An **executive support system (ESS)** lets senior executives access the firm's primary databases, often by touching the computer screen, pointing and clicking a mouse, or using voice recognition. In the typical ESS, users can choose from many kinds of data, such as the firm's financial statements and sales figures or stock market trends for the company and for the industry as a whole. Managers can start by looking at summaries, and then access more detailed information when needed.

Finally, an **expert system** is a computer program that imitates human thinking through complicated sets of "if-then" rules. The system applies human knowledge in a specific subject area to solve a problem. Expert systems are used for a variety of business purposes: to set credit limits for credit card applicants, to monitor machinery in a plant to detect potential problems or breakdowns, to arrange mortgage loans, and to design plant layouts. They are typically developed by capturing the knowledge of recognized experts in a field whether within a business itself or outside it.

LO 14.3 Outline how computer hardware and software are used to manage information.

COMPUTER HARDWARE AND SOFTWARE

It may be hard to believe, but only a few decades ago computers were thought of as exotic curiosities, used only for very specialized applications and understood by only a few people. The first commercial computer, UNIVAC I, was sold to the U.S. Census Bureau in the early 1950s. It cost $1 million, took up most of a room, and could perform about 2,000 calculations per second.[5] The invention of transistors and then integrated circuits (microchips) quickly led to smaller and more powerful devices. By the 1980s, computers could perform several million calculations per second. Now, computers perform billions of calculations per second, and some fit in the palm of your hand.

The first personal computers were introduced in the late 1970s and early 1980s. Then, the idea of a computer on every desk, or in every home, seemed unbelievable and not very likely. Today, computers have become a must-have for both businesses and households. Not only have computers become much more powerful and faster over the past 35 years, but they are also less expensive. IBM's first personal computer (PC), introduced in 1981, cost well over $5,000. Today, a PC can sell for less than $400.

Types of Computer Hardware

hardware all tangible, or physical, elements of a computer system.

Hardware consists of all tangible, or physical, elements of a computer system—the input devices, the components that store and process data and perform calculations, and the output devices that present the results to users. Input devices allow users to enter data and commands for processing, storage, and output. The most common input devices are the keyboard and mouse. Storage and processing components include the hard drive and various other storage components, such as DVD drives and flash memory devices. Flash memory devices are becoming increasingly popular because they are small and can hold large amounts of data. Some, called thumb drives, can even fit on a keychain. To gain access to the data they hold, users plug the drives into a USB (universal serial bus) port, standard on today's computers. Output devices, such as monitors and printers, are the hardware elements that transmit or display documents and other results of a computer system's work.

Different types of computers have varying memory capacities and processing speeds. These differences define four broad classifications: mainframe computers, midrange systems, personal computers, and hand-held devices. A mainframe computer is the largest computer system. It has the greatest storage capacity and the fastest processing speeds. Especially powerful mainframes called *supercomputers* can handle extremely rapid, complex calculations that involve thousands of variables, such as weather modelling and forecasting. Today's supercomputers can perform a trillion or more calculations per second.

Midrange systems consist of high-end network servers and other types of computers that can handle large-scale processing needs. They are less powerful than mainframe computers but more powerful than most personal computers. A **server** is the heart of a midrange computer network. It supports applications and allows networked users to share output devices, software, and databases. Many Internet-related functions at organizations are handled by midrange systems. Midrange systems are also commonly used in process control systems, computer-aided manufacturing (CAM), and computer-aided design (CAD).

server the heart of a midrange computer network.

Once the centre of the digital universe, a full-scale Windows or Mac OS personal desktop computer was the way most people accessed the Internet, wrote papers, played games, organized music and photos, and more. While some believe the PC is on its way to extinction and ownership rates have declined, PCs are still popular in homes, businesses, schools, and government agencies.

While millions of desktop computers remain on the job, laptops—including notebooks and netbooks—have surpassed desktop units in sales. The increasing popularity of these computers can be explained by smaller, lighter, more powerful computing, and by their improved displays, faster processing speeds, ability to handle more intense graphics, larger storage capacities, and more durable designs. Business owners, managers, salespeople, and students all benefit from their portability and instantaneous access to information.

Prices for full-size laptops, notebooks, and net-books vary greatly—a netbook can be purchased for an average of $350 to $500 or a MacBook Pro laptop for between $1,500 and $3,500. A netbook does not have the computing capacity of a larger, more expensive notebook, but it can perform basic tasks such as search, email, word processing, and spreadsheet calculations.

Hand-held devices such as smartphones are even smaller. The most popular smartphones today are powered by Google's Android and Apple's iOS mobile operating systems. Smartphones like the iPhone and Samsung's Galaxy essentially combine a mobile phone with more advanced computing capabilities than their predecessor, the basic cellphone. While smartphones can be terrific tools that boost productivity, some people overuse or even misuse them. See the "Career Kickstart" feature which describes some of the dos and don'ts of smartphone use in the business environment.

Two other devices—tablets and e-readers—are taking major market share from laptops. According to Pew Research Center's Internet and American Life Project, more than a third of U.S. adults now own a tablet.[6] In addition to the Apple iPad, the top selling tablet, there are a proliferation of tablet models on the market, including those from Google, Samsung, Amazon, and Sony. E-readers such as Amazon's Kindle continue to expand their market share. Currently, about 32 percent of U.S. adults own an e-reader. A hybrid device, called a phablet, is a cross between a smartphone and a tablet, with a screen larger than a smartphone but smaller than a

Using smartphones and tablets can boost productivity, but some people overuse or misuse them.

Jacob Wackerhausen/iStockphoto

CAREER KICKSTART

Courteous Communications via Mobile Devices

The number of smartphone users worldwide is expected to reach 4.5 billion over the next few years. With so many of us communicating instantly—and almost constantly—it is more important than ever to be courteous, or well-mannered, whether speaking or emailing on a hand-held device.

1. *Be aware of your surroundings—and your neighbours.* If you're in a meeting or another place where a phone conversation would be unsuitable, turn off your ring tone. If the call or email simply can't wait, excuse yourself and leave the room to respond.

2. *Lower your voice when taking a call in a public area.* If you are in an area that is quieter than your speaking voice, it's better to find another area more suitable for having a conversation.

3. *When sending email or texting, don't overabbreviate.* A business message can be short without being cute or, worse, hard to understand. It is just as easy to key in "See you at 3" as "cu@3."

4. *Before sending a text message or email, read it over carefully.* Typos and grammatical errors don't look professional in a business message.

5. *Be careful about your Facebook photos.* Now that smartphones let users link all their contact information, your photo may appear on the other person's phone when you call. And people beyond those on your Facebook friends list will see it. Be sure your photo is suitable for both friends and business callers.

Sources: "Smartphone Users Worldwide Will Total 1.75 Billion in 2014," eMarketer, accessed February 27, 2014, www.emarketer.com; Christopher Elliott, "E-Mail Etiquette for Wireless Devices," Microsoft Small Business Center, accessed February 25, 2014, www.microsoft.com; Taya Flores, "Cell Phone Etiquette Is Important," JC Online, accessed February 25, 2014, www.jconline.com; Mike Elgan, "Here Comes the New Cell Phone Etiquette," IT World, accessed February 25, 2014, www.itworld.com.

---

tablet. In the next few years, analysts predict that more than half of the smart connected devices sold will be tablets, followed by laptops and desktops. In a recent quarter, tablet sales surpassed desktop and laptop sales combined.[7]

In addition to smartphones, specialized hand-held devices are used in a variety of businesses for different applications. Some restaurants, for example, have small wireless devices that allow servers to swipe a credit or debit card and print out a receipt right at the customer's table. Drivers for UPS and FedEx use special hand-held devices to track package deliveries and accept delivery signatures. As each package is delivered, the information is transmitted to the delivery firm's network, and the sender can check online to see the delivery information and even the recipient's signature.

Computer Software

software all the programs, routines, and computer languages that control a computer and tell it how to operate.

Software includes all of the programs, routines, and computer languages that control a computer and tell it how to operate. The *operating system* is the software that controls the basic workings of a computer system. More than 90 percent of personal computers use a version of Microsoft's popular Windows operating system. Personal computers made by Apple use the Mac operating system. Most hand-held devices use either the Palm or Symbian operating system or a special version of Windows called Windows Mobile. But the Droid, iPhone, and BlackBerry models have their own operating systems. Other operating systems include Unix, which runs on many midrange computer systems, and Linux, which runs on both PCs and midrange systems.

Application software is a software program that performs the specific tasks that the user wants to carry out—such as writing a letter or looking up data. Examples of application software include Adobe Acrobat, Microsoft PowerPoint, and Quicken. **Table 14.1** lists the major categories of application software. Most application programs are stored on individual computers. But the future of applications software is constantly changing. Some believe much of it will become web-based, with the programs themselves stored in the "cloud," on Internet-connected servers. Others disagree, arguing that most computer users will not want to rely on an Internet connection to perform such tasks as preparing a spreadsheet using Microsoft Excel. The "Going Green" feature explains how some observers believe that cloud computing might help reduce greenhouse gases.

✓ ASSESSMENT CHECK

14.3.1 List two input and two output devices.

14.3.2 Why are notebook computers so popular?

14.3.3 What is software? List the two categories of software.

Table 14.1 Common Types of Application Software

TYPE	DESCRIPTION	EXAMPLES
Word processing	Programs that input, store, retrieve, edit, and print various types of documents.	Microsoft Word, Pages (Apple)
Spreadsheets	Programs that prepare and analyze financial statements, sales forecasts, budgets, and similar numerical and statistical data.	Microsoft Excel, Numbers (Apple)
Presentation software	Programs that create presentations. Users can create bulleted lists, charts, graphs, pictures, audio, and even short video clips.	Microsoft PowerPoint, Keynote (Apple)
Desktop publishing	Software that combines high-quality type, graphics, and layout tools to create output that can look as attractive as documents produced by professional publishers and printers.	Adobe Acrobat, Microsoft Publisher
Financial software	Programs that compile accounting and financial data to create financial statements, reports, and budgets; they perform basic financial management tasks such as balancing a chequebook.	Quicken, QuickBooks
Database programs	Software that searches and retrieves data from a database; it can sort data based on various criteria.	Microsoft Access, Approach
Personal information managers	Specialized database programs that allow people to track communications with personal and business contacts; some combine email capability.	Microsoft Outlook, Lotus Organizer
Enterprise resource planning	Integrated cross-functional software that controls many business activities, including distribution, finance, and human resources.	SAP Enterprise Resource Planning

GOING GREEN

CAN CLOUD COMPUTING ALSO BE "GREEN" COMPUTING?

The increase in cloud computing has some observers hoping it will also decrease the emission of greenhouse gases. But others are growing concerned that cloud computing will cause emissions to increase because it will lead to larger and larger data storage centres that use more energy.

The environmental organization Greenpeace issued the "Cool IT Challenge" to the IT sector. Greenpeace urges firms to reduce emissions by using renewable electricity to power their data centres. Greenpeace also wants firms to pressure utility companies to improve their access to renewable energy. In a report, Greenpeace said that IT energy solutions can even encourage the growth of local, decentralized energy centres as opposed to large grids. These smaller, local networks could result in better energy choices for consumers, improved energy efficiency, and greater use of renewable energy.

Greenpeace has published a chart that rates major data centres' use of power sources. Google's data centre in Oregon was the leading user of renewable energy: almost 51 percent of its energy comes from renewable sources, not from coal and nuclear power.

The Green Grid is a group of IT companies interested in improving energy efficiency. It launched a downloadable tool that helps IT professionals lower their overall energy use by using outside air and water to cool their data centres at little or no cost.

Even Greenpeace has come under fire for relying on coal and nuclear energy at some of its data centres, due to long-term agreements with local utilities. Gary Cook, one of the Cool IT Campaign's policy advisors, said, "We're definitely trying to run the greenest operation we can . . . We're in the process of reworking some of our IT infrastructure, and we'll clean that up."

Questions for Critical Thinking

1. Why do devices that rely on cloud computing, such as smartphones or the iPad, contribute to increased greenhouse gas emissions?

2. Will the data centres' voluntary actions be enough to lower greenhouse gas emissions? Why or why not?

Sources: Greenpeace, accessed May 22, 2010, www.greenpeace.org; The Green Grid, accessed May 22, 2010, www.thegreengrid.org; GreenerComputing Staff, "Green Grid Offers Tools for Free Data Center Cooling," *GreenBiz*, April 12, 2010, www.greenbiz.com /news/2009/04/12/green-grid-offers-tools-free-data-center-cooling; Rich Miller, "Greenpeace: Cloud Contributes to Climate Change," *Data Center Knowledge*, March 30, 2010, www .datacenterknowledge.com/archives/2010/03/30/greenpeace-cloud-contributes-to-climate-change; Matthew Wheeland, "Cloud Computing Is Efficient, But It's Not Green— Yet," *GreenBiz*, March 30, 2010, www.greenbiz.com/blog/2010/03/30/cloud-computing-efficient-but-not-green-yet; Rich Miller, "Greenpeace's Hosting: Not 'Truly Green,'" *Data Center Knowledge*, March 3, 2010, www.datacenterknowledge.com/archives/2010/03/03 /greenpeaces-hosting-not-truly-green.

COMPUTER NETWORKS

As mentioned earlier, nearly all computers today are linked to networks. In fact, if your PC has Internet access, you're linked to a network. Local area networks and wide area networks allow businesses to communicate, transmit and print documents, and share data. These networks require businesses to install special equipment and connections between office sites. But Internet technology has also been applied to internal company communications and business tasks, by using a ready-made network. Among these new Internet-based applications are intranets, virtual private networks (VPNs), and voice over Internet protocol (VoIP). Each has contributed to the effectiveness and speed of business processes, so we discuss them next.

Local Area Networks and Wide Area Networks

local area networks (LANs) computer networks that connect machines within limited areas, such as a building or several nearby buildings.

Most organizations connect their offices and buildings by creating **local area networks** (LANs), computer networks that connect machines within limited areas, such as a building or several nearby buildings. LANs are useful because they link computers and allow them to share printers, documents, and information. LANs also provide access to the Internet. **Figure 14.1** shows what a small-business computer network might look like.

wide area networks (WANs) computer networks that tie larger geographical regions together by using telephone lines and microwave and satellite transmission.

Wide area networks (WANs) tie larger geographical regions together by using telephone lines, microwave transmission, and satellite transmission. One familiar WAN is long-distance telephone service. Companies such as Bell Canada and TELUS provide WAN services to businesses and consumers. Firms also use WANs to conduct their own operations. Typically, companies link their own network systems to outside communications equipment and services for transmission across long distances.

Wi-Fi a wireless network that connects various devices and allows them to communicate with one another through radio waves.

Wireless Local Networks

A wireless network allows computers, printers, and other devices to be connected without the need for cables that physically link the devices. The current standard for wireless networks is called Wi-Fi, popularly thought to stand for *wireless fidelity*. **Wi-Fi is a wireless network that connects various devices and allows them to communicate with one another through radio waves.** Any PC that has a Wi-Fi receptor can connect with the Internet at so-called hot spots—locations with a wireless router and a high-speed Internet modem. There are hundreds of thousands of hot spots around the world. They are found in a variety of places, including college and university campuses, airports, libraries, and coffee shops. Some locations provide free access, while others charge a fee.

Many believe that Wi-Fi will soon be followed by *Wi-Max*. Unlike Wi-Fi's relatively limited geographic coverage area—generally around 90 metres—a single Wi-Max access point can provide coverage over many kilometres. In addition, cellphone service providers, such as Bell Canada and Rogers, offer broadband network cards for notebook PCs. These devices allow users to access the provider's mobile broadband network from nearly any location where cellphone reception is available.

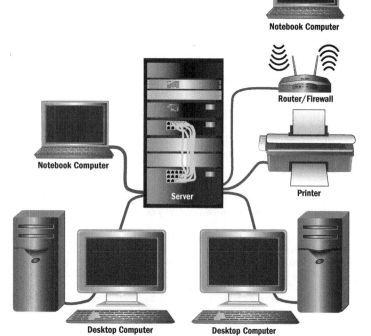

Notebook Computer

Router/Firewall

Printer

Notebook Computer

Server

Desktop Computer

Desktop Computer

FIGURE 14.1 A Local Area Network

Wi-Fi connections are often called *hot spots*—locations with a wireless router and a high-speed Internet modem. There are hundreds of thousands of hot spots around the world. They are found in a variety of places, including college and university campuses, airports, libraries, and coffee shops.

Intranets

One way to share information in an organization is to set up a company network similar to the Internet. This type of network is called an **intranet**. Intranets are similar to the Internet, but they limit access to authorized users, often an employee group. Intranet users access the system by entering a password. An intranet blocks outsiders who don't have valid passwords by using software and hardware known as a **firewall**. Firewalls limit data transfers to certain locations. They also track system use so that managers can identify threats to the system's security, including attempts to log on with invalid passwords. Highly advanced software will immediately alert system administrators to suspicious activities but will allow authorized personnel to use smart cards to connect from remote terminals.

Intranets solve the problem of linking different types of computers. Like the Internet, intranets can link computers that run different kinds of operating systems. Intranets are relatively easy and inexpensive to set up because most businesses already have some of the required hardware and software. For example, a small business can purchase a digital subscriber line (DSL) router and a few cables to create an intranet using phone jacks and internal phone lines. All the business's computers will be linked to each other and to the Internet.

Intranets also support teamwork among employees who travel or work from home. Any intranet member with the right identification, a PC, and an Internet connection can link to the intranet and gain access to group calendars, email, documents, and other files. Intranets can also be used for videoconferencing and other forms of virtual meetings. Jetstar, an airline serving the Asia-Pacific region, has more than 3,000 employees. But three-quarters of them—pilots, cabin crews, and airport staff—will never set foot in the home office. Pilots can visit the company's intranet to access the latest safety information, and home office employees can go online to update the staff directory and transfer paper forms. Corporate and staff communications are transmitted to all employees via Jetstar's intranet. These communications help to build a sense of community among people who may rarely meet in person.[8]

intranet a computer network that is similar to the Internet but limits access to authorized users.

firewall a type of security system for computers that limits data transfers to certain locations; it also tracks system use so that managers can identify threats to the system's security, including attempts to log on with invalid passwords.

Virtual Private Networks

virtual private networks (VPNs) secure connections between two points on the Internet.

To gain increased security for Internet communications, companies often turn to **virtual private networks (VPNs)**, secure connections between two points on the Internet. These VPNs use firewalls and programs that encrypt, or encode, data to make them more secure during transit. The data are then decrypted, or decoded at the receiving end. In very general terms, a VPN can include a range of networking technologies, from secure Internet connections to private networks from service providers like IBM. A VPN is cheaper for a company to use than leasing several of its own lines. It might take months to install a leased line in some parts of the world, but a new user can be added to a VPN in a day. Because a VPN uses the Internet, it can be wired, wireless, or a combination of the two.

VoIP

VoIP an alternative to traditional telecommunication services provided by companies such as Bell Canada and TELUS; uses the Internet instead of telephone lines to transmit messages.

VoIP stands for *voice over Internet protocol*. It is an alternative to traditional telecommunication services provided by companies such as Bell Canada and TELUS. The VoIP telephone is not connected to a traditional phone jack but is connected to a personal computer that has a broadband connection. Special software transmits phone conversations over the Internet, instead of through telephone lines. A VoIP user can access the phone as usual. People can use VoIP to place and receive calls to and from others who have traditional telephone connections (either landline or wireless).

A growing number of consumers and businesses are using VoIP, mainly because of its cost savings and extra features. As technology continues to advance, demand for VoIP has increased. Videotron provides VoIP service to Quebec customers, in addition to providing Internet and cable television services. Google announced it is developing its own VoIP service. The various VoIP providers are working together with the goal of creating a single VoIP standard to permit seamless roaming worldwide. This new standard might develop soon, especially since Microsoft acquired the global leader in VoIP technology—Skype.[9]

VoIP has many advantages. But there are also several potential downsides to replacing traditional telephony with Internet telephony. For one thing, an Internet phone service is only as reliable as the broadband connection. If your broadband connection goes out, so will your phone service. Also, without suitable protection, VoIP can expose a phone system to threats that can affect the rest of the Internet, such as worms and viruses.

✓ ASSESSMENT CHECK

14.4.1 What is a LAN?

14.4.2 What are the differences between an intranet and a VPN?

14.4.3 Briefly explain how VoIP works.

LO 14.5 Outline the security and ethical issues affecting information systems.

SECURITY AND ETHICAL ISSUES AFFECTING INFORMATION SYSTEMS

Many security and ethical issues affect information systems. Information systems are becoming more important as business assets; they are also becoming harder and more expensive to replace. Damage to information systems or theft of data can have disastrous results. When computers are connected to a network, a problem at any individual computer can affect the entire network. Two of the major security threats are cybercrime and so-called malware.

Cybercrime

Computers provide efficient ways for employees to share information. But they may also allow access to information by people who may have criminal intentions. Or they may allow access to private information by pranksters—who have no purpose other than to see whether they can break into a system. Common cybercrimes involve stealing or altering data in several ways:

- Employees or outsiders may change or create data to produce inaccurate or misleading information.

- Employees or outsiders may alter computer programs to create false information or illegal transactions or to insert viruses.

- Unauthorized people can access computer systems for their own benefit or knowledge or just to see if they can figure out how to get in.

Individuals, businesses, and government agencies are all vulnerable to computer crime. Computer hackers are unauthorized users. They sometimes work alone and sometimes work in groups. Hackers sometimes break into computer systems just to show that they can do it; other times, they have more disturbing reasons. A survey reported that although computer crimes have decreased slightly, many computer crimes may go undetected. Why? Because firms focus on discouraging hackers and blocking pornography but leave themselves open to cybercriminals who are developing increasingly advanced tools. Even Apple computers, which are normally protected from cybercrime, are becoming vulnerable: more and more Mac users now store data in the "cloud"—that is, on the Internet itself, not on their hard drives. Although there is no single uniform system for reporting cybercrime, the Internet Engineering Task Force (IETF) is working toward a common format that will have reliable time stamps, will be available in different languages, and will allow users to attach samples of malicious code. These automated tools will be able to analyze massive amounts of data much faster than human analysts.[10]

Information system administrators use two basic protections against computer crime: they try to prevent access to their systems by unauthorized users and they try to prevent the viewing of data by unauthorized system users. The simplest method of preventing access requires an authorized user to enter a password. The company may also install firewalls, described earlier. To prevent system users from reading sensitive information, the company may use encryption software, which encodes, or scrambles, messages. To read encrypted messages, users must use an electronic key to convert the messages to regular text. But, as fast as software developers invent new and more advanced protective measures, hackers seem to break through their defences. As a result, computer security is an ongoing battle.

Consumers with credit cards are particularly at risk from hackers. Luxury retailer Neiman Marcus discovered that hackers had breached its cyber-security system, which compromised customer credit card data. It is important for payment-processing companies used by major credit card companies to put protections in place so that consumer credit and debit card information remain safe.[11]

Another form of computer theft is as old as crime itself: theft of equipment. Because computers may contain important information for a business, employees need to be especially careful not to leave laptops unattended or within easy reach of others.

As computer hardware becomes smaller, it also becomes more at risk to theft. Hand-held devices, for instance, are particularly susceptible to theft. At an estimated cost of $30 billion annually, one in three robberies now involves smartphones.[12] Many notebook computers and hand-held devices contain special security software or passwords that make it difficult for a thief, or any unauthorized person, to access the computer's data. Find My iPhone was introduced for iOS users to locate their device and remotely delete data in the event it was lost or stolen. Apple updated its operating system to include software with an activation lock to prevent access to confidential information in the event of theft—similar to a kill switch feature.[13]

Luxury retailer Neiman Marcus is among those retailers who have faced a cybersecurity breach, compromising its customers' credit and debit card information.

© Kristoffer Tripplaar/Alamy

Computer Viruses, Worms, Trojan Horses, and Spyware

Viruses, worms, Trojan horses, and spyware are collectively referred to as **malware**—malicious software programs designed to infect computer systems. These programs can destroy data, steal sensitive information, and even make it impossible to operate a computer. Malware has been

malware any malicious software program designed to infect computer systems.

discovered in advertisements on major sites such as Yahoo and Google. Malware is proliferating; according to estimates, companies are spending more than $100 billion annually to deal with malware-related cyberattacks.[14] Law enforcement has made some progress against cybercrime. But some observers predict that cybercriminals may soon target social-networking sites such as Facebook and Twitter.[15]

viruses malicious software programs that attach themselves to other programs (called *hosts*) and change them or destroy data.

Computer **viruses** are malicious software programs that attach themselves to other programs (called *hosts*) and change them or destroy data. According to the computer security company Symantec, almost 3 million computer viruses are currently active worldwide.[16] Viruses can be programmed to become active immediately or to remain inactive for a period of time, and then later activate themselves and cause problems. A virus can reproduce by copying itself onto other programs stored on the same drive. It spreads as users install infected software on their systems or exchange files with others, usually by email, by accessing electronic bulletin boards, by trading disks, or by downloading programs or data from unknown sources on the Internet.

worm a small piece of software that uses a security hole in a network to replicate itself.

A **worm** is a small piece of software that uses a security hole in a network to replicate, or copy, itself. A copy of the worm scans the network for another machine that has a specific security hole. It copies itself to the new machine using the security hole and then also starts the same process of copying itself from that machine. Unlike viruses, worms don't need host programs to damage computer systems.

botnet a network of PCs that have been infected with one or more data-stealing viruses.

A **botnet** is a network of PCs that have been infected with one or more data-stealing viruses. Computer criminals tie the infected computers into a network, often without the owners being aware of it, and sell the botnet on the black market. The cybercriminals or others then use the botnet to commit identity theft, send spam, buy blocks of concert tickets for scalping, and attack the Internet itself. About 4,000 to 6,000 botnets are active today. Spanish authorities brought down the Mariposa botnet, the world's largest botnet to date—a network of 12.7 million infected computers. Some of the computers were inside *Fortune* 1000 companies and major banks. Although the authorities made some arrests, the creator of the Mariposa botnet has not been caught.[17]

Trojan horse a program that claims to do one thing but in reality does something else, usually something malicious.

A **Trojan horse** is a program that claims to do one thing but in reality does something else, usually something malicious. For example, a Trojan horse might claim to be a game. But when a user clicks on the Trojan horse to launch it, the program might erase the hard drive or steal personal data stored on the computer.

spyware software that gathers user information through the user's Internet connection without his or her knowledge, usually for advertising purposes.

Spyware is software that gathers user information through the user's Internet connection without his or her knowledge, usually for advertising purposes. Spyware applications are typically bundled with other programs downloaded from the Internet. Once installed, the spyware monitors user activity on the Internet and transmits that information in the background to someone else.

Attacks by malware are not limited to computers and computer networks. Users of smartphones have also been affected. Smartphone users have reported a sharp increase in viruses, worms, and other forms of malware.[18] A malware scare known as Backdoor AndroidOS.Obad.a is a Trojan horse that infects the handsets of unsuspecting users. It duplicates itself, installs additional malware, distributes malicious software to other phones via Bluetooth, and performs remote commands in the Android handset, while racking up enormous charges to premium-rate phone numbers.[19]

As viruses, worms, botnets, and Trojan horses become more complex, the technology to fight them must also become more complex. The simplest way to protect against computer viruses is to install one of the many available antivirus software programs, such as Norton AntiVirus and McAfee VirusScan. These programs also protect against worms and some Trojan horses. Antivirus software programs continuously monitor systems for viruses and automatically get rid of any they spot. Users should regularly update their antivirus software by downloading the latest virus definitions. Computer users should also install and regularly update antispyware programs because many Trojan horses are forms of spyware.

But management must begin to emphasize security at a deeper level: during software design, in corporate servers, at web gateways, and through Internet service providers. Because more than 90 percent of the world's PCs run on Microsoft operating systems, a single virus, worm, or Trojan horse can quickly spread among PCs. Individual computer users should carefully choose the files they load onto their systems, scan their systems regularly, keep their antivirus software up to date, and install only software from known sources. They should also be very careful when opening email attachments from unknown sources because many viruses, worms, and Trojan horses are spread that way.

Information Systems and Ethics

The scope and power of today's information systems raise many ethical issues and concerns. These ethical issues affect both employees and organizations. For example, organizations often have specific ethical standards and policies regarding the use of information systems by employees and vendors. These standards include obligations to protect system security and the privacy and confidentiality of data. Policies may also cover employees' personal use of computers and related technologies, both hardware and software.

Ethical issues also involve an organization's use of information systems. Organizations have an obligation to protect the privacy and confidentiality of data on employees and customers. Employment records contain sensitive personal information, such as bank account numbers. If this information is not protected, it could lead to identity theft. Another ethical issue is the use of computer technology to monitor employees while they are working. The "Solving an Ethical Controversy" feature debates the issue of employee monitoring.

 **ASSESSMENT CHECK**

14.5.1 Explain computer hacking.

14.5.2 What is malware?

14.5.3 How does a computer virus work?

SOLVING AN **ETHICAL** CONTROVERSY

Should Employers Monitor Employees' Internet Use?

According to an American Management Association/ePolicy Institute survey, two-thirds of employers monitor employees' use of the Internet. Technology now allows employers to check which websites their employees visit on company time, the pattern of keystrokes on individual computers, and the amount of time spent online. Employers can even use GPS-enabled phones to track employees.

For most employees, on-the-job access to the Internet and email is a necessity. In some workplaces, employees need to do a certain amount of Internet surfing for research purposes. A company's Facebook page can be either a powerful marketing tool or a liability if employees use their own social media sites to complain about the company.

Should employers monitor their employees' time online?

PRO

1. Surveys estimate that employees spend between one and two hours every day online for personal use. Some employees perform innocent tasks such as banking, but others visit inappropriate websites. Either way, those online hours mean lost productivity for the company.

2. Inappropriate use of office computers can leave a company vulnerable to hacking, viruses, and other security threats.

CON

1. Some employers are concerned that if they monitor employees, they could risk losing a workplace atmosphere of trust, commitment, and motivation.

2. Employees have a reasonable concern about privacy, especially if they have not been informed beforehand that their online activities are being monitored.

Summary

Although the law clearly gives employers the right to monitor computer activity, many debate the acceptable range of monitoring a worker's use of a company-provided device. Most analysts suggest that companies should establish clear policies on computer, Internet, and email use. They should train employees, have them sign a document stating that they understand the policies, and then trust their employees to do the right thing.

Sources: Pamela S. Stevens, "Employee Monitoring Software Review 2014," *Top Ten Reviews*, accessed March 20, 2014, http://employee-monitoring-software-review.toptenreviews.com; "How Do Employers Monitor Internet Usage at Work," *wiseGEEK*, accessed March 20, 2014, www.wisegeek.org/how-do-employers-monitor-internet-usage-at-work.htm; Susan M. Heathfield, "Electronic Surveillance of Employees," About.com, accessed March 20, 2014, http://humanresources.about.com/od/technology/a/surveillance.htm; Karen Codere, "Managing Social Media in the Workplace," *Business Ledger*, May 10, 2010, accessed March 20, 2014, http://dhbusinessledger.com/Content/Dot-com/Dot-com/Article/Managing-social-media-in-the-workplace/44/108/62; Laura Petrecca, "More Employers Use Tech to Track Workers," *USA Today*, March 17, 2010, accessed March 20, 2014, http://usatoday30.usatoday.com/money/workplace/2010-03-17-workplaceprivacy15_CV_N.htm.

DISASTER RECOVERY AND BACKUP

Even the most advanced computer information systems can be disrupted by natural disasters, power failures, equipment malfunctions, software glitches, human error, and terrorist attacks. These disruptions can cost businesses and other organizations billions of dollars. Even more serious outcomes can occur. For example, one study found that more than 93 percent of firms that lost their data centres for 10 days or more went bankrupt within six months.[20]

Disaster recovery planning is a critical function of all organizations. It refers to planning how to prevent computer system failures and planning how to continue operations if computer systems do fail. Disaster prevention programs can avoid some costly problems. The most basic precaution is routinely backing up software and data—at the organizational level and the individual level. But the organization's data centre cannot be the only place where critical data is stored because a single location is vulnerable to threats from both natural and human-caused disasters. As a result, offsite data backup is a necessity, whether in a separate physical location or online on the Internet itself. Companies that do online backups store the encrypted data in secure facilities that also have their own backups. The initial backup may take a day or more, but later backups will take far less time because they usually involve backing up only new or revised files.

According to security experts, an organization has five important tasks when considering offsite data storage. First is planning. The organization needs to decide what data need to be protected. Priority should be given to data that would lead to extreme legal or business consequences if it were lost. Second, a backup schedule must be set up and closely followed. Third, when data are transmitted offsite, they must be protected by the highest level of security possible. Fourth, care should be taken in selecting the right security vendor. Dozens of vendors offer different services in different areas of expertise. Finally, the backup system should be continually tested and evaluated.

INFORMATION SYSTEM TRENDS

Computer information systems are continually and rapidly changing. Firms that want to keep their information systems up to date must keep up to date with changes in technology. Some of the most significant trends in information systems include the growing demands of the so-called distributed workforce, the increased use of application service providers, on-demand computing, and cloud and grid computing.

The Distributed Workforce

As discussed in earlier chapters, many companies are relying more and more on a *distributed work-force*—employees who no longer work in traditional offices but work in *virtual offices,* including at home. Information technology (IT) makes a distributed workforce possible. Computers, networks, and other components of information systems make it possible for many workers to do their jobs almost anywhere. For example, none of JetBlue's reservations agents work in offices; they all work at home, connected to the airline's information system. JetBlue is not alone in its use of home-based workers. Boeing, Starbucks, Agilent Technologies, Sun Microsystems, and many other companies maintain virtual offices with thousands of workers. According to research, about 10 percent of North American full-time wage and salary workers work at home on any given day. Of the self-employed workforce, more than one-third work at home on any given day.[21] Statistics show that most at-home workers use computers and related technologies. Virtual offices can range from a mailing address, mail forwarding, and a phone answering service to a full office, usually leased by the month. The increasing demands of the distributed workforce will likely lead to more innovative and increasingly powerful information systems.

Application Service Providers

Many firms find that it makes sense to outsource at least some of their information technology functions. Because of the increasing cost and complexity of obtaining and maintaining information systems, many firms hire an **application service provider (ASP),** an outside supplier that provides both the computers and the application support for managing an information system. An ASP can simplify complex software for its customers

Continued technological advances in data storage and cloud computing allow businesspeople to work on their laptops, tablets, or smartphones from anywhere in the world.

so that it is easier for them to manage and use. When an ASP relationship is successful, the buyer can then devote more time and resources to its core businesses instead of trying to manage its information systems. Firms that use an ASP can also make their technology dollar stretch farther. Smaller companies who use an ASP can now access the kind of information power that was previously available only to larger organizations. Even large companies turn to ASPs to manage some or all of their information systems. Recently, Microsoft outsourced much of its internal information technology services to Infosys Technology to save money and to streamline, simplify, and support its services.[22]

Companies that decide to use ASPs should check the backgrounds and references of these firms before hiring one to manage critical systems. Customers should also ensure that the service provider has strong security measures to block computer hackers or other unauthorized access to the data, that its data centres are running reliably, and that adequate data and applications backups are maintained.

On-Demand, Cloud, and Grid Computing

Another trend is **on-demand computing,** also called *utility computing.* Instead of purchasing and maintaining expensive software, firms rent the software time from application providers. They pay only for their usage of the software, similar to purchasing electricity from a utility. On-demand computing is especially useful for firms that have annual peaks in demand or have seasonal increases in their use of an application. By renting the service they need only when they need it, customers can avoid buying software that is not needed frequently. By using on-demand computing, companies remain current with the most efficient software and avoid having to purchase huge upgrades.

Cloud computing uses powerful servers to store application software and databases. Users access the software and databases via the Web. They can use any Internet-connected device, such as a PC or a smartphone. The software as a service (SaaS) movement is an example of cloud computing. The "Hit & Miss" feature describes how Cisco Systems provides security for cloud-based applications.

Small and medium-size companies occasionally find themselves with jobs that require more computing power than their current systems offer. A cost-effective solution for these firms may be **grid computing,** a network of smaller computers running special software. The software breaks down a large, complex job into smaller tasks and then distributes the tasks to the networked computers. The software then reassembles the results of the individual tasks into the finished job. By combining multiple small computers, grid computing creates a virtual mainframe or even a supercomputer.

application service provider (ASP) an outside supplier that provides both the computers and the application support for managing an information system.

on-demand computing the use of software time from application providers; firms pay only for their usage of the software, not for purchasing or maintaining the software.

cloud computing the use of powerful servers that store application software and databases that users access by using any Internet-connected device, such as a PC or a smartphone.

grid computing a network of smaller computers that run special software.

✔ **ASSESSMENT CHECK**

14.7.1 What is an application service provider?

14.7.2 Explain on-demand computing.

Easy_Company/Getty Images, Inc.

HIT & MISS

Cisco Systems Tackles Cloud Security

More and more businesses are managing increasing amounts of email and storing increasing amounts of data. Many save money and physical space by turning to cloud computing and storage, including software as a service (SaaS). Instead of installing software on site, a business can use SaaS to access software over the Internet either by subscription or by using a "pay as you go" plan. These businesses also need to protect their databanks from computer crime. In a traditional local area network, security applications are relatively easy to set up at the network's borders. But this challenge is made more difficult by the borderless environment of cloud computing and because of increasing threats to online security.

Cisco Systems has responded by developing security applications for cloud-based computing. One application directs a business's web traffic to security towers located in 100 countries around the world. These locations use layers of antivirus and antimalware utilities to scan websites and quickly block access to any websites that have been infected.

Another application offers both cloud-based and on-site email security. The cloud-based application deletes spam and viruses. The on-site application provides data-loss prevention, email encryption, and other services. Another email encryption service provides cloud-based encryption for locally stored messages.

Other applications support security for off-site workers who use desktops computers, laptops, tablets, and smart-phones. One feature addresses the problem that occurs when an employee leaves a business. With one click of the mouse, an administrator can disable the departing employee's access to every SaaS application he or she ever used. And the administrator can use another click to set up access for a new employee.

As the vice-president and general manager of Cisco's security technology unit states, "Securing the cloud is highly challenging. But it is one of the top challenges that the industry must rise to meet."

Questions for Critical Thinking

1. What are some pros and cons of storing data "in the cloud"?

2. Why is it important to block a former employee's access to company data, email, or applications?

Sources: Company website, *News@Cisco* press release, accessed June 4, 2010, www.cisco.com; James Urquhart, "Cloud Computing and the Economy," *CNET News,* April 13, 2010, http://news.cnet.com; Margaret Steen, "Cloud Services and SaaS: A Smarter Way to Do Business," *Cisco News,* March 29, 2010, http://newsroom.cisco .com; Stuart Young, Andy Taylor, and James Macaulay, "Small Businesses Ride the Cloud: SMB Cloud Watch—U.S. Survey Results," Cisco Internet Business Solutions Group, February 2010, www.cisco.com; Mike Kirkwood, "Rulers of the Cloud: Will Cloud Computing Be the Second Coming of Cisco?" *ReadWriteWeb,* February 19, 2010, www.readwriteweb.com.

WHAT'S AHEAD

Part 5 was devoted to managing technology and information. Part 6 is about managing financial resources in contemporary business, and the next chapter, "Understanding Accounting and Financial Statements," focuses on accounting, financial information, and financing reporting. Accounting is the process of measuring, interpreting, and communicating financial information to enable people inside and outside the firm to make informed decisions. The chapter describes the functions of accounting and role of accountants; the steps in the accounting cycle; the types, functions, and components of financial statements; and the role of budgets in an organization.

RETURN TO INSIDE BUSINESS

Stock-Trak: Learning about the Stock Market through Simulation

A major competitive advantage for Stock-Trak is its use of real-time financial information to provide learners with a web-based stock market simulation. Price changes and analytical reports are sent online to users with little delay, only slightly behind the time that the same data and information are provided to real traders. Stock-Trak traders pay large subscription fees to receive this information so they can learn to make more intelligent trading decisions. The simulation provides a real-time learning experience that is as close to reality as the learner can expect to get. Stock-Trak is looking for ways to grow its business, such as by partnering with organizations that can deliver a large group of users.

QUESTIONS FOR CRITICAL THINKING

1. Which other organizations or groups should Stock-Trak consider partnering with? Why?

2. What other educational products or services could Stock-Trak develop?

SUMMARY OF LEARNING OBJECTIVES

LO 14.1 Distinguish between data and information, and discuss the role of information systems in business.

Businesspeople need to understand the difference between data and information. Data are raw facts and figures that may or may not be relevant, or meaningful, to a business decision. Information is knowledge gained from processing those facts and figures. An information system is an organized method for collecting, storing, and communicating past, present, and projected information on internal operations and external intelligence. Most information systems today use computer and telecommunications technology.

 ASSESSMENT CHECK ANSWERS

14.1.1 Distinguish between data and information. Data consist of raw facts and figures that may or may not be relevant to a decision. Information is the knowledge gained from processing data.

14.1.2 What is an information system? An information system is an organized method for collecting, storing, and communicating past, present, and projected information on internal operations and external intelligence.

LO 14.2 Describe the components and types of information systems.

When people think about information systems, they generally think of computer-based systems—information systems that use computers and related technologies. Computer-based information systems rely on four components: computer hardware, software, telecommunications and computer networks, and data resource management. The heart of an information system is its database, a centralized integrated collection of data resources. Information systems fall into one of two broad categories: operational support systems or management support systems. Operational support systems are designed to produce a variety of information for users. Examples include transaction processing systems and process control systems. Management support systems are designed to support effective decision making. They include management information systems, decision support systems, executive support systems, and expert systems.

 ASSESSMENT CHECK ANSWERS

14.2.1 List the four components of a computer-based information system. The four components of a computer-based information system are computer hardware, software, telecommunications and computer networks, and data resource management.

14.2.2 What is a database? A database is a centralized, integrated collection of data resources.

14.2.3 What are the two general types of information systems? Give examples of each. The two categories of information systems are operational support systems (such as transactions processing systems and process control systems) and management support systems (such as management information systems, decision support systems, executive support systems, and expert systems).

LO 14.3 Outline how computer hardware and software are used to manage information.

Hardware consists of all tangible, or physical, elements of a computer system, including input and output devices. Major categories of computers include mainframes, supercomputers, midrange systems, personal computers (PCs), and hand-held devices. Computer software provides the instructions that tell the hardware what to do. The operating system is the software that controls the basic workings of the computer. Other programs, called application software, perform specific tasks that users want to complete.

 ASSESSMENT CHECK ANSWERS

14.3.1 List two input devices and two output devices. Input devices include the keyboard and mouse. Output devices include the monitor and printer.

14.3.2 Why are notebook computers so popular? Notebook computers represent more than half of all new personal computers sold. Their increased popularity is due to better displays, lower prices, more rugged designs, increasing computing power, and slimmer designs.

14.3.3 What is software? List the two categories of software. Computer software provides the instructions that tell the hardware what to do. The two categories of software are the operating system and application software. The operating system is the software that controls the basic workings of the computer. Application software performs the specific tasks that users want to complete.

LO 14.4 Describe networking and telecommunications technology and the types of computer networks.

Local area networks connect computers within a limited area. Wide area networks tie larger geographical regions together by using telephone lines, microwave transmission, or satellite transmission. A wireless network allows computers to communicate through radio waves. Intranets allow employees to share information on a company network. Access to an intranet is restricted to authorized users and is protected by a firewall. Virtual private networks (VPNs) provide a secure Internet connection between two or more points. VoIP—voice over Internet protocol—uses a personal computer running special software and a broadband Internet connection to make and receive telephone calls over the Internet, instead of using traditional telephone networks.

 ASSESSMENT CHECK ANSWERS

14.4.1 What is a LAN? A LAN is a local area network, a computer network that connects machines within a limited area, such as a building or several nearby buildings.

14.4.2 What are the differences between an intranet and a VPN? An intranet is a computer network similar to the Internet. Unlike the Internet, access to an intranet is limited to employees or other authorized users. A virtual private network (VPN) is a secure connection between two points on the Internet.

14.4.3 Briefly explain how VoIP works. The VoIP phone is connected to a personal computer that has a broadband connection. Special software transmits phone conversations over the Internet. A VoIP user can place and receive calls to and from others who have traditional telephone connections (either landline or wireless).

LO 14.5 Outline the security and ethical issues affecting information systems.

Many security and ethical issues affect information systems. Two of the main security threats are cybercrime and malware. Cybercrimes range from hacking—unauthorized access to an information system—to the theft of hardware. Malware is any malicious software program designed to infect computer systems. Examples include viruses, worms, botnets, Trojan horses, and spyware. Ethical issues affecting information systems include the proper use of the systems by authorized users. Organizations also have an obligation to employees, vendors, and customers to protect the security and confidentiality of the data stored in information systems.

 ASSESSMENT CHECK ANSWERS

14.5.1 Explain computer hacking. Computer hacking refers to unauthorized people gaining illegal access to a computer system. Sometimes the hackers' purpose is just to see whether they can get into the system. Other times, hackers have more disturbing reasons, such as stealing or altering data.

14.5.2 What is malware? Malware is any malicious software program designed to infect computer systems.

14.5.3 How does a computer virus work? A virus is a program that attaches itself to another program (called a host). The virus then changes the host, destroys data, or even makes it impossible to operate the computer system.

LO 14.6 Explain how companies plan for, and recover from, information systems disasters.

Information system disasters may be caused by humans or may result from natural causes. Such disasters can cost businesses billions of dollars. The impact of a disaster can be decreased by routinely backing up software and data, both at an organizational level and at an individual level. Organizations should back up critical data at an offsite location. Some organizations may also want to invest in extra hardware and software sites, which can be accessed during emergencies.

 ASSESSMENT CHECK ANSWERS

14.6.1 What types of disasters are information systems vulnerable to? Even the most powerful and advanced computer information systems can be disrupted by natural disasters, power failures, equipment malfunctions, software glitches, human error, and even terrorist attacks.

14.6.2 List an organization's tasks when it is considering offsite data storage. The five tasks are planning and deciding which data to back up, establishing and following a backup schedule, protecting data when they are transmitted offsite, choosing the right vendor, and continually testing and refining the backup system.

LO 14.7 Review the trends in information systems.

Computer information systems are continually and rapidly evolving. Some of the most significant trends are the increasing demands of the distributed workforce, the increased use of application service providers, on-demand computing, and grid computing. Many people now work in virtual offices, including at home. Information technology makes this work arrangement possible. Application service providers allow organizations to outsource many of their IT functions. Instead of buying and maintaining expensive software, users of on-demand computing rent software time from outside vendors and pay only for their usage. Grid computing consists of a network of smaller computers running special software creating a virtual mainframe or even supercomputer.

 ASSESSMENT CHECK ANSWERS

14.7.1 What is an application service provider? An application service provider (ASP) is an outside vendor that provides both the computers and the application support for managing an information system. By using an ASP, the organization can effectively outsource some, or all, of its IT functions.

14.7.2 Explain on-demand computing. Instead of purchasing and maintaining expensive software, some organizations use on-demand computing. In this arrangement, software is rented from a vendor and the organization only pays for its actual usage.

BUSINESS TERMS YOU NEED TO KNOW

application service provider (ASP) 405

botnet 402

chief information officer (CIO) 390

cloud computing 405

computer-based information systems 391

data 390

database 392

decision support system (DSS) 393

executive support system (ESS) 394

expert system 394

firewall 399

grid computing 405

hardware 394

information 390

information system 390

intranet 399

local area networks (LANs) 398

malware 401

management information system (MIS) 393

management support systems 393

on-demand computing 405

operational support systems 393

process control systems 393

server 395

software 396

spyware 402

transaction processing systems 393

Trojan horse 402

virtual private networks (VPNs) 400

viruses 402

VoIP 400

wide area networks (WANs) 398

Wi-Fi 398

worm 402

REVIEW QUESTIONS

1. Distinguish between data and information. Why is this difference important to businesspeople who manage information?

2. What are the four components of an information system?

3. Describe the two different types of information systems, and give an example of how each type might help a specific business.

4. Explain decision support systems, executive support systems, and expert systems.

5. What are the major categories of computers? What is a server?

6. What is an intranet? Give specific examples of the benefits for firms that have their own intranets.

7. What steps can organizations and individuals take to prevent cybercrime?

8. How does a computer virus work? What can individuals and organizational computer users do to reduce the likelihood of acquiring a computer virus?

9. Why is disaster recovery important for businesses? Relate your answer to a natural disaster such as a hurricane or fire.

10. Describe four information system trends.

PROJECTS AND TEAMWORK APPLICATIONS

1. Suppose you've been hired to design an information system for a midsize retailer. Describe what that information system might look like, including the necessary components. Would the system be an operational support system, a management support system, or both?

2. Select a local company and contact the person in charge of its information system for a brief interview. Ask that individual to outline his or her company's information system. Ask the person what he or she likes most about the job. Did this interview make you more or less interested in a career in information systems?

3. Working with a partner, research the current status of Wi-Max. Prepare a short report on its growth, its current uses, and its future for business computing.

4. Your supervisor has asked for your advice. She isn't sure the company's information system needs any major safeguards because the company has very little web presence beyond a simple home page. But employees use email to contact suppliers and customers. List the threats that the company's information system is vulnerable to. What types of protection would you suggest?

5. Has your computer ever been hacked or attacked by a virus? What steps did you take to recover lost files and data? How would you prevent something similar from happening again?

WEB ASSIGNMENTS

1. **Enterprise resource planning (ERP).** SAP is one of the world's largest enterprise resource planning software companies. Visit the firm's website (www.sap.com) and click on "Customer Testimonials." Choose one of the customers listed and read its testimonial. Prepare a brief summary and explain how this exercise improved your understanding of the business applications of ERP software.

2. **Computer security.** Visit McAfee's website. Review the items for security awareness under "Threat Center" and discuss them in terms of how companies and consumers can prevent cybercrimes. www.mcafee.com/us/business-home.aspx

3. **Cloud computing.** IBM is one of the largest providers of cloud computing. Visit the IBM website (www.ibm.com) and click on "Solutions" and then select "Cloud computing." Print out the material and bring it to class to participate in a class discussion.

Note: Internet web addresses change frequently. If you don't find the exact sites listed, you may need to access the organization's home page and search from there or use a search engine such as Bing or Google.

PART 5: CASE STUDY Beau's All Natural Brewing Company
Using Technology to Manage Communications and Information

Without the array of communications technologies available at Beau's, employees would probably have a much harder time keeping track of sales, transportation logistics, and production scheduling. When Steve was told by some retailers they were out of stock and had nothing sell, he knew Beau's was missing sales opportunities they had already won but could not fulfill. Although delivery schedules worked out at the warehouses and supplemented with emergency deliveries to keep customers stocked worked well enough at the beginning, Steve knew the system was in need of better communications technologies between drivers, warehouses, and customer order takers.

The solution was a tablet device that delivered instructions to drivers while they were on their routes. Adjustments could be made to juggle delivery schedules and emergency deliveries in real time—and the high costs that went with modifications were reduced substantially. Technology allowed for better customer service, fewer headaches, and freed up resources for other tasks. According to Steve, "It was money well spent. We would have had an impossible time growing the distribution network using the old clipboard and cellphone technology. Today, with over 2,000 point-of-sale systems at restaurants, bars, Ontario Liquor Control Board Stores (LCBO) and warehouses in Ottawa, Trenton, and Toronto, the only way we can keep our drivers delivering what customers need, when they need it, is with an integrated online ordering system that connects with each driver through his mobile tablet. Our drivers are able to better serve and maintain contact with the customers they deliver to by making decisions and entering data on the go. We found through our system that by having our trucks carry some extra inventory, drivers were able to spontaneously fill empty shelves at LCBOs when competitors were late or unable to complete promised deliveries. As a result, we picked up 8% more sales simply because we had extra product available beyond what the LCBO had ordered for that delivery."

A second area where technology is enabling the company to serve customers better is through the Internet. Orders can be placed online and customers may choose to come by the brewery for pick up or have Beau's delivery service drop off orders at residences and pick up empty bottles for a fee in selected zones of Ottawa. The service is run in conjunction with BottleWorks, a charitable fundraiser for Operation Come Home. BottleWorks is a commercial empty-bottle pick-up service for local Ottawa restaurants, bars, hotels, condominiums, and conference facilities. It is a social enterprise that employs at-risk youth age 16 and up for a 12-week period to assist with bottle collection and administrative work.

As much as Beau's computerized systems can display reports on sales, expense, and other common requests for data and information, it does not provide information that would help the company with planning and understanding customer behaviour better. As Steve explained, "What would be really good to know is whether the customer who bought our beer today was a new customer or an

(continued)

established customer who is loyal to one of our brands. Does this customer buy only one or two of our brands or do they rotate through a wider variety of beers we are offering throughout the year? Many of our products are "seasonal" and won't be back until the season returns next year. We might be missing the opportunity to introduce a new "winner" brand but can't know from a short selling season. I wish I knew some of the answers to these questions."

Questions for Critical Thinking

1. How would you use technology do find out some of the answers to these questions?

2. After reviewing Beau's website at www.beaus.ca, evaluate the strengths and weaknesses from a customer information-gathering point of view.

3. How would you change the website to increase information flow to Beau's?

5 LAUNCHING YOUR. . .

INFORMATION TECHNOLOGY CAREER

Part 5, "Managing Technology and Information," consists of Chapter 14. This chapter discussed using computers and related technology to manage information. We discussed well-known technology companies such as Google and Oracle and many smaller organizations that use computer technology to manage information. These examples show that all organizations need to manage technology and information. The complexity and scope of technology and information are likely to increase in the years ahead. As a result, the demand for information systems professionals is expected to grow.

According to research, employment in occupations such as computer software engineering, software support specialists, and network systems administrators is expected to grow faster than the average for all occupations in the next decade. Of the top five occupations where employment is expected to grow the fastest over the next few years, two occupations are related to information systems.[1]

What types of jobs are available in information systems? What are the working conditions like? What are the career paths? Experience in information systems can lead to a wide variety of jobs. In some cases, you'll work in the information systems department of a business such as Enbridge. In other cases, you may work for a specialized information systems firm, such as IBM. A specialized firm provides information services to governments, not-for-profit organizations, and businesses.

Information systems is a popular business major, and many entry-level positions are available each year. Many information systems graduates spend their entire careers in this field, while some move into other areas. People who began their careers in information systems are well represented in senior management positions. Let's look briefly at some of the specific jobs you might find after earning a degree in information systems.

Technical support specialists are trouble shooters who monitor the performance of computer systems; provide technical support and solve problems for computer users; install, modify, clean, and repair computer hardware and software; and write training manuals and train computer users.

Network administrators design, install, and support an organization's computer networks, including its local area network, wide area network, Internet, and intranet systems. They provide administrative support for software and hardware users and ensure that the design of an organization's computer networks and all of the components fit together efficiently and effectively.

Computer security specialists plan, coordinate, and implement an organization's information security. They educate users about how to protect computer systems, install antivirus and similar software, and monitor the networks for security breaches. The role and importance of computer security specialists have increased in response to the growing number of attacks on networks and data.

CAREER ASSESSMENT EXERCISES IN INFORMATION SYSTEMS

1. Assume you're interested in a career as a systems administrator. Go to the following website: www.itworldcanada.com. Prepare a brief report outlining the responsibilities of a systems administrator, the employers that hire for these positions, and the educational background needed.

2. Examine the website for TradeInsight: www.tradeinsight.com. Read a few of the case studies. Write a brief report about how the firm's software helps clients to better understand their sales and marketing data.

15 | UNDERSTANDING ACCOUNTING AND FINANCIAL STATEMENTS

LEARNING OBJECTIVES

LO 15.1 Explain the functions of accounting and identify the three basic accounting activities.

LO 15.2 Describe the various types of accounting professionals.

LO 15.3 Discuss the foundation of the accounting system.

LO 15.4 Outline the steps in the accounting cycle.

LO 15.5 Explain the functions and major components of the four principal financial statements.

LO 15.6 Discuss how financial ratios are used to analyze a company's financial strengths and weaknesses.

LO 15.7 Describe the role of budgets in a business.

LO 15.8 Outline the accounting issues facing global business.

INSIDE BUSINESS

Cooking the Books

Imagine it is a few weeks after year end. The financial statements have been prepared by a team of experienced accountants. They've also been audited by another team of experienced auditors. This *must* mean that the statements are correct. After all, how complicated can accounting be? The numbers are either right or wrong.

These are common misconceptions—or misunderstandings—about the nature of accounting information. Accountants have quite a bit of flexibility when preparing financial statements, but they always need to stay within the limits of generally accepted accounting principles.

Accountants make choices about *when* to recognize, or record, revenue and expenses on the financial statements. For example, suppose the publisher of this textbook sells 100 copies of the textbook to your school bookstore with the option to return any books not purchased by students. When will the publisher's accountant recognize, or record, the revenue? Is it recognized when the books are delivered, or when the books are sold to students? Accountants also estimate how much bad debt or depreciation expense to charge against income in a given year. For example, when a company buys a delivery van, over how many years is the van depreciated? The more years the van is depreciated over, the lower the expense each year. Many people who prepare financial statements choose policies and make estimates at the high or low end of the acceptable ranges. Sometimes the decision comes down to an individual's personal motivations. Some individuals may want to increase their bonus, which may be tied to the company's net income; or they may want to lower their income taxes, which may also be based on net income.

Some financial statement preparers go far beyond the prescribed ranges. They commit fraud by changing the statements and providing false information for their personal gain. One well-known Canadian fraud case involved Livent co-founders Garth Drabinsky and Myron Gottlieb. Both were found guilty of forgery and defrauding their investors of more than $400 million. The two ran Livent, a theatre production company that produced some of Canada's best-known theatrical productions, including Canada's longest running musical at the time, *The Phantom of the Opera*. Part of the Livent scheme involved moving expenses from one period to another, or allocating expenses to certain shows that they did not relate to. Drabinsky was sentenced to seven years, and Gottlieb was sentenced to six years. They were released on $350,000 bail while waiting to file an appeal.

In the United States, the energy company Enron filed for bankruptcy in 2001. The Enron case was known as one of the world's biggest audit failures. Enron hid billions of dollars in debt by not recording it on the financial statements. Shortly after the Enron case, another fraud case was revealed. It was discovered that corporate executives at the telecommunications company WorldCom were also "cooking the books." They had been recording many expenses as assets and had inflated revenues by using creative accounting. These well-known accounting scandals resulted in the world's largest bankruptcies at the time.

These major fraud cases led to the creation of increased regulatory legislation, such as the Sarbanes-Oxley Act in the United States and Bill 198 in Canada. Canadian, American, and global companies are now required to spend billions of dollars to remain in compliance with these new legislations.[1]

CHAPTER 15 OVERVIEW

Accounting professionals prepare the financial information that organizations present in their annual reports. Whether you begin your career by working for a company or by starting your own firm, you need to understand what accountants do. You also need to understand why their work is so important in contemporary business.

Accounting is the process of measuring, interpreting, and communicating financial information to enable people inside and outside the firm to make informed decisions. In many ways, accounting is the language of business. Accountants gather, record, report, and interpret financial information in a way that describes the status and operation of an organization and aids in decision making.

Millions of men and women around the world are employed as accountants. In Canada, more than 200,000 people work as accountants or auditors.[2] Accounting is one of the most in-demand disciplines on university campuses. Part of the attraction is the availability of jobs and the high starting salaries for talented graduates. In Canada, salaries for Chartered Professional Accountants (CPAs) average more than $141,000 per year.[3]

This chapter begins by describing who uses accounting information. We then discuss business activities that involve accounting statements: financing, investing, and operations. Next, we explain the accounting process, define double-entry bookkeeping, and present the accounting equation. We then discuss how information about financial transactions is developed into financial statements. Next we look at the methods of interpreting these statements and the role of budgeting when planning and controlling a business. The chapter concludes with a discussion of the impact of financial information in global business.

accounting the process of measuring, interpreting, and communicating financial information to support internal and external business decision making.

LO 15.1 Explain the functions of accounting and identify the three basic accounting activities.

USERS OF ACCOUNTING INFORMATION

Both people inside an organization and people outside an organization use accounting information to help them make business decisions. **Figure 15.1** lists the users of accounting information and how they apply that information.

The major users of accounting information are managers at a business, owners, creditors (including banks), government agencies, and not-for-profit organizations. Accounting information helps them to plan and control daily and long-range operations. Business owners and boards of directors at not-for-profit groups also use accounting data to track managers' progress in operating the organizations. Union officials use accounting data in contract negotiations, and employees refer to it as they monitor their firms' productivity and profitability performance.

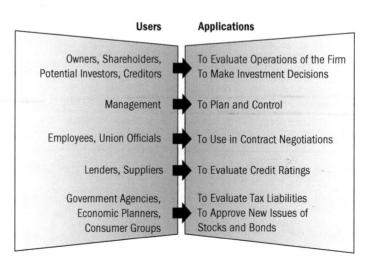

Users	Applications
Owners, Shareholders, Potential Investors, Creditors	To Evaluate Operations of the Firm To Make Investment Decisions
Management	To Plan and Control
Employees, Union Officials	To Use in Contract Negotiations
Lenders, Suppliers	To Evaluate Credit Ratings
Government Agencies, Economic Planners, Consumer Groups	To Evaluate Tax Liabilities To Approve New Issues of Stocks and Bonds

FIGURE 15.1 Users and Applications of Accounting Information

Some companies want employees to understand how their work affects the company's bottom line. These companies share sensitive financial information with their employees and teach them how to understand and use financial statements. People who support *open-book management* believe that allowing employees to view financial information helps them to better understand how their work contributes to the company's success, which, in turn, benefits the employees.

Outside a firm, potential investors evaluate accounting information to help them decide whether to buy a firm's shares. As we'll discuss later in the chapter, any company whose shares are traded publicly must report its financial results on a regular basis. That means that anyone can look up RONA's sales last year or how much money Tim Hortons made during the last quarter. Bankers and other lenders use accounting information to evaluate a potential borrower's financial soundness. The Canada Revenue Agency (CRA) and provincial tax officials use it to calculate a company's tax liability. Citizens' groups and government agencies use accounting information to assess the efficiency of such operations as Alberta Health Services, BC Hydro, and the Art Gallery of Ontario.

Accountants play important roles in business and in many other aspects of society. Their work influences each of the business environments discussed earlier in this book. Accountants clearly provide important information to help managers deal with the competitive and economic environments in which their companies do business.

Some other accounting contributions are less obvious, or less noticed, such as helping others to understand, predict, and react to the technological, regulatory, and social and cultural environments. For example, every year thousands of volunteers help Canadians complete their income tax returns. One of the largest organized programs is the Community Volunteer Income Tax Program (CVITP), organized by the CRA. Through this program, more than 16,000 volunteers help more than half a million Canadians complete their provincial and federal tax returns.

Accountants play an important role in business and other areas of society by providing services to businesses, individuals, government agencies, and not-for-profit organizations.

Business Activities Involving Accounting

The natural progression of a business begins with financing. All the steps after financing, including investing, lead to operating the business. All organizations, whether for-profit and not-for-profit, perform these three basic activities, and accounting plays a key role in each:

1. Financing activities provide necessary funds to start a business and expand it after it begins operating.

2. Investing activities provide valuable assets that are needed to run a business.

3. Operating activities focus on selling goods and services, but they also view expenses as important elements of sound financial management.

Brian Hill, CEO of Vancouver-based Aritzia, performed all three activities during the startup and growth of his high-fashion chain. Aritzia targets women between the ages of 15 and 30. Hill's success in Canada led to a major U.S. expansion. Hill could have tried to finance the expansion himself, as he had done before. But he wanted to avoid the financial risk that he had taken on earlier when Aritzia was growing. Hill decided to seek financing from Berkshire Partners, who took a majority stake in the company. Aritzia recently moved toward a more vertically integrated model. He chose this model to benefit from "a bigger piece of the pie" by cutting out a third-party retailer. He also made this choice for strategic reasons: Hill believes that part of Aritzia's success is that the company understands customers' needs. He feels that if he and his company are involved at the point of sale, they will have a better feel for the needs of the customers. This strategy has proven very successful thus far.[4]

ASSESSMENT CHECK

15.1.1 Define *accounting*.

15.1.2 Who uses accounting information?

15.1.3 What three business activities involve accounting?

LO 15.2 Describe the various types of accounting professionals.

ACCOUNTING PROFESSIONALS

Accounting professionals work in many areas in and for business firms, government agencies, and not-for-profit organizations. They can be classified as public accountants, management accountants, government accountants, and not-for-profit accountants.

Public Accountants

public accountant an accountant who provides accounting services to other organizations.

A **public accountant** provides accounting services to individuals or business firms for a fee. Most public accounting firms provide three basic services to clients: (1) auditing, or examining, financial records; (2) tax preparation, planning, and related services; and (3) management consulting. Because public accountants are not employees of a client firm, they can provide unbiased advice about a firm's financial condition.

Canada has hundreds of public accounting firms, but just a few firms attract the largest share of the industry. The four largest public accounting firms—Deloitte, Ernst & Young, KPMG, and PricewaterhouseCoopers—collect almost $5 billion annually from Canadian clients. In contrast, the Toronto-based Grant Thornton, the nation's fifth-largest accounting firm, has annual revenues of approximately $500 million.[5]

Some years ago, public accounting firms were criticized for providing management consulting services to the same firms they audited. Critics argued that when a public accounting firm does both—auditing and management consulting—a conflict of interest is created. This conflict of interest may weaken confidence in the quality of the financial statements that accounting firms audit. The bankruptcies of some high-profile firms increased pressure on public accounting firms to end the practice. Legislation also set strict limits on the types of consulting services auditors can provide. For example, an accounting firm that audits a company's books cannot provide any other services to that company, including tax services. As a result, three of the four largest public accounting firms either sold large portions of their consulting practices or created separate consulting companies. PricewaterhouseCoopers, for example, sold much of its consulting business to IBM. The accounting firms now focus on providing auditing and tax services.

As the "Hit & Miss" feature outlines, more and more public accountants are also being certified as *forensic accountants*. Some smaller public accounting firms have chosen to specialize in forensic accounting. These professionals and the firms that employ them focus on uncovering potential fraud in many different organizations.

Chartered Professional Accountants (CPAs) are Canada's most recognized group of professional accountants. They demonstrate their accounting knowledge by meeting provincial requirements for education and experience and by successfully completing thorough testing in accounting theory and practice, auditing, law, finance, strategy, and taxation. Other recognized accountants meet specified educational and experience requirements and pass certification exams to earn the title *Certified Fraud Examiner (CFE)* or *Certified Internal Auditor (CIA)*.

Management Accountants

An accountant who is employed by a business other than a public accounting firm is called a *management accountant*. A management accountant collects and records financial transactions and prepares financial statements used by the firm's managers in decision making. Management accountants provide timely, relevant, accurate, and concise information that executives can use to operate their firms more effectively and more profitably than without this input. A management accountant prepares financial statements and plays a major role in interpreting them. A management accountant should be able to provide answers to many important questions:

- Where is the company going?
- What opportunities are in the company's future?
- Will certain situations expose the company to excessive risk?
- Does the firm's information system provide detailed and timely information to all levels of management?

HIT & MISS

Forensic Accountants: Fraud Busters

When you think of an accountant, do you picture someone poring over stacks of ledgers or computer printouts, calculator in hand? Much of accounting *does* involve ledgers and printouts, but forensic accounting is a little different. Forensic accountants don't take a company's accounting numbers at face value—they are crime fighters who look at what's happening behind those numbers. Forensic accountants work in a growing field. They investigate such white-collar crimes as business fraud, improper financial report- ing, and illegal investment schemes.

Forensic accounting is accounting that is done in preparation for legal review. Forensic accountants take a skeptical view. They investigate below the surface of an organization's accounting system to find out what actually happened. They may also testify as expert witnesses if a case goes to trial. In Canada, forensic accountants typically need a professional accounting designation such as CPA and further training in investigative techniques. Forensic accountants may have a Certified Fraud Examiner (CFE) designation or a diploma in forensic accounting (DIFA).

Nortel Networks was once a large Canadian telecommunications company. It went through multiple financial statement restatements before completely collapsing. As a result, former CEO Frank Dunn, former CFO Douglas Beatty, and former corporate controller Michael Gollogly were charged with fraud, falsification of accounts and documents, and involvement in issuing a false prospectus. Such scandals can have far-reaching and disastrous effects on a firm. Nortel's stock once traded at as high as $124.50 per share and represented more than one-third of the TSE 300 index, the Toronto Stock Exchange's index of 300 influential stocks. After news broke on the accounting charges, Nortel stock became penny stock, trading at less than $1.00 per share. Nortel ceased operations in June 2009.

Al Rosen is one of Canada's best known (and possibly its most outspoken) forensic accountants. He said, "You can churn out all sorts of rubbish in quarterly and annual reports . . . and guess what the newspapers do with their databases? They take this crap, they do all this analysis, and they're playing with bogus numbers."

Questions for Critical Thinking

1. Describe how a shift in the economy has created a new career path for accounting students.

2. How can forensic accounting change the world of business?

Sources: "The Wild Ride of Canada's Most-Watched Stock," *CBC News*, February 27, 2008, accessed May 18, 2011, www.cbc.ca/news/background/nortel/stock.html; CICA, "The CICA Alliance for Excellence in Investigative and Forensic Accounting," accessed May 18, 2011, www.cica.ca/focus-on-practice-areas/forensic-accounting/the-alliance-for-excellence-in-investigative-and-forensic-accounting/index.aspx; "RCMP Lay Fraud Charges against Former Nortel Execs," *CTV News*, June 19, 2008, accessed May 18, 2011, www.ctv.ca/CTVNews/TopStories/20080619/rcmp_nortel_080619/; David Berman, "Lie Detector," *MoneySense*, December/January 2002, accessed May 18, 2011, www.canadianjusticereviewboard.ca/CJRB_director_Al_Rosen.htm.

Management accountants often specialize in different aspects of accounting. For example, a cost accountant decides on the costs of goods and services and helps to set their prices. An internal auditor examines the firm's financial practices to ensure that its records include accurate data and that its operations comply with federal, provincial, and local laws and regulations. A tax accountant works to minimize a firm's tax bill and handles its federal and provincial tax returns.

Management accountants are usually involved in the development and enforcement of organizational policies on such items as employee travel. As part of their job, many employees travel and accumulate frequent flyer miles and hotel reward points. Some organizations have strict policies over the personal use of these travel points, but many do not.

In recent years, the federal regulations for accounting and public reporting have changed. The need to adapt to the new regulations has increased the demand for management accountants. As a result, salaries for these professionals are rising.

Government and Not-for-Profit Accountants

Federal, provincial, and local governments also need accounting services. Government accountants and those who work for not-for-profit organizations perform professional services similar to the services provided by management accountants. Accountants in government and not-for-profit sectors are concerned primarily with how efficiently the organizations work to meet their objectives. Many government agencies employ accountants, including the CRA, the Canadian Security

✔ **ASSESSMENT CHECK**

15.2.1 List the three services offered by public accounting firms.

15.2.2 What tasks do management accountants perform?

Intelligence Service (CSIS), the Province of Manitoba, and the City of St. John's in Newfoundland and Labrador. The federal government employs hundreds of accountants.

Accountants also work for not-for-profit organizations, such as churches, labour unions, charities, schools, hospitals, and universities. The not-for-profit sector is one of the fastest-growing segments of accounting practice. More not-for-profits are publishing their financial information because donors want more accountability from these organizations. Donors are interested in how the groups spend the money they raise.

LO 15.3 Describe the foundation of the accounting system.

THE FOUNDATION OF THE ACCOUNTING SYSTEM

generally accepted accounting principles (GAAP) principles that outline the conventions, rules, and procedures for deciding on the acceptable accounting practices at a particular time.

Accountants need to provide reliable, consistent, and unbiased information to decision makers. To help them in this task, accountants follow guidelines, or standards, known as **generally accepted accounting principles (GAAP)**. These principles outline the conventions, rules, and procedures for deciding on the acceptable accounting and financial reporting practices at a particular time. GAAP includes International Financial Reporting Standards (IFRS), Accounting Standards for Private Enterprises (ASPE), accounting standards for not-for-profit organizations, accounting standards for pension plans, and accounting standards for governments.

All GAAP standards are based on several basic qualitative characteristics: consistency, relevance, representational faithfulness, reliability, timeliness, understandability, verifiability, and comparability. *Consistency* means that all data should be collected and presented in the same manner across all periods. Any change in how specific data are collected or presented must be noted and explained. *Relevance* states that all information being reported should be appropriate and assist users in evaluating financial information. *Representational faithfulness* means that financial information should reflect the substance of the economic activity during the reporting period. *Reliability* implies that the accounting data in financial statements are dependable and can be verified by an independent party, such as an outside auditor. *Timeliness* states that financial information should be made available within a time period that allows the financial information to be useful in decision making. *Understandability* requires that financial information be clearly presented to users. *Verifiability* means that other independent and knowledgeable individuals would agree that the financial information is fairly presented. Finally, *comparability* ensures that one firm's financial statements can be compared with those of similar businesses.

Accounting Standards Board (AcSB) the organization that interprets and modifies GAAP in Canada for private and not-for-profit businesses.

In Canada, the **Accounting Standards Board (AcSB)** is primarily responsible for evaluating and setting GAAP related to pension plans and to private and not-for-profit businesses. The Public Sector Accounting Board (PSAB) is responsible for accounting standards for governments.

Canadian public companies are required to use International Financial Reporting Standards (IFRS). These standards allow for financial statements to be more easily compared from country to country. This level of comparability is required because of the increase in worldwide trade. The idea of a uniform set of global accounting rules is gaining interest, mainly as a result of the expansion of the European Union and the signing of cross-national trade agreements, such as the North American Free Trade Agreement (NAFTA). Also, more investors are buying shares in foreign multinational corporations, and they need a practical way to evaluate firms in other countries. To assist global investors, more and more firms are reporting their financial information by using international accounting standards. This practice helps investors to make informed decisions.

International Financial Reporting Standards (IFRS) the standards and interpretations adopted by the IASB.

International Financial Reporting Standards (IFRS) are the standards and interpretations adopted by the **International Accounting Standards Board (IASB)**. The use of IFRS is widespread and growing. More than 120 countries require, permit the use of, or have a policy of working with IFRS, including India, Australia, Canada, Hong Kong, and member countries of the European Union.

International Accounting Standards Board (IASB) the organization that promotes worldwide consistency in financial reporting practices.

How does IFRS differ from ASPE? IFRS and ASPE share many similarities, but also have some important differences. For example, under ASPE firms report plant, property, and equipment on the balance sheet at the historical cost minus depreciation; under IFRS, firms have the option to report plant, property, and equipment on the balance sheet at current market value. The IFRS

CAREER KICKSTART

Tips for Complying with the Corruption of Foreign Public Officials Act

The Corruption of Foreign Public Officials (CFPO) Act is meant to prevent the bribery of foreign officials for the purpose of gaining or keeping business in another country. More companies now do business overseas, so they are naturally concerned about being at risk to violations of this law. Enforcement of this act is at an all-time high and is expected to remain high. Penalties are severe, including fines and prison time for anyone convicted. The following are some ways that global firms can improve their compliance and reduce their risk:

1. Assess your firm's risk under the CFPO Act, country by country. Does your firm do business with any government-owned foreign firms or with any foreign government officials? What are the risks of corruption and bribery?

2. Set up a policy for your firm's employees—in Canada and abroad—to comply with the CFPO Act. The policy should cover gifts and payments to foreign officials, charitable donations, accurate and complete records, and other areas at risk.

3. Train your employees in the policies of the CFPO Act. Include these policies in your company's overall compliance process. Have your human resources department make these policies part of new-employee orientation.

4. Have a compliance team in place to monitor compliance to the act and to be on the watch for potential risks. The team should include company lawyers, accountants, and auditors. The team should be empowered to make both in-house and external investigations.

5. Plan any international investigations carefully. Many foreign countries do not apply the attorney-client privilege to company lawyers and employees.

Sources: Department of Justice, "The Corruption of Foreign Public Officials Act: A Guide," May 1999, accessed May 27, 2011, www.justice.gc.ca/eng/dept-min/pub/cfpoa-lcape/index.html; "Foreign Corrupt Practices Act," Ernst & Young, accessed June 1, 2010, www.ey.com; U.S. Department of Justice, "Foreign Corrupt Practices Act: An Overview," accessed June 1, 2010, www.justice.gov; Gary Sturisky, "2010 Compliance Challenges: Three More Areas That Matter," *Corporate Compliance Insights,* March 4, 2010, accessed June 1, 2010, www.corporatecomplianceinsights.com; Brian Loughman, Aaron Marcu, and Kerry Schalders, "Top Ten Tips for FCPA Compliance," Association of Corporate Counsel, March 1, 2010, accessed June 1, 2010, www.acc.com; Nina Gross, "Foreign Corrupt Practices Act: Leading Practices to Consider," Deloitte, January 29, 2010, accessed June 1, 2010, www.deloitte.com.

option gives a clearer picture of the real value of a firm's assets. Many accounting experts believe that, overall, IFRS is less complicated than traditional GAAP and more transparent.[6]

In the United States, the **Financial Accounting Standards Board (FASB)** sets GAAP. The FASB is currently working with the IASB on a project to work toward IFRS. The United States is one of the few developed countries not currently using IFRS.

In response to accounting fraud and questions about the independence of auditors, the U.S. government enacted the Sarbanes-Oxley Act in 2002, commonly known as SOX. SOX then created the Public Company Accounting Oversight Board. This five-member board has the power to set audit standards and to investigate and approve the accounting firms that certify the books of publicly traded firms. All Canadian companies that have publicly traded stock or debt on a U.S. stock exchange must comply with SOX. In Canada, Bill 198 requires similar provisions as SOX for Canadian companies.

SOX and Bill 198 also added to the reporting requirements for publicly traded companies. For example, senior executives, including the chief executive officer (CEO) and chief financial officer (CFO), must personally certify that the financial information reported by the company is correct. As noted earlier, these additional requirements have increased the demand for accounting professionals, especially managerial accountants. One result of this increased demand has been higher salaries.

It is expensive for firms to meet GAAP standards and the requirements of SOX and Bill 198. For example, audits can cost millions of dollars each year. These expenses can be especially difficult for small businesses. Some people have suggested making changes to GAAP and SOX for smaller firms. They argue that some accounting rules were designed for larger companies. As a result, Canada has multiple sets of standards, such as the Accounting Standards for Private Enterprises (ASPE), which are set by the AcSB.

The **Corruption of Foreign Public Officials Act** is a federal law that prohibits Canadian citizens and companies from bribing foreign officials to win or continue business. The law was later extended to make foreign officials subject to penalties if they cause similar corrupt practices to occur within Canada or its territories. The "Career Kickstart" feature provides some tips on complying with this act.

Financial Accounting Standards Board (FASB) the organization that interprets and modifies GAAP in the United States.

Corruption of Foreign Public Officials Act a federal law that prohibits Canadian citizens and companies from bribing foreign officials to win or continue business.

 **ASSESSMENT CHECK**

15.3.1 Define *GAAP.*

15.3.2 What is the role played by the AcSB?

LO 15.4 Outline the steps in the accounting cycle.

accounting cycle the set of activities involved in converting information and individual transactions into financial statements.

THE ACCOUNTING CYCLE

Accounting deals with a firm's financial transactions with its employees, customers, suppliers, owners, and with bankers and various government agencies. For example, payroll cheques result in a cash outflow to employees. A payment to a supplier results in the delivery of needed materials for the production process. Customers use cash, cheques, and credit to purchase goods, which generate business funds to cover the costs of operations and to earn a profit. Prompt payment of bills keeps the firm's credit rating high and helps its future ability to earn a profit. Accountants gather data on individual buying and selling transactions and convert these data to financial statements through a process called the **accounting cycle**.

Figure 15.2 shows the activities involved in the accounting cycle: recording, classifying, and summarizing transactions. Any transaction that has a financial impact on the business, such as wages or payments to suppliers, should be recorded. These transactions are recorded in journals, which list the transactions in the order they occurred. Journal listings are then posted to ledgers. A ledger shows increases or decreases in specific accounts, such as cash or wages. Ledgers are used to prepare the financial statements, which summarize the financial transactions. Management and other interested parties use the resulting financial statements for many different purposes.

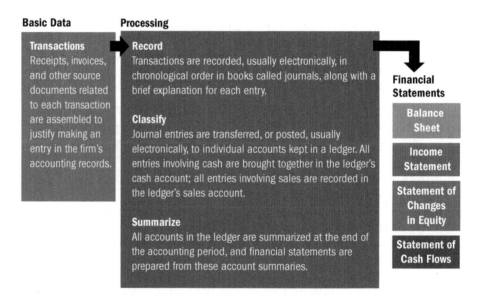

FIGURE 15.2 The Accounting Cycle

The Accounting Equation

asset anything with future benefit owned or controlled by a firm.

Three fundamental terms appear in the accounting equation: assets, liabilities, and owners' equity. An **asset** is anything with future benefit owned or controlled by a business. Assets include land, buildings, supplies, cash, accounts receivable (amounts owed to the business as payment for credit sales), and marketable securities.

Tangible assets, such as equipment, buildings, and inventories, are the most common assets. But a firm's most important assets may be its intangible assets, such as patents and trademarks. These assets are especially important for companies such as computer software firms, biotechnology companies, and pharmaceutical companies. For example, Johnson & Johnson—which has both biotechnology and pharmaceutical operations—reported more than $40 billion in intangible assets (including goodwill) in one recent year, out of a total of almost $133 billion in assets.[7]

Two groups have claims against the assets of a firm: creditors and owners. A **liability** of a business is anything owed to creditors—that is, the claims of a firm's creditors. When a firm borrows money to purchase inventory, land, or machinery, the claims of creditors are shown as accounts payable, notes payable, or long-term debt. Wages and salaries owed to employees are also liabilities (known as *wages payable* or *accrued wages*).

Owners' equity is the owners' initial investment in the business plus any profits that were not paid to owners. A strong owners' equity position is often used as evidence of a firm's financial strength and stability.

The **accounting equation** (also called the *accounting identity*) states that assets must equal liabilities plus owners' equity. This equation reflects the financial position of a firm at any point in time:

Tangible assets, such as buildings, equipment, and inventories, may look impressive. But they are sometimes less important to a company than its intangible assets, such as patents and trademarks.

$$Assets = Liabilities + Owners'\ Equity$$

Because financing comes from either creditors or owners, the right side of the accounting equation also represents the business's financial structure.

The accounting equation also illustrates **double-entry bookkeeping**—the process used to record accounting transactions. Because assets must always equal liabilities plus equity, each transaction must have two or more effects on the accounts. For example, if a company increases an asset, one of the following must also happen: another asset must decrease, a liability must increase, or owners' equity must increase. That is, if a company uses cash to purchase inventory, one asset (inventory) is increased while another asset (cash) is decreased by the same amount. Following the same idea, a decrease in an asset must be balanced by either an increase in another asset, a decrease in a liability, or a decrease in owners' equity. If a company uses cash to repay a bank loan, both an asset (cash) and a liability (bank loans) decrease by the same amount.

Two simple numerical examples will help to explain the accounting equation and double-entry bookkeeping.

First, assume the owner of a photo studio uses her own funds to buy a new camera system for $5,000. The accounting transaction would look like the following:

Increase plant, property, and equipment (an asset) by $5,000

Increase owners' equity by $5,000

So the left side of the accounting equation increases by $5,000 and is balanced by a $5,000 increase on the right side.

Second, assume a firm has a $100,000 loan from a bank and decides to pay it off using some of its cash. The transaction would be recorded as follows:

Decrease bank loan (a liability) by $100,000

Decrease cash (an asset) by $100,000

In this second example, the left side and right side of the accounting equation both decrease by $100,000.

liability a claim against a firm's assets by creditors.

owners' equity the funds that owners invest in the business plus any profits not paid to owners in the form of cash dividends.

accounting equation the relationship that should reflect a firm's financial position at any time: assets should always equal the sum of liabilities and owners' equity.

double-entry bookkeeping the process used to record accounting transactions; each individual transaction is always balanced by another transaction.

The relationship described by the accounting equation is the basis for developing the firm's financial statements. Three financial statements form the foundation: the balance sheet, the income statement, and the statement of changes in equity. The information in these statements is calculated using the double-entry bookkeeping system and reflects the basic accounting equation. A fourth statement, the statement of cash flows, focuses on the sources and uses of cash in a firm's operating, investing, and financing activities.

The Impact of Computers and the Internet on the Accounting Process

For hundreds of years, bookkeepers have manually recorded, or posted, accounting transactions as entries in journals. They then transferred the information, or posted it, to individual accounts listed in ledgers. Computers have simplified the process, making it both faster and easier. For example, point-of-sale terminals in retail stores perform several functions each time they record sales. These terminals recall product prices from a computer system's memory and keep inventory counts of individual items. They also do the data entry functions that were once entered manually.

Accounting software programs are used widely in both large and small businesses. They allow a do-it-once approach: A single sales entry is automatically converted into a journal entry, which is stored until needed. Decision makers can then instantly access up-to-date financial statements and financial ratios. Improvements in accounting software continue to make the process faster and easier. CPS is a Canadian company that sells and services machines. Recently CPS decided to use Sage 300 ERP and Sage CRM to integrate its databases and track its sales processes. This new system means that managers no longer need to wait for reports because they can access the data at any time. Those who use information on outside sales can now access and share information with management, accounting, and those who use inside sales figures. All the operational data is integrated with CPS's accounting data to reduce the number of duplicate entries.[8]

The accounting needs of entrepreneurs and small businesses differ from the needs of larger firms. Some accounting software programs, such as QuickBooks and Sage 50 (formerly Sage Simply Accounting), have been designed specifically for entrepreneurs and small businesses. To facilitate ease of use and maintenance, many cloud computing solutions have been introduced, like FreshBooks. Software programs designed for larger firms, such as products from Oracle and SAP, often need more sophisticated computer systems.

For firms that conduct business worldwide, software producers have introduced new accounting programs that handle all of a company's accounting information for every country where it operates. The software also handles other languages and currencies and can deal with the financial, legal, and tax requirements of each nation where the firm does business.

The Internet also influences the accounting process. Several software producers offer Web-based accounting products designed for small and medium-sized businesses. These products allow users to access their complete accounting systems from anywhere using a standard Web browser. The "Going Green" feature explains how Deloitte is integrating sustainability into its infrastructure and its business services.

✔ **ASSESSMENT CHECK**

15.4.1 List the steps in the accounting cycle.

15.4.2 What is the accounting equation?

15.4.3 Briefly explain double-entry bookkeeping.

GOING GREEN — DELOITTE EDUCATES ITSELF—AND OTHERS—ON SUSTAINABILITY

Deloitte is one of the Big Four accounting and auditing firms. Recently, the company made two decisions: to make its own internal operations greener and to offer its clients training in green practices. It seems logical that a firm specializing in financial reporting would enter the area of nonfinancial reporting as the business world begins to value green practices. Firms once thought of "going green" as good public relations but not so good financially. But many firms now see the importance of sustainability in an increasingly energy-limited world.

Kathryn Pavlovsky is a co-leader of Deloitte's Enterprise Sustainability Group. She says, "Nonfinancial reporting is evolving from voluntary communications to mandatory compliance, and the environmental regulatory and financial reporting worlds are

(continued)

converging." The move to add sustainable activities to a company's nonfinancial reporting has been encouraged by many factors: the recent recession, activism from shareholders, and changing consumer attitudes and behaviours. Also, technological advances have made green practices more realistic and affordable.

Deloitte's corporate responsibility policy declares that the company will "advocate the sustainable use of natural resources and the environment." The company began its internal greening campaign by surveying its employees. Called "How Green Is Your Footprint?" the survey measured "greenness" on an individual basis within the business environment. It then suggested how each employee could improve his or her performance. A second survey, "How Green Is Your *Other* Footprint?" helps employees to measure their sustainability practices at home.

Deloitte also established a Green Leadership Council (GLC) to maintain contact between the various company regions and management. The GLC educates employees about important green issues and promotes a unified message to all the company's offices. Deloitte employees now conduct virtual meetings and conferences whenever possible. When employees need to travel, the company travel arrangements include car rentals and hotel options considered to be green. Deloitte has also adopted Leadership in Energy and Environmental Design (LEED) standards when building new offices and retrofitting existing offices. The company focuses on purchasing supplies that have a minimal impact on the environment, and it has worked with its suppliers to reach greater levels of sustainability.

Deloitte's Center for Sustainability Performance (CSP) advises businesses on how to reduce their environmental impact and remain profitable. Among the areas covered are planning and strategy, revenue generation, tax incentives, and competitive branding. The CSP also explores sustainability opportunities for employees, offices, IT infrastructure, and communities. The CSP's activities include on-site training for client firms, research and development in sustainability measurement and reporting, publication of reports on these topics for corporate sustainability managers, and consulting and sales support.

One of the CSP's recent workshops for clients was "Sustainability Measurement and Reporting: Tools, Methods, and Metrics." The course was designed to help clients become familiar with the current methods for measuring and reporting their own sustainability. It also provided a preview of new developments in these areas. According to Mark W. McElroy, the CSP's director, the course covered "tools, methods, and metrics across all dimensions of corporate social responsibility and sustainability performance, including carbon, water, solid waste, social impacts, triple bottom line, and non-financial measurement and reporting in general, both from an enterprise and product life cycle perspective."

To further develop its internal greening efforts, Deloitte recently introduced its Green Sync tool. It is intended to promote employee and stakeholder involvement. Johanne Gelinas is a partner with Deloitte Canada's corporate responsibility and sustainability practice. She says, "Executives will always be challenged about where to spend time and resources. By adopting a strategic approach to corporate responsibility, they can start to identify environmental, social and governance initiatives that can also improve shareholder value."

Questions for Critical Thinking

1. Why would Deloitte find it relatively easy to expand from financial reporting to nonfinancial reporting?

2. How would you answer the question "How big is *your* carbon footprint?" What can you do to make your home or your workplace greener?

Sources: Deloitte, accessed June 1, 2010, www.deloitte.com; Deborah Fleischer, "Deloitte: Best Practices for Going Green," *Triple Pundit*, February 1, 2010, accessed June 1, 2010, www.triplepundit.com; Deborah Fleischer, "Deloitte: Green Training on Sustainability Measurement and Reporting," *Green Impact*, January 4, 2010, accessed June 1, 2010, http://greenimpact.com; "Deloitte Launches Center for Sustainability Performance," press release, August 10, 2009, accessed June 1, 2010, www.csrwire.com; Deloitte, "Sustainability & Climate Change," accessed May 17, 2012, www.deloitte.com/us/sustainability.

FINANCIAL STATEMENTS

LO 15.5 Explain the functions and major components of the four principal financial statements.

Financial statements provide managers with the information they need to evaluate the firm's profitability, its overall financial health, and its liquidity position—the ability to meet its current obligations and needs by converting assets into cash. Managers can base their decisions on information in the balance sheet, the income statement, the statement of changes in equity, and the statement of cash flows. Managers interpret the data in these statements so they can communicate the appropriate information to internal decision makers and to interested parties outside the organization.

Of the four financial statements, the only permanent statement is the balance sheet: Its amounts are carried over from year to year. The income statement, statement of changes in equity, and statement of cash flows are temporary statements because they are closed out at the end of each year and therefore are not cumulative in nature.

Public companies report their financial statements at the end of each three-month period and at the end of each fiscal year. Annual statements must be examined and verified by the firm's outside auditors. These financial statements are public information available to anyone. The "Solving an Ethical Controversy" feature discusses the problem of financial fraud.

— SOLVING AN **ETHICAL** CONTROVERSY —

Should Whistle-Blowers Be Rewarded?

The U.S. Sarbanes-Oxley Act of 2002 (SOX) and Canada's Bill 198 were intended to reduce fraud. Both require CEOs and CFOs to sign off on the accuracy of their companies' financial statements. But most reported fraud is revealed by anonymous whistle-blowers or by journalists, auditors, or others.

The Public Servants Disclosure Protection Act protects Canadians who report misconduct in the government. But unlike in the United States, this legislation does not financially reward whistle-blowers. In the United States, the False Claims Act allows citizens to file lawsuits alleging fraud against the federal government. The biggest settlements have involved hospital chains and drug manufacturers; the largest fine was $1.4 billion. Some whistle-blowers have collected almost $47 million in rewards. The U.S. Foreign Corrupt Practices Act (FCPA) may also result in huge rewards. But whistle-blowers are not always successful; some have been fired, forced to quit, or demoted.

Should whistle-blowers be rewarded for reporting financial fraud in Canada?

PRO

1. A recent survey found that "a strong monetary incentive to blow the whistle does motivate people with information to come forward."

2. People who commit fraud can face strict penalties, such as those outlined under SOX, Bill 198, the FCPA, and the Corruption of Foreign Public Officials Act. One survey reported that 83 percent of fraud examiners believe that internal corporate controls on fraud will actually decline.

CON

1. Some observers feel that some "whistle-blower-friendly" provisions of the FCPA in the United States may discourage accused firms from simply settling with the federal government and paying a fine to avoid costly legal procedures.

2. Not all whistle-blowers are innocent. A former UBS banker exposed tax evasion at the firm but was sentenced to prison because he did not reveal that he had participated in the fraud himself.

Summary

In the United States, legislation before Congress would require the Securities and Exchange Commission (SEC) to award whistle-blowers up to 30 percent of fines the government collects on the basis of "original information." Some observers worry that these changes could result in a "race to disclose" between companies that self-report and current or former employees. Canada has not seen any similar movements to financially reward whistle-blowers.

Sources: Parliament of Canada, "Bill C-25, The Public Servants Disclosure Protection Act," accessed June 3, 2011, www.parl.gc.ca/About/Parliament/LegislativeSummaries/bills_ ls.asp?ls=c25&Parl= 37&Ses=3; "Sarbanes-Oxley Can Help Curb Company Fraud," McGladrey, accessed June 1, 2010, http://rsmmcgladrey.com; Michael Connor, "Finance Reform Bill Could Increase Big Payouts to Whistleblowers," *Business Ethics*, May 2, 2010, accessed June 1, 2010, http://business-ethics.com; "Whistleblowers Making Money Thanks to Law," *NewsChannel8*, May 1, 2010, accessed June 1, 2010, http://cfc.news.8.net; Deloitte, "Poll: More Financial Statement Fraud Expected to Be Uncovered in 2010, 2011," *Corporate Compliance Insights*, April 28, 2010, accessed June 1, 2010, www.corporatecomplianceinsights.com; James Hyatt, "Who Detects Corporate Fraud? (Tip: It's Not Usually the SEC . . .)," *Business Ethics*, February 16, 2010, accessed June 1, 2010, http://business-ethics.com; Michael Rubinkam, "UBS Tax Evasion Whistle-Blower Reports to Federal Prison," *USA Today*, January 8, 2010, accessed June 1, 2010, www.usatoday.com; Free Advice, accessed August 13, 2014, http://employment-law.freeadvice.com/employment-law/employment-law/largest-whistleblower-lawsuit.htm.

A fiscal year does not need to be the same as the calendar year. Many companies set different fiscal years. For example, the Starbucks fiscal year runs from October 1 to September 30 of the following year. Nike's fiscal year consists of the 12 months between June 1 and May 31. By contrast, GE's fiscal year is the same as the calendar year, running from January 1 to December 31.

balance sheet a statement of a firm's financial position—what it owns and claims against its assets—at a particular point in time.

The Balance Sheet

A **balance sheet** (or *statement of financial position* under IFRS) shows a firm's financial position on a particular date. It is similar to a photograph of the firm's assets, liabilities, and owners' equity at a specific moment in time. Balance sheets must be prepared at regular intervals because a firm's managers and other internal parties often need this information every day, every week, or at least every month. External users, such as shareholders and industry analysts, may use this information less often, maybe every quarter (every three months) or once a year.

The balance sheet follows the accounting equation. On the left side of the balance sheet are the firm's assets—what it owns. These assets are shown in a downward order of liquidity. In other words, the assets with the highest ability to be converted to cash are shown first; that's why cash is always listed first on the asset side of the balance sheet. The assets represent how management has used its available funds.

On the right side of the equation are the claims against the firm's assets. Liabilities and owners' equity show the sources of the firm's assets. They are listed in the order they are due. Liabilities include the claims of creditors—the financial institutions or bondholders that have loaned the firm money; suppliers that have provided goods and services on credit; and others to be paid in the future, such as federal, provincial, and municipal tax authorities. Owners' equity represents the owners' claims against the firm's assets; in the case of a corporation, owners' equity represents the claims of shareholders. Owners' equity also includes any excess of all assets over liabilities.

Figure 15.3 shows the balance sheet for Diane's Java, a small coffee wholesaler. The accounting equation is illustrated by the three classifications of assets, liabilities, and owners' equity on the company's balance sheet. Remember, total assets must always equal the sum of liabilities and owners' equity. In other words, the balance sheet must always balance.

The balance sheet is the only permanent statement of the four financial statements. It shows the firm's financial position on a particular date, and its amounts are carried over from year to year.

The Income Statement

The **income statement** is a financial record of a company's revenues, expenses, and profits over a specific time period. In contrast, a balance sheet shows a firm's financial record at one specific point in time. You can think of the income statement as a video, while the balance sheet is more like a photograph. The income statement summarizes a firm's financial performance over a specific time period, usually a quarter (three months) or a year.

The income statement also helps decision makers focus on overall revenues and the costs needed to generate these revenues. Managers of a not-for-profit organization use the income statement to check whether the revenues from contributions and other sources will cover the organization's operating costs. Finally, the income statement provides many basic data used to calculate the financial ratios that managers use in planning and controlling activities. **Figure 15.4** shows the income statement for Diane's Java.

An income statement is also called a *profit-and-loss statement*, a *P&L statement*, or under IFRS a *statement of comprehensive income*. It begins with total sales or revenues generated during a year, quarter, or month. The following lines then deduct all of the costs related to producing the revenues. Typical costs include operating expenses, interest, and taxes. After all costs have been subtracted, the remaining net income may be distributed to the firm's owners (the shareholders, proprietors, or partners) or reinvested in the company as retained earnings. The final figure on the income statement—net income after taxes—is the so-called *bottom line*.

Keeping costs under control is an important part of running a business. But too often companies focus more on increasing revenue than on controlling costs. It doesn't matter how much money a company collects in revenues—it won't stay in business for long unless it earns a profit.

income statement a financial record of a company's revenues, expenses, and profits over a specific period of time.

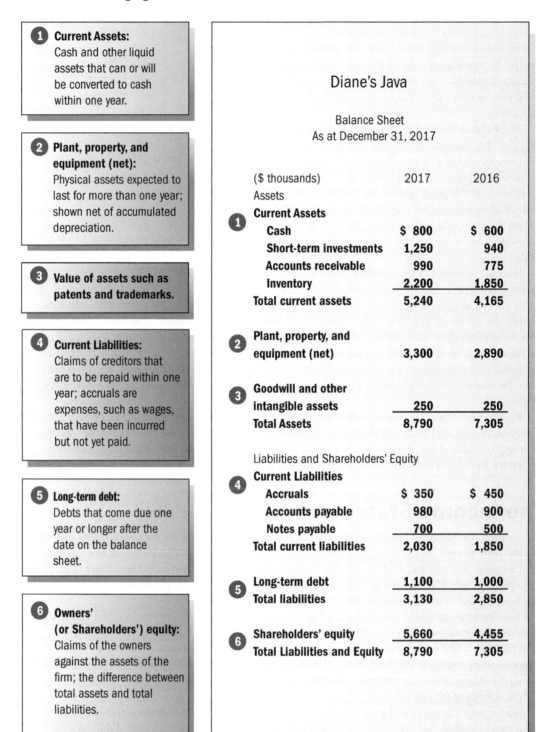

1 Current Assets:
Cash and other liquid assets that can or will be converted to cash within one year.

2 Plant, property, and equipment (net):
Physical assets expected to last for more than one year; shown net of accumulated depreciation.

3 Value of assets such as patents and trademarks.

4 Current Liabilities:
Claims of creditors that are to be repaid within one year; accruals are expenses, such as wages, that have been incurred but not yet paid.

5 Long-term debt:
Debts that come due one year or longer after the date on the balance sheet.

6 Owners' (or Shareholders') equity:
Claims of the owners against the assets of the firm; the difference between total assets and total liabilities.

Diane's Java

Balance Sheet
As at December 31, 2017

($ thousands)	2017	2016
Assets		
Current Assets		
Cash	$ 800	$ 600
Short-term investments	1,250	940
Accounts receivable	990	775
Inventory	2,200	1,850
Total current assets	5,240	4,165
Plant, property, and equipment (net)	3,300	2,890
Goodwill and other intangible assets	250	250
Total Assets	8,790	7,305
Liabilities and Shareholders' Equity		
Current Liabilities		
Accruals	$ 350	$ 450
Accounts payable	980	900
Notes payable	700	500
Total current liabilities	2,030	1,850
Long-term debt	1,100	1,000
Total liabilities	3,130	2,850
Shareholders' equity	5,660	4,455
Total Liabilities and Equity	8,790	7,305

FIGURE 15.3 Diane's Java Balance Sheet (Fiscal Year Ending December 31, 2017)

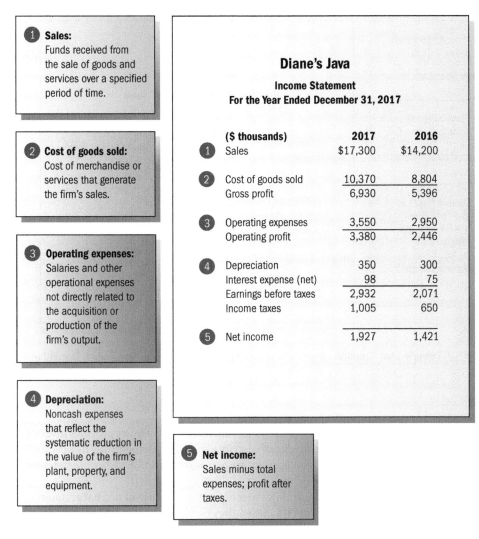

1 Sales:
Funds received from the sale of goods and services over a specified period of time.

2 Cost of goods sold:
Cost of merchandise or services that generate the firm's sales.

3 Operating expenses:
Salaries and other operational expenses not directly related to the acquisition or production of the firm's output.

4 Depreciation:
Noncash expenses that reflect the systematic reduction in the value of the firm's plant, property, and equipment.

5 Net income:
Sales minus total expenses; profit after taxes.

Diane's Java

Income Statement
For the Year Ended December 31, 2017

($ thousands)	2017	2016
1 Sales	$17,300	$14,200
2 Cost of goods sold	10,370	8,804
Gross profit	6,930	5,396
3 Operating expenses	3,550	2,950
Operating profit	3,380	2,446
4 Depreciation	350	300
Interest expense (net)	98	75
Earnings before taxes	2,932	2,071
Income taxes	1,005	650
5 Net income	1,927	1,421

FIGURE 15.4 Diane's Java Income Statement (Fiscal Year Ending December 31, 2017)

Statement of Changes in Equity

The **statement of changes in equity** is a record of the change in equity from the end of one fiscal period to the end of the next fiscal period. It uses information from both the balance sheet and income statement. A simplified example is shown in **Figure 15.5** for Diane's Java.

Note that the statement of changes in equity begins with the shareholders' equity that is shown on the balance sheet at the end of the prior year. Net income is added, and cash dividends paid to owners are subtracted. If owners contributed any additional capital, for example, through the sale of new shares, this amount is added to equity. If owners withdrew capital, for example, through the repurchase of existing shares, equity is reduced by that amount. All of the additions and subtractions, taken together, equal the change in owners' equity from the end of the previous fiscal year to the end of the current fiscal year. The new amount of owners' equity is then reported on the balance sheet for the current year.

statement of changes in equity a record of the change in equity from the end of one fiscal period to the end of the next fiscal period.

The Statement of Cash Flows

So far, we have looked at the balance sheet, the income statement, and the statement of changes in equity. Most firms prepare a fourth accounting statement—the **statement of cash flows**. All public companies must prepare and publish a statement of cash flows. Commercial lenders, such as banks,

statement of cash flows a record of the sources and uses of cash during a period of time.

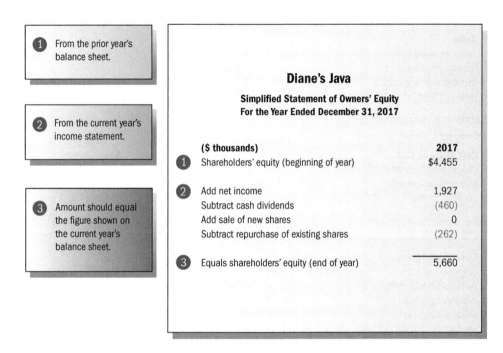

FIGURE 15.5 Diane's Java Simplified Statement of Changes in Equity (Fiscal Year Ending December 31, 2017)

often ask a borrower for a statement of cash flows. The statement of cash flows provides investors and creditors with information about a firm's cash receipts and cash payments for its operating, investing, and financing activities during an accounting period. **Figure 15.6** shows the statement of cash flows for Diane's Java.

Companies prepare a statement of cash flows because of the wide use of accrual accounting. **Accrual accounting** records revenues and costs when they occur, not when actual cash changes hands. As a result, the amounts may differ between what is reported as sales, expenses, and profits and the amount of cash that actually flows into and out of the business during a period of time. For example, companies depreciate fixed assets—such as machinery and buildings—over a specified period of time. In other words, companies reduce the value of the asset as the asset ages. Depreciation is reported as an expense on the firm's income statement (see item 4 in Figure 15.4), but it does not involve the movement of any cash. Depreciation is a noncash expense. That means that the amount a firm reports as net income (profits after tax) for a period actually understates the amount of cash the firm took in, less expenses. As a result, depreciation is added back to net income when calculating cash flow (see item 1 in Figure 15.6).

The lifeblood of every organization is its *cash flow*. Many former owners of failed firms blame poor cash flow for their company's downfall. Many people value the statement of cash flow. They believe that preparing it and having it examined by various people can help to prevent financial distress for otherwise profitable firms. Too many firms are forced into bankruptcy because they lack the cash needed to continue their day-to-day operations.

Even when bankruptcy is not an issue, the statement of cash flows can provide investors and others with vital information. For example, assume that a firm's income statement reports rising earnings. But, at the same time, the statement of cash flows shows that the firm's inventory is rising faster than its sales. This situation is often a signal that demand for the firm's products is dropping, which may, in turn, be a sign of financial trouble.

accrual accounting an accounting method that records revenues and expenses when they occur, not when cash actually changes hands.

 **ASSESSMENT CHECK**

15.5.1 List the four financial statements.

15.5.2 How is the balance sheet organized?

15.5.3 Define *accrual accounting*.

① Operating Activities: The nuts and bolts of day-to-day activities of a company carrying out its regular business; increases in accounts receivable and inventory are like uses of cash, while increases in accruals and accounts payables are like sources of cash; in financially healthy firms, net cash flow from operating activities should be positive.

② Investing Activities: Transactions to accumulate or use cash in ways that affect operating activities in the future; often a use of cash.

③ Financing Activities: Ways to transfer cash to or from creditors and to or from owners; can be either positive or negative.

④ Net Cash Flow: The sum of cash flow from operating, investing, and financing activities; a reconcilement of cash from the beginning to the end of the accounting period (one year in this example).

Diane's Java
Statement of Cash Flows
For the Year Ended December 31, 2017

($ thousands)	2017
Cash Flow from Operating Activities	
① Net income	$1,927
Depreciation	350
Change in accounts receivable	(215)
Change in inventory	(350)
Change in accruals	(100)
Change in accounts payable	80
Total cash flow from operating activities	1,692
② **Cash Flow from Investing Activities**	
Capital expenditures	(760)
Change in short-term investments	(310)
Total cash flow from investing activities	(1,070)
③ **Cash Flow from Financing Activities**	
Cash dividends	(460)
Sale/repurchase of shares	(262)
Change in notes payable	200
Change in long-term debt	100
Total cash flow from financing activities	(422)
④ Net Cash Flow	200
Cash (beginning of year)	600
Cash (end of year)	800

FIGURE 15.6 Diane's Java Statement of Cash Flows (Fiscal Year Ending December 31, 2017)

FINANCIAL RATIO ANALYSIS

Accounting professionals have important responsibilities beyond preparing financial statements. They also help managers interpret the statements by comparing data on the firm's current activities to data for previous periods and to data on other companies in the same industry. *Ratio analysis* is one of the most commonly used tools. It measures a firm's liquidity, profitability, and reliance on debt financing and how effectively management uses the firm's resources. This analysis also allows comparisons with other firms and with the firm's own past performance.

Ratios help managers by interpreting actual performance and making comparisons to what should have happened. Managers compare their firm's ratios with ratios of similar companies to understand their firm's performance compared with competitors' results. These industry standards are important measures and help to focus on problem areas—and areas of excellence. Ratios for the current accounting period can be compared with similar calculations for previous periods to spot developing trends. Ratios can be classified according to their specific purposes. The four major categories of financial ratios are summarized in **Table 15.1**. The ratios for Diane's Java for the 2016 and 2017 fiscal years are shown in **Table 15.2**.

Table 15.1 Major Categories of Financial Ratios

CATEGORY	RATIO	DESCRIPTION
Liquidity ratios	Current ratio	Current assets divided by current liabilities
	Quick (acid-test) ratio	Current assets (minus inventory and prepaid expenses) divided by current liabilities
Activity ratios	Inventory turnover	Cost of goods sold divided by average inventory
	Receivables turnover	Credit sales divided by average accounts receivable
	Total asset turnover	Revenue or sales divided by average total assets
Leverage ratios	Debt ratio	Total liabilities divided by total assets
	Long-term debt to equity	Long-term debt divided by owners' equity
Profitability ratios	Gross profit margin	Gross profit divided by revenue or sales
	Net profit margin	Net profit divided by revenue or sales
	Return on equity	Net profit divided by average owners' equity

Table 15.2 Financial Ratios for Diane's Java

FINANCIAL RATIO	2017 FISCAL YEAR	2016 FISCAL YEAR
Current ratio	2.58	2.25
Quick ratio	1.50	1.25
Inventory turnover	5.12	5.03
Receivables turnover	19.60	19.32
Total asset turnover	2.15	2.15
Gross profit margin	40.0%	38.0%
Net profit margin	11.1%	10.0%
Return on equity	38.1%	36.6%
Debt ratio	35.6%	39.0%
Long-term debt to equity	19.4%	22.4%

Liquidity Ratios

Liquidity ratios measure a firm's ability to meet its short-term obligations, such as loans, when they are due. An increase in liquidity reduces the likelihood that a firm will need to raise funds to repay loans. On the other hand, firms with low liquidity may have to choose between defaulting (failing to pay) and borrowing from high-cost lending sources to meet their short-term financial obligations.

Two commonly used liquidity ratios are the current ratio and the acid-test ratio, also called the quick ratio. The *current ratio* compares current assets to current liabilities. It provides executives with information about the firm's ability to pay its current debts as they mature or as payments are due. The current ratio of Diane's Java is computed as follows (unless indicated, all amounts from the balance sheet or income statement are in thousands of dollars):

$$\text{Current ratio} = \frac{\text{Current assets}}{\text{Current liabilities}} = \frac{5,240}{2,030} = 2.58$$

In other words, Diane's Java has $2.58 of current assets for every $1.00 of current liabilities. In general, a current ratio of 2:1 is considered to provide satisfactory liquidity. This rule of thumb, or guideline, must be considered along with other factors, such as the nature of the business, the season, and the quality of the company's management team. Diane's Java's management and others are likely to evaluate this ratio of 2.58:1 by comparing it with ratios for previous operating periods and with industry averages.

The *acid-test (or quick) ratio* measures the ability of a firm to meet its debt payments on short notice. This ratio compares quick assets—the most liquid current assets—against current liabilities. Quick assets generally consist of cash and equivalents, short-term investments, and accounts receivable. In general, quick assets equal total current assets minus inventory and prepaid expenses.

Diane's Java's current balance sheet lists total current assets of $5.24 million and inventory of $2.2 million. Therefore, its quick ratio is calculated as follows:

$$\text{Acid-test ratio} = \frac{\text{Current assets} - \text{Inventory} - \text{Prepaid expenses}}{\text{Current liabilities}} = \frac{(5,240 - 2,200 - 0)}{2,030} = 1.50$$

Because the traditional rule of thumb for an adequate acid-test ratio is around 1:1, Diane's Java appears to have a strong level of liquidity. However, the same cautions apply here as for the current ratio: The ratio should be compared with industry averages and data from previous operating periods to decide whether it is adequate for the firm.

Activity Ratios

Activity ratios measure how effectively management uses the firm's resources. One of the most frequently used activity ratios is the *inventory turnover ratio*. This ratio indicates the number of times merchandise moves through a business:

$$\text{Inventory turnover} = \frac{\text{Cost of goods sold}}{\text{Average inventory}} = \frac{10,370}{\left[(2,200 + 1,850)\right]/2} = 5.12$$

Average inventory for Diane's Java is calculated by adding the inventory as of December 31, 2017 ($2.2 million) to the inventory as of December 31, 2016 ($1.85 million) and dividing it by 2. Comparing the 5.12 inventory turnover ratio with industry standards provides a measure of the firm's efficiency. Note that inventory turnover can vary widely depending on the products a company sells and the industry it operates in.

When a company sells a large portion of its products on credit, it can learn useful information by measuring its *receivables turnover*. Receivables turnover can be calculated as follows:

$$\text{Receivables turnover} = \frac{\text{Credit sales}}{\text{Average accounts receivable}}$$

Because Diane's Java is a wholesaler, let's assume that all of its sales are credit sales. Average receivables equals the simple average of 2017's receivables and 2016's receivables. The receivables turnover for Diane's Java is calculated as follows:

$$\text{Receivables turnover} = \frac{17,300}{\left[(990+775)/2\right]} = 19.60$$

The average age of receivables is calculated by dividing 365 by the receivables turnover. The average age of Diane's Java's receivables is 18.62 days. Assume Diane's Java expects its retail customers to pay outstanding bills within 30 days of the date of purchase. Given that the average age of its receivables is less than 30 days, Diane's Java appears to be doing a good job collecting its credit sales.

Another measure of efficiency is *total asset turnover*. It measures the amount of sales generated by each dollar invested in assets. The calculations for Diane's Java's total asset turnover are as follows:

$$\text{Total asset turnover} = \frac{\text{Sales}}{\text{Average total assets}}$$

$$= \frac{17,300}{\left[(8,790+7,305)/2\right]} = 2.15$$

Average total assets for Diane's Java equals total assets as of December 31, 2017 ($8.79 million) plus total assets as of December 31, 2016 ($7.305 million) divided by 2.

Diane's Java generates about $2.15 in sales for each dollar invested in assets. Although a higher ratio generally shows that a firm is operating more efficiently, care must be taken when comparing firms that operate in different industries. Some industries require a higher investment in assets than other industries.

Profitability Ratios

Some ratios measure the organization's overall financial performance by evaluating its ability to generate revenues that are greater than its operating costs and other expenses. These measures are called *profitability ratios*. To compute these ratios, accountants compare the firm's earnings with total sales or investments. Over a period of time, profitability ratios may show the effectiveness of management in operating the business. Three important profitability ratios are *gross profit margin*, *net profit margin*, and *return on equity*:

$$\text{Gross profit margin} = \frac{\text{Gross profit}}{\text{Sales}} = \frac{6,930}{17,300} = 40.0\%$$

$$\text{Net profit margin} = \frac{\text{Net income}}{\text{Sales}} = \frac{1,927}{17,300} = 11.1\%$$

$$= \frac{\text{Net income}}{\text{Average equity}} = \frac{1,927}{\left[(5,660+4,455)/2\right]} = 38.1\%$$

All these ratios show positive evaluations of the current operations. For example, the net profit margin indicates that the firm realizes a profit of slightly more than 11 cents on each dollar of merchandise it sells. Although this ratio varies widely among business firms, Diane's Java compares well with wholesalers in general, which have an average net profit margin of around 5 percent. But, for a better interpretation of the results, this ratio, like the other profitability ratios, should be evaluated in relation to profit forecasts, past performance, or more specific industry averages. Similarly, although the firm's return on equity of almost 38 percent appears outstanding, any analysis should also consider the degree of risk in the industry.

Leverage Ratios

Leverage ratios measure how much a firm relies on debt financing. These ratios provide interesting information to potential investors and lenders. If management has taken on too much debt to finance the firm's operations, it may face difficulty in meeting future interest payments and repaying outstanding loans. As we discuss in Chapter 17, borrowing money does have advantages. But relying too much on debt financing may lead to bankruptcy. More generally, both investors and lenders may prefer to deal with firms whose owners have invested enough of their own money to avoid having to borrow funds. The *debt ratio* and the *long-term debt to equity* ratio help interested parties evaluate a firm's leverage:

Walmart Inc. President and CEO Doug McMillon addresses shareholders at a meeting and discusses various topics, including the company's return on equity. Return on equity is one measure of a company's profitability.

Rick Wilking/Reuters/Newscom

$$\text{Debt ratio} = \frac{\text{Total liabilities}}{\text{Total assets}} = \frac{3{,}130}{8{,}790} = 35.6\%$$

$$\text{Long-term debt to equity} = \frac{\text{Long-term debt}}{\text{Owners' equity}} = \frac{1{,}100}{5{,}660} = 19.4\%$$

When the debt ratio (the ratio of total liabilities to total assets) is greater than 50 percent, it shows that a firm is relying more on borrowed money than on owners' equity. Because Diane's Java's debt ratio is 35.6 percent, the firm's owners have invested considerably more than the total liabilities shown on the balance sheet. Also, the firm's long-term debt to equity ratio is only 19.4 percent, which shows that Diane's Java has only about 19.4 cents in long-term debt for every dollar in equity. The long-term debt to equity ratio also shows that Diane's Java hasn't relied much on borrowed money.

The four categories of financial ratios relate balance sheet and income statement data to one another, help management focus on a firm's strengths and weaknesses, and show the areas in need of further investigation. Large, multiproduct firms that operate in different markets use their information systems to update their financial ratios every day or even every hour. Each company's management must decide on a suitable review schedule to avoid the costly and time-consuming mistake of excessive monitoring.

Managers, investors, and lenders should pay close attention to how accountants apply accounting rules when preparing financial statements. GAAP gives accountants some flexibility in reporting certain revenues and expenses. Public companies are required to disclose, in footnotes to the financial statements, how the various accounting rules were applied.

✔ **ASSESSMENT CHECK**

15.6.1 List the four categories of financial ratios.

15.6.2 Define the following ratios: *current ratio*, *inventory turnover*, *net profit margin*, and *debt ratio*.

BUDGETING

The financial statements discussed in this chapter focus on past business activities. But these same financial statements also provide the basis for planning in the future. A **budget** is a planning and controlling tool. It is the organization's plan for how it will raise and spend money during a specific period of time. Specifically, it shows the firm's expected sales revenues, operating expenses, cash receipts, and cash expenses. It quantifies the firm's plans for a specified future period. The budget

LO 15.7 Describe the role of budgets in a business.

budget an organization's plans for how it will raise and spend money during a specific period of time.

can be thought of as a short-term financial plan. It becomes the standard that actual performance is compared against.

Budget preparation is often a time-consuming task. It may involve many people from various departments within the organization. The complexity of the budgeting process varies with the size and complexity of the organization. Large corporations such as Magna International, RBC, and Rogers maintain complex and sophisticated budgeting systems. Their budgets serve as planning and controlling tools and help managers to integrate their numerous divisions. Budgeting in both large and small firms is similar to household budgeting in its purpose: to match income and expenses in a way that accomplishes goals and schedules cash inflows and outflows.

The accounting department is an organization's financial centre. It provides much of the data for budget development. The overall master budget, or operating budget, is composed of many individual budgets for each of the firm's separate units. These individual budgets typically include the production budget, cash budget, capital expenditures budget, advertising budget, and sales budget.

Technology has improved the efficiency of the budgeting process. The accounting software products discussed earlier—like QuickBooks—all include budgeting features. The software modules designed for specific businesses are often available from third parties. Many banks now offer their customers personal financial management tools (PFMs) developed by software companies. One such tool is Quicken, Canada's most-used money management program from Intuit.[9]

One of the most important budgets prepared by firms is the *cash budget*. The cash budget tracks the firm's cash inflows and outflows. It is usually prepared each month. **Figure 15.7**

Birchwood Paper Company
Four-Month Cash Budget

($ thousands)	May	June	July	August
Gross sales	$1,200.0	$3,200.0	$5,500.0	$4,500.0
Cash sales	300.0	800.0	1,375.0	1,125.0
One month prior	600.0	600.0	1,600.0	2,750.0
Two months prior	300.0	300.0	300.0	800.0
Total cash inflows	1,200.0	1,700.0	3,275.0	4,675.0
Purchases				
Cash purchases	1,040.0	1,787.5	1,462.5	390.0
One month prior	390.0	1,040.0	1,787.5	1,462.5
Wages and salaries	250.0	250.0	250.0	250.0
Office rent	75.0	75.0	75.0	75.0
Marketing and other expenses	150.0	150.0	150.0	150.0
Taxes		300.0		
Total cash outflows	1,905.0	3,602.5	3,725.0	2,327.5
Net cash flow				
(Inflows − Outflows)	(705.0)	(1,902.5)	(450.0)	2,347.5
Beginnning cash balance	250.0	150.0	150.0	150.0
Net cash flow	(705.0)	(1,902.5)	(450.0)	2,347.5
Ending cash balance	(455.0)	(1,752.5)	(300.0)	2,497.5
Target cash balance	150.0	150.0	150.0	150.0
Surplus (deficit)	(605.0)	(1,902.5)	(450.0)	2,347.5
Cumulative surplus (deficit)	(605.0)	(2,507.5)	(2,957.5)	610.0

FIGURE 15.7 Four-Month Cash Budget for Birchwood Paper Company

illustrates a sample cash budget for Birchwood Paper, a small paper products company. The company has set a $150,000 target cash balance. The cash budget shows the months when the firm will need temporary loans—May, June, and July. It also shows the size of loan the company will need (close to $3 million). The document also shows that Birchwood will generate a cash surplus in August, when it can begin repaying the short-term loan. Finally, the cash budget produces a tangible standard against which to compare actual cash inflows and outflows.

✓ **ASSESSMENT CHECK**

15.7.1 What is a budget?

15.7.2 How is a cash budget organized?

INTERNATIONAL ACCOUNTING

LO 15.8 Outline the accounting issues facing global business.

Today, accounting procedures and practices must be adapted to work in an international business environment. For example, Air Canada generates more than half of its annual revenues from sales outside of Canada. Nestlé, the giant chocolate and food products firm, operates throughout the world. It derives 98 percent of its revenues from outside Switzerland, its home country. Global firms must reliably translate the financial statements of the firm's international affiliated firms, branches, and subsidiaries and convert data about foreign currency transactions to dollars. Also, foreign currencies and exchange rates influence the accounting and financial reporting processes of firms operating internationally.[10]

As market economies have developed in such countries as Poland and China, the demand for accountants has increased. The "Hit & Miss" feature describes recent developments in the accounting profession in China and Hong Kong.

(HIT) & MISS

Accounting: Hong Kong Meets China

Hong Kong was a British colony for almost 200 years. In 1997, Britain transferred Hong Kong to the People's Republic of China. China's rise to global power has led to difficulties in combining its financial environment with that of Hong Kong. Even after the transfer, Hong Kong and mainland China kept two separate accounting systems with different standards and different qualifying examinations. Hong Kong accounting is based on international standards and is conducted in English; Chinese accounting is not.

At the beginning of 2010, Hong Kong accepted Chinese accounting standards. This step shows China's growing attractiveness to international investors. It also advances China's ambition to be part of the international financial system. Until recently, the Chinese accounting system was known for its "book-cooking" scandals. As Hong Kong's transition to Chinese standards continues, Hong Kong accountants risk losing much of their business to Chinese firms.

Tim Lui is a tax partner at the Hong Kong branch of the worldwide accounting firm PricewaterhouseCoopers. He believes that in the short run, at least, Hong Kong accountants have a competitive edge because of their training and international perspective. Foreign investors will be glad to see that Chinese companies will be audited by large, international accounting firms. But he warns against

underestimating the Chinese market: "The mainland's development is robust and fast and the market is immense."

Another concern is that small and medium-sized Hong Kong accounting firms simply aren't big enough to succeed in China, especially in Shanghai, China's business and accounting centre. Robert Sawhney of SRC Associations Ltd., a Hong Kong accounting firm, urges smaller firms to market themselves more aggressively and to update their training strategies. He says, "There is substantial scope for Asian accounting firms to provide services to other organizations and in niche areas."

Questions for Critical Thinking

1. How might the mix of Chinese and internationally accepted accounting methods affect Chinese firms' operations and ethical standards?

2. What can Hong Kong accounting firms do to increase their business in mainland China?

Sources: Robert C. Sawhney, "The Competitiveness of Hong Kong & Asian Accounting Firms," White Paper, March 2010, www.srchk.com; "The Demand for Accountants Is Always There," *China Daily*, January 8, 2010; Alison Leung, "China Auditors Set to Take on Hong Kong Stock Market," *Reuters*, December 30, 2009.

Exchange Rates

As defined in Chapter 4, an exchange rate is the value of one country's currency in terms of the currencies of other countries. Currencies can be treated as if they are goods to be bought and sold. Like the price of any product, currency prices change according to supply and demand. But unlike many products, currency prices change daily—or more often. Exchange rate fluctuations, or ups and downs, complicate accounting entries and accounting practices.

Accountants who deal with international transactions must take care when recording their firms' foreign sales and purchases. Today's sophisticated accounting software helps firms handle all of their international transactions within a single program. An international firm's consolidated financial statements must show any gains or losses caused by changes in exchange rates during specific periods of time. Financial statements that cover operations in two or more countries need to treat fluctuations consistently to allow for comparison.

In Canada, GAAP requires firms to adjust their earnings to reflect changes in exchange rates. A weakening dollar generally increases the earnings of a Canadian firm that has international operations: The same units of a foreign currency will translate into more Canadian dollars. A strengthening dollar will have the opposite effect on earnings—the same number of units of a foreign currency will translate into fewer dollars. In one recent year, for example, currency fluctuations caused an $11 million drop in earnings from the same quarter of the previous year for PPG, the world's second-largest paint manufacturer.[11]

In Pakistan, a truck driver delivers Nestlé food products. Because the Swiss corporation operates around the world, its profits and its financial statements are affected by foreign exchange rates.

Ilyas Dean/NewsCom

 **ASSESSMENT CHECK**

15.8.1 How are financial statements adjusted for exchange rates?

WHAT'S AHEAD

This chapter describes the role of accounting in an organization. Accounting is the process of measuring, interpreting, and communicating financial information to interested parties both inside and outside the firm. The next two chapters discuss the finance function of an organization. Finance deals with planning, obtaining, and managing the organization's funds to accomplish its objectives in the most efficient and effective manner possible. Chapter 16 outlines the financial system, the system used to transfer funds from savers to borrowers. Organizations rely on the financial system to raise funds for expansion or operations. The chapter includes a description of financial institutions, such as banks; financial markets, such as the Toronto Stock Exchange; financial instruments, such as stocks and bonds; and the role of the Bank of Canada. Chapter 17 discusses the role of finance and the financial manager in an organization.

RETURN TO INSIDE BUSINESS

Cooking the Books

Many feel that accounting information is "black and white"—that is, it is either right or wrong with no in-between shades of grey. But as described in the stories of accounting fraud, many accountants and high-level executives risk stiff prison sentences when "cooking the books."

QUESTIONS FOR CRITICAL THINKING

1. How is it possible that what seems to be straightforward financial information can be altered by corporate executives who claim it conforms to GAAP?

2. Why do corporate executives risk prison sentences by preparing questionable financial statements?

SUMMARY OF LEARNING OBJECTIVES

LO 15.1 Explain the functions of accounting and identify the three basic accounting activities.

Accountants measure, interpret, and communicate financial information to people inside and outside the firm to support informed decision making. Accountants gather, record, and interpret financial information for management. They also provide financial information on the status and operations of the firm for evaluation by outside individuals, such as government representatives, shareholders, potential investors, and lenders. Accounting plays key roles in financing activities, which help to start and expand an organization; investing activities, which provide the assets a company needs to continue operating; and operating activities, which focus on selling goods and services and paying expenses incurred in regular operations.

✓ ASSESSMENT CHECK ANSWERS

15.1.1 **Define *accounting*.** Accounting is the process of measuring, interpreting, and communicating financial information that describes the status and operation of an organization and aids in decision making.

15.1.2 **Who uses accounting information?** Managers in all types of organizations use accounting information to help them plan, assess performance, and control daily and long-term operations. Outside users of accounting information include government officials, investors, creditors, and donors.

15.1.3 **What three business activities involve accounting?** The three activities involving accounting are financing, investing, and operating activities.

LO 15.2 Describe the various types of accounting professionals.

Public accountants provide accounting services to other firms or individuals for a fee. They perform the following activities: auditing, tax return preparation, management consulting, and accounting system design. Management accountants are employed by a firm, where they collect and record financial transactions, prepare financial statements, and interpret financial data for managers. Government and not-for-profit accountants perform many of the same functions as management accountants. But instead of dealing with profits and losses, they look at how effectively the organization or agency is operating.

✓ ASSESSMENT CHECK ANSWERS

15.2.1 **List the three services offered by public accounting firms.** The three services offered by public accounting firms are auditing, management consulting, and tax services.

15.2.2 **What tasks do management accountants perform?** Management accountants work for an organization. They are responsible for collecting and recording financial transactions and for preparing and interpreting financial statements.

LO 15.3 Discuss the foundation of the accounting system.

The foundation of the accounting system in Canada is GAAP (generally accepted accounting principles), a set of guidelines or standards that accountants follow. Companies that trade on a public stock exchange are required to use IFRS (International Financial Reporting Standards). Some basic qualitative characteristics of the financial statements are consistency, relevance, representational faithfulness, reliability, timeliness, understandability, verifiability, and comparability. The Accounting Standards Board (AcSB) is an independent body made up of accounting professionals. The AcSB is primarily responsible for evaluating, setting, and modifying GAAP.

✓ ASSESSMENT CHECK ANSWERS

15.3.1 **Define *GAAP*.** GAAP stands for generally accepted accounting principles. It is a set of standards, or guidelines, that accountants follow when recording and reporting financial transactions.

15.3.2 **What is the role played by the AcSB?** The Accounting Standards Board (AcSB) is an independent body made up of accounting professionals. It is primarily responsible for evaluating, setting, and modifying Canadian GAAP related primarily to private and not-for-profit organizations. Note that publicly accountable organizations are required to follow IFRS.

LO 15.4 Outline the steps in the accounting cycle.

The accounting process involves recording, classifying, and summarizing data about financial transactions. This information is used to produce financial statements for the firm's managers and other interested individuals. Transactions are recorded chronologically, in the order they occur, in journals; then posted in ledgers; and then summarized in accounting statements. Today, most of this activity takes place electronically. The basic accounting equation states that assets (what a firm owns) must always equal liabilities (what a firm owes creditors) plus owners' equity (the owners' investments in the firm). This equation also illustrates double-entry bookkeeping, the process used to record accounting transactions. In double-entry bookkeeping, each individual transaction must be balanced by another transaction.

✓ ASSESSMENT CHECK ANSWERS

15.4.1 **List the steps in the accounting cycle.** The accounting cycle involves the following steps: recording transactions, classifying the transactions, summarizing the transactions, and using the summaries to produce financial statements.

15.4.2 What is the accounting equation? The accounting equation states that assets (what a firm owns) must always equal liabilities (what a firm owes) plus owners' equity (the owners' investments in the firm). An increase or decrease in an asset must be balanced by an increase or decrease in liabilities, owners' equity, or both.

15.4.3 Briefly explain double-entry bookkeeping. Double-entry bookkeeping requires every transaction to be balanced by another transaction.

LO 15.5 Explain the functions and major components of the four principal financial statements.

The balance sheet shows a firm's financial position on a particular date. The three major classifications of balance sheet data are the elements of the accounting equation: assets, liabilities, and owners' equity. The income statement shows the results of a firm's operations over a specific time period. It focuses on the firm's activities—its revenues and expenditures—and the resulting profit or loss during the period. The major entries in the income statement are revenues, cost of goods sold, expenses, and profit or loss. The statement of changes in equity shows the change in owners' equity from the end of the previous year to the end of the current year. Finally, the statement of cash flows shows a firm's cash receipts and cash payments during an accounting period. It outlines the sources and uses of cash in the basic business activities of operating, investing, and financing.

 ASSESSMENT CHECK ANSWERS

15.5.1 List the four financial statements. The four financial statements are the balance sheet, the income statement, the statement of changes in equity, and the statement of cash flows.

15.5.2 How is the balance sheet organized? Assets (what a firm owns) are shown on one side of the balance sheet and are listed in a downward order based on their convertibility into cash. On the other side of the balance sheet are claims to assets, liabilities (what a firm owes) and owners' equity (the owners' investments in the firm). Claims are listed in the order in which they are due. For example, liabilities are listed before owners' equity. Assets always equal liabilities plus owners' equity.

15.5.3 Define *accrual accounting*. Accrual accounting records revenues and expenses when they occur, not when cash actually changes hands. Most companies use accrual accounting to prepare their financial statements.

LO 15.6 Discuss how financial ratios are used to analyze a company's financial strengths and weaknesses.

Liquidity ratios measure a firm's ability to meet its short-term obligations. Examples are the current ratio and the quick ratio, also called

the acid-test ratio. Activity ratios, such as the inventory turnover ratio, the accounts receivable turnover ratio, and the total asset turnover ratio, measure how effectively a firm uses its resources. Profitability ratios assess the overall financial performance of the business. Examples are the gross profit margin, the net profit margin, and the return on owners' equity. Leverage ratios, such as the total liabilities to total assets ratio and the long-term debt to equity ratio, measure the extent to which the firm relies on debt to finance its operations. Financial ratios help managers and outside evaluators compare a firm's current financial information with that of previous years and with results for other firms in the same industry.

 ASSESSMENT CHECK ANSWERS

15.6.1 List the four categories of financial ratios. The four categories of ratios are liquidity, activity, profitability, and leverage.

15.6.2 Define the following ratios: *current ratio, inventory turnover, net profit margin*, and *debt ratio*. The current ratio equals current assets divided by current liabilities; inventory turnover equals cost of goods sold divided by average inventory; net profit margin equals net income divided by sales; and the debt ratio equals total liabilities divided by total assets.

LO 15.7 Describe the role of budgets in a business.

Budgets are financial guidelines for future periods. They show a firm's expected sales revenues, operating expenses, cash receipts, and cash expenses. They reflect management's expected outcomes for the future and are based on plans that have been made. Budgets are important tools for planning and controlling. They provide standards against which actual performance can be measured. One important type of budget is the cash budget, which estimates cash inflows and outflows over a period of time.

 ASSESSMENT CHECK ANSWERS

15.7.1 What is a budget? A budget is a planning and control tool that reflects the firm's expected sales revenues, operating expenses, cash receipts, cash expenses.

15.7.2 How is a cash budget organized? Cash budgets are usually prepared monthly. Cash receipts are listed first. They include cash sales and the collection of past credit sales. Cash outlays, or cash expenses, are listed next. These include cash purchases, payment of past credit purchases, and operating expenses. The difference between cash receipts and cash outlays is net cash flow.

LO 15.8 Outline the accounting issues facing global business.

One accounting issue that affects global business is exchange rates. An exchange rate is the value of one country's currency in terms of the currencies of other countries. Daily changes in exchange rates affect the accounting entries for the sales and purchases of firms dealing in international markets. These fluctuations, or ups and downs, create either losses or gains for companies.

 ASSESSMENT CHECK ANSWERS

15.8.1 How are financial statements adjusted for exchange rates? An exchange rate is the value of one country's cur-

rency in terms of the currencies of other countries. Fluctuations, the ups and downs, of exchange rates create either gains or losses for global companies. Data about international financial transactions must be translated into the currency of the country where the parent company resides.

BUSINESS TERMS YOU NEED TO KNOW

accounting 416

accounting cycle 422

accounting equation 423

Accounting Standards Board (AcSB) 420

accrual accounting 430

asset 422

balance sheet 426

budget 435

Corruption of Foreign Public Officials Act 421

double-entry bookkeeping 423

Financial Accounting Standards Board (FASB) 421

generally accepted accounting principles (GAAP) 420

income statement 427

International Accounting Standards Board (IASB) 420

International Financial Reporting Standards (IFRS) 420

liability 423

owners' equity 423

public accountant 418

statement of cash flows 429

statement of changes in equity 429

REVIEW QUESTIONS

1. Define *accounting*. Who are the major users of accounting information?

2. What are the three major business activities where accountants play a major role? Give an example of each.

3. What does the term *GAAP* mean? Briefly explain the role of the Accounting Standards Board.

4. What is double-entry bookkeeping? Give a brief example.

5. List the four major financial statements. Which financial statements are permanent and which are temporary?

6. What is the difference between a current asset and a long-term asset? Why is cash typically listed first on a balance sheet?

7. List and explain the major items found on an income statement.

8. What is accrual accounting? Give an example of how accrual accounting affects a firm's financial statement.

9. List the four categories of financial ratios and give an example of each. What is the purpose of ratio analysis?

10. What is a cash budget? Briefly outline what a simple cash budget might look like.

PROJECTS AND TEAMWORK APPLICATIONS

1. Contact a local public accounting firm and set up an interview with one of the accountants. Ask the accountant about his or her educational background, why he or she was attracted to the accounting profession, and what he or she does during a typical day. Prepare a brief report on your interview. Do you want to learn more about the accounting profession? Are you more interested or less interested in a career in accounting after your interview? Why?

2. Suppose you work for a Canadian firm that has extensive operations in various countries. You are preparing your firm's

financial statements and you need to restate data from the various currencies to Canadian dollars. Which financial statements and which parts of these statements will be affected?

3. Identify two public companies operating in different industries. Collect at least three years' worth of financial statements for the firms. Calculate the financial ratios listed in Table 15.1. Prepare an oral report that summarizes your findings.

4. You've been appointed treasurer of a local not-for-profit organization. You want to improve the quality of financial reporting to

existing and potential donors. What kinds of financial statements do you ask the organization's accountant to prepare? Why do you think better-quality financial statements might help reassure donors?

5. Use the format of Figure 15.7 and adapt it to prepare your personal cash budget for next month. Keep in mind the following suggestions as you prepare your budget:

   a. *Cash inflows.* Your sources of cash include your payroll earnings, if any; gifts; scholarships; tax refunds; dividends and interest; and income from self-employment.

   b. *Cash outflows.* When estimating next month's cash outflows, include any of the following that may apply to your situation:

      i. Household expenses (rent or mortgage, utilities, maintenance, home furnishings, telephone/cellphone, cable TV, household supplies, groceries)

      ii. Education (tuition, fees, textbooks, supplies)

      iii. Work (transportation, clothing)

      iv. Clothing (purchases, cleaning, laundry)

      v. Automobile (auto payments, fuel, repairs) or other transportation (bus, train)

      vi. Insurance premiums
         • Renters (or homeowners)
         • Auto
         • Health
         • Life

      vii. Taxes (income, real estate)

      viii. Savings and investments

      ix. Entertainment/recreation (health club, vacation/travel, dining, movies)

      x. Debt (credit cards, instalment loans)

      xi. Miscellaneous (charitable contributions, childcare, gifts, medical expenses)

   c. *Beginning cash balance.* This amount can be based on a minimum cash balance you keep in your chequing account. It should include only the cash available for your use; investments in retirement plans should not be included.

WEB ASSIGNMENTS

1. **International Accounting Standards Board (IASB).** The IASB is responsible for setting and modifying international accounting rules. Go to the IASB's website (www.iasb.org); click on "About Us" and select "About the Organisation." Print out the material and bring it to class to participate in a class discussion on the IASB.

2. **Chartered Professional Accountant (CPA).** As noted in the chapter, many business professionals often seek the CPA designation. Visit the website of CPA Ontario (www.cpaontario.ca). Click on "Students/Education," and then "CPA Certification Program." What are the educational and experiential requirements to obtain a CPA? How many exams does a CPA candidate need to pass? What do these exams cover?

3. **Financial reporting requirements.** The chapter discussed the financial reporting requirements of Canadian companies, including public companies whose shares are traded on a stock exchange. Visit the website listed below and type in the name of a public company. Then click on "financials" to view the firm's current financial statements. Prepare a brief report comparing those statements to the ones shown in the chapter.

   www.google.com/finance

Note: Internet addresses change frequently. If you don't find the exact sites listed, you may need to access the organization's home page and search from there or use a search engine such as Bing or Google.

16 | THE FINANCIAL SYSTEM

LEARNING OBJECTIVES

LO 16.1 Outline the structure and importance of the financial system.

LO 16.2 List the various types of securities.

LO 16.3 Define *financial market* and distinguish between primary and secondary financial markets.

LO 16.4 Describe the characteristics of the major stock exchanges.

LO 16.5 Discuss how financial institutions are organized and how they function.

LO 16.6 Explain the functions of the Bank of Canada and the tools it uses to carry out these functions.

LO 16.7 Describe the regulation of the financial system.

LO 16.8 Describe the global financial system.

INSIDE BUSINESS

Canada Weathers the Credit Crisis

In 2008, much of the world's financial systems melted. But Canada's financial systems were largely unaffected. Europe, Greece, and Italy felt a significant impact of the global credit crisis. In the United States, interest rates were low and borrowing was high. The greater access to financing increased both the demand for housing and housing prices. U.S. banks became very aggressive. They tempted clients, including many high-risk clients, by offering very low down payments and low interest rates for the first few years of their mortgage. These mortgages were then packaged and sold to investors who felt assured that the collateral, or security, behind the mortgages (the homes) would reduce any risk of default on the mortgage. The main problem began after clients completed the first few years of low-interest mortgage payments. Their mortgage rates then increased, causing their monthly payments to also increase. Many clients were forced to default on their payments or sell their homes. The increase of homes on the market led to a reverse effect on prices—the "bubble" burst. The result was a high proportion of "toxic" mortgages, which had a higher value than the homes themselves. For example, homes valued at less than $250,000 had mortgages of more than $500,000. This situation was a disaster for creditors. Some lost half or more of their investment.

Why weren't Canadians affected in the same way? And why were Canadian banks rated the strongest in the world by the World Economic Forum? For starters, Canada's financial system is much more regulated than the U.S. banking system. And, by nature, Canadians tend to be less financially aggressive than Americans. Canadian banks have many more checks and balances related to confirming income, job status, and sales contracts. Canadian *consumers* also carry less debt on average than Americans (20 percent versus 26 percent, respectively). That explains why Canadians had fewer subprime mortgages: one in twenty in Canada versus one in six in the United States.

In Canada, housing values just before the 2008 financial crisis were about 200 percent of what they were in 1989, compared with 260 percent in the United States. During the crisis, the value of U.S. homes dropped to approximately 220 percent of their 1989 values, while little change was felt in Canada. The same type of housing bubble is highly unlikely in Canada because Canadians are generally financially conservative, both on the buyer's side and the lender's side. As a result, Canadian homes are rarely valued at less than their mortgage, which was a problem for Americans after the housing bubble burst. The Canada Mortgage and Housing Corporation (CMHC) is owned by the Canadian government. It insures mortgages for higher-risk clients who have low down payments.

Finally, Canadians receive no tax incentive for having a mortgage, whereas mortgage interest is a tax deduction in the United States, providing another reason for Americans to have a mortgage. In Canada, "a mortgage is seen as something you want to get rid of as fast as possible," says Peter Dungan, an economist at the Rotman School of Management at the University of Toronto. It is clear that no single factor preserved the financial system in Canada during the financial meltdown. Instead, a combination of financial conservatism and government policy helped Canadians to weather the crisis.[1]

CHAPTER 16 OVERVIEW

Businesses, governments, and individuals often need to raise capital, or money. For example, suppose a businessperson forecasts a sharp increase in sales for the coming year. This expected sales increase requires additional inventory. If the business lacks the cash to purchase the needed inventory, it may turn to a bank for a short-term loan. On the other hand, some individuals and businesses have incomes that are greater than their current expenses. They may want to earn interest on the extra funds. For example, suppose your income this month is $3,000, but your expenses are only $2,500. You can deposit the extra $500 in a bank account and receive interest.

The two transactions described above are small parts of what is known as the **financial system**, the mechanism by which money flows from savers to users. Almost all businesses, governments, and individuals participate in the financial system. A well-functioning financial system is vital to a nation's economic health. The financial system is the topic of this chapter.

We begin by describing the financial system and its components in more detail. We then outline the major types of financial instruments, such as bonds and stocks (also known as shares). Next we discuss financial markets, where financial instruments are bought and sold. We then describe the world's major stock markets.

Next, banks and other financial institutions are described in depth. We detail the structure and responsibilities of the Bank of Canada and the tools it uses to control the supply of money and credit. The chapter concludes with an overview of the major laws and regulations affecting the financial system and a discussion of today's global financial system.

financial system the mechanism by which money flows from savers to users.

LO 16.1 Outline the structure importance of the financial system.

UNDERSTANDING THE FINANCIAL SYSTEM

Households, businesses, government, financial institutions, and financial markets together form what is known as the financial system. A simple diagram of the financial system is shown in **Figure 16.1**.

On the left are savers—those who have excess funds. For different reasons, savers choose not to spend all of their current income, so they have a surplus of funds. Users are the opposite of savers; their spending needs are greater than their current income, so they have a shortfall. They need to obtain additional funds to make up the difference. Savings are provided by some households, businesses, and the government, but some other households, businesses, and the government are borrowers. Households may need money to buy automobiles or homes. Businesses may need money to purchase inventory or build new production facilities. Governments may need money to build highways and courthouses.

In Canada, households are generally net savers. That means that, as a whole, households save more money than they use. Businesses and governments are net users. That means that they generally use more funds than they save. You may be surprised that households provide most of the net savings in the Canadian financial system. After all, Canadians do not have a reputation for being thrifty. The savings rate of Canadian households is low compared with the savings rates in other countries, but Canadian households still save billions of dollars each year.

How much an individual saves depends on many factors. One of the most important factors is the person's age. As people age, they often move from being net borrowers to being net savers.

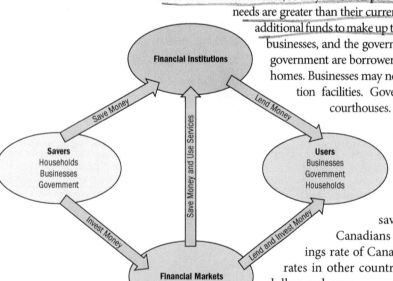

FIGURE 16.1 Overview of the Financial System and Its Components

When you graduate from university or college and begin a career, you likely have very little savings. In fact, you may be in debt. In the early years of your career, you may spend more than you make as you buy major assets, like a home. In these early career years, your *net worth*—the difference between what you own and what you owe—is very low and may even be negative. But as your career progresses and your income rises, you will begin to build financial savings to fund retirement and other needs. Your net worth will also increase. It will continue to increase until you retire and begin drawing on your retirement savings.

Funds can be transferred between savers and users in two ways: directly and indirectly. A direct transfer means that the user raises the needed funds directly from savers. Direct transfers *do* occur, but most funds flow through either financial markets or financial institutions. For example, assume a local school district needs to build a new high school. The district does not have enough cash to pay for the school construction costs, so it sells bonds to investors (savers) in the financial market. The district uses the funds from the sale to pay for the new school. In return, the bond investors receive interest each year for the use of their money.

The other way that funds can be transferred indirectly is through financial institutions— for example, through a commercial bank such as TD Canada Trust or Scotiabank. The bank pools, or combines, customer deposits and uses the funds to make loans to businesses and households. These borrowers pay the bank interest, and the bank, in turn, pays its depositors interest for the use of their money.

The accompanying "Going Green" feature describes how TD Bank has started to transform all its branches so that they will be "carbon neutral."

✔ ASSESSMENT CHECK

16.1.1 What is the financial system?

16.1.2 In the financial system, who are the borrowers and who are the savers?

16.1.3 List the two most common ways that funds are transferred between borrowers and savers.

GOING GREEN — TD BANK: "AS GREEN AS OUR LOGO"

TD Bank's square, green logo is a familiar sight from Vancouver to Florida. TD Bank announced that it was the first North American bank to go carbon neutral in the United States. The bank achieved carbon neutrality by reducing waste, using alternative sources of energy, and building environmentally friendly buildings from sustainable materials. With 1,300 branches, or "stores," TD has used its resources to pursue an aggressive "green" policy.

To demonstrate its goal of carbon neutrality, TD bank unveiled a new prototype store. The 3,800-square-foot building is designed to reduce energy use by 50 percent compared with earlier models. Each new store will make up to 20 percent of its own electricity through solar panels on the roof. To keep interior temperatures comfortable, the windows will have specially coated glass that reflects or absorbs heat energy. Sensors will control lighting over the course of the day. The drive-through facility will feature a translucent solar canopy. Outside, the landscaping will include drought-resistant plants and water-efficient plumbing.

Among other measures, TD Bank has bought a block of wind energy large enough to run its 2,300 automated teller machines (ATMs). It plans to encourage its customers to save energy by signing up for online banking and paperless statements. TD Bank has also located many of its branches near public transportation.

TD Bank's first fully green office opened in Queens Village, New York. Since opening this branch, TD has opened 71 LEED (Leadership in Energy and Environmental Design) Certified branches, including one branch in Florida that generates more electricity than it uses. The bank eventually plans to have all of its offices meet LEED standards.

In Canada, TD Financial Group has established the TD Friends of the Environment Foundation. It has provided over $66 million to support more than 22,000 environmental projects and programs.

Fred Graziano, TD Bank's head of regional commercial banking, says, "We're taking the environment seriously and we strongly believe this is the right thing to do for our business, customers, employees and the community. We want TD Bank to be as green as our logo."

Questions for Critical Thinking

1. Why does "going green" make good business sense for TD Bank?

2. Think about your own banking practices. What steps can you take to be greener?

Sources: TD Bank, accessed February 22, 2012, www.tdbank.com; James Comtois, "TD Bank's First Green Branch Sprouts in Queens," *Oram's New York Business.com*, February 22, 2012, www.crainsnewyork.com; Patrick Lo, "TD Bank Goes Carbon Neutral," *Green Street Journal*, March 16, 2010, www.gsjournal.com; "TD Bank Goes Carbon Neutral, Unveils 'Green Store' Prototype," *Environmental Leader*, February 22, 2012, www.environmentalleader.com; "TD Bank, America's Most Convenient Bank, Announces It's Now Carbon Neutral and Unveils New 'Green Store' Prototype Design," press release, February 18, 2010, http://multivu.prnewswire.com; TD Friends of the Environment Foundation, "Helping Canadians Make a Difference," accessed July 4, 2011, www.fef.td.com/about.jsp; TD Bank, accessed August 13, 2014, www.tdbank.com/aboutus/about_us.html and https://fef.td.com/about-us/.

securities financial instruments that represent the obligations of the issuers to provide the purchasers with the expected stated returns on the funds invested or loaned.

TYPES OF SECURITIES

When businesses and governments borrow funds from savers, they provide different types of guarantees for repayment. **Securities**, also called financial instruments, represent the obligations of the issuers—businesses and governments—to provide the purchasers with the expected or stated returns on the funds invested or loaned. Securities can be grouped into three categories: money market instruments, bonds, and shares (also known as stock). Money market instruments and bonds are debt securities. Shares are units of ownership in public corporations, such as Sun Life Financial, Hudson's Bay, and Bell Canada Enterprises.

Money Market Instruments

Money market instruments are short-term debt securities issued by governments, financial institutions, and corporations. All money market instruments mature within one year from the date of issue. The issuer pays interest to the investors for the use of their funds. Money market instruments are generally low-risk securities and are purchased by investors when they have surplus cash. Examples of money market instruments include Canadian Treasury bills, commercial paper, and bank certificates of deposit.

Treasury bills are short-term securities issued by the Canadian Treasury and backed by the full faith and credit of the Canadian government. Treasury bills are sold with a maturity date of 30, 90, 180, or 360 days and must be a minimum of $1,000. They are virtually risk free and are easy to resell. Commercial paper refers to securities sold by corporations, such as TELUS. These securities mature in 1 to 270 days from the date of issue. Although commercial paper is slightly riskier than Treasury bills, it is generally considered to be a very low-risk security.

A certificate of deposit (CD) is a time deposit at a financial institution, such as a commercial bank, a savings bank, or a credit union. The sizes and maturity dates of CDs vary and can often be tailored to meet the needs of purchasers. CDs of $100,000 or less per depositor are insured by the Canada Deposit Insurance Corporation (CDIC). CDs in larger denominations are not federally insured but can be sold more easily before they mature.

Bonds

Bondholders are creditors of a corporation or government body. A firm may sell bonds to obtain long-term debt capital. Federal, provincial, and municipal governments also acquire funds through bonds. Bonds are issued in various denominations, or face values, usually between $1,000 and $25,000. Each issue indicates the rate of interest and the maturity date. The rate of interest to be paid to the bondholder is stated as a percentage of the bond's face value. The maturity date is the date when the bondholder will be paid the bond's full face value. Bondholders are creditors. That means their claim on the firm's assets must be satisfied before any claims of shareholders if the firm enters into bankruptcy, reorganization, or liquidation.

Types of Bonds

A prospective bond investor can choose among several types of bonds. The major types of bonds are summarized in **Table 16.1**. *Government bonds*, such as Canada Savings Bonds, are bonds sold by the Canadian government. Government bonds are backed by the full faith and credit of the Canadian government, which means they are the least risky of all bonds. The Treasury sells bonds that mature in 2, 5, 10, and 30 years from the date of issue.

Municipal bonds are bonds issued by municipal governments. Two types of municipal bonds are available: corporate bonds and mortgage-backed corporate bonds. Corporate bonds include a diverse group of bonds. They often vary depending on the collateral—the property pledged by the borrower—that backs the bond. For example, a *secured bond* is backed by a specific pledge of company assets. These assets are the collateral, just like a home is collateral for a house mortgage. However, many businesses also issue unsecured bonds, called *debentures*. These bonds are backed only by the financial reputation of the issuing corporation.

Table 16.1 Types of Bonds

ISSUER	TYPES OF SECURITIES	RISK	SPECIAL FEATURES
Government of Canada (government bonds)	Canada Savings Bonds: Mature in 10 years, but can be cashed at any time.	Government bonds carry virtually no risk.	Affordable: can be purchased for as little as $100
Provincial and local governments (municipal bonds)	General obligation: Issued by provincial or local governmental units with taxing authority; backed by the full faith and credit of the province or municipality where the bonds are issued.	Risk varies, depending on the financial health of the issuer. Risk is generally very low.	
Corporations	Secured bonds: Bonds that are backed by specific assets.	Risk varies depending on the financial health of the issuer.	A few corporate bonds are convertible into common shares of the issuing company.
	Unsecured bonds (debentures): Bonds that are backed by the financial health and reputation of the issuer.	Most corporate bond issues are rated in terms of credit risk (AAA or Aaa is the highest rating).	
Financial institutions	Mortgage-backed securities	Generally very low risk.	They pay monthly income consisting of both interest and principal.

The second type of bonds are mortgage-backed corporate bonds, also called *mortgage-backed securities (MBSs)*. These bonds are backed by a pool, or group, of mortgage loans purchased from lenders, such as chartered banks. As borrowers make their mortgage payments, these payments are "passed through" to the holders of the securities. MBSs are very safe because all mortgages in the pool, or group, are insured by CMHC. In the United States, during the period of approximately 2004 to 2008, similar securities were issued. But these securities consisted of so-called *subprime mortgages*, loans made to borrowers with poor credit ratings. Many of these securities turned out to be risky and, in part, triggered what became known as the *credit crisis* that began in 2008. The extent of the crisis forced the U.S. government to undertake a massive bailout of the financial system. The Office of Financial Stability—part of the U.S. Treasury department—was created to purchase poor-quality mortgage-backed securities from financial institutions.

Quality Ratings for Bonds

Two factors affect the price of a bond: its risk and its interest rate. Bonds vary in terms of their risk. Bond investors use a tool called a *bond rating* to assess the risk of a bond. Several investment firms rate corporate and municipal bonds. In Canada, the Dominion Bond Rating Service (DBRS) provides bond ratings. The best-known bond rating organizations are Standard & Poor's (S&P), Moody's, and Fitch. **Table 16.2** lists the S&P bond ratings. Moody's and Fitch use similar rating systems. Bonds with the lowest level of risk are rated AAA. As ratings descend, risk increases. Bonds with ratings of BBB and above are classified as *investment-grade bonds*. Bonds with ratings of BB and below are classified as *speculative bonds* or *junk bonds*. Junk bonds attract investors because they offer high interest rates in exchange for greater risk. Today, junk bonds pay about 50 percent more in interest than investment-grade corporate bonds. The recent credit crisis generated a great deal of criticism toward the ratings companies. This criticism centred on the conflict of interest from ratings companies also advising companies on how to structure their bond offerings.

The second factor affecting the price of a bond is its interest rate. All other things being equal, the higher the interest rate, the higher the price of a bond. But often everything else is *not*

Table 16.2   Standard & Poor's Bond Ratings

Investment Grade	Highest	AAA	Extremely strong capacity to meet financial commitments; highest rating
		AA	Very strong capacity to meet financial commitments
		A	Strong capacity to meet financial commitments, but somewhat susceptible to adverse economic conditions and changes in circumstances
		BBB	Adequate capacity to meet financial commitments, but more subject to risk during poor economic conditions
		BBB–	Considered lowest investment grade by market participants
Speculative Grade		BB+	Considered highest speculative grade by market participants
		BB	Less vulnerable in the near term but faces major ongoing uncertainties to adverse business, financial, and economic conditions
		B	More vulnerable to risks from poor business, financial, and economic conditions but currently has the capacity to meet financial commitments
		CCC	Currently vulnerable and dependent on favourable business, financial, and economic conditions to meet financial commitments
		CC	Currently highly vulnerable
		C	A bankruptcy petition has been filed or similar action taken, but payments of financial commitments are continued
	Lowest	D	Payment default on financial commitments

Note: Standard & Poor's occasionally assigns a plus or minus following the letter rating. For instance, AA+ means that the bond is higher quality than most AA bonds but hasn't quite met AAA standards. Ratings below C indicate that the bond is currently not paying interest.
Source: Standard & Poor's Rating Services, "Credit Ratings Definitions and FAQs," accessed February 22, 2012, www.standardandpoors.com/ratings/definitions-and-faqs/en/us#def_1; Standard & Poor's, accessed August 13, 2014, http://img.en25.com/Web/StandardandPoors/SP_CreditRatingsGuide.pdf.

equal: The bonds may not be equally risky, or one bond may have a longer maturity date. Investors must evaluate the individual characteristics of each bond.

Another important influence on bond prices is the *market interest rate*. Bonds pay fixed rates of interest. That means that as market interest rates rise, bond prices fall. The opposite is also true: As market interest rates fall, bond prices rise. For example, the price of a 10-year bond that pays 5 percent per year would fall by about 8 percent if market interest rates rose from 5 percent to 6 percent.

Most corporate and municipal bonds are callable, as are some government bonds. A *call provision* allows the issuer to redeem, or cash, the bond before its maturity at a specified price. Not surprisingly, issuers tend to call bonds when market interest rates are declining. For example, suppose the City of Toronto had $50 million in bonds outstanding with a 5 percent annual interest rate. It would pay $2.5 million annually in interest. Now, suppose interest rates fall to 3 percent. The city may decide to call the 5 percent bonds by repaying the principal from the proceeds, or funds, from the newly issued 3 percent bonds. Calling the 5 percent bonds and issuing 3 percent bonds will save the city $1 million a year in interest payments. The savings in annual interest expense should be greater than the cost of retiring the old bonds and issuing new bonds.

Shares

common shares the basic form of corporate ownership

The basic form of corporate ownership is **common shares**. Purchasers of common shares are the true owners of a corporation. Holders of common shares vote on major company decisions, such as purchasing another company or electing a board of directors. In return for the money they invest, holders of common shares expect to receive some sort of return.

This return can be cash dividend payments, expected increases in the value of the shares, or both. Dividends vary widely from firm to firm. As a general rule, faster-growing companies pay less in dividends because they need more funds to finance their growth. As a result, investors expect shares that pay little or no cash dividends to show a greater increase in value compared with shares paying larger cash dividends.

Sometimes unexpected events can have a major effect on dividends and share prices. On March 8, 2014, Malaysian Airlines flight MH370 disappeared with 259 passengers and crew aboard. Later that year, on July 17, 2014, Malaysian Airlines flight MH17 was shot down over Ukraine. These events have led to a decrease in the share price of Malaysian Airlines of over 35 percent, the virtual elimination of the likelihood of dividends, along with the privatization of the airline.[2]

Investors who hold common shares benefit from a company's success. But they also risk losing their investments if the company fails. If a firm dissolves, claims of the creditors must be satisfied before shareholders receive anything. Because creditors have the first (or senior) claim to assets, holders of common shares are said to have a residual claim on company assets.

The market value of a share is the price that shares are currently selling for. For example, Apple's share price varied between $64 and $99 per share in the 12-month period ending August 13, 2014.[3] What leads to a share's market value? The answer is complicated. Many factors can cause share prices to move up or down. In the long run, share prices tend to follow a company's profits.

Preferred Shares

In addition to common shares, a few companies also issue preferred shares. Holders of preferred shares receive preference in the payment of dividends. TransCanada and Bombardier are examples of firms that have issued preferred shares. Also, if a company is dissolved, holders of preferred shares have claims on the firm's assets that are ahead of the claims of holders of common shares. On the other hand, holders of preferred shares rarely have voting rights. Also, they are paid fixed dividends, regardless of how profitable the firm becomes. Preferred shares are legally classified as equity, but many investors consider preferred shares to be more like a bond than common shares.

Convertible Securities

Companies may issue bonds or preferred shares that include a conversion feature. Such bonds or shares are called *convertible securities*. This feature gives the bondholder or holder of preferred shares the right to exchange the bond or preferred shares for a fixed number of common shares. Convertible bonds pay lower interest rates than bonds without conversion features, which helps to reduce the issuing firm's interest expenses. Investors are willing to accept lower interest rates because they value the possibility of additional gains if the price of the firm's shares increase. For example, at a price of $61 per share, Peabody Energy's convertible bond would have a common share value of at least $1,043 ($61 × 17.1). If the price of Peabody's common shares increases by $10 per share, the value of the convertible bond will increase by at least $171.

✓ **ASSESSMENT CHECK**

16.2.1 What are the major types of securities?

16.2.2 What areas of the government issue bonds?

16.2.3 Why do investors purchase common shares?

FINANCIAL MARKETS

Securities are issued and traded in **financial markets**. There are many different types of financial markets. One of the most important differences is between primary and secondary markets. In the **primary markets**, firms and governments issue securities and sell them initially to the general public. A company may sell a bond or issue shares to the investing public when it needs capital to purchase inventory, expand a plant, make major investments, acquire another firm, or pursue other business goals. For example, RUSNANO planned to sell $1.7 billion in bonds to pay for expansion and new projects.[4]

In a share offering, investors are offered the opportunity to purchase ownership shares in a firm and to participate in a firm's future growth, in exchange for providing the firm's current capital.

LO 16.3 Define *financial market* and distinguish between primary and secondary financial markets.

financial markets markets where securities are issued and traded.

primary markets a financial market where firms and governments issue securities and sell them initially to the general public.

At the Toronto Stock Exchange, current share prices are displayed.

When a company offers shares for sale to the general public for the first time, it is called an *initial public offering (IPO)*. Many of these offerings were from Asian companies.[5] The "Hit & Miss" feature describes an American company's IPO.

Both for-profit corporations and government agencies also rely on primary markets to raise funds by issuing bonds. For example, the federal government sells Treasury bonds to finance some of the federal expenses, such as interest payments on outstanding federal debt. Provincial and local governments sell bonds to finance capital projects, such as the construction of sewer systems, streets, and fire stations.

Announcements of new bond and share offerings appear daily in business publications such as *The Globe and Mail* and the *Financial Post*. These announcements are often in the form of a simple black-and-white ad called a *tombstone*.

Securities are sold to the investing public in two ways: in open auctions and through investment bankers. Almost all securities sold through open auctions are Government of Canada securities. Sales of most corporate and municipal securities are made through financial institutions like TD Securities. These

 & MISS

A Major Spinoff for Citigroup

Not long ago, the U.S. banking company Citigroup was involved in not just banking but also other interests, including insurance. Following the financial crisis, Citigroup's CEO, Vikram Pandit, began to dispose of some of these holdings. He wanted to slim the company down to its original core banking business by focusing on large institutions and wealthy individuals. The trend in Canada has been the opposite: Major Canadian banks are now entering the insurance sector and adding to their core banking business.

Primerica Inc. was one of the Citigroup holdings to go. Based in Duluth, Georgia, Primerica sells life insurance, mutual funds, and other financial products door to door. Its middle-class customers earn from $30,000 to $100,000 a year. Primerica never fit well with the rest of Citigroup—and Primerica's 100,000 fiercely independent salespeople liked it that way. As the financial crisis worsened, some of Primerica employees suggested cutting ties with Citigroup.

Citigroup tried to sell Primerica but could not find a buyer willing to pay the asking price. So Citigroup announced that it would spin off Primerica. Primerica would issue an IPO and sell shares in the company for the first time. Primerica planned to sell 18 million shares at $12 to $14 a share. Under the terms of the IPO, Citigroup would take all the profits and keep Primerica's existing accounts. Primerica would be a smaller company but it would keep any new policies. John Addison and Rick Williams, the co-CEOs of Primerica, said, "We're going to be a smaller, faster-growing company going forward."

The IPO went better than expected. Primerica sold more than 21 million shares at almost $20 each. Addison and Williams feel that the company's focus has contributed to its success. "No one else has our business model," said Williams. "No one else focuses on the middle-income, middle market like we do." Analysts took the IPO's success as a sign that both the life insurance industry and the market were recovering from the recession.

Questions for Critical Thinking

1. Visit the websites of Citigroup and Primerica. Why do you think these two companies did not work well together?

2. Although Citigroup failed to find a buyer for Primerica, the IPO was very successful. Why do you think it was so successful?

3. Can you see a similar sale in one of Canada's larger financial institutions, such as RBC Financial Group or TD Bank Financial Group? If so, which line of business can you see being spun off?

Sources: Primerica, accessed June 21, 2010, www.primerica.com; Citigroup, accessed June 21, 2010, www.citigroup.com; Kerri Shannon, "Citigroup Spin-Off Primerica Boasts Strong Stock Debut in Hot IPO Market," *Money Morning*, April 4, 2010, http://moneymorning.com; "Primerica IPO a Success as Shares Jump," *CNBC*, April 1, 2010, www.cnbc.com; Maria Aspan and Clare Baldwin, "Citi Spinoff Primerica Soars on Hopes for Economy," Reuters, April 1, 2010, www.reuters.com; David Enrich, "An IPO of Primerica Will End a Citi Era," *Wall Street Journal*, November 6, 2009, www.online.wsj.com.

institutions purchase the issue from the firm or government and then resell the issue to investors. This process is known as *underwriting.*

Financial institutions underwrite shares and bond issues at a discount. That means they pay the issuing firm or government less than the price that financial institutions charge investors. This discount is compensation for the financial institution's services, including the risk financial institutions take on when they underwrite a new security issue. The discount is often negotiable, but usually averages about 5 percent for all types of securities. The size of the underwriting discount is generally higher for share issues than for bond issues. For example, underwriting discounts for IPOs are generally between 7 and 10 percent.

Corporations and governments are willing to pay for the services provided by financial institutions because they are financial market experts. The underwriter typically locates buyers for the issue and advises the issuer on several details: the general characteristics of the issue, its pricing, and the timing of the offering. Several financial institutions commonly perform the underwriting process. The issuer selects a lead, or primary, financial institution, which forms a syndicate consisting of other financial institutions. Each member of the syndicate purchases a portion of the security issue and resells it to investors.

Media reports of share and bond trading are most likely to refer to trading in the **secondary market**, a collection of financial markets where previously issued securities are traded among investors. The corporations or governments that originally issued the securities being traded are not directly involved in the secondary market. The issuers do not make payments when securities are sold, and they do not receive any proceeds when securities are purchased. For example, the Toronto Stock Exchange (TSX) is a secondary market. The secondary market handles four to five times the dollar value of securities than are handled in the primary market. Each day, millions of shares worth billions of dollars are traded on the TSX.[6] The characteristics of the world's major stock exchanges are discussed in the next section.

secondary market a collection of financial markets where previously issued securities are traded among investors.

✔ **ASSESSMENT CHECK**

16.3.1 What is a financial market?

16.3.2 Distinguish between a primary and a secondary financial market.

16.3.3 Briefly explain the role of financial institutions in the sale of securities.

UNDERSTANDING STOCK MARKETS

LO 16.4 Describe the characteristics of the major stock exchanges.

Stock markets, or exchanges, are probably the best-known of the world's financial markets. In these markets, shares of stock are bought and sold by investors.

stock markets (exchanges) markets where shares of stock are bought and sold by investors.

The Toronto Stock Exchange

The Toronto Stock Exchange, or TSX, is Canada's largest stock exchange. For a company's shares to be traded on the TSX, the firm must apply for a listing and meet certain listing requirements. The firm must continue to meet requirements each year to remain listed on the TSX. Corporate bonds are also traded on the TSX, but bond trading is less than 1 percent of the total value of securities traded on the TSX during a typical year.

Foreign Stock Markets

The *New York Stock Exchange (NYSE)* is sometimes referred to as the "Big Board." The NYSE is the most famous stock market and one of the oldest stock markets in the world. Shares traded on this exchange represent most of the largest, best-known companies in the United States and have a total market value of more than $16 trillion. The NYSE is the world's largest stock market.

The *NASDAQ Stock Market* is the world's second-largest stock market. It is very different from the NYSE. NASDAQ stands for National Association of Securities Dealers Automated Quotation System. It is actually a computerized communications network that links member investment firms. It is the world's largest intranet. All trading on NASDAQ takes place through its intranet, not on a trading floor.

All trading on NASDAQ takes place through its intranet, not on a trading floor.

MONIKA GRAFF/UPI/Landov

Stock markets can be found throughout the world. Almost all developed countries and many developing countries have stock exchanges. For example, stock exchanges are located in Mumbai, Helsinki, Hong Kong, Mexico City, and Paris. One of the largest stock exchanges outside the United States is the London Stock Exchange. The London Stock Exchange was founded in the early seventeenth century. It lists over 2,600 stock and bond issues from more than 60 countries around the world. Trading on the London Stock Exchange takes place using a NASDAQ-type computerized communications network.

The London Stock Exchange is the most international of all stock markets. It handles about two-thirds of all cross-border trading in the world, such as the trading of shares of Canadian companies outside of Canada. Institutional investors in Canada may trade TSX-listed shares or NASDAQ-listed shares in London.

Stock markets around the world are closely interconnected. As a result, changes in one country's economy can affect other countries, as explained in the "Hit & Miss" feature.

HIT & MISS

How News Lifts—or Sinks—Shares around the World

The growth of computerized trading has closely connected all the developed nations and many developing nations. A snapshot of the world markets shows how events in one country can affect stock markets everywhere.

Canada was not hit very hard by the global recession of 2008 to 2012. But this recession was the worst in U.S. history since the Great Depression. The Canadian recession was not as damaging as the recessions in the early 1980s or the early 1990s. Still, former Finance Minister Jim Flaherty decided to set up an economic action plan.

In the spring of 2010, Americans grew hopeful that their country was starting to climb out of the recession. The U.S. Federal Reserve announced that although American households were not spending as much as before the recession, the U.S. economy was slowly improving. Some companies were making a profit because of rising consumer demand. Earlier in the recovery, some companies had made money by cutting their costs. The share prices increased in some U.S. companies, like Apple. The computer company Hewlett-Packard announced that it was buying the smartphone maker Palm.

America seemed to be emerging from the credit crisis. But the credit crisis hit Greece, which has had major challenges paying off its debts. As a member of the European Union, Greece had adopted the euro as its currency. Other euro countries, such as Spain and Portugal, also faced financial troubles. Standard & Poor's reduced the bond rating of all three countries.

As Greece tried to recover amid violence and political turmoil, it adopted drastic measures: Government spending was reduced on social programs even though the public protested. Prime Minister George Papandreou said that the public sector was "overly grown, overly expensive." He told Greeks that he hoped the austerity program would "give us a cushion" that will "give us quite a bit of money."

Questions for Critical Thinking

1. Why would a financial crisis on the other side of the world affect the Canadian economy? Why was the Canadian economy less affected by the global financial crisis than the United States?

2. What has happened in Greece, Spain, and Portugal? Have they recovered from their economic crises? Why was Germany expected to help bail out other Eurozone countries from the debt crisis?

3. When Standard & Poor's downgraded the U.S. debt, what was the effect on the Canadian economy in 2011?

Sources: Mark Rohner, "Greece Ahead of Targets, Will Not Default, Papandreou Says," *Bloomberg Businessweek*, February 22, 2012, www.businessweek.com; European Union, accessed February 22, 2012, http://europa.eu; Will Swarts, "Stocks Surge as Earnings Stay Robust," *SmartMoney*, April 29, 2010, www.smartmoney.com; Christine Hauser, "Stocks Higher as Earnings Lift Sentiment," *New York Times*, April 28, 2010, www.nytimes.com; Reuters, "Earnings Lift World Stocks, Greece Stays in Focus," *Economic Times*, April 21, 2010, http://economictimes.indiatimes.com; Spyros Economides, "Viewpoint: The Politics of Greece's Economic Crisis," *BBC News*, June 17, 2011, accessed July 6, 2011, www.bbc.co.uk/news/world-europe-13805391; Department of Finance Canada, "Budget 2009: Canada's Action Plan," January 27, 2009, accessed July 6, 2011, www.fin.gc.ca/n08/09-011-eng.asp; Tavia Grant, "Was Canada's Recession 'Average'?" *Globe and Mail*, May 6, 2010, accessed July 6, 2011, www.theglobeandmail.com/report-on-business/economy/was-canadas-recession-average/article1535179/.

ECNs and the Future of Stock Markets

For years a so-called *fourth market* has existed. The fourth market is the direct trading of exchange-listed stocks off the floor of the exchange. Until recently, trading in the fourth market was limited to institutional investors who were buying or selling large blocks of shares.

The fourth market has begun to open up to smaller, individual investors through markets called *electronic communications networks* (ECNs). In ECNs, buyers and sellers meet in a virtual stock market and trade directly with one another. ECNs have become a significant force in the stock market in recent years. The TSX now uses the services of Savvis to facilitate its ECN.[7]

Investor Participation in the Stock Markets

Most investors aren't members of the TSX or any other stock market; they need to use the services of a brokerage firm to buy or sell shares. Two examples of brokerage firms are Edward Jones and TD Waterhouse. Investors establish an account with the brokerage firm and then enter orders to trade shares. The brokerage firm handles the trade for the investor and charges the investor a fee for the service. Some investors phone in their orders or visit the brokerage firm in person. But today, most investors use their computers to trade stocks online. The requirements for setting up an account vary from broker to broker. Selecting the right brokerage firm is one of the most important decisions investors make.

The most common type of order is a *market order*. This order instructs the broker to obtain the best possible price—the highest price when selling and the lowest price when buying. If the stock market is open, market orders are filled within seconds. Another popular type of order is called a *limit order*. It sets a price ceiling when buying or a price floor when selling. If the order cannot be filled when it is placed, the order is left with the exchange's market maker, a firm who is always ready to buy or sell a specific share at a publicly quoted price. It may be filled later if the price limits are met.

> **✓ ASSESSMENT CHECK**
>
> **16.4.1** What are the world's two largest stock markets?
>
> **16.4.2** What makes the London Stock Exchange unique?
>
> **16.4.3** Explain the difference between a market order and a limit order.

FINANCIAL INSTITUTIONS

> **LO 16.5** Discuss how financial institutions are organized and how they function.

One of the most important parts of the financial system is its **financial institutions**. They are an intermediary between savers and borrowers. They collect funds from savers and then lend the funds to individuals, businesses, and governments. Financial institutions improve the transfer of funds from savers to users by increasing the efficiency and effectiveness of the process. Financial institutions make it easier for savers to earn more and for users of funds to pay less. It is difficult to imagine how any modern economy could function without well-developed financial institutions. Think about how difficult it would be for a business to obtain financing or for an individual to purchase a new home without using a financial institution. Borrowers would need to identify and negotiate terms with each saver individually.

Traditionally, financial institutions have been classified into depository institutions and non-depository institutions. Depository institutions accept deposits that customers can withdraw on demand. Examples of depository institutions include commercial banks, such as CIBC, RBC, TD Canada Trust, and Scotiabank. Nondepository institutions include life insurance companies, such as Manulife Financial; pension funds, such as the Ontario Teachers' Pension Plan; and mutual funds. Together, Canadian financial institutions have trillions of dollars in assets. **Figure 16.2** illustrates the number and types of major financial institutions in Canada.

financial institutions intermediaries between savers and borrowers that collect funds from savers then lend the funds to individuals, businesses, and governments.

Commercial Banks

Commercial banks are the largest and probably the most important financial institutions in Canada and in most other countries. In Canada, the 28 domestic banks and other foreign-based financial institutions manage assets of more than $4.0 trillion. Commercial banks offer the most services of any financial institution. These services include a wide range of chequing and savings

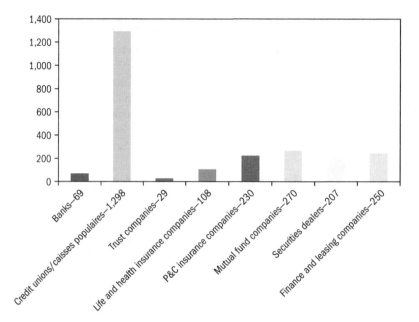

FIGURE 16.2 Financial Institutions in Canada

Note: P&C insurance companies refer to profit and casualty insurance companies.

Source: Department of Finance Canada, "The Canadian Financial Services Sector," accessed July 6, 2011, www.fin.gc.ca/toc/2002/fact-cfss_-eng.asp.

The Royal Bank of Canada (RBC) is Canada's largest financial institution.

Fred Lum/The Globe and Mail/The Canadian Press

deposit accounts, consumer loans, credit cards, home mortgage loans, business loans, and trust services. Commercial banks also sell other financial products, including securities and insurance.[8] Within the past few years, the number of domestic banks increased significantly from 14 to 23.

How Banks Operate

Banks raise funds by offering customers a variety of chequing and savings deposits. The banks then pool, or combine, these deposits and lend most of them out in the form of consumer and business loans. At the end of a recent year, banks held several billion dollars in deposits and outstanding loans.[9] Banks lend a great deal of money to households and businesses for a variety of purposes. Banks currently hold approximately 75 percent of residential mortgages and more than $900 billion in commercial loans.[10] Commercial banks are an especially important source of funds for small businesses. When banks evaluate loan applications, they look at the borrower's ability and willingness to repay the loan. Occasionally, banks reject loan applications.

Banks make money mostly because the interest rate they charge borrowers is higher than the rate of interest they pay depositors. Banks also make money from other sources, such as fees they charge customers for using chequing accounts and ATMs.

After the recent credit crisis, many small business owners have suffered because banks have begun pulling their lines of credit; the "Career Kickstart" feature offers some suggestions if this happens to you.

Electronic Banking

Each year, more and more funds move through electronic funds transfer systems (EFTSs). EFTSs are computerized systems for conducting financial transactions over electronic links. Millions of businesses and consumers now pay bills and receive payments electronically. For example, most

CAREER KICKSTART

What to Do When Your Credit Gets Pulled

For years banks have issued business credit cards to small business owners. The cards come with a line of credit of usually several thousand dollars or more. The line of credit gives these businesses a safety net in case of a late payment from a client or some other emergency. After the credit crisis hit, banks began to either call those loans in or limit the credit lines to the amount currently outstanding. As a result, millions of small business owners lost that safety net. The Canadian Federation of Independent Businesses (CFIB) reported that 20 percent of small and medium-sized business owners had their applications for credit rejected. In some cases, their credit lines had been decreased or their requests to extend their loans had been denied. Here are some steps to consider if this situation happens to you:

1. Be careful not to use all credit you have left; doing so could have a negative impact on your credit score.

2. Make your current monthly payment as quickly as possible, either online or by phone.

3. Obtain debt counselling to learn how to better manage your debt. Use a trusted organization like Credit Canada (www.creditcanada.com).

4. If possible, pay down your existing credit card debt. But if you know you'll need money in the short term, weigh that need against your credit score before you write the cheque.

5. Keep careful track of your credit score. Equifax Canada and TransUnion Canada provide free credit reports.

Sources: Federal Trade Commission, "Credit and Your Consumer Rights," accessed June 21, 2010, www.ftc.gov; Sam Thacker, "Steps to Take When Your Credit Line Is Pulled," *All-Business*, accessed June 21, 2010, www.allbusiness.com; Jeffrey Weber, "What to Do When Your Credit Limit Is Decreased," SmartBalanceTransfers.com, March 4, 2010, www.smartbalancetransfers.com; Julie Bennett, "What to Do When the Bank Pulls Your Line of Credit," *Entrepreneur*, February 2010, www.entrepreneur.com; Industry Canada, *Supporting Small Business Innovation: Review of the Business Development Bank of Canada*, accessed July 28, 2011, www.ic.gc.ca/eic/site/ic1.nsf/vwapj/E-BDC.pdf/$file/E-BDC.pdf; Equifax, accessed July 28, 2011, www.econsumer.equifax.ca/index_en.html?transaction_id5100aca537487668e726bba5aaf22a4; TransUnion, accessed July 28, 2011, www.transunion.ca/.

employers directly deposit employees' paycheques into their bank accounts instead of issuing paper cheques. Today, nearly all social assistance payments and other federal payments are sent as electronic data, not as paper documents.

One of the original forms of electronic banking, the automated teller machine (ATM), continues to grow in popularity. ATMs allow customers to make bank transactions at any time by inserting a bank issued electronic card into the machine and entering a personal identification number (PIN). Networked systems enable ATM users to access their bank accounts all across Canada and throughout the world. Customers can use a debit card to pay for purchases directly from their chequing or savings account. All major retailers and even smaller sized merchants offer customers the option to pay by debit card, and some even go further and offer additional cash withdrawals, known as cash back, from the customer's bank account. Consumers enjoy the convenience of debit cards, while at the same time it eliminates the problem of bad cheques for retailers. There were approximately 4.9 billion debit card transactions in Canada in 2014 alone.[11]

Online Banking

Today, many consumers do some or all of their banking online. Data shows that Canadians were the highest users of Internet banking (see **Figure 16.3**). Canadians can choose from two types of online banks: Internet-only banks, such as PC Financial, and traditional bricks-and-mortar banks that also have websites, such as RBC and CIBC. The main reason people use online banking is for convenience. Customers can transfer money, check their account balances, and pay bills, and even deposit cheques via their smartphones.

Deposit Insurance

Most commercial bank deposits are insured by the **Canada Deposit Insurance Corporation** (CDIC), a federal agency. If a CDIC-insured bank fails, its depositors are paid in full by the CDIC up to $100,000. The CDIC was formed in 1967 to build public confidence in the banking system.

Canada Deposit Insurance Corporation (CDIC) the federal agency that insures deposits at commercial and savings banks.

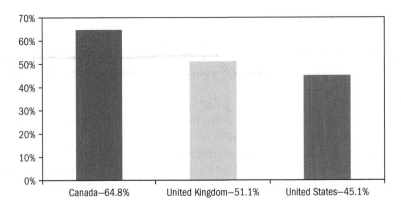

FIGURE 16.3 Online Banking Usages

Source: Comscore, "Top 10 Countries by Online Banking Penetration," accessed August 14, 2014, www.comscore.com/Insights/Data-Mine/
Top-10-Countries-by-Online-Banking-Penetration.

Before deposit insurance, banks often experienced so-called *runs*, where people rushed to withdraw their money, often because of a rumour about the bank's unstable financial condition. As banks experienced more and more withdrawals in a short period, they would reach a point where they were unable to meet all the demands for cash and closed their doors. The remaining depositors who could not get to the bank on time often lost most of their money. Deposit insurance shifts the risk of bank failures from individual depositors to the CDIC. Banks can still fail today, but no insured depositor has ever lost any money within the insurable limit.

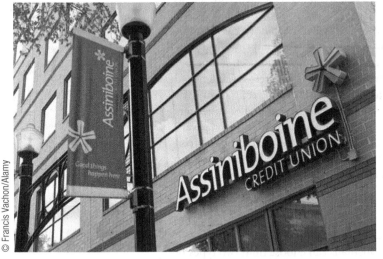

Credit unions are growing in popularity. The Credit Union Central of Canada is a good place to start when looking for a credit union in your area.

Credit Unions

Commercial banks are the largest depository financial institution in Canada, but credit unions also serve a significant segment of the financial community. Today credit unions offer many of the same services as commercial banks, so despite the strength of the "big banks," many consumers opt to do their banking with smaller financial institutions that offer more personal service.[12]

Credit unions are cooperative financial institutions that are owned by their depositors, all of whom are members. More than 5 million Canadians belong to one of the nation's approximately 320 credit unions. Combined, credit unions have more than $162 billion in assets.[13] The number of credit unions in Canada has decreased in recent years because of their efforts to merge to gain economies of scale.[14] Edmonton-based Servus Credit Union partnered with 20 credit unions across Alberta to launch province-wide inter-credit union banking services.[15]

Credit unions are designed to serve consumers, not businesses. Credit unions raise funds by offering members several different chequing and saving accounts. Credit unions then lend these funds to members. Because credit unions are not-for-profit institutions, consumers often prefer them over commercial banks and other financial institutions: Credit unions often pay higher rates of interest on deposits, charge lower rates of interest on loans, and charge fewer fees. Deposits at credit unions are insured at the provincial level. The Prince Edward Island Credit Union Deposit Insurance Corporation insures deposits at credit unions in the province of Prince Edward Island. It works essentially the same way that the CDIC does.

Nondepository Financial Institutions

Nondepository financial institutions accept funds from businesses and households, and then invest most of these funds. Generally, these institutions do not offer chequing accounts (demand deposits). Three examples of nondepository financial institutions are insurance companies, pension funds, and finance companies.

Insurance Companies

Households and businesses buy insurance to transfer risk from themselves to the insurance company. The insurance company accepts the risk in return for a series of payments, called *premiums*. Underwriting is the process insurance companies use to determine whom to insure and how much to charge. During a typical year, insurance companies collect more in premiums than they pay in claims. After they pay their operating expenses, they invest the difference. Insurance companies are a major source of short- and long-term financing for businesses. Life insurance companies have total assets of more than $615 billion. They invest their funds in everything from bonds and stocks to real estate.[16] Examples of life insurers include Canada Life and Manulife Financial.

Pension Funds

Pension funds provide retirement benefits to workers and their families. They are set up by employers and are funded by regular contributions from employers and employees. Because pension funds have predictable long-term cash inflows and very predictable cash outflows, they invest heavily in assets, such as common stocks and real estate. The Canada Pension Plan (CPP) fund has assets of more than $219 billion. The recovery of global markets led to total investment income of $31.7 billion after the financial crisis era. The fund's current asset mix consists of 31 percent in Canadian assets and 69 percent in foreign investment assets with only 28.4 percent of total assets in less risky bonds. Since the financial crisis, the asset mix has shifted to include more foreign investment and fewer Canadian assets.[17]

Finance Companies

Consumer and commercial finance companies offer short-term loans to borrowers. Two examples are Ford Credit and John Deere Capital Corporation. A commercial finance company supplies short-term funds to businesses that use their tangible assets as collateral for the loan. These tangible assets can include inventory, accounts receivable, machinery, or property. A consumer finance company plays a similar role for consumers. Finance companies raise funds by selling securities or by borrowing funds from commercial banks. Many finance companies, such as Toyota Financial Services, are actually subsidiaries of a manufacturer. Toyota Financial Services finances dealer inventories of new cars and trucks. It also provides loans to consumers and other buyers of Toyota products.

Mutual Funds

One of the most significant types of financial institutions today is the mutual fund. *Mutual funds* are financial intermediaries that raise money from investors by selling shares. They then use the money to invest in securities that meet the mutual fund's objectives. For example, a share-based mutual fund invests mainly in common shares. Mutual funds have become extremely popular over the last few decades. Canada's almost 3,000 mutual funds have over a trillion dollars in assets, up from $125 billion in the early 1990s. One reason for this growth is the increased popularity of registered retirement savings plans (RRSPs) and similar types of retirement plans. In a recent poll, 49 percent of Canadians chose to invest their RRSP assets in mutual fund shares. This amount has increased in recent years as the economy recovers from the financial crisis.[18]

Mutual fund investors are indirect owners of a portfolio of securities. As the value of the securities owned by the mutual fund changes, the value of the mutual fund's shares will also change. Investment income, such as bond interest and stock dividends, is passed through to mutual fund shareholders.

Just less than half of mutual fund assets are invested in company shares. Money market mutual funds are also popular. These funds invest in money market instruments like commercial paper. Money market funds have total assets of just over $2.6 trillion.[19]

 **ASSESSMENT CHECK**

16.5.1 What are the two main types of financial institutions?

16.5.2 What are the primary differences between commercial banks and credit unions?

16.5.3 What is a mutual fund?

LO 16.6 Explain the functions of the Bank of Canada and the tools it uses to carry out these functions.

THE ROLE OF THE BANK OF CANADA

Bank of Canada (the Bank) the central bank of Canada.

Created in 1935, the **Bank of Canada (the Bank)** is the central bank of Canada and an important part of the nation's financial system. The Bank, once privately owned, became a government-owned Crown corporation in 1938. The Bank of Canada has four basic responsibilities: regulating monetary policy, designing and issuing bank notes, regulating the financial system, and managing funds for the federal government and other clients.

Monetary Policy

The Bank's most important function is regulating monetary policy, which means controlling the supply of money and credit. The Bank's job is to make sure that the money supply grows at a suitable rate, allowing the economy to expand and inflation to remain in check. If the money supply grows too slowly, economic growth will slow, unemployment will increase, and the risk of a recession will increase. If the money supply grows too rapidly, inflationary pressures will build. The Bank uses its policy tools to push interest rates up or down. If the Bank pushes interest rates up, the growth rate in the money supply will slow, economic growth will slow, and inflationary pressures will ease. If the Bank pushes interest rates down, the growth rate in the money supply will increase, economic growth will pick up, and unemployment will fall.

The two common measures of the money supply are called M1 and M2. M1 consists of currency in circulation and the balances in bank chequing accounts. M2 equals M1 plus balances in some savings accounts and money market mutual funds. **Figure 16.4** shows the approximate composition of the M2 money supply.

The Bank has two major policy tools for controlling the growth in the supply of money and credit: the discount rate and open market operations. The *discount rate* is the interest rate at which the Bank makes short-term loans to member banks. The discount rate is often referred to as the bank rate. A bank might need a short-term loan if transactions leave it short of reserves. If the Bank wants to slow the growth rate in the money supply, it increases the bank rate. This increase makes it more expensive for banks to borrow funds. Banks, in turn, raise the interest rates they charge on loans to consumers and businesses. The end result is a slowdown in economic activity. Lowering the bank rate has the opposite effect.

The second policy tool, and the one used more often, is *open market operations*, the technique of controlling the money supply growth rate by buying or selling Canadian government securities. If the Bank buys government securities, the money it pays enters circulation, where it increases the money supply and lowers interest rates. When the Bank sells government securities, money is taken out of circulation and interest rates rise. When the Bank uses open market operations it uses as its benchmark, or guideline, the so-called *overnight rate*—the rate at which banks lend money to each other overnight. **Table 16.3** shows how the tools used by the Bank can either stimulate or slow the economy.

The Bank has the authority to use selective credit controls when the economy is growing too rapidly or too slowly. These credit controls include the power to set margin requirements—the percentage of the purchase price of a security that an investor must pay in cash when making credit purchases of shares or bonds.

The Bank can also inject capital into the financial system in response to a financial crisis. For example, during the credit crisis in the United States, which began in 2008, the U.S. Federal Reserve (the American equivalent to the Bank of Canada) pumped hundreds of billions of dollars into the financial system. The Federal Reserve even came to the rescue of AIG, a major U.S. insurance company, by purchasing some of the firm's shares. In Canada, the Bank kept interest rates at historical lows during the global financial crisis.

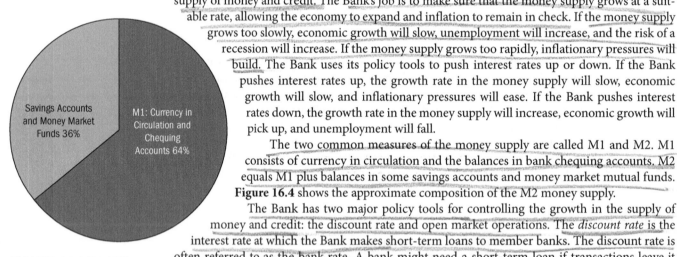

FIGURE 16.4 Total M2 Money Supply

Source: Statistics Canada, "Exchange Rates, Interest Rates, Money Supply and Stock Prices, 2007–2011," accessed August 21, 2014, www.statcan.gc.ca/tables-tableaux/sum-som/l01/cst01/econ07-eng.htm.

Table 16.3 Tools Used by the Bank of Canada to Regulate the Growth in the Money Supply

TOOL	BRIEF DESCRIPTION	IMPACT ON THE GROWTH RATE OF THE MONEY SUPPLY	IMPACT ON INTEREST RATES AND THE ECONOMY	FREQUENCY OF USE
1. Bank rate	The interest rate that the Bank of Canada charges banks for loans.	An increase in the bank rate slows the growth rate in the money supply.	An increase in the bank rate pushes interest rates up and slows economic growth.	Used only with open market operations.
2. Open market operations	The buying and selling of government securities to increase or decrease bank reserves.	Selling government securities reduces bank reserves and slows the growth rate in the money supply.	Selling government securities pushes interest rates up and slows economic growth.	Used frequently.

Transactions in the foreign exchange markets also affect the Canadian money supply and interest rates. The Bank can lower the exchange value of the dollar by selling dollars and buying foreign currencies. It can also raise the dollar's exchange value by doing the opposite—buying dollars and selling foreign currencies. When the Bank buys foreign currencies, the effect is the same as buying securities: the purchase of foreign currencies or securities increases the reserves in Canada's banking system. In contrast, selling foreign currencies is like selling securities: It reduces bank reserves.

Historically, the Bank also influenced the money supply by controlling the *reserve requirement*. The reserve requirement was the percentage of cash that banks were required to maintain for immediate withdrawal by customers. The lower the reserve requirement, the more the money supply could increase. For example, if you deposited $10,000 at your local bank and the reserve requirement was 3 percent, the bank would then likely lend out $9,700 to someone else (perhaps to purchase a car). The purchaser (the borrower) would then give the $9,700 to the seller of the car who would deposit it in the bank. At this point, the money supply related to the initial deposit is $19,700 (the initial $10,000 plus the $9,700 also in the bank). This process would continue, increasing the money supply further. The original deposit of $10,000 would have a potential impact on the money supply of $333,333 ($10,000/3%). In 1992, the Bank of Canada removed the reserve requirement. Banks now decide themselves the proportion of deposits to keep on hand.

✔ **ASSESSMENT CHECK**

16.6.1 What is the Bank of Canada?

16.6.2 List the two main tools the Bank uses to control the supply of money and credit.

REGULATION OF THE FINANCIAL SYSTEM

LO 16.7 Describe the regulation of the financial system.

It is probably not surprising that many parts of the financial system must comply with government regulation and are supervised by government agencies. After all, the financial system is very important to how our economy works.

Bank Regulation

Banks are among the nation's most heavily regulated businesses. The main purpose of bank regulation is to ensure public confidence in the safety and security of the banking system. Banks are critical to the overall functioning of the economy. For example, a collapse of the banking system can have disastrous results. Under the Bank Act, the federal government is responsible for regulating the banking sector. Several regulatory bodies are involved in regulating Canadian banks, including the Department of Finance, the Bank of Canada, the Office of the Superintendent of Financial Institutions (OSFI), and the CDIC. Some regulation is also at the provincial level because of the many lines of business that a commercial bank or credit union may be involved in.[20]

Government Regulation of the Financial Markets

At the provincial level, regulation of Canadian financial markets is primarily administered by organizations such as the Manitoba Securities Commission or the Ontario Securities Commission. These provincial organizations are in turn coordinated by the Canadian Securities Administrators (CSA) to reduce duplication of efforts and provide consistency. But, in the end, responsibility is in the hands of the various provincial bodies.

insider trading use of material, nonpublic information about a company to make investment profits.

One area that provincial regulators pay particular attention to is insider trading. **Insider trading** is defined as the use of material, nonpublic information about a company to make investment profits. Examples of material, nonpublic information include a pending merger or a major oil discovery. Releasing information on these activities before they occur could affect the firm's share price. The definition of insider trading goes beyond corporate insiders—people such as the company's officers and directors. It includes lawyers, accountants, investment bankers, and even reporters—anyone who uses nonpublic information to profit in the stock market at the expense of ordinary investors. Although some actions or communications are clearly insider trading, other activities are more difficult to pin down. As a result, all employees of public companies must keep in mind what is and is not permitted.

Industry Self-Regulation

The securities markets are also heavily self-regulated by professional associations and the major financial markets. The securities industry understands that rules and regulations are designed to ensure fair and orderly markets. The rules and regulations also promote investor confidence and benefit all participants. Two examples of self-regulation are the rules of conduct established by professional organizations and the market surveillance techniques used by the major securities markets.

Market Surveillance

All securities markets use a variety of methods to spot possible violations of trading rules or securities laws. In Canada, the Toronto Stock Exchange (TSX) wants to promote integrity and fairness in all trading across equity marketplaces. The TSX outsources market surveillance to an independent third party—the Investment Industry Regulatory Organization of Canada (IIROC). IIROC's surveillance functions include real-time monitoring of trading activity: A team of experts watch all equity trades as they occur to ensure compliance with the securities trading rules. IIROC is equipped with an experienced team and a dedicated surveillance facility with advanced technology. It monitors company news, stock charts, and chat room activity to detect volume and price anomalies. IIROC also monitors timely disclosure of material information by publicly traded businesses to ensure they comply with Universal Market Integrity Rules (UMIR). State-of-the-art technology and monitoring systems allow IIROC to track trading behaviour in real time and collect evidence needed to pursue cases relating to violations, such as insider trading and manipulative activity.[21] Self-regulation by the financial industry has been an important part of securities market regulation. But some argue that the industry can never truly regulate itself effectively in today's market environment. The "Solving an Ethical Controversy" feature debates the pros and cons of industry self-regulation.

 **ASSESSMENT CHECK**

16.7.1 Who regulates banks?

16.7.2 Define *insider trading*.

SOLVING AN **ETHICAL** CONTROVERSY

Can the Securities Market Regulate Itself?

"Those of us who have looked to the self-interest of lending institutions to protect shareholders' equity, myself included, are in a state of shocked disbelief."

That's what was said by Alan Greenspan, former chair of the Federal Reserve Board in the United States, in his testimony before Congress after the credit crisis. He had long supported the idea that the market could always be trusted to regulate itself and should be left free to do so. But with his words, he rejected that policy. The crisis brought an end to a Wall Street bubble that had done well, partly due to unlimited, unregulated speculation. Stricter government regulation of the financial industry seems very likely.

Can the securities market be trusted to regulate itself?

PRO

1. Regulation of the securities market will give the government too much power over private industry.

2. The mere idea of regulation has made some institutions change their behaviour voluntarily. For example, some banks have announced that they will eliminate overdraft fees for consumer accounts.

3. Self-regulation can lead to greater investor confidence.

CON

1. Some analysts feel that existing government regulation is too lax. They believe that the government, which is supposed to regulate the financial industry, was too lenient with some large financial institutions.

2. The TSX has one body that both approves company listings and enforces the rules. Most other exchanges, such as the NYSE and London Stock Exchange, have two separate bodies, one for each purpose.

3. Self-regulation leads to a loss of independence.

Summary

Public disapproval of the securities market is likely to continue as long as people continue to feel the effects of the financial crisis in their everyday lives, especially in the United States. The government has considered new, stricter regulations on financial institutions. Some argue that those regulations are unnecessary and could even be harmful.

Sources: Bill Singer, "Analyzing a Troubling Wall Street Double Standard," *Corporate Compliance Insights*, May 4, 2010, www.corporatecomplianceinsights.com; Felix Salmon, "How the SEC Cracks Down on Unethical Behavior," Reuters, April 20, 2010, http://blogs.reuters.com; Peter Hamby, "DNC Ad: Wall Street Lobbyists Trying to Block Reform," *CNN*, April 20, 2010, http://politicalticker.blogs.cnn.com; Roger Lowenstein, "*The End of Wall Street* by Roger Lowenstein: Book Excerpt," *Bloomberg Businessweek,* April 8, 2010, www.businessweek.com; Andrew Ross Sorkin, "Extreme Makeover, Wall Street Edition," *New York Times*, April 1, 2010, http://dealbook.blogs.nytimes.com; Charles H. Green, "Fixing What Ails Wall Street: Ethics, or Incentives?" Trusted Advisor Associates, September 21, 2009, http://trustedadvisor.com; Tim Kiladze, "TSX Regulation a Conflict of Interest: Report," *Globe and Mail*, July 29, 2010, accessed July 28, 2011, www.theglobeandmail.com/globe-investor/tsx-regulation-a-conflict-of-interest-report/article1653215.

THE FINANCIAL SYSTEM: A GLOBAL PERSPECTIVE

LO 16.8 Describe the global financial system.

Not surprisingly, the global financial system is becoming more and more integrated each year. As we've noted, financial markets exist throughout the world. Shares of Canadian firms trade in other countries, and shares of international companies trade in Canada. Financial institutions have also become a global industry. Major Canadian banks—such as CIBC, RBC, and Scotiabank—have extensive international operations. They have offices, lend money, and accept deposits from customers throughout the world.

Of the 50 largest banks in the world (measured by total assets), only three are Canadian: RBC, TD Bank, and the Bank of Nova Scotia. The largest of the three, RBC, ranks thirty-seventh. Besides the three Canadian banks on the list, the other 47 are based in Belgium, China, France, Germany, Italy, Japan, the Netherlands, Switzerland, the United Kingdom, and other parts of the world. The world's largest bank, the Industrial & Commercial Bank of China, has over $3.2 trillion in assets. Many of these international banks also operate worldwide, including in Canada.[22]

The effects of financial globalization are evident in Canada. Canada's growing cultural diversity has led to an increase in other banking models. Many other financial models exist around the world, including the interest-free Islamic system of banking. Special banks are needed to address the financial needs of devout Muslims who cannot be involved in interest-based transactions, including home mortgages. Islamic finance companies such as Guidance Financial, Hakim Wealth Management, the Islamic Credit Union of Canada, and Ijara Canada provide financial products to the previously underserved niche market of Islamic finance. Globally, financial institutions, including HBSC, Citigroup, and Lloyds Bank, have seen their assets grow at an annual rate of more than 20 percent in this emerging market. Currently their assets total more than $4 trillion worldwide. In recent years, many new initiatives were created because of this rapidly growing market. For example, Standard & Poor's has launched the S&P/TSX 60 Shariah Index, which is a version of the S&P/TSX 60 that complies with Islamic law.[23]

Almost all nations have some sort of a central bank, similar to the Bank of Canada. Examples include the U.S. Federal Reserve (the Fed), the Bank of England, the Bank of Japan, and the European Central Bank. These central banks have a similar role to that of the Bank of Canada—controlling the money supply and regulating banks. Policymakers at the

In Frankfurt, Germany, a sculpture of the euro—the symbol for the European Union's currency—stands outside the headquarters of Europe's central bank. The 12 gold stars represent all the peoples of Europe.

HSBC Amanah was set up to serve the unique financial needs of the Muslim community.

Bank of Canada often respond to changes in the U.S. financial system by making similar changes to the Canadian system. For example, if the Fed pushes U.S. interest rates lower, central banks in Canada, Japan, and Europe may also push their interest rates lower. These changes can influence events in countries around the world. When Canadian and European interest rates are low, they decrease the cost of borrowing for Canadian and European firms but increase the amount of money available for loans to borrowers in other countries, such as Chile and India.

✓ **ASSESSMENT CHECK**

16.8.1 Where do Canadian banks rank compared with international banks?

16.8.2 Do other countries have organizations that play roles similar to those played by the Bank of Canada?

WHAT'S AHEAD

This chapter explored the financial system, a key part of the Canadian economy and a process that affects many aspects of contemporary business. The financial system is the process by which funds are transferred between savers and borrowers. It includes securities, financial markets, and financial institutions. The chapter also described the role of the Bank of Canada and discussed the global financial system. In the next chapter, we discuss the finance functions of a business, including the role of financial managers, financial planning, asset management, and sources of short- and long-term funds.

RETURN TO INSIDE BUSINESS

Canada Weathers the Credit Crisis

The financial crisis has had a significant impact on global financial markets. Countries significantly affected include the United States, Greece, Italy, Australia, Brazil, Russia, and many more.

QUESTIONS FOR CRITICAL THINKING

1. How can financial institutions and countries prevent another major financial crisis?

2. Why was Africa not as affected by the financial crisis as most of the rest of the world?

SUMMARY OF LEARNING OBJECTIVES

LO 16.1 Outline the structure and importance of the financial system.

The financial system is the process by which funds are transferred between those who have excess funds (savers) and those who need additional funds (users). Savers and users are individuals, businesses, and governments. Savers expect to earn a rate of return in exchange for the use of their funds. Financial markets, financial institutions, and financial instruments (securities) make up the financial system. Although direct transfers are possible, most funds flow from savers to users through the financial markets or financial institutions, such as commercial banks. A well-functioning financial system is vital to the overall health of a nation's economy.

✓ **ASSESSMENT CHECK ANSWERS**

16.1.1 What is the financial system? The financial system is the mechanism by which funds are transferred between those

who have excess funds (savers) and those who need additional funds (users).

16.1.2 In the financial system, who are the borrowers and who are the savers? Savers and borrowers are individuals, businesses, and governments. Generally, individuals are net savers, meaning they spend less than they make. Businesses and governments tend to be net borrowers.

16.1.3 List the two most common ways that funds are transferred between borrowers and savers. The two most common ways funds are transferred are through the financial markets and through financial institutions.

LO 16.2 List the various types of securities.

Securities, also called *financial instruments*, represent the obligations of the issuers—businesses and governments—to provide purchasers with the expected or stated returns on the funds invested or loaned. Securities can be classified into three categories: money market instruments, bonds, and shares. Money market instruments and bonds are debt instruments. Money market instruments are short-term debt securities and tend to be low-risk securities. Bonds are longer-term debt securities and pay a fixed amount of interest each year. Bonds are sold by the Canadian government (Canada Savings Bonds), provincial and local governments (municipal bonds), and corporations. Mortgage-backed securities are bonds backed by a pool, or group, of mortgage loans. Most municipal and corporate bonds have risk ratings. Common shares represent ownership in corporations. Investors who hold common shares have voting rights and a residual claim on the firm's assets.

 ASSESSMENT CHECK ANSWERS

16.2.1 What are the major types of securities? The major types of securities are money market instruments, bonds, and shares.

16.2.2 What areas of the government issue bonds? Bonds are issued by the federal, provincial, and municipal governments.

16.2.3 Why do investors purchase common shares? Investors purchase common shares for two reasons. One reason is to receive dividends, which are cash payments made to share-holders by the firm. The other reason is the potential price increase of the shares.

LO 16.3 Define *financial market* and distinguish between primary and secondary financial markets.

A financial market is a market where securities are bought and sold. The primary market for securities serves businesses and governments that want to sell new security issues to raise funds. Securities are sold in the primary market either through an open auction or through a process called *underwriting*. The secondary market handles transactions of pre-viously issued securities between investors. One example of a second-ary market is the Toronto Stock Exchange. The business or government that issued the security is not directly involved in secondary market transactions. The secondary market handles about four to five times the dollar value of securities than are handled in the primary market.

 ASSESSMENT CHECK ANSWERS

16.3.1 What is a financial market? A financial market is a market where securities are bought and sold.

16.3.2 Distinguish between a primary and a secondary financial market. The primary market for securities serves businesses and governments that want to sell new security issues to raise funds. The secondary market handles trans-actions of previously issued securities between investors.

16.3.3 Briefly explain the role of financial institutions in the sale of securities. Financial institutions purchase new securities issues from corporations or provincial and munici-pal governments, and then resell the securities to investors. The institutions charge a fee for their services.

LO 16.4 Describe the characteristics of the major stock exchanges.

The best-known financial markets are the stock exchanges. Stock exchanges can be found throughout the world. Canada's largest stock exchange is the Toronto Stock Exchange, or TSX. The world's two largest stock exchanges are the New York Stock Exchange and NASDAQ. Both are located in the United States. The NYSE is bigger when measured in terms of the total value of shares traded. Larger and better-known companies dominate the NYSE. The NASDAQ stock market is an electronic market where buy and sell orders are entered into a computerized communication system. Most of the world's major stock markets today use similar electronic trading systems. Electronic trading may be the future for stock markets.

 ASSESSMENT CHECK ANSWERS

16.4.1 What are the world's two largest stock markets? The world's two largest stock markets are the New York Stock Exchange and the NASDAQ Stock Market.

16.4.2 What makes the London Stock Exchange unique? The London Stock Exchange is the most international of the world's stock markets. A large percentage of the shares traded there are not from British firms.

16.4.3 Explain the difference between a market order and a limit order. A market order instructs the investor's broker to obtain the best possible price when buying or selling securities. A limit order sets a maximum price (if the investor wants to buy) or a minimum price (if the investor wants to sell).

LO 16.5 Discuss how financial institutions are organized and how they function.

Financial institutions act as intermediaries between savers and users of funds. Depository institutions accept deposits from cus-tomers that can be exchanged for cash on demand. Examples of depository institutions are commercial banks, savings banks, and credit unions. Commercial banks are the largest and most impor-tant of the depository institutions. They offer the widest range of services. Savings banks are a major source of home mortgage loans. Credit unions are not-for-profit institutions that offer financial services to consumers. The Canada Deposit Insurance Corporation is a government agency that insures deposits at these financial institutions. Nondepository institutions include pension funds and insurance companies. Nondepository institutions invest a large portion of their funds in stocks, bonds, and real estate. Mutual funds are another important financial institution. These companies sell shares to investors and, in turn, invest the proceeds in securities. Many individuals today invest a large portion of their retirement savings in mutual fund shares.

 ASSESSMENT CHECK ANSWERS

16.5.1 What are the two main types of financial institutions? The two major types of financial institutions are depository institutions (those that accept chequing and similar accounts) and nondepository institutions.

16.5.2 What are the primary differences between commercial banks and credit unions? Today, commercial banks and credit unions offer many of the same services. Commercial banks lend money to businesses and to individuals. Credit unions lend money mostly to individuals, usually in the form of home mortgage loans.

16.5.3 What is a mutual fund? A mutual fund is an intermediary that raises money by selling shares to investors. It then pools, or combines, investor funds and purchases securities that meet the mutual fund's objectives.

LO 16.6 Explain the functions of the Bank of Canada and the tools it uses to carry out these functions.

The Bank of Canada (the Bank) is the central bank of Canada. The Bank regulates monetary policy, designs and issues bank notes, regulates the financial system, and manages funds for the federal government and other clients. It controls the supply of credit and money in the economy to promote growth and control inflation. The Bank's main tools include the bank rate and open market operations. Selective credit controls and purchases and sales of foreign currencies also help the Bank manage the economy.

 ASSESSMENT CHECK ANSWERS

16.6.1 What is the Bank of Canada? The Bank of Canada is Canada's central bank. It is responsible for regulating the financial system, providing banking-related services for the federal government, acting as the banker's bank, designing and issuing bank notes, and setting monetary policy.

16.6.2 List the two main tools the Bank uses to control the supply of money and credit. The two main tools are the bank rate and open market operations.

LO 16.7 Describe the regulation of the financial system.

Commercial banks, savings banks, and credit unions in Canada are heavily regulated by federal banking authorities. Banking regulators require institutions to follow sound banking practices. They have the power to close noncompliant banks. In Canada, financial markets are regulated primarily at the provincial level. Markets are also heavily self-regulated by the financial markets and professional organizations. Provincial regulatory bodies set the requirements for both primary and secondary market activity. They ban a number of practices, including insider trading. They also require public companies to disclose financial information regularly. Professional organizations and the securities markets also have rules and procedures that all members must follow.

 ASSESSMENT CHECK ANSWERS

16.7.1 Who regulates banks? All banks are regulated by the federal government.

16.7.2 Define *insider trading*. Insider trading is defined as the use of material, nonpublic information to make an investment profit.

LO 16.8 Describe the global financial system.

Financial markets exist throughout the world and are increasingly interconnected. Investors in other countries purchase Canadian securities, and Canadian investors purchase foreign securities. Large Canadian banks and other financial institutions have a global presence. They accept deposits, make loans, and have branches throughout the world. Foreign banks also operate worldwide. The average European or Japanese bank is much larger than the average Canadian bank. Almost all nations have a central bank that performs the same roles as the Bank of Canada. Central bankers often act together, raising and lowering interest rates to control economic conditions.

 ASSESSMENT CHECK ANSWERS

16.8.1 Where do Canadian banks rank compared with international banks? Banks in Asia and Europe are generally much larger than Canadian banks. Only three of the world's 50 largest banks are based in Canada.

16.8.2 Do other countries have organizations that play roles similar to those played by the Bank of Canada? Yes, almost all nations have central banks that perform many of the same functions as the Bank of Canada.

BUSINESS TERMS YOU NEED TO KNOW

Bank of Canada (the Bank) 460

Canada Deposit Insurance
Corporation (CDIC) 457

common shares 450

financial institutions 455

financial markets 451

financial system 446

insider trading 462

primary markets 451

secondary market 453

securities 448

stock markets (exchanges) 453

REVIEW QUESTIONS

1. What is the financial system? Why is it rare for funds to be directly transferred from savers to users?

2. What is a security? Give several examples.

3. List the major types of bonds. What is a mortgage-backed security?

4. What are the differences between common shares and preferred shares?

5. Explain the difference between a primary financial market and a secondary financial market.

6. Why are commercial banks and credit unions classified as depository financial institutions? How do commercial banks differ from credit unions?

7. Why are life insurance companies, pension funds, and mutual funds considered financial institutions?

8. Briefly explain the role of the Bank of Canada. List the tools it uses to control the supply of money and credit.

9. What methods are used to regulate banks? Why are Canadian chartered banks also regulated by the CDIC?

10. Explain how the Bank of Canada works with other central banks to affect exchange rates.

PROJECTS AND TEAMWORK APPLICATIONS

1. Collect current interest rates on the following types of bonds: Canada Savings Bonds, AAA-rated municipal bonds, AAA-rated corporate bonds, and BBB-rated corporate bonds. Arrange the interest rates from lowest to highest. Explain the reasons for the ranking.

2. You've probably heard of Canada Savings Bonds. You may even have received some bonds as a gift. What you may not know is that there are *two* different types of Canada Savings Bonds. Do some research and compare the two types of bonds. What are their features? What are their pros and cons? Which of the two bonds do you prefer?

3. Working with a partner, assume you are considering buying shares of RONA or the Home Depot. Describe how you would analyze the two companies' shares to decide which you would buy.

4. Working in a small team, identify a large bank. Visit that bank's website and look up its most recent financial statements.

Compare the bank's financial statements to those of a nonfinancial company, such as a manufacturer or retailer. Report on your findings.

5. Assume you're investing money for retirement. What investment criteria are the most important to you? Go to the MSN Money website (http://money.msn.com). Click the "Tools" tab, and select "Fund Picks". Then use the filter on the right side of your screen to find funds that meets your criteria. Identify at least three mutual funds that most closely meet your criteria. Choose one of the funds and research it. Answer the following questions:

a. What was the fund's average annual return for the past five years?

b. How well did the fund perform relative to its peer group and relative to an index such as the S&P 500?

c. What are the fund's 10 largest holdings?

WEB ASSIGNMENTS

1. **Online stock trading.** To learn more about online trading, visit the website of a brokerage firm that offers online trading, such as BMO InvestorLine (www.bmoinvestorline.com) or Scotia iTRADE (www.scotiaitrade.com). Most electronic brokerage firms also offer a trading demonstration. Use the demonstration to see how to obtain price information or company news, place buy or sell orders, and check account balances. Make some notes about your experience and bring them to class to participate in a class discussion.

2. **Banking statistics.** Visit the Bank of Canada web page listed below. Access the most recent year you can find and answer the following questions:

   a. How many commercial banks were operating at the end of the year? How many credit unions were operating?

   b. What were the total assets of commercial banks and credit unions at the end of the year?

   c. How many commercial banks had assets greater than $2 billion at the end of the year? How many commercial banks had assets of less than $300 million at the end of the year? www.bankofcanada.ca/publications/bfs/?page_moved=1.

3. **The Bank of Canada.** Go to the website of the Bank of Canada (www.bankofcanada.ca). Locate information on the Bank of Canada's board of directors. Prepare a short report on the 14-member board. Who are the current members? What are their backgrounds? When were they appointed? When do their terms expire?

Note: Internet Web addresses change frequently. If you don't find the exact sites listed, you may need to access the organization's home page and search from there or use a search engine such as Bing or Google.

Pressmaster/Shutterstock/Getty Images

17 | FINANCIAL MANAGEMENT

LEARNING OBJECTIVES

LO 17.1 Explain the role of financial managers.

LO 17.2 Describe the parts of a financial plan and the financial planning process.

LO 17.3 Outline how organizations manage their assets.

LO 17.4 Discuss the two major sources of funds for a business and capital structure.

LO 17.5 Identify sources of short-term financing for businesses.

LO 17.6 Discuss long-term financing options.

LO 17.7 Describe mergers, acquisitions, buyouts, and divestitures.

INSIDE BUSINESS

The Wooing of Ratiopharm

Nearly all Canadians know that it is cheaper to buy a generic drug—an over-the-counter drug such as ibuprofen—than the brand-name version, such as Aleve or Advil. Pharmaceutical companies know this, too. Canadian patents on brand-name drugs expire after 20 years. After a patent runs out, a drug company loses its exclusive right to manufacture the brand-name version of the product it has spent time, research, and money to develop. As patents have expired, generic-drug companies have opened all over the world, from Germany to India. The result has been a huge growth in the pharmaceutical industry. Apotex Inc. is Canada's largest generic-drug manufacturer. Every year it produces more than 300 generic pharmaceuticals for more than 85 million individual prescriptions.

Many big pharmaceutical companies have expanded by buying manufacturers of generic drugs. The decision to buy another firm can be difficult. Financial managers need to carefully forecast the expected increase in profits and then weigh that benefit against the costs of acquisition. But these forecasts are not certain, and success is never guaranteed.

In one recent case, several companies wanted to buy a generic-drug maker. They were like gentlemen suitors presenting themselves to an attractive potential bride. In a modern, electronic twist, their courtship was concluded in less than three months. Ratiopharm, based in Ulm, Germany, is one of the world's five largest producers of generic drugs. It specializes in drugs that treat cardiovascular and respiratory disorders, diseases of the central nervous system, and other illnesses. It also deals with medicines that prevent infections. When the family that owned Ratiopharm announced the company was up for sale, several big pharmaceutical firms were interested. That list was then narrowed down to three: Pfizer Inc., based in New York City; Teva Pharmaceutical Industries of Israel; and Actavis of Iceland.

Ratiopharm was especially attractive because Germans buy more generic drugs than other Europeans, and Ratiopharm was the second-biggest seller of generics in Germany. The companies sent their executives to Ulm to explain why Ratiopharm should accept their offer. Some analysts thought that Ratiopharm's decision would depend on which company promised to keep the greatest number of jobs at Ratiopharm.

Pfizer or its subsidiaries manufacture over-the-counter brands from Advil and ChapStick to Centrum vitamins and Robitussin; prescription drugs for women's health, cardiovascular disease, and cancer; and veterinary medicines. One analyst suggested that buying Ratiopharm would help Pfizer move its brand-name products into the worldwide generic market when their patents expire. It would also allow Pfizer to expand into developing markets. Pfizer's bid for Ratiopharm was €3 billion (almost $4 billion). After Pfizer's presentation, Ratiopharm's management wrote a letter to the company's employees, saying "The bidder emphasized the high efficiency of Ratiopharm's domestic and foreign production sites and told the meeting it was ready to make investments in Ulm."

Teva was already the world's largest producer of generic pharmaceuticals. Acquiring Ratiopharm would make Teva the leading generic-drug maker in Europe and the second-biggest in Germany. According to one analyst, Teva aimed to preserve both Ratiopharm's workforce and its locations in Germany. Teva offered €3.63 billion ($4.7 billion).

The Icelandic company Actavis had about 10,000 employees in 40 countries, making it about the same size as Ratiopharm. It also had about the same sales figures as Ratiopharm. Despite being heavily in debt, Actavis made an offer of about €3.32 billion ($4.37 billion).

Analysts had predicted that Ratiopharm would not make a decision quickly, but Teva soon made an announcement. It would acquire Ratiopharm for €3.63 billion. Shlomo Yani, Teva's president and CEO, announced that Ratiopharm would strengthen Teva's presence "in key European markets, most notably in Germany, as well as rapidly growing generic markets such as Spain, Italy and France."[1]

CHAPTER 17 OVERVIEW

Previous chapters discussed two basic functions that a business must perform. First, the company must produce a good or service or contract with suppliers to produce a good or service. Second, the firm must market its good or service to prospective customers. This chapter introduces a third, equally important function: A company's managers must ensure that the company has enough money to perform its other tasks successfully, in both the present and the future, and that these funds are invested properly. The company must have enough funds to buy materials, equipment, and other assets; pay bills; and compensate employees. This third business function is **finance**—planning, obtaining, and managing the company's funds to accomplish its objectives as effectively and efficiently as possible.

An organization's financial objectives include meeting expenses, investing in assets, and maximizing its overall worth, which is often measured by the value of the firm's common shares. Financial managers are responsible for meeting expenses, investing in assets, and increasing profits to shareholders. Solid financial management is critical to the success of a business. You can look at the news any day and find examples of firms that may have offered good products to the marketplace but failed because funds were improperly managed.

This chapter focuses on the finance function of organizations. It begins by describing the role of financial managers, their place in the organizational hierarchy, and the increasing importance of finance. Next, we outline the financial planning process and the parts of a financial plan. Then the discussion focuses on how organizations manage assets as efficiently and effectively as possible. We compare the two major sources of funds: debt and equity. Next, we introduce the concept of leverage. The major sources of short-term and long-term funding are described in the following sections. A description of mergers, acquisitions, buyouts, and divestitures concludes the chapter.

finance the business function of planning, obtaining, and managing the company's funds to accomplish its objectives as effectively and efficiently as possible.

LO 17.1 Explain the role of financial managers.

THE ROLE OF THE FINANCIAL MANAGER

financial managers the executives who develop and carry out their firm's financial plan and decide on the most appropriate sources and uses of funds.

Organizations face intense pressures today. As a result, organizations need to measure and reduce the costs of their business operations. They also need to maximize their revenues and profits. **Financial managers are the executives who develop and carry out their firm's financial plan and decide on the most appropriate sources and uses of funds.** They are among the most vital people on the corporate payroll.

Figure 17.1 shows the finance function of a typical company. At the top is the chief executive officer (CEO). The chief financial officer (CFO) usually reports directly to the company's CEO or chief operating officer (COO). In some companies, the CFO is also a member of the board of directors. In the case of the software maker Oracle, both the current CFO and the former CFO serve on that company's board; the former CFO chairs the board. Moreover, CFOs often serve as independent directors on other firms' boards, such as TELUS, Tim Hortons, or Microsoft. As noted in Chapter 15, the CFO and the firm's CEO must both certify the accuracy of the firm's financial statements.

Three senior managers often report directly to the CFO. The titles can vary, but these three executives are commonly called the *vice-president of financial management* (or *planning*), the *treasurer,* and the *controller*. The vice-president of financial management or planning is responsible for preparing financial forecasts and analyzing major investment decisions related to new

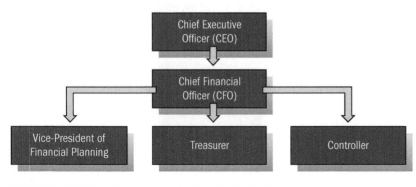

FIGURE 17.1 The Finance Organization at a Typical Firm

products, new production facilities, and acquisitions. The treasurer is responsible for all of the company's financing activities, including cash management, tax planning and preparation, and shareholder relations. The treasurer also works on the sale of new security issues to investors. The controller is the chief accounting manager. The controller's functions include keeping the company's books, preparing financial statements, and conducting internal audits. The "Hit & Miss" feature explains the increasing importance of financially sound IT management.

The growing importance of financial professionals is reflected in the number of CEOs who have been promoted from financial positions. For example, Indra Nooyi, CEO of PepsiCo, and Jim Marsh, CEO of the British telecommunications company Cable and Wireless, both served as their firm's CFO prior to assuming the top job. The importance of finance professionals is also reflected in CFOs' salaries. A survey by the executive compensation consulting firm Equilar found the median annual salary for CFOs of *Fortune* 500 companies to be around $3.76 million.[2] The CFO of the investment firm Berkshire Hathaway is actually paid more than the company's famous chairperson, Warren Buffett.[3]

In their jobs, financial professionals continually balance risks with expected financial returns. *Risk* is the uncertainty of gain or loss; *return* is the gain or loss that results from an investment over a specified period of time. Financial managers try to maximize the wealth of their firm's shareholders by striking the right balance between risk and return. This balance is called the

Jin Lee/Bloomberg/Getty Images, Inc.

The importance of financial professionals is reflected in the growing number of CEOs who have been promoted from financial positions. Indra Nooyi, CEO of PepsiCo, served as CFO prior to assuming the top job.

HIT & MISS

Apptio Calculates the Cost of Information Technology

Software as a service (SaaS) is growing. Many companies are making the change to cloud computing to save money and increase efficiency. But is cloud computing always more economical and efficient? Until recently, there was no reliable way to find out.

Apptio provides hosted Internet technology solutions, including its Technology Business Management package. Recently, Apptio introduced its new Cost Transparency Template. This template generates formulas a company can use to calculate how much more—or less—it would cost to invest in cloud computing compared with other options, including traditional in-house hardware and storage. Among Apptio's clients are BNP Paribas, Starbucks, Hallmark, and Expedia. Jeff Day, Apptio's director of marketing, says "We see that cloud computing is going to change the way IT leaders think about how they manage IT."

Saint Luke's Health System has 1,200 doctors among its 9,000 employees in 11 hospitals. The chief information officer, Debe Gash, wanted to get rid of all nonessential IT-related costs. A spending-analytics tool from Apptio helped Gash and her team save millions of dollars. The tool works by highlighting unnecessary or duplicate spending. For example, Saint Luke's had too many desktop software licences, two full-time employees who dealt only with spam management,

and large expenses related to electronic storage. Those expenses were reduced or eliminated, and funds are now redirected to pay for needed programs, such as electronic health records. "We were surprised at the efficiencies we were able to derive from getting those insights," Gash said.

In the future, IT managers will need to understand how the cloud works and whether it will be more cost effective than other in-house or external systems. Day says, "The greatest inhibitor of the cloud is a lack of understanding. IT leaders need better systems and tools to perform accurate analysis."

Questions for Critical Thinking

1. Why have companies recently become so concerned with cost management?

2. Why might it be difficult for very large companies to keep accurate account of spending on such items as computer hardware and software licences?

Sources: Apptio, accessed June 24, 2010, www.apptio.com; Denise Dubie, "IT Cost Management and the Cloud," *Network World,* April 13, 2010, www.networkworld.com; Bob Evans, "Global CIO: St. Luke's CIO Saves Millions with Apptio's Help," *InformationWeek,* April 6, 2010, www.informationweek.com; Brian Carlson, "Top 5 Financial Management Predictions for 2010," *CIO,* February 2, 2010, www.cio.com.

risk–return tradeoff the process of maximizing the wealth of the firm's shareholders by striking the right balance between risk and return.

risk–return tradeoff. For example, a firm that relies heavily on borrowed funds may increase the return (in the form of cash) to shareholders. But the more money a firm borrows, the greater the risks to shareholders. An increase in a firm's cash on hand reduces the risk of being unable to meet unexpected cash needs. But cash alone does not earn much, if any, return. Firms that fail to invest their surplus funds in an income-earning asset—such as in securities—reduce their potential return or profitability. This chapter provides many examples of the risk–return tradeoff.

Every financial manager must balance risks and returns. For example, in the late 1990s Airbus had to make a major decision: whether to begin development and production of the giant A380 jetliner, the world's largest jetliner. The development costs for the aircraft were first estimated at more than $10 billion. But before committing to such a huge investment, financial managers weighed the potential profits of the A380 against the risks of investing in the aircraft's development. Airbus's future was on the line. It decided to go ahead with the development of the A380. The company spent more than $15 billion on research and development. The A380 entered commercial service a few years ago. Airbus currently has orders for approximately 318 A380 jetliners at a list price of more than $359 million each. The Airbus A380 has been a success thus far with more than 151,000 revenue flights and an average daily utilization greater than 13 hours.[4]

Financial managers must also adapt to changes in the financial system. The recent credit crisis has made it more difficult for some companies to borrow money from traditional lenders like banks. As a result, many firms have scaled back their expansion plans or are looking for funding from other sources, such as commercial financing companies. Financial managers must also adapt to internal changes.

✓ **ASSESSMENT CHECK**

17.1.1 What is the structure of the finance function at the typical firm?

17.1.2 Explain the risk–return tradeoff.

LO 17.2 Describe the parts of a financial plan and the financial planning process.

financial plan a document that specifies the funds needed by a firm for a period of time, the timing of cash inflows and outflows, and the most appropriate sources and uses of funds.

FINANCIAL PLANNING

Financial managers develop their organization's **financial plan**, a document that specifies the funds needed by a firm for a given period of time, the timing of cash inflows and outflows, and the most appropriate sources and uses of funds. *Operating plans* are short-term financial plans that focus on no more than a year or two in the future. *Strategic plans* are financial plans that have a much longer time horizon, up to five or ten years.

A financial plan is based on forecasts of several items: production costs, purchasing needs, plant and equipment expenses, and sales activities for the period covered. Financial managers use forecasts to decide on the specific amounts needed and the timing of expenses and receipts. They build a financial plan based on the answers to three questions:

1. What funds will the firm require during the planning period?

2. When will the firm need additional funds?

3. Where will the firm obtain the necessary funds?

Some funds flow into the firm when it sells its goods or services, but funding needs vary. The financial plan must reflect both the amounts and timing of inflows and outflows of funds. Even a profitable firm may face financial difficulties when it needs funds but sales are slow, when the volume of its credit sales increases, or when customers are slow in making payments.

In general, preparing a financial plan consists of three steps. The first step is a forecast of sales or revenue over some future time period. This projection is the key variable in any financial plan: without an accurate sales forecast, the firm will have difficulty accurately estimating other variables, such as production costs and purchasing needs. The best way to forecast sales depends on the type of business. For example, a retailer's CFO might begin by looking at the current sales per store. The CFO would look at the near future, including expected sales growth and any planned store openings or closings. This information can provide a forecast of sales for the next period.

If the company sells merchandise through other channels, such as online, the forecast is adjusted to include those additional channels.

Next, the CFO uses the sales forecast to decide on the expected level of profits for future periods. This longer-term projection involves estimating expenses such as purchases, employee compensation, and taxes. Many expenses are the result of sales. For example, the more a firm sells, generally the more it purchases. The CFO should also decide what portion of these profits will likely be paid to shareholders in the form of cash dividends.

After coming up with the sales and profit forecast, the CFO then needs to estimate how many additional assets the firm will need to support the projected sales. For

Costco's *asset intensity* is lower than that of a typical manufacturing business.

Justin Sullivan/Getty Images, Inc.

example, an increase in sales might mean the company needs additional inventory, faster collection of accounts receivable, or even a new plant and equipment. Depending on the type of industry, some businesses need more assets than other businesses to support the same amount of sales. The technical term for this greater requirement is *asset intensity*. For example, the chemical manufacturer DuPont has approximately $4.98 in assets for every dollar in sales. In other words, for every $100 increase in sales, the firm needs about $498 of additional assets. The warehouse retailer Costco is less asset intensive. It needs only about $0.29 in assets for every dollar in sales. In other words, Costco would need an additional $29 of assets for every $100 of additional sales. This difference is not surprising; manufacturing is a more asset-intensive business than retailing.

A simplified financial plan illustrates these steps. Assume a growing company is forecasting that sales next year will increase by $40 million to $140 million. After estimating the company's expenses, the CFO believes that after-tax profits next year will be $12 million, and the firm will pay nothing in dividends. The projected increase in next year's sales will require the firm to invest another $20 million in assets. Because increases in assets represent a use of funds, the company will need an additional $20 million in funds. The company's after-tax earnings will contribute $12 million, and the remaining $8 million must come from outside sources. The financial plan tells the CFO how much money will be needed and when it will be needed. Using this knowledge, and knowing that the firm has decided to borrow the needed funds, the CFO can then begin negotiations with banks and other lenders.

The cash inflows and outflows of a business are similar to the cash inflows and outflows of a household. The members of a household depend on weekly or monthly paycheques for funds, but their expenses may vary greatly from one pay period to the next. The financial plan should indicate the amount and timing of funds flowing into and out of the organization. One of the largest business expenses is employee compensation.

A good financial plan also includes financial control. Financial control is a process of comparing actual revenues, costs, and expenses with the forecasted amounts. This comparison may show differences between projected and actual figures. It is important to discover any differences early so quick action can be taken.

Bill Morrison is the CFO of GENCO Marketplace, a business that liquidates, or sells off, other companies' excess inventory. GENCO buys inventory that is not selling well, then resells the inventory to wholesalers. In turn, the wholesalers sell the inventory to discount retailers. GENCO is

✓ **ASSESSMENT CHECK**

17.2.1 What three questions does a financial plan address?

17.2.2 Explain the steps involved in preparing a financial plan.

always careful about the cost of freight, including fuel, because GENCO pays the transportation costs of taking the goods from their current location to where they will be liquidated. Some excess inventory is seasonal. For example, when a retailer has winter coats left over in June, GENCO will buy those coats, hold them in inventory, and sell them to a wholesaler in the fall when demand for winter coats increases. But the longer a product remains unsold, the harder it is to liquidate, even at a deep discount. In all cases, Morrison or members of his team need to prepare a financial plan that takes into account both the benefits and risks of buying the merchandise.[5]

LO 17.3 Outline how organizations manage their assets.

MANAGING ASSETS

As noted in Chapter 15, assets consist of what a firm owns. But assets also represent uses of funds. To grow and prosper, companies need to obtain additional assets. Sound financial management requires assets to be acquired and managed as effectively and efficiently as possible. The "Career Kickstart" feature offers tips for managing assets.

Short-Term Assets

Short-term assets are also called current assets. These assets consist of cash and assets that can be or are expected to be converted into cash within a year. The major current assets are cash, marketable securities, accounts receivable, and inventory.

Cash and Marketable Securities

The major purpose of cash is to pay for day-to-day expenses. It is similar to individuals who keep a balance in their chequing accounts to pay bills or buy food and clothing. Most organizations try to keep a minimum cash balance so they have funds available for unexpected expenses. As noted earlier, cash earns little if any return; most firms invest their excess cash in *marketable securities*. These are low-risk securities that either have short maturities or can be easily sold in secondary

---

CAREER KICKSTART

Tips for Managing Assets

These are challenging times for all businesses, whether one-person startups or large corporations. One of the most difficult problems is controlling costs. Here are some tips for managing assets—physical, financial, and human—while focusing on both short-term demands and long-term planning:

1. *Define your goals and objectives.* Be realistic when working out the resources you will need to meet both your immediate needs and your long-term plans. If you need to borrow money, be aware that credit is currently very tight and can be difficult to access.

2. *Examine your expenses.* You may find some areas where you can reduce or eliminate unnecessary expenditures, such as travel or discretionary spending. Which makes more financial sense for your company—cloud computing or traditional hardware and storage?

3. *Communicate with all your associates.* Be sure that your employees, suppliers, and clients know what is happening with your business. When people hear nothing, especially during difficult times, they often assume the worst has happened.

4. *Cultivate your human assets.* Identify your valued employees and let them know that they are important to the business. In difficult times, companies often try to hire talented personnel from their competitors. Again, communication is important. If your best employees hear nothing from you, they may also assume the worst has happened—and they may be more willing to leave for what may seem to be better opportunities elsewhere.

5. *Have at least one backup plan.* Your goals and objectives may not work out the way you expected them to. You may plan for a certain amount of receivables, but they may suddenly decrease. If possible, keep sufficient financial reserves available to see the company through the unexpected. That way, you may be able to turn disaster to your advantage.

Sources: "Managing Assets in Volatile Times: Nine Ways CFOs Can Adapt to Changing Financial Markets," Deloitte, accessed June 24, 2010, www.deloitte.com; Fred Jennings and R. W. Beck, "Leveraging Enterprise Value with Asset Management," *Utility Products,* January 14, 2010, www.elp.com; Daniel Solin, "Seven Shocking Tips to Boost Your Returns by 400% (or More)," *DailyFinance,* January 1, 2010, www.dailyfinance.com.

markets. Money market instruments (described in Chapter 16) are popular choices for firms that have excess cash. The cash budget, which we discussed and illustrated in Chapter 15, is one tool for managing cash and marketable securities. The cash budget shows expected cash inflows and outflows for a period of time. The cash budget shows which months the firm will have surplus cash and will be able to invest in marketable securities and which months it will need additional cash.

Critics of some companies' budgeting practices argue that some firms hoard cash. Recently, Cisco Systems had more than $35 billion in cash and marketable securities. But firms may have good reasons for holding large amounts of cash and marketable securities. For example, they may be planning to use these funds soon to make a large investment, pay dividends to shareholders, or repurchase outstanding bonds.

Accounts Receivable

Accounts receivable are uncollected credit sales. They can represent a significant asset. The financial manager's job is to collect the funds owed to the firm as quickly as possible while still offering sufficient credit to customers to attract and generate increased sales. In general, a more liberal credit policy means higher sales but also increased collection expenses, higher levels of bad debt, and a higher investment in accounts receivable.

Management of accounts receivable is composed of two functions: deciding on an overall credit policy and deciding which customers will be offered credit. Formulating a credit policy involves deciding whether the firm will offer credit and, if so, what terms of credit to offer. For example, will a discount be offered to customers who pay in cash? The overall credit policy is often the result of competitive pressures or general industry practices. If all your competitors offer their customers credit, your firm will likely also need to offer credit. The second aspect of a credit policy is deciding which customers will be offered credit. Managers must consider the importance of the customer and the customer's financial health and repayment history.

One simple tool for assessing how well receivables are being managed is to calculate the accounts receivable turnover over two or more time periods in a row. We showed how this ratio is calculated in Chapter 15. If the receivables turnover shows signs of slowing, it means that, on average, credit customers are paying later. This trend may need further investigation.

Inventory Management

For many firms, like retailers, inventory represents the largest single asset. For example, at the home furnishings retailer Bed Bath & Beyond, inventory makes up about 49 percent of total assets. Even for nonretailers inventory is an important asset. At the heavy-equipment manufacturer

At Bed Bath & Beyond, inventory is the most valuable asset. Managing inventory can be a costly and highly complicated task, especially for retailers.

Caterpillar, inventory is almost 12 percent of total assets. On the other hand, some types of firms, such as electric utilities and transportation companies, have no inventory. Most firms carry inventory, and their proper management of inventory is vital to the business's success.

Managing inventory can be complicated. The cost of inventory includes more than just the cost of acquiring goods. It also includes the costs of ordering, storing, insuring, and financing inventory. In addition, businesses take on the costs of stockouts and the costs of lost sales due to insufficient inventory. Financial managers try to minimize the cost of inventory. But production, marketing, and logistics also play important roles in determining proper inventory levels. The production considerations of inventory management were discussed in Chapter 10. In Chapter 12, we outlined the marketing and logistics issues surrounding inventory.

Trends in the inventory turnover ratio (described in Chapter 15) can be early warning signs of difficulties ahead. For example, when inventory turnover has been slowing for several quarters in a row, inventory is rising faster than sales. This situation may suggest that customer demand is slowing. The firm may need to take action, such as reducing production or increasing promotional efforts.

Capital Investment Analysis

In addition to current assets, firms also invest in long-lived assets. Unlike current assets, long-lived assets are expected to produce economic benefits for more than one year. These investments often involve large amounts of money. For example, as noted earlier in the chapter, Airbus invested more than $15 billion in development of the A380. In another example, Target Corporation commenced its expansion into Canada, buying out the store leases of 220 Zellers stores for $1.83 billion. Target invested over $10 million per store in long-lived assets to support the opening of the 133 stores that it opened.[6]

Capital investment analysis is the process financial managers use when deciding whether to invest in long-lived assets. Firms make two basic types of capital investment decisions: expansion and replacement. The A380 and Target investments are examples of expansion decisions. Replacement decisions involve upgrading assets by substituting new assets for older assets. A retailer like Walmart might decide to replace an old store with a new Supercentre, as it did in Concord, Ontario. Walmart Canada also plans to increase to 395 stores in the near future, spending some $500 million on remodelling, expansion, moving, and adding additional locations.[7]

Financial managers must estimate all the costs and benefits of a proposed investment. This task can be very difficult, especially for extremely long-lived investments. Companies should only pursue those investments that offer an acceptable return—measured by the difference between benefits and costs. Target's financial managers believed that the benefits of expanding into Canada outweighed the high cost. The expansion would allow Target to begin an international strategic expansion project. When deciding whether to expand into Canada, Target's financial managers would have considered the expected profit and the strategic benefits from the expansion. Despite aggressive attempts to win customers, Target's Canadian operations resulted in a loss of $941 million before interest and taxes, likely leading to the replacement of its Canadian president Tony Fisher in the same year that Target's CEO Gregg Steinhafel was replaced by the board after a devastating data breach. However, despite Target's aggressive capital expenditures it was still forced to discontinue operations less than two years after entering the Canadian market as it overestimated the expected profits that its Canadian operations would generate.[8]

Managing International Assets

Today, firms often have assets worldwide. Air Canada generates more than half of its annual sales outside of Canada.[9] Most sales for Unilever and Nestlé occur outside their home countries (the Netherlands and Switzerland, respectively). Managing international assets creates several challenges for financial managers. One of the most important challenges is dealing with exchange rates.

As we discussed in several other chapters, an exchange rate is the rate at which one currency can be exchanged for another currency. Exchange rates can vary widely from year to year, which creates a problem for any company that has international assets. For example, assume a Canadian firm has a major subsidiary in the United Kingdom. Assume that the U.K. subsidiary earns an annual profit of £750 million. Over the past five years, the exchange rate between the Canadian dollar and the British pound has varied between 2.061 (dollars per pound) and 1.5353.[10] This means the dollar value of the U.K. profits ranged from $1.55 billion to $1.15 billion.

Many global firms are involved in activities that reduce the risks associated with exchange rate ups and downs. Some of these activities are complicated, but if done correctly they can reduce or even eliminate the risks associated with changes in the value of foreign currencies. Reducing the risks of exchange rate fluctuations will improve the financial performance of the firm, which can have a positive impact on its share price.

SOURCES OF FUNDS AND CAPITAL STRUCTURE

LO 17.4 Discuss the two major sources of funds for a business and capital structure.

The use of debt for financing can increase both the potential for return and the potential for loss. Recall the accounting equation introduced in Chapter 15:

$$\text{Assets} = \text{Liabilities} + \text{Owners' Equity}$$

When this equation is viewed from a financial management perspective, it shows that there are only two types of funding: debt and equity. *Debt capital* consists of funds obtained through borrowing. *Equity capital* consists of funds provided by the firm's owners when they reinvest their earnings, make additional contributions, liquidate assets, issue shares to the general public, or raise capital from outside investors. The mix of a firm's debt and equity capital is known as its **capital structure**.

capital structure the mix of a firm's debt and equity capital.

Companies often take very different approaches to choosing a capital structure. As the company uses more debt, the risk to the company increases: The firm needs to make the interest payments on the money borrowed, regardless of the amount of cash flow coming into the company. Choosing more debt increases the fixed costs a company must pay, which makes a company more sensitive to any change in sales revenues. Debt is frequently the least costly method of raising additional financing dollars, which is why it is so frequently used.

Different industries choose varying amounts of debt and equity to use when financing. Information provided by Datamonitor shows the automotive industry has debt ratios (the ratio of liabilities to assets) of more than 60 percent for both Toyota and Honda and more than 85 percent for Ford. These companies are primarily using debt to finance their asset expenses. Companies such as McDonald's and Starbucks use only 57 percent debt and 61 percent debt, respectively. The mixture of debt and equity a company uses is a major management decision.[11]

Leverage and Capital Structure Decisions

Raising needed cash by borrowing allows a firm to benefit from the principle of **leverage**, increasing the rate of return on funds invested by borrowing funds. The key to managing leverage is to ensure that a company's earnings remain larger than its interest payments, which increases the leverage on the rate of return on shareholders' investment. Of course, if the company earns less than its interest payments, shareholders lose money on their original investments.

leverage increasing the rate of return on funds invested by borrowing funds.

Figure 17.2 shows the relationship between earnings and shareholder returns for two identical imaginary firms that choose to raise funds in different ways. Leverage Company obtains 50 percent of its funds from lenders who purchase company bonds. Leverage Company pays 10 percent interest on its bonds. Equity Company raises all of its funds through sales of company stock.

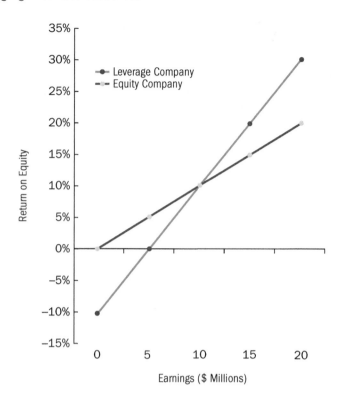

FIGURE 17.2 How Leverage Works

Note: The example assumes that both companies have $100 million in capital. Leverage Company consists of $50 million in equity and $50 million in bonds (with an interest rate of 10 percent). Equity Company consists of $100 million in equity and no bonds. This example also assumes no corporate taxes.

Notice that if earnings double, from $10 million to $20 million, the returns to the shareholders of Equity Company also double—from 10 percent to 20 percent. But returns to shareholders of Leverage Company more than double—from 10 percent to 30 percent. But leverage can also work in the opposite direction. If earnings fall from $10 million to $5 million (a decline of 50 percent), returns to shareholders of Equity Company also fall by 50 percent—from 10 percent to 5 percent. By contrast, returns to shareholders of Leverage Company fall from 10 percent to zero. Thus, leverage increases potential returns to shareholders but also increases risk.

Another problem with borrowing money is that relying too much on borrowed funds may reduce management's flexibility in future financing decisions. If a company raises equity capital this year and needs to raise funds next year, it will probably be able to raise either debt or equity capital. But if it raises debt capital this year, it may be forced to raise equity capital next year.

Equity capital also has downsides. Because shareholders are owners of the company, they usually elect the board of directors and vote on major company issues. But when new equity is sold, the control of the existing shareholders is weakened and the outcome of these votes could potentially change. One sensitive subject today between companies and shareholders is whether shareholders should be able to vote on executive pay packages. The "Solving an Ethical Controversy" feature discusses this issue.

Another downside of equity capital is that it is more expensive than debt capital. First, creditors have a senior claim to the assets of a firm before the shareholders' claims. Because of this advantage, creditors will accept a lower rate of return than shareholders will. Second, the firm can deduct interest payments on debt, reducing its taxable income and its tax bill. In contrast, dividends paid to shareholders are not tax deductible. A key part of the financial manager's job is to weigh the upsides and downsides of debt capital and equity capital, and then create the most suitable capital structure for the firm.

SOLVING AN **ETHICAL** CONTROVERSY

Executive Pay: Should Shareholders Decide the Salaries of CEOs?

While the world was suffering through the recent financial crisis and its aftermath, the news media were reporting on the huge salaries of CEOs and other top executives at large corporations.

At a Royal Dutch Shell annual meeting, shareholders voted down a proposed executive compensation package. In response, the company announced it would freeze executive pay and base its bonuses on performance. The new CEO received a salary 20 percent lower than that of the previous CEO. The company said that the changes would "demonstrate appropriate restraint in the current economic environment." "Say-on-pay" voting by shareholders has become increasingly common—and controversial.

Should company shareholders help decide how much top executives are paid?

PRO

1. Publicly held corporations are owned by their shareholders, who should have the opportunity to vote on compensation for top executives. Robert E. Denham and Rajiv L. Gupta, co-chairs of the Conference Board's Task Force on Executive Compensation, said "Shareholders . . . and the public deserve to see executive compensation programs that serve shareholders' interests and are explained to shareholders."

2. Some analysts believe that lopsided pay structures played a role in the financial crisis in the United States. Federal Reserve Chair Ben Bernanke said "Compensation practices at some banking organizations have led to misaligned incentives and excessive risk-taking."

CON

1. Shareholders may not necessarily know what appropriate pay is. Many do not have the time or resources to do their own analysis and to judge whether a pay program is suitable or whether it promotes a risk-taking, get-rich-quick mentality in executives.

2. Shareholders recently turned down the chance to vote on executive pay at companies such as Johnson & Johnson and Dow Chemical. Many shareholders prefer to discuss pay structures with management and board members before voting.

Summary

The Ontario Securities Commission has long been considering making it a requirement for companies to give shareholders a say on executive compensation. This approach would begin to position Canada in line with many European countries and in the direction of the United States, where "say-on-pay" regulations are either currently in place or are in the planning stage.

Sources: Alix Stuart, "Reform Bill Mandates Say on Pay," CFO.com, June 29, 2010, www.cfo.com; Jim Kuhnhenn and Alan Fram, "Congress Agrees on Financial Oversight," *Philadelphia Inquirer,* June 26, 2010, www.philly.com; Ann Yerger, "Red Flags for Say-on-Pay Voting," Harvard Law School Forum on Corporate Governance and Financial Regulation, May 18, 2010, http://blogs.law.harvard.edu; A. G. Laffey, "Executive Pay: Time for CEOs to Take a Stand," Harvard Business Review, May 2010, http://hbr.org; Bryant Ruiz Switzky, "CEO Compensation Down in 2009," Washington Business Journal, May 7, 2010, http://washingtonbizjournals.com; "Shell Shareholder 'Rebellion' Leads to New Limits on Executive Pay, Bonuses," *Huffington Post,* February 26, 2010, www.huffingtonpost.com; Helen Coster, "The State of the CEO in 2010," *Forbes,* January 21, 2010, www.forbes.com; David R. Butcher, "Cracking Down on Excessive Executive Pay," IMT Industry Market Trends, October 29, 2009, http://news.thomasnet.com; Danielle Arbuckle, "Should Shareholders Have a Say on Executive Pay?" Wallet Pop, accessed August 2, 2011, www.walletpop.ca/blog/2011/01/19/should-shareholders-have-a-say-on-executive-pay/; Lexpert, "Executive Compensation: High Risk for the Status Quo," accessed August 21, 2014, www.lexpert.ca/magazine/article/executive-compensation-high-risk-for-the-status-quo-2567/.

Mixing Short-Term and Long-Term Funds

Financial managers face another decision: deciding on the suitable mix of short-term and long-term funds. Short-term funds consist of current liabilities, and long-term funds consist of long-term debt and equity. Short-term funds are generally less expensive than long-term funds, but they expose the firm to more risk. This risk occurs because short-term funds need to be renewed, or rolled over, frequently. Short-term interest rates can be unstable. For example, during a recent 12-month period, rates on commercial paper, a popular short-term financing option, ranged from a high of 4 percent to a low of less than 1 percent.[12]

Because short-term rates move up and down frequently, the interest expense on short-term funds can vary greatly from year to year. For example, if a firm borrows $50 million for 10 years at 5 percent interest, its annual interest expense is fixed at $2.5 million for the entire 10 years. On the

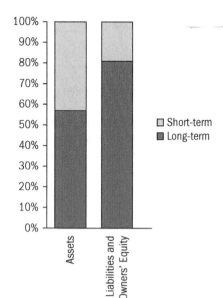

FIGURE 17.3 Johnson & Johnson's Mix of Short-Term and Long-Term Funds

Source: Data from Johnson & Johnson balance sheet, Yahoo! Finance, accessed August 15, 2014, http://finance.yahoo.com/q/bs?s=JNJ+Balance+Sheet&annual.

other hand, if the firm borrows $50 million for one year at a rate of 4 percent, its annual interest expense of $2 million is fixed for only that year. If interest rates increase the following year to 6 percent, then $1 million will be added to the interest expense bill. Another potential risk of relying on short-term funds is availability. Even financially healthy firms can occasionally find it difficult to borrow money.

Because of the added risk of short-term funding, most firms choose to finance all of their long-term assets, and even a portion of their short-term assets, by using long-term funds. Johnson & Johnson is typical of this choice. **Figure 17.3** shows 2013 balance sheet data from the company that divides out the short-term and long-term assets, and the short-term and long-term funds.

Dividend Policy

In addition to decisions regarding capital structure and the mix of short-term and long-term funds, financial managers also make decisions regarding a firm's dividend policy. *Dividends* are periodic cash payments to shareholders. The most common type of dividend is paid quarterly and is often called a *regular dividend*. Occasionally, firms make one-time special dividend payments or extra dividend payments, as Microsoft did some years ago. Earnings that are paid in dividends are not reinvested in the firm and don't contribute additional equity capital.

Firms are under no legal obligation to pay dividends to shareholders. Although some companies pay generous dividends, others pay nothing. Until 2010, Starbucks never paid a dividend to its shareholders. In contrast, 3M has paid dividends for 30-plus consecutive years; during that time, the amount of the dividends has more than quadrupled. Companies that pay dividends try to increase the amount of dividends paid or, at the very least, hold the amount of the dividends steady from year to year. But in rare cases firms must cut or eliminate dividends. After the major oil spill in the Gulf of Mexico in 2010, BP announced it was cancelling dividend payments for the first quarter and suspending those payments to shareholders for the second and third quarters of their fiscal year.[13]

Attendees arrive for BP's 2011 annual general meeting—its first after the oil spill in the Gulf of Mexico in 2010. As a result of the oil spill, BP announced it was cancelling dividend payments for the first quarter and suspending them for the second and third quarters of its year.

Many factors are considered when deciding on a company's dividend policy. One factor is the firm's investment opportunities. Suppose a firm has numerous investment opportunities and wants to finance some or all of them through equity funding. It will likely pay little, if any, of its earnings in dividends. Shareholders may actually want the company to retain earnings, because if they are reinvested the firm's future profits, and the value of its shares, will increase faster. By contrast, a firm with more limited investment opportunities generally pays more of its earnings in dividends.

In addition to dividends, some firms buy back a portion of their outstanding shares. The Home Depot, for example, has repurchased more than $1 billion worth of shares over the past few years. Generally, shares are purchased on the secondary markets. The main purpose of share buy-backs is to raise the market value of the remaining shares, which benefits the shareholders.

✓ ASSESSMENT CHECK

17.4.1 Explain the concept of leverage.

17.4.2 Why do firms generally rely more on long-term funds than short-term funds?

17.4.3 What is an important factor in deciding on a firm's dividend policy?

SHORT-TERM FUNDING OPTIONS

LO 17.5 Identify sources of short-term financing for businesses.

An organization may discover that its cash needs are greater than its available funds. Retailers generate surplus cash for most of the year, but they need to build up inventory during the late summer and fall to get ready for the holiday shopping season. They often need funds to pay for this merchandise until the holiday sales generate revenue. They can then use the incoming funds to repay the amount they borrowed. In this kind of situation, financial managers often look to short-term sources of funds. Short-term sources of funds are repaid within one year. The three major sources of short-term funds are trade credit, short-term loans, and commercial paper. Large firms often rely on a combination of all three sources of short-term financing.

Trade Credit

Trade credit is extended by suppliers when a firm receives goods or services and agrees to pay for them at a later date. Trade credit is common in many industries such as retailing and manufacturing. Suppliers ship billions of dollars of merchandise to retailers each day and are paid at a later date. Without trade credit, the retailing sector would probably look much different—with fewer selections. To record trade credit, the supplier enters the transactions as an account receivable, and the retailer enters it as an account payable. Canadian Tire Corporation currently has more than $1.8 billion of accounts payable on its books.[14] The main upside of trade credit is its easy availability. The main downside to trade credit is that the amount a company can borrow is limited to the amount it purchases.

What is the cost of trade credit? If suppliers do not offer a cash discount, trade credit is effectively free. For example, assume a supplier offers trade credit under the terms net 30. These terms mean that the buyer has 30 days to pay. In other words, companies are borrowing $100 and repaying $100 in 30 days. The effective rate of interest is zero. But some suppliers offer a discount if they are paid in cash. If a discount is offered, trade credit can get expensive. Assume that a 2 percent discount is offered to cash buyers. If buyers do not take the discount, they have 30 days to pay. If the buyer does not pay cash, the terms are the same as borrowing $98 today and repaying $100 in 30 days. The annual interest rate on such a loan is more than 24 percent.

Short-Term Loans

Loans from commercial banks are a significant source of short-term financing for businesses. Businesses often use these loans to finance inventory and accounts receivable. For example, a small manufacturer of ski equipment has its highest sales in late fall and early winter. To meet this demand, it begins building inventory during the summer. The manufacturer also needs to finance accounts receivable (credit sales to customers) during the fall and winter. It takes out a bank loan during the summer. As the inventory is sold and as accounts receivable are collected, the firm repays the loan.

Borrowers can choose from two types of short-term bank loans: lines of credit and revolving credit agreements. A line of credit specifies the maximum amount the firm can borrow over a period of time, usually a year. The bank is under no obligation to actually lend the money. It will lend the money, but only if funds are available. Most lines of credit require the borrower to repay the original amount, plus interest, within one year. In contrast, a revolving credit agreement is basically a guaranteed line of credit—the bank guarantees that the funds will be available when needed. Banks typically charge a fee on top of interest for revolving credit agreements.

The cash budget is an important tool when deciding on the size of a line of credit. The cash budget shows the months when additional financing will be needed or when borrowed funds can be repaid. For example, assume the ski manufacturer's cash budget indicates that it will need $2.5 million from June through November. The financial manager might set up a line of credit with the bank for $2.8 million. The extra $300,000 is added to cover any unexpected cash outflows.

Commercial finance companies also make short-term loans to businesses. Most bank loans are unsecured, which means that no specific assets are pledged as collateral, or security. Loans from commercial finance companies are often secured by using accounts receivable or inventory as collateral.

Factoring is another form of short-term financing that uses accounts receivable. The business sells its accounts receivable at a discount to either a bank or a finance company—which is called a *factor*. The cost of the transaction depends on the size of the discount. Factoring allows the firm to convert its receivables into cash quickly without worrying about collections.

The cost of short-term loans depends on the interest rate and the fees charged by the lender. Some lenders also require the borrower to keep *compensating balances*—5 to 20 percent of the outstanding loan amount—in a chequing account. Compensating balances increase the effective cost of a loan because the borrower does not have full use of the amount borrowed.

For example, suppose a firm borrows $100,000 for one year at 5 percent interest. The borrower will pay $5,000 in interest (5 percent × $100,000). If the lender requires that 10 percent of the loan amount be kept as compensating balance, the firm has use of only $90,000. But because the firm will still pay $5,000 in interest, the effective rate on the loan is actually 5.56 percent ($5,000/$90,000).

Commercial Paper

ASSESSMENT CHECK

17.5.1 What are the three sources of short-term funding?

17.5.2 Explain trade credit.

17.5.3 Why is commercial paper an attractive short-term financing option?

Commercial paper is a short-term IOU sold by a company; it was briefly described in Chapter 16. Commercial paper is usually sold in multiples of $100,000 to $1 million and has a maturity date that ranges from 1 to 270 days. Most commercial paper is unsecured. It is an attractive source of financing because large amounts of money can be raised at interest rates that are usually 1 to 2 percent less than the interest rates charged by banks. At the end of a recent year, almost $1.15 trillion in commercial paper was outstanding.[15] Although commercial paper is an attractive short-term financing option, only a small percentage of businesses can issue it. Access to the commercial paper market has traditionally been limited to large, financially strong corporations.

LO 17.6 Discuss long-term financing options.

SOURCES OF LONG-TERM FINANCING

Funds from short-term sources can help a firm meet its current needs for cash or inventory. But a larger project or plan, such as buying another company or investing in real estate or equipment, usually requires funds for a much longer period of time. Unlike short-term financing, long-term financing is repaid over many years.

Organizations acquire long-term financing from three sources. The first source is long-term loans from financial institutions such as commercial banks, life insurance companies, and pension funds. A second source is bonds—certificates of indebtedness—sold to investors. A third source is equity financing acquired by selling shares in the firm or reinvesting company profits. The "Going Green" feature describes how new investment vehicles are being created to reflect some investors' interests in corporate sustainability.

A KNIGHT IN SHINING CAPITALISM

The words *clean* and *capitalism* are not often used together in the same sentence. Many think of capitalism in a negative sense. But can large corporate companies operate under the concept of "clean capitalism"?

Corporate Knights (CK) is a Toronto-based company that understands that many investors have changing objectives. CK publishes an annual "clean capitalism" report. It uses objective measures to assess the environmental, social, and governance (ESG) practices of some of Canada's largest companies. Executives, regulators, investors, and other stakeholders consult this $2,495 report to assess the sustainability practices of these companies. CK also publishes a list of the top 100 companies in the "Global 100 Most Sustainable Corporations in the World." Canadian companies that made the list for 2014 include Tim Hortons (#22), Bombardier Inc. (#24), Teck Resources Limited (#44), and Bank of Montreal (#49). Westpac Banking Corporation of Australia was ranked number one.

CK is currently developing a global collection of clean capitalism passive investments to help investors who want to invest in companies that practise clean capitalism.

CK is responding to investors who want to evaluate companies both on their financial performance and on their "extra-financial" performance, including activities that support the environment, labour, and human rights. The measurement of ESG practices by a single organization allows investors to compare various companies. Many believe that these extra-financial measures can significantly influence a company's long-term performance and affect its true overall value.

Questions for Critical Thinking

1. Why does "going green" make good business sense for large corporations?

2. How do ESG practices affect a company's market value and long-term financial potential?

Sources: Corporate Knights, "Clean Capitalism," accessed August 15, 2014, www .corporateknights.com/report/united-states-clean-capitalism-report-2012; "2012 Global 100 Most Sustainable Companies: The Full List," accessed March 6, 2012, www .global100.org/; Corporate Knights, "Toronto-Based Clean Capitalism Media Company Closes Investment Round to Launch Capital Markets Division," press release, November 16, 2011, accessed March 6, 2012, http://huffstrategy.com/MediaManager/release/ Corporate-Knights/31-12-69/Toronto-based-clean-capitalism-media-company-closes-investment-ro/2386.html.

Public Sale of Shares and Bonds

Public sales of securities, such as shares and bonds, are a major source of funds for corporations. These sales provide cash inflows for the issuing firm and either a share in its ownership (for a share purchaser) or a specified rate of interest and repayment at a stated time (for a bond purchaser). Because many shares and bonds are traded in the secondary markets, shareholders and bondholders can easily sell these securities. During the recent European debt crisis there was a massive slowdown in European bond sales. During this time, foreigners flocked to Canadian bonds which had an AAA rating. This led to foreign sales of Canadian bonds reaching a record $16.7 billion in May 2012.[16] Public sales of securities can vary quite a bit from year to year depending on conditions in the financial markets. For example, bond sales tend to be higher when interest rates are low.

In Chapter 16, we discussed how most companies sell securities publicly through investment bankers using a process called *underwriting*. Investment bankers purchase the securities from the issuer and then resell them to investors. The issuer pays a fee to the investment banker, called an *underwriting discount*.

Private Placements

Some new share or bond issues are not sold publicly but are offered instead to a small group of major investors such as pension funds and insurance companies. These sales are referred to as *private placements*. Most private placements involve corporate debt issues. More than $120 billion in corporate bonds were sold privately in a recent year in the United States.[17]

It is often cheaper for a company to sell a security privately than publicly. Private placements are subject to fewer government regulations because registration with the Canadian Securities Administrators is not required. Institutional investors such as insurance companies and pension funds buy private placements because they typically carry slightly higher interest rates than publicly issued bonds. In addition, the terms of the issue can be designed to meet the specific needs of both the issuer and the institutional investors. Of course, the institutional investor gives up liquidity, or ease of cashability, because privately placed securities do not trade in secondary markets.

Venture Capitalists

Venture capitalists business firms or groups of individuals that invest in new and growing firms in exchange for an ownership share.

Venture capitalists are an important source of long-term financing, especially for new companies. **Venture capitalists** are business firms or groups of individuals that invest in new and growing firms in exchange for an ownership share. They typically raise money from wealthy individuals and institutional investors and invest these funds in promising firms. Venture capitalists also provide management consulting advice and funds. In exchange for their investment, venture capitalists become part owners of the business. If the business succeeds, venture capitalists can earn large profits.

One of Canada's largest venture capital firms is Covington Funds. Covington was established in 1994. It has invested in several sectors, including technology and health care. One of the many companies that Covington has invested in is Golf Town. Covington currently manages more than $300 million in assets.[18]

Private Equity Funds

Private equity funds are similar to venture capitalists. They are investment companies that raise funds from wealthy individuals and institutional investors. They then invest those funds in both public and privately held companies. Unlike venture capital funds, which tend to focus on small startup companies, private equity funds invest in all types of businesses, including mature companies. For example, Onex Corporation, a private equity fund, recently bought three of Boeing's parts manufacturing plants for $1.5 billion.[19] Often, private equity funds invest in transactions that take public companies private, also known as leveraged buyouts (LBOs). In these transactions, discussed in more detail in the next section, a public company reverts to private status. The "Hit & Miss" feature profiles another large private equity fund, Harvest Partners.

A variation of the private equity fund is the so-called *sovereign wealth fund*. Sovereign wealth funds are owned by governments. They invest in a variety of financial and real assets, such as real

HIT & MISS

Harvest Partners Grows Its Investments

Is it possible to have too much money to spend in too little time? Harvest Partners and other private equity firms had just a few years to invest about $500 billion.

Harvest Partners is a private equity firm that specializes in leveraged buyouts and growth financing. It focuses on companies in North America and Western Europe. The firm manages funds emphasizing private equity and debt investments. Harvest Partners makes equity investments of $50 million to $200 million in companies with revenues of between $100 million and $750 million. It prefers to be a control investor by becoming a partner in the companies it finances. Those companies tend to be middle-market firms that need investment to adapt to changing times and markets.

Private equity firms usually have three to six years to reinvest the funds they have raised from client investors. If they cannot or do not reinvest during that time, they must return the money. During the boom years, Harvest Partners raised $815 million from client investors. They had reinvested about $293 million. The firm then faced a deadline to reinvest the remaining $522 million.

Not all private equity investments are successful. Harvest Partners had owned the equity of the Natural Products Group (NPG), a manufacturer of organic shampoos and soaps. When NPG went bankrupt, Harvest Partners lost its entire investment.

Recently Harvest Partners joined MTP Energy Management to invest $80 million in Regency Energy Partners, a middle-market natural gas company. Michael DeFlorio is a senior managing director of Harvest Partners. He said that Regency "embodies our investment strategy focused on exceptionally managed . . . midstream service providers participating in the most promising resource plays in the industry."

Questions for Critical Thinking

1. Describe some of the risks faced by a firm like Harvest Partners.

2. Why do you think Harvest Partners and other equity firms are required to invest their clients' funds within a limited time?

Sources: Harvest Partners, accessed June 24, 2010, www.harvpart.com; "Harvest Partners," profile from *Bloomberg Businessweek*, accessed June 24, 2010, http://investing.businessweek.com; Julie Cresswell, "On Wall Street, So Much Cash, So Little Time," *New York Times*, June 23, 2010, www.nytimes.com; Emily Thornton, "LBO Firms Can't Spend $503 Billion as Deadlines Loom (Update 1)," Bloomberg.com, March 10, 2010, www.bloomberg.com; Brian Baxter, "The Bankruptcy Files: Curtain Drops on Movie Gallery, Air America Loses Frequency," *AM Law Daily*, February 4, 2010, http://amlawdailytypepad.com; "Harvest Partners, MTP Energy Invest in Regency Energy Partners," iStockAnalyst, September 7, 2009, www.istockanalyst.com; Find the Best, "Harvest Partners," accessed August 15, 2014, http://private-equity.findthebest.com/l/781/Harvest-Partners.

The television series *Dragons' Den* popularizes entrepreneurs and their search for long-term financing.

estate. Sovereign wealth funds generally make investments that are based on the best risk–return tradeoff. But their investment decisions are also influenced by political, social, and strategic considerations.

Chinese sovereign wealth funds have recently made several purchases in Canada. The China Investment Corporation made several large investments in major Canadian resource companies and the Alberta oil sands. PetroChina Company paid $5.44 billion for a 50 percent stake in Encana Corporation's natural gas assets in Western Canada. China Petrochemical Corporation paid $4.65 billion recently to buy a part of Syncrude Canada Ltd., a company that produces bitumen from Alberta oil sands projects.[20] The assets of the 10 largest sovereign wealth funds are shown in **Figure 17.4**. Together, these 10 funds have more than $5 trillion in assets.

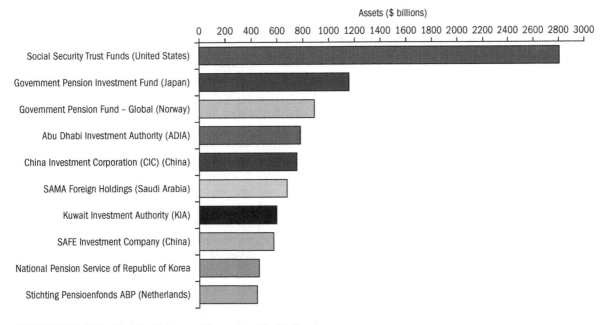

FIGURE 17.4 The World's 10 Largest Sovereign Wealth Funds

Source: Data from Sovereign Wealth Fund Institute, "Sovereign Wealth Fund Rankings," June 2015. Accessed August 20, 2015, www.swfinstitute.org/fund-rankings/.

Hedge Funds

Hedge funds are private investment companies that are available only to qualified large investors. In recent years, hedge funds have become a significant presence in Canadian financial markets, though they have the same relative representation in the United Kingdom and the United States. Before the recent recession, some analysts estimated that Canadian hedge funds and hedge fund–related products totalled more than $30 billion. More recently, hedge fund providers have begun selling these funds, in the form of mutual funds, to smaller investors for as little as $1,000.[21] Hedge funds also make large investments in noninvestment-grade bonds, also known as junk bonds. Globally, hedge funds are estimated to have total assets of more than $2.7 trillion.[22] Traditionally, hedge funds, unlike venture capitalists and private equity funds, did not make direct investments in companies; instead, they usually preferred to purchase existing shares and bond issues.

LO 17.7 Describe mergers, acquisitions, buyouts, and divestitures.

MERGERS, ACQUISITIONS, BUYOUTS, AND DIVESTITURES

Chapter 5 briefly described mergers and acquisitions. A *merger* is a transaction where two or more firms combine into one company. In an *acquisition*, one firm buys the assets of another firm and assumes that firm's obligations. Chapter 5 listed the classifications of mergers and acquisitions: vertical, horizontal, and conglomerate. It also noted that many of these transactions involve large sums of money. A recent example is AT&T's $49 billion acquisition of DirecTV. In this section, we focus on the financial implications of mergers and acquisitions, buyouts, and divestitures.

A merger includes a buyer and a seller. The seller is often referred to as the *target*. Financial managers evaluate a proposed merger or acquisition in much the same way they evaluate any large investment—by comparing the costs and benefits. To acquire another company, the buying firm typically needs to offer a premium for the target's shares—in other words, a price higher than the current market price. For example, AT&T paid $95 for each share of DirecTV, a premium of almost 30 percent over the existing price.[23]

tender offer a proposal made by a firm to the target firm's shareholders specifying a price and the form of payment.

When the buyer makes what is known as a **tender offer** for the target's shares, it specifies a price and the form of payment. The buyer can offer cash, securities, or a combination of the two. The AT&T offer to DirecTV shareholders was a combination of $28.50 in cash and AT&T stock valued at $66.50 per share. The tender offer can be friendly, meaning it is backed by the target's board of directors, or unfriendly. Shareholders of both the buyer and target must vote to approve a merger.

Setting a premium requires the financial manager to estimate the benefits of a proposed merger. These benefits can include the cost savings from economies of scale, reduced workforces, or the buyer getting a bargain price for the target's assets. Sometimes a buyer finds that the most cost-effective method of entering a new market is simply to buy an existing company that serves the market. Johnson & Johnson has a long history of making such acquisitions. When it decided to enter the contact lens market several years ago, Johnson & Johnson bought Vistakon, the firm that invented disposable contact lenses under the brand name Acuvue. *Synergy* is the term used to describe the benefits produced by a merger or acquisition. It refers to the idea that the combined firm is worth more than the buyer firm and the target firm are worth individually.

Leveraged buyouts, or LBOs transactions where public shareholders are bought out and the firm reverts to private status.

Leveraged buyouts, or LBOs, were briefly introduced in the preceding section. In an LBO, public shareholders are bought out and the firm reverts to private status. The term *leverage* refers to the financing of many of these transactions with high degrees of debt—often more than 75 percent. Financial companies provide financing for many LBOs. LBO activity decreased sharply during the recent economic downturn. As the economy began to recover, LBO activity increased. According to Standard & Poor's, LBO financing recently grew to $13.6 billion, about 15 times the amount from the same time a year before.[24]

Why do so many LBOs occur? One reason is that private companies enjoy benefits that public companies do not. Private companies are not required to publish financial results, are subject to less regulatory supervision, and are not pressured to produce short-term profits. Some argue that LBOs, because of the high degree of debt, require management to use more discipline to control costs. Although LBOs do have advantages, history has shown that many companies that go private appear as public companies several years later.

In a sense, a **divestiture** is the reverse of a merger. That is, in a divestiture, a company sells its assets, such as subsidiaries, product lines, or production facilities. Two types of divestitures exist: selloffs and spinoffs. In a *selloff,* assets are sold by one firm to another. For example, when Shell Canada decided to focus its resources on "other options," it sold its stake in the Mackenzie Valley Pipeline project in the Northwest Territories and other assets in the region. When asked for a statement, the chairperson of the Aboriginal Pipeline Group said, "We're sure that there's . . . a lot of companies out there that would love to step up to the plate and take over." Similarly, Calgary-based Suncor Energy sold its natural gas assets, located in Trinidad and Tobago, for $396 million. Centrica Plc took ownership of all the assets, allowing Suncor to focus on other aspects of its core business.[25]

The other type of divestiture is a *spinoff.* In this transaction, the assets sold form a new firm. For example, Motorola announced that it was splitting into two publicly traded firms. The parent company will handle its core business of mobile converged devices, digital home entertainment devices, and video voice and data solutions. The spinoff firm will handle heavy-duty two-way radios, mobile computers, public security systems, wireless network infrastructure, and other business-oriented goods and services. Both organizations will continue to use the Motorola brand name, with the parent company now named Motorola Mobile Devices and Home. Motorola shareholders will receive shares of the new company, Motorola Enterprise Mobility and Networks. Bell Canada also recently spun off its regional small-business operations and rural portions of its residential wire line business to Aliant.

Firms divest assets for several reasons. Sometimes divestitures result from previous acquisitions that didn't work out as well as expected. In early 2001, America Online and Time Warner merged to create AOL Time Warner, Inc. Nine years later, Time Warner announced it was spinning off AOL. The merger is now considered one of the worst mistakes in corporate history. It had failed to generate the expected synergies between the two companies. Shortly after the merger, AOL had 27 million subscribers; more recently, that number had shrunk to about 6.3 million.

In other cases, a firm makes a strategic decision to focus on its core businesses. It then decides to divest any assets that fall outside this core. That was the explanation that Motorola gave when criticized that the company had become too large and after its mobile-device business was taken over first by Nokia, then Samsung, and then Apple. A similar explanation was given by Bell Aliant CEO Karen Sheriff. She explained that the company had sold xwave to Bell to "focus on our core priorities such as fibre-to-the home, improve our balance sheet and ensure long-term value to our investors."

divestiture the sale of assets by a firm.

 **ASSESSMENT CHECK**

17.7.1 Define *synergy*.

17.7.2 What is an LBO?

17.7.3 What are the two types of divestitures?

WHAT'S AHEAD

Contemporary Business concludes with several appendices. Appendix A contains additional case studies. Appendix B outlines the main legal issues concerning business. It reviews the types of laws, the regulatory environment of business, and the core of business law, including discussions of contract law and property law. Appendix C examines risk management and insurance. It describes the concept of risk, alternative ways of dealing with risk, and the various kinds of insurance available to businesses and individuals. Appendix D discusses some of the important areas of personal financial planning, such as budgeting, credit, and retirement planning, and Appendix E describes how to write an effective business plan. An additional appendix, Appendix F, features video case studies with accompanying videos. This appendix is available in WileyPLUS Learning Space. Appendix G, which discusses career searches and options to help you prepare for your future in business, is available on the textbook's companion website at www.wiley.com/go/boonecanada.

RETURN TO INSIDE BUSINESS

The Wooing of Ratiopharm

Financial managers make key decisions related to a company's most liquid asset—cash.

QUESTIONS FOR CRITICAL THINKING

1. When making a key investment decision, what projections do management need to prepare?

2. What key external factors can affect the reliability of a manager's financial forecasts?

SUMMARY OF LEARNING OBJECTIVES

LO 17.1 Explain the role of financial managers.

Finance deals with planning, obtaining, and managing a company's funds to accomplish its objectives efficiently and effectively. The major responsibilities of financial managers are developing and carrying out financial plans and deciding on the most appropriate sources and uses of funds. The chief financial officer (CFO) heads a firm's finance organization. Three senior executives reporting to the CFO are the vice-president of financial management, the treasurer, and the controller. When making decisions, financial professionals continually balance risks with expected financial returns.

 ASSESSMENT CHECK ANSWERS

17.1.1 What is the structure of the finance function at the typical firm? The head of the finance function of a firm usually has the title of chief financial officer (CFO) and generally reports directly to the firm's chief executive officer. Reporting to the CFO are the treasurer, the controller, and the vice-president of financial management.

17.1.2 Explain the risk–return tradeoff. Financial managers try to maximize the wealth of their firm's shareholders by striking the right balance between risk and return. Often, the decisions that involve the highest potential returns expose the firm to the greatest risks.

LO 17.2 Describe the parts of a financial plan and the financial planning process.

A financial plan is a document that specifies the funds needed by a firm for a given period of time, the timing of cash inflows and outflows, and the most appropriate sources and uses of funds. The financial plan addresses three questions: What funds will be required during the planning period? When will funds be needed? Where will funds be obtained? Three steps are involved in the financial planning process: forecasting sales over a future period of time, estimating the expected level of profits over the planning period, and deciding on the additional assets needed to support the additional sales.

 ASSESSMENT CHECK ANSWERS

17.2.1 What three questions does a financial plan address? The financial plan addresses three questions: What funds will be required during the planning period? When will funds be needed? Where will funds be obtained?

17.2.2 Explain the steps involved in preparing a financial plan. The first step is to forecast sales over a future period of time. Second, the financial manager must estimate the expected level of profits over the planning period. The final step is to decide on the additional assets needed to support the additional sales.

LO 17.3 Outline how organizations manage their assets.

Assets consist of what a firm owns. They also represent the uses of its funds. Sound financial management requires assets to be acquired and managed as effectively and efficiently as possible. The major current assets are cash, marketable securities, accounts receivable, and inventory. The goal of cash management is to have enough funds to meet day-to-day transactions and pay for any unexpected expenses. Excess cash should be invested in marketable securities, which are low-risk securities with short maturity dates. Accounts receivable are uncollected credit sales. Managing accounts receivable involves collecting funds owed to the firm as quickly as possible while also offering enough credit to customers to attract and generate increased sales. The main goal of inventory management is to minimize the overall cost of inventory. Production, marketing, and logistics also play roles in determining proper inventory levels. Capital investment analysis is the process financial managers use when deciding whether to invest in long-lived assets. This process involves comparing the benefits and costs of a proposed investment. Managing international assets poses additional challenges for the financial manager, including the problem of fluctuating exchange rates.

 ASSESSMENT CHECK ANSWERS

17.3.1 Why do firms often choose to invest excess cash in marketable securities? Cash in hand earns no rate of return. Excess cash should be invested in marketable securities. Marketable securities are low-risk securities that have short maturity dates and can be easily sold in the secondary markets. As a result, they are easily converted into cash when needed.

17.3.2 What are the two aspects of accounts receivable management? The two aspects of accounts receivable management are deciding on an overall credit policy (whether to offer credit and, if so, what terms of credit to offer) and deciding which customers will be offered credit.

17.3.3 Explain the difference between an expansion decision and a replacement decision. An expansion decision involves decisions about offering new products or building or acquiring new production facilities. A replacement decision considers whether to replace an existing asset with a new asset.

LO 17.4 Discuss the two major sources of funds for a business and capital structure.

Businesses have two sources of funds: debt capital and equity capital. Debt capital refers to funds obtained through borrowing, and equity capital consists of funds provided by the firm's owners. The mix of debt and equity capital is known as the firm's capital structure, and the financial manager's job is to find the proper mix. Leverage is a technique of increasing the rate of return on funds invested by borrowing. But leverage also increases risk. Also, relying too much on borrowed funds may reduce management's flexibility in future financing decisions. Equity capital also has its downsides. When additional equity capital is sold, the control of existing shareholders is weakened. In addition, equity capital is more expensive than debt capital. Financial managers also face decisions concerning the suitable mix of short-term and long-term funds. Short-term funds are generally less expensive than long-term funds but expose firms to more risk. Financial managers are also involved in deciding the firm's dividend policy.

 ASSESSMENT CHECK ANSWERS

17.4.1 Explain the concept of leverage. Leverage is a technique of increasing the rate of return by borrowing funds. But leverage also increases risk.

17.4.2 Why do firms generally rely more on long-term funds than short-term funds? Although short-term funds are generally less expensive than long-term funds, short-term funds expose the firm to additional risks. The cost of short-term funds can vary greatly from year to year. In addition, short-term funds can sometimes be difficult to obtain.

17.4.3 What is an important factor in deciding on a firm's dividend policy? The main factor in deciding on a firm's dividend policy is its investment opportunities. Firms with

more profitable investment opportunities often pay less in dividends than firms that have fewer such opportunities.

LO 17.5 Identify sources of short-term financing for businesses.

The three major short-term funding options are trade credit, short-term loans from banks and other financial institutions, and commercial paper. Trade credit is extended by suppliers when a firm receives goods or services and agrees to pay for them at a later date. Trade credit is relatively easy to obtain and costs nothing unless a supplier offers a cash discount. Loans from commercial banks are a significant source of short-term financing and are often used to finance accounts receivable and inventory. Loans can be either unsecured or secured. In unsecured loans, no assets are pledged as collateral, or security. In secured loans, accounts receivable or inventory are pledged as collateral. Commercial paper is a short-term IOU sold by a company. Large amounts of money can be raised through the sale of commercial paper, usually at interest rates lower than those charged by banks. Access to the commercial paper market is limited to large, financially strong corporations.

 ASSESSMENT CHECK ANSWERS

17.5.1 What are the three sources of short-term funding? The three sources of short-term funding are trade credit, short-term loans from banks and other financial institutions, and commercial paper.

17.5.2 Explain trade credit. Trade credit is extended by suppliers when a buyer agrees to pay for goods and services at a later date. Trade credit is relatively easy to obtain and costs nothing unless a cash discount is offered.

17.5.3 Why is commercial paper an attractive short-term financing option? Commercial paper is an attractive financing option because large amounts of money can be raised at interest rates that are usually lower than the interest rates charged by banks.

LO 17.6 Discuss long-term financing options.

Long-term financing is repaid over many years. Organizations acquire long-term financing from three sources: long-term loans from financial institutions, bonds sold to investors, and equity financing. Public sales of securities, such as shares and bonds, are a major source of funds for corporations. These securities can generally be traded in secondary markets. Public sales can vary quite a bit from year to year depending on the conditions in the financial markets. Private placements are securities—new share or bond issues—sold to a small number of institutional investors. Most private placements involve debt securities. Venture capitalists are an important source of long-term financing for new companies. If the business succeeds, venture capitalists can earn large profits. Private equity funds are investment companies that raise funds from wealthy individuals and institutional investors. They then invest the funds in both public and private companies. Unlike venture capitalists, private equity funds invest in all types of businesses. Sovereign wealth funds are investment companies owned by governments.

 ASSESSMENT CHECK ANSWERS

17.6.1 What is the most common type of security sold privately? Corporate debt securities are the most common type of security sold privately.

17.6.2 Explain venture capital. Venture capitalists are important sources of funding, especially for new companies. Venture capitalists invest in new companies by taking an ownership position. If the business succeeds, venture capitalists can earn large profits.

17.6.3 What is a sovereign wealth fund? A sovereign wealth fund is a government-owned investment company. These companies invest in a variety of financial and real assets, such as real estate. Although most investments are based on the best risk–return tradeoff, investment decisions are also influenced by political, social, and strategic considerations.

LO 17.7 Describe mergers, acquisitions, buyouts, and divestitures.

A merger is a transaction where two or more firms combine into one company. An acquisition is a transaction where one company buys another. A merger includes a buyer and a seller (called the *target*). The buyer offers cash, securities, or a combination of the two in return for the target's shares. Mergers and acquisitions should be evaluated the same way any large investment is evaluated—by comparing the costs with the benefits. *Synergy* is the term used to describe the benefits a merger or acquisition is expected to produce. A leveraged buyout (LBO) is a transaction where shares are purchased from public shareholders and the company reverts to private status. LBOs are usually financed with large amounts of borrowed funds. Private equity companies are often major financers of LBOs. Divestitures are the opposite of mergers—companies sell their assets such as subsidiaries, product lines, or production facilities. A selloff is a divestiture where assets are sold to another firm. In a spinoff, a new firm is created from the assets divested. Shareholders of the divesting firm become shareholders of the new firm.

 ASSESSMENT CHECK ANSWERS

17.7.1 Define *synergy*. *Synergy* is the term used to describe the benefits produced by a merger or acquisition. It refers to the idea that the combined firm is worth more than the buyer firm and the target firm are worth individually.

17.7.2 What is an LBO? An LBO—a leveraged buyout—is where public shareholders are bought out and the firm reverts to private status. LBOs are usually financed with large amounts of borrowed money.

17.7.3 What are the two types of divestitures? The two types of divestitures are selloffs and spinoffs. In a selloff, assets are sold by one firm to another firm. In a spinoff, a new firm is created from the assets divested. Shareholders of the divesting firm become shareholders of the new firm.

BUSINESS TERMS YOU NEED TO KNOW

capital structure 479	financial managers 472	leveraged buyouts (LBOs) 488	venture capitalists 486
divestiture 489	financial plan 474	risk–return tradeoff 474	
finance 472	leverage 479	tender offer 488	

REVIEW QUESTIONS

1. Explain the risk–return tradeoff and give two examples.

2. Describe the financial planning process. How does asset intensity affect a financial plan?

3. What are the main considerations when deciding on an overall credit policy? How do the actions of competitors affect a firm's credit policy?

4. Why do exchange rates pose a challenge for financial managers at companies that operate internationally?

5. Discuss the idea of leverage. Use a numerical example to illustrate the effect of leverage.

6. What are the advantages and disadvantages of debt financing and equity financing?

7. Compare and contrast the three sources of short-term financing.

8. Define *venture capitalist*, *private equity fund*, *sovereign wealth fund*, and *hedge fund*. Which of the four invests the most money in startup companies?

9. Briefly describe the mechanics of a merger or acquisition.

10. Why do firms divest assets?

PROJECTS AND TEAMWORK APPLICATIONS

1. Assume you would like to start a business. Create a rough financial plan that addresses the three financial planning questions listed in the text.

2. Working with a partner, assume that a firm needs $10 million in additional long-term capital. It currently has no debt and $40 million in equity. The firm's options are issuing a 10-year bond (with an interest rate of 7 percent) or selling $10 million in new equity. You expect next year's earnings will be $5 million before interest and taxes. (The firm's tax rate is 35 percent.) Prepare a memo outlining the advantages and disadvantages of debt financing and equity financing. Using the numbers provided, prepare a numerical illustration of leverage similar to Figure 17.2.

3. Your new small business has grown, but it now needs a large amount of capital. A venture capital firm has agreed to provide the money you need. In return, the venture capital firm will own 75 percent of the business, and you will be replaced as CEO by someone chosen by the venture capitalist. You will be considered the founder of the company and the chairperson of the board. Are you willing to take the money in return for losing control over your business? Why or why not?

4. Working in a small team, select three publicly traded companies. Visit each firm's website. Find the part of the website that includes information for investors. Review each firm's dividend policy. Does the company pay dividends? If so, when did it begin paying dividends? Have dividends increased each year, or have they had ups and downs from year to year? Is the company currently repurchasing shares? Has it repurchased shares in the past? Prepare a report to summarize your findings.

5. As noted in the chapter, one of the most unfortunate mergers in corporate history involved Time Warner and America Online. Research this merger. Why did analysts expect it to be successful? Why did it fail? What has happened to AOL since then? What are some examples of failed Canadian mergers?

WEB ASSIGNMENTS

1. **Jobs in financial management.** Visit the website listed below to explore careers in finance. How many people currently work as financial managers? What is the projected increase in employment over the next 10 to 20 years? What is the average level of compensation? www.servicecanada.gc.ca/eng/qc/job_futures/statistics/0111.shtml

2. **Capital structure.** Go to the website listed below to access recent financial statements for Canadian Tire. Access the most recent annual report and locate the balance sheet. What is the firm's current capital structure (the relationship between debt and equity)? Has it changed over the past five years? Why would Canadian Tire choose this capital structure? http://corp.canadiantire.ca/EN/Investors/FinancialReports/Pages/AnnualReports.aspx

3. **Mergers and acquisitions.** Using a news source such as the CBC (www.cbc.ca) or The Globe and Mail (www.theglobeandmail.com), search for an announcement of a recent merger or acquisition. An example would be Whitecap Resources Inc.'s recent acquisition of Western Canadian oil and gas properties from Imperial Oil Ltd. (a link is shown below). Print out the articles and bring them to class.

   www.theglobeandmail.com/report-on-business/industry-news/energy-and-resources/imperial-oil-sells-some-western-canada-assets-to-whitecap-for-855-million/article17515518/

Note: Internet Web addresses change frequently. If you don't find the exact sites listed, you may need to access the organization's home page and search from there or use a search engine such as Bing or Google.

PART 6: CASE STUDY Beau's All Natural Brewing Company

Financing Growth

Finances are at the heart of understanding a business and the decisions that managers make to start and then grow their business. Entrepreneurs need to calculate a starting budget that will allocate sufficient spending of funds for the company to establish itself. Inadequate financing to get the business started properly is a primary reason why many new businesses fail to launch. Once operational, the budget should then reflect the generation of cash flow that will eventually pay for all operating costs and provide profits to finance expansion of the business.

Steve and Tim Beauchesne began Beau's All Natural Brewing Company with a loan and Tim's capital totalling $300,000. The loan was tied to the leather finishing plant and land he owned—the primary assets guaranteeing repayment. Until Beau's showed sufficient positive cash flow from actual operations, the amount of bank debt would be limited to the value of the collateral they had—the plant. Any other sources of debt financing could come from those willing to lend without any guarantees of security, such as good friends and family.

On the equity side, Steve and Tim wanted to keep ownership of the company to themselves and the decision-making control that comes with 100 percent ownership. Rather than accept new investors willing to provide cash in exchange for shares in the now well-established brewery, Steve and Tim are maintaining their ability to manage the firm the way they have from the start—guided by the principles discussed in Part 3 of this case study.

In their first year of operation Beau's produced and sold 30,000 litres of beer; eight years later the company is selling 3.5 million litres—a 100 times increase. Steve believes that on average Beau's operating numbers are competitive with the industry. He estimates that Beau's net profit runs about 7 to 10 percent of sales. Production costs are the major expense, running between 40 to 50 percent of sales. Marketing, distribution, and selling expenses each run about 12 percent.

Growth in sales has averaged 40 to 50 percent in each of the last few years, and Beau's has used the profits generated to expand plant facilities to scale up beer production as the company prepares for increasing sales in the Quebec and Northeastern U.S. markets. Financing the costs of expanding into these new markets as well as the growth in the Ontario market has come from internally generated profits and more bank debt. As Steve explains,

It's pretty simple and keeps us under control as well. Each year we go to our bank with our financial statements, show them our profits for the past year, and they lend us about twice whatever those profits are. We can plan our growth based on what we know our profits are going to be. So those new tanks we installed were bought with some borrowed money along with some of our internally generated profits. And next year the sales from those additional tanks will help us finance future expansion. But to do that we have to hire new salespeople and cover their expenses as they introduce our beer to retail customers. That costs! There's lots of people who haven't discovered our beer yet and we are working our way to them as fast as we can.

Questions for Critical Thinking

1. Should Beau's consider growing faster by taking in equity funding from investors?

2. How else could Beau's finance growth without giving up equity?

6 LAUNCHING YOUR . . .

ACCOUNTING OR FINANCE CAREER

Part 6, "Managing Financial Resources," describes the finance function in organizations. Finance deals with planning, obtaining, and managing an organization's funds to accomplish its objectives in the most effective way possible. In Chapter 15, you read about accounting firms and the variety of large and small public and private organizations that generate and use accounting data. In Chapter 16 we discussed the financial system, including the various types of securities, financial markets and institutions, the Bank of Canada, financial regulators, and global financial markets. In Chapter 17 we examined the role that financial managers play in an organization; financial planning; short-term and long-term financing options; and mergers, acquisitions, buyouts, and divestitures. In both Chapters 16 and 17 we described the finance functions of a variety of businesses, governments, and not-for-profit organizations. As Part 6 illustrates, finance is a diverse profession and includes many different occupations. According to Human Resources and Skills Development Canada (which is now known as Employment and Social Development Canada), over the next decade most finance-related occupations are expected to experience slightly better-than-average employment growth. And employment in several finance occupations is expected to grow much faster than average. Employment in the financial investment industry should be strong for two reasons: the globalization of securities markets and the large number of baby boomers in their peak earning years who have funds to invest.[1]

In most business schools, accounting and finance are popular majors among undergraduates. Many accounting graduates start their careers working for a public accounting firm. At first, their job duties may include auditing or tax services, usually working with more senior accountants. As their careers progress, accounting graduates may take on more supervisory responsibilities. Some may move from public accounting firms to take accounting positions at other organizations. Many accounting graduates spend their entire careers in these fields, while others move into other areas. Let's look briefly at some of the specific jobs you might find after earning a degree in accounting.

Public accountants perform a broad range of accounting, auditing, tax, and consulting services for their clients, which include businesses, governments, not-for-profit organizations, and individuals. Auditing is one of the most important services offered by public accountants, and many accounting graduates begin their careers in this field. Auditors examine a client's financial statements and accounting policies to make sure they conform to all applicable standards and regulations. Public accountants either own their own businesses or work for public accounting firms. Many public accountants are Chartered Professional Accountants (CPAs). To become a CPA, you must meet educational and experience requirements and pass a number of examinations.

Many accountants work for an organization other than a public accounting firm. They record and analyze financial information and financial statements for their organizations. Management accountants are also involved in budgeting, tax preparation, cost management, and asset management. Internal auditors verify the accuracy of their organization's internal controls and check for irregularities, waste, and fraud.

Combining finance with accounting is a common choice for a double major. Individuals who have degrees in finance also enjoy relatively high starting salaries. A recent survey found that the average starting salary for a person with an undergraduate degree in finance was nearly $40,000 per year and could be as high as $94,391 per year.[2]

All organizations need to obtain and manage funds. They employ finance professionals to handle these tasks. Financial institutions and other financial services firms employ a large percentage of all finance graduates. These businesses provide important finance-related services to businesses, governments, and not-for-profit organizations. Some graduates with finance degrees take jobs with financial services firms such as Royal Bank Financial Group and Scotia Capital. Others begin their careers working in the finance departments of businesses in other industries, such as Canadian Tire, Bell Canada, governments, or not-for-profit organizations. You may begin your career by evaluating commercial loan applications for a bank, analyzing capital investments for a business, or helping a not-for-profit organization decide how to invest its endowed funds. Finance professionals often work as members of a team that advises top management. Some individuals spend their entire careers working in finance-related occupations; others use their finance experience to move into other areas of the firm. The chief financial officer—the most senior finance executive—holds one of the most important jobs in any organization. Today, an increasing number of CEOs began their careers in finance.

Finance is a diverse, exciting profession. Here are a few of the specific occupations you might find after earning a degree in finance.

Financial managers prepare financial reports, direct investment activities, raise funds, and carry out cash management strategies. Computer technology has reduced the time needed to produce financial reports. Many financial managers spend less time preparing reports and more time analyzing financial data. All organizations employ financial managers. About 30 percent of all financial managers work for financial services firms such as commercial banks and insurance companies.[3] Specific responsibilities vary depending on the job title. For example, credit managers supervise the firm's issuing of credit, establish credit standards, and monitor the collection of accounts receivable. Cash managers control the flow of cash receipts and disbursements to meet the needs of the organization.

Most *loan officers* work for commercial banks and other financial institutions. They find potential clients and help them apply for loans. Loan officers usually specialize in commercial, consumer, or mortgage loans. Loan officers often act in a sales role by contacting individuals and organizations about their need for funds and trying to persuade them to borrow the funds from the loan officer's institution. As a result, loan officers often need marketing skills in addition to their finance skills.

Security analysts generally work for financial services firms such as Sunlife Financial or Manulife Financial. Security analysts review economic data, financial statements, and other information to predict the outcome for securities such as common shares and bonds. They recommend investment strategies to individual investors and institutional investors. Many senior security analysts hold a chartered financial analyst (CFA) designation. Obtaining a CFA requires a specific educational background, several years of related experience, and a passing grade on a thorough, three-stage examination.

Portfolio managers manage money for an individual client or an institutional client. Many portfolio managers work for pension funds or mutual funds; they make investment decisions to benefit the funds' beneficiaries. Portfolio managers generally have extensive experience as financial managers or security analysts, and many are CFAs.

Personal financial planners help individuals make decisions related to insurance, investments, and retirement planning. Personal financial planners meet with their clients, assess their needs and goals, and make recommendations. Approximately 30 percent of personal financial planners are self-employed. Many hold certified financial planner (CFP) designations. Obtaining a CFP requires a specific educational background, related experience, and passing a thorough examination.

CAREER ASSESSMENT EXERCISES IN ACCOUNTING AND FINANCE

1. CPA Canada is a professional organization for the public accounting profession. Visit the organization's website (www.cpacanada.ca). Review the information on CPA Canada standards and examinations. Write a brief summary on what you learned about how to become a CPA.

2. Suppose you are interested in a career as a security analyst. You've heard that the CFA is an important designation and can help enhance your career. Visit the CFA's website (www.cfainstitute.org) to learn more about the designation. What are the requirements to obtain a CFA designation? What are the professional benefits of having a CFA designation?

3. Arrange for an interview with a commercial loan officer at a local bank. Ask the loan officer about his or her educational background, what a typical day is like, and what the loan officer likes and does not like about the job.

4. TD Waterhouse offers financial planning services to individuals and organizations. Visit the firm's careers website (www.td.com/careers). Review the material and write a brief summary of what you learned about being a personal financial planner. Are you interested in a career as a financial planner? Why or why not?

APPENDIX A
ADDITIONAL CASES

Part 1 Business in a Global Environment

Case Study 1 Vancity: On Top of Its Game

What makes a great organization? Well, if winning multiple national awards is a positive signal, Vancity Credit Union is definitely on the right path! Vancity was on Mediacorp Canada Inc.'s list of Canada's Top 100 Employers for 2013, Canada's top family-friendly employers, and British Columbia's top employers for 2013, and it was one of Canada's Top 30 Greenest Employers. In 2012, Vancity was also ranked number two on the Corporate Knights Best 50 Corporate Citizens in Canada. What does Vancity do right to deserve all this external recognition?

Keeping Employees Happy and Healthy

This Vancouver-based cooperative was founded in 1946; it began with only $22 in total assets, aiming to lend money to those the banks ignored. Today it is Canada's largest credit union, with over 2,565 employees and more than $17.1 billion in assets. As a member-owned credit union, it provides a complete range of financial services to its 492,000 members. Vancity continues to be committed to its original purpose and values: working with people and communities to help them thrive and prosper, all the while operating with integrity, innovation, and responsibility.

Vancity acknowledges that a healthy and committed workforce is the reason it is able to sustain productivity and financial success within a competitive industry. Vancity provides its employees with the opportunity to help set corporate policies and procedures that impact both their work and home life. At work, employees enjoy business casual dress, listening to music while they work, participating on Vancity sports teams, and attending a host of social events.

Vancity has other family-friendly programs as well. For example, the cooperative understands that if an employee has a young child, it may be necessary to build a workday that allows for flexibility. This positive approach recognizes the challenges of balancing work and life commitments and empowers employees to create the right environment to thrive at both.

The organization offers several alternative work options, including telecommuting, flexible hours, shortened workweeks (fewer hours with less pay), and compressed workweeks. Employees are given full pay for working 35 hours a week.

Over the years and primarily driven by the employees' desire for personal development, Vancity has initiated a number of programs to help employees adopt a plan for a healthier life. Programs have included opportunities to work with employee assistance program (EAP) providers for developing personal plans for health and wellness.

Vancity offers a competitive pay and benefits program that includes dental and life insurance, three to six weeks of annual vacation, maternity and paternity leave top-ups, and care days that can be used for personal and family illness or injury. Other rewards include tuition reimbursement, retirement planning, and reduced rates on personal financial services such as mortgages and loans. Employees also have a chance to attend Vancity's cooperative studies program in Italy, where co-ops are well established.

Vancity has a young corporate culture—the average age of its employees is 40, and 94 percent of its new recruits are under 40. Even its CEO, Tamara Vrooman, was only 39 when she took the helm in 2007. The cooperative once threw a party for 2,200 employees and guests, and hip-hop dancers and a slam poet entertained the crowd until 3 a.m. Young employees organized the event for their peers. "We're interested in creating energy, we're interested in having people connect," Vrooman says. "And young people tell us that's an important part of the entire employee experience that they come to Vancity to enjoy."

There are some challenges in human resources, too. Every year the cooperative surveys employees, and it did not meet its targets for employee engagement for three years in a row, which it blamed partly on workforce and budgetary reductions. The employee engagement target is set at 75 percent, but in those years it did not reach beyond 64 percent. "The Executive Leadership Team's compensation is tied to achieving this significant stretch target, reflecting how important it is we improve employee engagement and their pivotal role and responsibility in making this happen," Vancity said in its annual accountability report to members.

In response to the first disappointing employee survey, the cooperative held focus groups with 120 employees, who said they were concerned, among other things, that individual goals were not aligned with those of the organization; that work processes, tools, and resources were not streamlined to improve efficiency; and that managers lacked support to manage performance effectively. To reengage employees, Vrooman said Vancity would increase investment in training and development, renew the organization's IT infrastructure, and provide employees with growth opportunities by focusing on new areas. Among other things, the organization examined its process for conducting employee performance reviews; as a result, it clarified the process, told managers to focus on ongoing employee coaching, and provided employees with online training and support materials to help them improve in areas identified during their performance reviews. It then planned on examining its monetary and nonmonetary compensation strategies.

Keeping the Organization Healthy

Vancity uses a triple bottom line business model; it is driven to achieve financial success but also focuses on environmental and social sustainability. Vancity is in a healthy financial position with rising membership because it takes an innovative approach in serving the financial needs of its members. It was the first Canadian financial institution to offer mortgages to women, the first to use traditional media to market directly to the gay and lesbian community, the first North American credit union to receive an R1 rating from the Dominion Bond Rating Service, and the first financial institution to offer its own socially responsible mutual fund.

Vancity's vision to achieve positive social change has succeeded through a number of programs, such as one called Shared Success. Through this program, Vancity gives back each year a significant portion of net profits (generally 30 percent) to members and to communities. Since the program was introduced, a total of $221 million has been shared with members and redistributed as community grants and other funding initiatives. Among the grant recipients was Just Beginnings Flowers, a not-for-profit florist that provides jobs to people with barriers to employment, which was selected to provide victory ceremony bouquets for the 2010 Winter Olympics in Vancouver. Other successful Vancity programs include its Pigeon Park Savings program, which provides banking services to the poor, and Each One, Teach One, which trains selected employees to teach basic financial literacy skills to newcomers to Canada.

A focus on giving back to the community makes decision making in a credit union more challenging, since maximizing shareholder profit is not the only goal. Vancity managers take leadership training in values-based decision making. An employee survey found that 95 percent said they feel great about the organization's corporate social responsibility approach.

"What makes a credit union is that we are community-based," Vrooman says. "We make decisions locally, we get to know our members, we live and work where they live and work, and when you start to expand beyond that we need to make sure that we keep the key thing that differentiates us from a large bank, which is the local decision-making. That's the biggest challenge: how to keep the credit union niche while you grow."

Starting in 1995, before doing so was popular, Vancity focused on its own environmental performance. Vancity achieved its target of being the first carbon-neutral North American–based financial institution. Through its climate change strategy, Vancity has supported innovative partnerships involving public transportation and green building projects. It also invests in organizations doing climate change work.

The organization is also a strong supporter of women. For example, among its recent board of directors, five of nine directors, including the chair, were women.

Banking on the unbankable is one of the cornerstones of the Vancity story, and today this financial institution continues to look for ways to improve. Vrooman, who was given an accolade herself by being named by the *Vancouver Sun* as one of British Columbia's most influential women in business, says, "We're owned by our members, who have a say in the way our organization is run and a vested interest in how we do things, and we're accountable to them to deliver positive financial, social and environmental returns." And deliver they do—that and win awards!

Questions for Critical Thinking

1. What is Vancity's competitive advantage over other types of financial institutions?

2. Who are Vancity's stakeholders and what value does the organization create for them?

3. Vancity's financial position allows it to take innovative approaches to meeting the needs of its members. If you were a competitor, would you try to emulate Vancity's innovative approach? Why or why not?

4. What new initiatives is Vancity Credit Union undertaking right now for its employees and members?

Sources: Vancity website, www.vancity.com; "Vancity Recognized as One of Canada's Top 100 Employers," news release, October 15, 2010; Nick Rockel, "Luring Young Talent Sets Stage for the Future," *The Globe and Mail*, June 1, 2010; *Vancity 2008–2009 Accountability Report*; Brian Morton, "Vancity's Net Income Near Record Level," *Vancouver Sun*, July 12, 2010, p. B6; Frances Bula, "The Queen of Vancity," *News and Features Vancouver*, September 1, 2009; Regan Ray, "Q&A: Vancity's Tamara Vrooman," *Canadian Business*, November 19, 2007; "B.C.'s Top 100 Influential Women," *Vancouver Sun*, October 29, 2010; "Vancity Believes We Can All Be Wealthy; New Accountability Report from One of Canada's Top Three Corporate Citizens," news release, July 8, 2010; Jobs at Vancouver City Savings Credit Union, eluta.ca; Canada's Top 100 Employers, "BC's Top Employers 2013" and "Canada's Greenest Employers 2013", www.canadastop100.com; Ingenious Awards 2013 website, https://ingeniousawards.ca/panel; The 2012 Best 50 Corporate Citizens of Canada website, www.corporateknights.com/node/1559.

Case Study 2 Patagonia: Leading a Green Revolution

How has Patagonia managed to stay both green and profitable at a time when the economy is tough, consumers are tight for cash, and "doing the profitable thing" is not necessarily doing the right thing? Are Patagonia's business practices good for outdoor enthusiasts, good for the environment, or just good for Patagonia?

Twelve hundred Walmart buyers, a group legendary for their tough-as-nails negotiating tactics, sit in rapt attention in the company's Bentonville, Arkansas, headquarters. They're listening to a small man in a mustard-yellow corduroy sportcoat lecture them on the environmental impact of Walmart's purchasing choices. He's not criticizing the company, per se—*he's criticizing them*. Yet when he finishes speaking, the buyers leap to their feet and applaud enthusiastically.

Such is the authenticity of Yvon Chouinard. Since founding Patagonia in 1972, he's built it into one of the most successful outdoor clothing companies, and one that is steadfastly committed to environmental sustainability.

It's hard to discuss Patagonia without constantly referencing Chouinard, because for all practical purposes the two are one. Where Chouinard ends, Patagonia begins. Chouinard breathes life into the company, espousing the outdoorsy athleticism of Patagonia's customers. In turn, Patagonia's business practices reflect Chouinard's insistence on minimizing environmental impact, even at the expense of the bottom line.

Taking Risks to Succeed

For decades Patagonia has been at the forefront of a cozy niche: high-quality, performance-oriented outdoor clothes and gear sold at top price points. Derided as *Pradagonia* or *Patagucci* by critics, the brand is aligned with top-shelf labels like North Face and Royal Robbins. Patagonia clothes are designed for fly fishermen, rock climbers, and surfers. They are durable, comfortable, and sustainably produced. And they are not cheap.

It seems counterintuitive—almost dangerous—to market a $400 raincoat in a tough economy. But the first thing you learn about Yvon Chouinard is that he's a risk taker. The second thing you learn is that he's usually right.

"Corporations are real weenies," he says. "They are scared to death of everything. My company exists, basically, to take those risks and prove that it's a good business."

And it is a good business. With estimated 2011 revenues of $400 million, up from $333 million the previous year, Patagonia succeeds by staying true to Chouinard's vision. "They've become the Rolls-Royce of their product category," says Marshal Cohen, chief industry analyst with market research firm NPD Group. "When people were stepping back, and the industry became copycat, Chouinard didn't sell out, lower prices, and dilute the brand. Sometimes, the less you do, the more provocative and true of a leader you are."

Chouinard concurs. "I think the key to surviving a conservative economy is quality," he says. "The number one reason is that in a recession, consumers stop being silly. Instead of buying fashion, they'll pay more for a multifunctional product that will last a long time."

Ideal Corporate Behaviour

Chouinard is not shy about espousing the environmentalist ideals intertwined with Patagonia's business model. "It's good business to make a great product, and do it with the least amount of damage to the planet," he says. "If Patagonia wasn't profitable or successful, we'd be an environmental organization."

In many ways, Patagonia is an environmental organization. The company publishes online a library of working documents, *The Footprint Chronicles*, that guides employees in making sustainable decisions in even the most mundane office scenarios. Its mission statement: "Build the best product, cause no unnecessary harm, use business to inspire and implement solutions to the environmental crisis." Patagonia revamped *Footprints* in 2012 and included a world map that shows where all of Patagonia's products are made, profiles of the social and environmental practices of key suppliers and mills, and profiles of key independent partners.

Patagonia's solutions extend well beyond the lip service typically given by profitable corporations. The company itself holds an annual environmental campaign, a recent one being *Our Common Waters*.

Chouinard has co-founded a number of external environmental organizations, including 1% For the Planet, which secures pledges from companies to donate 1 percent of annual sales to a worldwide network of nearly 2,400 environmental causes. To date, almost 1,480 companies participate, raising more than $50 million since 2002.

The name comes from Patagonia's 30-year practice of contributing 10 percent of pre-tax profits or 1 percent of sales—whichever is *greater*—to environmental groups each year. Whatever you do, don't call it a handout. "It's not a charity," Chouinard flatly states. "It's a cost of doing business. We use it to support civil democracy."

Another core value at Patagonia is providing opportunities for motivated volunteers to devote themselves to sustainable causes. Employees can leave their jobs for up to two months to volunteer full time for the environmental cause of their choice, while continuing to receive full pay and benefits from Patagonia. And every 18 months, the company hosts the Tools for Grassroots Activists Conference, where it invites a handful of participants to engage in leadership training, much of it derived from the advocacy experiences of Patagonia management. Patagonia of Japan team members also contributed to cleanup efforts following the devastating March 2011 earthquake and subsequent tsunami.

Growing Green

Patagonia has demonstrated a remarkable ability to thrive despite the unplanned obsolescence of several of its key products. What makes this even more notable is that Chouinard is often the force driving his own bestsellers out of the marketplace.

Chouinard Equipment, Ltd., Patagonia's precursor, was a successful vendor in the nascent rock climbing community. Chouinard himself was well known on the circuit, having made the first successful climbs of several previously unconquered Californian peaks. For more than a decade Chouinard had been hand forging his own steel pitons (pegs driven into rock or ice to support climbers) that were far more durable than the soft iron pitons coming from Europe. Because his pitons could be used again and again, climbing was suddenly more affordable and less of a fringe activity.

But during a 1970 ascent of El Capitan in California, Chouinard saw that the very invention that brought his company success was also irreparably damaging the wilderness he so loved. Though Chouinard Equipment's pitons brought more climbers into the sport, the climbers tended to follow the same routes. And the constant hammering and removal of steel pitons was scarring the delicate rock face of these peaks.

Ignoring the fact that pitons were a mainstay of their success, Chouinard and partner Tom Frost decided to phase themselves out of the piton business. Two years later, the company coupled a new product—aluminum chocks that could be inserted or removed by hand—with a 14-page essay in their catalogue on the virtues of *clean climbing*. A few months later, demand for pitons had withered and orders for chocks outstripped supplies.

Fast forward nearly 20 years. Chouinard Equipment spinoff Patagonia is a booming manufacturer of outdoor clothing. And though it had seen success with products woven with synthetic threads, the majority of its items were still spun with natural fibres like cotton and wool. Patagonia commissioned an external audit of the environmental impact of its four major fibres, anticipating bad news about petroleum-derived nylon and polyester.

Instead, the company was shocked to learn that the production of cotton, a mainstay of the American textile market for hundreds of years, had a more negative impact on the environment than any of its other fibres. The evidence was clear: destructive soil and water pollution, unproven but apparent health consequences for fieldworkers, and the astounding statistic that 25 percent of all toxic pesticides used in agriculture are spent in the cultivation of cotton.

To Chouinard and Patagonia, the appropriate response was equally clear: Source organic fibres for all 66 of their cotton clothing products. They gave themselves until 1996 to complete the transition, which was a manageable lead time of 18 months. But due to the advanced nature of fashion production, they had only four months to lock in fabric suppliers. Worse, at the time there wasn't enough organic cotton being commercially produced to fill their anticipated fabric needs.

Taking a page from their own teaching on grassroots advocacy, Patagonia representatives went directly to organic cotton farmers, ginners, and spinners, seeking pledges from them to increase production, dust off dormant processing equipment, and do whatever it would take to line up enough raw materials to fulfill the company's promise to its customers and the environment.

Not surprisingly, Patagonia met its goal, and every cotton garment made since 1996 has been spun from organic cotton.

Sustaining Momentum

At 74, Chouinard can't helm Patagonia forever. But that's not to say he isn't continuing to find better ways for Patagonia to do business.

"I think entrepreneurs are like juvenile delinquents who say, 'This sucks. I'll do it my own way,'" he says. "I'm an innovator because I see things and think I can make it better. So I try it. That's what entrepreneurs do."

Patagonia's current major project is its Common Threads initiative. To demonstrate that it's possible to minimize the number of Patagonia clothes that wind up in landfills, the company is committing to making clothes built to last, fixing wear-and-tear items for consumers that can be repaired, and collecting and recycling worn-out fashions as efficiently and responsibly as possible.

"It'll be in the front of the catalog—our promise that none of our stuff ever ends up in a land-fill," Chouinard says. "We'll make sure of it with a liberal repair policy and by accepting old clothing for recycling. People will talk about it, and we'll gain business like crazy."

It's doubtful that Chouinard will ever stop thinking about how Patagonia can responsibly innovate and improve. "Right now, we're trying to convince zipper companies to make teeth out of polyester or nylon synths, which can be recycled infinitely," he says. "Then we can take a jacket and melt the whole thing down back to its original polymer to make more jackets."

Despite his boundless enthusiasm for all things green, Chouinard admits that no process is truly sustainable. "I avoid using that word as much as I can," he says. He pauses for a moment and adds: "I keep at it, because it's the right thing to do."

Questions for Critical Thinking

1. Patagonia has a history of putting sustainability ahead of profits. Based on what you learned about Patagonia's ideals, how do you think the company determines what possible ventures will be both business practical and environmentally friendly?

2. What could Patagonia do today to make sure that Yvon Chouinard's ideals become a permanent part of the company's culture after he leaves the company?

3. It seems Yvon Chouinard is never satisfied. He comes to you and asks for a proposal on a new—"forward looking"— sustainability agenda for the firm. What would you include in this agenda to stretch the firm beyond what it is already doing, and why?

4. Business decisions can be a compromise between ethics and profitability. Could ethics lose out to greed even in a company with the idealism of Patagonia? See if you can find a decision that appeared to or could put profits ahead of the company's publicly stated environmental goals. Explain why you think that company made this decision and the competing factors you believe were involved.

Sources: Patagonia website, www.patagonia.com, "The Footprint Chronicles," "Environmentalism: Our Common Waters," "Environmental Internships," "Tools for Grassroots Activists Conference," and "Our History," "Introducing the Common Threads Initiative"; Monte Burke, "Wal-Mart, Patagonia Team to Green Business," *Forbes*, May 6, 2010; Kent Garber, "Yvon Chouinard: Patagonia Founder Fights for the Environment," *U.S. News*, October 22, 2009; Diana Random, "Finding Success by Putting Company Culture First," *Entrepreneur*, April 19, 2011; Jennifer Wang, "Patagonia, from the Ground up," *Entrepreneur*, May 11, 2010; 1% For the Planet, www.onepercentfortheplanet.org/en; Kristall Lutz, "What Makes Patagonia 'The Coolest Company on the Planet': Insights from Founder Yvon Chouinard," Opportunity Green, January 27, 2011; Takayuki Tsujii, "A Look Back: Following the Devastation of Tohoku Region Pacific Coast Earthquake," The Cleanest Line, March 11, 2012.

Case Study 3 Canarm Ltd.: Creating Innovation within by Always Looking Outward

Where can you find a wholesaler; an agricultural equipment manufacturer; and a heating, ventilation, and air conditioner manufacturer all in one company? Visit Canarm Ltd., located in Brockville, Ontario.

From humble beginnings, Canarm Ltd. developed into a global marketer and manufacturer of lighting, air moving, and related products, supplying residential, agricultural, and industrial markets. Its customers include wholesalers, retailers, and distributors. The privately owned and operated company has five satellite manufacturing plants in Ontario and one in Illinois, as well as a distribution centre in Montreal. Canarm has over 300 full-time employees.

History

The company started in 1934 as Danor Manufacturing Co. Ltd., a small sheet metal shop in Gorrie, Ontario, making agricultural metal products such as hog troughs and turkey feeders. In 1963, the operation moved to a new 275-square-metre (3,000-square-foot) factory in Brockville, Ontario, the site of the company's current corporate offices.

In the late 1950s and early 1960s, instead of running loose in the fields, pigs and chickens were confined to large barns. This created a need for farmers to remove gases, odours, and heat from the barns, which created an opportunity for Danor to add barn exhaust fans to its product line.

During one of its down cycles, Danor decided to diversify its fan market to include commercial and industrial customers. During the process of trying to break into this new market, a supplier suggested the company consider acquiring a long-established Montreal business whose electrical products ranged from fans and heaters to compact kitchens and hose dryers. A deal was struck, and shortly after the Montreal and Brockville facilities were combined. Truckloads of machinery were transferred from Montreal to Brockville, with several product lines discontinued so everything could squeeze into one location.

In the 1970s, Danor's fan business branched out into the residential market and saw success for several reasons. First, energy conservation and efficiency became a high priority, and many customers asked for slow-moving ceiling fans to push the hot air gathered at the ceiling back to floor level. The company found manufacturers in Hong Kong and started importing industrial ceiling fans for a growing market throughout the 1970s. Second, the 1980s saw a spike in prime interest rates to 22 percent, resulting in commercial buyers making far fewer purchases. The Hong Kong manufacturers now had an excess capacity and were desperate to sell product. Third, by replacing metal blades with wooden ones and painting the fan brown, a more decorative look opened up new markets for ceiling fans with restaurants and homeowners.

The need to develop retail chains and ceiling fan and lighting showrooms to sell these products led to the creation of Canarm Ltd. in 1980 through the merger of Danor and Canadian Armature Works. In 1986, Canarm purchased a Montreal ceiling fan company, which became its main distribution centre for imported products and also provided a Quebec sales office and showroom. In 1990, Canarm entered the retail lighting market, and now has one of the most extensive lighting lines in North America.

Always Putting the Customer First Makes the Company Number One!

The secret to Canarm's success has and continues to be its innovative and nimble nature, which is reflected throughout the company—its front-line employees and its leaders, its products, and its strategic approach to growth. At the core of this innovative nature is the company's unrelenting focus on its customers' needs. "Everything starts and ends with the customer here at Canarm," says company president James Cooper. "We always listen to our customers and look for ways to make it easier for them to use our products," says Cooper, who himself recently invented Easy Connect, a mounting bracket that makes changing a light fixture easy. As further evidence of just how nimble Canarm is, within three days of Cooper sharing the idea with his team, they provided him with a prototype.

Cooper has more than 25 years of experience at Canarm and has been in the president's role since 2007. Under his leadership, Canarm was named one of Canada's Best Managed companies in 2012. However, he is quick to deflect credit to the company's employees. "I will start by saying Canarm is extremely fortunate to have the best people," says Cooper. "Our business model is very unique. Our strategy was to build the perfect three-legged stool. Our acquisition trail over the past 10 years was to strengthen the legs of the stool." Canarm's growth strategy, and an investment of $85 million, resulted in a series of mergers and acquisitions since 2003 in fluorescent lighting products, axial fans, blowers, heat exchangers, roof exhausters, and other equipment servicing the HVAC (heating, ventilating, and air conditioning) and livestock confinement equipment markets. This has strengthened Canarm's strategic position and provided additional manufacturing resources to support growing customer demand in North America and abroad for its consumer, commercial, and agricultural markets. Canarm has also built solid business relationships in China over the past 25 years. The company's operations, centred in Zhongshan, China, include 14 manufacturing sites and a showroom. From there, the company manages engineering, quality, and logistics, to ensure consistent quality and on-time delivery. Canarm imports parts and motors from China that arrive in Vancouver and are shipped cross-country by rail for assembly as fans, lights, and heating and ventilation systems at the company's plants in Brockville; Laval, Quebec; and Arthur, Ontario.

In 2013, Canarm increased its efforts to create growth through cross-pollination of its business units, with all three coming together for strategic planning, which has been "vital to our past success and is critical to our future," says Cooper. "Our retail lighting guys have a lot of expertise and capabilities related to lighting. Well, guess what? It gets dark every day in the hog industry or the HVAC industry," says Cooper. "So they're working together on new ideas. It's the people who make it happen. Once they get excited, you just stand back and watch it grow." The company has successfully balanced the need for organizational structure with the ability to remain agile and innovative to adapt to this ever-changing marketplace.

Questions for Critical Thinking

1. What drives the development of new products at Canarm?

2. How important were the mergers with other companies in the evolution of the company?

3. How might Canarm develop yet another category of products either through a merger or cooperation with another firm?

4. Research other business activities and markets that might fit the current organization well.

Sources: Canarm Ltd. Website, www.canarm.com; Inside View–Business Directory, "Canarm" Alexandra Lopez-Pacheco, "Canarm Ltd.: Unique Business Model Glows with Innovation, Nimbleness," *Financial Post*; "James A. Cooper: Will the Company Spend to Expand?" *Financial Post*, March 11, 2013; Leeds-Grenville website, www.leedsgrenville.com/en/invest/profile/majoremployers.asp; Doreen Barnes, "Brockville Chamber Honours Best in Business for 2012," *St. Lawrence EMC News*, November 15, 2012; Nick Gardiner, "Layoffs Averted at Canarm," *Brockville Recorder*, May 31, 2012.

Case Study 4 McCain Foods: Global Fries— Good in Any Language

What do you get when you mix the lowly potato with a passion for growth? The answer is as close as your freezer! McCain Foods Limited, maker of frozen fries, pizzas, appetizers, and entrees, is one of Canada's most famous world brands. The maker of Canada's favourite French fries was started in 1957 in Florenceville, New Brunswick, by brothers Wallace and Harrison McCain, with one plant, 30 employees, and sales of just over $157,000. Over 50 years later, McCain employs over 20,000 people at 57 facilities worldwide generating over $6 billion in sales. Currently producing nearly one-third of the world's French fries for fast-food giants McDonald's and KFC, McCain also supplies frozen products for restaurants and grocery stores in over 166 countries.

How did a homegrown Canadian company become an international success story? Co-owner Harrison McCain had always been interested in emerging markets as a way to grow and expand the business. McCain embraces multicultural experiences and traditions, which translate into new ways of thinking and doing business. Based on this principle, McCain pursued global expansion with passion; he focused on entering new markets through a variety of strategies, including direct selling, joint ventures, acquisitions of existing local businesses, and greenfield developments by building new production facilities. Currently, McCain has 57 manufacturing facilities on six continents, 45 of which are outside Canada.

One major advantage McCain had was the success of its largest client, McDonald's. Harvard's James L. Watson, author of *Golden Arches East: McDonald's in East Asia*, states that the secret to McDonald's global popularity has almost certainly been its French fries, which he writes are "consumed with great gusto by Muslims, Jews, Christians, Buddhists, Hindus, vegetarians, communists, Tories, marathoners, and armchair athletes." McDonald's fries made from McCain products have resonated with local tastes across the globe.

Globalization: Successes and Challenges

Like many in the North American food industry, McCain has struggled over the past few years with a slowed U.S. economy, the high Canadian dollar, the increased cost of fuel, and low-priced competition from Europe. While most of the company's revenue is generated in the United States, Canada, the United Kingdom, and Australia, emerging countries such as China and India are becoming increasingly important to McCain's future profitability. To compensate for decreasing demand in North America, where fast-food suppliers are increasingly under scrutiny for rising obesity rates, McCain is focusing on strengthening its share in foreign markets, especially Asia.

With a population of over 1.3 billion people China is an attractive market, but success was not guaranteed for McCain. China, the world's largest potato producer, often uses potatoes in traditional dishes, but the average annual per capita consumption of fries is less than 100 grams. Compare that with the 13 kilograms that the average Canadian consumes per year and McCain had one tough market to crack. Back in 1988, McCain was hesitant to get into China; the Chinese market, while exciting, wasn't strong enough to warrant setting up operations. McCain's clients KFC and McDonald's were just breaking into China, but neither was doing well enough to warrant McCain's investment in on-the-ground operations.

Yet by 1995 McCain became interested again as China's economy started to emerge. Practising a "beachhead" strategy, McCain began in 1997 by developing a salesforce in Shanghai to start building relationships with fast-food chains such as McDonald's and KFC, as well as hotel chains and grocery stores, to further expand its sales base and introduce a range of products to Chinese consumers. By 2005 McCain had built its own processing plant surrounded by land on which Chinese farmers had been growing potatoes for centuries. McCain employs mostly local workers at its processing plant in Harbin. Facility managers and line workers are largely hired from within the local community and are sent abroad to be educated in the McCain culture. Joining other production facilities on six continents, McCain's investment in China responded to rising demand from its restaurant and retail markets and helped solidify the company's position as a major supplier to the Chinese market.

In September 2012, McCain Foods announced plans to double capacity in its Harbin, China, potato processing plant, and in early 2013 the company announced that it plans to invest an additional $69 million to double capacity of its potato processing plant at Mehsana in Gujarat, India. It appears McCain's strategic bet on global expansion is paying off. Based on 2012 sales, McCain Foods is the thirtieth-largest private company in Canada.

Questions for Critical Thinking

1. Identify the potential risks in the global business environment that McCain Foods would have to be aware of and manage in regard to its international expansion.

2. What challenges might Canadian managers at McCain face when interacting with their Chinese business colleagues?

3. Much of McCain's global success seems to be closely tied to the success and efforts of its clients, McDonald's and KFC. Describe another globalization strategy that McCain Foods might have used to expand into China using only its own brand name.

4. Identify, through research, the specific cultural differences between China, India, and Canada that could impact how McCain Foods carries out operations.

Sources: McCain Foods Limited website, www.mccain.com, "Our Company," "History," "Worldwide," and "McCain Food's Global Corporate Social Responsibility Report Fiscal 2009"; Grant Catton, "Repeat Issuer McCain Gets Funds via HSBC & BNP," *Private Placement Letter, 27*, no. 35 (August 31, 2009): 3; Rebecca Penty, "McCain's Passion for China; Growth: French Fry Producer Is After a Lion's Share of the Asian Country's Fast Food Market," *The Telegraph-Journal*, Saint John, February 6, 2010, C1; Rebecca Penty, "McCain to Cut Potato Sourcing by 20 Per Cent; Food: Low Demand, High Loonie, Leftover Crop and Competition behind Cutbacks," *The Telegraph-Journal*, Saint John, March 16, 2010, B1; John Greenwood, "McCain Hopes Busy Chinese Like Fries; Asian Expansion," *National Post*, February 26, 2008, FP1; Danielle Flavelle, "McCain to Build Fry Plant in China; Wants to Solidify Its Market There. Joins Influx of Foreign Firms," *Toronto Star*, June 24, 2004, D1; Ben Shingler, "McCain's New Plant Has Latest Bells and Whistles; French Fries Company Looking to Strengthen Its Share of Foreign Markets," *The Telegraph-Journal*, Saint John, September 5, 2008, B1; "McCain Foods Limited Announces the Expansion of its Harbin, China Potato Processing Plant," Reuters, September 19, 2012; "McCain Foods to Invest 350 Crore in Gujarat Unit," *The Economic Times*, January 14, 2013; "2012 Rankings of Canada's 350 Biggest Private Companies," *Report on Business Magazine*, June 28, 2012.

Part 2 Starting and Growing Your Business

Case Study 5 Lululemon Athletica: Successful Yogis Want to Make the World a Better Place

Who would base a business on selling $100 yoga pants? Dennis "Chip" Wilson did just that in 1998, when he founded Lululemon Athletica Inc., a Vancouver-based yoga-inspired athletic clothing company. Lululemon sought employees who had an entrepreneurial spirit and are innovative, risk takers, open to learning new things, and comfortable taking responsibility. And it has worked!

Where Ideas Come From

As a student, Wilson was a top swimmer and solid football player, and found that athletic clothing was generally poorly made with lots of bad seams and not enough stretch. He got involved in designing technical athletic fabrics by founding Westbeach, a surf, skate, and snowboard clothing company. Later, discovering yoga in Vancouver, he became an enthusiastic practitioner, leading to the founding of Lululemon Athletica Inc. The trendy brand—a household name in Canada and growing in popularity in the United States and Australia—has been described as one of Canada's most successful companies. Chip's wife, Shannon Wilson, a competitive athlete, is the lead clothing designer and has been a key player in the company's growth.

Building the Business

The first Lululemon store opened in Vancouver in 2000 with the Wilsons teaching yoga courses and selling their own designed yoga pants. Taking the lessons learned as founder of Westbeach, Chip Wilson realized that to maximize his vision for Lululemon, he needed complete control of the brand—from pricing to quality of product. So instead of selling through wholesalers, right from the start Lululemon designed, manufactured (or managed that process through partners), then sold products in its own retail locations. After starting out as a privately owned venture, the company became publicly traded in 2007 to raise funds to fuel its expansion. Within a few short years, the company has grown to over 200 stores, including expanding heavily in the United States, with revenue now over $1 billion.

Entrepreneurs must successfully deal with control and management issues when their firms grow. Initially, Wilson, a University of Calgary economics graduate, ran every facet of the company as it grew rapidly into an international retailer. However, he recognized his own limitations. When Lululemon reached revenue of $100 million in the mid-2000s, Wilson hired people with more expertise than he had in certain areas of managing a company of that size.

Then, in January 2012, he relinquished his role as chief innovation and brand officer, handing the leadership reins to Christine Day, who had been Lululemon's CEO since 2008. Wilson remained as the company's chairman but was no longer involved in the company's daily operations. He said, "I could have my ego around being the CEO or the head guy, but I knew that wouldn't serve me. So really a big part of success is sometimes just getting out of the way once the base has been set." Wilson's decision proved to be a wise one—from March 2009 to May 2012, Lululemon shares rose an incredible 3,637 percent in value! In 2012, Christine Day was named *Report on Business* magazine's CEO of the year. Even during the economic downturn, when other specialty clothing retailers were struggling in the challenging economy, Lululemon's revenues and profits consistently rose. The only struggle for Lululemon was keeping up with the demand for its fashionable and form-fitting athletic wear and accessories. Lululemon truly appeared unstoppable.

It's About More Than Just Money

Lululemon is dedicated to promoting a healthy lifestyle, and the company's culture is described as laid-back, community-oriented, and self-motivational. Lululemon's Manifesto, found on the company website, offers 31 tips on improving health and life, including "If (Lululemon) can produce products to keep people active and stress-free, we believe the world will become a much better place."

In keeping with tip number 12 on the Lululemon Manifesto—"friends are more important than money"—Wilson personally supports many charitable causes. Among these is the charity he and his wife, Shannon, started called Imagine1Day, with a goal of bringing primary education to 80 percent of children in Ethiopia by 2020. In December 2012, Chip and Sharon committed a donation of $8 million to help fund a new design school with a focus on high-tech clothing at Kwantlen Polytechnic University in Vancouver. Lululemon also allots $2,700 per store to give to charities or events in their community, with store employees getting to decide where the money goes.

Chip Wilson's passion to make better-quality and more comfortable athletic clothes enabled him to create a successful and highly profitable company. As a tip on Lululemon's Manifesto states, "If your passion is not there, your brain won't work at it 24/7." Passion has also enabled Wilson to achieve tremendous personal financial success at age 56. With a net worth of $2.9 billion, he was listed number 10 in Canada on the *Forbes* billionaires list. As well, it has allowed the Wilsons to make significant contributions to society through their charitable work.

Handling Setbacks

One of the tips on Lululemon's Manifesto states, "Life is full of setbacks. Success is determined by how you handle setbacks."

In March 2013, Lululemon encountered a major setback. Product quality issues resulted in the recall of about 17 percent of its popular women's black yoga pants, made with its proprietary "luon" fabric, due to unacceptable sheerness. The product's failure to meet Lululemon's technical specifications was not caught during internal quality testing, but was noticed only after the product was stocked in its retail stores. Consumers—or "guests," as the company calls them—who bought these yoga pants after March 1, 2013, could return the product to stores for a full refund or exchange. However, it was estimated that the recall would cost Lululemon $12 million to $17 million in revenue in the first quarter of 2013, and $45 million to $50 million for the rest of the year. On a conference call with investors, Lululemon CEO Christine Day said, "This has been a challenging time for all of us. Disappointing our guests and shareholders and falling short of our own expectations is not something we take lightly and we deeply regret."

As companies grow and expand their manufacturing capacity, it can be a challenge for its management to continue to keep tight control on all aspects of the product's production. When Lululemon Athletica Inc. opened its first store in the Kitsilano neighbourhood of Vancouver in 1998, Lululemon's factory was just a 20-minute bike ride from the store. However, as the company grew, it formed global manufacturing partnerships to support its need for both capacity and technical capability, and collaborated with other brands in the industry on issues such as environmental responsibility and factory auditing standards, and sharing global best practices for supporting its factory partners. Today Lululemon has a global supply chain, with production outsourced to factories in Canada, the United States, Peru, China, Taiwan, South Korea, Israel, India, Bangladesh, Indonesia, Malaysia, Cambodia, Sri Lanka, Vietnam, and Switzerland.

The material involved in the March 2013 recall, luon, a combination of nylon and Lycra spandex fibres, is manufactured in factories in Vietnam and Taiwan. Immediately after the discovery of the quality problem, Lululemon began an investigation into the cause of the sheerness of the product, reporting that it was not the result of having changed manufacturers or the quality of ingredients. Lululemon also added more stringent quality controls and began diversifying its supplier base. As well as impacting revenue, the quality issue also affected Lululemon's inventory, resulting in a shortage of some styles available to its customers. However, the issue also has the potential to jeopardize the reputation of the company known for its high-quality products, as the luon pants weren't the only product involved: Lululemon also encountered unacceptable sheerness with swimsuits and light-coloured pants. This setback opens an avenue for the company's competitors to cut into Lululemon's market share.

Soon after the yoga pant recall, Day announced she was stepping down as CEO, though didn't give reasons why. Lululemon's future success will be partially determined by how well it handles these kinds of setbacks.

Questions for Critical Thinking

1. What entrepreneurial traits and personal characteristics does Dennis "Chip" Wilson display?

2. What are some of the reasons Lululemon Athletica Inc. did not succumb to the statistically high failure rate of businesses within the first five years of operation?

3. How would you ensure future success of Lululemon?

4. What new challenges does Lululemon face today?

Sources: Lululemon website, , www.lululemon.co; Lululemon, "Black Luon Pants Shortage Expected," news release, March 18, 2013; Michael Mink, "Chip Wilson's Design Made Lululemon a Winner," Investors.com, June 8, 2012; Sunny Freeman, "Lululemon Founder Chip Wilson Steps Down from Management, Will Stay on Board," *Toronto Star*, January 6, 2012; "Lululemon Tries IPO on for Size," *National Post*, March 21, 2007; Mae Anderson, "Lululemon Says No Need for 'Downward Dog' Demo for Yoga Pants Refund," *Financial Post*, March 2, 2013; Colleen Leahey, "Lululemon CEO: How to Build Trust Inside Your Company," *Fortune*, March 16, 2012; "#847: Chip Wilson," *Forbes*; Kim Peterson, "Why Gap Wins in Lululemon's Pants Crisis," *MSN Money*, March 27, 2013; "Lululemon: Yoga Pants Recall Will Hurt 2013 Results," *CBS Money Watch*, March 21, 2013; Richard Blackwell, "'I Am Not the Culture of Lululemon,' Outgoing CEO Christine Day Says," *Globe and Mail*, June 13, 2013.

Case Study 6 G Adventures Canada: The Path Less Travelled

Organizations have cultures, but do they have personalities? If so, do businesses take on the personalities of their founders? Some would say Apple's innovativeness and tremendous success was a reflection of Steve Jobs's incredible imagination, fearlessness, and perfectionist nature. G Adventures Canada founder Bruce Poon Tip walks to the beat of a different drum, and so does the adventure travel company he founded.

Seemingly born to be an entrepreneur, at age 14 Bruce Poon Tip won a gold medal in the prestigious Junior Achievement youth business program. At age 16, he was fired from Denny's restaurant after two weeks and dismissed from McDonald's before his training was complete because of his maverick style that didn't fit with the corporate culture of those organizations. Donning a backpack and setting out to explore the world, his business acumen and personal drive fuelled a visionary, high-growth company and a new travel category: small-group tours to off-the-beaten-path destinations.

In 1990, at age 23, Poon Tip founded G Adventures (formerly Gap Adventures) with a passion to deliver authentic travelling experiences for those who craved a vacation that went beyond coach tours, cruise ships, and all-inclusive resorts. When the banks weren't willing to provide a loan, Poon Tip maxed out his two credit cards. G Adventures is now a leader in adventure travel, with offices around the world, offering small-group experiences in over 100 countries. It has grown to become the world's largest eco-tour operator.

Twenty years after founding the company, Poon Tip's belief in its core values are as strong as ever. The company culture is driven by five core values: We love changing people's lives, lead with service, embrace the bizarre, create happiness and community, and do the right thing.

Poon Tip is passionate about changing the lives of the more than 100,000 customers who travel with G Adventures annually. His belief that change is the key to innovation, and people are the key to change, has him encouraging his customers and 1,500 employees worldwide to explore the road less travelled. His company has led the travel industry in customer service by developing unprecedented benefits such as no single-traveller supplements and 24/7 service.

Poon Tip was determined to build a business that could change the world by doing the right thing every time—including hiring locals to have a positive impact on the local economy. And instead of a traditional human resources department, Poon Tip created the Culture Club, where people with the job title "Karma Chameleons" focus on raising company morale worldwide, and the Talent Agency, where staff are dedicated to recruiting and talent management. Poon Tip believes that the company's culture is its brand—and that culture begins with employees. In the last stage of hiring, G Adventures puts candidates through a "culture fit" interview, asking them, for example, "If you were to be stuck on a desert island for five years, what three things would you not bring?" Once hired, staffers at the Basecamp (company headquarters in Toronto) can run a campaign to be elected by co-workers as "mayor" of the company, get involved in the company's charitable projects, and attend an annual weekend retreat, during which Poon Tip once spoke to employees for seven hours about his vision for the company. Annual staff turnover is 5 percent, whereas it is typically around 35 percent in the travel industry. Poon Tip's constant focus on respect and unbridled enthusiasm keeps G Adventures focused on what matters most—community, people, and cultural exchange.

Poon Tip is also passionate about sustainability and philanthropy. Calling his business a social enterprise, he is committed to a "quadruple bottom line" instead of a "triple bottom line"—that is, corporate social responsibility, environmental responsibility, leading with service, and innovation. In 2003, Poon Tip founded the not-for-profit Planeterra Foundation to make a positive difference around the world and to demonstrate his determination to lead his industry in sustainable tourism and community development. The Planeterra Foundation has close to 40 projects worldwide, supporting communities in education, healthcare, environment, and social development—where travellers have the opportunity to visit.

In 2013, G Adventures entered into a $1.3 million partnership with the Multilateral Investment Fund—the leading source of development funding for Latin America and the Caribbean. G Adventures is the only privately owned travel company to receive such a grant. It will build five new long-term, sustainable tourism projects over three years in Latin America.

Poon Tip has demonstrated how travelling with a conscience can fulfill one's purpose while being a highly profitable endeavour. He believes that tourism travel will double in the next decade and therefore that "tourism as usual" is not enough. He believes business models need to adapt to changing societal concerns to create "tourism as a force for good." Poon Tip believes that responsible travel is about personal integrity: people have changed the way they live at home—from recycling to eating more locally grown foods—and they shouldn't suspend their beliefs when they go on vacation.

The list of Poon Tip's awards for leadership and entrepreneurship is impressive. He was the recipient of the Ethics In Action Award, World Savers Award by the prestigious *Condé Nast Traveler* magazine, and the Travel and Leisure Global Vision Leadership Award for "voluntourism." He has also received the Global Traders Leadership award for his groundbreaking ideas in exporting and international business. Poon Tip has also been honoured twice as the Ernst & Young Entrepreneur of the Year. G Adventures has been named one of Canada's 50 Best Managed Companies for six consecutive years, and a Top 100 Employer.

Poon Tip is a sought-after speaker, making over two dozen public appearances a year. He has shared his views on sustainability and tourism at the TED Whistler and TED Bangkok events, as well as at several United Nations forums.

Poon Tip's passion, authenticity, and maverick personality is strongly reflected in his company. He has proven that you can live your values and be profitable too!

Questions for Critical Thinking

1. How would you describe Bruce Poon Tip's personality? How does his personality influence the company's culture and its core values?

2. Describe how Poon Tip's personality has had an influence on his company's success.

3. In what specific ways does G Adventures's low staff turnover directly impact the organization's revenue and profits?

4. What type of customer does G Adventures most appeal to? Do you think this focus would have an effect on its potential to broaden and diversify its user base?

5. How might another company—one that is having difficulty retaining its employees—draw from G Adventures's approach to develop a company "personality" that is as equally engaging?

6. Research news reports on how recent economic conditions have affected the travel industry. Does G Adventures have special strengths that help it deal better than other travel companies with challenges such as those posed by a declining economy? If so, describe these strengths.

Sources: World Green Tourism website; "Travel Style: Bruce Poon Tip," *Johnny Jet*, March 22, 2012; Todd Henneman, "Is HR at Its Breaking Point?" *Workforce*, April 5, 2013; Joanna Pachner, "The Gospel According to Bruce," ProfitGuide.com, October 7, 2011; Elisa Birnbaum "In Conversation with Bruce Poon Tip," *SeeChange Magazine*, December 4, 2012; "Bruce Poon Tip Founder Gap Adventures," TEDx Toronto [video], 2012; Sean Stanleigh, "Tourism Program for Latin America," *The Globe and Mail*, April 4, 2013.

Part 3 Management: Empowering People to Achieve Business Goals

Case Study 7 Electronic Arts: Inside Fantasy Sports

Electronic Arts (EA) is one of the largest and most profitable video game makers. Exclusive contracts with professional sports teams have enabled it to dominate the sports gaming market. But as gaming has shifted from consoles to laptops, phones, and tablets, it is struggling to stay relevant. The question is: Can EA regain the pole position in a crowded and contentious market?

Founded in 1982 by William "Trip" Hawkins, who once worked at Apple Computer, EA quickly gained merit for its detail-oriented sports titles that worked on Nintendo and Sega platforms. Although EA also received good reviews for its strategy and fighting games, its focus (and heart) was on the gridiron, diamond, court, or any other playing surface. According to former EA Sports marketing chief Jeffrey Karp, EA wanted to be "a sports company that makes games."

Ad Revenue In, Ad Revenue Out

Word of mouth may still be the most trusted form of advertising, and EA has always depended on fans to spread its gaming gospel. But in a highly competitive—and often lucrative—gaming market, EA knows better than to skimp on brand building: It spends over two to three times as much when marketing and advertising a title as it does developing it. EA knows its audience; it promotes heavily to readers of both gaming and sports magazines.

The realism of EA's graphics sets it apart from competitors. However, the energy and talent used to depict that realism would be wasted if EA games didn't include the one element fans most want to see: likenesses of their favourite players. Top athletes aren't cheap. Players such as Sidney Crosby, Tiger Woods, and Jarome Iginla expect a tidy sum to promote any product, including video games that use their likenesses. EA spends $100 million annually— three times its ad budget—to license athletes, players' associations, and teams. Anything but cheap, though you'll likely not hear EA complaining about the 15 million digital and physical copies of *FIFA Soccer 2011* it sold in one year, netting $150 million in revenue in the first week alone.

Losing Ground in a Crowded Market

Until recently, EA's devotion to sports games was a winning asset—it dominated the market as the world's largest video game publisher. But over a few short years, the gaming market radically changed. Now EA finds itself in third place behind two strong competitors whose successes represent areas in which EA needs a powerplay to stay in the game.

Blame the Wii. Or *Guitar Hero*, the iPad, and Facebook. All of these new platforms led popular interest in gaming away from complex sports games played with standard controllers to new types of games and new ways of interacting with consoles that sense movement or are portable. Nintendo's Wii has been tremendously popular, and although EA has several successful titles for the platform, many of the top games are produced by Nintendo itself.

Emerging nearly parallel with the Wii was the popularity of *Guitar Hero* and *Rock Band*. It didn't take long for casual gamers to take up plastic guitars and drum sets, leaving their traditional controllers to gather dust. Small gaming shop Harmonix pulled double duty in this market, first publishing *Guitar Hero*, then selling it to EA adversary Activision only to follow up with the arguably better *Rock Band* series. EA came to the party late; sensing the market for rock-along music games was sufficiently saturated, it resorted to striking a deal with Harmonix to help distribute *Rock Band*.

And then there's Apple. Not long after the iOS App Store debuted in the summer of 2008, specifications improved in iOS devices to make them serious mobile gaming machines. At the same time, Facebook was coming into its own as a destination for simple but time-swallowing games. Together these platforms heralded a new way of acquiring and playing games in which EA had little to no experience: digital distribution. Quick on the draw was Zynga, an upstart publisher that quickly dominated Facebook games with Farmville and Frontierville, among others.

As of press time, EA was the third-place games publisher behind Activision and Zynga. EA knows that the road to riches is paved with recurring sales. And though it has released annual versions of many of the popular sports titles for some time, it hadn't done so for the growing market of massive multiplayer online games (MMOG), which Activision has been lucratively exploiting for years with *Call of Duty* and *World of Warcraft*. EA's entry into the MMOG fray was *Star Wars: The Old Republic*.

There are some bright spots for EA. It has been remarkably successful in creating new franchises, which has historically been difficult in the sequel-heavy video game market. EA's successes include *Mass Effect*, a sci-fi action series that has sold over 7 million units, and *Dead Space*, a survival horror series that sold over 4 million units. The company has also seen continued success with older franchises: *Battlefield 3* has shipped over 12 million units. EA has also launched *The Sims Social*, a popular Facebook game that has performed well against titles from Zynga.

And the company is showing signs that it's shifting gears to compete successfully in the new social gaming landscape. It recently spent $300 million to snatch up social gaming developer Playfish, and it also brought *Madden NFL Superstars* to Facebook, where it has been intensely popular. Origin, EA's digital distribution business, offers profile management, the ability to connect with friends via chat, and integration of scores and game stats to social media and online gaming sites. As of last count, 9.3 million users installed Origin, earning EA more than $100 million and helping it to do battle with rival online platform Steam.

Playing for Keeps

In March 2013, EA's chief executive officer, John Riccitiello, resigned after having overseen a near-two-thirds loss in the company's market value since he became CEO in 2007, saying he held himself accountable for missed operational targets. Under Riccitiello's watch, EA grew its digital and mobile games businesses, but as well as experiencing financial losses, the company had high-profile product launch glitches when its servers were unable to handle user demand for a new title, preventing gamers from accessing the game for days.

Some analysts feel that Riccitiello's tenure is a textbook case of how not to run a company in an innovation-driven sector. Video games depend on in-house innovation. However, rather than create new experiences, many felt that EA merely chased trends.

The company's financial health has significant repercussions for Electronic Arts (Canada) Inc., which employs more than 2,000 people at four locations. In April 2013, EA laid off 170 people in its Montreal development unit and announced the closure of two of its Vancouver studios as part of the company's worldwide restructuring around priorities in new technologies and mobile. In total, the global layoffs affected approximately 10 percent of EA's workforce.

Despite its wild success in the video game market, Electronic Arts faces substantial challenges to its power by competing game companies, the cost of doing business, and even dissatisfied gamers. Can EA overcome these threats and continue producing the sports franchises that brought the company considerable success?

Questions for Critical Thinking

1. How much of the blame lies with the leadership of the company, and why?

2. How should EA change its strategic plan to regain lost business?

3. How should EA be reorganized to deal with its new plan?

4. Should EA include partnerships with other firms or organizations in its new plan?

5. Describe the characteristics of the ideal leader you would hire for the firm.

6. What is the latest in Electronic Arts's quest to regain its former glory as the top gaming publisher? How well is EA positioned for future competitive advantage? Overall, is EA's executive team "on top of its game?"

Sources: Electronic Arts website, www.ea.com, "FIFA 12 for iPad and iPhone"; Electronic Arts Investor Relations, "Investor Presentation"; "EA's Chief Creative Officer Describes Game Industry's Re-Engineering," *Venture Beat*, August 26, 2009; Eric Fisher, "EA Sports to North America: Even If You Don't Necessarily Love Soccer, You'll Still Love New 'FIFA 12' Game," *Sports Business Journal Daily*, September 26, 2011; Ben Fritz, "Viacom Sold Harmonix for $50, Saved $50 Million on Taxes," *Los Angeles Times*, January 4, 2011; Christopher Grant, "Jobs: 1/3 of iPhone App Store Launch Apps Are Games," *Joystiq*, July 10, 2008; Dean Takahashi, "Zynga Confirms It Hired EA's Jeff Karp as Marketing and Sales Chief," *Venture Beat*, August 21, 2011; Chris Morris, "Video Game Faceoff: EA vs. Activision," *CNBC*, February 11, 2010; Matt W., "Mass Effect Sales Top 7 Million," *The Sixth Axis*, April 22, 2011; "Electronic Arts F1Q11 Earnings Call Transcript," *Seeking Alpha*, August 4, 2010; Jake Denton, "News: Battlefield 3 Ships 12 Million Copies," *Computer and Video Games*, November 30, 2011; Alex Pham, "The Sims Social Bests Farmville as Second-Largest Facebook Game," *Los Angeles Times*, September 9, 2011; Tom Senior, "Origin Is Doing Quite Well: 9.3 Million Registered Users, $100 Million Revenue since Launch," *PC Gamer*, February 2, 2012; Malathi Nayak, "Electronic Arts CEO Quits as Stumbling Game Maker Misses Targets," *Globe and Mail*, March 19, 2013; Peter Nowak, "5 Reasons Electronic Arts Is in Big Trouble (Which Is Bad News for Canada)," *Canadian Business*, March 20, 2013; Gillian Shaw, "Electronic Arts Closing PopCap and Quicklime in Latest Layoffs to Hit Vancouver's Gaming Sector," *Vancouver Sun*, April 25, 2013.

Case Study 8 The Ottawa Hospital: Employee Engagement during Times of Organizational Change

The origins of The Ottawa Hospital, a not-for-profit, publicly funded, university teaching hospital, date back to 1845 when a building was purchased for $240 to house the Ottawa General Hospital. In 1922 and 1924, respectively, the Grace Hospital and Ottawa Civic Hospital opened, and the Riverside Hospital opened in 1967. In 1998, an amalgamation of the services of the Ottawa Civic, General, Grace, and Riverside hospitals formed The Ottawa Hospital. Today, The Ottawa Hospital is recognized as one of the largest and most important research and teaching hospitals in Canada, with 1,300 physicians and 12,085 staff at its three sites.

Engaged Employees Are Key to Quality Patient Care

There are few sectors where having engaged and satisfied employees matters more than in healthcare, where the need for skilled and empathic workers can be a matter of life and death. In Canada, 70 percent of healthcare costs go to employee salaries. As healthcare costs continue to rise, hospitals across the country are looking for ways to do more with less, and are finding that paying attention to employee engagement could be one way to do that.

Consider the example of The Ottawa Hospital. In 2009, hospital leadership grew concerned with lower patient satisfaction ratings and decided to take a hard look at its vision. The hospital restated its vision: "To provide each patient with the world-class care, exceptional service and compassion we would want for our loved ones." "We learned quickly that in order to even think about success in our goals we needed a very active and engaged workforce that included all 12,000 employees and 1,300 physicians," says Ottawa Hospital president and CEO Dr. Jack Kitts.

Taking a cue from its patient surveys, the hospital undertook its first employee and physician engagement survey. That survey had a response rate of 75 percent—a good indication that employees had something to say. Staff said they wanted the hospital to improve performance management, to make employee wellness a priority, and to provide further career opportunities. The hospital set up committees to consider these concerns. The efforts seem to be working. Dr. Kitts says the hospital has seen significant improvement in these areas since 2009, but more remains to be done. "If we can improve employee engagement," Dr. Kitts says, "we have no doubt that our patient satisfaction scores will go up, our quality and safety indicators will go up, and we'll become one of the top performing hospitals."

High employee engagement is driven by leadership quality, effective rewards, and strong workplace culture and values, enabling productivity and the support of performance and development.

Engaged employees are committed to their employer, satisfied with their work, and willing to give extra effort to achieve the organization's goals. The Ottawa Hospital has a strong leader in Dr. Kitts, who is known for his inclusive, team-oriented strategic leadership, his passion to ensure delivery of quality patient-centred care, and the development and mentoring of physician leaders.

Adopting Evidence-Based HR Practices

A decade ago, hospitals put the focus on creating healthier workplaces, linking the physical and emotional health of workers to high-quality patient care. Now, taking a more comprehensive, strategically focused approach, hospitals recognize the need to move beyond workplace health promotion programs and also focus on the work environment to improve both performance and quality of care. An Ontario Hospital Association–NRC Picker Employee Experience Survey, involving over 10,000 employees in 16 Ontario hospitals, examined how job, work environment, management, and organizational factors influence levels of engagement among healthcare employees. The findings confirmed that a high level of employee engagement is related to retention, patient-centred care, patient safety, culture, and employees' positive assessments of the quality of care or services provided by their team. Echoing private sector research that shows strong correlations between employee engagement scores and customer experiences, hospitals now recognize the positive relationship between staff satisfaction and patient satisfaction. To support this new direction in evidence-based human resource practices, the Ontario Hospital Association created the Quality Healthcare Workplace Model that integrates a healthy workplace, human resources, quality, and patient safety goals within a performance-focused framework.

Facing Changes and Fiscal Challenges

As hospitals strive to improve employee engagement, the Ontario government, as part of its goal to eliminate the deficit, has looked at ways to reduce public spending on healthcare. Shifting from 7 percent average annual growth of healthcare funding during 2006 to 2010, healthcare funding growth was reduced to 2 percent per year for three years beginning in 2012. In addition, as part of the Ontario government's healthcare reform program, the funding model for hospitals was changed, and more funding for patient care has shifted to community-based facilities, such as medical clinics, home care services, long-term care facilities, and not-for-profit organizations. Most impacted by this reform are hospitals, which saw a reduction to 0 percent growth in their base funding.

To respond, The Ottawa Hospital began looking at the makeup of its workforce, aiming to better match the skills of various health professionals—from registered nurses to social workers—with the needs of patients. Dr. Kitts stated that the projected budget shortfall was "the catalyst to move this forward at an accelerated rate . . . We don't believe that the way we provide service today is achieving the best in quality or the least in cost," Dr. Kitts says. "So we are going to change the way we deliver service." It determined the skills and scope of practice for all healthcare workers. It then went through each unit of the hospital to identify the needs of the typical patient and match staff skills to needs. As an example, changes in technology make it possible for lower-paid technicians to provide dialysis to kidney patients under certain circumstances, a treatment that has traditionally been done by registered nurses. In another cost-cutting move, the hospital was considering moving some diagnostic services to community clinics, where they can be done more cheaply.

As a result of the funding cuts, The Ottawa Hospital had to reduce its annual operational costs by $31 million to balance its $1.04 billion budget for the year. To do so, the hospital announced in January 2013 that it was cutting 290 full-time jobs, including 90 nurses, 100 administrative staff, and 100 people categorized as other health professionals, such as physiotherapists, psychologists, and social workers. The planned staff cuts will save nearly $22 million, with the other $9 million in savings expected to come from increased revenue and reduced supply costs. Aiming to show good "bedside manners" with staff, Dr. Kitts and other administrators spent a morning informing the affected unions of the cuts and held open forums with all hospital staff to notify them about the pending layoffs. Administrators were hopeful that very few people would lose their jobs, promising to move as many of the affected employees as possible into the 600 full-time positions that were vacant at that time, and would also offer early retirement to some staff. Dr. Kitts also stressed that patient care wouldn't suffer as a result of the cuts, and he didn't expect hospital wait times to rise. "(The goal) is to achieve quality care at the least cost," said Dr. Kitts.

Questions for Critical Thinking

1. The Ottawa Hospital is working on processes to better "engage" employees for improved job satisfaction, which leads to greater patient satisfaction in the delivery of quality patient care, while at the same time being forced to execute a workforce reduction plan to reduce costs to balance its annual operational budget. In what ways can strong employee engagement help with the layoff situation? Conversely, how might the layoffs affect employee engagement?

2. Describe and discuss how Dr. Kitts and his management team are practising the major responsibilities of human resource management by undertaking the initiative of examining its staff mix to better match the skills of various health professionals with the needs of patients.

3. In what ways will employee layoffs at The Ottawa Hospital affect the culture of the organization? Discuss ways that hospital management has and can further avoid or minimize negative effects on its culture during this time.

4. Research the reaction of CUPE, the public sector union representing healthcare workers, to layoffs in healthcare facilities across Canada. Discuss some of the issues your research revealed that HR managers and hospital CEOs have to work through with employees and unions when circumstances beyond their control require a reduction and realignment of its workforce.

Sources: "Canada's 50 Best Employers: The Top Perks, Programs and Initiatives Inside Our Best Workplaces," *Maclean's*, October 18, 2012; The Ottawa Hospital website, www.ottawahospital.on.ca, "Our Vision" and "Our Leadership Team"; Graham Lowe, "How Employee Engagement Matters for Hospital Performance," *Healthcare Quarterly* 15, no. 2 (2012): 29–39; "Ontario Nurses Association Submission on 2013 Pre-Budget Consultations to the Standing Committee on Finance and Economic Affairs," March 22, 2013; "Ottawa Hospital to Cut 290 Jobs," *CTV News*, January 30, 2013; Chris Hofley, "Ottawa Hospital Cuts 290 Full-Time Jobs to Trim $31 Million," *Ottawa Sun*, January 30, 2013; Don Butler, "Job Cuts Won't Harm Patient Care, Says Ottawa Hospital CEO," *Ottawa Citizen*, January 30, 2013.

Case Study 9 Canada's Team of the Century: 1972 Summit Series

Team Canada 1972 was voted the Canadian "team of the century." When talking about the iconic hockey series in which Canada beat the Russians, many people remember the all-important goal in the final seconds of the last game. Yet Team Canada's story is really about the greatest comeback in hockey history by a team that just would not give up. What lessons can managers learn from this incredible success story?

The Summit Series was the first competition between the Soviet national team and a Canadian team of professional NHL players. The Soviets had recently become the dominant force in international competitions, overtaking Canada. With this hockey rivalry and with the Summit Series being played at the height of the Cold War, it aroused intense feelings of nationalism in both countries.

With the first seven games resulting in a series draw (the third game ended in a tie), it was only during the last 34 seconds of the eighth and final game that the outcome was finally decided. While the winning goal was an important one for all of Canada, if the players hadn't worked together as a team in the other games, they wouldn't have been positioned to win.

Recruiting the Team

Harry Sinden, who had been head coach of the Boston Bruins, was named Team Canada coach and general manager in the summer of 1972, leaving him only a few weeks to organize the team for the September series. Selecting the best players was the easiest part; convincing them to interrupt their off-season proved more challenging. "I don't think anyone in Canada, including the players, realized the significance of the series at the time," said Sinden. "Also, the players felt they had proven they were the top in their field during past NHL seasons; they had little motivation to play against the Soviets."

Sinden's first job was to convince those selected of the importance of the series and the impact it could have on their careers. He played to their sense of national pride. Coining the name "Team Canada" helped, as did showing players film footage of world championships in which he had played. It also helped that the media had started to focus on the series. When the 1972 Team Canada players were announced, the entire hockey world was certain of Canadian victory, and an eight-game sweep was predicted.

Team Canada and most of the sports media were therefore shocked when the Soviet team won the opening game, 7–3. The Soviet team had proven superior in their conditioning, discipline, and game plan. According to Pat Stapleton, Team Canada defenceman, there had been another major difference between the two teams: "The Soviets had long been practising and playing together as a team; whereas, as members of various NHL teams, we had been playing against each other as competitors," Stapleton said. "We needed time to get to know each other's strengths and get to the point where we began to trust each other as teammates rather than as competitors."

Canada won the second game 4–1, with the third game ending in a tie (4–4). When the Soviets won game four (5–3) in Vancouver, taking a two-to-one game lead, the fans booed Team Canada as they left the ice. The captain, Phil Esposito, passionately scolded the fans on post-game national television. The Vancouver episode left Team Canada disheartened. However, Esposito's outburst fired up his teammates (and the nation), and the experience helped galvanize the team. Stapleton said, "Much of what makes a team successful is the players developing instinct and intuition for the game. We were up against a team that played a different style than we were used to, so it was taking a little time for us to develop the intuition and instinct we needed to make risky split-second decisions." He added, "Hockey is played *on the ice*—and you should never underestimate the competition!"

Creating a High-Performance Team

According to Stapleton, one of Team Canada's biggest challenges was building the trusting relationships that are key to a cohesive team. When they trained in Toronto, many of the players were local and went home after practice. It was only when the team headed overseas for the last four games in the USSR and they spent all their time together that they started to bond. They first stopped in Sweden, spending 10 days together training hard; there the players began to understand each other's strengths and trust each other on the ice.

But when the series resumed in Moscow, the Soviets won game five, leaving Team Canada with the daunting task of having to win all three remaining games. As the exhausted and dejected Team Canada players skated off the ice, the few thousand Canadian fans who had made the trip to Moscow stood up and sang "O Canada" at the top of their lungs.

Coach Sinden had chosen 35 star players for Team Canada with the intent that they would each play at least one game. Now, with the series on the line in every game, Sinden knew he had to choose the best 19 to continue. "We had to pick our team, and if somebody hadn't yet played, we were just going to have to break our promise," he recounted. "People who weren't playing were upset about it." But leaders emerged, Sinden said, who helped the group work through this conflict, convincing the disgruntled players that "this series is bigger than all of us" and that they had to pull together, whether they got ice time or not, and win the series for Canada.

The Canadians then started to develop a team mindset, recognizing which of their skills they could deploy to make the whole team stronger, and how they could best serve the team and accomplish the collective goal. "Each player was prepared to do whatever was required, even if it meant working in obscurity, for the good of the team," said Stapleton. Most of the players on Team Canada who played very little or not at all cheered on their teammates in their street clothes from the stands and behind the bench.

The team developed in other ways. For example, the Soviets' game was becoming very predictable. Sinden and Assistant Coach John Ferguson created an environment conducive to the Canadians adapting their playing style to neutralize the Soviets' strengths. Of Sinden, Stapleton said, "As the leader, Harry left the 'on-the-ice' decisions up to us players; he never passed judgement, he empowered us to figure out how to complement each other, to get the job done." The Canadians also began to draw on emotion, heart, and the will to win.

Team Canada won games six and seven. On the day of the eighth and final game, things almost came to a stop across Canada as people watched the game at home, at school, or at work. Until the men's hockey gold medal game of the 2010 Winter Olympics, the 1972 Summit Series was the most-watched sporting event in the history of Canadian television. In dramatic fashion, Canada won the final game, overcoming a two-goal Soviet lead after two periods by scoring three in the third. As the country sat on edge, the final goal was scored by Paul Henderson, with only 34 seconds left in the game!

"After the game, the entire team gathered in the locker room—those who had played and those who had not, everyone feeling equally part of the team. Emotions were running very high! Their burden was lifted; they would return to Canada as the world's best," Sinden said. Back in Canada, Team Canada was greeted by the prime minister in Montreal, then went on to Toronto, where fans lined the highway from the airport, in a rainstorm, to welcome them home.

Over the decades, the legacy of the Summit Series has grown, making it not just an important hockey moment, but also one of the most significant cultural events in Canadian history. Team Canada 1972 holds the rare distinction of being the only sports team inducted into Canada's Sports Hall of Fame, and it was named the greatest team of the twentieth century in a poll by the Canadian Press.

Questions for Critical Thinking

1. From the information provided in the case, identify aspects of Team Canada's development in each of the five phases of the team's life cycle: forming, storming, norming, performing, and adjourning.

2. Referencing the textbook material, describe the actions by Head Coach Harry Sinden that contributed to team cohesiveness.

3. Although Team Canada was led and managed by both a head and an assistant coach, in what way could it be described as a *self-managed team*? Can you provide examples of *distributed leadership* as described in the case?

4. When the 1972 Team Canada players were announced, the entire hockey world was certain of Canadian victory. However, as Pat Stapleton said, "Hockey is played *on the ice*—and you should never underestimate the competition!" Discuss how this "perception" and "action" understanding also relates to business organizations and highlight a business example. How do you ensure that perceptions (either negative or positive) do not overshadow the importance of the underlying actions that need to be done?

5. Which characteristics of high-performing teams were reflected in Team Canada 1972 and also in the gold medal men's and women's hockey teams at the 2010 Olympics in Vancouver and the 2014 Olympics in Sochi?

Sources: Interview with Team Canada 1972 Head Coach and General Manager Harry Sinden, August 8, 2013, and Pat Stapleton, defenceman, Team Canada 1972, July 30, 2013; Andrew Podnieks, *Team Canada 1972: The Official 40th Anniversary Celebration* (Toronto: Fenn/McClelland & Stewart, 2012); 1972 Summit Series website, www.1972summitseries.com; Ted Blackman, "Esposito Booed, Raps Ungrateful Fans," *Montreal Gazette*, September 9, 1972, 25; "The Canada-Russia Summit Series: 40th Anniversary Special: Dispatches from Montreal Hockey Legends Red Fisher and Ted Blackman," *Montreal Gazette* (2012); Mary Janigan, "Hockey Sidetracked City for Three Hours as Fans All Over Stayed Riveted to Screens," *Montreal Gazette*, September 29, 1972, 1.

Case Study 10 Toyota: Looking Far into the Future

By borrowing the best ideas from North American brands and innovating the rest itself, Toyota has become a paragon of auto manufacturing efficiency. Its vehicles have been widely known for their quality and longevity—and Toyota's sales numbers are once again the envy of the North American Big Three, as it recently regained the global sales crown. Toyota had slipped as low as third following the natural disasters in Japan and Thailand that hurt production and demand. Here is how Toyota became so efficient at producing high-quality automobiles, and yet it is still facing challenges.

Buy Domestic?

There used to be a sentiment encouraging Canadian and U.S. car buyers to purchase domestic models built and assembled in North America. Those who still tout the movement to buy domestic have likely done a good bit of head-scratching over how to classify Toyota—a Japanese company operating in Ontario that employs Canadian workers and that uses Canadian- and American-made parts to produce vehicles sold across North America. What to think when this Japanese brand achieves a product quality superior to long-known North American brands and surges ahead of General Motors and Ford to rank number one in global auto sales? Yet Toyota, the model automotive manufacturing company, is still facing its own quality challenges.

Quality by Design

Toyota's success and growth in the North American auto market have been based on strategies honed since the 1950s to earn and retain customer satisfaction by producing superior vehicles within a highly efficient production environment. From the home office to factories to showrooms, two core philosophies guide Toyota's business: (1) creating fair, balanced, mutually beneficial relationships with both suppliers and employees; and (2) strictly adhering to a just-in-time (JIT) manufacturing principle.

Over the decades, other North American auto manufacturers developed relationships with their suppliers that emphasized tense competition, price cutting, and the modification of suppliers' production capacities with the changing needs of the domestic market. Year after year, parts suppliers had to bid to renew contracts in a process that valued year-to-year price savings over long-term relationships. Domestic manufacturers, notorious for changing production demands mid-season to comply with late-breaking market dynamics or customer feedback, forced suppliers to turn to double or triple shifts to keep up with capacity and thus avoid the problems—quality slips, recalls, line shutdowns, layoffs—that ultimately slow the final assembly of vehicles. When a carmaker doesn't know what it wants, suppliers have little chance of keeping up. This system of industry dynamics proved susceptible to new approaches from Japanese competitors.

Toyota's model of supply chain management displayed an exclusive commitment to parts suppliers, well-forecast parts orders that were not subject to sways in the market, and genuine concern for the success of suppliers. Supply chain relationships among Asian manufacturers are based on a complex system of cooperation and equity interests.

Visiting other North American auto plants and seeing months' worth of excess parts waiting to be installed taught Toyota the benefit of having only enough supplies on hand to fulfill a given production batch. Toyota plans its production schedules months in advance, dictating regularly scheduled parts shipments from its suppliers. Suppliers benefit by being able to predict long-range demand for products so they can schedule production accordingly. This builds mutual loyalty between suppliers and the carmaker—almost as if suppliers are part of Toyota. The fit and finish in Toyota vehicles is precise because its suppliers can afford to focus on the quality of their parts. And consumers notice: Toyota vehicles consistently earned high marks for customer satisfaction and retained their resale value better than almost any other brand.

Keep It Lean

Early Toyota presidents Toyoda Kiichiro and Ohno Taiichi are considered the fathers of the Toyota Production System (TPS), known widely by the JIT moniker or as "lean production." Emphasizing quality and efficiency at all levels, it drives nearly all aspects of decision making at Toyota.

Simply put, TPS is "all about producing only what's needed and transferring only what's needed," said Teruyuki Minoura, senior managing director at Toyota. "The answer is a flexible system that allows the line to produce what's necessary when it's necessary. If it takes six people to make a certain quantity of an item and there is a drop in the quantity required, then your system should let one or two of them drop out and get on with something else."

To achieve maximum efficiency, workers at Toyota plants must be exceptionally knowledgeable about all facets of a vehicle's production so they are able to change responsibilities as needed. "An environment where people have to think brings with it wisdom, and this wisdom brings with it *kaizen* [the notion of continuous improvement]," noted Minoura. "If asked to produce only one unit at a time, to produce according to the flow, a typical line worker is likely to be flummoxed. It's a basic characteristic of human beings that they develop wisdom from being put under pressure." However, kaizen also has to compete with the pressure of Mother Nature. The earthquake and subsequent tsunami that occurred in 2011 in Japan took a heavy toll on Toyota's supply chain and hurt its overall production of vehicles.

Keeping Up with the Times

No vehicle represents Toyota's focus on continuous improvement and innovation better than the wildly successful hybrid, the Prius. A niche car when introduced in Japan in 1997, Prius is now the world's third-bestselling car, recently topping the 3 million mark. Toyota now offers 18 hybrid passenger models in over 80 countries, accounting for 15 percent of total Toyota sales.

On the other hand, no Toyota vehicle has come to represent the challenges of adapting to a changing sales landscape more than its Tundra pickup truck. Toyota built a Tundra plant in Texas to prove that its trucks were as North American as those made by the Big Three. But truck sales began to decline as the price of oil rose. Contractors and builders began to think twice about new pickup purchases; the Tundra plants began to run well under capacity. To try to turn things around, Toyota was betting heavily on its 2014 Tundra model. Based on feedback from focus groups, designers and production paid more attention to power and capacity and less to style and comfort.

Yet quality, and in turn Toyota's reputation, has suffered in the past. Toyota is still dealing with the fallout from negative publicity when it recalled 7.6 million vehicles because of acceleration problems, which led to dozens of accidents and some deaths in the United States. Toyota's reputation for quality took another hit when influential magazine *Consumer Reports* pulled its recommendation on Toyota's popular flagship Camry sedan, plus the RAV4 and Prius v due to poor front crash test results. Toyota's number 2 safety technology officer says, "From a production point of view, it requires a drastic change. So it requires time." As in all things in the fast and flexible world of operations management, time is the essence of success.

Questions for Critical Thinking

1. How could Toyota's competitors draw from kaizen to gain efficiencies in their supply chain management?

2. What problems might a manufacturing firm face when trying to implement and use the just-in-time systems successfully used at Toyota?

3. How must employees' concerns fit in with production tinkering at Toyota?

4. Given the bad news from *Consumer Reports*, what customer relationship management initiatives would you suggest Toyota undertake?

5. Toyota has had to face the same quality challenges that its North American competitors (GM, Chrysler, and Ford) have been facing. Do some investigation on how automobile manufacturers are incorporating quality into their cars and into their image. Who now is doing the best job on both questions?

Sources: Toyota website, www.toyota.com; "Toyota Outsells GM, Ford Posts Eye-Popping Loss," *U.S. News & World Report*, July 24, 2008; M. Reza Vaghefi, "Creating Sustainable Competitive Advantage: The Toyota Philosophy and Its Effects," Mastering Management Online (October 2001), accessed at www.ftmastering.com; "Top 10 SUVs, Pickups and Minivans with the Best Residual Value for 2005," Edmunds.com; Toyota Motor Corporation, "Making Things: The Essence and Evolution of the Toyota Production System," and "The 'Thinking' Production System: TPS as a Winning Strategy for Developing People in the Global Manufacturing Environment"; Alex Taylor III, "The Birth of the Prius," *CNN Money*, February 24, 2006; Rick Newman, "Toyota's Next Turn," *U.S. News & World Report*, June 16, 2008; Greg Keenan, "Trigger-Happy Toyota Recalls 1 Million Corolla, Matrix Vehicles," *The Globe and Mail*, August 26, 2010; Robert E. Cole, "No Big Quality Problems at Toyota?" *Harvard Business Review* blog, March 9, 2010, http://blogs.hbr.org; Yoko Kubota, "Toyota Keeps Top Spot in Global Auto Sales Rankings, Outselling GM, VW," *The Globe and Mail*, October 28, 2013; Deepa Seetharaman, "Toyota Redesigns 2014 Tundra to Appeal to Truck Buyers," Reuters, February 7, 2013; Brad Tuttle, "Toyota Prius: Niche Car No More," *Time*, May 29, 2012; Tiffany Kaiser, "Toyota's Prius Hybrid Crosses 3 Million Unit Threshold in Worldwide Sales," *DailyTech*, July 5, 2013, www.dailytech.com; Jeremy Cato, "Toyota Stumbles on One Crash Test; Still Rated 'Reliable,'" *The Globe and Mail*, October 31, 2013.

Part 4 Marketing Management

Case Study 11 Zara International: Fashion at the Speed of Light

At the announcement of her engagement to Spain's Crown Prince Felipe, Letizia Ortiz Rocasolano wore a chic white trouser suit; within a few weeks, hundreds of European women sported the same look. Welcome to fast fashion, a trend that sees clothing retailers frequently purchasing small quantities of merchandise to stay on top of emerging trends. In this world of "hot today, gauche tomorrow," no company does fast fashion better than Zara International. Shoppers in 78 countries, including Canada, have taken to Zara's knack for bringing the latest styles from sketchbook to clothing rack at lightning speed and reasonable prices.

In Fast Fashion, Moments Matter

Because style-savvy customers expect shorter and shorter delays from runway to store, Zara International employs a stable of more than 200 professionals to help it keep up with the latest fashions. It takes just two weeks for the company to update existing garments and get them into its stores; new pieces hit the market twice a week.

Defying the recession with its cheap-and-chic Zara clothing chain, Zara's parent company Inditex posted strong sales gains. Low prices and a rapid response to fashion trends are enabling it to challenge Gap, Inc., for top ranking among global clothing vendors. The improved results highlight how Zara's formula continued to work even in the downturn. The chain specializes in lightning-quick turnarounds of the latest designer trends at prices tailored to the young—about $27 an item. Louis Vuitton fashion director Daniel Piette described Zara as "possibly the most innovative and devastating retailer in the world."

Inditex Group shortens the time from order to arrival by using a complex system of just-in-time production and inventory reporting that keeps Zara ahead. Their distribution centres can have items in European stores within 24 hours of receiving an order, and in American and Asian stores in under 48 hours. "They're a fantastic case study in terms of how they manage to get product to their stores so quick," said Stacey Cartwright, executive vice-president and CFO of Burberry Group PLC. "We are mindful of their techniques."

Inditex's history in fabrics manufacturing made it good business sense to internalize as many points in the supply chain as possible. Inditex controls design, production, distribution, and retail sales to optimize the flow of goods without having to share profits with wholesalers or intermediary partners. Customers win by having access to new fashions while they're still fresh off the runway. During a Madonna concert tour in Spain, Zara's quick turnaround let young fans at the last show wear Madonna's outfit from the first one.

Twice a week Zara's finished garments are shipped to logistical centres that simultaneously distribute products to stores worldwide. These small production batches help the company avoid the risk of oversupply. Because batches always contain new products, Zara's stores perpetually energize their inventories. Most clothing lines are not replenished. Instead they are replaced with new designs to create scarcity value—shoppers cannot be sure that designs in stores one day will be available the next.

Store managers track sales data with handheld computers. They can reorder hot items in less than an hour. This lets Zara know what's selling and what's not; when a look doesn't pan out, designers promptly put together new products. According to Dilip Patel, managing director for Inditex, new arrivals are rushed to store sales floors still on the black plastic hangers used in shipping. Shoppers who are in the know recognize these designs as the newest of the new; soon after, any items left over are rotated to Zara's standard wood hangers.

Inside and out, Zara's stores are specially dressed to strengthen the brand. Inditex considers this to be of the greatest importance because that is where shoppers ultimately decide which fashions make the cut. In a faux shopping street in the basement of the company's headquarters, stylists craft and photograph eye-catching layouts that are emailed every two weeks to store managers for replication.

Zara stores sit on some of the world's glitziest shopping streets—including New York's Fifth Avenue, near the flagship stores of leading international fashion brands—which make its reasonable prices stand out. "Inditex gives people the most up-to-date fashion at accessible prices, so it is a real alternative to high-end fashion lines," said Luca Solca, senior research analyst with Sanford C. Bernstein in London. That is good news for Zara, as many shoppers trade down from higher-priced chains.

Catfights on the Catwalk

Zara is not the only player in fast fashion. Competition is fierce, but Zara's overwhelming success (sales were US$13.6 billion in 2012) has the competition scrambling to keep up. San Francisco-based Gap, Inc., which had been the largest independent clothing retailer by revenue until Zara bumped them to second place in 2009, posted a 21 percent decline in the first half of 2011 and had plans to close 700 stores by the end of 2013. Only time will tell if super-chic Topshop's entry into the American market will make a wrinkle in Zara's success.

Some fashion analysts are referring to this as the democratization of fashion: bringing high(er) fashion to low(er)-income shoppers. According to James Hurley, managing director and senior research analyst with New York–based Telsey Advisory Group LLC, big-box discount stores such as Target and Walmart are emulating Zara's ability to study emerging fashions and knock out look-alikes in a matter of weeks. "In general," Hurley said, "the fashion cycle is becoming sharper and more immediately accessible."

But making fashion more accessible can have its costs: Zara faced some controversy last year when Brazilian authorities discovered and shut down a São Paulo sweatshop run by AHA, one of Zara's contractors. Inditex denied knowledge of the working conditions, but it acknowledged that the conditions in the sweatshop ran counter to its code of conduct and compensated the affected workers.

A Single Fashion Culture

With a network of over 1,600 stores around the world, Zara International is Inditex's largest and most profitable brand, bringing home 77 percent of international sales and nearly 67 percent of revenues. The first Zara outlet opened shop in 1975 in La Coruña. It remained solely a Spanish chain until opening a store in Oporto, Portugal, in 1988. The brand reached the United States and France in 1989 and 1990 with outlets in New York and Paris, respectively. Zara went into mainland China in 2001, India in 2009, and Australia in 2011.

Essential to Zara's growth and success are Inditex's 100-plus textile design, manufacturing, and distribution companies that employ more than 92,000 workers. The Inditex group began in 1963 when Amancio Ortega Gaona, chairman and founder of Inditex, got his start in textile manufacturing. After a period of growth, he assimilated Zara into a new holding company, Industria de Diseño Textil. Inditex has a tried-and-true strategy for entering new markets: start with a handful of stores and gain a critical mass of customers. Generally, Zara is the first Inditex chain to break ground in new countries, paving the way for the group's other brands, including Pull and Bear, Massimo Dutti, and Bershka.

Inditex farms out much of its garment production to specialist companies, located on the Iberian Peninsula, which it often supplies with its own fabrics. Although some pieces and fabrics are purchased in Asia—many of them not dyed or only partly finished—the company manufactures about half of its clothing in its hometown of La Coruña, Spain. H&M, one of Zara's top competitors, uses a slightly different strategy. Around one-quarter of its stock is made up of fast-fashion items that are designed in-house and farmed out to independent factories. As at Zara, these items move quickly through the stores and are replaced often by fresh designs. But H&M also keeps a large inventory of basic, everyday items sourced from cheap Asian factories.

Inditex CEO Pablo Isla believes in cutting expenses wherever and whenever possible. Zara spends just 0.3 percent of sales on ads, making the 3 to 4 percent typically spent by rivals seem excessive in comparison. Isla disdains markdowns and sales, as well.

Few can criticize the results of Isla's frugality. Inditex opened 358 new stores by the end of Q3 2011 and was simultaneously named Retailer of the Year during the World Retailer Congress meeting. Perhaps most important in an industry predicated on image, Inditex secured bragging rights as Europe's largest fashion retailer by overtaking H&M. According to José Castellano, former deputy chairman of Inditex, the group plans to double in size in the coming years while making sales of more than US$15 billion. He envisioned most of this growth taking place in Europe—especially in trend-savvy Italy.

Fashion of the Moment

Although Inditex's dominance of fast fashion seems virtually complete, it isn't without its challenges. For instance, keeping production so close to home becomes difficult when an increasing number of Zara stores are far-flung across the globe. "The efficiency of the supply chain is coming under more pressure the farther abroad they go," notes Nirmalya Kumar, a professor at London Business School.

Inditex launched its Zara online store in the United States in the fall of 2011, offering free two- to three-day shipping and free returns in the model of uber-successful eretailer Zappos. A Zara application for the iPhone has been downloaded by more prospective clients in the United States than in any other market, according to chief executive Pablo Isla—more than a million iPhone users in just three months. Beginning in 2010, Zara rolled out its online store in 16 European countries and plans to progressively add the remaining countries where Zara operates. Analysts worry that Inditex's rapid expansion may bring undue pressure to its business. The rising number of overseas stores, they warn, adds cost and complexity and is straining its operations. Inditex may no longer be able to manage everything from Spain. But Inditex wasn't worried. By closely managing costs, Inditex said its current logistics system could handle its growth for several more years.

José Luis Nueno of IESE, a business school in Barcelona, says that Zara is here to stay. Consumers have become more demanding and more arbitrary, he says—and fast fashion is better suited to these changes. But is Zara International trying to expand too quickly? Do you think it will be able to introduce a new logistics system able to carry it into another decade of intense growth?

Questions for Critical Thinking

1. What do all Zara customers want?

2. What does the Zara brand mean to customers around the world?

3. How are Zara's customers different than other fashion-oriented shoppers?

4. How can Zara control unwanted inventories?

5. Gather the latest information on competitive trends in the apparel industry and the latest actions and innovations of Zara. Is the firm continuing to do well? Is it adapting in ways needed to stay abreast of both its major competition and the pressures of a changing global economy?

Sources: Inditex website, www.inditex.com, "Inditex: Who We Are: Concepts: Zara," Inditex press kit, "Inditex FY2010 Results," "Our Group," "Who We Are," "Inditex: Our Team," and Inditext 2012 Annual Report; "Inditex Recognized as International Retailer of the Year at the World Retail Congress," news release, March 10, 2011; "The Future of Fast Fashion," *The Economist*, June 16, 2005; "Zara Grows as Retail Rivals Struggle," *Wall Street Journal*, March 26, 2009; "Zara, a Spanish Success Story," *CNN*, June 15, 2001; Cecile Rohwedder and Keith Johnson, "Pace-Setting Zara Seeks More Speed to Fight Its Rising Cheap-Chic Rivals," *Wall Street Journal*, February 20, 2008, B1; "Zara: Taking the Lead in Fast-Fashion," *BusinessWeek*, April 4, 2006; Dana Mattioli and Kris Hudson, "Gap to Slash Its Store Count," *Wall Street Journal*, October 14, 2011; Diana Middleton, "Fashion for the Frugal," *Florida Times-Union*, October 1, 2006; Stephen Burgen and Tom Phillips, "Zara Accused in Brazil Sweatshop Inquiry," *The Guardian*, August 18, 2011; Zara España, S.A. "Hoover's Company Records," February 14, 2012; "Shining Examples," *The Economist*, June 17, 2006; "Ortega's Empire Showed Rivals New Style of Retailing," *The Times*, June 14, 2007; "Zara Launches Online Shopping in the USA," *College Fashion*, September 7, 2011; Christopher Bjork, "Zara Has Online Focus for US Expansion Inditex Says," *Dow Jones Newswires, March* 17, 2010; "Zara Arrived in Australia with a Flagship Store on Sydney's Most Prominent Shopping Street," Inditex news release, April 19, 2011; Walter Loeb, "Zara's Secret to Success: The New Science of Retailing," *Forbes*, October 14, 2013.

Case Study 12 Hudson's Bay Company: From Fur to Fendi

After 300 years, Canada's oldest retailer knows a thing or two about change. Older than the country it serves, Hudson's Bay Company (HBC) has remained a landmark institution in Canada, navigating its way from rural outposts to over 600 locations and nearly 60,000 associates located in every province. Known best for its flagship department store Hudson's Bay (formerly The Bay), HBC also operates Home Outfitters in Canada and U.S. retail chain Lord & Taylor.

Despite its long and glorious past, all is not well at Canada's historic company. Leadership changes, increased competition, a fragmenting retail market, and plummeting sales have plagued HBC well into the new millennium. Will HBC be able to successfully weather the seas of change, or will it sink into history?

History

Two centuries before Confederation, a pair of European explorers discovered a wealth of fur in the interior of Canada accessible by an inland sea, Hudson's Bay. In 1670, with permission from the King of England, trading began, and HBC traded goods and furs in a few forts and posts around James Bay and Hudson Bay throughout the first century. Later, competition forced HBC to expand into Canada's interior, and a string of outposts grew up along river networks that would eventually become the modern cities of Winnipeg, Calgary, and Edmonton.

By the end of the nineteenth century, changing tastes caused the fur trade to lose importance, while western settlements and the gold rush introduced new clientele to HBC—ones who paid in cash, not fur. Trading posts gave way to sales shops with a greater selection of goods, transforming HBC into a modern retail organization. During this time, HBC also started selling homesteads to newly arrived settlers, eventually diversifying into a full-scale commercial property holding and development organization. Shipping and natural resources, particularly oil and gas, were important sidelines.

Challenges

Fast forward to the 1980s. The pace of HBC's retail acquisition and the economic downturn left the company with major debt and caused it to rethink its priorities. Like many other firms at the time, HBC decided to return to its core business. Nonstrategic assets were sold, as were the company's last natural resource holdings. Strategic expansion followed to strengthen its share of the market with the acquisition of other retailers, such as Kmart Canada.

Since the 1980s, the company has continued to navigate its way through the wake of a weakened economy, changing consumer tastes, and intense competition. The popularity of big-box stores, such as Walmart, Old Navy, and Future Shop, changed consumer behaviour away from department store shopping, forcing retailers like The Bay and Zellers to compete on selection of merchandise and price.

With its reputation for unfocused collections of merchandise, shabby stores, and unhelpful sales staff, HBC tried a number of strategies to entice customers back. Some strategies, such as the HBC Rewards program and online shopping, have been successful; however, other strategies haven't fared as well. Early in 2001, it tried to reinvent itself with a more fashionable image for The Bay and reduced the focus on steep discounts. The economy, and frustrated customers, forced it to abandon the move and return to its value-based focus. To try to remain competitive with other low-cost retailers, HBC diversified, although unsuccessfully, through Designer Depot/Style Depot, which operated from 2004 to 2008.

After remaining a Canadian company for over 330 years, HBC was bought in 2006 by U.S. financier Jerry Zucker. He sought to revive the firm by focusing on improving operations and customer satisfaction. In 2008, after Zucker's death, HBC was bought by U.S. private equity firm NRDC Equity Partners, which also owned the U.S. department store chain Lord & Taylor. NRDC's strategy was once again to revitalize HBC with better brands and better service.

Under NRDC's leadership, The Bay quickly focused on reattracting customers by dropping over 60 percent of its former brands and relaunching "The Room," a plush VIP suite at one of its

Toronto locations, with high-end designers such as Armani, Ungaro, and Chanel. Despite the economic downturn in 2008 and while other organizations were laying off workers, The Bay was in the black.

Another coup for HBC was becoming the official clothing outfitter for the Canadian Olympic Team. The $100 million deal made HBC the clothing provider for the 2006, 2008, 2010, and 2012 games. The HBC apparel for the 2010 Winter Olympics in Vancouver was extremely popular, and new customers and those who hadn't shopped at The Bay in years flocked back to snap up hoodies, coats, hats, and the iconic red mittens as fast as the merchandise could be put on the shelves. HBC's Olympic sponsorship has been renewed through 2020.

HBC continued its revitalization strategy by redesigning and renovating stores; offering a higher-end assortment of fashionable brands such as Juicy Couture, Theory, and Hugo Boss; and expanding ecommerce. The company also hoped to capitalize on its history with a redesigned Signature Line, adding a modern twist to HBC classics such as its striped "point" blankets, sweaters, coats, canoes, trapper hats, and maple syrup, reminiscent of its early trading days.

Moving Forward

As HBC continued its reinvention, former CEO Richard Baker spearheaded a number of initiatives to make the retailer the country's top seller of women's shoes, along with introducing more British-based "cheap-chic" Topshop store-within-stores, and by 2014 its downtown Toronto flagship store was to feature New York–based Kleinfeld Bridal salon of *Say Yes to the Dress* reality-show fame.

However, the company faces increased competition from U.S. retailers. "Cheap-chic" retailer Target, which opened 124 stores across Canada in 2013, many in locations formerly occupied by the Zellers retail chain, was one example. It's interesting to note that Target Corporation bought about 220 of the struggling Zellers Inc. chain from HBC in 2011, intending to convert 100 to 150 of them to its Target banner, and eventually planned to have more than 200 Target outlets in Canada within 10 years. Target failed to catch on with Canadian consumers and closed operation in 2015. HBC will also face further competition from Seattle-based upscale department store chain Nordstrom Inc., which planned to expand into the Canadian market between 2014 and 2016. Nordstrom's first Canadian stores opened at Chinook Centre in Calgary and Rideau Centre in Ottawa in 2015 with more scheduled to open soon after.

Undaunted, the iconic Hudson's Bay Company continues its evolution after many years of change and innovation in the Canadian retail landscape. In spring 2013, the company celebrated its past, present, and anticipated future by unveiling a rebranding of its company and store logos, replacing "The Bay" with its classic full name. "We're very proud to say that Hudson's Bay is continuing to advance in 2013, not only with our new business ventures, but with our updated look," says Tony Smith, creative director at HBC. "We've taken what is a very meaningful two-pronged approach to the redesign: maintaining our heritage while modernizing the new Hudson's Bay Company. It's a throwback to our remarkable history and an image for the direction we're heading in."

Based on its recent successes, HBC seems to be on the right track, but will it be enough to make it once again a premier Canadian shopping destination, or is it too late to revive the historic department store?

In July 2013, HBC "rolled the dice" and bought upscale department chain Saks Inc. for US$2.9 billion. While some observers called it risky, there is agreement that this bold move will help HBC defend its turf in Canada against the arrival of big foreign players.

Questions for Critical Thinking

1. Describe the competitive retail landscape HBC faces in Canada today.

2. What strategic moves would you suggest to HBC as it tries to find a place in the retail environment?

3. What are Hudson's Bay Company's current major strengths that provide it with a competitive advantage? What are its current major weaknesses?

4. What types of things should HBC's top management be doing with respect to the company's employees to ensure successful strategy implementation?

5. Are there other successful chains in the world that Hudson's Bay could learn from by examining their innovative strategic path? If so, which ones, and why?

Sources: Hudson's Bay Company website, www.hbc.com, "About" and "History"; Marina Strauss, "HBC Tries to Build on Olympic Momentum," *The Globe and Mail*, August 23, 2012; Kristin Laird, "The Bay, RBC Renew Olympic Sponsorship," *Marketing*, October 28, 2011; Marina Strauss, "New-Look Hudson's Bay Pushes Retail Growth Plan," *The Globe and Mail*, April 7, 2013; Marina Strauss and Jacquie McNish, "With Target, Canada's Retail Landscape Set for Massive Makeover," *The Globe and Mail*, August 24, 2012; "Nordstrom Expands Canadian Footprint to Yorkdale Mall," CBC News, April 8, 2013; "Hudson's Bay Celebrates Its Past, Present and Future with Modern New Logo," news release, March 6, 2013; Mark Anderson, Keith Howlett, Richard Talbot, and Lindsay Meredith, "Subject: Hudson's Bay Co.: Venerable Department Store and Discount Retailer. Problem: More Dynamic Competitors Are Eating Its Market. Question: Can CEO George Heller Beat Off the Big-box Innovators?" *National Post*, July 2002, 29; Rachel Giese, "The Bay's Cinderella Moment," *Canadian Business*, November 23, 2009, 42; "New Owner of The Bay Says No Major Layoffs Planned," *Canada AM*, January 27, 2006; David George-Cash, "Hudson's Bay Co. Owner Dies, Wife Takes Key Role," *Canwest News*, April 13, 2008; David Moin, "Brooks on The Bay Watch," *WWD*, October 19, 2009, 5; David Moin, "Hudson's Bay Scores with Olympics," *WWD*, March 2, 2010, 19; Marina Strauss, "HBC's Wares Get Hot with the 'Coolness' Factor," *The Globe and Mail*, February 27, 2010, B.4.

Case Study 13 Luxury Brands Market to Millennials

Chanel. Armani. BMW. Cartier. These long-established, high-end brands are interested in Generation Y, also known as the Millennials—those born during the 1980s to the mid-2000s. The newest challenge these once-exclusive brands face is marketing to this age group.

According to a recent American marketing survey, which also applies to Canada, Millennials are the "largest consumer group in U.S. history," even bigger than the baby-boom generation, the previous record holders. The 70 million to 85 million Millennials make up 25 percent of the American population. They are the most ethnically diverse population group ever and the age group that is the least limited by gender stereotypes. They spend more than $200 billion a year on purchases. As they enter the workforce and set up their own households, their spending power will overtake the soon-to-retire baby boomers.

Even more important is how Millennials receive information and communicate. Unlike any previous generation, they have grown up with digital technology. They take for granted such things as cellphones, video games, and other high-speed electronic devices and media. They are used to having instantly available information and communication. A survey by the Pew Research Center notes that 75 percent of Generation Y use social media, compared to 50 percent of Generation X (those born between 1961 and 1981) and 30 percent of baby boomers (those born between 1946 and 1964).

Millennials are very aware of the value of what they buy. The marketing survey found that 65 percent of female Millennials and 61 percent of male Millennials describe themselves as brand conscious. But the marketing tools of heritage and exclusivity, which have traditionally been used to promote prestige brands, mean little to Millennials. Instead, they value quality, authenticity, and image. They shun anything that resembles self-promotion in either brands or people, including prominently displayed corporate logos.

Burberry, a maker of high-end clothing and accessories established in 1836, recently began an ambitious multimedia effort to reach Millennials. One of the company's first moves was to hire Emma Watson, an actress famous for playing the role of Hermione Granger in the Harry Potter movies. Watson, a Millennial born in 1990, was the new face of Burberry's spring–summer campaign. In addition to promoting its business through traditional print advertising and its website, Burberry has also used live streaming and 3D filming of its fashion shows. Burberry also hired the photo blogger Scott Schuman, known as the Sartorialist, to launch a special website, Art of the Trench, to promote its classic trench coat. Burberry's Facebook page calls Art of the Trench "a living celebration of the trench coat and the people who wear it." The website, essentially a social networking blog, invites owners to submit photos of themselves wearing their trench coats—and to submit videos to its YouTube channel. Links allow visitors to "view details," "like," "share," and "leave comments" on the photos. They can also sort the photos by popularity, gender, styling, trench colour, and weather. The site features music by the Maccabees, White Lies, and other groups, with links to their websites. Burberry's chief executive officer, Angela Ahrendts, said, "Attracting the Millennial customer to luxury started two years ago—I said that we can either get crushed or ride the greatest wave of our life."

Scott Galloway of New York University's School of Business says, "Gen Y goodwill is arguably the closest thing to a crystal ball for predicting a brand's long-term prospects. Just as Boomers drove the luxury sector for the last 20 years, brands that resonate with Gen Y, whose purchasing power will surpass that of Boomers by 2017, will be the new icons of prestige."

Questions for Critical Thinking

1. Millennials are brand conscious but generally dislike conspicuous, flashy brand logos. How might these likes and dislikes affect a company's brand equity?

2. Burberry is basing its product strategy on how Millennials use the Internet and social media, not on the preferences of their parents. Will this difference in strategy continue as the Millennials mature? If so, how might Burberry change its product strategy?

Sources: Burberry website, http://us.burberry.com; Art of the Trench, http://artofthetrench.com; Sharalyn Hartwell, "Millennials Love Brands, Not Branding," Examiner.com, May 6, 2010; Scott Galloway, "Gen Y Prestige Brand Ranking," May 3, 2010, http://l2thinktank.com/Gen_Y_Report.pdf; Pew Research Center, "The Millennials: Confident. Connected. Open to Change," February 24, 2010; Jessica Bumpus, "Millennial Burberry," *Vogue*, March 3, 2010; Suzy Menkes, "Marketing to the Millennials," *New York Times*, March 2, 2010.

Part 5 Managing Technology and Information

Case Study 14 Technology Drives Zipcar's Success

As a member of Zipcar, the world's largest car-sharing service, consumers avoid the costs associated with car ownership: gasoline, insurance, maintenance, and parking. Based in Cambridge, Massachusetts, Zipcar was founded by two moms who met when their children were in the same kindergarten class. Prior to its launch, Zipcar raised $75,000, most of which was spent to develop technology. Today, Zipcar is owned by Avis Budget and offers self-service, on-demand cars by the hour or day. The company provides automobile reservations to its 850,000 members and offers more than 10,000 cars in urban areas, on college campuses, and at airports worldwide.

With a seamless user experience, it may be difficult for Zipsters (the company's name for its members) to realize the complex technology that goes into making the car-sharing service so user friendly. Zipcar relies on a number of different technologies, including mobile, web, telematics, radio-frequency identification (RFID), operational information administration systems, and phone and interactive voice response systems for support and customer service. In addition, there are teams responsible for the company's security infrastructure, mobile app development, and auto maintenance to make sure its fleet of vehicles is ready for members.

At the heart of Zipcar's technologies is an operational administration system. As a data-driven company, Zipcar relies heavily on information to make company decisions and manage assets. The system enables the company to manage its physical assets—its vehicles—in many locations worldwide. The system provides data about car utilization, when and how people are driving, specific locations, hours used, and miles driven. Using the data, analytics are performed that allow the company to optimize utilization levels. This type of information is valuable for making strategic decisions about supply and demand, including when and where to place cars, the models and types to use, and when to change them.

The technology in the cars provides information that allows the company to understand how its cars are being used. Zipcar has created a telematics board for each vehicle with GPS and RFID, which supplies geographic, customer, and utilization information. Using transponders, the RFID technology works with a card reader physically placed on the car's windshield. After the customer makes a reservation either on the web or via a mobile device, the RFID card is used to enter and exit any Zipcar. This technology identifies the user and his or her car reservation. Once the car is unlocked, the key is in the car attached to a tether on the steering column. The user will also find a toll pass (members pay for tolls) and a gas card (price of gas is included in the rental fee).

Because of Zipcar's technology, the keys can be left in the car without concern of theft. When a user enters or exits a car, hours, usage, and mileage are uploaded to a central computer via a wireless data link. However, for privacy purposes, the location of the vehicle is not tracked. In addition, all cars are equipped with a "kill" function, which allows the company to prevent theft. For security purposes, the car opens only to the designated user. With a mobile device, a user is able to unlock and lock the car and honk its horn, which helps determine a car's location.

Because 98 percent of Zipcar users have smartphones, mobile and web applications are integral to interfacing with customers. At the heart of the Zipcar's car sharing is a self-serve transaction that allows a user to find, reserve, and access a specific car at a specific location at a specific time. The information is then sent wirelessly to the car, and Zipcar members use their Zipcard to open the car door. Once the car is returned and locked, billing is finalized and information is made available to the member.

Although it is rare that Zipsters interact directly with someone from the company because reservations happen via mobile device or online, providing superior service when something goes wrong requires technology. Dedicated phone systems and customer support systems are crucial for things like on-the-road issues. The Zipcar phone system identifies users who are calling, their reservations, and the cars they are driving, so that timely support and problem solving can happen quickly. Technology also supplies information about the vehicle's service history, which helps with troubleshooting and service.

As transportation needs continue to change, Zipcar is working to improve its technology base. The company remains committed to assessing consumer transportation and parking needs for business and personal use. Zipcar is focused on understanding and assessing trip-type needs, whether it is an errand for a few hours, an afternoon at the beach, or a business meeting. Using various technologies, the company has created a seamless experience for consumers who desire alternatives to car ownership. So, the next time you decide to reserve a Zipcar and drive to the beach for the day, you will have a strong support system at the ready thanks to the company's focus on technology.

Questions for Critical Thinking

1. What type of data does Zipcar use to make decisions on behalf of its customers? Its operations? How does the data used to make customer decisions differ from the data used to make decisions related to operations? Discuss.

2. Discuss how Zipcar manages and deals with information security. What are some of the issues the company faces with regard to security?

3. What information does Zipcar use to manage its fleet? What information is used to decide which types of cars to purchase, how they will be used, and where they will be located? How might weather patterns or seasonality impact the types and number of cars the company purchases?

4. Discuss how Zipcar leverages technology to acquire new members. Based on its segmentation of consumers, businesses, and college students, discuss the various technologies used to identify the relevant target audiences and the types of messages conveyed to each of them.

Sources: Zipcar website www.zipcar.com, "Zipcar Overview" and "How to Zip"; Chris Ready, "Zipcar Rolls Out One-Way Service with Guaranteed Parking," *Boston Globe*, May 2, 2014; Mark Rogowsky, "Zipcar, Uber, and the Beginning of Trouble for the Auto Industry," *Forbes*, February 8, 2014; Carol Hymowitz, "Zipcar Founder Robin Chase on Starting Buzzcar and a Portugal Venture," *Bloomberg Businessweek*, August 8, 2013.

Part 6 Managing Financial Resources

Case Study 15 Canadian Pacific: All Dedicated, Hard-Working Railroaders Aboard!

Canadian Pacific (CP), one of Canada's oldest and most iconic companies, is headquartered in Calgary. The railway company has over 15,000 employees and owns approximately 22,500 kilometres (14,000 miles) of track all across Canada and into the United States, stretching from Montreal to Vancouver. Its freight rail network also serves major cities in the United States, such as Minneapolis, Detroit, Chicago, and New York City. CP recently underwent a downsizing that required creative ways to keep employees motivated in a competitive industry.

A Prestigious Past

Canadian Pacific (CP) was incorporated on February 16, 1881. Less than five years later, Canada was united when the rail line to the Pacific coast was completed with the driving of the "last spike" at Craigellachie, British Columbia, on November 7, 1885. Canadian Pacific became Canada's first transcontinental railway. Primarily a freight railway, however, CP was for decades the only practical means of long-distance passenger transport in many regions of Canada. It was instrumental in the settlement and development of Western Canada and has become one of the largest and most powerful companies in Canada.

Over the years, as Canada's rail industry expanded because of immigration, settlement of the west, and our burgeoning natural resources, the CP workforce became heavily unionized and the company became more bureaucratic. The workplace culture meant there were few incentives for employees to excel. That all changed when business developments and the new economy resulted in a leaner CP that was able to better compete in the challenging transportation industry. And key to this transformation was employee motivation.

A New Hill to Climb

In the spring of 2012, the railway's largest shareholder, Pershing Square Capital Management, pushed for leadership change at CP, feeling that the company was underperforming. Pershing Square Capital launched a successful proxy battle, resulting in several board members and the CEO being replaced. The new CEO, industry veteran Hunter Harrison, is an American and the retired CEO of the other company that dominates Canadian rail traffic—Canadian National Railway Company.

Harrison took over in June 2012 and began a major restructuring plan to make the company more streamlined and efficient. In the fall of 2012, CP began to reduce its rail network. Among other things, the company increased the length of its trains, resulting in the need for 195 fewer locomotives and 3,200 fewer leased freight cars. Leaner operations also require fewer employees, so in December 2012 Canadian Pacific announced it was cutting almost a quarter of its workforce over four years, as Harrison aggressively cut costs to create a more competitive railway. Approximately 1,700 jobs were eliminated by the end of 2012 through layoffs, attrition, and the use of fewer contract positions, with up to a total of 4,500 jobs to be cut by 2016—representing about 23 percent of CP's 19,500 employees and contractors. "This is clearly, initially, a cost-takeout story," he told financial investors at a presentation in New York. "We were clearly, in my view, top heavy," he added, noting that three in ten employees were in non-union management positions. "That's far too much."

The company also reviewed its property costs and real estate holdings and decided to move its headquarters out of leased, downtown Calgary office space and relocate by 2014 to a building it already owned in a rail yard on the outskirts of town.

Getting Back on Track

Motivating employees is challenging in any environment, but especially so in a company that is downsizing. Remaining employees often have to work harder, and they may wonder if they'll be the next one to lose their job. How did CP handle this common problem?

Throughout the restructuring, management let employees know there was a place for them if they were willing to move into different positions. The company also made a commitment to training and to focusing on the opportunities for learning new skills. But first, CP had to get over the common hurdle of a company culture that stressed the status quo. "There's some degree of it being a cultural issue. There was lack of a sense of real urgency. You know, headquarters and the top sort of sets the tone for the rest of the organization," Harrison said. "But we have said we're not going to lose good people if they want to work. If where they are now doesn't fit necessarily, we've said, 'If you're willing to be cross-trained, trained in another discipline, and you're mobile and able to move, you've got a job.' If you're stuck in some area, and you won't move, and you don't want to do anything but what you're doing and you don't want to be trained, you're probably going to have look somewhere else to work."

The company also went to work to motivate employees to improve customer service. Instead of focusing on customer service agents, CP encourages and empowers staff in the field to solve problems for customers. "We have had a huge customer service department of about 650 people. You show me a group that has a customer service department of 650 and I'll show somebody who's got bad service," Harrison said. "So, what we said is those aren't the important people. The people we need to get impassioned about service is the people on the ground who are providing the service. So rather than have this huge bureaucracy where if something goes wrong in Toronto and the person is next door to the operating personnel, rather than have the customer call Winnipeg to create a lot of bureaucracy and take a week to get back to the customer, what we're doing is trying to produce a passion about service with everybody on the ground and recognize the commitments we have to do and that's where our customer service department is going to be—on the ground. If those people don't provide the kind of customer service we say we're going to do, then we're going to have somebody else do it."

CP's decision to move its headquarters from downtown Calgary to a suburban location was partly intended to improve morale. "I think it helps the culture and it saves us money. It's going to save us about $17 million or $18 million annually, and I think over time it's a better environment for the employees," Harrison said. "It's going to be much more functional and nicer for the employees to work in. Workout centres and an outdoor track. It's a way to take those people out of headquarters and kind of let them be out there and see what the business is all about. It's not about downtown bank buildings and glass towers. It's about railroading, and they can look out and see track and interface with the people who run the railroad."

Some of the employees who were let go didn't meet company expectations. Harrison said, "75 to 80 percent-plus" of CP was "dedicated, hard-working railroaders," but "some people weren't doing [their jobs] appropriately." He added, "Our culture is a culture of holding people accountable and applying consequences, both good and bad."

By spring 2013, Harrison was facing criticism for his hard-driving approach to running Canadian Pacific. But his numbers spoke for themselves. Harrison delivered a record first-quarter result in April, and said CP was en route to a record year of earnings for its shareholders. By June 2013, the value of CP shares had more than tripled since Pershing Square Capital Management had taken its initial shareholdings in the railway in September 2011. In its 2013 first-quarter earnings announcement, CP listed "controlling and removing unnecessary costs from the organization, eliminating bureaucracy and continuing to identify productivity enhancements" as keys to its success.

Questions for Critical Thinking

1. What accounting information would help management make decisions about what and where to make cuts to operating costs?

2. What accounting information should be used to measure the success of the transition?

3. What impact on employee engagement could result from Harrison's approach to reduce bureaucracy and "produce a passion about service with everybody on the ground and recognize the commitments we have to do"? Likewise, what might be the impact on employee engagement of his plan to move headquarters from downtown to the rail yard in order to "take those people out of headquarters and kind of let them be out there and see what the business is all about"?

4. Harrison used a cost-cutting strategy that focused heavily on employee accountability. What management systems would you need in place before you could initiate a performance-based program such as the one Harrison used?

5. Find out how Canadian Pacific is doing now. Have Harrison's restructuring plans continued to achieve the desired improved results for CP's shareholders? Have there been any negative aspects to his aggressive approach to cut costs and improve efficiency at CP?

Sources: Canadian Pacific Railway website, www.cpr.ca, "Our Past, Present, and Future"; Library and Archives Canada, "Ties That Bind: A Brief History of Railways in Canada"; Ian Austen, "Ackman Wins Proxy Fight at Canadian Pacific," *New York Times*, May 17, 2012; Guy Dixon, "CP Cuts Deep as Hunter Harrison Makes His Mark," *Globe and Mail*, December 4, 2012; Scott Deveau, "Straight-Talking CP Rail CEO Opens Up about Company Overhaul, Job Cuts," *Financial Post*, December 5, 2012; Brady Yauch, "CP Rail CEO Harrison Fixing 'Permissive' Culture," *Business News Network*, May 27, 2013; Scott Deveau, "Share Sale Could Signal CP Rail Shift," *Financial Post*, June 4, 2013; RolandBerger Strategy Consultants, "The Optimal Setup of a Rail System—Lessons Learned from Outside Europe," Munich (August 31, 2012).

Case Study 16 Globalive Communications Corp.: Winds of Change in the Telecom Industry

Founded in 1998, Globalive Communications' mission was to introduce superior telecommunications products and services. Since then, the company has introduced a suite of telecom services including long-distance telephone, high-speed Internet, and VoIP (voice over Internet protocol) services. It is probably best known for its WIND Mobile cellphone service. Globalive has become a leading provider in Canada and abroad to over 1 million consumer and corporate clients. Globalive takes a long-term view and disciplined approach, and its success has stemmed largely from a willingness to take calculated risks, be innovative, and engage consumers in discussing what type of services they want. Globalive has been recognized through numerous awards, including Canada's 50 Best Managed Companies for nine consecutive years, Canada's Fastest Growing Company in 2004, *Canadian Business*'s Top 30 Best Workplaces in Canada, Canadian Technology 50 Hottest Startups, and Canada's Fastest Growing Wireless Carrier. Globalive's founder, Anthony Lacavera, has been recognized as one of Canada's Top 40 under 40.

Setting Sail

In 1998, using money he made developing company websites while a student at the University of Toronto along with $25,000 from Royal Bank's small-business loan program, Anthony Lacavera started Globalive Communications Corp. "I didn't know anything about telecommunications," he laughed, but someone who worked at Bell told his father, who in turn told Lacavera, there was going to be a deregulation of Canada's telecom market. "That's when I got the idea to start Globalive."

Toronto-based Globalive's approach has been to break down the market into smaller segments and identify growth opportunities. The company looks at unique and niche markets and explores what technologies are not currently offered by the competition that it can develop. The company started as a long-distance reseller focused on the hotel sector—an underserviced niche business. With a new and unknown company, Lacavera drove across Canada, visiting hotels and pitching the business. Starting with Canadian Pacific Hotels in 2000, he soon had 2,500 hotels as clients.

However, when the telecommunications industry imploded in the early 2000s, Globalive nearly went out of business. Lacavera realized he had to diversify the company, and so Globalive went into the home phone, teleconference, and Internet businesses by identifying service gaps and offering those services to customers. The company did very well, boasting sales of $160 million in 2007, but telecommunications infrastructure was getting more difficult to access. Lacavera was faced with a decision: either sell the company or find a major investor and go into the wireless business. He decided on the latter, and within six months he had secured $700 million in financing from Egypt-based Orascom Telecom Holding. Lacavera said, "I flew to Cairo for a 15-minute meeting that turned into dinner."

Tacking into the Wind

Financing secured, Globalive was ready to enter the mobile phone market. In 2008, Industry Canada held an auction to sell some of the advanced wireless spectrum—public radio frequencies needed for cellular communication—to open up competition in the wireless market. Lacavera bought a significant amount of spectrum. However, when Globalive set out in 2009 to launch its new cellphone startup called WIND Mobile, the Canadian Radio-television and Telecommunications Commission (CTRC), which regulates the telecommunications industry, determined that the company failed to meet Canadian ownership rules. Under CRTC rules, a telecom carrier is eligible to operate in Canada as long as it is a Canadian-owned and controlled corporation. Globalive Communications and WIND Mobile were mostly funded from outside. Therefore, from the CRTC's perspective, Globalive was owned and controlled by a foreign company—Globalive's investor, Egyptian Orascom Telecom Holding. Stunned by the CRTC ruling, Globalive had no choice but to delay WIND Mobile's launch. Later that year, the Government of Canada, which had indicated two years earlier its intention to allow greater foreign competition in Canada's telecom sector, overruled the CRTC decision. The Canadian government declared that Globalive Communications Corp. satisfied conditions as a Canadian-owned and controlled company, allowing WIND Mobile to launch its service.

With the regulatory issues behind him, Lacavera decided to approach the wireless sector in a unique way by asking Canadians, through a website called WirelessSoapbox.com, what they would like to see in the next wireless company in Canada, and promised to develop WIND's services based on this feedback. Lacavera says this collaborative initiative was "a first in Canada" and that by opening itself up to all comments, including negative ones, Globalive had a head start in determining what consumers wanted. "We knew there was widespread consumer frustration, so we created WirelessSoapbox.com and invited Canadians to share their ideas, thoughts and opinions on all things wireless. And they did—in huge numbers," Lacavera said.

Working with an extraordinary amount of consumer feedback, Globalive launched WIND Mobile in December 2009—Canada's first new national wireless carrier in over a decade. Lacavera said, "We have no contracts with our customers and no early cancellation penalties. We have to earn their business every day." With WIND's customer-focused service and products, the company has been growing at about 10 percent every three months. WIND Mobile is now Canada's fourth-largest wireless carrier, with services in Ontario, Alberta, and British Columbia, and serves over 600,000 subscribers.

Plotting an Upwind Course

In March 2012, the Canadian government stated that it would change foreign ownership rules to encourage the type of foreign investment that was made in WIND Mobile, lifting the stringent conditions it imposes on telecom companies as long as each one makes up less than 10 percent of Canada's overall market. The government felt that lifting the conditions would result in greater competition, which would benefit consumers through enhanced service, further innovations, and lower costs. "I feel really good about approaching our investors and new potential investors that can back us now with confidence that all of our regulatory and legal issues are fully and finally behind us," said Lacavera.

However, one of the biggest challenges for WIND Mobile continues to be a market dominated by three large phone and cable companies—Rogers Communications Inc., TELUS Corp., and BCE Inc.'s Bell Canada—which together control 95 percent of the market. Lacavera also knows that a significant portion of Globalive's market is due to consumer discretionary spending, and when the economy is in a downturn, consumers spend less on items such as mobile phone services.

Lacavera said that WIND was going "on the offense" after its regulatory and legal problems related from its foreign ownership structure were settled. "It's never been more clear that new entrants have to work together. We can't get enough spectrum in the next auction, so we have to find ways to partner," Lacavera said. He stressed that WIND was taking other steps to position itself for growth. In June 2012, WIND began looking at developing strategic partnerships with regional telecommunications and cable companies to grow distribution and coverage on its network and share costs on network infrastructure. Lacavera says, "There's no easy way to start and grow a company. All those clichés about hard work and focus are true. Despite daily disappointments and mistakes, I always kept my eye on the big goal."

Today, Globalive companies include Yak Communications, One Connect, Canopco, and Globalive Carrier Services. In 2013, Globalive announced that Orascom Telecom Holding would indirectly acquire a 99.3 percent stake in WIND Mobile and that Lacavera would step down as WIND's CEO. True to his entrepreneurial roots, Lacavera planned to launch another division, Globalive Capital. "Now that I am confident WIND Mobile Canada is on a course for long-term success, I can focus on launching Globalive Capital to make targeted investments in companies that share my entrepreneurial vision and continue to support innovation through new and emerging entrepreneurs," he said.

Lacavera attributes Globalive's success to its consistent strategy. "Our biggest advantage is that we are prepared to grow in a profitable, sustainable way. Our strength has been low management turnover and a strong, cohesive and consistent strategy. We believe that the drivers of our success have been the right team and a consistent and disciplined approach. We are very focused on continuing to build and enhance our corporate culture and ensuring our people have a similar attitude and approach to problems and are willing to learn from others," he said.

Questions for Critical Thinking

1. Describe the key financial decisions that Anthony Lacavera faced in the startup of Globalive and later in the creation and divestiture of WIND Mobile.

2. Do you think Orascom's early investment in WIND Mobile was a good one, given the legal and regulatory environment at the time?

3. Globalive operates in a risky environment. What action did Lacavera undertake to increase the probability of making good decisions under risky conditions when launching WIND Mobile?

4. WIND's competitors are also making decisions that will impact the success of the company. How would you gather information from the environment so that you have good data from which to make good decisions?

5. What are the latest changes occurring in the telecommunications industry? How is Globalive responding to these changes? Where is WIND Mobile today? What new initiatives is Lacavera undertaking? How is Globalive stacking up in relation to the company's competitors?

Sources: View from the Top: Arcus Innovation Leaders Series, "How Business Leaders Use Innovative Approaches to Shape Their Strategies," www .arcusgroup.ca/innovation_globalive.html; Globalive website, http://globalive.com, "Globalive Named One of Canada's Best Managed Companies Nine Years in a Row"; "Globalive CEO Harnesses WIND Power," *Ontario Business Report*; Grant Robertson, "Globalive Fails Ownership Test: CRTC," *Globe and Mail*, October 29, 2009; "Government of Canada Varies CRTC Decision on Globalive," Canada News Centre news release, December 11, 2009; Globalive, "Orascom Telecom to Acquire AAL Corporation Interest in WIND Mobile Canada; Anthony Lacavera to Step Down as CEO of WIND Mobile Canada, Plans to Launch Globalive Capital in 2013," news release, January 18, 2013; "Globalive Wins Wireless Fight with Public Mobile," *CBC News*, April 26, 2012; Rita Trichur, "Wind 'on Offense,' Globalive Considers Partnerships," *Globe and Mail*, June 6, 2012.

Case Study 17 SunOpta Divests to Grow

SunOpta Inc. focuses on integrated business models in the natural and organic foods and natural health products markets. SunOpta Inc. is based in Brampton, Ontario, and has three business units, including the well-known SunOpta Food Group. This division specializes in sourcing, processing, and packaging natural and organic food products.

On June 14, 2010, SunOpta Inc. announced that it had completed the divestiture of the company's Canadian food distribution assets to United Natural Foods Inc. (UNFI) and UNFI Canada Inc. The food distribution assets included in the divestiture were part of the SunOpta Distribution Group (SDG), but SunOpta did not give up all of its operations. SunOpta ensured that it retained the natural health products distribution and manufacturing assets—which represent the balance of the assets in SDG.

SunOpta was pleased that this divestiture resulted in no jobs lost. All employees involved in the Canadian food distribution operations were offered employment with UNFI (the leading distributor of natural, organic, and specialty foods in the United States).

But the question remains—why the divestiture? This divestiture was done purely for growth. SDG explains that for fiscal 2009, SDG brought in revenues of US$237.3 million. In the same period, its Canadian food distribution operations alone generated revenues of US$169.6 million and raised positive operating earnings. But the natural health products operation was a different story. Despite its revenues of US$67.7 million, this sector had negative operating earnings because of the cost of relaunching some of its natural health product brands. SunOpta could not continue without divesting.

Steve Bromley, the president and CEO of SunOpta, was not discouraged. Instead, he was optimistic about the growth opportunities the divestiture could bring. "Completing this divestiture is an important step in our strategy to focus on our core food manufacturing platform, strengthening our balance sheet and positioning the company for the future," he commented. Again, Bromley showed his employee-focused mindset: "Once again we want to express our sincere appreciation to our dedicated employees for their years of hard work and dedication and wish them continued success under UNFI's leadership."

It appeared that everyone involved in the deal was pleased with the outcome, which is unusual in these types of divestitures. Steve Spinner, the president and CEO of UNFI, was more than pleased about the divestiture. He commented, "We are very happy to have closed this acquisition as it represents the latest step in our strategy to grow our business in the Canadian market and we look forward to working closely with our new UNFI Canada associates." United Natural Foods Inc. carries and distributes more than 60,000 products to more than 17,000 customer locations across North America.

SunOpta continued with its divestures well after the sale to UNFI. In May 2011, SunOpta sold some of its equipment for processing frozen fruit to Cal Pacific Specialty Foods for $1.8 million. "This divestiture is another step in simplifying our frozen fruit business model to focus on value-added private label frozen fruit products for the retail and food service channels and improve long-term profitability," said Bromley. Similar to earlier divestitures, SunOpta plans to reinvest the funds from the divestiture in growth projects.

Questions for Critical Thinking

1. What are some of the reasons that companies divest their assets?

2. How can SunOpta's divestitures assist the company in meeting its growth prospects?

Sources: SunOpta website www.sunopta.com, "SunOpta Completes Divestiture of Canadian Food Distribution Assets," press release, June 14, 2010, www.newsfilecorp.com/release.aspx?id=540; SunOpta website; UNFI, "About Us."

APPENDIX E
DEVELOPING A BUSINESS PLAN

What's Next? A New Business Model for Restaurants

You're probably familiar with buying airline tickets and concert tickets in advance—but what about a restaurant meal? We're not talking about a fast-food chain; we're talking about a fine dining restaurant. Usually, restaurant customers walk in the door and hope to find a vacant table; if they plan ahead, they might call for a reservation. But the idea of purchasing advance tickets for a restaurant is new to most of us.

Grant Achatz is a well-known chef and restaurant owner. He has a new restaurant called Next—based on a new kind of business plan. Instead of taking reservations, the restaurant sells tickets. The plan makes sense. Next will probably be as popular as Achatz's other restaurant, Alina, which is sold out many weeks in advance. "We now pay three or four reservationists all day long to basically tell people they can't come to the restaurant," explains Achatz. When customers purchase tickets in advance, they are assured of a ready table just as they would with a reservation. Achatz and his partner, Nick Kokonas, will be able to save the costs of the full-time reservation staff. They plan to pass along savings like this to their diners. Selling tickets "allows us to give an experience that is actually a great value," notes Achatz.

Diners who want a meal at Next simply visit the restaurant's website. They can look at the menu, which changes four times a year, and then lock into the fixed price for the entire six-course meal. They can also choose to dine at peak or off-peak hours, which will be reflected in the ticket price. For example, a table at 9:30 on a Tuesday night will cost less than a table at 8:00 on Saturday night. Meals range from $45 to $75, with wine and other beverages costing extra. A service charge—instead of a traditional tip—is included in the ticket price. This way, Achatz and Kokonas can distribute the gratuities among the staff as they see fit.

Achatz is known to offer unique dining experiences that many customers are willing to pay for. Next offers patrons a total experience in the cuisine of a specific place and time. It isn't just a theme; it's an experience that re-creates an era, with everything researched by Achatz and his team. The first offering was based on Paris in 1912, with Escoffier-era cuisine prepared, cooked, and served down to the last detail. When the menu changes, every three months, the chef may choose recipes that take diners to postwar Sicily or a fantasy of Chinese cuisine in the year 2020.

In the same way that sports fans buy season tickets, customers of Next can purchase a year's subscription to Next. That way they lock in the price and are guaranteed a reserved table for each of the seasonal menus. Achatz believes that once people get used to the idea of a prepaid meal, they will enjoy the experience. The dinner is paid for, and there's no fumbling for the wallet. "There's no transaction in the restaurant at all," Achatz points out. "So you can literally come in, sit down, start your experience, and when you're done, you just get up and leave."[1]

Many entrepreneurs and small-business owners write business plans to help them organize their businesses, get them up and running, and raise money for expansion. In this appendix, we cover the basics of business planning: what business plans are, why they're important, and who needs them. We also explain the steps involved in writing a good plan and the major elements it should include. Finally, we cover additional resources to get you started with your own business plan—to help you bring your unique ideas to reality with a business of your own.

APPENDIX E OVERVIEW

WHAT IS A BUSINESS PLAN?

You may wonder how the millions of different businesses operating throughout the world today got their start. Many of them got started with a formal business plan. A *business plan* is a written document that defines what a company's objectives are, how these objectives will be achieved, how the business will be financed, and how much money the company expects to bring in. In short, it describes where a company is, where it wants to go, and how it intends to get there.

Why a Business Plan Is So Important

A well-written business plan serves two key functions:

1. It organizes the business and validates (or gives justification for) its central idea.

2. It summarizes the business and its strategy to obtain funding from lenders and investors.

First, a business plan gives a business formal direction, whether it is just starting, going through a phase of growth, or struggling. The business plan forces the principals—the owners—to do some thorough planning, to think through the realities of running and financing a business. In their planning, they consider many details. How will inventory be stored, shipped, and stocked? Where should the business be located? How will the business use the Internet? And most important, how will the business make enough money to make it all worthwhile?

A business plan also gives the owners a well-thought-out blueprint, or plan, to refer to when daily challenges come up. It also acts as a benchmark by which successes and disappointments can be measured. A solid business plan will sell the potential owner on the real possibilities of the idea. In some cases, the by-product of developing the plan is demonstrating to a dreamy person that he or she is trying to start a business that won't work. In other words, the process of writing a plan benefits a would-be businessperson as much as the final plan benefits potential investors.

Finally, a business plan communicates the business's strategy to financiers who may fund the business. A business plan is usually required to obtain a bank loan. Lenders and venture capitalists need to see that the business owner has thought through the critical issues and has presented a promising idea before they will consider investing. After all, they're really interested in whether investing in the business will bring them significant returns.

Who Needs a Business Plan?

Every business owner who expects to be successful needs a business plan. Some people mistakenly believe that they need a business plan only if it will land on the desk of a venture capitalist or the loan committee of a bank. Others think that writing a plan is unnecessary if their bank or lending institution doesn't need it. But these people miss the point of planning. A business plan acts as a map to guide the way through the often tangled roads of running a business. Every small-business owner should develop a business plan because it empowers that person to take control.

HOW DO I WRITE A BUSINESS PLAN?

Developing a business plan should mean something different to everyone. Think of a business plan as a clear statement of a business's identity. A construction company has a different identity from a newly launched magazine, which has yet a different identity from a restaurant hoping to expand its share of the market. Each business has unique objectives and processes, and each faces different obstacles.

At the same time, good business plans contain some similar elements no matter who the business owner is, what he or she sells, or how far the owner is into the venture. A smart business owner shapes the elements of a business plan into a professional and personal representation of the firm's needs and goals. The plan should also be realistic in its assessment of the risks and obstacles specific to the business, and then present solutions for overcoming them.

Because the document is important, it takes time to collect needed information and organize it. Don't be misled into believing that you will simply sit down and begin writing. Before any writing begins, the business owner must become an expert in his or her field. Gathering important information about the company and the market will make the writing easier and faster. The following items are some critical pieces of information that you should have on hand:

- The company's name, legal form of organization, location, financial highlights, and owners or shareholders (if any).

- Organization charts, list of top managers, consultants or directors, and employee agreements.

- Marketing research, customer surveys, and information about the company's major competitors.

- Product information, including goods and services offered; brochures; patents, licences, and trademarks; and research and development plans.

- Marketing plans and materials.

- Financial statements (both current and forecasted).

The business owner also must do a lot of soul searching and brainstorming to answer important questions necessary to build a healthy business. **Figure E.1** lists some critical questions to ask yourself.

Once you have answered these questions, you can begin writing the document. It can be between 10 and 50 pages long. The length of the plan depends on the complexity of the company, whether the company is a startup (established companies have longer histories to detail), and how the plan will be used. Regardless of size, the document should be well organized and easy to use, especially if the business plan is intended for external uses, such as to secure financing. Number all pages, include a table of contents, and make sure the format is attractive and professional. Include two or three charts or graphs, and highlight the sections and important points with headings and bulleted lists. **Figure E.2** outlines the major sections of a business plan.

The following paragraphs discuss the most common elements of an effective business plan. When you need additional instruction or information, refer to the "Resources" section at the end of the appendix.

Executive Summary

The primary purpose of an executive summary is to interest readers so that they want to learn more about the business. An *executive summary* is a one- to two-page snapshot of what the overall business plan explains in detail. Consider it a business plan within a business plan. By expressing enthusiasm and energy, the summary should capture the reader's imagination. Describe your strategy for succeeding in a positive, intriguing, and realistic way. Briefly yet thoroughly answer the first questions anyone would have about your business: who, what, why, when, where, and how. Financiers always turn to the executive summary first. If it isn't well presented or is missing the

**Take a few minutes to read and answer these questions.
Don't worry about answering in too much detail at this point.
The questions are preliminary and
intended to help you think through your venture.**

1. In general terms, how would you explain your idea to a friend?

2. What is the purpose or objective of your venture?

3. What service are you going to provide, or what goods are you going to manufacture?

4. Is there any significant difference between what you are planning and what already exists?

5. How will the quality of your product compare with competitive offerings?

6. What is the overview of the industry or service sector you are going to enter? Write it out.

7. What is the history, current status, and future of the industry?

8. Who is your customer or client base?

9. Where and by whom will your good or service be marketed?

10. How much will you charge for the product you are planning?

11. Where is the financing going to come from to initiate your venture?

12. What training and experience do you have that qualifies you for this venture?

13. Does such training or experience give you a significant edge?

14. If you lack specific experience, how do you plan to gain it?

FIGURE E.1 Self-Evaluation Questions

proper information, they will quickly move on to the next business plan in the stack. The executive summary is also important to people funding the business with their own resources. The business plan channels their motivations into a clear, well-written mission statement. It is a good idea to write the executive summary last because it will almost always be revised again, when the business plan takes its final shape.

To write an effective executive summary, focus on the issues that are most important to your business's success, and save the supporting information for the body of the business plan. The executive summary should describe the firm's strategy and goals, the good or service it is selling, and the advantages it has over the competition. It should also give a quick overview of how much money will be required to launch the business, how the money will be used, and how the lenders or investors will recoup their funds.

Introduction

The introduction follows the executive summary. After the executive summary has offered an attractive overview, the introduction should begin to discuss the fine details of the business. It should include any material the upcoming marketing and financing sections do not cover. The introduction should describe the company, the management team, and the product in detail. If one

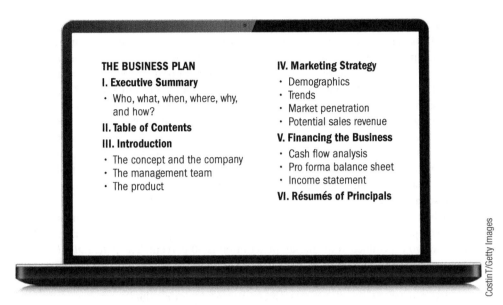

FIGURE E.2 Outline of a Business Plan

of these topics is particularly noteworthy for your business, you may want to present that topic as its own section. Listen to what you write and respond as the plan takes shape.

Include basic information about the company—its past, present, and future. What are the company's roots, what is its current status, and what actions does it need to take to achieve its goals? If you are starting a company, include a description of the evolution of the concept. Be sure to tie all of the business's goals and plans to the industry it will operate in, and describe the industry itself.

A business doesn't run itself, of course. People are the heart of a business, so write an interesting profile of the business's management team. Who are the key players and how does their experience support the company's goals? Describe their—or your, if you are a sole proprietor (an owner–operator)—education, training, and experience, and highlight and refer to résumés included later in the plan. Be honest—not all businesses are started by experts. If you lack demonstrated experience in a certain area, explain how you plan to gain experience.

Also describe the product, which is the driving force behind the venture. What are you offering, and why is it special? What are the costs of the service or the price tag on the good? Analyze the features of the offering and the effect these features have on the overall cost.

Marketing Strategy

Next comes the marketing strategy section. The *marketing strategy* describes the market's need for the item and the way the business will fulfill it. Marketing strategies are not based on informal projections or observations. They are the result of a careful market analysis. Putting together a marketing strategy allows the business owner to become familiar with every aspect of the particular market. If done properly, it will allow you to define your target market and position your business within that sector to get its share of sales.

The marketing strategy will include discussing the size of the customer base that will want to purchase your good or service and the projected rate of growth for the product or category. Highlight information on the demographics of your customers. *Demographics* are statistical characteristics of the segment of the market, such as income, gender, and age. What types of people will purchase your product? How old are they, and where do they live? What is their lifestyle like? For example, someone starting an interior design business will want to report how many homeowners live within a certain distance from the firm and their median income. Of course, this section of the marketing analysis will be quite different for a company that does all of its business online. You will want to know the types of people who will shop at your website, but your discussion won't be limited to one geographic area. It is also a good idea to describe the trends in your product category. Trends are consumer and business tendencies or patterns that business owners can use to gain market share.

The marketing strategy should also detail your distribution, pricing, and promotional goals. Discuss the average price of your offering and the reasons behind the price you have chosen. How do you intend to let your potential customers know that you have a product to sell? How will you sell it—through a catalogue, in a retail location, online, or maybe a combination of all three? The effectiveness of your distribution, pricing, and promotional goals will determine the extent to which you will be able to gain market share.

Competitors are another important part of your marketing strategy. What companies are already selling products similar to yours? Include a list of your competitors to show that you know exactly who they are and what you are up against. Describe what you think are their major strengths and weaknesses and how successful they have been within your market.

Also include the *market penetration*, which is the percentage of total customers who have purchased a company's product. For example, if there are 10,000 people in your market, and 5,000 have purchased your product, your market penetration is 50 percent. The *potential sales revenue*, also an important figure to include, is the total revenue of a company if it captured 100 percent market penetration. In other words, this figure represents the total dollar value of sales you would bring in if everyone who is a potential customer purchased your product.

Financing the Business

The goal of a business is to make money. Everything in the business plan lays the foundation for the *financing section*. Business owners should not skip this section even if they are not seeking outside money. It is crucial to have an accurate financial analysis to get financing, but it also is a necessary exercise for business owners funding the venture themselves. The financing section shows the cost of the product, operating expenses, expected sales revenue and profit, and the amount of the business owner's personal funds that will be invested to get the business up and running. The financial projections should be encouraging but also accurate and based on realistic assumptions. The owner should be able to defend the numbers projected.

Any assumptions made in the body of the business plan should be tied into the financial section. For example, if you think you will need a staff of five, your cash flow analysis should explain how you are going to pay them. A cash flow analysis, a required section of a financial analysis, shows how much money will flow through your business throughout the year. It helps you plan for staggered purchasing, high-volume months, and slow periods. Your business may be cyclical or seasonal; the cash flow projection lets you know whether you need to arrange a line of credit to cover periodic shortfalls. An income statement is another critical document. The income statement is a statement of income and expenses your company has taken on over a period of time.

Remember that leaving out important details can reduce your credibility, so be thorough. The plan must include your assumptions about the conditions under which your business will operate. It should cover details such as market strength; date of startup; sales buildup; gross profit margin; equipment, furniture, and fixtures required; and payroll and other key expenses that will affect the financial plan. In addition, a banker will want a pro forma balance sheet, which provides an estimate of what the business owns (its assets), what it owes (its liabilities), and what it is worth (the owner's equity). Refer to chapters 15, 16, and 17 of *Contemporary Business* for additional details on accounting, financial statements, and financial management.

Résumés of Principals

The final element of the business plan is the inclusion of the résumés of the principals behind the business: the management team. Each résumé should include detailed employment information and accomplishments. Consider expanding on the traditional résumé by including business affiliations, professional memberships, hobbies, and leisure activities, but only if this information applies to your business.

Whichever method you choose to develop a business plan, make sure that *you* develop the plan. It should sound as though it was written by the entrepreneur, not by some outside "expert."

RESOURCES

Whether a person has been in business for decades or is just starting out, many resources are available. A tremendous amount of material can help business owners write effective business plans. The biggest task is narrowing down the resources to the ones that are right for you. The Internet offers many sound business-planning tools and advice, much of which are free. You can look up different examples and opinions, which is important. Remember that no one source will match your situation exactly. Your library and career centre also offer many resources. Following are some helpful resources for business planning.

Books

Dozens of books describe how to write a business plan. Examples include the following:

- Edward Blackwell, *How to Prepare a Business Plan*, 5th ed. (London: Kogan Page Ltd., 2011).
- Michael Gerber, *The E-Myth Enterprise: How to Turn a Great Idea into a Thriving Business* (New York: Harper Collins, 2010).
- Mike McKeever, *How to Write a Business Plan*, 11th ed. (Berkeley, CA: Nolo Press, 2012).
- John W. Mullins, *The New Business Road Test: What Entrepreneurs and Executives Should Do Before Writing a Business Plan*, 3rd ed. (Financial Times/Prentice Hall, 2012).
- Steven D. Peterson, Peter E. Jaret, and Barbara Findlay Schenck, *Business Plans Kit for Dummies*, 4th ed. (Wiley, 2013).
- Hal Shelton, *The Secrets to Writing a Successful Business Plan: A Pro Shares a Step-by-Step Guide to Creating a Plan That Gets Results* (Rockville, MD: Summit Valley Press, 2014).
- Paul Tiffany, Steven D. Peterson, and Nada Wagner, *Business Plans for Canadians for Dummies*, 2nd ed. (Wiley, 2012).

Websites

- *Entrepreneur, Inc.* and *Business Week* magazines offer knowledgeable guides to writing a business plan. *Entrepreneur*'s website also contains sample business plans.

  www.entrepreneur.com

  www.inc.com

  www.bloomberg.com

- If you are hoping to obtain funding with your business plan, it is a good idea to become familiar with what investors are looking for. The following are professional associations for the venture capital industry:

  www.cvca.ca/ (Canadian Venture Capital & Private Equity Association)

  www.nvca.org (National Venture Capital Association)

  www.sbia.org (Small Business Investor Alliance)

  www.bdc.ca/EN/bdc-capital/venture-capital/Pages/venture-capital.aspx (Business Development Bank of Canada - BDC Capital)

Software

Business-planning software can help to give an initial shape to your business plan. But a word of caution if you write a business plan using a software template—bankers and potential investors, such as venture capitalists, read so many business plans that the plans that are based on templates may sink to the bottom of the pile. Also, if you aren't looking for funding, using software can undercut a chief purpose of writing a plan—learning about your unique idea. Think twice before you deprive yourself of that experience. Remember, software is a tool. It can help you get started, stay organized, and build a professional-looking business plan, but it can't actually write the plan for you.

Associations and Organizations

Many government and professional organizations provide assistance to would-be business owners. Here is a partial list:

- The Business Development Bank of Canada (BDC) is Canada's business development bank providing Canadian businesses with flexible financing, venture capital, and consulting services.

  www.bdc.ca/Pages/SplashPage.aspx

- The U.S. Small Business Administration offers planning materials, along with other resources.

  www.sba.gov/category/navigation-structure/starting-managing-business

- The SBA also has a centre specifically designed for female entrepreneurs.

  www.sba.gov/content/women-owned-businesses

PROJECTS AND TEAMWORK APPLICATIONS

1. Visit the website for Next Restaurant at www.nextrestaurant.com to learn more about the restaurant's innovative method of selling tickets in advance. Think of another business that doesn't usually sell tickets in advance—yet. Write a brief plan for converting that business to the pre-selling business model. Why do you think this business would be successful? What might be the drawbacks?

2. Do you dream of starting your own business? Take your idea and answer as many of the self-evaluation questions in **Figure E.1** as you can. Share your answers with the class. Then file your answers away to read at a future date—either when you have graduated from college or university or when you think you are ready to pursue your own business.

3. Write the executive summary portion of the business plan for your potential business. You may use the answers to the questions in **Figure E.1** to help you get started.

GLOSSARY

accounting the process of measuring, interpreting, and communicating financial information to support internal and external business decision making.

accounting cycle the set of activities involved in converting information and individual transactions into financial statements.

accounting equation the relationship that should reflect a firm's financial position at any time: assets should always equal the sum of liabilities and owners' equity.

Accounting Standards Board (AcSB) the organization that interprets and modifies GAAP in Canada for private and not-for-profit businesses.

accrual accounting an accounting method that records revenues and expenses when they occur, not when cash actually changes hands.

acquisition an agreement in which one firm purchases another.

advertising paid nonpersonal communication usually targeted at large numbers of potential buyers.

affective conflict a disagreement that focuses on individuals or personal issues.

affinity program a marketing effort sponsored by an organization that targets people who share common interests and activities.

angel investors wealthy individuals who invest directly in a new venture in exchange for an equity stake.

application service provider (ASP) an outside supplier that provides both the computers and the application support for managing an information system.

asset anything with future benefit owned or controlled by a firm.

balance of payments the overall money flows into and out of a country.

balance of trade the difference between a nation's exports and imports.

balance sheet a statement of a firm's financial position—what it owns and claims against its assets—at a particular point in time.

balanced budget a situation where total revenues raised by taxes and fees equal the total proposed government spending for the year.

Bank of Canada (the Bank) the central bank of Canada.

bankruptcy the legal nonpayment of financial obligations.

benchmarking the process of looking at how well other companies perform business functions or tasks and using their performance as a standard for measuring another company's performance.

board of directors the governing body of a corporation.

botnet a network of PCs that have been infected with one or more data-stealing viruses.

brand a name, term, sign, symbol, design, or some combination that identifies the products of one firm and shows how they differ from competitors' offerings.

brand equity the added value that a respected and successful name gives to a product.

brand name the part of a brand that is made up of words or letters that form a name. It is used to identify a firm's products and show how they differ from the products of competitors.

branding the process of creating in consumers' minds an identity for a good, service, or company; a major marketing tool in contemporary business.

breakeven analysis the pricing-related technique used to calculate the minimum sales volume a product must generate at a certain price level to cover all costs.

budget an organization's plan for how it will raise and spend money during a specific period of time.

budget deficit a situation where the government spends more than it raises through taxes.

budget surplus the excess funding when government spends less than it raises through taxes and fees.

business all profit-seeking activities and enterprises that provide goods and services necessary to an economic system.

Business Development Bank of Canada (BDC) a governmental agency that assists, counsels, and protects the interests of small businesses in Canada.

business ethics standards of conduct and moral values regarding right and wrong actions in the business environment.

business incubator a local program designed to provide low-cost, shared business facilities to small startup companies.

business intelligence a field of research that uses activities and technologies for gathering, storing, and analyzing data to make better competitive decisions.

business law those parts of law that most directly influence and regulate the management of business activity.

business plan a formal document that details a company's goals, methods, and standards.

business product or business-to-business (B2B) product a good or service purchased to be used, either directly or indirectly, in the production of other goods for resale.

Canada Deposit Insurance Corporation (CDIC) the federal agency that insures deposits at commercial and savings banks.

capital production inputs consisting of technology, tools, information, and physical facilities.

capital structure the mix of a firm's debt and equity capital.

capitalism an economic system that rewards firms for their ability to perceive and serve the needs and demands of consumers; also called the private enterprise system.

category advisor the individual that the business customer assigns as the major supplier to deal with all the other suppliers for a project. The category advisor also presents the entire package to the business buyer.

cause advertising a form of institutional advertising that promotes a specific viewpoint on a public issue as a way to influence public opinion and the political process.

cause marketing marketing that promotes a cause or social issue, such as preventing child abuse, anti-littering efforts, and stop-smoking campaigns.

Central America–Dominican Republic Free Trade Agreement (CAFTA-DR) an agreement among the United States, Costa Rica, the Dominican Republic, El Salvador, Guatemala, Honduras, and Nicaragua to reduce tariffs and trade restrictions.

chief information officer (CIO) the executive responsible for managing a firm's information systems and related computer technologies.

classic entrepreneur a person who sees a business opportunity and sets aside resources to gain access to that market.

cloud computing the use of powerful servers that store applications software and databases that users access by using any Internet-connected device, such as a PC or a smartphone.

co-branding a cooperative arrangement where two or more businesses team up to closely link their names on a single product.

code of conduct a formal statement that defines how an organization expects its employees to resolve ethical issues.

cognitive conflict a disagreement that focuses on problem- and issue-related differences of opinion.

collective bargaining the process of negotiation between management and union representatives.

co-marketing a cooperative arrangement where two businesses jointly market each other's products.

common law laws that result from judicial decisions, some of which can be traced to early England.

common shares the basic form of company ownership; shares that give owners voting rights but only residual claims to the firm's assets and income distributions.

communication a meaningful exchange of information through messages.

communism an economic system where all property is shared equally by the people in a community under the direction of a strong central government.

compensation the amount employees are paid in money and benefits.

competition the battle among businesses for consumer acceptance.

competitive differentiation the unique combination of organizational abilities, products, and approaches that sets one company apart from its competitors in the minds of customers.

competitive pricing a strategy that tries to reduce the emphasis on price competition by matching other firms' prices and by focusing their own marketing efforts on the product, distribution, and promotional elements of the marketing mix.

computer-aided design (CAD) a process used by engineers to design parts and entire products on the computer. Engineers who use CAD can work faster and with fewer mistakes than those who use traditional drafting systems.

computer-aided manufacturing (CAM) a computer tool that a manufacturer uses to analyze CAD output and the steps that a machine must take to produce a needed product or part.

computer-based information systems information systems that use computer and related technologies to store information electronically in an organized, accessible manner.

computer-integrated manufacturing (CIM) an integrated production system that uses computers to help workers design products, control machines, handle materials, and control the production function.

conflict the outcome when one person's, or one group's, needs do not match those of another, and one side may try to block the other side's intentions or goals.

conflict of interest a situation in which an employee must choose between a business's welfare and personal gain.

conglomerate merger a merger that combines unrelated firms, usually with the goal of diversification, increasing sales, or spending a cash surplus to avoid a takeover attempt.

consumer behaviour end consumers' activities that are directly involved in obtaining, consuming, and disposing of products, and the decision processes before and after these activities.

consumer orientation a business philosophy that focuses first on consumers' unmet wants and needs, and then designs products to meet those needs.

Consumer Price Index (CPI) a measurement of the monthly average change in prices of goods and services.

consumer product or business-to-consumer (B2C) product a good or service that is purchased by end users.

consumerism public demand that a business consider the wants and needs of its customers when making decisions.

contract a legally enforceable agreement between two or more parties regarding a specified act or thing.

controlling the function of assessing an organization's performance against its goals.

cooperative advertising allowances that marketers provide to share with channel partners the cost of local advertising of their firm's product or product line.

copyright legal protection of written or printed material such as books, designs, cartoons, photos, computer software, music, and videos.

core inflation rate the inflation rate after energy prices and food prices are removed.

corporate culture an organization's collection of principles, beliefs, and values.

corporate philanthropy an organization's contribution to the communities where it earns profits.

corporation a legal organization with assets and liabilities separate from the assets and liabilities of its owners.

Corruption of Foreign Public Officials Act a federal law that prohibits Canadian citizens and companies from bribing foreign officials to win or continue business.

cost-based pricing calculating total costs per unit and then adding markups to cover overhead costs and generate profits.

countertrade a barter agreement whereby trade between two or more nations involves payment made in the form of local products instead of currency.

creative selling a persuasive type of promotional presentation.

creativity the capacity to develop novel solutions to perceived organizational problems.

credit receiving money, goods, or services on the basis of an agreement between the lender and the borrower that the loan is for a specified period of time with a specified rate of interest.

critical thinking the ability to analyze and assess information to pinpoint problems or opportunities.

cross-functional team a team made up of members from different functions, such as production, marketing, and finance.

cyclical unemployment the joblessness of people who are out of work because of a cyclical contraction in the economy.

data raw facts and figures that may or may not be meaningful to a business decision.

data mining the use of computer searches of customer data to detect patterns and relationships.

data warehouse a customer database that allows managers to combine data from several different organizational functions.

database a centralized integrated collection of data resources.

debt financing borrowed funds that entrepreneurs must repay.

decision making the process of seeing a problem or opportunity, assessing possible solutions, selecting and carrying out the best-suited plan, and assessing the results.

decision support system (DSS) an information system that gives direct support to businesspeople during the decision-making process.

deflation the opposite of inflation, occurs when prices continue to fall.

delegation the managerial process of assigning work to employees.

demand the willingness and ability of buyers to purchase goods and services.

demand curve a graph of the amount of a product that buyers will purchase at different prices.

demographic segmentation dividing markets on the basis of various demographic or socioeconomic characteristics, such as gender, age, income, occupation, household size, stage in family life cycle, education, or ethnic group.

departmentalization the process of dividing work activities into units within the organization.

devaluation a reduction in a currency's value in terms of other currencies or in terms of a fixed standard.

directing guiding and motivating employees to accomplish organizational goals.

discrimination biased treatment toward a job candidate or employee.

distribution channels the paths that products—and their legal ownership—follow from producer to consumers or business users.

distribution strategy a plan that deals with the marketing activities and institutions that get the right good or service to the firm's customers.

diversity the blending of individuals of different genders, ethnic backgrounds, cultures, religions, ages, and physical and mental abilities to enhance a firm's chances of success.

divestiture the sale of assets by a firm.

double-entry bookkeeping the process used to record accounting transactions; each individual transaction is always balanced by another transaction.

downsizing the process of reducing the number of employees within a firm by eliminating jobs.

dumping selling products in other countries at prices below production costs or below typical prices in the home market to capture market share from domestic competitors.

economics the social science that studies the choices people and governments make when dividing up their scarce resources.

embargo a total ban on importing specific products or a total stop to trading with a particular country.

employee benefits additional compensation—such as vacation time, retirement savings plans, profit-sharing, health insurance, gym memberships, child and elder care, and tuition reimbursement—paid entirely or in part by the company.

employee separation a broad term for the loss of an employee for any reason, voluntary or involuntary.

Employment Equity Act (EEA) an act created (1) to increase job opportunities for women and members of minority groups and (2) to help end discrimination based on race, colour, religion, disability, gender, or national origin.

empowerment giving employees shared authority, responsibility, and decision making with their managers.

end-use segmentation a marketing strategy that focuses on the precise way a B2B purchaser will use a product.

entrepreneur a person who seeks a profitable opportunity and takes the necessary risks to set up and operate a business.

entrepreneurship the willingness to take risks to create and operate a business.

equilibrium price the current market price for an item.

equity financing funds invested in new ventures in exchange for part ownership.

equity theory an individual's perception of fair and equitable treatment.

European Union (EU) a 28-nation European economic alliance.

event marketing marketing or sponsoring of short-term events such as athletic competitions and cultural and charitable performances.

everyday low pricing (EDLP) a strategy of maintaining continuous low prices instead of using short-term price cuts such as cents-off coupons, rebates, and special sales.

exchange control a restriction on importing certain products or a restriction against certain companies to reduce trade and the spending of foreign currency.

exchange process an activity in which two or more parties trade something of value (such as goods, services, or cash) that satisfies each other's needs.

exchange rate the value of one country's currency in terms of the currencies of other countries.

executive support system (ESS) an information system that lets senior executives access the firm's primary databases, often by touching the computer screen, pointing and clicking a mouse, or using voice recognition.

expansionary monetary policy a plan to increase the money supply to try to decrease the cost of borrowing. Lower interest rates encourage businesses to make new investments, which leads to employment and economic growth.

expectancy theory the process people use to evaluate the likelihood that their efforts will lead to the results they want and the degree to which they want those results.

expert system a computer program that imitates human thinking through complicated sets of "if-then" rules.

exports domestically produced goods and services sold in other countries.

external communication a meaningful exchange of information through messages sent between an organization and its major audiences.

factors of production four basic inputs for effective operation: natural resources, capital, human resources, and entrepreneurship.

fair trade a market-based approach of paying higher prices to producers for goods exported from developing countries to developed countries in an effort to promote sustainability and to ensure the people in developing countries receive better trading conditions.

finance the business function of planning, obtaining, and managing the company's funds to accomplish its objectives as effectively and efficiently as possible.

finance charge the difference between the amount borrowed and the amount repaid on a loan.

Financial Accounting Standards Board (FASB) the organization that interprets and modifies GAAP in the United States.

financial institutions intermediaries between savers and borrowers that collect funds from savers and then lend the funds to individuals, businesses, and governments.

financial managers the executives who develop and carry out their firm's financial plan and decide on the most appropriate sources and uses of funds.

financial markets markets where securities are issued and traded.

financial plan a document that specifies the funds needed by a firm for a period of time, the timing of cash inflows and outflows, and the most appropriate sources and uses of funds.

financial system the process by which money flows from savers to users.

firewall a type of security system for computers that limits data transfers to certain locations; it also tracks system use so that managers can identify threats to the system's security, including attempts to log on with invalid passwords.

fiscal policy a plan of government spending and taxation decisions designed to control inflation, reduce unemployment, improve the general welfare of citizens, and encourage economic growth.

flexible manufacturing system (FMS) a production facility that workers can quickly change to manufacture different products.

foreign licensing agreement an international agreement in which one firm allows another firm to produce or sell its product, or use its trademark, patent, or manufacturing processes, in a specific geographical area, in return for royalties or other compensation.

franchise a contract-based agreement in which a franchisee can produce and/or sell the franchisor's products under that company's brand name if the franchisee agrees to the operating terms and requirements.

franchisee the individual or business firm purchasing a franchise.

franchising a contract-based business arrangement between a manufacturer or other supplier, and a dealer, such as a restaurant operator or retailer.

franchisor the firm whose products are sold to customers by the franchisee.

frequency marketing a marketing initiative that rewards frequent purchases with cash, rebates, merchandise, or other premiums.

frictional unemployment the joblessness of people in the workforce who are temporarily not working but are looking for jobs.

General Agreement on Tariffs and Trade (GATT) an international trade accord that has greatly reduced worldwide tariffs and other trade barriers.

generally accepted accounting principles (GAAP) principles that outline the conventions, rules, and procedures for deciding on the acceptable accounting practices at a particular time.

geographical segmentation dividing an overall market into similar groups on the basis of their locations.

global business strategy the offering of a standardized, worldwide product and the selling of it in basically the same way throughout a firm's domestic and foreign markets.

goal-setting theory the idea that people will be motivated to the extent to which they accept specific, challenging goals and receive feedback that shows their progress toward goal achievement.

grapevine an internal information channel that passes information from unofficial sources.

green marketing a marketing strategy that promotes environmentally safe products and production methods.

grid computing a network of smaller computers that run special software.

gross domestic product (GDP) the sum of all goods and services produced within a country during a specific time period, such as a year.

guerrilla marketing innovative, low-cost marketing efforts designed to get consumers' attention in unusual ways.

hardware all tangible, or physical, elements of a computer system.

health insurance insurance that pays for losses due to illness or injury.

home-based businesses firms operated from the residence of the business owner.

horizontal merger a merger that joins firms in the same industry for the purpose of diversification, increasing customer bases, cutting costs, or expanding product lines.

human resource management the function of attracting, developing, and retaining employees who can perform the activities needed to meet organizational objectives.

human resources production inputs consisting of anyone who works, including both the physical labour and the intellectual inputs contributed by workers.

hyperinflation an economic situation marked by soaring prices.

imports foreign goods and services purchased by domestic customers.

income statement a financial record of a company's revenues, expenses, and profits over a specific period of time.

inflation rising prices caused by a combination of excess consumer demand and higher costs of raw materials, component parts, human resources, and other factors of production.

infomercials a form of broadcast direct marketing; 30-minute programs resemble regular TV programs, but sell goods or services.

information knowledge gained from processing data.

information system an organized method for collecting, storing, and communicating past, present, and projected information on internal operations and external intelligence.

infrastructure the basic systems of a country's communication, transportation, and energy facilities.

insider trading use of material nonpublic information about a company to make investment profits.

institutional advertising messages that promote concepts, ideas, or philosophies. It can also promote goodwill toward industries, companies, organizations, or government entities.

insurance a contract in which the insurer, for a fee, agrees to reimburse an insured firm or individual a sum of money if a loss occurs.

integrated marketing communications (IMC) the coordination of all promotional activities—media advertising, direct mail, personal selling, sales promotion, and public relations—to produce a unified customer-focused message.

integrity behaving according to one's deeply felt ethical principles in business situations.

International Accounting Standards Board (IASB) the organization that promotes worldwide consistency in financial reporting practices.

International Financial Reporting Standards (IFRS) the standards and interpretations adopted by the IASB.

international law the numerous regulations that govern international trade.

International Monetary Fund (IMF) an organization created to promote trade, eliminate barriers, and make short-term loans to member-nations that are unable to meet their budgets.

International Organization for Standardization (ISO) an international organization whose mission is to develop and promote international standards for business, government, and society. The aim is to improve and encourage global trade and cooperation.

intranet a computer network that is similar to the Internet but limits access to authorized users.

intrapreneurship the process of promoting innovation within the structure of an existing organization.

inventory control a function that balances the costs of storing inventory with the need to have stock on hand to meet demand.

joint venture a partnership between companies for a specific activity.

judiciary the branch of government that is responsible for applying laws to settle disagreements; also known as the court system.

just-in-time (JIT) system a broad management philosophy that reaches beyond the narrow activity of inventory control to affect the entire system of production and operations management.

labour union a group of workers who organize themselves to work toward common goals in the areas of wages, hours, and working conditions.

law the standards set by government and society in the form of either legislation or custom.

law of large numbers the idea that seemingly random events will follow predictable patterns if enough events are observed.

leadership the ability to direct or inspire people to reach goals.

LEED (Leadership in Energy and Environmental Design) a voluntary certification program administered by the Canada Green Building Council, aimed at promoting the most sustainable construction processes available.

leverage increasing the rate of return on funds invested by borrowing funds.

leveraged buyouts (LBOs) transactions where public shareholders are bought out and the firm reverts to private status.

liability a claim against a firm's assets by creditors.

life insurance a type of insurance that protects people against the financial losses that occur with premature death.

lifestyle entrepreneur a person who starts a business to reduce work hours and create a more relaxed lifestyle.

lifetime value of a customer the revenues and intangible benefits (such as referrals and customer feedback) from a customer over the life of the relationship, minus the amount the company must spend to acquire and serve that customer.

listening receiving a message and interpreting its intended meaning by grasping the facts and feelings the message conveys.

local area networks (LANs) computer networks that connect machines within limited areas, such as a building or several nearby buildings.

logistics the process of coordinating flow of goods, services, and information among members of the supply chain.

macroeconomics the study of a nation's overall economic issues, such as how an economy maintains and divides up resources and how a government's policies affect its citizens' standards of living.

make, buy, or lease decision choosing whether to manufacture a needed product or part in-house, buy it from an outside supplier, or lease it.

malware any malicious software program designed to infect computer systems.

management the process of achieving organizational goals through people and other resources.

management by objectives (MBO) a structured approach that helps managers to focus on reachable goals and to achieve the best results based on the organization's resources.

management information system (MIS) an information system designed to produce reports for managers and other professionals.

management support systems information systems that are designed to provide support for effective decision making.

market segmentation the process of dividing a total market into several relatively similar groups.

marketing an organizational function and set of processes for creating, communicating, and delivering value to customers and for managing customer relationships in ways that benefit the organization and its stakeholders.

marketing concept a companywide consumer focus on promoting long-term success.

marketing mix a blending the four elements of marketing strategy—product, distribution, promotion, and pricing—to satisfy chosen customer segments.

marketing research the process of collecting and evaluating information to support marketing decision making.

Maslow's hierarchy of needs a theory of motivation proposed by Abraham Maslow. According to the theory, people have five levels of needs that they try to satisfy: physiological, safety, social, esteem, and self-actualization.

mass production a system for manufacturing products in large quantities by using effective combinations of employees with specialized skills, mechanization, and standardization.

materials requirement planning (MRP) a computer-based production planning system that ensures a firm has all the parts and materials it needs to produce its output at the right time and place and in the right amounts.

merger an agreement in which two or more firms combine to form one company.

microeconomics the study of small economic units, such as individual consumers, families, and businesses.

mission statement a written description of an organization's overall business purpose and aims.

missionary selling an indirect form of selling where the representative promotes goodwill for a company or provides technical or operational assistance to the customer.

mixed market economy an economic system that draws from both private enterprise economies and planned economies, to different degrees.

monetary policy a government plan to increase or decrease the money supply and to change banking requirements and interest rates to affect bankers' willingness to make loans.

monopolistic competition a market structure where large numbers of buyers and sellers exchange distinct and differentiated (dissimilar) products so each participant has some control over price.

monopoly a market situation where a single seller controls trade in a good or service, and buyers can find no close substitutes.

multidomestic business strategy a plan to develop and market products to serve different needs and tastes in separate national markets.

multinational corporation (MNC) a firm with many operations and marketing activities outside its home country.

national debt the money owed by government to individuals, businesses, and government agencies who purchase Treasury bills, Treasury notes, and Treasury bonds.

natural resources all production inputs that are useful in their natural states, including agricultural land, building sites, forests, and mineral deposits.

nearshoring the outsourcing of production or services to locations near a firm's home base.

net worth the difference between an individual's or a household's assets and liabilities.

nonpersonal selling forms of selling such as advertising, sales promotion, direct marketing, and public relations.

North American Free Trade Agreement (NAFTA) an agreement among the United States, Canada, and Mexico to break down tariffs and trade restrictions.

not-for-profit corporations organizations whose goals do not include pursuing a profit.

not-for-profit organizations organizations whose primary aims are public service, not returning a profit to their owners.

objectives guideposts by which managers define the organization's desired performance in such areas as new-product development, sales, customer service, growth, environmental and social responsibility, and employee satisfaction.

odd pricing a pricing method that uses uneven amounts to make prices appear to be less than they really are.

offshoring the relocation of business processes to lower-cost locations overseas.

oligopoly a market situation where relatively few sellers compete and high startup costs act as barriers to keep out new competitors.

on-demand computing the use of software time from application providers; firms pay only for their usage of the software, not for purchasing or maintaining the software.

operational support systems information systems designed to produce a variety of information on an organization's activities for both internal and external users.

order processing a form of selling used mostly at the wholesale and retail levels; involves identifying customer needs, pointing out products that meet those needs, and completing orders.

organization a structured group of people working together to achieve common goals.

organization marketing a marketing strategy that influences consumers to accept the goals of and organization, receive the services of an organization, or contribute in some way to an organization.

organizing the process of blending human and material resources through a formal structure of tasks and authority: arranging work, dividing tasks among employees, and coordinating them to ensure plans are carried out and goals are met.

outsourcing using outside vendors to produce goods or fulfill services and functions that were previously handled in-house or in-country.

owners' equity the funds that owners invest in the business plus any profits not paid to owners in the form of cash dividends.

partnership an association of two or more persons who operate a business as co-owners by voluntary legal agreement.

patent legal protection that guarantees an inventor exclusive rights to an invention for 20 years.

penetration pricing a strategy that sets a low price as a major marketing tactic.

performance appraisal evaluation of and feedback on an employee's job performance.

person marketing efforts that are designed to attract the attention, interest, and preference of a target market toward a person.

personal financial management the study of the economic factors and personal decisions that affect a person's financial well-being.

personal financial plan a guide to help a person reach his or her desired financial goals.

personal selling the most basic form of promotion: a direct person-to-person promotional presentation to a potential buyer.

physical distribution the actual movement of products from producer to consumers or business users.

place marketing an attempt to attract people to a particular area, such as a city, state, or country.

planned economy an economic system where business ownership, profits, and resource allocation are shaped by a plan to meet government goals, not goals set by individual firms.

planning the process of looking forward to future events and conditions and deciding on the courses of action for achieving organizational goals.

point-of-purchase (POP) advertising displays or demonstrations that promote products when and where consumers buy them, such as in retail stores.

positioning a concept whereby marketers try to establish their products in the minds of customers by communicating to buyers the meaningful differences about the attributes, price, quality, or use of a good or service.

preferred shares shares that give owners limited voting rights and the right to receive dividends or assets before owners of common shares.

prestige pricing setting a relatively high price to develop and maintain an image of quality and exclusiveness.

price the exchange value of a good or service.

primary markets financial markets where firms and governments issue securities and sell them initially to the general public.

private enterprise system an economic system that rewards firms for their ability to identify and serve the needs and demands of customers.

private property the most basic freedom under the private enterprise system; the right to own, use, buy, sell, and hand down land, buildings, machinery, equipment, patents, individual possessions, and various intangible kinds of property.

privatization the conversion of government-owned and -operated companies to privately held businesses.

problem-solving team a temporary combination of workers who gather to solve a specific problem and then disband.

process control systems operational support systems that monitor and control physical processes.

product a bundle of physical, service, and symbolic attributes designed to satisfy buyers' wants.

product advertising messages designed to sell a particular good or service.

product liability the responsibility of manufacturers for injuries and damages caused by their products.

product life cycle the four basic stages in the development of a successful product—introduction, growth, maturity, and decline.

product line a group of related products that share physical similarities or are targeted toward a similar market.

product mix the assortment of product lines and individual goods and services that a firm offers to consumers and business users.

product placement a form of promotion where marketers pay placement fees to have their products featured in various media, from newspapers and magazines to television and movies.

production the use of resources, such as workers and machinery, to convert materials into finished goods and services.

production and operations management the process of overseeing the production process by managing the people and machinery that convert materials and resources into finished goods and services.

production control creating well-defined procedures for coordinating people, materials, and machinery to provide the greatest production efficiency.

productivity the relationship between the number of units produced and the number of human and other production inputs needed to produce them.

product-related segmentation dividing consumer markets into groups that are based on benefits sought by buyers, usage rates, and loyalty levels.

profitability objectives common goals that are included in the strategic plans of most firms.

profits rewards for businesspeople who take the risks involved to offer goods and services to customers.

promotion the function of informing, persuading, and influencing a purchase decision.

promotional mix the combination of personal and nonpersonal selling that marketers use to meet the needs of a firm's target customers and to effectively and efficiently communicate its message to them.

property and liability insurance a general category of insurance that protects against losses due to a number of perils, such as fire, accident, and theft.

psychographic segmentation dividing consumer markets into groups with similar attitudes, values, and lifestyles.

public accountant an accountant who provides accounting services to other organizations.

public relations an organization's communications and relationships with its various public audiences.

publicity the nonpersonal stimulation of demand for a good, service, place, idea, event, person, or organization by unpaid placement of information in print or broadcast media.

pulling strategy promotion of a product by generating consumer demand for it, mainly through advertising and sales promotion appeals.

pure competition a market structure where large numbers of buyers and sellers exchange similar products, and no single participant has a large influence on price.

pushing strategy personal selling to market an item to wholesalers and retailers in a company's distribution channels.

quality the state of being free of deficiencies or imperfections.

quality control measuring output against quality standards.

quota a limit set on the amounts of particular products that can be imported.

recession a cycle of economic contraction that lasts for six months or longer.

recycling reprocessing of used materials for reuse.

regulated monopoly a firm that is granted exclusive rights in a specific market by a local, provincial, or federal government.

relationship era the business era where firms seek to actively promote customer loyalty by carefully managing every interaction.

relationship management the collection of activities that build and maintain ongoing, mutually beneficial ties with customers and others.

relationship marketing developing and maintaining long-term, cost-effective exchange relationships with partners.

restrictive monetary policy a plan to reduce the money supply to control rising prices, overexpansion, and concerns about overly rapid economic growth.

retailers distribution channel members that sell goods and services to individuals for their own use, not for resale.

risk uncertainty about loss or injury.

risk management calculations and actions a firm takes to recognize and deal with real or potential risks to its survival.

risk–return tradeoff the process of maximizing the wealth of the firm's shareholders by striking the right balance between risk and return.

rule of indemnity the requirement that the insured cannot collect more than the amount of the loss and cannot collect for the same loss more than once.

salary pay calculated on a periodic basis, such as weekly or monthly.

sales law the law governing the sale of goods or services for money or on credit.

sales promotion forms of promotion such as coupons, product samples, and rebates that support advertising and personal selling.

Sarbanes-Oxley Act of 2002 U.S. federal legislation designed to deter and punish corporate and accounting fraud and corruption. It is also designed to protect the interests of workers and shareholders by requiring enhanced financial disclosures, criminal penalties for CEOs and CFOs who defraud investors, and safeguards for whistle-blowers. The act also established a new regulatory body for public accounting firms.

seasonal unemployment the joblessness of workers in a seasonal industry.

secondary market a collection of financial markets where previously issued securities are traded among investors.

securities financial instruments that represent the obligations of the issuers to provide the purchasers with the expected stated returns on the funds invested or loaned.

seed capital the initial funding needed to launch a new venture.

self-managed team a work team that has the authority to decide how its members complete their daily tasks.

serial entrepreneur a person who starts one business, runs it, and then starts and runs more businesses, one after another.

server the heart of a midrange computer network.

sexism discrimination against members of either sex, but usually against women.

sexual harassment unwelcome and inappropriate actions of a sexual nature.